Sixth Edition

Advertising Copywriting

Sixth Edition

Advertising Copywriting

Philip Ward Burton

School of Journalism
Indiana University

NTC Business Books
a division of *NTC Publishing Group* • Lincolnwood, Illinois USA

Published by NTC Business Books, a division of NTC Publishing Group.

Library of Congress Catalog Card Number: 88-62909
Manufactured in the United States of America.

9 0 RA 9 8 7 6 5 4 3 2 1

Contents

Foreword

Advertising Copywriting has always remained within arm's-reach of my typewriter. There's Mr. Roget. Mr. Webster. And Mr. Burton. These three gentlemen have kept me out of trouble for years. And although Mr. Webster and Mr. Roget never asked me to write forewords for their books, Mr. Burton did. And of the three, he's the one I owe the most.

Through his book, I can relive my career, chapter by chapter. When I got my first job writing about the glamorous world of potato blight, I reread the pages on agricultural advertising. When I "moved up" to write about rebuilt washer transmissions, I reached for Burton's thinking on trade advertising. And when I finally walked into an agency that was doing 90 percent TV, I closed my office door and became an instant expert on television terms.

This is a college book that serves long, long after college. A book so broad that it gives a working knowledge of every aspect of copywriting. So focused that it gives details on structure and timing. A book that's as big as a 50-year campaign and as small as a 10-second spot.

I have carefully avoided calling *Advertising Copywriting* a textbook, though it is what I consider the most definitive text on copywriting. And it is certainly a book. To put those two words together implies that the reading is going to be tedious and stuffy. I referred to the "coffee factor" when I was in school. How many cups does it take to get through a chapter of a textbook?

Happily, here the answer is zero. Each chapter begins with a scenario of advertising people in action. It's involving. It's fun. It reads like a story. Like any great copywriter, Mr. Burton has you "hooked" before you know it. And he never lets you down. The facts are presented in a style that's lively and lucid. All in all, this book is just plain good reading.

The Sixth Edition has changed in many ways from the Fifth. The chapters on television, research, fashion, law, and direct response advertising have undergone major revisions to keep the reader current. The illustrations, storyboards, and photos have all been updated, reflecting some of the best advertising out there.

The good news is that much of the book is unchanged. This spanking new Sixth Edition holds the same time-tested advertising principles that are found in my frayed and tired Fourth Edition. A solid foundation of learning provided by a man who knows how to teach. A man who knows how to turn students into professionals.

A man who introduced me to advertising. So hold the phone, Mr. Webster. Save the telex, Mr. Roget. This foreword belongs to Mr. Burton. You opened up new words. He opened up new worlds.

Mary Beth Reed
Vice President and Creative Director
Foote, Cone & Belding Communications, Inc.

Preface

Interesting and significant changes have occurred in advertising since the Fifth Edition of this book was published. In television, the 15-second commercial has become a factor. Newspapers have adopted the standard advertising unit (SAU). Merger-mania has been running wild in the world of big agencies. Direct response advertising is in a boom stage. In contrast, network television slides steadily downward.

While all this change has been occurring, what changes have occurred in advertising copywriting? The answer? No profound changes.

Advertising copywriting remains a largely anonymous activity. Still, advertising copywriters continue to have more chance for personal expression than any other workers in advertising. What they say in their headlines, body copy, and illustrations—and the ideas they conceive—reflects their personalities whether the copy is deft or clumsy; inventive or stylized; eloquent or dull; persuasive or lackluster; enthusiastic or plodding.

While those in media and other forms of advertising are wrenched about by drastic changes, the advertising copywriter finds that the appeals and approaches that worked twenty years ago are still effective today.

It is striking to see how much about advertising copywriting is timeless and constant. Most of the suggestions made many years ago by such masters as John Caples, for example, apply today. Likewise, many suggestions that appeared in the First Edition of this book are valid today.

Copywriters write for people. Because basic "people" appeals stay largely constant, a book that recognizes this fact is not going to discard all the original material in succeeding editions.

When you write advertising copy, you continue to learn more about it—what works, what doesn't. You never stop learning, no matter how long you write.

This nonstop learning process is true in the teaching of advertising copywriting. As more students sit in your classrooms, you learn more about what subject matter arouses student interest, or makes them yawn. You find out how presenting subject matter makes such a difference. In this new edition, accordingly, there are some new truths about teaching advertising copywriting, as well as writing it.

To be able to teach such writing is a true talent. Some immensely skilled practitioners cannot do this. They cannot succeed with students because they cannot think like students. So often, theirs is an intuitive ability, based on quick, swift, and accurate judgments. For them, it is difficult, if not impossible, to work with uninformed, plodding learners. Yet, much of a book on advertising copywriting must be addressed to these plodders. Step by step it must bring them along, and so must the teacher.

So it must be granted that books about advertising copywriting retain much of the old in the new editions. Still, in this new edition of *Advertising Copywriting,* there is much that is new. There is, in fact, something new in each chapter. This includes new text material, new examples, new illustrations, new captions, new subheads. Outdated material has been dropped.

Some chapters especially reflect the new such as those about research, television, and advertising law. This last has been greatly strengthened because it is so important to the working copywriter to keep his clients from running afoul of regulatory bodies and the courts.

In the Fifth Edition there was some emphasis on the importance of campaigns and campaign thinking by the copywriter. There is much more emphasis on this subject in the Sixth Edition.

There are, for example, many instances where as many as three or four illustrations are included for one advertiser that show how a campaign theme and look were carried out in succeeding advertisements. Sometimes these may all be print advertisements. Sometimes broadcast commercials. Other times a combination of print and broadcast. In one instance, a direct response campaign is included.

More Advertising Council advertisements are included in this Sixth Edition than in the Fifth. This has been done for two reasons: (a) To recognize, and call attention to, the important contributions made by the Advertising Council and by those who contribute to its efforts. (b) Because Advertising Council advertising is so well done—thoughtful, important, often dramatic, and expertly written.

What's the net result of the changes that have been made in the Sixth Edition? A more useful book for the student and practitioner. A more teachable book for teachers.

Summing up: While retaining much that appeared in the other editions, the Sixth Edition offers new material that will help make the book even more appealing to those concerned with the teaching or writing of advertising copy.

ACKNOWLEDGMENTS

When you're writing a new book, or doing another edition of a book, it's humbling to realize how much you depend on others to help you. You will see below scores of names of people who contributed in one way or the other to the Sixth Edition of Advertising Copywriting. *In most cases, these people supplied print and broadcast material. Their furnishing of such material does not, however, necessarily mean that they endorse or approve the content of the book. Regardless, their help has been valuable and is deeply appreciated.*

Special thanks to:

Stephen R. Bergerson, J.D., of Kinney & Lange. Mr. Bergerson, a practicing attorney with a vast experience in laws affecting communications, advertising, and marketing, made significant changes and additions in the chapter "Advertising Law and the Copywriter." As I told him, he put so much into improving the chapter that I would have been unable to pay him had he been charging for his time. His contribution was made simply because seeing that advertising and marketing adhere to legal standards is a never-ending crusade with him.

Scott Purvis, President of Gallup & Robinson, and **William F. Greene,** Director of Research of this leading firm in advertising and marketing research, made many suggestions for the chapter "A Copywriter's Helper: Research." When I had incorporated these numerous suggestions into the chapter, I felt much more comfortable with the chapter.

Mary Beth Reed, Vice President and Creative Director, Foote, Cone & Belding Communications, Inc., reviewed the two television chapters: "Television: Advertising's Powerhouse" (Parts A and B). Working as she is with television at the highest levels, she was able to update material, winnow out much material and, in short, sharpen both chapters. The result is that the chapters better reflect current television advertising thinking and practice.

You will find in the following list the names of people and firms whose material is found throughout the Sixth Edition. Once more, I thank them: Abel, Edmund, W., Wellman Thermal Systems Corporation; Atseff, Larry, Alert Marketing, and Ogilvy & Mather Sales Promotion Services; Beard, Charles M., Telemecanique, Inc.; Bond, Patti, John Hancock Insurance; Booth, Linda, Ogilvy & Mather Direct; Brouette, Rosanne, Goody, Berlin & Silverstein; Burgess, Mark N., AT&T International Long Distance; Calderon, Marc, *Antiques*; Caminiti, Joseph, Starch INRA Hooper, Inc.; Cannon, Robert E.; Channellock, Inc.; Casteel, John M., Dow Corning Corporation; Collins, Joseph T., McGraw-Hill Research; Comer, Gary, Lands' End, Inc.; Continental Airlines; Currie, Douglas, Van Air Systems, Inc.; Davidson, Marty, *Vanity Fair*; DiGennaro, Rose Ann, Conde Nast Publications, Inc.; Drake, Ron, Backer Spielvogel Bates, Inc.; Dretzer, H., *Barron's*; Dunaway, James, Newspaper Advertising Bureau, Inc.; Evans, Ray, *Farm Journal*; Feeney, Kevin, Amax Coal Company; Friedman, John T., The Advertising Council, Inc.; Gibbs, Jospeh F., United Gilsonite Laboratories; Graham, F. J., Unison; Guise, B., Shop Vac; Hamilton, Vanessa, The Advertising Council, Inc.; Hartnett, Catherine, L. L. Bean, Inc.; Hauptman, Don, Don Hauptman, Inc.; Holmloe, Richard M., Lockwood Products, Inc.; Jackson, Laura, Quaker Oats Company; Jackson, Ted, Nissan Industrial

Equipment Company; Jacobsen, Joanna L., Encyclopaedia Britannica, U.S.A.; Katzel, Jeanine A., *Plant Engineering;* Kempe, David K., The Upjohn Company; Kinelski, Robert, Glenbrook Laboratories; Knight, Wayne, Velux-America, Inc.; Koop, Ellen G., Project Software & Development, Inc.; Kosich, C. M., Texaco Refining and Marketing; Kruse, Anna, Bullock's Department Store; Kunz, Peggy, Xerox Corporation; Lucero, Belinda, Del Monte Corporation; Mahler, Kenneth, Good Life Designs; Malloy, W. E., Parke-Davis; Marcus, Edward, Adria Laboratories; Matthews, James, Nuway Distributors, Inc.; McCollum, Toney R., Duracell U.S.A.; McKenzie, Scott C., Bearings, Inc.; Miller, William F., Kwikset Corporation; Munsell, William, Creswell, Munsell, Fultz & Zirbel; Newbury, Gerry, SMW Systems, Inc.; Norton, Jeffrey, Jeffrey Norton Publishers, Inc.; Orton, Lyman, The Vermont Country Store; Rand, Lenora, Marshall Field's; Reed, George, Jr., Professional Golf Car Corporation; Rein, Michael A., E & J Gallo Winery; Richards, Leona M., Northwestern Steel and Wire Company; Rogers, Richard L., Readex, Inc.; de Ryss, Janice, Chiat/Day, Inc.; Sample, William R., Abbott Pharmaceuticals, Inc.; Sammut, Charles P., VISA International; Phillips 66 Company; Schieling, Beth, Roerig, a division of Pfizer Pharmaceuticals; Simpson, Norman, Richards Of Course Advertising; Smith, R. S., The Eureka Company; Soderstrom, Jan, VISA U.S.A., Inc.; Spellman, Leo, Steinway & Sons; Stauderman, Albert B., Bird, Bonette, Stauderman, Inc.; Stearns, Ben, Creswell, Munsell, Fultz & Zirbel; Stockton, B.C., Oscar Mayer Foods Corporation; Story, Chris, Bloomhorst, Story, O'Hara; Story, James, Bloomhorst, Story, O'Hara; Stout, William T., Stout, Wallwork & Hindson, Inc.; Tilton, G. F., Texaco Refining and Marketing; Tobin, Michael, United Parcel Service; Vickers, Nancy M., Hershey Chocolate Corporation; Vickery, Shelly, Beckman Industrial; Vose, Marcia, Vose Galleries of Boston, Inc.; Weidner, Rick, *Successful Farming*; Weiss, Judy, *Vanity Fair*; Wiese, Nancy J., Xerox Corporation; Williams, Don, Don Williams Advertising; Williams, Donald J., Lands' End, Inc.; Wilson, Lynn E., 3M Commercial Office Supply Division; Wulfman, Ellen S., Signature Advertising.

COPYWRITING

What You Can Expect to Learn by Reading a Book about It

You'll find it's a *Yes* and *No* situation.

Yes—you can learn to distinguish good copy from bad copy. You will learn the dos and don'ts that can save you time and trouble on the job.

Yes—you can learn the terminology of the field of copywriting and of advertising.

Yes—you can learn what motivates people to buy and what appeals to use.

Yes—you can learn the technical requirements that are peculiar to the different media so that you can proceed confidently whether you're writing a 10-second television commercial, a 4-color magazine spread, or a 24-sheet outdoor poster.

Yes—you can learn the special requirements of the different forms of advertising, such as retail, mail order, industrial, professional, trade, and others.

Yes—you can learn what a copywriter must know about research and law, and how a copywriter can write copy that is in keeping with the tenets of consumerism, yet can sell efficiently for the advertiser.

Yes—you can learn how a copywriter cooperates with, and learns from, artists and production people.

—but—

No—you cannot learn from a book the ability to come up with an inspirational idea that forms the basis of an outstanding campaign, or of a memorable, award-winning advertisement. Some people have a heaven-sent ability to think creatively and originally. They have this, book or no book. A copywriter can be trained but there are some who are naturals. They are born with the ability to spark original ideas just as there are artists, poets, and musicians whose talent shines through almost from birth.

No—you cannot learn from this, or any book, how to write first-draft copy speedily and under pressure. Such speed is learned on the job and is developed from constant practice.

A book on copywriting can point you in the right direction. It can give you a helping hand in a course in advertising copywriting, and it can help you significantly during those first days on the job. It can help you even after you've had working experience because all writers need to go back to the fundamentals occasionally.

There may be moments when you experience doubt and insecurity. Perhaps this book can help you get through such moments. If it does, it will have justified itself.

1

COPYWRITING

It's Tough, It's Fun, It's a Never-ending Challenge

You snap on your desk lamp. Dusk is settling. Out your window you see the commuters scurrying for transportation. What a day! One rush job after another. On top of that, a copy conference that swallowed two precious hours. You've just called home to tell them to eat dinner without you.

Worst of all, not a single ad you've written in the last two days has been approved, not even that 30-second TV for the automotive client, a commercial you know is your very best. Oh, well, that's life in the trenches. No percentage in griping. Let's try again. . . .

At such moments, you wonder why you refused that insurance job, or the chance to take management training in the department store. Yet, despite the discouragement, you know in your heart that you're glad you're in copy. You do have moments of depressing failure, but if you had wanted a job that didn't have ups and downs, you'd have elected to be a bank teller or a retail sales clerk.

It's Part of the Business Scene

Purple drapes, a cathedral-like hush, and sweet violin music playing softly in the background—these were provided (the story goes) to create the right mood for one temperamental advertising-agency copywriter in the fabulous 1920s.

During this period, when advertising billings were beginning to zoom, copywriters could do no wrong. If they wanted mood background, the indulgent advertisers let them have it. The copywriter was a favorite actor in a dizzy drama of lush profits.

Today's copywriters are likely to be less coddled than the copywriters who worked during the period from the end of World War I until the 1929 crash. They were credited then with the sensitivity of any other "artiste." They were littérateures who condescended to work at the prosaic job of selling soap, automobiles, and washing machines.

When the crash came, advertising emerged from the golden haze. The era of advertising research began. Advertising became a serious, painstaking business instead of a madcap adventure. Copywriters pulled down the purple drapes and looked out soberly upon the smoky city below. They were no longer artists with taken-for-granted temperamental rights. They were businesspeople.

Not all copywriters, admittedly, have given up the idea that they are apart from the ordinary businesspeople. Generally, however, most of today's copywriters think of themselves as businesspeople—not artists.

Slogans Play a Minor Role

Most people in the general public have only the vaguest idea of a copywriter's work and some of these ideas have been colored by exaggerations of motion pictures and trashy novels that "tell the truth" about the advertising business.

Very deep-rooted is the idea that the usual copywriter is a glib "sloganeer." A sizable portion of the public, including many businesspeople who should know better, think of copywriting in terms of writing clever slogans. Such persons, wanting to enter the advertising and the copywriting field, believe that they can "turn out slogans." The fact that "99 and-$^{44}/_{100}$% pure," "Say it with flowers," and others have become a part of the American vernacular has helped create the illusion that copywriting is basically slogan writing.

The duties of a copywriter, although practically unknown to most persons, do not discourage advertising aspirants. Persons who might, for example, question their ability to do satisfactory work in the research department or the media department of a company will apply very confidently for a copywriter's position. Without advertising knowledge or experience, applicants will try unhesitatingly to enter this tough, competitive field. When their applications are received indifferently or without too much serious consideration, the applicants are hurt and amazed.

Writing Ability May Not Be Enough

Just what is there about copywriting which makes it seem easy and desirable? The answer is that there is almost 100 percent ignorance among nonadvertising folk of just what copywriters are supposed to do—and what they get paid for doing it. They have no comprehension of the hard work and supplementary knowledge that must accompany a copywriter's expected ability in writing.

Advertising managers, like newspaper editors, are continually squashing the hopes of applicants who have little else in their personal sales kit than an alleged flair for writing. Because of letter-writing ability or a succession of A's on high school or college themes, the youthful men and women of self-asserted literary merit feel that writing advertising or newspaper copy is merely an extension of the writing they have already done.

People think they can write because everyone has to write at one time or another. How many times have you looked at an advertisement and said to yourself, "And they call that copywriting! Why didn't they do it this way?" The world is filled with people who feel they could do a better job of writing advertisements than the persons who make their living as copywriters. Under the delusion that they "could do it better," the uninitiated approach the copywriting field eagerly and confidently.

What's Tougher to Write—a News Story or an Advertisement?

Reporting and copywriting demand ability, knowledge, and experience far beyond a surface facility in writing. Requirements for the two occupations are similar in some points. In both, for instance, it is vital to understand people and to use that understanding in the fashioning of lucid material.

A copywriter, like a reporter, must be analytical, observant, and thorough. Each has specialized knowledge for the work. Where, for example, the aspiring reporter might find it advantageous to obtain a background in political science and labor economics, the future copywriter might acquire a knowledge of sociology and mass psychology.

Despite certain points of similarity between the two occupations, it is perhaps more difficult to prepare for a copywriter's job than for that of a reporter. A journalism school, granted normal intelligence and aptitude on the part of the student, can teach the student the newswriting formulas. Having mastered the rather stylized forms of newswriting, the intelligent journalism school graduate can do a creditable beginning job for most newspapers.

The fact that copywriting is less precise than newswriting and less amenable to "formula" writing makes the task of teaching copywriting in school somewhat more arduous. Take the writing of crime stories. Reporters who have worked a police beat have developed a format for crime stories. Depending on their ability they can work within this format, but essentially they follow a definite writing pattern. Their work is made easier and faster if they follow the pattern.

You have no such formula to help you in copywriting. You cannot use as a crutch any mechanical style of writing to make your job easier. Each advertisement is custom built to time or space requirements and to the product.

What makes your preparation for copywriting work even more difficult is the fact that the copywriter must know business matters. Before you sit down at the typewriter, you should have a background of business experience that enables you to write copy intelligently and competently. The knowledge of selling, of merchandise, or of general business procedure gained from this experience gives you confidence.

The copywriter adds another element to writing that is not present in the news story. This is the element of persuasion. Whereas the reporter gives the facts without embellishment, the copywriter, while also giving facts, must add words and sentences that will cause readers to take action.

Words must create a mood, an excitement, and a desire for the goods or services. A mere recital of facts is not enough. Copy must sell, as well as tell. As anyone knows who has done face-to-face selling, persuading a reluctant prospect to a course of action can be difficult. Yet this is what the copywriter must do in advertisements.

To sum up, copywriting, like reporting, demands much more than facility with words. Whether it is more difficult to become a good copywriter than a good reporter is debatable, but there is no debating the assertion that copywriting calls for hard and extensive preparatory work.

Anonymity: The Copywriter's Lot

Although copywriters may write top-flight copy, develop slogans, trade names, and descriptive phrases that become a part of the nation's idiom, they may never be identified with their work. Copywriters are anonymous. They are among the thousands who do their jobs day after day—efficiently and unknown. Here again the copywriter is removed from the class of the artiste.

Not for the copywriter is the acclaim of the byline newspaper reporter or of the motion picture scenario

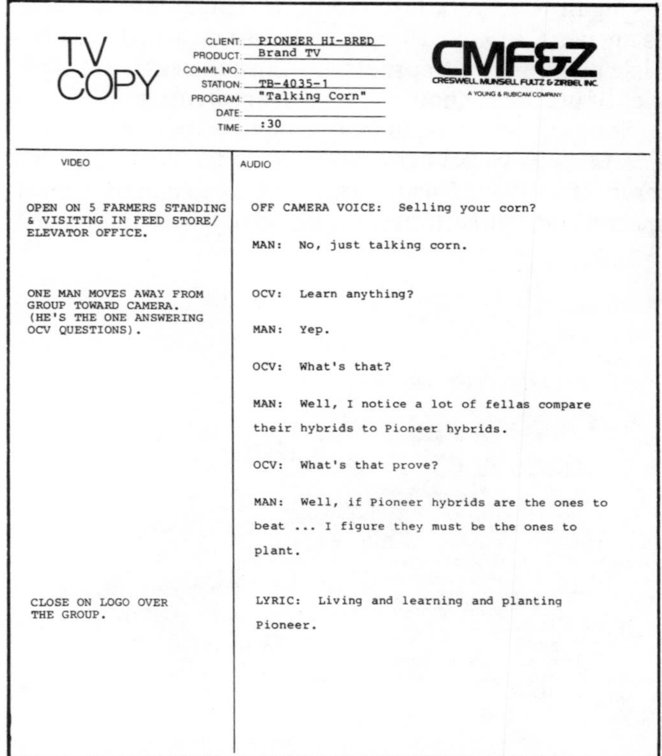

TV COPY

CLIENT: PIONEER HI-BRED
PRODUCT: Brand TV
COMML NO:
STATION: TB-4035-1
PROGRAM: "Talking Corn"
DATE:
TIME: :30

CMF&Z
CRESWELL MUNSELL FULTZ & ZIRBEL INC
A YOUNG & RUBICAM COMPANY

VIDEO	AUDIO
OPEN ON 5 FARMERS STANDING & VISITING IN FEED STORE/ ELEVATOR OFFICE.	OFF CAMERA VOICE: Selling your corn? MAN: No, just talking corn.
ONE MAN MOVES AWAY FROM GROUP TOWARD CAMERA. (HE'S THE ONE ANSWERING OCV QUESTIONS).	OCV: Learn anything? MAN: Yep. OCV: What's that? MAN: Well, I notice a lot of fellas compare their hybrids to Pioneer hybrids. OCV: What's that prove? MAN: Well, if Pioneer hybrids are the ones to beat ... I figure they must be the ones to plant.
CLOSE ON LOGO OVER THE GROUP.	LYRIC: Living and learning and planting Pioneer.

Figure 1–1. Television commercial addressed to farmers. Copywriters don't always write about consumer products. An important field is agricultural advertising. Writers in this type of advertising must have the right touch with farm talk.

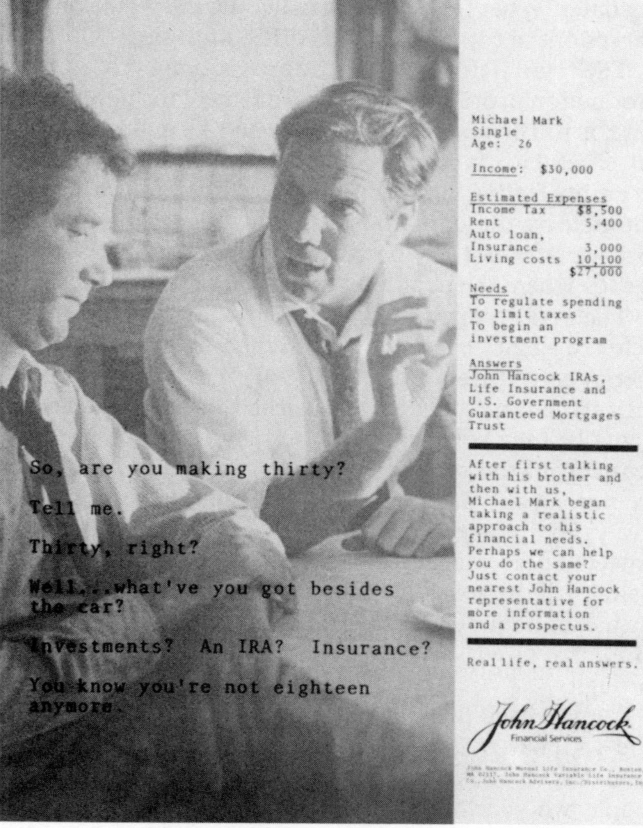

Figure 1–2. Selling advertisement with a strong service slant. In this advertisement, which is part of a campaign using print and television, the copy performs a useful function by demonstrating the need for financial planning. It is the kind of advertisement a writer is proud to have written.

writer. If the only satisfaction you get out of writing is the glow you feel when people talk about your work, then copywriting will give you only limited satisfaction because the only people who will know what you have written are those who are associated with you in business. As a copywriter you are just another salesperson peddling merchandise and ideas.

How Much Will You Be Paid?

Salaries for copywriters are generally thought to be much higher than they are. Although top agency copywriters draw very high pay, many beginning copywriters start with salaries lower than those paid in less demanding jobs.

Skill in copywriting, however, is rewarded as well as in any other business activity. Some advertising agency copy chiefs, to illustrate, are paid huge salaries, but for every high-salaried person there are hundreds of copywriters who earn modest salaries. The high salaries paid to relatively few copywriters have, unfortunately, been so widely publicized that the beginner is led into thinking that all copywriters are paid bountifully.

If you are able to check the salaries paid to copywriters in the different kinds of advertising activity—retail, agency, newspaper, business concerns, or radio—you will soon discover that such copywriters are paid no better and no worse than are persons of comparable skill in most other fields of business activity. A few make the top-bracket figures—most make average salaries.

Hurry! Hurry! Hurry!

Like the newspaper reporter, copywriters are hounded by deadlines. If they are nervous types, they will find the work taxing. Day after day, month after month, they will be hurried, always conscious of publishing or broadcasting dates. What field of advertising is most trying on the nerves of the copywriter? It is difficult to say.

The retail field, in which the artists, copywriters, and production people are just a step ahead of the publishing date, is full of worry for persons who like to do thoughtful, careful work. As one retail copywriter said, "There's an empty feeling in turning out copy this way. I'm always haunted by the consciousness that this hurried, rush-rush work is not my best work. I'd like to work in an agency where the deadlines are farther apart."

The retail copywriter typically sighs for the green fields of agency copywriting. All the way down the line, agency copywriters are envied. But what is the situation with the agency copywriter? Is the job relatively easy? Actually, they voice almost exactly the same complaint heard from the retail copywriters. True, the deadlines are not usually daily deadlines, but they are seemingly always behind the schedule. Then, there is always the unexpected presentation, the new account, or the quick revision. All these call for hurry-up writing dashed off to the accompaniment of the impatient jigging of the copy chiefs or clients waiting for the copywriter to get through.

Copywriting provides little quiet, leisurely writing. The copywriter is a businessperson who writes under hard-driving business conditions for other businesspeople who have no time for creative temperament. Copywriters produce work quickly—and good work, too, or out they go.

Still, many successful copywriters feel that they do their very best work when under extreme pressure. Like athletes, you may often find inspiration when circumstances force you to do the "impossible." If you're the type who can rise to the urgency of the moment, you will find the pressure stimulating.

You'd Better Be in Good Shape

The drain on the copywriter's creative talent is considerable. Where a successful magazine writer might make a good living turning out a few articles or stories a year and have a chance to rest up between efforts, copywriters must turn out a quantity of good writing daily. Each day they search for new ways to write headlines, body copy, commercials, and direct-mail pieces.

If you, as a copywriter, are assigned miscellaneous accounts, you must adjust yourself rapidly to each new product that you write about. You are expected to give a fresh twist to your copy in order that you may satisfy the probing and skeptical examination by executives of the client company. Such quantity writing puts a great strain on your freshness and originality.

The working hours of copywriters are likely to be irregular. When an emergency arises (and emergencies are always arising), you are expected to stay on the job day and night until your part of the work is done. Overtime is a part of creative work. Then, too, as a conscientious copywriter, you are likely to take your work with you wherever you go.

As you walk down the street, you may see new uses for the products that you write copy about. You jot down the ideas before they escape you. At night you squirm in your bed, musing over a new approach for a current campaign. Finally, unable to get back to sleep, you snap on the light, sketch the idea, and wait impatiently for morning in order that you may give your sizzler the test of daylight examination.

The combination of irregular hours and work which creates nervous tension makes good health an important requisite for copywriters. Obviously, you don't need the muscles of a Samson, but if you can bounce out each day fresh and vigorous—all the better. Health and an ability to take each new assignment as it comes are important in the profession.

Unless you reach top levels, you cannot expect pampering in your working conditions. You are more likely, as an average copywriter, to work in a crowded little cubicle piled high with proofs, unfinished work, and samples of products about which you are writing.

Some copywriters, in fact, seem to work best in an office that many persons might consider hopelessly littered. If you're the usual copywriter, you cannot expect specialized work to bring specialized working condi-

Figure 1–3. Professional advertisement aimed at medical doctors. Copywriters for such advertising must know the vocabulary of the medical field and should be totally accurate with facts. A background in science, especially biology, is almost mandatory for such writing. Look in the second of the chapters on "Business, Professional, and Agricultural Advertising" (Chapter 16) for other examples of professional advertising.

tions. Although your work may be important, you are just part of the business of creating advertising that will sell, and you carry on your function in a business office.

A Number of Psychic Satisfactions

Up to this point, the "cold water" approach has been employed in discussing the career of a beginning advertising copywriter. Any copywriting book must describe the negative aspects. Such frankness is necessary because of the general misconceptions regarding copywriting. When you start your first copywriting job, you should do so eagerly but not with a feeling that you are about to enter a never-never land divorced from the usual business world.

Before discouraging you further, however, it is only sensible to point out that there are agreeable sides to the life of a copywriter. To those who can stand the pace, the work is deeply satisfying. Copywriters may grumble, threaten to quit, fight with the boss, but they know deep down that it would be difficult to find any other work that they would like so well.

The lure of the copywriter's job is a compound of various factors. Some of these factors mean more to one person than to another. You, for example, might experience a never-ending thrill in the creative side of the work. Seeing your copy in *Reader's Digest* or the *New Yorker* or your commercial over a national network—these moments are your bonus for the hours of word-hammering.

Reading your words in print is a satisfaction whether they appear in a country weekly, a huge metropolitan daily, or a national magazine. Although much of the copywriter's work is mere common sense put into selling words, some efforts fall into the classification of sheer creativeness. Such work is a joy to perform, never routine, always satisfying.

You Perform a Useful Service

Copywriters might derive satisfaction from the important part they have in the movement of goods. They realize that all the manufacturing skill and marketing genius behind a product are wasted unless their words convince the customers they should buy the product. To these copywriters comes a sense of usefulness in the business picture, the feeling that they are "movers of goods."

This feeling of being useful is vital to the copywriter. Your work is better if you can feel that it is of service in the social and economic sense. Admittedly, the utility of many products is so questionable that you feel no glow in having written the copy that makes goods move from the producer to the consumer.

On the other hand, if the product is beneficial to the user, you are gratified that you can inform users about the product and that you can cause them to buy it. One of your real pleasures is to see the sales curve rise as a result of a successful advertisement or series of advertisements. You soon discover that if your copy doesn't sell, it represents so much wasted effort. The successful copywriter and the sales department are never far apart.

If you feel that you are part of business, if you see your work as contributing to the marketing pattern, you are likely to be a better copywriter. You then see the marketing pattern as it is concerned with the product research and sales plans behind the goods advertised. You include in your working knapsack some knowledge of the manufacturing difficulties and even the legal aspects such as the patent rights, trademark details, and regulations affecting the distribution of the products you write about.

You Owe It to Others to Do a Good Job

You are aware, too, of the many things that happen after you have punched out copy on your typewriter. You know that untruths or careless wording may cause trouble with such groups as the Federal Trade Commission, the Better Business Bureau, or the Food and Drug Administration. Possibly your words might cause consumer "kickback" which will make the sales department storm and ask angrily, "Who wrote this?"

Copy, you realize, is a sharp-edged business tool, part of the marketing process involving you, salespeople, wholesalers, retailers, consumers, manufacturers, research people, and all others engaged in business. You have an obligation to all of these and especially to the consumers who, like you, are entitled to honest, competently written copy in order that they may make the best possible use of their money when they purchase goods.

In a sense, you must also look upon yourself as a merchant who has goods to sell. Your words either take the place of salespeople or make the salesperson's job more productive by acting as the door opener. They tell the truth about the goods, but they tell the truth persuasively—so much so that the reader is given a reason to buy. Again, you must, above all, become a part of the vital business of moving goods.

Don't Just Sit in Your Office

The feeling of being a "merchant" must be especially strong in the department store copywriter. True, some of these writers merely sit passively in their tiny offices in the advertising department. By preference, these "sitters" deal with goods—not with people, and not with the big, dynamic selling process of modern retailing. They become wrapped up in their task of writing words—countless words—about merchandise. Such copywriters are not businesspeople/writers. They have the writer's viewpoint only. It is not enough.

The retail copywriter—the good one—must be a part of the retail business. If you write newspaper advertisements for an aggressive department store, you have the privilege of learning merchandising in its most vigorous form. Some of the best copy in any business activity is turned out daily at such stores as Marshall Field & Company, Macy's, and Bullock's.

Do the men or women copywriters turning out these words learn to do so by spinning them out in their offices, far removed from the bargain hunters in the basement? No! These writers become a part of the business scene. They get out of their offices and into the store.

They talk to buyers. From them they can learn merchandising, fashions, trade talk, prices, and customer likes and dislikes. The topnotch retail copywriters learn the jobs of other people in the store, too. The salespeople, in direct contact with the customers, can provide much grist for copy.

A personal service shopper can be pumped for comments made by customers. In the retail trade, the learning of all the functions and services of a department store is known as acquiring the "whole-store" viewpoint. The acquisition of such a viewpoint by you, the retail copywriter, is a part of your training as a businessperson and hence—a better copywriter.

Copy's the Vital Last Link in the Chain

If you have become a good copywriter, you will derive satisfaction from your standing in the business community and in the firm for which you work. Although it has been pointed out that good copywriters are not coddled as artists, they are definitely treated with respect as an important working professional.

If you are in an agency, you are one of a relatively small group of specialists. To picture this, assume that XYZ agency has lined up a new account through the work of its new-business person. The account executive who is to service the account has been approved. The agency's financial stability and business integrity have been found satisfactory by the client.

Despite the foregoing—the fast-talking and persuasive new-business person, the charming and efficient account executive, the firm's unquestioned integrity—all these will mean nothing if the agency cannot, through you, furnish good selling copy. Copy is a last and very important link in the manufacturer–agency–consumer chain. As the welder of the link, you are an important person. Yours is the final responsibility.

A retail copywriter has the same sort of prestige. The men and women who write the copy for Ohrbach's, Wanamaker's, Lord & Taylor's, and Bloomingdale's are solidly established in the business community. In addition to having developed the ability to write selling copy, they have stored in their brains an accumulation of valuable knowledge about products, merchandising, and other general business facts.

So long as advertising is used in the mass distribution of goods, there will be need for skilled copywriters, especially in retail advertising—the biggest field of all. Mediocrity in copywriting brings the usual reward of mediocrity. Skill in the profession enables you, the possessor, to name your ticket in the advertising world.

ANNCR: Think for a minute what could happen if every one of us gave just five hours a week, if we gave just 5 percent of what we earn to the causes we say we care about. It could add up to the biggest, most effective volunteer effort this country has ever seen. And we could accomplish things that, right now, we only dream about. Just five hours. Just 5 percent. It's not that much to give. But what we could get back is immeasurable. A public service of Independent Sector and the Ad Council.

Figure 1–4. Straight commercial. As you've read in this chapter, "Good copy serves a vital function." Certainly this is true of copywriters who donate their time and skill to write public service radio commercials such as this.

Five Final Points

Now that you have been pummeled by rules, warned against this, and told to do that, you might think back over what has been said. If you do, you'll find that the following are some of the principal conclusions:

1. **There is no easy road to copywriting ability.** Throughout the book we have made an effort to deglamorize copywriting. You were told that copywriting is not Hollywoodish; that as a copywriter you will not be a petted, pampered artist. You will be a businessperson in a business office. You'll be important—yes. You will not, however, have special prerogatives and working condi-

Figure 1–5. Industrial advertisement using long copy and full details. Such advertising is far different from the often frothy and superficial consumer advertising for such products as soaps, perfumes, cereals, and hair lotions. This copy is addressed to people who weigh every word before they make important buying decisions.

tions. If you think of yourself always as a businessperson, you'll be better off.

You're expected to know how to write, but you must remember that your writing is a tool of business, not a stepladder to literary prominence. If copywriting ability were easy to acquire, there'd be no need for this book, for advertising copy courses, for the slow apprentice system so often found in agencies and retail stores—nor would copywriters be paid so well. But copywriting is not easy to learn. It's an exacting craft which a very few learn easily and the great majority learn through trial and error, perseverance, and instruction. Some never learn it.

2. **Skill in one kind of copywriting does not automatically transfer to other types of copywriting.** Competent copywriters can usually write all kinds of copy. Agency copywriters, for example, because they handle diversified accounts, often attain proficiency in almost every type and style of copy. The fact remains, however, that a person who has done nothing but radio or television copy has learned techniques different from those of the copy person who has spent all the time on magazine or newspaper copy. The retail writer who began in department store copywriting and has remained in it is in a little world of her own which has its own problems.

Even within the same field, there are pronounced differences. In Chicago, for example, Carson, Pirie, Scott & Company, the widely known department store, develops the "Carson" copy approach. Copy and art treatment are distinctive enough to identify advertisements as "Carsons" advertisements, establishing the store's character and individuality unmistakably. The store's copy people, ever mindful of their great rival, Marshall Field & Company, strive constantly to be different from Field's.

The same thing is true of nearly all big cities—big stores through their copy and art treatment build up individuality. Thus a successful writer for one store may be so thoroughly indoctrinated into certain copy techniques that she must consciously adapt herself to the general approach used by another store if she changes jobs.

Then, look at mail-order and fashion copy. The first is stripped of nonsense. It's direct, detailed, and slugs the message home. The customer gets up from the floor groggy with facts. He knows just how to order. He probably even knows how many seams were put in that pair of overalls he's asked about. Fashion copy, on the other hand, is normally light, fluffy, and inclined to substitute atmosphere for facts. Perhaps each writer could take over the other's job. In a good many cases, however, it is doubtful that such a switchover could be made without considerable flexibility on the part of the copywriter.

As a last warning on the point that a certain adjustment is needed in order to switch from one kind of copy to another—think about the industrial magazine advertising writer. Consider the technical knowledge needed to write industrial advertisements. Think again, then, of your fashion writer, or your average writer of consumer copy. The airy, nonsensical touch of the fashion copywriter would be out of place in a hard-selling advertisement for steam boilers. Some writers can do both types of copy. Others never can.

3. **Copy research, like copywriting, has no final answer.** You will notice that this book treats copy testing as if it were capable of blowing up at any time. Copy testing and other forms of research *are* explosive. Some of the most violent advertising arguments are concerned with research methods.

If you pick up the idea that we don't espouse any one kind of copy testing, that we find some good and bad points in all the methods, that we think copy testing is very important, and that you should learn some of the methods—then the research section did its job.

Most of all, we hope that you will decide, after finishing the chapter, that you will always keep an open mind about copy testing, always looking for the good and bad points of each system.

4. **Education, work experience, and personality are important elements in copywriting success.** Although there are and have been successful copywriters with no more education than one might pick up from McGuffey's Fourth Grade Reader, education—especially college education—is an advantage to copywriters. Certain courses of study are more suited to a copywriting career than others, but this doesn't mean a copywriter can't profit from almost any course of study.

Although advertising, newswriting, and such courses are directly applicable to a copy career, a course in history, economic geography, or sociology might provide a background that could be very useful some day.

As for work experience, we depart from American tradition by suggesting that you try several jobs. Work experience is ideally composed of writing and selling, with an accent on diversity of experience. A sort of composite reporter-salesperson may have floated before your eyes as the ideal precopywriter. That's our ideal, too.

Quite a stress must be placed on the copywriter's personality. Of course, you can find some good copy people who shy from human contact. They're the exceptions. Unless you like people and share the usual enthusiasms, annoyances, and disappointments of most people, you are handicapped as a copywriter.

And, too, if you are overly sensitive to criticism of your work, you'll suffer as your fellow workers or bosses roughly and caustically criticize what you consider your choicest copy.

5. **Your conscience and good taste should make you an "honest" copywriter.** There have been so many high-sounding and painfully moral treatises turned out under the title of "Honesty in Advertising" that we've decided to be different. We assume that you have been well indoctrinated into the ethics of truth and honesty in advertising. Our approach is to point out that it's just plain silly to write untruthful copy.

   On one side, you have the law ready to pounce if you transgress. We hope very earnestly that the sections involving points about which the Federal Trade Commission is very sensitive will help you avoid trouble with that body. On the other side are the consumers of your products. Their buying power is an effective inducement to honesty. Sooner or later the cheat and fraud is discovered; and when that happens sales are lost.

   We will discuss the practical inducements to honest advertising. When you are dealing with the public—the very young and the very old, the shrewd and the feeble-minded, the very poor and the very rich—your own conscience, also, should dictate honesty. In your person-to-person contacts you wouldn't cheat a subnormal or a charity case out of one cent, yet, through their copy, some of your fellow copywriters can bilk thousands of people. It's a matter of extending your conscience beyond what you're writing and visualizing the undiscerning people who will buy your product because you tell them to. The saying "Let your conscience be your guide" can be most apropos in this instance—only be sure to put your conscience in order before you write copy.

As a closing note, remember that nowhere will we say, "This is the way and the only way to write copy." If you put any of the book's principles to work, remember that each copy job is just a little different from the one before it. Understand what we say and then make allowances and adjustments when you apply our ideas to your individual situation. Among the copywriter's greatest assets are flexibility and skill in adjusting to the needs of the individual copy assignment.

And remember: Keep smiling no matter what they do to your copy.

2

What Is Copy?

Depends on Who Is Speaking

If you can define copy *in one concise sentence, you'll have succeeded where most people fail. Usually, the definitions of the word simply reflect the standpoint of the persons offering the definitions. Consider, for example, the following:*

A critic: "Copy is composed of words that cause people to buy what they don't need."

A printer: "Copy is the word we use to describe the whole ad—printed message, artwork, headlines, etc."

A print advertisements writer: "Copy is the printed message whatever the medium in which it appears."

A television advertising writer: "Copy consists of the words (audio) that accompany the pictures in television commercials."

Go beyond these workers in the field (and the critic) and you will be given many more definitions for this seemingly simple word. There are those, for example, who give the classic definition of copy, "salesmanship in print."

Opposing the "salesmanship in print" adherents are those who say that advertising copy that does not present a product to the public for purchase and does not offer reasons why the reader or viewer should buy is not salesmanship but subtle persuasion and an impression builder.

Those who thus define copy say that the salesmanship-in-print definition is too narrow—that it reduces the advertising person to the role of merchandise peddler. They point to advertising's place in the total marketing process. Advertising properly used is, they assert, a force for mass consumer education and a tool for effecting social change. It is almost insulting to copywriters, they add, to assume that their only interest in writing copy is to sell something or somebody.

This latter group would probably accept one definition of advertising as any paid-for communication that stirs a person to think or to do something. Purchasing of a product may be just one result of such communication.

Despite the argument that swirls about the salesmanship-in-print definition, it hardly seems questionable that the overall objective of almost all advertising copy is to sell. Rarely is an advertisement found that does not have a sales motive somewhere behind its writing. True, as one looks at many advertisements, it is difficult to find any obvious sales message. Many advertisements, for example, that appear in print media or in broadcast media are written to build a feeling of goodwill, to strengthen public opinion, or to break down a possible negative public opinion. Such advertisements, often called "institutional advertisements," normally do not offer products or services for sale.

The copy, nevertheless, is selling copy just as surely as is product-selling copy. It is merely selling something different. If you are a salesperson and you invite a customer or a prospective customer to dinner, to play golf, or to see a ball game, you are engaged in a form of selling. Perhaps you aren't actually clinching your order—possibly you make no attempt to talk business—but you are selling your company or yourself, or both. The impression you create in the mind of your client is almost certain to have an important bearing upon the ultimate signing of the order.

So it is with advertising copy. In almost any type of advertisement you are asked to write, remember that you have something to sell to your readers. Otherwise, there would be little reason to spend thousands of dollars, or anything at all, for the space or time in which to deliver your message.

Much More than Salesmanship in Print

Can we, accordingly, agree that copy is merely salesmanship in print? Is that as far as the definition goes? No—it isn't half-defined—especially as far as you, the copywriter, are concerned.

Copy can be the voice of the advertiser, boasting about the product, shouting its merits in bald, unlovely terms, damning the competition, gaining attention through sheer weight of words and extravagant claims, making the most noise.

Or copy can be the voice of a friend—a trusted adviser offering help to the consumer in purchasing problems—clear, arresting, interesting, honest.

Copy can be the enthusiasm of salespeople—echoing their words, reflecting their pride in their products, opening doors for them, easing their jobs. It can be your contribution to the merchant who knows what he wants to say but doesn't know how to say it. It can be a primer for the dealer, the jobber, and the distributor—a means of preconditioning their selling. Copy can be an instrument of better living, easier living, happier living. Through copy that stimulates mass sales, the whole economy of a field of enterprise may be improved.

Newswriters and Advertising Writers View Copy Differently

To newspaper reporters, copy is simply the text of a story. This text is usually their sole responsibility. They needn't worry about headlines, subheads, typography, illustrations.

Advertising copywriters consider everything that appears in an advertisement as copy. When you are asked to prepare copy for an advertisement, you are expected to write everything required for the complete advertisement. If you are asked, "Is the copy ready?" it is expected that you have completed headline, subheads, body text, captions, blurbs, signatures, and even copyright notices. To you, copy means every word appearing in your finished advertisement, depending upon its format.

In an informal working session, however, sometimes "copy" will mean nothing more than the headline, main body text, and possibly a subhead.

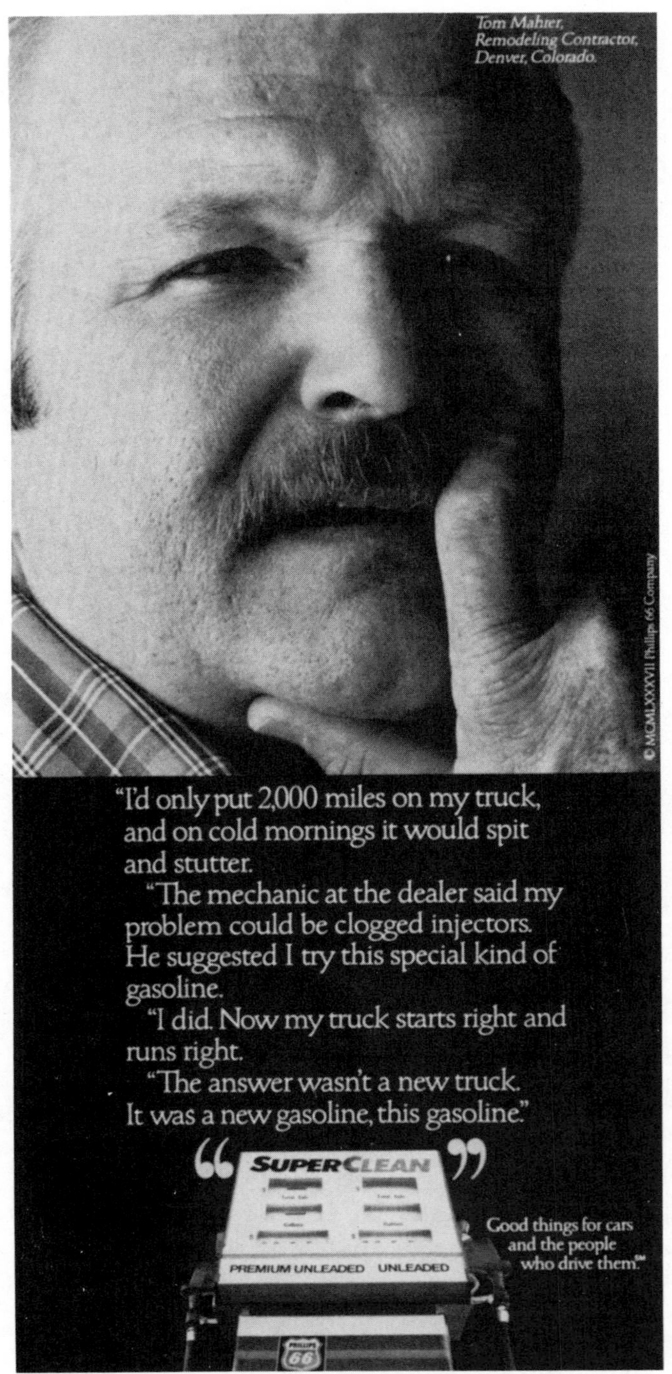

Figure 2–1. Use of reverse type. It is usually sensible to avoid heavy use of reverse type (white on black) because it cuts readership. In small-space advertisements, however, reverse type will make the ads stand out on the page. This advertisement uses reverse correctly: (a) there is not too much of it; (b) the type size is big enough for easy reading; and (c) spacing is generous between lines.

Copy's Elements

Occasionally you will find one advertisement that contains all the different elements of copy. This is rare. Normally, your advertisements will be made up of two or three of the common copy elements. There is certainly no rule of thumb by which you can predetermine exactly which elements you'll use and which you'll not need.

When preparing a campaign for a client or a prospective client, a copywriter may often need but two elements of the complete advertisement in order to convey the basic campaign idea or approach. These elements are the headline and the illustration.

A number of layouts may be prepared that show the client different headlines and illustrations. If the client approves the campaign idea, as demonstrated in these layouts, the copywriter will then supply the body copy for the advertisements, plus the subheads, or captions, or other elements needed to complete the advertisements.

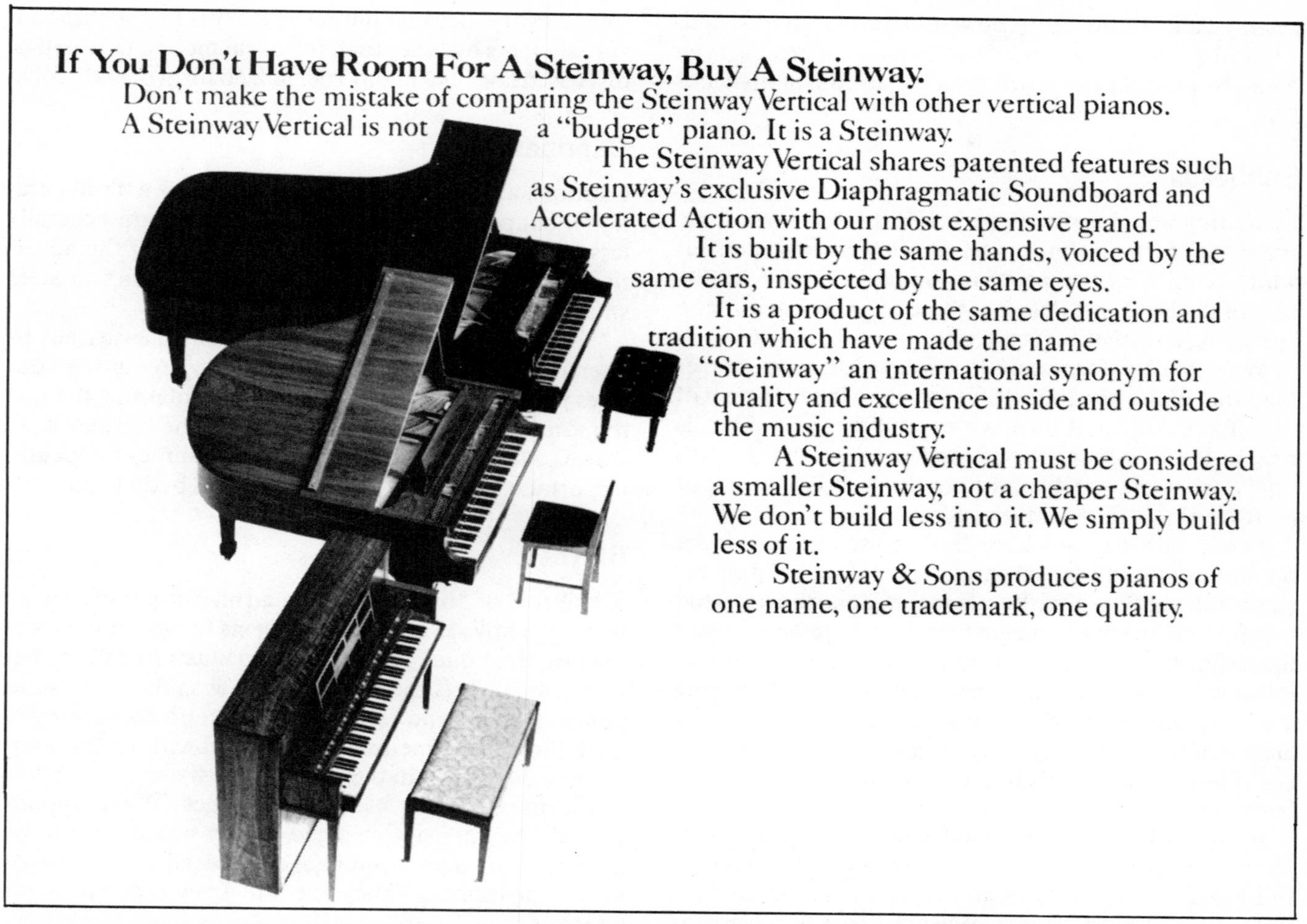

If You Don't Have Room For A Steinway, Buy A Steinway.

Don't make the mistake of comparing the Steinway Vertical with other vertical pianos. A Steinway Vertical is not a "budget" piano. It is a Steinway.

The Steinway Vertical shares patented features such as Steinway's exclusive Diaphragmatic Soundboard and Accelerated Action with our most expensive grand.

It is built by the same hands, voiced by the same ears, inspected by the same eyes.

It is a product of the same dedication and tradition which have made the name "Steinway" an international synonym for quality and excellence inside and outside the music industry.

A Steinway Vertical must be considered a smaller Steinway, not a cheaper Steinway. We don't build less into it. We simply build less of it.

Steinway & Sons produces pianos of one name, one trademark, one quality.

Figure 2–2. Catalog copy for a prestige product. Starting off with a challenging headline, this advertisement in clear language informs prospects of the quality that marks all products manufactured by the advertiser.

Main Headline

Any reader of news stories or magazine material is aware of headlines that use larger type than any of the material underneath. Often the reader sees these headlines tied up with illustrations, the combination attracting maximum reader attention. In advertisements, you will use headlines in the same manner as the story editors do.

Normally, the headline of an advertisement will present a selling idea or will otherwise serve to intrigue the prospective purchaser into a further and more exhaustive reading of your advertisement.

Headlines can and do fall into many varied patterns. It is not necessary, for instance, for a headline to be big. Some headlines—notably in newspaper advertisements—are set in very large type and in general resemble regular newspaper headlines. Others, however, may be quite small in type size and qualify as headlines by their leading position in the advertisement.

Still another common form of headline is the blurb or balloon, in which a character is supposed to be speaking. Headlines do not even have to say anything. A company name, for instance, might be used as a headline. So might a familiar brand or signature. But practically all advertisements have headlines of one sort or another, and their primary function is to attract immediately the attention of the reader.

Overline

In some instances, you'll see an advertisement that is topped by a combination that looks like the following:

> Cut heating costs this winter.
>
> *(This is an overline. It is usually set in smaller type than the main headline that follows.)*
>
> A new MIDAS furnace control can slash fuel bills by 40%.
>
> *(This is the main headline.)*

As you see, the overline, often called a "lead-in," is placed over the main headline and is almost always in smaller type. In the foregoing example the copywriter may have found that putting the two lines together would have forced the use of smaller type in order to fit the headline in the space. In smaller type the attention-getting value of the headline would have been lessened. Thus, the first line was made an overline. Then big type could be used for the words required for the main headline.

Subheads

In writing an advertisement you will often have some important facts you wish to telegraph to your reader, but which require more space than you care to use in the display of the headline. Possibly, these facts are not quite so appealing as attention attracters.

When such information is displayed in type smaller than that of the headline, yet larger than the body text of the advertisement, it is known as a "subhead." Subheads may be three or four lines of copy underneath the headline, or they may be display lines throughout the text or in other places in the advertisement.

In our nation of quick readers who so often are more picture minded than print minded, the subhead serves an important function. It tells the readers quickly what is coming in the copy and enables them to judge whether they want to continue. In most advertisements, nothing is lost if the subhead causes readers to skip the following copy. Usually, the headline and illustration, plus the signature of the advertiser, have already enabled the readers to judge whether it's in their self-interest to read the body copy.

A subhead, on the other hand, will normally lure readers into the following copy. In the case of very long copy, it will break up type masses and make the advertisement look easier to read. This is especially true of advertisements that do not sell products but instead talk about the company or its point of view. These institutional advertisements, or "corporate" advertisements, usually obtain low readership. Well-written subheads can help make the advertisements look more interesting.

In some places, particularly in department store and other retail advertising operations, subheads are also known as "captions." This is not usually the case, however. Caption normally has a meaning all its own, as will be discussed shortly.

Body Copy

Sometimes "body copy" is called "body text." Either way, it is the main message of your advertisement. Your selling is done in the body copy. Here is where you reason with the reader and show how persuasive you can be. Your body copy, if you structure your writing properly, is an extension of the idea conveyed initially by the headline and the illustration.

You have probably heard salespeople talk about "getting a foot in the door." Well, your headline is your foot. The body copy is the follow-through on that foot. Some advertisements actually have no body copy, from a technical standpoint. That is, they contain no major unit of type. Advertisements built around a comic-strip style, picture-and-caption advertisements, and others fall into this category. Because the entire story is told in these advertisements by other than the usual means, they will be discussed later as a highly specialized form of body copy.

Captions

Captions are the small units of type used with illustrations, coupons, and special offers. They are generally less important to the main selling points of the advertisement than body copy and are usually set in type sizes smaller than the body text.

Now and then you will want to plan an entire advertisement in picture-and-caption style, presenting your sales points by illustrating them and explaining them at the same time, much the way a magazine handles news stories. Here, of course, the caption assumes far greater importance and must be considered as body text.

Blurbs

A "blurb," or "balloon," is the advertising profession's term for copy set up so that it seems to be coming from the mouth of one of the characters illustrated in the advertisement. It is most often used, as is the caption, to punch across some secondary feature in the story you are telling, but sometimes it too can constitute the complete body text, as in the comic-strip style.

Blurbs are often used as headlines. When so employed, they are not changed in any way except to be displayed in larger-sized type and placed at the head of the advertisement. They are still known as blurbs or balloons.

Boxes and Panels

You'll hear copywriters and artists referring regularly to "boxes" or "panels." These, as their names imply, are simply captions which obtain greater attention value by being placed in special display positions. A "box" is a caption around which a rule has been lined, singling it out from other copy.

A "panel" is a solid rectangle of black or color, in the center of which is the caption, either in white or "reverse" type, or centered in white space. Boxes and panels are usually used in advertisements using such features as coupons, special offers, and contest rules. These will often be set apart from the rest of the advertisement by means of such devices. Boxes should be used sparingly.

Slogans, Logotypes, and Signatures

At times you may write copy for a company that insists on the use of its slogan in every advertisement. Too, almost all advertisers logically demand that their company name be displayed in its familiar form. This display of the company name, seal, or trademark is called a "logotype" and is a common part of most advertisements. The term is often abbreviated in advertising jargon to "logo," "sig," or "sig cut." Copyright notices, too, are often required for legal reasons and must be included in all copy prepared for such advertisers.

An important point to remember is that *everything* that appears in print in an advertisement must appear on the copy sheets that the copywriter prepares. These sheets serve as a guide to the artists and typographers and other production people who will be working on the advertisement after the copywriter has finished. If the copywriter leaves some element out of the copy, the whole advertisement may be held up later and a publication date missed because the advertisement may need to be reset.

One way to make sure of including the various elements is to set up the copy neatly and logically on the copy sheet by labeling the different elements on the side. Many copywriters are sloppy in their execution. An example of an ideal copy sheet is shown in Figure 2–3. If all copy sheets were handled in this manner, there would be fewer mistakes in production.

Headline: Small boys, delivery men, plumbers, and husbands with dirty shoes—they're murder on floors.

Subhead: Protect the finish with Enduro Wax.

Copy: When you apply Enduro, you'll see gleaming floors immediately. And over the *long* run you'll have a scuff-proof finish that lasts and lasts. In fact, the finish is so hard that you'll probably never again need to pay out money for floor refinishing expenses.

Floor-wrecking crews of small boys? Bring 'em on.

Illustration: Pictures and captions.

1. Small boys jumping up and down on kitchen floor.
2. Delivery man dropping crate.
3. Plumber working at sink.
4. Husband coming in from the rain.

(Somewhere in layout is a can of Enduro Paste Wax prominently displayed.)

Figure 2–3. This shows the way to set up copy for easy reading.

Requirements for Broadcast Copy

The requirements for broadcast copy in radio and television will be discussed in more detail later. The same attention to form must be observed in writing radio commercials and in preparing material for television. In the latter, the writers must think in two dimensions: sight and sound. They encounter an entirely different vocabulary from that used for print. Because, in many advertising agencies, copywriters create broadcast commercials as well as print advertisements, they must be equally familiar with the terminology and form required in this kind of advertising.

Later, as you will see, much of what has been said in this chapter will apply to other forms of print such as leaflets, folders, and catalogs.

Copywriters: Good Writers or Hacks?

Many copywriters are competent, but routine, writers. Still others are first-rate writers by any standard. Copywriting, if done well, is one of the most exacting forms of writing. It requires not only a command of the language but also an ability to coordinate persuasive, colorful writing with music, photography, artwork, printing, engraving, vocal intonations, and acting.

All this skill and coordination takes place within stern limitations of time or space. Copywriting thus requires the writer to be precise, clear, and persuasive in relatively few words compared to most other forms of writing (always excepting poetry, of course). Furthermore, the good copywriter brings to the craft a knowledge of psychology, salesmanship, merchandising, marketing, and purchasing habits.

Like any writer you try to make each piece of copy as perfect as possible, but "perfect" often means that what you have written has produced sales rather than memorable prose. Many of the best advertisements will never win writing awards, but they'll make the cash registers sing.

In most copy you strive for sales, not literary recognition. Instead of concentrating on literary excellence, you're thinking of the copy's suitability to the media used, the market for the product, and selling points. Often "fine" writing would be incompatible with a nuts-and-bolts type of product, or service, being sold.

Yet, there are times when your copy can be almost poetic in its execution; other times it will be prosaic and businesslike. The following examples were aimed carefully at their audiences. Each is executed well, but note the total difference in writing style.

> Reclaim Camelot, and set it towering over a Hampton's beach. Or relocate Rome's Castel Sant' Angelo, from the Seven Hills it has guarded for 1800 years, to the sands of Fire Island or Malibu. Then, the fate of a sandcastle being what it is, watch it crumble.
>
> *"Safe upon the solid rock the ugly houses stand: Come and see my shining palace built upon the sand!"*
>
> Like Edna St. Vincent Millay, you may have noticed that reality is not always a preferred alternative. Certainly not when you are sitting on a beach, gazing across the water, thinking . . .
>
> About the office? Car repairs? What's for dinner? No. If you have read and pondered well the lessons of SANDCASTLES, you will be on the verge of a magical endeavor of will and imagination, a ceremony of inevitability.

In the following is another example of the more lyrical form of copywriting, writing that reaches for expression rather than a recital of product facts. The product is a necklace.

> Intricate sculpture that dazzles like the night sky. Ablaze with fiery crystals. Accented by crystal teardrops that shatter the light into a thousand flames dancing to the beat of your every movement. Here at last is a necklace designed to put you in the spotlight.

Caples on copy.

On headlines:

"Headlines make ads work. The best headlines appeal to people's self interest, or give news. Long headlines that say something outpull short headlines that say nothing. Remember that every headline has one job. It must stop your prospects with a believable promise. All messages have headlines. In TV, it's the start of the commercial. In radio, the first few words. In a letter, the first paragraph. Even a telephone call has a headline. Come up with a good headline, and you're almost sure to have a good ad. But even the greatest writer can't save an ad with a poor headline. You can't make an ad pull unless people stop to read your brilliant copy."

On word power:

"Simple words are powerful words. Even the best educated people don't resent simple words. But they're the only words many people understand. Write to your barber or mechanic or elevator operator. Remember, too, that every word is important. Sometimes you can change a word and increase the pulling power of the ad. Once I changed the word 'repair' to 'fix' and the ad pulled 20% more!"

On first drafts:

"Overwriting is the key. If you need a thousand words, write two thousand. Trim vigorously. Fact-packed messages carry a wallop. Don't be afraid of long copy. If your ad is interesting, people will be hungry for all the copy you can give them. If the ad is dull, short copy won't save it."

On directness:

"Get to the point. Direct writing outpulls cute writing by a big margin. Don't save your best benefit until last. Start with it, so you'll have a better chance of keeping your reader with you. Don't stop by just telling people the benefits your product offers. Tell them what they'll miss if they don't buy it. If you have an important point to make, make it three times: in the beginning, the middle, the end. At the end, ask for action. If people are interested enough to read your ad, they want to know what to do. Tell them."

On humor:

"Avoid it. What's funny to one person isn't to millions of others. Copy should sell, not just entertain. Remember there's not one funny line in the two most influential books ever written: the Bible and the Sears catalog."

On changing times:

"Times change. People don't. Words like 'free' and 'new' are as potent as ever. Ads that appeal to a reader's self interest still work. People may disagree about what self improvement is important, but we all want to improve ourselves. Ads that offer news still work. The subjects that are news change, but the human curiosity to know what's new doesn't. These appeals worked fifty years ago. They work today. They'll work fifty years hence."

Figure 2–4. In this excerpted material from a 1978 *Wall Street Journal* advertisement is contained basic advice by John Caples, famous copywriter. Every advertising writer—beginner or veteran—can profit from following these maxims. Some might feel differently about the use of humor, but there are many who feel as Mr. Caples does in this respect.

Sultry, sophisticated. And very, very rich.

Contrast the following copy.

Balances heaviest, bulkiest loads with incredible ease! Can't tip or spill! Essential for every gardener or homeowner. Gets more done in less time with much less effort. Precise balance of this cart carries the load—NOT YOUR ARMS! So you avoid the back strain and heart-straining effort of an ordinary wheelbarrow or those small-wheeled inadequate carts. The Garden Way Cart rolls so easily, it practically seems self-propelled, even with very heavy loads . . . like manure. And its extra heavy duty construc-

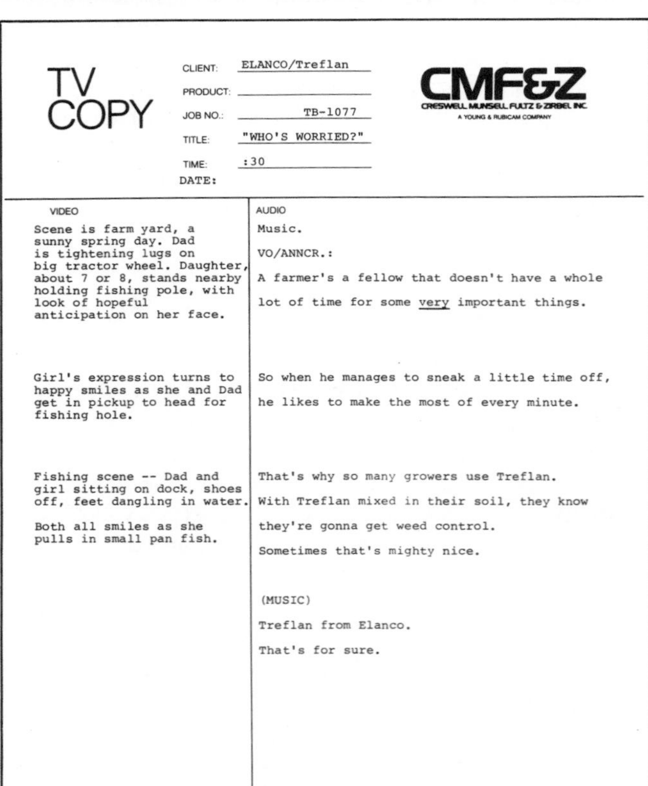

TV COPY

CLIENT: ELANCO/Treflan
PRODUCT:
JOB NO.: TB-1077
TITLE: "WHO'S WORRIED?"
TIME: :30
DATE:

CMF&Z
CRESWELL, MUNSELL, FULTZ & ZIRBEL INC.
A YOUNG & RUBICAM COMPANY

VIDEO	AUDIO
Scene is farm yard, a sunny spring day. Dad is tightening lugs on big tractor wheel. Daughter, about 7 or 8, stands nearby holding fishing pole, with look of hopeful anticipation on her face.	Music. VO/ANNCR.: A farmer's a fellow that doesn't have a whole lot of time for some very important things.
Girl's expression turns to happy smiles as she and Dad get in pickup to head for fishing hole.	So when he manages to sneak a little time off, he likes to make the most of every minute.
Fishing scene -- Dad and girl sitting on dock, shoes off, feet dangling in water. Both all smiles as she pulls in small pan fish.	That's why so many growers use Treflan. With Treflan mixed in their soil, they know they're gonna get weed control. Sometimes that's mighty nice. (MUSIC) Treflan from Elanco. That's for sure.

Figure 2–5. Television commercial aimed at farmers. In creating such a commercial the copywriter and the artist work as a team because the video is just as important as the audio, and sometimes more important.

CURIOSITY CAN'T BE TAUGHT. BUT IT CAN BE SPARKED.

There is, as every teacher and parent inevitably discovers, a curious truth to curiosity: It often defies their best efforts to inspire it. At the same time, many of these same teachers and parents can tell of magic moments when, prodded by new facts or fresh experiences, youngsters suddenly awaken. Aroused, they become eager to know all we can teach.

That's why, since 1976, we've funded and distributed films about economics, science and mathematics. Their purpose is to encourage learning. And to show where learning can lead.

Already, millions of students have seen "American Enterprise" and "The Search for Solutions." Very soon, many will be seeing "The Challenge of the Unknown."

If you'd like to find out more about these films, write to: Phillips Petroleum Company Phillips Educational Films Bartlesville, Oklahoma 74004.

Of course, we can't promise to ignite the curiosity of every young person who sees these films. But we can hope to set off sparks. And who knows how brightly they might burn.

Phillips Petroleum Company

Figure 2–6. Institutional advertisement that proves that there is a place for first-rate, thoughtful writing in advertising. This advertisement is one of a series that performs a public service.

> tion makes it easy to carry up to 400 lbs. Many owners actually claim that their cart feels LIGHTER when fully loaded!

The first two are ethereal and interpretive. They are concerned with mood instead of fact. The third is informative and uses common sense in its approach. Would you say the writing in the first advertisements was better than that in the third?

Ask that question of laypeople and they'd probably answer "Yes." They would be impressed by the color of the words, the sensory appeal, the emotion. Advertising people, however, would say "To each his own." They would mean that the third advertisement was just right for the product and the market. To attempt the approach of the first advertisements in the third advertisement could be detrimental to sales.

It is possible that the copywriter who wrote the third advertisement devoted more time and thought to the copy than did the copywriter who turned out the first. The writing you do must be tailored with precise craftsmanship to fit the job in hand.

Judgment and versatility are other attributes that stand high among the requirements of good copywriting. As an agency copywriter, especially, you will be expected not only to pace your copy correctly, but to write copy which differs in approach and feeling as radically as do the foregoing three examples.

It should be pointed out that some agencies and many retail establishments and mail-order houses consider the neophyte copywriter little more than a space filler. In other words, you may start to work for a company whose policy will not permit you to do much creative thinking on your own for some time.

During the preliminary phases of your training, you may be asked simply to write the body text, captions, or other parts of advertisements for which the major planning has already been done by others. No attempt is made here to determine whether this system is better or worse than that which calls for the beginner to jump into the business of thinking out entire advertisements right from the start.

Both have produced, and are still producing, successful copywriters. It is somewhat a question of temperament. Some copywriters like to have their assignments blueprinted for them—others find their satisfaction in being their own copy architects.

Creative Satisfaction: Just One of Many Rewards

To spin something out of your mind, as in creative work, is exciting. Then, to see the idea on the television screen, to hear it on radio, or to see it in a four-color magazine spread is deeply satisfying. That excitement and pleasure never disappear completely, and shouldn't. But as a copywriter you're concerned with something more than a personal satisfaction.

There is the effect of what you've created on that big market reached by the media, on the sales curves of your clients, on their salespeople, on the retail stores that sell their goods. If you think beyond those words that you've committed to paper, you'll see that there's another creative thrill to be obtained as an advertising copywriter, one that matches or even outdoes that of many writing artists whose work touches very few people.

One evidence of the right of advertising copywriting to be considered a legitimate example of writing art is in the number of writers of contemporary literature who began as advertising copywriters—especially as advertising agency copywriters. The exactness, the economy of phrasing, the requirement for subtle shadings in word meanings have given many copywriters the precise training they needed for their subsequent literary efforts.

It is not surprising then to discover how many well-known writers spent their early years behind a copywriter's desk. A few of these are Richard Powell, Cameron Hawley, Sinclair Lewis, and Sherwood Anderson. Many successful writers have, like Richard Powell and Cameron Hawley, produced best-selling novels or plays while they were still employed in advertising. These accomplishments are beyond most copywriters who find all the creative challenge they need in turning out good copy day after day. It is not recommended that persons enter the copywriting field as a preparation for producing literary works. It is true, nonetheless, that numerous literary people have found such preparation valuable.

One agency head had this to say about copywriters who write outside of their copywriting jobs:

> Let 'em moonlight as poets, novelists, or free-lance article writers. Just so they don't drain themselves so much creatively that they have nothing left for their copy jobs, I'm all for it. It's sort of a two-way street. Working in copy can make someone a better poet or novelist. And doing literary stuff can make copywriters better ad writers. All I ask is that they don't do these literary productions on company time.

Most copywriters find all the creative satisfaction and challenges they seek in the daily writing of good advertising. They don't *need* to do outside writing in order to satisfy their creative urges. They are fulfilled on the job and that, they will tell you, is why they like their work so much.

If, on the other hand, your training in copywriting leads to other forms of writing, count this as an extra reward—a reward, as was said, that has been enjoyed by many copywriters.

3

YOU LEARN QUICKLY THAT ADVERTISING IS JUST ONE PART OF THE MARKETING MIX

Foster Coleman, a veteran account executive for the Morrow agency, put his hand in a friendly fashion on the shoulder of Ira Mulvey, the agency's newest copywriter. "Look, Ira. Don't be upset but I have to say that your copy shows a certain lack of marketing know-how.

"You write well but around here we don't think copy's going to do the job unless it stems from an ever-present awareness of marketing—things such as pricing, sales aims, distribution channels, packaging, demographics.

"Try again, but this time think of marketing objectives, not just sparkling words."

Although this book deals almost entirely with copywriting and the copywriter's duties, you should understand some of the marketing questions that must be investigated and answered before your advertising copy can be fully effective. You must know the basic sales strategy because it establishes a definite set of boundaries into which you fit your writing and the planning of your writing.

You may never have much to do with the establishment of the basic sales strategy unless you happen to work on a new product promotion; or possibly the product is one that needs a complete promotional overhauling. In either case, you might sit in on meetings during which the sales setup of the company is established or reorganized. Usually, however, you will do most of your creative work for organizations which have been operating profitably and whose sales strategy is well established.

Part of your job will consist of studying this policy. You will need to understand why it was established. Such understanding will be accomplished through a thorough examination of what might be termed "the Three P's": the product, the prospects, and the purchases. To write effective copy, you must know your three P's well. Whatever product you're writing about, consider it in the light of the following analysis.

P Is for Product

Does the Product Fill a Definite Need or Desire?

An automatic washing machine, for example, fills a definite need. Several, in fact. It enables a person to wash the family's clothes cleaner, with less effort, in less time, and with less wear and tear on the clothes. If a person had been taking the laundry out prior to the purchase of the automatic washing machine, such a machine will also save money. Thus, an automatic home laundry can fill five basic needs.

Perfume or shaving lotion, on the other hand, does not fill a specific need. It does fill a very strong natural desire felt by many people to be attractive. People use these products to fulfill a wish—to feel better groomed.

Then there are products that fall in between. For some, they fill a need. For others, they fill a desire. Such a product is the CB radio that caused a buying wave in the mid-70s. Only a relative few in the population really *needed* CB radios, but millions *desired* them and this latter group formed a vast market. Other products that fall into this in-between status include snowmobiles and ten-speed bicycles. They are needed by few and desired by many.

Almost all successful products fill either a need or a desire. Unfortunately, however, a continuous flow of products on the market fills neither need nor desire. These are usually spawned by "mad" inventors or by others whose imagination is spent on fashioning the inventions—not in figuring out a real use for their creations.

Without seeking competent advice from persons experienced in marketing, they blindly rush into production "before someone steals the idea." Their reasoning, if it may be called that, seems to run something like this: "There's no product on the market like it! Therefore, it's bound to be a best seller!" They fail to see the reason there is no similar product—*because there's no real need or desire for one.* Typical of this type of "predoomed" product would be a left-handed shoehorn. Such a gadget might amuse you, but you wouldn't buy it. The marketer of such a product would soon run out of prospects because it fills neither need nor desire.

Just the same, there is—and undoubtedly will continue to be—a constant flow of novelty products which manufacturers introduce with the full knowledge that—because they do not fill any lasting need or desire—the products can only hope to enjoy flash sales over a short period and then almost die out.

The objective is to whip up a desire for the product through its novelty. If it catches on, sales skyrocket; but they usually plummet a short time later as illustrated by "soapless" soap bubbles, hula hoops, and pet rocks which piled up sales for a brief time and then were seen no more.

Such products come and go. They're freaks and not to be likened to the normal, stable products that are your primary concern as an advertising person. Once it has been established that your product fills a valid need or desire, the next thing you should want to know is:

Are Most Users Satisfied with the Product?

It is a fundamental of marketing that a product must live up to the buyers' expectations if it is to be a successful repeat-sale item.

Living up to expectations is probably even more important in the case of low-cost, nondurable products. Bread, hair oil, soft drinks can't attain sustained success, no matter how sound your advertising may be, unless a good percentage of buyers constantly and quickly repeat their purchases when the initial purchase needs replacement.

In the case of the printing press, it is important to the continued success of the manufacturer that the product live up to its claims. Repeat orders for $300,000 printing presses, however, would come at very long intervals. Few printers would make such a huge investment without first finding out from companies already owning similar presses whether they were satisfactory—thus the buyer of such an item would be satisfied in advance of purchase that the product was all right.

Regardless of the nature of a product, then, it must represent honest value if it is to obtain lasting success. Next, you will want to know:

Does the Product Possess Any Exclusive Features of Benefit to the User?

The answer to this question is important. When your product does possess exclusive advantages over competition, it often will give you an advantage over the copywriters working on the competitive accounts—a knockout punch they don't have.

Crest toothpaste, with fluoride, is an example. It was a success from the start, vaulting into first place almost overnight. Polaroid's instant camera offered another exclusive benefit that made the copywriter's job easy. The remote control device introduced on Zenith television sets is still another product exclusive to which the public responded. The lesson? Give people a *meaningful* exclusive benefit and they'll buy.

Other "firsts" or product exclusives were the Ford convertible hardtop, Sanka coffee (caffeine removed), and the original mentholated cigarettes. Speaking of mentholated cigarettes, although you may not recall when they were first marketed, you certainly have been aware of the results of imitation. The first mentholated cigarettes were followed by a parade of new cigarettes featuring everything from dry ice to crème de menthe.

Many products have exclusive features. Unless, however, their advantages are rather obvious to prospective buyers, these exclusives may be difficult to write about and thus far less effective as selling tools. That a product differs from competitive ones does not mean, of course, that the difference necessarily will sell more merchandise—the difference must be a definite plus value of demonstrable importance to the buyer.

Be careful that you are not lulled into a pleasant dream by the glowing description you may get of a product from its maker. Human nature being what it is, almost any advertiser may be overly enthusiastic about what is offered, endowing the product with advantages that actually don't exist outside the imagination. Only your own close study of the product, independent laboratory tests, or large-scale sampling studies can give an unbiased comparison between two or more similar products, insofar as possible consumer reaction and your copy approach are concerned.

Such laboratory tests or samplings, though they may be fairly expensive, often prove to be excellent investments. If, as a result, the product lives up to expectations, buyers will respond more readily to copy backed by impartial comparisons than to copy filled with unproved claims.

For instance, the car that delivers greater *proved* mileage; the washing machine that has *proved* it uses less hot water; or the tire that has *proved* it lasts longer gives the advertisers powerful material for advertisements.

Is the Product or Service "Positioned" Correctly?

Positioning a product simply means that you and others concerned with product promotion examine that product to determine just what it is you are offering, and to what kind of people, and how you want these people to think of the product. Out of these three findings is born much of your creative strategy.

Few products are intended for everyone. In today's market segmentation, there are specific products for specific groups and subgroups. Advertising is directed to them. The same is true of services. A bank, for example, might position itself as the "young family" bank that aims at those who are buying homes and furnishings, taking loans, and are generally on the way up—and going into debt to get there.

In the same city, another bank is positioned as a "solid, conservative, business-oriented" institution. Its advertising and media choices (no radio stations featuring rock, country western, or bluegrass) zero in on the older, more affluent group. The stress in advertising is on the bank's understanding of the needs of business people and investors.

So it goes. First, you determine what your product really is and what needs it will satisfy. After this, you position it in relation to your prospects. At that point, you can more surely find an advertising strategy that will convince the prospects that the product is suited to their needs and that it will answer their problems better than competing products.

This separation from the competition is vital. Thus you might well call "positioning" a search for the product's proper identity in the marketplace.

One of the problems in positioning is that it is becoming increasingly difficult to change a consumer's mind about ideas that have been drilled into that consumer over a long period. Thus, when you position your product as better than the outstanding leader in the field, whether the leader is in computers, airlines, or rental cars, the consumer resists your positioning of superiority.

Accordingly, your copy should not be obvious in trying to change the consumer's mind but should relate your client's position to that of the leader without making a frontal assault on the leader. Disbelief follows such an attack if the leader has firmly implanted a reputation for unquestioned excellence in the field.

P Is for Prospects

When you have examined the foregoing product considerations, you will have explored only one area of the precopy approach. Now that you have thought about the product, what about the people you hope will buy your goods instead of your competitor's? You must know these people equally well.

In many instances, you will know clearly who your best prospects are. In many others, what you may consider obvious may be wrong. You might think that men would be your best prospects for men's shirts. You may find that they are not. To your surprise you may find that so many wives shop for their husbands that women buy more men's shirts than men do.

Never ride a wild conclusion when determining who are your best prospects. Get the facts—from actual sales studies. Find out:

Are Your Best Prospects Men or Women?

For maximum effectiveness, your copy must be aimed at your best prospects—not at just anyone. Certain copy approaches appeal especially to men, others to women. When you write to women, for example, your copy should be consistently directed only to women if it is going to be fully effective. If, as with cigarettes, both sexes are large buyers, your copy will be written to appeal to both.

When you're communicating with women, for example, your knowledge of certain feminine characteristics is helpful. Women pay attention to small details, tend to personalize more than men, and seem to have a more sharply developed sensory feeling when they are shopping. They buy, you might say, with their senses. This is apparent in their sensitivity to irritating noises in machinery. "Noiselessness" sells them.

As for male-directed copy, the writer must recognize the changing role of the man, largely due to the fact that 50 percent of women are now in the working force. Males have become more domestic. In U.S. households, men are taking on many of the responsibilities and interests once almost entirely the province of women.

Men are doing much of the family shopping, cooking, dishwashing, laundry work, vacuuming, and taking care of the children. In the past, copy people have usually written copy for most household products with the 18–35-year-old feminine market wholly in mind. Now such copy must reflect the more important role of the man in the selection of household goods and in the running of a household. Those caricatures of the bungling husband are less and less pertinent.

To sum up: Decide whether your product will appeal to men, women, or to both men and women. Having determined this, key your writing to fit the group.

Are They Young, Middle-aged, or Old?

And why is this knowledge of value? Because, as people grow older—as they proceed from grade school, to high school, to college, to business, to marriage, to family, to middle age, and possibly on to grandparenthood—both their needs and desires for products change. (Children, certainly, are your best potential customers for bubble gum. Children are your worst prospects for automobiles—the law and the family budget see to that.)

Young married couples buy the largest percentage of baby necessities, but they put up strong resistance to the cemetery-lot salesperson. People over 35 years of age are fine prospects for home improvement products but would laugh if you tried to sell them boxing gloves or popsicles. So birthdays are important—not only to the people themselves but also to the copywriters who can make money out of birthdays if they key their copy to the age.

Because of our aging population, with growing and significant numbers in the 65-and-older grouping, marketers and copywriters are taking a fresh look at what this market buys and how advertising should be written to them.

When you read about men and women as prospects, you learned that men are assuming a changing role in the household. Likewise, the "geriatric set," as it is somewhat condescendingly termed, has changed, too. Older people are in better health than in the past and lead longer, more vigorous lives. When you write advertising addressed to this group, you must recognize this change from the one-time sedentary retiree to the older person of today who, in many cases, plays tennis, cycles, skis, takes luxury vacation trips and, generally, defies the stereotype of those who have reached the so-called golden years.

While you may continue to sell these people dentures and tonics for "tired blood," you'll also sell them a host of products that would at one time have seemed out of place for this market. It's a market that has developed political power, buying power, and a group awareness. Unless you wish to alienate the market, you no longer write as if a 65-year-old's idea of the full life is to occupy a rocker on the front porch and watch the cars go by.

Are Your Best Prospects Rich, Poor, or Average?

Who, would you say, would be your best prospects if you were writing an advertisement for fur coats—women of wealth, women of average means, or working women? The answer to that question would depend on what kind of fur coats you were writing about! You'd know that Park Avenue or Gold Coast women would be your best bets for ermine evening wraps. You'd know, too, that the Park Avenue prospect would shudder at the low-priced, dyed-rabbit coat that a store clerk would go without lunches to buy. Sex, age, and income thus are important factors in the movement of many types of merchandise.

One warning: Income level isn't a sure guide to what people will buy. Education and taste must be considered. A long-haul truck driver and many skilled blue-collar workers (such as machinists, tool and die makers, pipefitters) make handsome annual incomes—more than many college teachers and other better-educated white-collar workers. This superior income, however, doesn't necessarily mean that the blue-collar worker will buy all the same goods and services as the white-collar workers, nor will the blue-collar worker respond to the same language and appeals. Once more, the copywriter is forced to study market characteristics carefully to gauge the proper writing approach.

Copywriters, and everyone else in marketing, will often be hazy when asked to define what is meant by such terms as rich, poor, and average. If you *are* hazy, then your copy may reflect your ignorance of the buying potential and expectations of the prospects to whom your copy is directed.

It is not easy, however, to obtain clear-cut explanations of the income classes because they shift constantly, especially in times of financial stress. Government sources provide the income levels of each income group. Because any figures provided here might change markedly by the time the book is published, specific figures are not presented. As a copywriter you can obtain these figures. In place of them, here are general observations that are pertinent.

- Those persons described as *affluent to rich* usually make up about 10 percent of the nation's households. Persons in this group tend to be middle-aged, or older.
- In the middle-income group are about 70 percent of the households. This group takes in a wide range of incomes from the lower middle-income to the upper middle-income persons. At the upper level of the middle-income group, individuals are likely to be middle-aged. At the lower end of the group, individuals are younger.
- The *poor to poverty* level includes about 20 percent of U.S. households and, in general, individuals are older. This group has a substantial number of the retired, the out-of-work, and elderly women living alone.

Where Do Most of Your Prospects Live?

If your product is burglary insurance, your best prospects would be among city dwellers, because statistics show that a huge percentage of burglaries occur in cities. Small-town people, on the other hand, would probably be more interested in your copy story on home canning equipment than would urbanites. Farm families, logically, are your audience if you're writing about agricultural equipment.

Again, you may say, "But all those things are obvious." You're right. Throughout this entire chapter you have been given examples that would be obvious to any thinking person. Why? Because when you and the next person and the next person write copy, you tend to forget what was once so obvious to you. You forget the simple truths—the obvious thinking that makes your copy sell. You get so wrapped up in technique and the ultra refinements of the copywriter's art that you forget these obvious truths and facts that sell merchandise.

This section, accordingly, has not endeavored to be subtle. You have been told, "When writing to women, then write exclusively to women." "When writing about a home canning product, then write primarily to small town or country dwellers." If you learn these obvious stratagems early in your copy career—and remember them—you'll be a better copywriter.

To show how the obvious can be overlooked, wouldn't you think that it would be a waste of money for an advertiser to take large space in California newspapers to warn motorists to "Get Set Now for Winter's Sub-Zero Blasts!"? But one major advertiser did just that. The illustration showed Old Man Winter blowing an icy breath. It failed, however, to chill the sun-tanned spines of Californians.

The copy pushed antifreeze, tire chains, high-powered heaters, and other arctic equipment—all of which the average Californian has as much use for as for Florida oranges—unless he plans to spend the entire winter skiing in the Sierras.

Remember where your prospect lives. Location has a direct bearing on lifestyle and often affects wants or needs.

What Are Your Prospects' Tastes—in Reading, in TV, in Radio?

If you have been able to determine the sex, age, income, and habitat of your prospects, you have covered some of the important points of their private lives. You will still want to know something about their preferences in reading and in TV and radio. What kinds of newspapers and magazines do they usually read? Do they read the *New York Times, Harper's, Fortune,* and the *Wall Street Journal,* or perhaps a tabloid newspaper, *Playboy,* and *Variety?*

Naturally, you can find out much about reading tastes by closely examining various publications read by your prospects. Another great help is the "Publisher's Editorial Profile" that heads each listing in *Standard Rate and Data Service* magazine section. These profiles give you a strong clue as to the nature of the publication and the readers of that publication. To provide an example, here's a profile for the magazine *Family Circle.*

> *Family Circle* is edited for women who enjoy their role as family manager. Editorial is intended to fulfill women's needs for information, advice, tools and shortcuts by providing regular features on subjects such as health, diet, nutrition, careers, travel, children, food, entertaining, decorating, remodeling, fitness, beauty and fashion. Book-bonuses, mini-magazines, pull-out sections, and regional features address the active lifestyles of women today.

When they watch television, do they lean toward high drama or low comedy, sports, news, or sitcoms? In radio listening, are they likely to be hearing your commercials in the car driving home from work or at home doing the ironing?

In cross-section studies of potential consumers, the equal appeal of a product to different groups often necessitates diversified radio or television advertising. This wide appeal is particularly true of products such as cereals, which are equally enjoyed by children and adults. You'll agree that a cereal television commercial written for use on a show produced for young children is not likely to have much selling appeal for viewers of an adult TV show.

How Much Do Your Prospects Already Know about the Product?

Are most of your best prospects already familiar with the product, as most people are now familiar with home permanents, for instance? Or is it a new product, whose utility or other benefits must be clearly explained as videodiscs originally had to be explained? How much potential buyers know about the product, and how well they know it, will definitely affect your copy.

Starting your copy in either case will give you certain difficulties. If your product is well known, you either say the same thing over and over again hoping to sell through repetition, or work for new ways to start your copy. If you use this latter technique, copy will "start" out of your inventiveness and your application of the P's. You'll strain to give an old story a new fascination in each advertisement.

On the other hand, your problem with a new product is that you can assume so little. You're not entirely sure of your prospects because you cannot tell by any previous sales record, as in the case of an already marketed product, how the consumers react to your product and copy message. The reader will not know your product name, how it works, what it's made of, who makes it, and just what it will do for the buyer.

You must explain and sell, and you must do your best to gauge the readers' interest in and knowledge of the type of product you are advertising. If they are already acquainted with the type of product, for instance, it will make your copy job easier even if your product is being put on the market for the first time.

It may mean that you will need to do less selling of the *need* for the product. Advertising of similar products may have given your type of product an acceptability to the general public. Thus you may start off your copy confident that you don't need to stress the need for the product so much as the qualities of your product that make it superior to other similar ones on the market.

P Is for Purchases

You now have arrived at the point where you may think you have done enough analyzing to enable you to create campaigns that will ring the cash registers of every store selling your product. Perhaps you're eager to get your ideas down on paper—but wait just a minute. You may know a good deal about your product. You may know fairly well the people who should be your best prospects. There are still, however, some important points you haven't touched that affect the actual buying of the product.

Where Do Customers Buy the Product?

Early in their careers copywriters must recognize that most people are *not* particularly anxious to buy the products for which they're writing copy. During World War II, when shortages existed, a single whisper from a salesperson to a friend could have sold a carload of nylon stockings. That's because there weren't enough nylons to go around.

Normally, in peacetime there's more than enough of all commodities. There's plenty of your product and plenty of your competitors'. The public, under normal conditions, won't react to your selling message with a fraction of the mad greed they displayed for nylon stockings years ago.

Today is not enough to sell people merely on the desirability of your product. You must be a sort of remote-control Pied Piper and lure them from their easy chairs right down to the store. You must make it as easy as possible for them to buy. Unless the product is one that is so well established that everyone knows where to buy it, you'll want to write where it is sold—whether at drug stores, hardware stores, grocery stores, or all three.

Never leave any question open because, unless you're selling diamond rings for a dollar, few people will be so anxious to purchase your product that they will be willing to go out and search for a place that handles it. Tell your readers or listeners where they can buy it. And be as specific as possible. Don't rely on such empty phrases as "sold by leading stores everywhere" or "get it at your nearest dealer's."

The first of these statements possibly has some vague value as advertising. It may enhance the prestige of the product in the minds of a small percentage of prospects. Some people may reason, if they take the trouble, that if leading stores carry it, it must be good. But this type of statement is sometimes no more than an expression of wishful thinking on the part of the advertiser, and it often backfires to his disadvantage.

To illustrate, picture a man reading a shoe advertisement in a national magazine. The shoes look good to him, and he wants to buy a pair. The advertisement explains that he can get them "at better stores coast to coast." He concludes from the phrase that Macy's carries this particular brand. Certainly, Macy's is a "better store," so he goes down to Macy's. He finds that Macy's doesn't carry the brand in which he's interested, and what happens? While in Macy's he eyes a pair of shoes by a different maker and decides to buy them instead.

The copywriter who wrote the shoe advertisement that appealed to this man actually ended up making a sale for a competitive brand. Wouldn't it have been much wiser if this manufacturer (as so many do) had clearly listed the dealers in the classified section of the phone book and advised readers to "see the classified section of your phone book for name of your nearest dealer"? Or run in the advertisement a list of stores in the country that sell the shoes? Or provide a free "800" number?

Similarly, the phrase "get it at your nearest dealer's" is meaningless if a prospect doesn't have any idea where the nearest dealer is—perhaps seventy-five miles away for all the reader may know. You have to *tell* where to buy all but the most commonplace products. If your brand is available only at Safeway Stores, *say* so. If all good stores carry it, *say* so. If the name and address of the nearest dealer is obtained by calling a telephone number, *say* so. If the item can be ordered by mail, *say* so. In short, do everything in your power to make it easy for the prospect to buy.

Are the Purchases Primarily Seasonal or for Special Occasions?

Most products sell well all year round. Many are sold as seasonal items. You'd know that snow shovels, Christmas tree lights, and ice skates aren't bought in June; and you wouldn't be surprised that lawn mowers, flower seeds, and sun shades would sell poorly in winter.

But what about electric light bulbs? Do they sell equally well throughout the year? Offhand, if you didn't stop to analyze it, you might well answer yes to that question. But, because it is dark earlier in winter—which means more use of electricity and more burned-out bulbs—sales are naturally greater during the winter months.

Similarly, you might reason that because people must know the time every day, watches wouldn't be subject to any sharp rises and falls in sales. But you'd be wrong because watches—and perfume, jewelry, and candy, to name but a few items—are largely bought as gifts for Christmas, graduations, birthdays, and wedding anniversaries. Thus they are referred to as "special occasion" items.

Why is it important that you know whether the products for which you are writing copy sell more readily in one period than another? Or are bought primarily as gifts? The answer is—to help you avoid misdirecting your copy.

Suppose you are an agency copywriter and you are assigned to write copy on watches. The contact person, or account executive in charge of the account, is so familiar with the peculiarities of the market that he or she may take it for granted that you know the slant your copy should take. Without knowing that most people receive their watches as gifts, you might naturally assume that your primary objective would be to persuade readers to buy a watch for personal use. In actual practice, you'd probably have much better results if you told them the watch would make a wonderful gift for a coming graduation.

If there's the slightest question in your mind as to whether a product falls into one of these specialized categories, ask, don't guess, in order that you can be sure you're aiming at the right market. Be humble and remember that although you might think candy bars sell in about the same volume every month of the year, actually they don't.

Is Purchase Premeditated or Impulsive?

Any major purchase, such as a car, fur coat, refrigerator, or stereo disc player, is usually made only after lengthy consideration. Before buying, people usually debate their actual need for a new stove. They ask themselves if, instead of buying a new sofa, they might not have their old sofa repaired. In the purchase of an automobile, there is usually a long deliberation as to the family's ability to pay for a car.

Even after a decision has been made to buy the super-deluxe, they still take their time before actually making the purchase. Almost any major purchase is made slowly. The buyers shop around, comparing one VCR against several others; one food processor against its competitors.

Such sales are made only after the buyer has weighed the facts. Thus they are termed "premeditated purchases" to differentiate them from what are known as "impulse purchases." In this latter classification falls such merchandise as chewing gum, soft drinks, cigarettes—and any and all other goods people normally buy without going through the long process of reasoning that precedes a planned purchase.

Typical impulse buyers are the persons who insert coins in Coke dispensers in a service station. They drive in to get gasoline; but when they see the Coca-Cola cooler, they decide to have a cool drink. This purchase is completely impulsive.

To show the extent of impulse buying, various researchers interested in grocery-buying habits have pointed out that more than 50 percent of women shoppers buy one-third of their groceries on impulse. Does your product come within this one-third group?

You should learn into which category a product falls if you hope to attain maximum effectiveness in your copy. You can be flippant and capricious—and deal in generalities—in an advertisement for a bubble bath. The technique changes when you're persuading a person to part with thousands of dollars for a Cadillac. This person wants fact, not foolishness—sincerity, not flippancy.

How Does the Price of Your Product Compare with Prices Charged by Competitors?

If buyers have a choice between two products of equal merit, the lower-priced product almost always is the one selected. Product loyalty vanishes in the face of lower prices. Should you doubt this, watch how the person making up a grocery list marks down for purchase those products that are on "special" that day.

Price, especially in times of economic distress, is an important factor in the selling of merchandise. You are handicapped if you don't know how the price of your product compares with the prices of competitive goods. If your price is appreciably higher, then you will want to explain, as convincingly as you can, why it's higher. If it's lower, you'll want to tell your readers or listeners that they not only can get good service from your product, but also that they save money by buying it rather than some other make.

A Copywriting Tool: Psychographics

For the marketing person, demographics (groupings by age, ethnic composition, income, etc.) are vital and, as you have read, they are important to the copywriter, too. Psychographics, in contrast, are more useful to the copywriter than the marketing person. That's because psychographics, concerned with lifestyles, social roles, personality traits, and personal values, are more abstract and thus of less use to the marketer in defining markets. On the contrary, the copywriter finds them useful in devising copy appeals.

Psychographic groupings are subject to variations, according to the authority you refer to. Following is one such breakdown of groupings resulting from an extensive research project.[1]

Female groups
The Conformist
The Puritan
The Drudge
The Free Spender
The Natural, Contented Woman
The Indulger
The Striving Suburbanite
The Career Seeker

Male groups
The Quiet Family Man
The Traditionalist
The Ethical Highbrow
The Pleasure-oriented Man
The Achiever
The He-Man
The Sophisticated Man
The Discontented Man

Although the names of these groups give a clue as to the group characteristics, it is useful to a copywriter to obtain a full description of the traits of group members (or to fashion such a description from observation and experience). Here are descriptions of two of the foregoing groups that demonstrate the usefulness of psychographic analysis when one is writing copy.

> **The Career Seeker (Female)**
> These are women who are likely to reject the housewife role in favor of a career. They tend to feel liberated, like to cultivate their intellects, and want to feel important in life. They are impulsive buyers, spend money freely, and like attractive things.
>
> It is the best-educated group, with the highest socio-economic status; and although 83 percent of them are married, they have the lowest proportion of marrieds among them.

1. "Psychographics, A Study of Personality, Life-Styles, and Consumption Patterns." Newspaper Advertising Bureau Study. Sponsored by the Newsprint Information Committee, 1973.

The He-Man
He is gregarious, likes action, seeks an exciting and dramatic life. Thinks of himself as capable and dominant. Tends to be more of a bachelor than a family man, even after marriage. Products he buys and brands preferred are likely to have a "self-expressive" value, especially a "Man of Action" dimension.

Well-educated, mainly of middle socio-economic status; the youngest of the male groups.

Another Help: Values and Lifestyles Systems (VALS)

Coming after psychographics, VALS offers some similar ideas in its delineations of lifestyles. As devised by the Stanford Research Institute, VALS breaks the population into four groups and nine types. These groups and types are categorized not only by lifestyle, but also by buying style.

One of the groups, for example, is made up of those persons described as "Need-Driven." One of the important types is named the "Achievers." (Look for a fuller description of the groups and types in the appendix and the chapter on research.)

Those who have utilized VALS include many important corporations and advertising agencies. In comparing VALS with psychographics, proponents say that VALS relates better to demographics and can be applied to a greater variety of products.

Know Your Market's Segments

Closely allied with positioning, discussed earlier, is segmentation that is involved with all three of the P's. This term refers to breaking the total market into units of various types. Segmentation has many definitions and appears in many forms, as you will discover in reading the numerous articles and books on the subject.

Sometimes the segmentation breakdown is geographic. Regional magazines recognize this form of segmentation. Then there is Zip Code marketing that can be geographic and demographic in enabling the marketer to zero in on certain areas and certain demographic groupings.

For the copywriter, the demographic segmentations are more important. It is important to know that people of similar interests tend to cluster and that they tend to exhibit common buying habits and attitudes. Such people will likewise have similar goal-related characteristics.

Another segmentation is by rate of usage of a product. The market, accordingly, may be broken down into heavy users of a product, light users, and potentially heavy or light users among those not presently users.

Usage might have ethnic overtones. For example, a study[2] of rice consumption in New York City has shown that Puerto Ricans and blacks consumed a huge proportion of the rice sold in the market.

In Miami, Florida, Cubans consumed 66 percent of the rice. In Los Angeles, the high consumption of rice was among Mexican-Americans and blacks, while in San Francisco the product was consumed largely by Orientals and blacks.

Mayonnaise, the study revealed, had a consumption index of 24 in Des Moines, 204 in Atlanta. Likewise, regular coffee, with a national average of 15.1 percent, was consumed at a 3.7 percent level in Portland, Oregon, but reached a 34.6 percent level in Charlotte, North Carolina.

These variations, of intense interest to the marketing and sales departments of the manufacturer, will ultimately be of concern to the copywriter who shapes an approach to what market research has revealed—especially if markets are developed on a section-by-section basis.

Still another segmentation breakdown is psychographic, referring to the lifestyles or personality characteristics of buyers within the segment. According to psychographics, the market might be described in such terms as: religion-obsessed, radical chic, buttoned-down-conservative, macho, white-Anglo-Saxon-Protestant, executive, militant, activist, women's lib, ski bum, hippie, back-to-nature, and in a myriad of other ways.

Some of these are easily defined and thus easy to write to; others have blurred profiles that make it more difficult for the copywriter to write to them effectively.

Although segmentation is more directly pertinent to the marketing strategist than the copywriter, it is, nonetheless, one more factor in your search for understanding of those complex, fascinating prospects to whom you address your copy messages. The more you understand of such matters as positioning and segmentation, the more confident you can be in your writing. Some aspects of segmentation and positioning you already know through observation and experience; others you learn as you go along.

For instance, an example of segmentation in the sports field is provided by the Spalding company, which has divided tennis players into several types. A special racket has been designed for each type, such as those who play a power game, a forcing game, a percentage game, and an anticipation game. A copywriter writing for such equipment is provided with much on which to base a copy approach.

Then, there is J.C. Penney, which bases its long-range planning on developing selected market segments, but which puts merchandising and promotional emphasis on young married couples whose income is above average because both are working.

Segmentation is possibly most obvious in the media. By their nature, media have always segmented the market except for the very general media (most of which have disappeared). Magazine titles reveal the segmentation—*Scientific American, Hot Rod, Golf Digest.* Today, media are segmenting their markets more than

2. Harry Wayne McMahan, "Baptists Researching $1,000,000 'Peace of Mind' TV Campaign," *Advertising Age,* December 20, 1976, p. 20.

ever in order to serve the needs of special demographic groups. Direct mail, too, has always aimed at specific market segments, possibly more pronouncedly than any other medium.

Get Some Facts on Your Own

If copywriters collected personally all the data needed for an analysis similar to the one presented, they would be taking too much time from the writing job. No copywriter would be expected to gather it all. Much of it may have been already well established by previous experience with the given product. Most of the rest will come from research studies.

You can take an active part by doing what has for many years been popularized as "The Hat Trick." That is, you should put on your hat and go out to do some firsthand research on your own hook. Make a representative number of the interviews yourself. Ask questions—not among your own friends, but of the ordinary people on the street.

Talk to dealers and wholesalers. Talk to people who use your product and like it. Find out why they like it. Talk to people who have tried your product but now use something else. Find out why they didn't like your product. Do "The Hat Trick"—often and thoroughly.

Your study of the basic strategy is now completed. You have done enough personal research to give you a good feel of the problem.

You now have what seem to be all the pertinent facts.

You have determined what seem to be your best selling points. You've identified what seem to be your best prospects. And you've come to a decision on how best to reach these prospects.

You are ready now to start building a good, sound advertising program that will sell more of your goods to more and more people.

Writing Strategy Evolves from Copy Platform

A dictionary definition of *strategy* is "employing plans toward a goal." A plan for advertising, if it involves a campaign, is almost always expressed in a written presentation. Sometimes it is called a "copy platform" and may take weeks, or months, to work out. It can be very long but usually is short, a mere outline, in fact. Brevity is desirable. If the plan is very long, it is more difficult to use on a day-to-day basis. Also, it can be subject to more misinterpretation.

You may be certain that if a client and the advertising agency have developed a plan, or copy platform, through weeks or months of hard work, you will, if you're a copywriter, deviate from the plan at your peril. It is your guide until a new plan has been worked out.

Although creative plans, copy platforms, and enunciations of copy strategy differ, all have certain common points. Following are three examples: Creative Planning Guide, Creative Strategy, and Written Advertising Plan. Any one of them will be useful in helping you determine the direction of your creative efforts, no matter what it is called.

Creative Planning Guide

1. Overall, what do we want to accomplish: Increased sales? Bigger share of market? Favorable

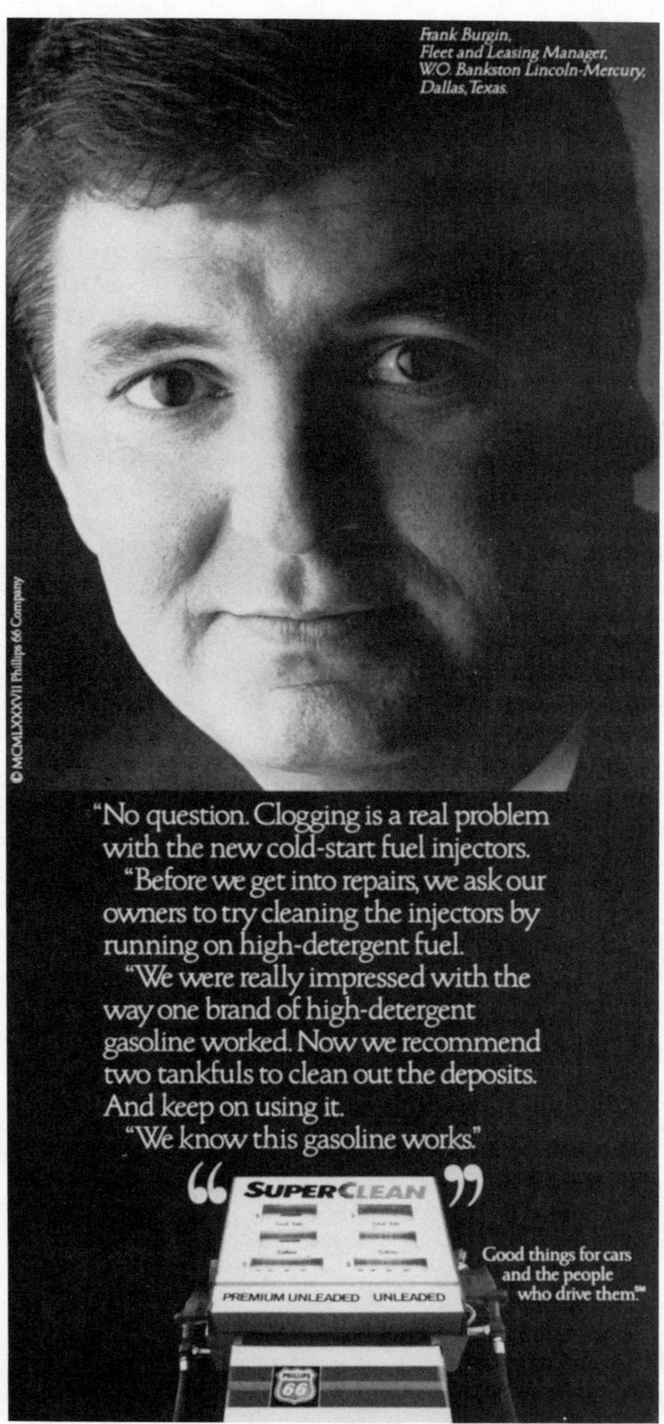

Figure 3–1a. Campaign approach. In this, and Figures 3–1b and 3–1c, the advertiser achieves strong identification with similar illustrations, copy, and the identifying symbol at the bottom of each advertisement. After several such advertisements, readers will be able to tell at a glance who is advertising.

opinion toward company, or product? A change of public attitude toward company, or product?
2. To whom are we addressing our message?
3. What do we have to offer that is unique? If we have nothing unique, what is our strongest selling point? Supporting points?
4. What media will carry our advertising?
5. How do we position our product (or service)?
6. What is the best creative strategy—hard sell? Soft persuasion? Strong identification approach?

Creative Strategy

1. Objective—what the advertising should do
2. Target audience—who the consumer is
3. Key consumer benefit—why the consumer should buy your product
4. Support—a reason to believe in that benefit
5. Tone and manner—a statement of the product "personality"[3]

3. Kenneth Roman and June Maas, *How to Advertise* (New York: St. Martin's Press, 1976), p. 3.

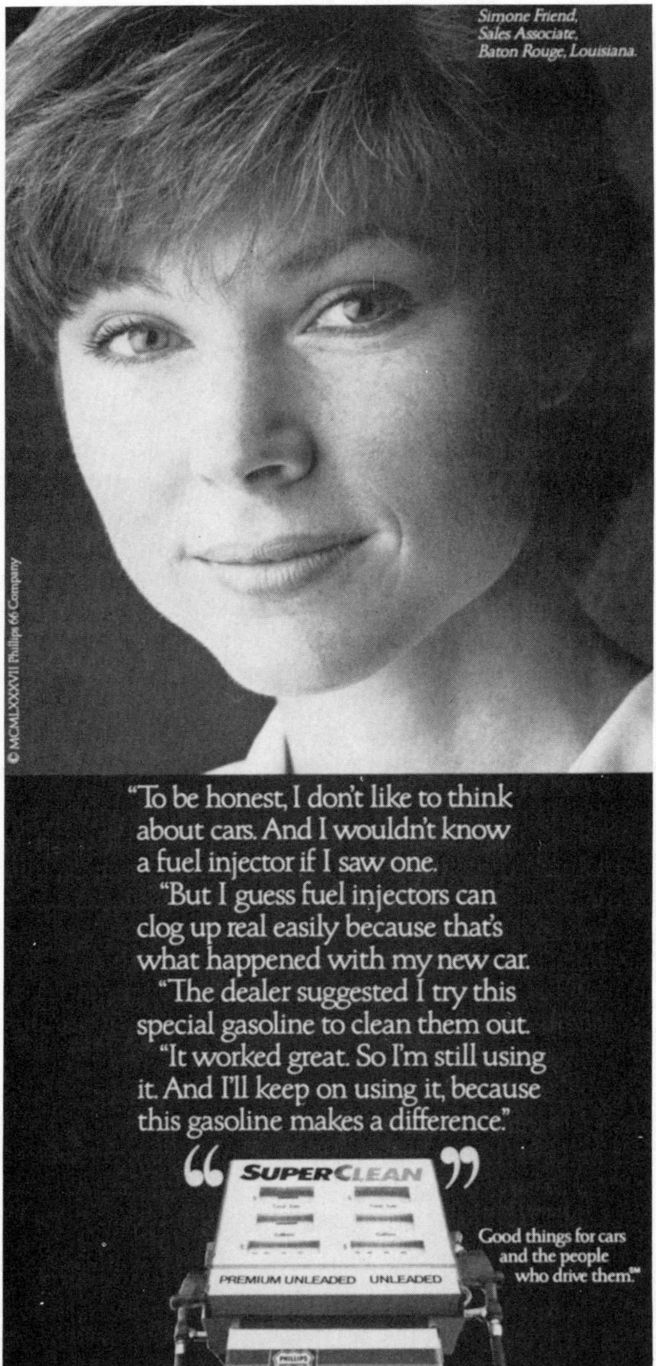

Figure 3–1b. Campaign advertisement.

Figure 3–1c. Campaign advertisement.

"NOT YOUR CAR"
:30 Radio (Live)

ANNCR (Live): If your car's not running the way you want it to, (Dealer name) thinks you should know that the problem may not be your car . . . it may be your gasoline.

The solution? Use new Phillips 66 **SuperClean™** Unleaded or **SuperClean™** Premium Unleaded. Both grades of Phillips 66 **SuperClean™** unleaded gasolines will clean your car's fuel injectors or carburetor and keep them clean with continuous use.

Come by (Dealer name and location) to try **SuperClean™** unleaded gasolines—the clean-up and keep clean gasolines from Phillips 66.

Figure 3–2a. Campaign commercial. Elsewhere in this chapter you've seen three print advertisements in this campaign (Figures 3–1a–c). Here is a radio commercial that is part of the series. Notice that the commercial gives the listeners the name and address of the local dealer. This carries the print advertisements one step further.

"YOU SHOULD KNOW"
:30 Radio (Live)

ANNCR (Live): If your new fuel-injected car is running like an old clunker, (Dealer name) thinks you should know that many gasolines don't have enough detergent to keep your car's engine clean and running smooth.

But with new Phillips 66 **SuperClean™** Unleaded or **SuperClean™** Premium Unleaded, you can clean up your car's fuel injectors and keep them clean with continuous use.

See (Dealer Name and Location) today, for **SuperClean™** unleaded gasolines—the clean-up and keep clean gasolines from Phillips 66.

Figure 3–2b. Campaign commercial. Notice that in writing campaign commercials or print advertisements, you include similar points but introduce them differently. This is a writing challenge in long-running campaigns.

Written Advertising Plan

1. Statement of advertising objectives
2. Written advertising strategy
3. List of reasons for buying
4. Product positioning statement
5. Creative blueprint[4]

Before You Write, Develop a Theme

Once the basic sales strategy for any product or service is established, the next step is to develop a *campaign* theme. This is the vehicle in which you deliver your selling points to the public. It's the central idea—the imaginative spark plug—that will give your advertisements continuity, recall value, and thus, extra selling power.

Your theme is the lifeline of your campaign, and its development will largely be your responsibility as the copywriter. So take your time: make sure you develop a good theme. The success of the entire campaign may well hinge on the effectiveness of your theme.

Copywriters working the national level almost always are looking for big ideas, or themes, that can be repeated in many advertisements as part of the long-run campaign. Even on the local level, the copywriters for such organizations as banks and dairies will work mightily to come up with a strong campaign theme that will be used many times with effectiveness.

The writer who consistently presents campaign themes or ideas is the one who shoots ahead in advertising, not the one who thinks only in terms of "one-shotters." In the following material you will be given some suggestions for utilizing certain basics from which powerful advertising themes spring.

4. Steuart Henderson Britt, ed., *Marketing Manager's Handbook* (Chicago: Dartnell Corporation, 1973), p. 935.

You have already determined from your basic strategy planning *why* people might buy yours and similar products, *what* they want and expect for their money. Your first interest is to develop a theme that will, over a long period, influence a large number of people to want and buy your product instead of that of a competitor. To accomplish this you want to appeal to their own selfish interests.

Another point about campaigns. Good ones should not be changed quickly unless your product itself is changed significantly, or some other truly major change has occurred. Too often an advertiser using an outstanding campaign changes it to meet the challenge of competitive advertising. If the campaign is productive, its effective life span may be years.

An advertiser, alas, frequently tires of a campaign long before the public does or, as said, deserts the campaign in order to counter a campaign of a rival product. There are two ways to thwart this tendency by the advertiser: (a) Develop a long-range campaign theme that will result in advertisements that wear well; (b) supply campaign advertisements that will utilize the theme in a fresh, engaging way in advertisement after advertisement.

These two stratagems are evident in such long-lasting campaigns as those for Volkswagen, Maytag, Marlboro, and Keebler. Maintain such quality in the advertisements you produce and the advertiser won't dare to change what has worked so well.

Consumer Drives and Your Copy

You may ask, "Aren't the basic human appeals used by a copywriter simply the means by which I can satisfy consumer drives?"

That question cannot be posed, nor answered, unless you understand "drives" to mean urgent, basic, or instinctual needs. Sometimes such drives may also be

"NO TUNE-UP"
:30 Radio (Live)

ANNCR (Live): If your new car's not running as you want it to, bring it to (Dealer name), before you take it in for a tune-up. Because your problem may be that your gasoline doesn't have enough detergent to keep your engine clean and running smooth. But with new Phillips 66 **SuperClean™** Unleaded or **SuperClean™** Premium Unleaded, both grades have the same strong detergent action that cleans up your car's fuel system and keeps it clean with continuous use.

Come by (Dealer name and location) to try new **SuperClean™** unleaded gasolines—the clean-up and keep clean gasolines from Phillips 66.

Figure 3–2c. Campaign commercial. You've seen two other commercials in this series. Notice once more that although the basic theme is similar, the writer has made the approach different enough to avoid boring listeners.

defined as culturally acquired concerns, interests, or longings.

Human beings do what they do because of certain stimuli. It's unlikely, however, that in your daily work you'll talk learnedly of drives and stimuli. Instead, you will usually refer to basic human appeals, or simply "advertising appeals."

Nevertheless, each of us is motivated every day by psychological stimuli, either consciously or subconsciously. You hope, when you write, that your copy will trigger the stimuli that lead to buying action. To accomplish such action you draw upon your understanding of human appeals.

You are not limited when you write to the basic, or primary, appeals of hunger, thirst, and the sex drive, nor do you need to worry because some psychologists insist that all human appeals stem from fear, love, or hunger. What appeals you'll use will be up to you because lists of appeals are numerous, as are the varying opinions of psychologists. When trying to decide on a definitive list of basic human appeals, it is too limiting to utilize only the truly basic, or primary, appeals. On the other hand, some authorities offer lists of twenty-four such appeals or more. A copywriter will find such long lists unworkable.

It may be understood, therefore, that no one list of basic human appeals has been agreed upon by everyone. You are offered the following list, ample enough to be useful, but brief enough for convenience. Each appeal is powerful enough to supply the stimuli previously referred to and each may be found in advertisements, some more than others, of course.

In studying these products and relating their sales stories to the basic appeals, you will again be aware that almost all of them employ multiple appeals. In many cases one appeal can be made unmistakably dominant. Many advertisements, however, seem to put equal stress on two or more appeals.

A Goodyear tire advertisement might, through illustration and headline treatment, put over a smashing stress on fear. The copy will carry out this theme but will do so through a strong appeal to family love. The father will be urged to protect his wife and children against the hazards of a blowout. A copy section at the bottom of the advertisement emphasizes a strong third point—economy.

In many products you will find it possible to develop a theme that will intermingle appeals so that it is difficult to say just which is dominant. In one advertisement, for example, the headline reads, "How to be safe—and save 31¢ on our flashlight batteries." Which is stronger—the appeal to fear or to acquisitiveness?

Although it is difficult and sometimes impossible to develop a theme which falls unmistakably into one appeal classification, it is best to try to come as close to this goal as possible. A "shotgun" theme which embraces several appeals may often fail to carry out your basic sales strategy by weakening the punch of your copy message.

All advertising, of course, is not built on such attention-catching themes. All advertising, however—even one-time insertions—should be built on a central theme that appeals to the prospect through one or more basic human interests. *The important thing to remember is to choose the appeal or appeals that will have the greatest interest for the greatest number of your prospects.*

Utilize These Basic Human Appeals

As you go over the following basic appeals, evaluate each one as it applies to yourself. Not until you do this can you fully appreciate the wide extent of their power in influencing people to buy the goods you have to sell.

You will discover something more in going over these appeals—that they often overlap. Thus an advertisement will contain several basic appeals. Possibly all of them are equally strong, or it may be that one appeal clearly dominates.

Acquisitiveness. Desire for money, power, prestige, efficiency, material possessions
Comfort. Desire for physical comfort, rest, leisure, peace of mind
Convenience. Desire to eliminate work, to do tasks more easily
Curiosity. Desire for any kind of new experience
Egotism. Desire to be attractive, popular, praised
Family Affection, Togetherness, and Happy Home Life. Desire to do things as a family unit, to please members of the family, to help children in their growing years
Fear. Of pain, death, poverty, criticism; loss of possessions, beauty, popularity, and loved ones
Health. Desire for good health, longevity, youthful vigor.
Hero Worship. Desire to be like people we admire
Kindness, Generosity, and Unselfishness. Desire to help others, our country, our church

Backer Spielvogel Bates

SCRIPT/COPY ☒ TV ☐ RADIO ☐ PRINT

Client: Xerox — Date: March 29, 1988 — Page 1 Of 2
Product: Corporate — Title: "World"
Job No./Ad #: — Code # OXCP 0140 — Length :45
Author(s): — Revision #:

AS PRODUCED

VIDEO	AUDIO
Open MS office, 2 men rush to desk	MUSIC (SINGERS):
CU of fingers on keyboard	TO WRITE
CU of electronic page on monitor	THE WORDS
CU finger on mouse	AND MAKE THE PLANS
CU of electronic page	THAT BRING
MS of group looking at monitor	THE FUTURE
CU of man looking at printed document	IN SIGHT.
MS female officer in classroom	TO TAKE THOSE DREAMS
CU finger on copier button	AND SET THEM DOWN...
CU paper coming out of conference room copier	SET THEM IN
MS officer handing out copies	A WHOLE NEW LIGHT.
	ANNCR (VO):
MS man at drafting table	FROM ORIGINAL
MS man pulling paper out of copier	TO COPY,
CU man looking at monitor	ELECTRONIC,
CU copy out of jet printer	TO PRINT,
CU woman looking at monitor	WHAT YOU SEE

Legal Approval — Date — Client Approval — Date

Backer Spielvogel Bates

SCRIPT/COPY ☒ TV ☐ RADIO ☐ PRINT

Client: Xerox — Date: March 29, 1988 — Page 2 Of 2
Product: Corporate — Title: "World Lift"
Job No./Ad #: XECP BF/87/26 — Code # OXCP 0141 — Length :30
Author(s): J. Colasurdo — Revision #:

AS PRODUCED

VIDEO	AUDIO
CU of paper coming out of printer	COPY,
CU paper going through sorter	FILE, DISTRIBUTE
MS of architect pulling copy out of engineering copier	AND MAKE
MS of architect holding up copy	YOUR OUTPUT OUTSTANDING
MS man at desk taking paper from telecopier	DOCUMENT PROCESSING
SUPER: Xerox	FROM TEAM XEROX.
	MUSIC (SINGERS):
SUPER: Xerox	WE DOCUMENT THE WORLD
We Document the World	

Legal Approval — Date — Client Approval — Date

Figure 3–3a. Television script—part of a campaign.

Backer Spielvogel Bates

SCRIPT/COPY ☒ TV ☐ RADIO ☐ PRINT

Client: Xerox — Date: March 29, 1988 — Page 1 Of 2
Product: Corporate — Title: "World/Non-Lift"
Job No./Ad #: XECP BF/87/26 — Code # OXCP 0200 — Length :30
Author(s): J. Colasurdo — Revision #:

AS PRODUCED

VIDEO	AUDIO
Fade up on CU, woman's fingers on computer keyboard.	Song: TO WRITE THE WORDS
Cut to CU of data on computer screen.	
Cut to CU of man's face in surgical mask and headcover.	AND MAKE THE PLANS
Cut to WS of computer operator at terminal in foreground with operating theatre, surgery in progress in background.	THAT BRING THE FUTURE IN SIGHT.
Cut to WS of female executive in office. She is in the process of faxing photo image of a sculpture piece.	TO SHOW THE WORLD IT CAN SEE IT S DREAMS Woman: (Under) IT'S ON IT S WAY.
Cut to CU of FAX image being printed out of receiving terminal.	
Cut to WS of man at receiving FAX terminal in foreground. An art gallery is in background. Man takes the FAX copy from terminal.	Song: SEE THEM IN A WHOLE NEW LIGHT. Man: (Under) QUITE HANDSOME.
Cut to CU of Xerox lazer printer recording image of a map.	Anncr/Copy: FROM ORIGINAL
Cut to CU of colating section of copying machine. Xerox logo is on individual copies being colated.	TO COPY,

Legal Approval — Date — Client Approval — Date

Backer Spielvogel Bates

SCRIPT/COPY ☒ TV ☐ RADIO ☐ PRINT

Client: Xerox — Date: March 29, 1988 — Page 2 Of 2
Product: Corporate — Title: "World/Non-Lift"
Job No./Ad #: XECP BF/87/26 — Code # OXCP 0200 — Length :30
Author(s): J. Colasurdo — Revision #:

AS PRODUCED

VIDEO	AUDIO
Cut to CU of computer screen. Screen shows image of a chart.	ON SCREEN,
Cut to CU of this same chart emerging from printing terminal.	OR ON PAPER.
Cut to CU of man's face lit up by the glow of computer screen.	WHAT YOU SEE
Cut to CU of a color bar-chart on computer screen.	IS WHAT WE DO.
Cut to a moving graphic of Xerox logo inside mock copier.	TEAM XEROX.
Cut to CU of man's hand pressing button on computer.	LEADERSHIP IN DOCUMENT PROCESSING
Cut to WS of office activity in a bank setting. Woman hands a stack of documents to man.	WITH MACHINES AND SYSTEMS THAT MAKE OUTPUT OUTSTANDING. Man: (Under) THANKS!
Cut to black and white optical title:	Song:
Xerox. We Document the World.	WE DOCUMENT THE WORLD.

Legal Approval — Date — Client Approval — Date

Figure 3–3b. Television script—part of a campaign.

Backer Spielvogel Bates ☒TV ☐RADIO ☐PRINT

SCRIPT/COPY

Client Xerox | Date March 29, 1988 | Page 1 Of 2

Product Corporate | Title "World Lift"

Job No./Ad # XECP BF/87/26 | Code # OXCP 0141 | Length :30

Author(s) J. Colasurdo | Revision #

AS PRODUCED

VIDEO	AUDIO
Open on CU of fingers on keyboard	SINGERS: TO WRITE
CU to electronic image - financial folio	THE WORDS
MS office workers looking at computer screen	AND MAKE THE PLANS THAT
CU of papers coming out of conference copier	BRING THE FUTURE
CU of Naval officer handing out copies	IN SIGHT
	ANNCR (VO):
CU man working at drafting table	FROM ORIGINAL
MS man taking copy out of engineering copier	TO COPY
CU of copy coming out of ink jet printer	ELECTRONIC TO PRINT
CU of woman facing monitor	WHAT YOU SEE
CU of paper coming out of desk-top copier	IS WHAT WE DO
CU of mock copier Pulls back to reveal "Xerox"	XEROX. THE LEADER IN DOCUMENT PROCESSING
CU of finger pressing copier button	ALL THE MACHINES
CU electronic image building on monitor screen	AND SYSTEMS TO CREATE,

Legal Approval Date Client Approval Date

Backer Spielvogel Bates ☒TV ☐RADIO ☐PRINT

SCRIPT/COPY

Client Xerox | Date March 29, 1988 | Page 2 Of 2

Product Corporate | Title "World Lift"

Job No./Ad # XECP BF/87/26 | Code # OXCP 0141 | Length :30

Author(s) J. Colasurdo | Revision #

AS PRODUCED

VIDEO	AUDIO
CU of paper coming out of printer	COPY,
CU paper going through sorter	FILE, DISTRIBUTE
MS of architect pulling copy out of engineering copier	AND MAKE
MS of architect holding up copy	YOUR OUTPUT OUTSTANDING
MS man at desk taking paper from telecopier	DOCUMENT PROCESSING
SUPER: Xerox	FROM TEAM XEROX.
	MUSIC (SINGERS):
SUPER: Xerox	WE DOCUMENT THE WORLD
We Document the World	

Legal Approval Date Client Approval Date

Figure 3–3c. Television script—part of a campaign.

Love and Sex. Desire for romantic love, normal sex life
Mental Stimulation. Desire to improve mind, to broaden mental horizons
Pleasure. Desire for fun, travel, entertainment, enjoyment in general
Sensory Appeals. Desire for any stimulus received through any of the five senses

To show how the foregoing may be used in developing advertising campaign themes, the table on pages 32–34 presents a list of familiar products whose advertising consistently reflects one or more of these basic appeals. You will recognize immediately the association between the appeal and the product sales story, even though, through the years, different words and different slogans and copy approaches have been used to express the idea.

Industrial Copywriters Learn S.I.C. Numbers to Determine Their Audience

Demographics, psychographics, VALS, and lifestyles give way to Standard Industrial Classifications (S.I.C.) numbers when the industrial copywriters want to find out who will be reading their copy. You will find such numbers listed for the publications that appear in the "Industrial" section of *Standard Rate and Data Service.* Refer to these if you wish to know just who might be reading those industrial advertisements you're writing.

Use of the Standard Industrial Classifications numbers is indispensable to anyone who wishes to know precisely the extent and character of the business market. It is especially useful to the advertiser who is deciding whether a certain business publication will reach more prospects than another.

Using a system of coding devised by the Division of Statistical Standards of the U.S. Bureau of the Budget, the S.I.C. assigns appropriate manufacturing industry code numbers to all industries in the entire field of business activity.

So important is the system the federal government adopted it as a standard basis for the collection and presentation of statistics relating to the U.S. economy. Industrial data, gathered and reported by the federal government according to S.I.C. groups, include as a partial list some of these important classifications:

1. Number of manufacturing plants in operation
2. Value of products shipped
3. Value added by manufacture
4. Employment in the manufacturing industries
5. Hours worked and wages earned by manufacturing employees
6. Value of materials consumed
7. Expenditures for new plant and equipment
8. Value of fuels and electric energy consumer

Each division of industry—agriculture, manufacturing, transportation, finance, government, and others—is

Backer Spielvogel Bates ☒ TV ☐ RADIO ☐ PRINT

SCRIPT/COPY

Client	Xerox	Date	March 29, 1988	Page 1	Of 3
Product	Corporate	Title	"WYSIWWD"		
Job No./Ad #	XECP BF/87/27	Code #	OXCP 0162	Length	:30
Author(s)	Schancupp/Smith	Revision #			

AS PRODUCED

VIDEO	AUDIO
CAMERA OPTICAL TITLES	
Fade up on CU lazer printer recording image of a map	Sound effects of office environment and computers play over picture throughout, with intermittent silence over optical titles.
Cut to ECU of finger pressing button on computer mouse	THERE IS NO COPY OR MUSIC.
Cut to a color bar graph being generated from ink jet printer	
Cut to ECU letters being typed onto paper in typewriter	
CUT TO TITLE: Whether it's	
CUT TO TITLE: printed	
CUT TO TITLE: on paper,	
Cut to ECU finger pressing "Print" button on conference copier	
Cut to ECU hand removing document from conference copier tray	

Legal Approval Date Client Approval Date

Backer Spielvogel Bates ☒ TV ☐ RADIO ☐ PRINT

SCRIPT/COPY

Client	Xerox	Date	March 29, 1988	Page 2	Of 3
Product	Corporate	Title	"WYSIWWD"		
Job No./Ad #	XECP BF/87/27	Code #	OXCP 0162	Length	:30
Author(s)	Schancupp/Smith	Revision #			

AS PRODUCED

VIDEO	AUDIO
Cut to MS Navy classroom. A woman is standing in front of a chart drawn on screen of conference copier	
Woman turns to distribute papers to students	
CUT TO TITLE: seen	
CUT TO TITLE: on a screen,	
Cut to ECU of a man's face illuminated by computer screen	
Cut to ECU electronic image coming up on computer screen	
CUT TO TITLE: a perfect	
CUT TO TITLE: copy	
Cut to CU of a document being printed out of computer	
CUT TO TITLE: or a brilliant	
CUT TO TITLE: original,	

Legal Approval Date Client Approval Date

Figure 3–3d. Television script—part of a campaign. In this unusual commercial, the writer departed from the format used in three other commercials shown in this chapter (Figures 3–3a through 3–3c). No music or copy are used. Sound effects and video carry this message.

assigned an industry code based on its major activity. This is assigned according to the product or groups of products produced, handled, or serviced.

Under S.I.C., industries are classified by two-digit, three-digit, and four-digit classification. The two-digit classifications are very broad in that they refer to industries as a whole. As the digit numbers grow larger, the industries in question are narrowed down to help the marketer refine specific prospects. Here is how the system works in the case of one type of market:

S.I.C. Number	*Industry Definition*
33	Primary metal industries
3311	Blast furnaces

Using the foregoing as an example, the advertiser who was content to get figures on the industry as a whole would use the two-digit classification. If however, the advertiser made components for blast furnaces, the two-digit classification would be too broad. Thus the four-digit breakdown would be useful.

To give you further examples of how industry classifications become more precise as they go from two digits to four digits, examine the following listings:

19 Ordnance and accessories
192 Ammunition, except for small arms
1921 Artillery ammunition

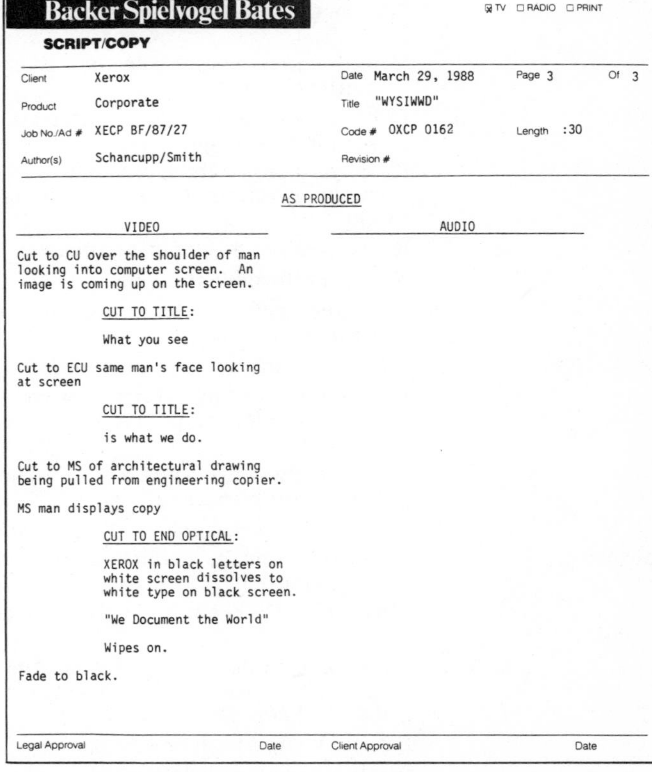

Backer Spielvogel Bates ☒ TV ☐ RADIO ☐ PRINT

SCRIPT/COPY

Client	Xerox	Date	March 29, 1988	Page 3	Of 3
Product	Corporate	Title	"WYSIWWD"		
Job No./Ad #	XECP BF/87/27	Code #	OXCP 0162	Length	:30
Author(s)	Schancupp/Smith	Revision #			

AS PRODUCED

VIDEO	AUDIO
Cut to CU over the shoulder of man looking into computer screen. An image is coming up on the screen.	
CUT TO TITLE: What you see	
Cut to ECU same man's face looking at screen	
CUT TO TITLE: is what we do.	
Cut to MS of architectural drawing being pulled from engineering copier.	
MS man displays copy	
CUT TO END OPTICAL: XEROX in black letters on white screen dissolves to white type on black screen.	
"We Document the World"	
Wipes on.	
Fade to black.	

Legal Approval Date Client Approval Date

35 Machinery (except electrical)
351 Engines and turbines
3511 Steam engines and turbines

Advertisers find that many publishers will break down their circulation figures into three-digit and four-digit subscribers in order that the users of the publications can approach their marketing planning intelligently.

When publications put their listings in *Standard Rate and Data Service,* they not only break their circulation into S.I.C. industries but also show how many executives and what types of executives are being reached in each S.I.C. category.

An important side result of the standardization represented by the use of S.I.C. numbers in circulation breakdowns is the possibility it presents for the use of computers in media analysis.

While the uses of S.I.C. figures are almost limitless in marketing and advertising—such as coding consumer lists, laying out sales territories, projecting samples—their special values to the advertiser-marketer are (a) helping determine which industries should be cultivated with special vigor because of the high sales potential; (b) helping select business publications for advertising schedules; and (c) giving the copywriters the target audience for their copy.

In the first case, an industrial marketer is helped greatly if he or she knows, for example, that 85 percent of inquiries resulting from an advertisement came from plants in S.I.C. 3555, printing trades machinery. Then again, if marketing information is needed, a mail questionnaire can be precoded by four-digit S.I.C. numbers before mailing. Returns will then enable the industrial marketer to classify products precisely.

As for the second case (selection of business publications), the circulation broken down by S.I.C. and by the number of executives reached in each classification gives the advertiser-marketer precise information on which to base media selection.

Third, not only will copywriters know the number of executives reached by the publications but also what **kind** of executives—plant operating engineers, safety engineers, plant managers, presidents, purchasing agents, and other management types. Having such information enables copywriters to focus their copy messages.

U.S.P., Suffering Points, and Point of Difference

Some years ago Rosser Reeves, a prominent advertising agency executive, stirred the advertising world with his book *Reality in Advertising.* In this short book he made a

Appeal	*Headline of advertisement*	*Product or service*	*Advertiser*
Acquisitiveness	How to enjoy your salary long after you've stopped working.	Personal finance planning	IDS Financial Services
	"I'm an easy guy to satisfy. I only want the best."	GMC truck	General Motors
	Your dream of owning a Jaguar just came a little closer to reality.	Jaguar automobile	Jaguar Cars, Inc.
	Life insurance that helps you keep up with the Dow Joneses.	Variable appreciable life plan	Prudential Company
Comfort	Keep warmer in winter, cooler in summer, with money saving Window Quilt.	Insulating shades	Appropriate Technology Corporation
	Relaxation is a matter of perspective.	Caribbean cruises	Holland American Lines
	Think comfortable thoughts.	Shoes	Tretorn
	The Lane Recliner. Comfort to enjoy for a lifetime.	Easy chair	Action Industries
Convenience	All your beauty needs in one bottle.	Baby oil	Johnson & Johnson
	How to buy a gift from Cartier, when your plane leaves in 50 minutes from Kennedy.	*Package* magazine	Condé Nast Publications, Inc.
	First, there was the 2-minute egg. Now meet the 2-minute turkey.	Butterball turkey	Swift/Eckrich
	Introducing the gas self-cleaning oven.	Gas oven	Modern Maid Company
Curiosity	A new world awaits you in a new travel magazine.	*Traveler* magazine	Condé Nast Publications, Inc.
	This is only the cover . . . you should see the rest.	Caribbean cruises	Windjammer Barefoot Cruises, Ltd.
	Get valuable information on collecting fine wines including *which* wines to buy and *how much* to pay.	Magazine	Wine Spectator
	Expand your natural horizons.	Books	Nature Book Society
Egotism	Small colleges can help you make it big.	College enrollment	Council of Independent Colleges

Appeal	*Headline of advertisement*	*Product or service*	*Advertiser*
	The crystal is exclusive to us. The porcelain could be exclusive to you.	Baccarat crystal	Garrard Jewellers
	What does it take to be the best?	University enrollment	Hofstra University
	Exquisite. The diamonds, the classic designs and the woman who wears them.	Diamond jewelry	BEST Company Jewelers
Family Affection, Togetherness, and Happy Home Life	The family is more important than the family room.	Furniture	Ethan Allen Galleries
	Patent 2,823,421 has changed the way you look at your children.	Mylar® polyester film	Du Pont
	Listen to your mother.	AT&T phone	Sears Roebuck and Company
	Family affair.	Vacationer's guide	Lee Island Coast
Fear	Nuclear energy helps keep us from reliving a nightmare.	Booklet on energy independence	U.S. Committee for Energy Awareness
	Why be gray when you can be yourself?	Haircolor lotion	Loréal®
	One less thing to worry about.	Automobile	Hyundai
	"I don't intend to grow old gracefully . . . I intend to fight it every step of the way."	Cosmetic	Oil of Olay
Health	Fight cavities with a stick.	Sugarless gum	Warner-Lambert Company
	Now you can put your hay fever to sleep while you stay awake.	Anti-allergy product	Merrell Dow Pharmaceuticals, Inc.
	Finally: A sophisticated weapon in the war against plaque.	Plaque removal instrument	Dental Research Corporation
	Take control of your life.	Health center program	Palm-Aire Hotel & Spa
Hero Worship	In her own words, Teri Garr tells you why you should eat new thicker, creamier Yoplait.	Yogurt	Yoplait, U.S.A., Inc.
	Dennis Conner. Cardmember since 1983.	Charge card	American Express
	Give your favorite sports heroes a home.	Action posters	*Sports Illustrated*
	When Grandma Moses was in her 70s, she wanted to keep busy. So she took up painting.	Restaurant	Denny's
	The most unforgettable women in the world wear Revlon.	Complexion makeup	Revlon, Inc.
Kindness, Generosity, and Unselfishness	Commitment is supporting something you believe in.	Little League program	CNA Insurance
	For the cost of a morning coffee break, you can break the cycle of poverty for one small child.	Foster child sponsorship	Foster Parents Plan
	Animals wouldn't burn your home. Don't burn theirs.	Smokey the Bear	Advertising Council
	Four reasons why Upjohn's commitment to improving the quality of life is greater than ever.	Medicine	Upjohn
Love and Sex	Love at First Sight.	Sun glasses	Foster Grant
	"Laughter, Tears, Passion, Friendship, Love."	Diamonds	De Beer
	Romance on a Grand Scale.	Hotel	Grand Cypress Resort
	"I chose my crystal because of the way it came to life in candlelight. The same reason he chose me."	Crystal	Towle
Mental Stimulation	The New Encyclopaedia Britannica . . . it gives you something to talk about. And think about.	Books	Encyclopaedia Britannica, Inc.
	How to become a Straight-A Student.	Book	Publishers Choice
	European Travel & Life. A Wealth of Uncommon Knowledge.	Magazine	*European Travel & Life*
	With this sophisticated equipment, you can monitor the world for just 31 cents a day.	Newspaper	*Christian Science Monitor*
Pleasure	Pleasure on a Grand Scale.	Hotel	Grand Cypress Resort
	Great Tennis! Great Fun!	Tennis camp	All American Sports

Appeal	Headline of advertisement	Product or service	Advertiser
	The Greatest Adventure of a Lifetime could be 22¢ away.	Travel	Government of India Tourist Office
	When you're on top, you should enjoy the view.	Luxury apartment	Buckingham Towers
Sensory Appeals	Fragrances for the mind, body, and soul.	Perfume	Princess Marcella Borghese
	A.1. makes stuffed peppers taste even peppier.	Steak sauce	Nabisco Brands
	Why buy a limp excuse for a pickle when you can crunch a Claussen pickle?	Pickles	Claussen Pickle Co.
	Turn an innocent salad into a sinful indulgence.	Salad dressing	Marie's Specialty Brands
	The taste is warm. The feeling is delicious.	Cognac	Courvoisier

number of powerful points that caused endless discussion in advertising circles. One of the most important phrases to come from that book was *unique selling proposition,* or *U.S.P.*

To paraphrase from the definition in the book, the *U.S.P.* is a proposition each advertisement makes that is powerful, unique, and not offered by the competition. Sometimes the uniqueness lies in the product or in a claim that is made for the product. An example of the latter was Colgate's "Cleans your breath while it cleans your teeth."

What you must do in those minutes or hours before writing your copy is to look for the U.S.P. Sometimes it jumps right out at you. Consider the attributes of the four following products:

Product No. 1: A power lawn mower that cuts tall grass evenly even when the grass is soaking wet.
Product No. 2: Canned cream that tastes exactly like real cream.
Product No. 3: An alarm clock that plays the Brahms's "Lullaby."
Product No. 4: A magnesium tray that polishes silver without rubbing.

Can you always find a distinct U.S.P. in a product or service? No. If you're ingenious enough, however, you may be able to devise a unique claim such as that mentioned for Colgate. But suppose you can't seem to dig out any usable U.S.P.? Here is where you might rely on the suffering points approach.

A *suffering point* is the need of the consumer that possession of the product will satisfy. Remember that people do not buy products; they buy uses of the product that will take care of some problem they have. A product may take care of a consumer's suffering points without having U.S.P.

A product may start out offering a U.S.P. but then, when other products offer the same attribute, end up simply offering a suffering point. For example, after Teflon-coated frying pans became common, these products still answered a suffering point—the tendency of food to stick to frying pans.

Another suffering point, voiced by millions of nonprofessional painters, was the dripping of the paint and its regrettable habit of running down the paintbrush when the brush was held above shoulder level. DuPont's Lucite answered this problem.

Look for the suffering points in every product you advertise and bring them up humanly and believably. Suffer with the reader. Sympathize. Let him or her know that you appreciate the problem and then tell how your product solves that problem.

In the following you will read a headline and a section of body copy for an electric knife sharpener. This material demonstrates the suffering point principle at work:

Headline: Don't let a dull carving knife spoil the effect of that perfect roast.

Subhead: Keep knives sharp always with a Keen-Edge electric sharpener.

Copy: Few sights are more trying than seeing your husband hacking the picture-roast you just took out of the oven. You can avoid this sorry situation by making sure your carving knives are always sharp. Your Keen-Edge sharpener will see to that while, at the same time, it pampers your finest cutlery.

Twin aluminum oxide wheels—exclusive in this DeLuxe model—ensure scratchless sharpening while Keen-Edge's simple operation guarantees that the least mechanically minded person in your family can hone to razor sharpness any kind of knife you have. In the *kitchen,* paring, slicing, cutting chores are made easier, whether it's potatoes, tomatoes, or apples. And in the *dining room* your husband can do his stuff as a master carver whether you're serving turkey, Long Island duck, or Chateaubriand steak.

A quick inspection of the foregoing copy example shows that a number of suffering points have been answered:

- The hacking of a good-looking roast

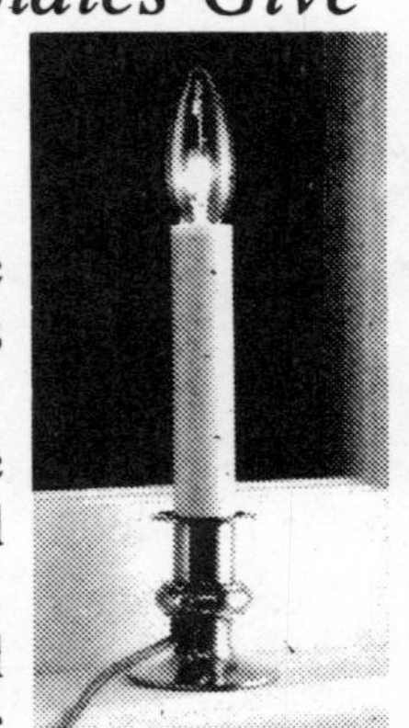

Figure 3–4. Effective small space advertisement. In this example, the copy uses the "suffering point" principle by mentioning a common failing of window candles—that they fall over easily. At the top, the headline sets a holiday note for a product sold chiefly at the Christmas season. According to the advertiser, this advertisement pulled very well, but magazine advertising for such a product normally would not bring the sales generated through catalog offerings.

- The scratching of fine cutlery in the sharpening process
- The difficulty of sharpening silver for an unskilled person

And then we come to the *point of difference.* While this would seem to be another way of saying U.S.P., it isn't necessarily. It may not be a U.S.P. that makes your product different from your competition's but merely a somewhat superior quality or product feature that makes it sharper, longer lasting, cheaper to run. It could be a brighter picture tube in the television set or a more sensitive tuning device.

Because advertising is so very competitive, it makes sense to ask: "What do we have that's different? Is there a point of difference?"

If you hear the answer "There *is* no point of difference," you may be excused if you feel a sinking sensation because you now face a difficult job in making your product stand out.

If you are told that there is a difference and the difference is important, you will probably stress the difference in the headline, opening copy, and the illustration. That difference might not be unique as in a U.S.P. but it is enough to make your product stand out and to make it sensible for you to stress it.

If the difference is not very important, it simply becomes one of the selling points of the advertisement. If it's important enough to be considered a U.S.P. of the product, the copywriter will usually build the whole advertisement around it because, of course, the best point of difference is a U.S.P.

The most powerful type of advertisement has a strong U.S.P. slammed home to the reader by having it stressed in headline, illustration, and opening copy. Yet, too often, we see advertisements that stress the most powerful point in headline and illustration but neglect it in the opening copy, or push it in headline and opening copy but let the illustration go off in another direction.

All advertisements should have three-way power—headline, illustration, and opening copy working together. What is astonishing is how many professional copywriters ignore this principle. Don't ever forget it! Give each advertisement you write **three-way** power.

4

WORKING PARTNERS

Artists and Copywriters

Gwen Taylor looked hopefully at Ed Pankow sitting across the desk from her. "Any ideas, Ed? Guess you know that the ad manager at Merchant's Trust is a short-copy type. More than four lines and he gets nervous. Says that people simply aren't interested in reading bank advertising."

"So," Ed broke in, "what you're looking for is an illustration that'll grab the reader with or without copy?"

"That's about it."

In this little episode we have a situation that occurs frequently. Instead of full copy, the necessary illustration will provide impact, grab the reader's attention, and carry the story. Teamwork by the copywriter and the artist is needed to produce a powerful, effective advertisement.

Copywriters constantly have this experience. Like Gwen, they're quick and deft with words but outstanding illustration ideas often elude them. They know from readership studies—and experience—that good copy and headlines aren't always enough. A striking, or at least competent, illustration is needed for campaign success. Poor illustrations can doom advertisements no matter how good the copy. On the contrary, a brilliant series of illustrations can ensure the selling success of a campaign for which the copy might be quite ordinary.

There is no sure way to determine whether the effectiveness of any piece of advertising is based on copy or art. One can very rarely stand by itself. Advertising graveyards are full of the gravestones of copywriters and artists who never learned the fundamental fact of teamwork.

It *is* teamwork—between you and your art associates—that will result in sound, selling advertisements, properly executed for maximum impact upon readers. There is no room for the "I-can-do-it-alone" technique. If you learn quickly how to get along with your art people, you will have taken a major step toward your creative goal.

How Deeply Should Artists Be Involved in Copy?

Some excellent artists have strayed from their creative field and have assumed positions of importance in executive capacities other than art direction. A few have become heads of advertising agencies, large and small. Others are in charge of the advertising activities of department stores and other retail operations.

The varied and complex business matters which you, as a copywriter, must know to do your part of the creative job properly have less bearing upon the work of your art director, though many of them have definite bearing upon the general layout and character of the advertisement itself. Proper emphasis, for example, of certain sales points or policy matters are most often not a part of the art director's responsibility but yours. If the art director is interested in these matters—fine, but they are "musts" for you.

Suggest, but Don't Take Over, When Working with Artists

Probably the most common error that copywriters make in attempting to cooperate with artists is to assume too much responsibility in "art direction."

Most copywriters usually resent art colleagues telling

them how to write copy, or criticizing the manner in which it has been written.

Yet, that same writer, who has written the headline, has suggested an illustration and made an amateurish sketch to show what the illustration will look like and will sometimes dictate exactly how the artist should proceed.

Advice may be offered on the artwork style, typography, lettering, and borders. Perhaps there will be an insistence on photography when the artist believes that drawings will be better. Layouts are rejected on which the artist has spent hours. The reason? The copywriter's statement, "Personally, I prefer something just a little different" or "The client won't buy these."

All this delay and extra work and pointless dictation results in a copywriter–artist relationship that is a source of irritation and the cause of poor work.

Remember that you are not an art director. There is no doubt that you can and should offer valuable suggestions about your layouts. From you, the art director must obtain all the essential information about what elements are most important to the ultimate selling job.

From you will be gained the background of the problem, background which must be understood to get the proper feeling for the work. Once this information is imparted, then it's time to let the artist proceed unhindered. A better layout will result if the artist's imagination is permitted to function freely without interference by unwanted advice from you.

The goal is to produce advertising of which you can both be proud—you of the thinking behind the advertisement and the power and clarity of the selling ideas, and the artist of the physical execution of these ideas.

Art directors will welcome suggestions from you upon which they may improvise. Artists see, in you, art of another sort. Most of them will admit that they're glad they aren't faced with the responsibility of conceiving the original copy ideas. Artists are, after all, specialists in translating those ideas to layouts and illustrations and they are much better at it than any copywriter or group of copywriters.

Regardless of the type of copy work you do, if your art associates realize that you consider the creation of advertising a job of close and friendly teamwork—if you can establish a method of joint operation with them—you will discover a richness in the routine of your daily work that many copywriters never find. Such richness will help produce good advertisements.

The success of your career as a copywriter depends in a large measure upon your knowledge of human psychology. Don't let that knowledge apply only to the people who read your advertisements. It will pay off fully in your dealings with your art directors.

How Much Do You Need to Know about Art?

Beginners in copywriting generally feel that a thorough working knowledge of art and layout is a good thing for them to have. Some young men and women, aspiring to be advertising writers, even study art in art schools to better grasp the problems they think will be confronting them.

It may be better for copywriters to know nothing at all of art than to know just enough to make them think they know a lot. Alexander Pope's "A little learning is a dangerous thing" applies very well here.

This is certainly true from the standpoint of economy of effort. Wherever you work—agency, department store, retail shop, direct-mail, or mail-order house—you will have available the services of men and women trained in making layouts and supervising artwork.

They take your ideas and make attractive and compelling layouts from them. If you, the copywriter, have a wide knowledge of art and layout, you will tend to spend time which should be spent in copywriting, making rough layouts that will neither be used nor appreciated by the artists. After all, no two artists will ever see a layout job exactly the same way.

Far better to set your ideas down on paper, *write* your suggestions for illustrations; supply the other necessary elements, such as headlines and subheads; and then forget them until you have something to look at done by a specialist. Then, if you have suggestions to make—if you would prefer to see some slightly different style of handling and you really feel that your criticisms are justified for the good of the advertisement—then is the time to take them up.

You'll get along better that way with the person it's most important to get along with. You'll have more time for your own job, copywriting. Also, copywriters' roughs often make lazy artists. They are tempted merely to "dress up" copywriters' ideas instead of applying their specialized knowledge of layout to designing the advertisement as it should be designed.

Assuming that you have reasonably sensible taste, all you need to know about art is what you will normally learn working with and around artists.

Most of your important relationships with the art department, wherever you work, will be concerned with print advertising.

Many advertising agencies, however, maintain specially trained and talented art directors whose duties are entirely confined to television visualization. In no phase of creative advertising is a person expected to be so versatile and flexible as in the creating of television "storyboards." (Although concentration in this chapter is on the need for copywriter–artist cooperation in turning out good print advertising, the importance of TV creation must be mentioned here, but full discussion will be given in the television chapters.)

Certain important fundamentals of art which can influence the success of your advertising will be covered very briefly here. Other than learning these few basic facts and terms, however, you'd better be a copywriter first and an artist last.

Types of Layouts[1]

An idea for a proposed print advertisement may be presented for approval by a client with a drawing called a "layout."

A layout, as its name implies, is the physical grouping of all the elements in an advertisement, as originally conceived by the artist. There are several types of layouts: thumbnail sketches, roughs, finished, and comprehensives.

Thumbnail Sketches

The type of layout often used in advertising operations that has the least drawing detail is called the "thumbnail sketch." This is a very rough layout done in one-half or one-fourth size, or even smaller, by the artist, and is normally used when you are considering several different ideas for a new campaign.

From thumbnail sketches, it is possible for you and your art director to determine quickly whether an idea has possibilities. You may find, however, that the various units won't fit and that it would be a waste of time to go into further layout attempts.

Rough Layouts

When you have decided upon a headline, subheads, captions, and illustrative suggestion for an advertisement, you will present the artist with this material, pointing out which selling points are to get the main emphasis, and in what sequence the other elements of the advertisement should logically follow.

From this information, the artist will then arrange the advertisement in an orderly, balanced manner, roughing in your headline and making a very rough sketch of your illustrative suggestion (or a different one, if it will work better).

This is called a "rough layout" or "visual," and from it you can determine whether the final job will maintain the place you desire, will focus proper attention on the right parts of your message, and, in general, whether your idea is going to jell.

During your early years as a copywriter, you may be working under a copy chief or supervisor, with whom you will be required to clear your ideas before passing them on to members of the art department.

When the artist has made the rough layout, you will then discuss it with your superiors, and the three of you will decide whether it is okay to proceed or whether more roughs are needed. Possibly, especially if you are working in an advertising agency, the rough layout or layouts will also be shown to others who are working on the account—contact people, account executives, and on some occasions even representatives of the client's advertising department.

Figure 4–1. Thumbnail sketches. By executing thumbnails (and even a nonartist can do so), it is possible to experiment quickly with a number of different layout combinations. The art doesn't need to be expert because the purpose is to juggle elements until the best combination is achieved.

Finished and Comprehensive Layouts

Once the rough layout is approved by all those who are concerned with its formative stages, the artist is ready to do a "finished layout" or "comprehensive layout." Such layouts are more complete than "roughs." Lettering is done rather carefully and pictures may be sketched. The client can obtain an accurate idea from the layout of just what the printed advertisement will look like.

The "comprehensive" is a layout which carries the elements of the advertisement into a more refined stage. It serves two purposes. One is to present the elements to the people who have the final say in okaying them for publication. Two is to solicit new business or to present an entirely new departure for an old campaign.

When advertisements are presented formally, all major elements in the advertisement appear as nearly as possible the way they will actually look in the printed advertisement. Because most of your clients will not possess the trained imagination of you and your art director, they may be unable to visualize the published advertisement from a rough layout. In finished and comprehen-

1. In the following section you will find four sets of "Before" and "After" advertisements. These will demonstrate that almost always it is possible to improve layouts by incorporating simple changes. Judicious use of white space is especially important in achieving more attractive advertisements. Also important is the arranging of elements that will make it easier for the shopper to read the advertisement.

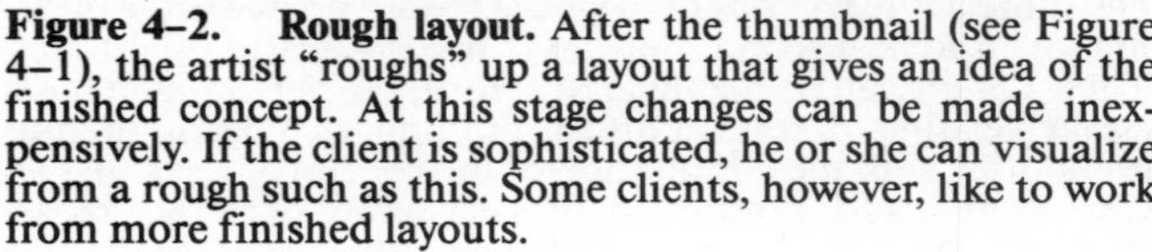

Figure 4–2. Rough layout. After the thumbnail (see Figure 4–1), the artist "roughs" up a layout that gives an idea of the finished concept. At this stage changes can be made inexpensively. If the client is sophisticated, he or she can visualize from a rough such as this. Some clients, however, like to work from more finished layouts.

Figure 4–3. Comprehensive layout. All the elements are presented well enough in the comprehensive to furnish an excellent idea of the printed advertisement. Comprehensives require much art time and can be expensive. Usually, few changes will be made—preferably none.

sive layouts, therefore, the standard procedure is to letter in carefully the headlines, subheads, and caption headings, and to include a fairly accurate sketch of the illustration.

The comprehensive must be accurate enough to be followed easily by two more persons who turn out advertisements: the commercial artist who creates the finished artwork or photograph; those who handle the printing and engraving and who must know exactly how to position the elements mechanically.

Comprehensive layouts are done with precision because of their use in presenting a new campaign idea or soliciting new business. They are usually "slick" enough to give a graphic idea of how the final job should look. When you ask an artist to make a comprehensive layout, the artist will very often ask you, "*How* comprehensive?"

Then, according to the nature of the job, the production time element, and other considerations, you will describe just how far the artist is expected to go. A five- or six-word headline for a comprehensive layout can be lettered in by a good lettering person in a few minutes, but where you wish to show an exact type style or other precision lettering, the job may require several hours.

In some places, the rule is that you should spend your time writing body copy and captions while the layout is being made, so that your entire advertisement will be ready for study at the same time. You can then take up any final copy polishing while the finished or comprehensive layout is with the art department.

This "rule" depends, however, on the situation. As mentioned in a preceding chapter, you may, when presenting campaign ideas, merely write headlines and suggest ideas for the main illustrations. The body copy can be done later.

If, however, you know what you want to write and you have done the needed background thinking and investigation, you may prefer to write all the copy in the advertisement before you give it to the artist, along with your illustration ideas. If you do, the artist will know how much space is to be occupied by the copy and can do the layout accordingly.

Sometimes, when the layout technique for a campaign has already been decided upon, you will write the same amount of copy for every advertisement because the illustration size will be the same in every instance and the space for the copy will not vary from advertisement to advertisement.

Thus, you might set your typewriter or word processor to write fifteen lines of sixty-five characters. While writing copy to such exact specifications can be irksome to some copywriters, the practice results in copy that will fit precisely into space allotted.

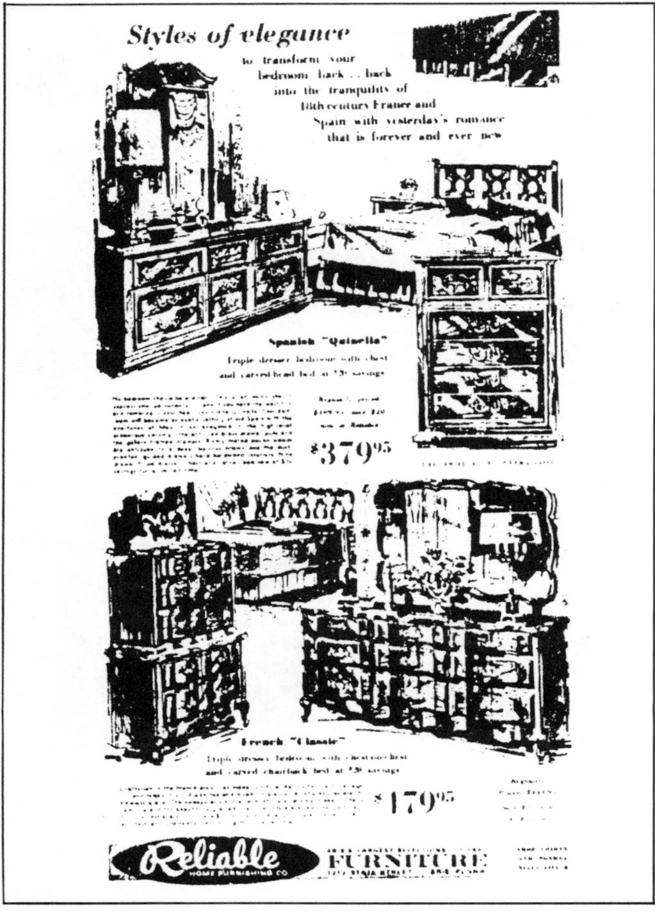

Figure 4–4a. **Before.** Here is a layout that is well organized in the way it has grouped the two styles of furniture—Spanish and French. You will see, however, in the "After" version that an even more pleasing layout can be achieved.

Courtesy of the Newspaper Advertising Bureau from *How to Make a Good Ad Better.*

Figure 4–4b. After. As one change from the "Before" example, more white space is used giving the advertisement a pleasing, open look. Second, line art is used instead of halftones. Thus, details can be highlighted. Third, the new version has a clever headline that is set off for full impact. Fourth, there is less clutter with the elimination of the picture of the store, an element that adds nothing to the sales power of the advertisement. Most of all, this reworked layout demonstrates the role of white space in achieving attractive advertisements.

Courtesy of the Newspaper Advertising Bureau from *How to Make a Good Ad Better.*

Steps in Print Production

After the layout and copy for your advertisement have been okayed by all those whose approval is necessary, it is ready for production.

Production of any advertisement requires the following procedure:

1. The art director calls in whatever type of commercial free-lance artist is needed to make the final art unless there is someone on the staff who can do the finished art. Usually this requires a specialist in some phase of art, depending upon whether the illustration is to be a careful line drawing in ink, a painting, a cartoon, a photograph, or a wash drawing. (See glossary at end of chapter.)

   Your art director could possibly do this artwork, but it is normally the job of a specialist, and in any event the art director probably wouldn't have the time to do this in addition to other duties. In many agency operations it is the custom for the art directors to farm out the actual artwork in this manner.

   Although some retail advertising departments use the farming out method also, most have staff artists who do the final artwork. Except in rare cases, it is the function of the art director to supervise the creation of the final art. The director may ask your opinion on certain points, and you certainly are privileged to offer any suggestions you may have, but the responsibility for the job rests with the art department.
2. Art directors, in most cases, are also responsible for the direction of typesetting. They will make, or have made, what is called a "type mechanical"—a tissue-paper tracing of the area into which type is to be set. This is attached to the piece of copy to be sent to the printer and shows the printer exactly how wide and how deep to set the type, specifies the type face and size to be used, and gives the printer all other specific instructions on the job.

Figure 4–5a. Before. Every lamp in the store is on sale, a point not made unmistakably in the first layout. There is another problem with this layout that is solved in the following "After" version.

Courtesy of the Newspaper Advertising Bureau from *How to Make a Good Ad Better.*

Figure 4–5b. After. There's no lack of clarity here. It's obvious that *every* lamp is on sale. It's more important to convey that point than to show a few styles. Likewise, the layout follows the principle of offering a dominant element. In the "Before" version there is nothing for the eye to focus on. In the new version we have more impact and excitement.

Courtesy of the Newspaper Advertising Bureau from *How to Make a Good Ad Better.*

3. Once the artwork is completed and okayed and copy is set and okayed, the job passes on to the engraver, who makes the plates from which the advertisement is printed. (With the advent of computers and word processors much work these days is camera-ready, eliminating much of the need for traditional printing methods that marked the hot-type era.) This, again, in most operations is watched carefully by the art director.

In many large advertising agencies and retail operations, there are subdepartments which specialize in mechanical production and which are responsible for all printing and engraving. Even where there are such experts on hand, however, the supervision of the production of the advertisement remains in the hands of the art director.

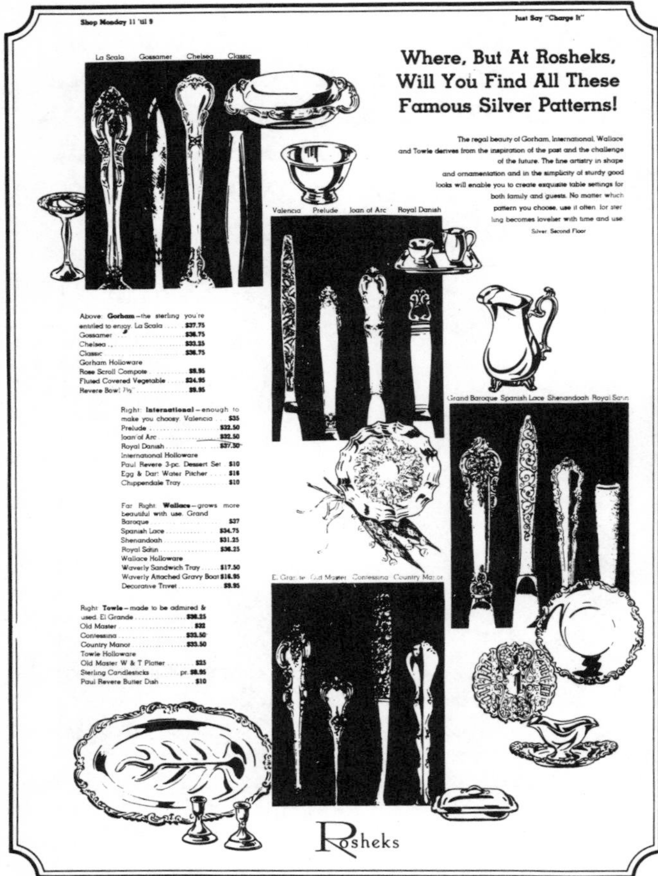

Figure 4–6a. Before. In this instance, the layout artist followed accustomed practice in displaying the product groupings in a reverse-C eyeflow pattern but notice in the "After" example, how the new layout has made reading the advertisement even simpler for the reader.

Courtesy of the Newspaper Advertising Bureau from *How to Make a Good Ad Better.*

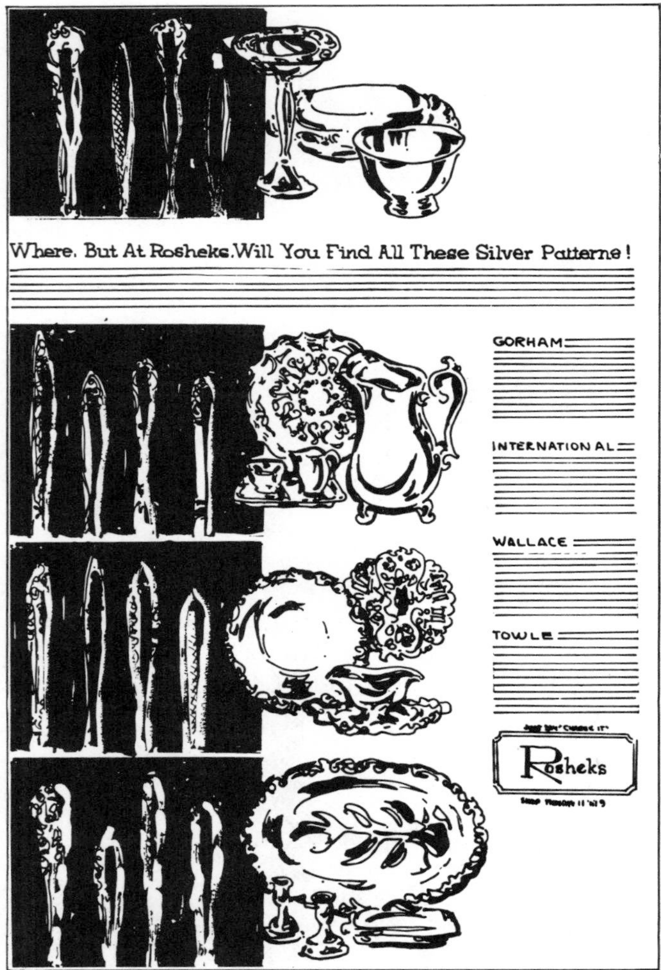

Figure 4–6b. After. Now we have an "easier" advertisement to read. Also, the re-do gives more space to the item, enabling the reader to examine the patterns more clearly. The headline, too, stretches across the advertisement creating more impact than the headline in the "Before" version, where it is tucked away in the upper corner for low visibility. In version "After," as pleasing as it is, it is possible that the reader might hesitate before deciding which copy block pertains to which of the four illustrations.

Courtesy of the Newspaper Advertising Bureau from *How to Make a Good Ad Better.*

What You Need to Know about Mechanical Production

As in the case of art, you do not need to be an authority on production. It would take years of working closely with printers and engravers to give yourself even the most modest background in the lore of that field.

You can and should, however, have a "working knowledge" of the operations of these trades. You should learn exactly what happens to your advertisements after they gain the okay of your superiors and/or clients.

You should know the fundamentals of hot type and cold type printing, engraving, the use and production of electrotypes, and other mechanics of typesetting. You should be familiar with various styles of typefaces. It will help you find what can be done to obtain special effects in the printing of your advertisements.

You won't often be called upon to use this information, but it will help you to know just what you can expect in the way of reproduction of your ideas, and to know what is and is not possible from a production standpoint. Also, some copy jobs call for more production knowledge than others.

Know Typography but Don't Use Too Many Typefaces

A common mistake of beginning copywriters is to call for too many typefaces. Let the art department or production people make these selections. Neither they, nor you, should use a full array of typefaces in an advertisement.

Most of the time you won't be expected to specify type, but when you do, the knowledge is useful, as the following comments demonstrate. The first is from a young woman copywriter in a large department store:

> Because the copywriter here does have a "finger in the pie" as far as layout and typefaces are concerned, a sound knowledge of typography is invaluable. I recall that in school I talked my way out of the typography requirement. . . . I rue the day now. To show how type knowledge is always with us, we use a different advertising approach for our basement departments than for the upstairs sections. Typefaces are different along with artwork.

Another woman copywriter wrote:

> On my very first day I was asked to indicate type to be used—faces and sizes. Furthermore, I had to make it fit. I was certainly glad I had that one course in typography and that I had learned copyfitting.

Knowing How to Fit Copy Is Vital

A favorite expression of printers (who tend to think that copypeople are ignoramuses about production) is "Space isn't elastic, you know. Write your copy to the space."

Hard-boiled printers won't hide their exasperation if you've written 350 words to fit into a 50-word space. Get it right the first time. At first you may need to use a copyfitting method to be sure. After you've picked up experience, you can estimate quickly whether your copy will fit.

You can learn in a few minutes the character-count method of copyfitting. It will pay off when you stare at your layout and wonder whether the space allotted for copy will take 50, 100, or 150 words. There are methods other than the character-count system for use in copyfitting. Learn some method so that you'll be able to save yourself the painful job of rewriting copy just because you had no idea of how much copy you could write for the space allowed.

The following simple method enables you to fit type if you know the size of the space to be filled:

1. Find an advertisement that has (a) type of the size you think is suitable for the advertisement you are preparing, and (b) the kind of spacing between lines you want.
2. Now count the characters (including spaces and punctuation marks) per inch on the line of type you have selected as suitable. Then multiply by the number of inches in the line that you are going to use in *your* advertisement. (Thus if there are sixteen characters to the inch, you can set your typewriter at fifty-six if your line is to be 3½ inches.)
3. Next, measure how many lines of this type will fit into a vertical inch. In Step 1(b), you selected an example that was suitably spaced (leaded) between lines. When you measure, you find that the lines so spaced fit eight lines to the vertical inch. (Thus if the space to be filled is four vertical inches, you will be typing thirty-two lines of copy, each line having fifty-six characters.)

Another simple method is to utilize a "type specimen" book that shows type in different faces and different sizes. Using this book, you can follow the procedure described in the foregoing section.

Guidelines for Typography

The following guidelines were condensed from an approximately 1,100-word staff memo at Benton & Bowles:

> There are exceptions to every one of the following guidelines, but, on the other hand, there is a good solid reason behind each. In general, the rules of typography follow custom. We find that what we are most accustomed to read is what we read most comfortably and easily.

1. A line should be 1½ to 2 alphabets long. The longer the line, the harder it is for the eye to follow.
2. Body text should not be set in smaller than 10-point. Some folks wear glasses.
3. Use one typeface throughout, for display lines and text. This is an esthetic consideration. An ad looks more homogeneous, less busy, less distracting, when so set.
4. A long copy block must be broken up! This is one rule you will hardly ever want to break.
5. Avoid setting the body copy in reverse whenever possible. Reverse type will cut down readership.
6. If the paragraph leads are not indented, more leading is required between paragraphs.
7. Don't print text over tint blocks. It's harder to read that way.
8. Don't print the text over illustration or design element. It is a signal to the reader that the copy really isn't very important.
9. Use lowercase instead of caps in display lines. Lowercase is more legible.
10. Body copy should always have an even left-hand margin for easier reading.
11. When there are several copy elements, align them wherever possible. This is to avoid a cluttered, busy look to an ad.
12. Use numerals instead of bullets when possible.
    a. All bullets do is to signal that you have a list.
    b. Numbers do the same job better, add interest, make your list seem more important.
13. Never run a picture without a caption. (Well, hardly ever.)
14. Try to run a cutline under every main illustration.
15. Don't be afraid of "widows!"
16. Use normal punctuation. Commas, semicolons, periods, and dashes serve a useful purpose in guiding the reader through your copy. Leaders (those nasty little dots . . .) usually are merely a crutch for proper punctuation. In addition, they make copy look messy and uninviting.
17. Don't overdo the bangs. Exclamation points are often the refuge of the writer who can't think up exciting thoughts.
18. Keep your sentences short. They make copy look less formidable. They lend a feeling of urgency and conviction.
19. Use italics sparingly. Italics are good for occasional emphasis. A lot of italics in a piece of copy make it look paler and weaker, instead of adding impact.

Figure 4–7a. Before. Although this layout sets out the different elements in an orderly way, the theme of the advertisement—Beat the Tax—is somewhat lost.

Courtesy of the Newspaper Advertising Bureau from *How to Make a Good Ad Better.*

Figure 4–7b. After. In this re-do, the "Beat the Tax" theme is dramatically highlighted in big type set in a reverse block. Furthermore, the whole layout has a cleaner, more open look. Because this is a once-a-year, important merchandising event, it is played up; but the individual items and prices are played down. Certainly, with the new layout treatment, no one will miss the theme.

Courtesy of the Newspaper Advertising Bureau from *How to Make a Good Ad Better.*

20. Sans serif type is better in display than in text. That's because this cleaner, more modern-looking face is easy to read in big size, not so easy in running text.

Color: When to Use It

Sometimes you *can't* use color. Very small space units in magazines and newspapers don't qualify for color. Yet, these small advertisements often pull readership and sales very effectively. This is one answer to the question whether you "must" use color. Obviously, you must not.

Still, research shows consistently that, all things being equal, color advertisements perform better than black and white advertisements. Common sense will tell you, for example, that the subject matter of an advertisement is important in making the color decision. Draperies, color film, floor covering, food products are just a few of the categories that cry for color. They are sold through color.

Other advertisers whose products don't necessarily require color for selling effectiveness use color simply for added attention value.

Full color isn't always needed. Occasionally, instead of calling for a four-color treatment, you will do better to use one color in order to focus on an important element in the advertisement, a new lipstick shade, for example.

Packages Take Center Stage

Although no one denies the importance of headlines, body copy, and illustrations, the most important single element in hundreds of advertisements is the package. If your product comes in a bottle, carton, package or some other container, you and the artist should plan to make the package the "hero" in the layout. It should be big enough to have impact and should be placed for utmost prominence.

Consumers may forget your headline when they're in the supermarket or drugstore but they *must* remember the package. Package design is an art. Once that design has been approved, the advertising must give it featured billing. This does not mean that you will very often ask that the package be the *only* illustration in the advertisement because readership studies reveal that this technique tends to obtain low attention. It *does* mean that in building the layout the artist is ever conscious of the placement and prominence to be given the package. It is not an element to be inserted as an afterthought.

Such featuring of the package is vital in all media—magazines, newspapers, outdoor, transit, and television. Even radio commercials use such phrases as "Look for it in the bright blue and white package on your grocer's shelves." If such an announcement has been preceded by strong featuring of the package in print advertisements, the radio commercial is thus enhanced.

Question: Should You Use Photographs or Artwork?

Photography is most often going to be used in advertising illustration because of its realism. This is true whether you are concerned with consumer or business advertising. Thus, under normal circumstances you will call for, or expect, photography for your advertising illustrations.

Still, artwork *is* used and may be suitable if:

- **Exaggeration is desirable,** as in the case of some high-fashion advertising in which the models have a fashionably elongated look never found in real life.
- **A schematic, or cross section, is wanted,** as may be the case in an industrial advertisement aimed at engineers.
- **A seasonal illustration is needed** in the off-season, such as a snow scene in the summer or a farm spring-plowing scene in the harvest season.
- **It is difficult, or impossible, to find the right people as models for photography.** These might be current people or historical figures.
- **Speed is important.** It may take a long time to get the proper photographic shot, but a good artist can sketch what is needed quickly and on order.
- **Cartoon treatment is desired.** This treatment might be especially suitable for comic page advertising or for advertising to children.
- **Way-out mood, or atmosphere, is needed.** Horror, exclusiveness, or satire may often be conveyed more starkly or subtly through artwork.

Figure 4–8. Small space advertisement using reverse type. Often it is desirable when using small advertisements to set them in reverse type but only if the type is readable and there isn't too much of it. Because of the use of reverse in this instance, the advertisement will stand out even on a page where there are larger advertisements.

Suggestions for Doing Rough Layouts

Here are some suggestions if you are a copywriter who works in small organizations—agencies, companies, or retail stores—which expect you to do rough layout work.

1. Make sure you supply a dominant element, something for the reader's eyes to focus upon and to attract his attention. This element will usually be the illustration, but sometimes it can be a big headline. Above all, avoid making layouts that have no impact because you've cluttered them with a number of different elements of equal size.
2. Make your headlines and illustrations competitive in size and character with other advertising. This suggestion is especially important when your advertisement is to be on a big newspaper page with advertisements that are equal in size, or even bigger.

   One way to tell whether your advertisement's elements *are* competitive is to mount your layout on a page with other display advertisements. Then put the page on the floor, or pin it up on a wall cork- board. You'll see quickly if you've made such elements as the headline, illustrations, logotype, or price figures big enough to compete.

   In most advertisements, make the logotype big enough, or distinctive enough, to stand out. Now and then the mood of the advertisement or the nature of the product is such that the logo can be relatively small. Usually, however, it must be commanding enough to ensure that readers know the advertiser, or the product, being advertised.
3. Keep copy elements out of illustration area—items such as headlines, subheads, price figures. When such elements intrude into the illustration area, they distract from the illustration and they give a cluttered feeling to the advertisement.

Figure 4–9. Illustration using artwork. Although photography dominates in advertising illustrations, there are times when artwork might be preferable. This is one of them. Artwork can evoke a mood. In this instance, the soaring grace of the ballerina is captured in art. There is no need to be literal. Feeling is more important and art conveys feeling admirably.

4. Don't play tricks with copy and headlines by putting them in circles, wavy lines, upside down, or in odd shapes. Such tricks will cost you extra typesetting charges. Furthermore, whatever attention value you achieve will be offset by loss of readership and by the annoyance felt by many readers who don't like it when the advertiser makes the message hard to read.
5. Favor the 3-to-5 proportion in layouts. Artists, from ancient times, have preferred the 3-to-5 proportion. Except for unusual circumstances they shun squarish shapes; long, narrow shapes; or wide, shallow shapes. An advertisement 6 in. by 10 in. exemplifies the 3-to-5 proportion. Furthermore, the 3-to-5 proportion fits nicely into the "pyramid" construction of newspaper pages. In fact, a wide, shallow advertisement may be rejected by newspapers because it is not suitable for the pyramid construction. Examine Figure 4–11 to see why this would be so.

You, Your Artist, and the Campaign Look

While, at times, in national advertising you may devise advertisements that are not part of a campaign, most are part of a series that carry out a theme. This same theme may be used for a half year or a year, or it may go on indefinitely.

In order to identify advertisements in your campaign and make them stand out, you employ certain techniques in copy and art. In copy, each advertisement will feature a writing style, an individual use of words, a distinctive headline approach, copy of a certain length, and, possibly, the use of subheads or a slogan.

It is your artist, however, who will make the greatest contribution to the campaign resemblance in advertisement after advertisement. The two of you will collaborate in achieving this resemblance. This is truly a team effort because there has to be complete agreement before you launch a long-term campaign. Here are some of the art elements to consider; these elements involve typography, as well.

1. If you use color, use similar colors in all advertisements. Type style likewise should be consistent. Don't change families of type.
2. Slogans and trademark characters (if either is used) should be in the same location and should be of the same size.
3. A distinctive logo (product or company name) should look exactly the same in every advertisement and usually should be in the same location. This is certainly one of the most important requirements for the campaign resemblance and product or company identification.
4. A well-designed border can call immediate attention to a campaign advertisement, but this is usually more true if the campaign features advertisements of less than a page.
5. Headlines and illustrations that look alike consistently mark the campaign advertisements instantly. This resemblance is created by using main headlines of the same length and type size, and illustrations of the same size and character. Character, in this instance, refers to the subject matter used and style of art or photography.
6. Copy blocks should be of the same size and usually, but not always, follow the same arrangement or placement.
7. Balance of the layout will be consistent once you have decided whether it should be formal or informal.

The result of the planning that you and your artist have done should be a series of advertisements that are so distinctive that readers will eventually be able to name the advertiser or product instantly without reading the body copy or even seeing the logotype. Most important, to repeat, is the incorporation of these various elements in the same way until (and if) it is decided that it's time to create a new campaign.

Production and Art Terms

Terms supplied here are used constantly, whether in preparation of newspaper, magazine, retail, agency, or

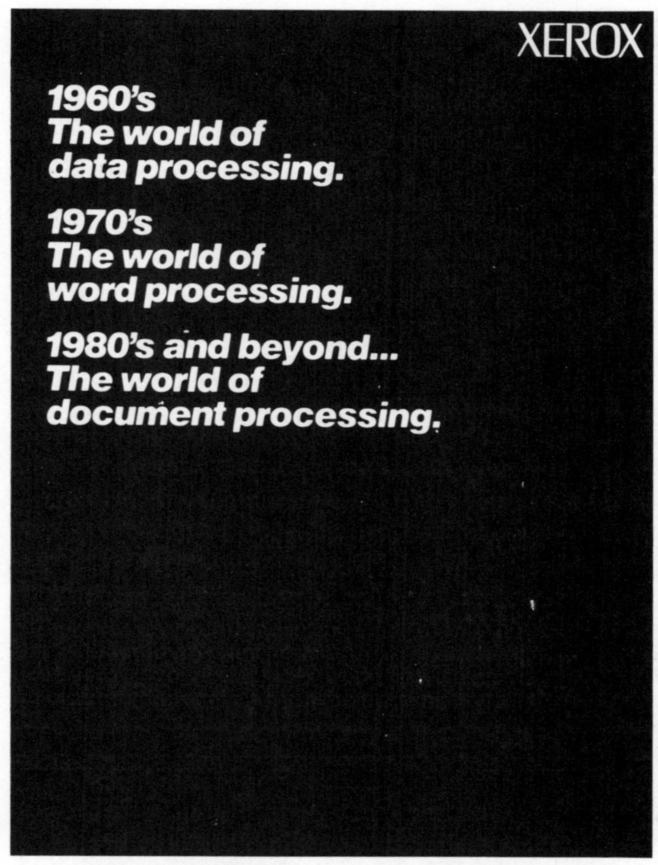

Figure 4–10a. Campaign advertisement. Occasionally, the creative team may decide to eliminate an illustration as in this case. Considerable impact is achieved with the white printing on the solid black background.

Figure 4–10b. Campaign advertisement. See Figure 4–10a for another advertisement in the campaign. Once again the creative team decided on a different format. This time a dominant illustration was omitted in favor of small illustrations accompanied by copy explaining the uses of the ten products pictured. The technique is effective when you have many products to sell and much to say about each one.

other advertisements. There are many other production terms for print advertising, and television requires that you learn another extensive set of production terms.

Working daily with print and production terms will soon give you an easy facility with the terminology, something that doesn't seem possible when you read about them in a book.

Agate. In the early days of newspapers this was a popular size of type that fit fourteen lines to the vertical inch. Later, newspapers charged national advertisers by the agate line, but this was changed when newspapers adopted the standard advertising unit (SAU) for measuring space and assessing costs. Under the new arrangement, national as well as local advertisers are charged by the column inch.

Air Brushing. Blowing a liquid pigment onto photographs or wash drawings. Results in smooth, tinted surfaces.

Ben Day Processing. A medium for use in photomechanical engraving for adding tints, shading, or stippling to line engravings. The important result is that it gives line plates a halftone tonal appearance. Its use eliminates hand shading of a drawing, thus avoiding irregularities. The ordinary method of indicating on the drawing the portions to be shaded is to attach a transparent flap upon it and mark the areas of each Ben Day with appropriate colors.

Bleed. Printed matter runs right to edge of page. This creates an illusion of size and gives a natural appearance. It may add to cost—about 10 to 15 percent in some magazines. It is usually not available in regular press runs of newspapers.

Body Type. Refers to type sizes generally used for the composition of body matter. The sizes are 6 to 14 points.

Box. An element composed of four rules which has art or type inside. Should not be used too often because it gives advertisement a mechanical appearance. Good occasionally, however, to focus attention on that part of the advertisement.

Broadside. This is a large printed sheet used as a circular and folded into a size that can be used for mailing. It differs from a folder in that its printed matter runs across the sheet, regardless of the fold.

Camera-ready Copy. A paste-up that's ready to be photographed by the platemaker. It is the last step before actual production.

Figure 4–10c. Campaign advertisement. Two other advertisements in this series appear in this chapter. See Figures 4–10a, b. Like the others, this one uses the black bar across the top with the company name prominently displayed. Unlike the other two, this one uses people, but once more lets the campaign theme-line substitute for a conventional headline. Despite distinct differences in all three advertisements, campaign identity has been clearly established by the use of words and layout technique.

Camp Art. This is art that is self-consciously so bad that it has become acceptable, especially in youthful circles. It has a strong element of humor.

Carbro. A carbro is a photographic print in full color, as distinguished from a black-and-white print that has been retouched in color. Carbros are ideal for use as artwork on subjects that are likely to require retouching or idealization. They are not as satisfactory for "snapshot" or "candid" color illustrations because of the length of exposure time needed.

Cold Type Composition. Copy composed for photomechanical reproduction by means other than the use of metal type; usually by the typewriter or computer printer.

Column Inch. Local and national advertisers use column inches to measure the size of advertisements and thus are charged for the number of column inches they use. A column inch is one inch deep and one column wide no matter how wide the column. A newspaper utilizing the change to SAU is typically 6 columns wide by 21 inches deep for a total of 126 column inches to the page. Magazine advertisements, incidentally, are measured and charged for in terms of page units such as a page, quarter page, half page, and so forth.

Combination Plate. The combining of a halftone and line plate in one engraving.

Contrast. A difference in tonal values in an illustration which gives strong highlights and shadows.

Crib File. Also called "swipe" file. This is a collection of illustrative material filed by advertising artists. The files are usually crammed with many advertisements that may be under different headings such as "Babies," "Animals," "Machinery." If the artist is stuck, he can refer to the file for ideas. He can use what he finds as a point of departure, or he may lift the idea bodily.

Crop. To cut off or trim an illustration to make it fit into a space.

Cut. Any plate used for printing.

Display Type. Larger type, usually starting with 14 points, that is used for heads and subheads and other material that is to stand out.

Electrotype. A duplicate of an original engraving or type form. These are used when the same advertisement is to appear in various publications and save the expense of making separate engravings for each. "Electros," as they are called, are useful for long runs, for color work, and for fine engravings. They are electrolytically reproduced from the original type and/or engraving. They are expensive to make and costly to ship because of their weight.

Engraving. A metal plate of copper or zinc upon which is etched the lines from which an advertisement is reproduced.

Face. The printing surface of a piece of type is called its face. The same word is used to describe a style of type.

Font. A complete assortment or font of any one size and style of type. It contains all the characters—capitals, small capitals, lowercase letters, numerals, punctuation marks, and so forth.

Highlight. Light areas in an illustration. Term is used very frequently in photographic work and is understood to be the opposite of shadow.

Insert. A page, either type matter or illustration, printed separately from the regular sections and tipped in later between the pages. In newspapers these are often called color preprints.

Island Position. An advertisement is in this position when it is entirely surrounded by editorial matter. Such positions are found most often in magazines.

Leading. The spacing between lines of type that is achieved by the placing of metal strips between the lines. It varies by a point system such as 2-point leading, 3-point leading. If there is no leading, the type is described as "set solid."

Line Drawing. Drawings made with pen and black ink are commonly called line drawings. In this class are included drawings made in line, stipple, or brush strong enough in color to be reproduced in the line etching process. In line drawing there is no continuous blending of color from light to dark as in photographs or wash drawings. It consists of solid blacks and pure whites.

Lowercase. The small letters in a font of type as distinguished from the capital letters.

Masking. The use of material to protect or block out certain areas on a proof or plate.

Mechanical. When a client approves copy, a "mechanical" is made which explains to the typographers the typefaces required and the position of copy in the advertisement. The mechanical is really a tracing of the layout in outline form. The art director dictates the style of type which in his judgment will be consistent with the design of the page. The copy is measured by actual count of characters that can fit into the space allotted on the mechanical. The typographer follows this mechanical exactly.

Montage. Refers to the putting together into a single unit of several photographs or drawings. The term is also used in television when several scenes are shown together or follow each other in rapid succession.

Mortise. A mortise is a place in an engraving where part of the plate has been cut out to insert type or other illustrative material. Mortising is the cutting away of the part of the block, usually in a space that has been left for the insertion of type matter.

Mounted Plate. An engraving plate which is mounted "type high" (0.9186 of an inch). The mount may be metal or wood.

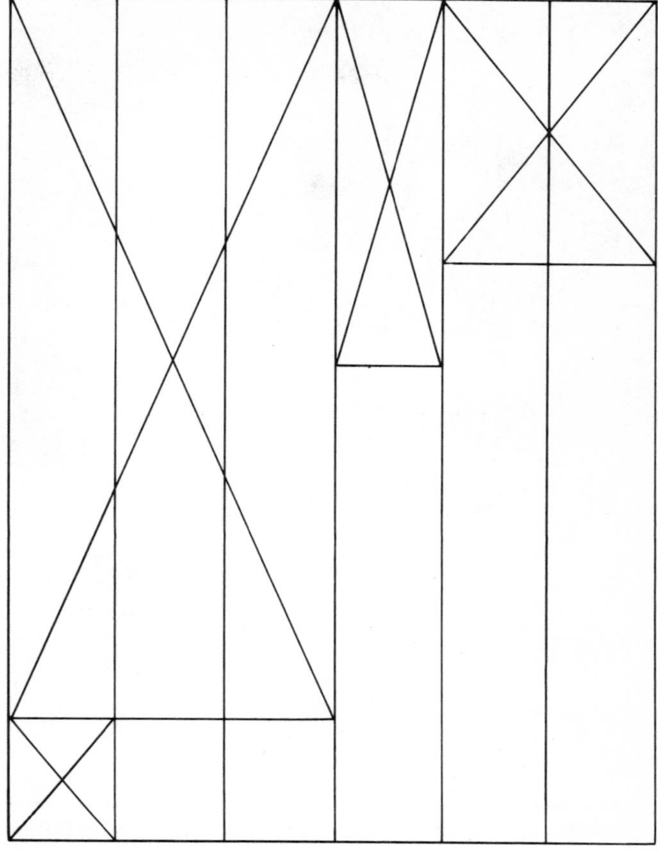

Figure 4–11. Newspaper "dummy." A dummy, such as shown here, is worked up by the page makeup person on a newspaper. It is used to indicate the placement of advertising and news material. Advertising goes in first and is marked by the X's. News material goes into the areas not marked with an X. Most often newspapers build the so-called pyramid design for pages from left to upper right. This type of makeup favors layouts that are vertical rectangles rather than squares. Also, pyramid design normally rules out advertisements that are wider than they are deep. Such advertisements—wide shallow advertisements—are hard to fit into pyramid page construction. Although almost any vertical rectangle can be fit into a pyramid construction, the ideal proportion of an advertisement is 3 to 5 (incidentally, in giving the dimensions of an advertisement, always give the width first).

Opaque. A water-soluble paint applied to negatives to block out areas by making them nontransparent.

Overlay. In producing layouts, sometimes alternate suggestions and ideas for arrangements of headlines, copy, or illustration may be desired. A transparent overlay is made and attached to the original, showing these alternates. Very often overlays are made on drawings or paintings to show the engravers the position of lettering, type, or supplementary art to be superimposed when engravings are being made.

Paste-up. When various pieces of art, lettering, design, and typography are ready for final assembly, a paste-up of these units is necessary for positioning. This paste-up is necessary for two reasons:

1. To give the art director a chance to make any necessary adjustments because of changes, correc-

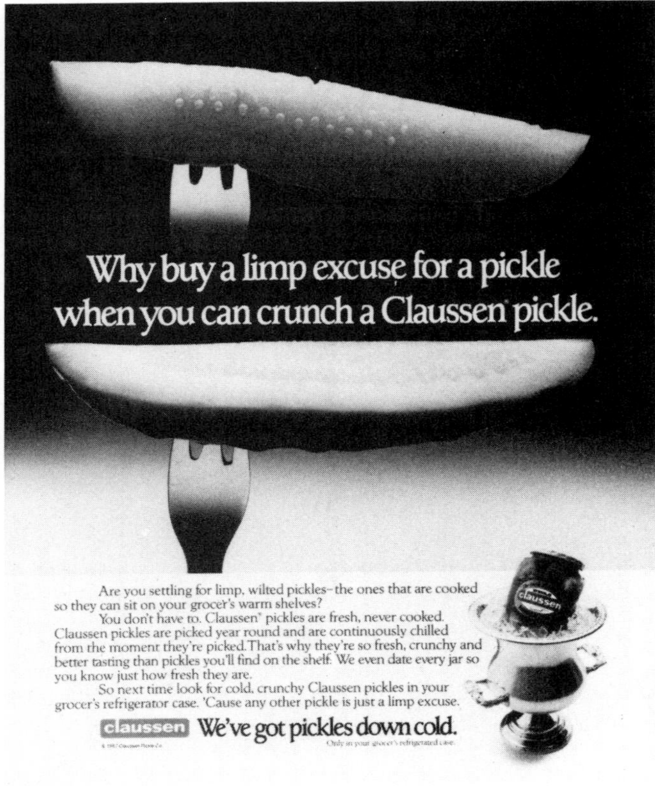

Figure 4–12. Striking illustration with indirect question headline. This attention-getting illustration demonstrates that it isn't always necessary to have people in illustrations. No reader can ignore the message of the advertisement nor fail to respond to the sensory appeal of the illustration. This appeal is enhanced by the words in the headline such as "limp excuse" and "crunch."

Photographs courtesy of Oscar Mayer Foods Corporation. Claussen is a registered trademark of Oscar Mayer Foods Corporation.

tions, or additions to art or copy after original layout was made.

2. To get the client's approval. If artwork is made up of a number of separate pieces, it shows the advertisement as a unit.

Pica. In printing, a pica equals 12 typographical points or 1/6 inch. On a typewriter the key size is either pica or the small elite size.

Progressive Proofs. Made from separate plates used in color-process work to show the printing sequence and the result after each additional color has been applied. They are furnished to the printer by the engraver.

Reproduction Proofs. Often called "repro proofs," these are proofs of great sharpness. They can be used for reproduction.

Retouch. Change a negative or photograph through art techniques. May eliminate or tone down such sections.

Reverse Plate. A line plate in which the whites come out black and vice versa. Thus the letters will normally be white against a black background. Such technique is especially useful in small advertisements that must flag

THE ADVERTISING COUNCIL Ad Council

We don't know how to solve every problem in the community, but we know the people who do.

WHERE THERE'S A NEED, THERE'S A WAY.

Thanks to you it works for all of us.

Figure 4–13. All-type advertisement with long headline. Although the use of an illustration is desirable for most advertisements, occasionally it can be eliminated in favor of using a long, attention-getting headline such as this.

Courtesy of the Advertising Council.

attention. Don't use this technique for long copy because it is difficult to read.

Run-in. To set type without paragraph breaks or to insert new copy without making a new paragraph.

Scaling. Working out measurements for art that is being reduced, or enlarged, to fit a space.

Scratchboard Drawing. Drawing made by scratching a knife across a previously inked surface.

Script. Script lettering will sometimes bring distinctiveness to headlines or other text as well as provide a style of lettering to harmonize with a special design or special space. It is a continuous form of letters into words. Typographers are able to set type designed especially to imitate a hand-lettered script character.

Self-mailer. A direct-mail piece that can be mailed without an envelope.

Set Solid. Type composed with no lead between the lines.

SpectaColor. This is an advertisement printed by rotogravure in another plant for later use in a newspaper. Unlike a preprint advertisement, a SpectaColor advertisement has clearly defined margins.

Stock Art. This is art that usually falls in many categories, listed alphabetically, that the artist may draw upon for particular situations. Many companies supply books of stock shots that may be found in the offices of artists. If the artist wants a certain shot, he orders it by number and gets back a glossy photograph for a modest price. The danger is that some other agency may be ordering the same shot at the same time for use in the same publication.

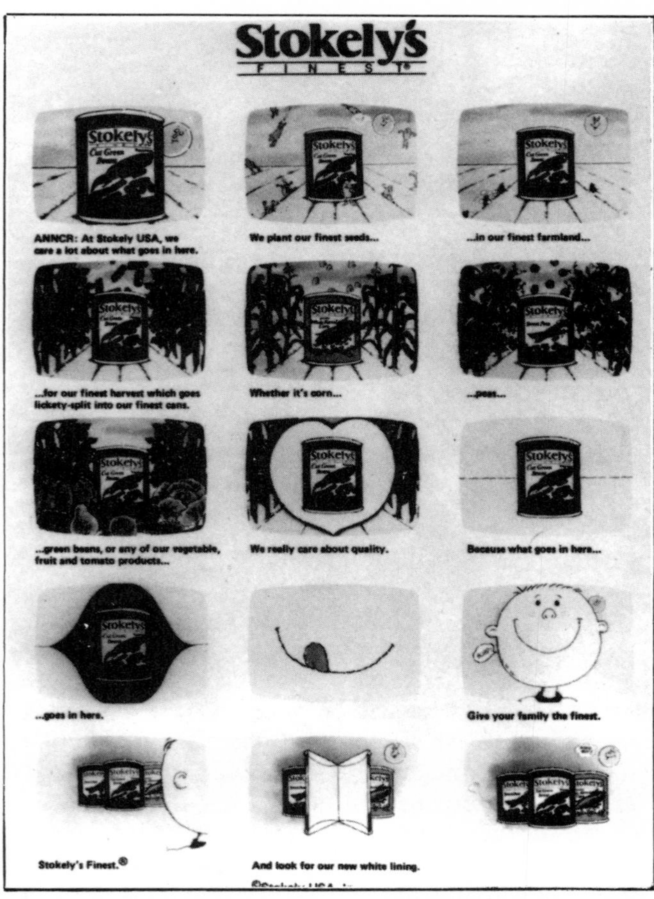

Figure 4–14. Antimated television commerical. Artwork takes many forms—in this case animation, an especially demanding form.

Strip-in. Patch placed in an engraving containing correction for original plates. The metal is cut away and new metal, engraved with the correction, is inserted and locked in.

Tooling. Hand-cutting of white areas in engraving for retouching purposes.

Wash Drawing. A drawing in sepia, India ink, or transparent colors. The color or shading is "washed" on as with a brush. Suitable for halftone. Most wash drawings are made in "black and white"—that is, they are made on white drawing board usually in tones of color running from black to very light grays or pure white in the highlights. An opaque pigment is used in making an opaque wash drawing.

The composition is first worked up in masses or all over and then the artist adds lights and shade as may be necessary to emphasize the right detail. This ability to place emphasis where needed makes wash drawings better than photographs for many types of products—especially where great detail is needed.

Widow. A very short line carried over to the top of a newspaper column or magazine page. Sometimes a copywriter will be asked to rewrite a piece of copy in order that the widow can be avoided and a full-length line used instead.

Attract Readers with These Illustration Techniques

Illustrations are as boundless as the imaginations of artists. No one knows for certain what illustration will succeed or fail. Still, some subject matter of illustrations seems to have a consistent appeal. A few approaches are listed here in case sometime you're groping for a direction to go:

- People pull better than things. Generally, an illustration featuring a person or persons—especially if something interesting is being done by the person or persons—will pull better readership than illustrations that feature an object such as the product, package, or something else that is inanimate.

  This suggestion isn't always pertinent in industrial advertising, however, because industrial readers may well be more interested in an illustration of a piece of machinery, or in a blueprint, or schematic drawing.
- Babies, puppies, kittens, and animals in general have pulling power. Studies are available that tell which animals pull better than others. For example, because many people dislike cats, a cat isn't always the best choice to feature.
- Men tend to pay more attention to advertisements featuring men, and women are more attracted to advertisements featuring women. As you can imagine, there are numerous exceptions to this observation. Furthermore, as an observation, it is much more pertinent when the person in the illustration is shown doing something interesting and/or relevant to the interests of the readers—male or female, as the case may be.
- Occasionally an all-type advertisement works well. By the nature of the type and the editorial tone of the advertisement, the type serves almost as an illustration. The all-type approach is used when an announcement of an important development or of a dramatic new product or service is needed. Because illustrations are so very important as attention-getters and for actual selling, it is generally better to use an illustration but, occasionally, you may choose the all-type technique. If you do, make it look as much like surrounding editorial material as possible with a big headline and news-type appearance.
- Celebrities pull well when featured in advertisements. Here again, it is necessary to qualify. Results are better if the celebrity can be connected in some way with the product or service advertised—such as a sports star and athletic equipment, or a situation such as the one in the Volkswagen advertisement that showed a 7′ 2″ basketball star riding comfortably in the small car.

  Just showing the celebrity isn't enough. The celebrity should be doing something interesting, relevant (to the reader), or both. Thus, if you had to choose between showing the product by itself or a celebrity by himself or herself, in most cases you'd choose the former because the product should be the "hero"; and the use of a celebrity is employed only to enhance that product-as-hero status.

5

GET YOUR ADVERTISEMENTS OFF TO A FAST START WITH POWERFUL HEADLINES

Part A

Lisa Cameron, advertising manager for a leading cosmetics firm, gazed reprovingly at Trevor Novak, account executive for the Creative Designs advertising agency.

"Trevor, like me, you've probably grown up with that axiom that 80 percent of the selling power of an ad is in the headline. Would you agree?"

"Sure, I agree that headlines are important but whether the 80 percent figure's right, who knows?"

"Regardless, let's look at this head your people have put on this ad. Where's the sell? Where's the attention-getting? Where's the identification for our product and company? This is a label, not a headline. Frankly, I'm disappointed."

Now, let's switch to Jack Campbell.

Jack Campbell is a nervous type. Although he boasts about his reading of magazines and newspapers, the truth is that he's a "skimmer" where advertisements are concerned. Unless advertisers can catch his attention with headlines and subheads, they can scratch our Mr. Campbell as a prospect. A quick flick of his gaze is all they get for their carefully prepared advertisements.

Mrs. Campbell, although she runs the household and works at a parttime job, spends much more time on advertising than does her husband. But with her double duties, she has no time to waste. The advertiser's task is to get busy Mrs. Campbell, and others like her, to hesitate before going on to the next advertisement.

In either situation, the advertiser relies on headlines to flag the reader and to create enough interest to force that pausing over the advertisement. The headline doesn't *convince* the reader, that comes later. It says in effect, "Here's something interesting," "Here's news," "Here's a useful item," "Here's something profitable for you," or "Here's an easy way to do something."

When you've written your headline, you've taken your first step toward the sale. It's a vital step because if you fail to attract Mr. or Mrs. Campbell to your advertisement or your message, you're out of the action completely. You must get that initial attention and that initial sparking of interest.

Headline or Illustration—Which Is More Important?

Arguments between copywriters and artists about which does the better job of gaining the reader's attention—the headline of the advertisement or the illustration—fail to settle the issue. Sometimes the illustration is the principal attention-getter. Sometimes the headline wins.

Actually, you have only three ways of shouting "Stop and Read" to your prospects:

- Headline alone
- Illustration alone
- A combination of both

You will find that—often enough to be called standard technique—this last method will prove to be most logical. Headlines fall into certain categories or types. You will see how, in each type, the words and illustration are usually so closely allied that often neither the copywriter nor the artist could tell you which was the original thought.

Your relationship to your art associates is one, as already discussed, that can and will have an important bearing upon the success you attain. Functioning as a team, you can contribute immeasurably to the quality of the work the other turns out.

Good Headlines Don't Come Easily

Most copywriters will tell you that once they've worked up a good headline, the rest of the copy seems to fall in line. The creating of a clever or sales-producing headline is usually sheer hard work, and you'll never know before you start a headline-writing session how long it will take you to write the one that satisfies you.

Occasionally, the very first headline that rattles off your typewriter or word processor may be what you use. Then again, you may work for hours or days without results. Most of the time you'll write many heads to get the one you'll finally use. You'll drop words, add words, change words, and shuffle words until finally the headline falls in place. Yet, you often end with the feeling that somewhere within you an even better headline is crying for release.

Headlines Should Give Advertisements a Fast Start

For much of your creative time you will be writing headlines that must *start to sell at once,* at the same time that they are attracting attention. You will often use as attention-getting means the "sales appeals" of your product. You must stop your audience by offering something they want, thus inviting their interest in further exposition of those appeals.

For example:

An Irish Stole to Keep You Warm

No literary talent was needed to fashion this headline but it will interest anyone shopping for the product, and that counts more than high literary quality.

In contrast is this next headline for a hotel advertisement:

An exquisite escape from the humdrum

Here we have a different writing style that can be effective for hotels, restaurants, travel, fashion clothing, and a host of other products and services. The headline this time *does* have a literary air.

Most copywriters prefer writing unusual headlines. They seldom get this chance. Day in and day out, your job will be much more prosaic than that. It will be a matter of stating the facts, stating the facts, stating the facts.

Headline writing varies a great deal with types of markets and types of media. The same techniques that are successful in one may not work well in others. Certain specialized principles apply to each of these fields—fashion, direct mail, catalog, trade and industrial, and retail newspaper advertising.

For the moment, consider only the agency copywriter who has a client with a product of national distribution, normal appeal, and reasonable price, and whose problem is to write headlines that will sell the product to the general public through magazine or national newspaper advertising.

Direct or Indirect Headlines: Which to Use?

In reviewing types of headlines that will be presented in the succeeding pages, keep in mind the differences between direct and indirect selling. *All* advertising headlines definitely fall into one of those two selling categories, regardless of which type of approach or appeal is used.

A "direct-selling" headline uses one or more of the primary sales features of your product as both attention-getters and sales-influencers. An "indirect-selling" headline merely stops the reader to get him to read past the heading.

The two examples given previously illustrate the point:

An Irish Stole to Keep You Warm

This headline represents direct selling. An outstanding and desired feature gains immediate interest. The other headline:

An exquisite escape from the humdrum

sells a thought but nothing specific or direct.

You may ask, "When do you use a direct-selling approach, and when an indirect one?" That depends almost entirely upon what you have to sell. If you can discover features in your product strong enough to arouse interest and stimulate sales response, then, by all means, headline them.

If you can attract your reader by telling him of the specific advantages your product has over others, you have a good chance to make an actual sale. He is enough interested in what you have to offer to read further. If, however, he must be caught by a nonselling device, you still aren't sure you won't lose him when you present your sales story.

As you review the types of headlines, note how many

of them may be used directly or indirectly. Only in the "news" and in the "slogan, label, logotype" headlines will you find that either one or the other is a must. Those two, by their very nature, call for direct selling.

Headline Types

Everyone who writes about advertising will probably give you a list of headline types. You'll find one here. It may be shorter than some and longer than others. It isn't given as the *ONLY* list but as a means of helping you visualize different types of headlines by their creation and function. Sometime when you just can't come up with a good headline—consult the list. It may suggest a new direction to try.

One point you should realize is that most headlines may fall into more than one classification. For example, the "stole" advertisement previously quoted can be classed as a news and direct benefit head while the hotel headline can be classed as emotional or curiosity.

Except for a headline here and there that seems to defy classification, the following headline list covers headlines that you are likely to write. Sometimes a headline has no real meaning in itself because its meaning is clear only when the reader looks at the illustration.

News	Offbeat
Emotional	Curiosity
Direct benefit	Hornblowing
Directive	Slogan, label, and logotype

News

A news headline can be described as the workhorse of advertising because it's used so much, and it *should* be because readers are looking for new products, new features, new services, new prices. In a sense, every advertisement contains news, but writers may elect to use headlines that aren't clearly news-type headlines for a variety of advertisements.

The true news headline is unmistakable. It presents a strong feature in a clear, brisk, no-nonsense manner. To be sure that the readers are aware of the fact that news is being presented, the writer may use the word "new," or "introducing," or "announcing." (A danger here is that advertisement after advertisement in some magazines uses one or more of these words to the point of saturation. You might well aim at conveying the idea of new without using these words.)

A typical news headline follows:

**Finally!
Ocean cruises for land lovers**

By using the word "finally," the writer gave the headline a news flavor by conveying the development of a long-awaited event.

Rate the headlines you see in magazines and newspapers. Judge how quickly, clearly, and forcefully they give selling facts. Grade them on how well they attract attention while starting the selling of the product or service. Notice whether they are believable, another must.

Be sure your product or service *deserves* a news headline. When you plan on using a news approach, determine quickly whether or not you really have a news story. Headlines announcing new features, sensational developments, unheard-of low prices, or any of the other selling points must be backed up. You cannot afford to write a headline that will attract the attention of your readers because of its news value and then fail to gain conviction as you develop your later copy.

If you announce "a new amazingly low price," be sure that your price *is* amazingly low—not just lower than the highest-priced product in the same field, but low clear across the board.

Here, for example, are two headline news story, each offers a statistic or presents a different degree of that "believability."

**Doctors prove 2 out of 3 women
can have lovelier skin in just 14 days.**

Without question, a headline designed to attract the attention of a majority of women, young and old. It tells them something they wish to know, something that they'd like to believe, and doesn't appear to be too impossible. Furthermore, it is a headline which can be backed up by factual evidence, presented in a straightforward manner.

Now consider this statement:

**50% Faster!
200% Smoother!**

That's a headline about a razor—a product with which most men feel familiar. Now it is within reason to suppose that male readers of that headline will believe the "extra speed" promise. The nature of the razor seems to make that possible, even though the average man would have trouble believing he could actually cut his shaving time in half.

It's doubtful, too, if the second part of that headline ever attracted anything more than a hearty laugh—200% smoother! In the first place, it's a quality that can. hardly be measured. Secondly, the average man is a cynic when the percentage figures climb too high. "Shaves smoother" is a statement to be accepted. "Shaves 200% smoother" asks for disbelief. Be careful in your presentation of news. *It must be believed if it's going to sell.*

In writing news headlines it is well to be wary of words such as "amazing," "new," "sensational," "what you've been waiting for," and others. There is nothing wrong with using these words and phrases if they are true. Many copywriters, however, avoid them because they feel they have been overused—clichés that have lost their selling value.

Where a product (or its characteristics) is in reality "amazing" or "sensational" news to the reader, it is reasonable selling technique to say so.

The copywriter can back up "amazing" not only by stating the facts which make it so, but also by presenting the testimony of several men who agree. The whole feeling of the headline is one of important news that is supported with dignity and credibility.

On the other hand, here is another news headline:

New . . . A history-making advance in the annals of electric clockmaking!

Sounds as if the least you could expect would be a clock that ran by radar or played Brahms. But, on reading further, the "history-making" advance turned out to be a simple improvement in design.

This is a classic case of overselling, a gross misuse of the news headline. On the contrary, here are a few news headlines that are believable, as well as newsworthy:

New life for your financial future

New pastry pockets.
Turn ordinary stuff into hot stuff.

At last. A way to keep warm
no matter how cold it is.

Now, you can have extra crispy
hash browns in minutes

Announcing the Barbizon Tower suites

The new Spanish-language magazine
you can hear

All of the foregoing avoided the use of words such as "amazing" and "sensational." None used exclamation points. All had strong news value. None is subtle because you don't have to be subtle (in fact, you shouldn't be) when you must impart quickly some interesting news about a product or service.

Figure 5–1. News-direct benefit headline featuring advertiser's name. Straight-line copy that follows this headline is packed with selling information. Notice the use of artwork instead of photography in the illustration. In its light-hearted approach, the artwork relieves the seriousness usually surrounding consideration of the purchase of a prestigious reference work.

Reprinted with permission of Encyclopaedia Britannica, Inc.

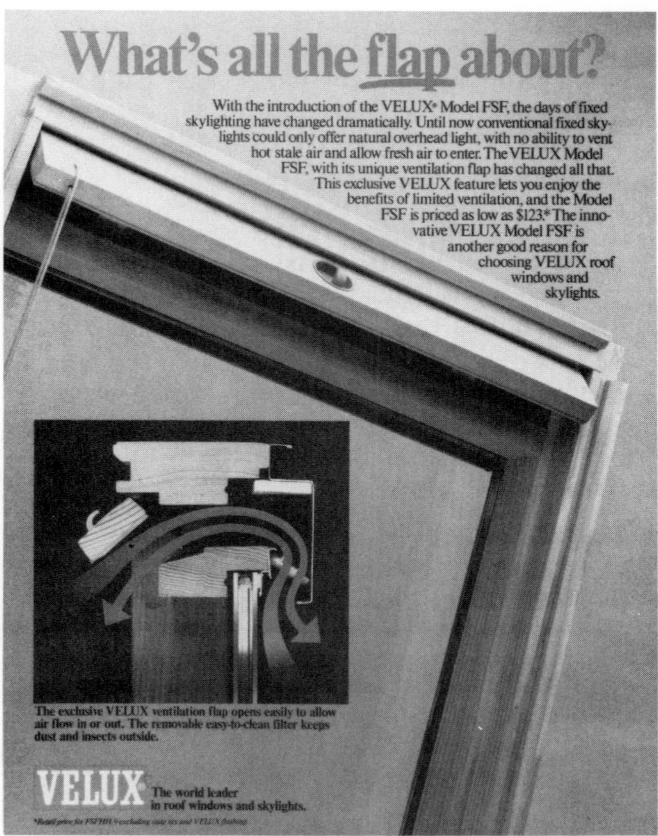

Figure 5–2. Question headline. Indirect questions such as this command immediate attention and involve the reader in the straight-line copy that follows.

Emotional

A common approach to headline writing is to appeal directly to the emotions of the reader. It could probably be argued that all selling, in headlines, in copy, and in artwork, does this in varying degrees.

Unlike the news headline, which usually is used only in making a direct sales presentation, the emotional headline can be either direct or indirect. These two headlines illustrate this point.

Beautiful lingerie—
you'll both enjoy the romance
(direct)

But will he want a second date?
(indirect—for a mouth wash)

In one, though it makes capital of strong emotional appeal, both visually and in the headline, a claim is advanced. In the other, the headline has no direct-selling virtues. It does have sales value, in that it sets up a situation which, in itself, is representative of the campaign strategy. But, as a headline, it sells only curiosity and attention value.

Both headlines capitalize on the reader's interest in anything that can be linked to personal problems. Certainly love and pride are two strong emotions with which to lure the reader into further examination of the advertisements.

It will be obvious to you that certain products, or types of products, lend themselves particularly well to emotional approaches, and you will find that the emotional approach is used in their advertising. Your job is one of interpretation.

Almost all products used in the intimate daily lives of both men and women are well adapted to this type of approach. In the campaigns behind toothpaste, soap, perfume, tobacco, hair tonic, shaving cream, deodorants, and similar items, you will find emotional appeals headlined.

If you are selling an automobile, a cigarette, or a typewriter, a straight emotional headline will be used less frequently.

Most of us are emotional about our health: frightened, joyful, worried, uncertain, apprehensive. Thus, many emotional headlines have a health base such as this unusual example:

Love can make your ears ring, your heart sick, leave you breathless, and wreck your health.

So can wisdom teeth.

Many headlines featuring emotional appeals represent statements from either real or imaginary people. It is easier for the reader to identify himself with a person of some resemblance to himself, who is saying something familiar, than with the impersonal words of an advertiser. Furthermore, your reader is much more ready to apply the sales psychology to himself if someone else is "guilty," than if you come right out and tell him he has terrible teeth or bad breath.

One of the most important points to remember in writing headlines with an emotional slant is that they must be realistic. Don't put words in the mouths of characters in your headline that your reader would not say himself. The more human and down-to-earth you can make your headlines, the more attention you will get, and the more believability. If you were the reader, what would *you* think of the following headlines?

It's Grape Nuts for me; they're crammed with nutritious goodness for me and my family.

I like Kool-Aid because it tantalizes my taste buds.

Every bite of Mrs. Jones's fudge is pure eating pleasure.

Looking at the foregoing headlines analytically, as you just have, you undoubtedly reject them. Yet, time after time, you see such statements in print or hear them delivered by characters on television or radio.

On the other hand, a testimonial-type headline of the emotional type can be very effective if it creates a sympathetic reaction in the readers such as the following headline for a product aimed at elderly women:

Main head: "My brown aging spots were so embarrassing,
I tried to hide my hands when people were around."
Subhead: And then she discovered Fade-Kreme.

It should not be assumed that all good headlines of an emotional approach must be testimonial types or purport to be the words of actual people. There are many ways to reach the reader's emotions—and most of them are good, provided they are based on sound psychology.

You have much more latitude in writing emotional headlines than is possible with the news approach. For example, no woman would actually believe that any lotion on her hands would render her sweetheart "helpless." Still this headline attracts attention. It is not intended by the copywriter to be taken literally by readers, and they realize that. But they associate the exaggeration with the fact that hand lotion makes hands soft, and soft hands are appealing.

Certain types of emotional headline writing must be done with special care. Insurance, at least life insurance, represents one of the most common fields of advertising in which the emotional approach is used. Yet, because the subject is anything but frivolous, and because the investment involved is more than the price of a bar of soap, great care must be taken to stick to the facts.

A few examples of emotional headlines demonstrate the many directions they can take:

Relive the romance of the Riviera

A gift for lovers

Beautiful memories aren't all you'll bring home

**Carlos knows hunger and fear.
Help him find security and love.**

**Experience those enchanting childhood
years all over again**

**Don't suffer the anguish of
a blotchy complexion**

Even industrial advertisements can use emotional headlines occasionally. An advertisement for a safety system might appeal to a plant manager's pride in cutting down-time caused by accidents. Another advertisement may use a head and illustration that stress how the advertiser's farm machinery has made life better in a Third World drought-area.

A final note on emotional headlines. In many instances, only your headline (and possibly your illustration) will be emotional. The body copy might be quite factual. Emotion causes reaction. It's a stopper, an attention-getter. Once that attention has been obtained through the headline, its job is done. (Actually, it is quite difficult to maintain an emotional tone throughout an entire advertisement, at least if you're selling a product or service. This point is made later in the chapter on fashion writing, where it is explained that fashion advertisements frequently use emotion in headlines but may be literal and almost cold in the body copy.)

Direct Benefit

In general, a direct benefit headline is also a news headline, and often it can be called a hornblowing headline in that it trumpets some outstanding quality of the product or service. By definition it is a simple statement of the most important benefit offered by the product. An example:

Q-Vel® prevents nighttime leg cramps

When you have a strong benefit such as this, why be cute or clever or subtle? Why try to arouse curiosity? Your most powerful selling weapon is, in this instance, a straightforward statement of fact.

In today's ingredient-conscious world, the following direct benefit head carries a strong message for the reader. Set in big type, it commands heavy readership.

**Wesson Oil is 100% Pure Vegetable Oil.
No chemicals.
No preservatives.
No coloring agents.**

Two more observations can be made about this head-

When confronted with a mental illness, families experience a wide range of emotional responses. From outrage to shame and denial. They often blame victims for causing worry, embarrassment, family strife. And they often blame themselves.

But mental illness is no one's fault. Least of all those afflicted. It's a serious medical illness that affects one in four families—afflicting 35 million Americans from all walks of life.

Recognizing the warning signs and seeking treatment for your loved one can be the first steps to reducing family fears and confusion. And to actually healing the sickness. Today, mental illness need not be hopeless.

Learn more. For an informative booklet, write: The American Mental Health Fund, P.O. Box 17700, Washington, D.C. 20041. Or call toll free: 1-800-433-5959. In Illinois, call: 1-800-826-2336.

Learn to see the sickness. Learning is the key to healing.

THE AMERICAN MENTAL HEALTH FUND Ad Council

Figure 5–3. Emotional advertisement with quotation headline. A blunt headline and an illustration that tugs at the heartstrings rivet attention for this advertisement. While the headline and illustration are emotional to command attention, the following copy is straight-line, rational copy that presents a commonsense analysis of mental illness and what can be done about it.

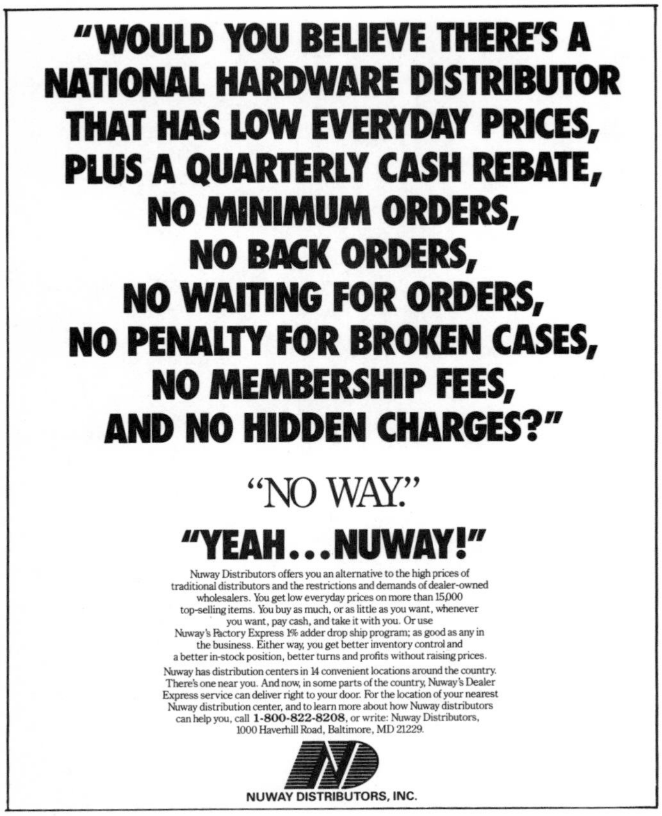

"WOULD YOU BELIEVE THERE'S A NATIONAL HARDWARE DISTRIBUTOR THAT HAS LOW EVERYDAY PRICES, PLUS A QUARTERLY CASH REBATE, NO MINIMUM ORDERS, NO BACK ORDERS, NO WAITING FOR ORDERS, NO PENALTY FOR BROKEN CASES, NO MEMBERSHIP FEES, AND NO HIDDEN CHARGES?"

"NO WAY."

"YEAH...NUWAY!"

Nuway Distributors offers you an alternative to the high prices of traditional distributors and the restrictions and demands of dealer-owned wholesalers. You get low everyday prices on more than 15,000 top-selling items. You buy as much, or as little as you want, whenever you want, pay cash, and take it with you. Or use Nuway's Factory Express 1% adder drop ship program; as good as any in the business. Either way, you get better inventory control and a better in-stock position, better turns and profits without raising prices.

Nuway has distribution centers in 14 convenient locations around the country. There's one near you. And now, in some parts of the country, Nuway's Dealer Express service can deliver right to your door. For the location of your nearest Nuway distribution center, and to learn more about how Nuway distributors can help you, call **1-800-822-8208**, or write: Nuway Distributors, 1000 Haverhill Road, Baltimore, MD 21229.

NUWAY DISTRIBUTORS, INC.

Figure 5–4. Trade advertisement that insures attention through the use of an unusually long, interesting headline.

line. One is the use of the product name. There are some advertising authorities who declare that *every* headline should carry the name of the product or advertiser. Although this statement is extreme, it is true that flagging readers with product or company name in headlines will result in higher identification for either, and better "Advertiser Associated" figures in Starch readership figures described in the chapter on advertising research.

The second observation is that the use of the subheads strengthened an already powerful and seemingly complete headline.

Beginning copywriters, thinking that they must always be clever, shun direct benefit headlines as unimaginative and dull. They forget that a strong benefit is never uninteresting to the reader who reads advertisements for benefits, not for cleverness and entertainment which are strictly by-products.

People in the car-buying mood will find it fascinating if you tell them directly in the headline that the car you're selling has front wheel drive that will provide better winter driving handling. Nothing dull about this to anyone who drives in the snowbelt.

Suppose you have no special advantage over a competing product. Should you, as so many copywriters do, avoid the direct benefit headline in favor of pure cleverness? Not so. You can still use the direct benefit headline, but you will combine it with a twist, an interesting phrase, or a different way of expressing the benefit. In that way you can satisfy your urge to be clever while simultaneously giving the reader a strong reason to buy.

A way to be simultaneously clever, while offering a direct benefit, is to be clever (but obscure) in the main headline and to offer your direct benefit in the main subhead as is demonstrated in the following:

Main headline: Farberware found that the best way to get something done is to go around in circles.

Main subhead: The Farberware Convection Oven. A cooler, cleaner, faster,
and more economical way
to cook.

Another example of a copywriter's finding an interesting way to headline a direct benefit is offered by an advertisement for a rich-looking but relatively inexpensive carpeting. The writer might have written a headline that said:

Here's carpeting that looks expensive but costs little.

Although this headline would attract readers and sales, the copywriter preferred a headline that would express the benefit with more flair and imagination. The headline actually used was:

Bigelow's sculptured elegance for the woman who likes to feel extravagant—but isn't.

Notice once again the use of the company (and product) name in the headline.

A third example of a direct benefit headline that uses the name of the product and incorporates an interesting—and in this case, humorous—twist is the following:

**TASTER'S CHOICE® makes fresh coffee in seconds.
Our competition is still boiling.**

Other examples of direct benefit headlines:

**Gore-Tex® Fabrics
Keep you warm and dry
Regardless of what falls
Out of the sky**

**Speak a foreign language in 30 days
or your money back**

**100 pages of free advice for anyone
wishing to visit Alaska**

6

GET YOUR ADVERTISEMENTS OFF TO A FAST START WITH POWERFUL HEADLINES

Part B

Leaning back in her executive-type swivel chair, Lois Shafer mulled over the kind of headline to write for the agency's tire account. To her surprise, she realized how long it had been since she had consciously thought of headline classification.

As an experienced copywriter she simply wrote headlines; she didn't bother to classify them. Now, however, she was devoid of ideas for a headline approach; she hoped such ideas might be spurred if she mentally reviewed the classes of headlines she had learned as a beginning copywriter.

In your case, as the reader of this book, you've already been given some types of headlines such as news, emotional and direct benefit. Here are some additional types that can be useful as thought-starters.

Directive	Hornblowing
Offbeat	Slogan, Label, Logotype
Curiosity	

While the foregoing are largely self-explanatory, you may stumble a bit over offbeat.

Directive

Salespeople know that prospects must be nudged to get them to act. A command or directive headline provides this "nudge." Although retail advertisers use this type of headline frequently, national advertisers also make strong use of it because it imparts a vitality to headlines and because such headlines spur decision making.

Directive headlines alternate between outright commands and suggestions, with more of the latter being used. It is difficult to decide that dividing point where a suggestion becomes a command. For example, the following might be called commands:

Learn French on your own

Don't let Lisa become a street child

In contrast, the following alternate between suggestion and outright command:

Before you crack, do this

Moving? Make sure *Reader's Digest* goes with you.

Go on, cut. You'll be brilliant. Armstrong guarantees it.

Check the mirror. Have you been telling yourself a little white lie?

Whatever you call your directive headlines—command or suggestion—they seldom call for immediate action but they *do* indicate that some action should be taken. When Greyhound tells you, *Next time take the bus and leave the driving to us,* the company is thinking of some future time. They do not envision hundreds of people leaping from their chairs and rushing down to the bus station. If immediate action *is* taken, it will more likely be from directive headlines in retail advertising than national advertising. Retailers depend upon and expect quick response. The directive headline helps achieve this.

To demonstrate the popularity of the directive headline, here are some picked up in a quick perusal of two magazines:

Grace your home with beautiful books

Own the sword that crowned 25 kings

Exercise more with less

Stop burglary before it starts

Give up the single life

Don't just sit there. Do something!

Start each day with a smile

Let Princess take you to the best of Europe

Try a little tenderness
(for meat)

Sail the ageless, cageless Amazon

Return to tradition

Don't buy a big tiller for a small job

Offbeat

Although most of the headlines you write may be based upon common sense and will, consequently, fall into the news, direct benefit, or directive types, you may find it desirable to try an offbeat headline.

When you do, you will, for a brief time, be that kind of copywriter shown in motion pictures or television. You'll let your imagination run freely. For the moment, you forget common sense. But first, what is offbeat? In advertising it's used frequently to describe almost anything that defies easy definition.

Offbeat describes a headline that's unconventional and uses for its appeal something that may have no apparent relationship to the advertised product.

Usually, you will use the offbeat headline for a product that has few important competitive advantages. There may be nothing newsy about the product, nor can it be sold through emotion. Your offbeat headline will cause readers to linger when they read, long enough, you hope, to check out your illustration and body copy.

If you have a good story that can be told effectively through use of a straightforward headline, then *don't* use an offbeat headline. It's an infrequently used device, but beginning copywriters with a yearning to be "creative" tend to use it too much.

Examples of offbeat headlines follow. Notice as you look over these and other offbeat headlines that sometimes the meaning is clear when you combine the headline with the illustration. In most cases, however, the reader must go into the body copy to understand the headline fully. If you *have* succeeded in making the reader delve into the body copy, you can consider that your offbeat experiment has been successful.

Roads Scholar
(for a car that has an axle that "thinks for itself")

If you can't see the beauty of *Sporting News,* our new sales rep may have to adjust your eyesight
(Illustration shows scowling 280-pound NFL lineman.)

Rush hour traffic in New Zealand
(Illustration shows flock of sheep blocking a lonely New Zealand road.)

Hotline
(for an airline)

Wow. Wow. Wow.
(Each "Wow" is used with three different illustrations of a remodeled home.)

Curiosity

Anyone who is even moderately perceptive will notice that all of the foregoing examples of offbeat headlines arouse curiosity.

Offbeat headlines usually arouse reader curiosity about nothing in particular, or about nothing that is instantly obvious. Curiosity headlines, in contrast, arouse curiosity about the product or service they are advertising.

Example:

Hartman has an interesting angle on luggage The right angle
(Illustration shows luggage standing on end.)

"What is Hartman talking about?" would be your response to this headline-illustration combination. It is reasonable to suppose you would read the copy to find out.

Another curiosity-impelling headline:

At Saab, This Is What We Call A Beautiful Car.
(Illustration shows a Saab that has been smashed in an accident.)

Like a good curiosity headline, this one offers the unexpected, such as the famous Volkswagen headline of years ago that simply said "Lemon." It would be a strong-willed reader who could resist reading the copy to discover why Saab finds beauty in a wrecked car. Remember: Give the reader something unexpected to ponder when you write a curiosity headline.

An effective device for writing a curiosity headline is to tell just enough of a story via a quotation to pique reader interest. An example is this headline for a Gulf Oil advertisement that was accompanied by an elaborate motion picture set of an old hotel building.

"This is the set where they shot 'Hello Dolly!' What you can't see is us pumping oil behind it."

Both curiosity and offbeat headlines are methods of indirect selling, one a little less indirect than the other. Both should be used when the same general conditions prevail as far as the product's characteristics and appeals are concerned.

If you have any means of direct selling at your command—any logical, believable approach to the reader's interest through a straightforward presentation—*use it.* If you have not, if you are selling an idea, an institution, or a product which fails to offer any attention-getting appeals, then it is good copywriting to examine the other means of approach.

Examples of curiosity headlines:

It's headed for your face at 119 MPH. How does it feel?
(Illustration shows hockey goaltender at the net.)

Your search for a perfect cup of coffee ended in Gayle, Sweden, more than 100 years ago.

The Russians were here! The Russians were here!

Some people don't even tell their best friends about us

Discover a little bit of Europe on Madison at 69th

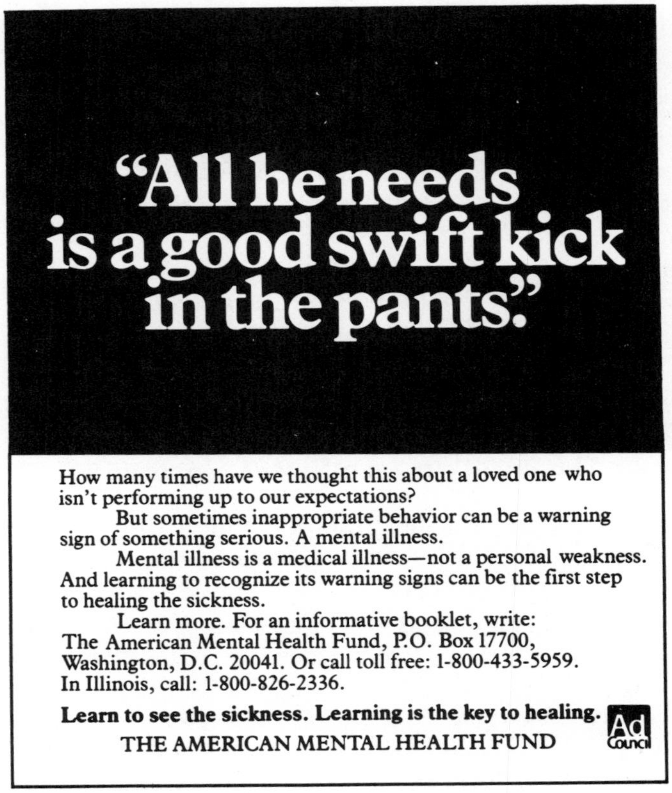

"All he needs is a good swift kick in the pants."
How many times have we thought this about a loved one who isn't performing up to our expectations?
But sometimes inappropriate behavior can be a warning sign of something serious. A mental illness.
Mental illness is a medical illness—not a personal weakness. And learning to recognize its warning signs can be the first step to healing the sickness.
Learn more. For an informative booklet, write: The American Mental Health Fund, P.O. Box 17700, Washington, D.C. 20041. Or call toll free: 1-800-433-5959. In Illinois, call: 1-800-826-2336.
Learn to see the sickness. Learning is the key to healing.
THE AMERICAN MENTAL HEALTH FUND
Ad Council

Figure 6–1. Offbeat headline. An ordinary, mild sort of headline would lack the jarring effect of this offbeat type. The writer deliberately chose to write a headline that would shake the readers out of their indifference to an important problem.
Courtesy of the Advertising Council.

One of our best ideas is a lot of hot air.
Every plant has those spaces where cold air from the outside chills the bones of those on the inside. That's why we designed this new heavy-duty forced convection heater. It is ideal for environments where people need high velocity discharge. It's built to be tough, season after season, with flexible mounting options for ceiling or wall installation and swivel and tilt capability.
Wellman Thermal Systems Corp., One Progress Road, Shelbyville, IN 46176, Telephone: (317)392-5329.
WELLMAN
Keeping the heat on industry
Circle 395 on Post Card

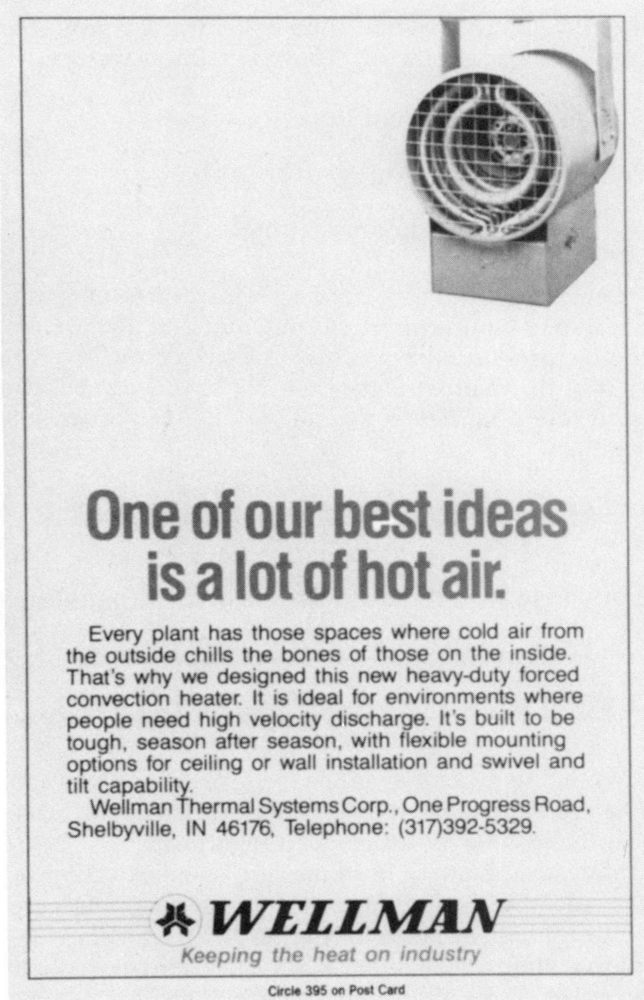

Figure 6–2. Offbeat headline for an industrial advertisement. In an industrial magazine this unusual headline will get more attention than a more conventional type. If you read the body copy of this advertisement, you see that the headline is quite relevant to point being made.

Look what just came into bloom

Could a cat that eats supermarket pet food take this test and land on its feet?

Hornblowing

Gallup & Robinson, the research organization, gives low marks to what they call "Brag and Boast" headlines. Furthermore, every beginning copywriter is told to go easy on superlatives and to avoid outright boasting. Yet, that same writer will see hundreds of such headlines in printed media. Why is this?

One answer, of course, is the natural pride felt by someone offering a product or service. All of us tend to boast a bit about ourselves, those we care for, or about our possessions. A maker of a product is no different. Furthermore, it can well be that the maker's product or service *is* superior in a significant way. Why shouldn't this superiority be called to the attention of prospects?

There are different shadings in the hornblowing headline. Some such headlines are outright boasts that have little grace or charm. They may simply trumpet:

Most luxurious

The finest ever built

Incomparable!

Other headlines may stress an honest pride of craftsmanship. Manufacturers *do* put much of themselves into the products they make, or those offering services try mightily to provide the best service that can be rendered. Here are some typical *pride of craftsmanship* headlines:

Oil of Olay. Amazing. And still ahead of its time.

For those who demand the best workmanship

Often imitated . . . never duplicated

When it looks this good—it's got to be Dansk

When this type of headline is used, the product had *better* be superlative and the body copy should make clear the reasons for the claimed superiority.

Many hornblowing headlines are based on claims to "the only," No. 1 status, or exclusivity. If such claims are true, the use of the hornblowing headline is not only sensible but almost mandatory in this competitive world. If you're No. 1, it's absurd not to let your prospects know this fact. Americans respect product leaders, reasoning that a product that's tops in its field must be good. Hertz has exploited its leadership for years while Avis has done the best it can in building up the theme "We're No. 2 so we try harder." You can assume that Avis has deep yearnings to be No. 1 and that the minute the firm

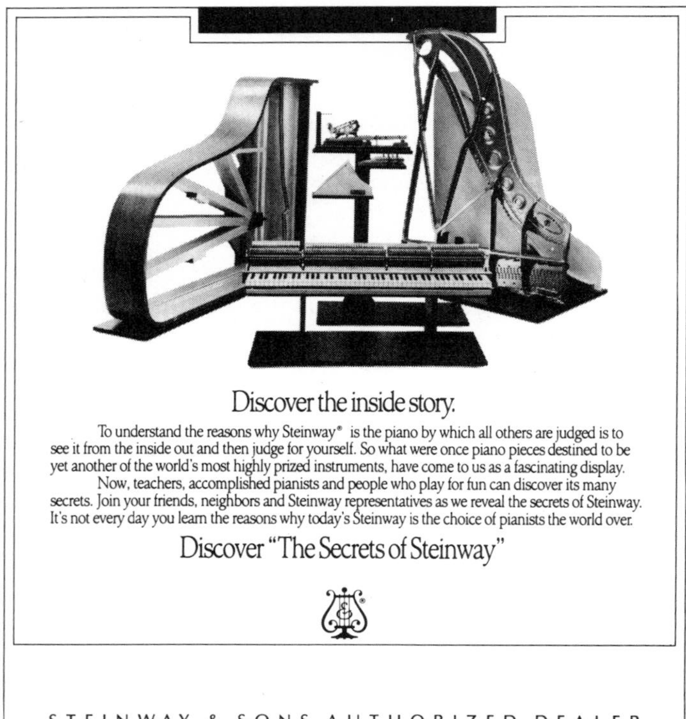

Figure 6–3. Curiosity headline. A powerful inducement for reading the body copy of this advertisement is provided in the combination of a curiosity headline and the unusual illustration.

reached this level the headlines on its advertisements would shout the message to the car-renting public.

Here are some headlines that stress *"the only," No. 1 status,* or *exclusivity.*

For buttery taste no margarine can match

There is no other store in the world like Hammacher Schlemmer. And no other catalog.

The world's most efficient peppermill.

The first dry dog food that's like a homemade meal.

One of the problems with using some of the foregoing headlines is that you may be called upon to defend your claim. When you say "only" or "No. 1," you are being specific and when you're specific in a claim you may be asked by the Federal Trade Commission, or some other legal body, to document your claim. Such action may result from complaints of outraged customers.

Advertisers not being sure of No. 1 status or not wanting to exploit such status may still utilize powerful hornblowing headlines based on opinion. Anyone making a product or offering a service is usually entitled, without worry about legal action, to express a strong opinion about the worth of that product or service. In the following are hornblowing headlines based on *opinion:*

You're not fully clean unless you're Zestfully clean

This new car will change the way you measure world-class luxury

Perhaps the most lavish catalogue of 18th-century reproductions ever published

The Ritz-Carlton has always been synonymous with culture

The kind of car Mercedes might have built if they were a little more frugal and a lot more inventive

Although legally the foregoing headlines are safe enough, the question is "Are they believable?" This question of believability is a problem with hornblowing headlines generally, with the possible exception of the headlines that are obviously capable of proof such as those that claim No. 1 standing or "only" status. Likewise, a hornblowing headline that says specifically . . .

14 ways better than a wheelbarrow. Easier and more enjoyable to use.

carries credibility lacking in the following headlines that the reader senses are backed by nothing specific:

Everything the grand resort hotels used to be . . . we still are.

Molla. Something a little bit different—and a lot better.

Fashionberry. The true essence of elegance.

While, as you have seen, many hornblowing headlines serve a legitimate purpose, many are written because the copywriter didn't work hard enough to find a more creative and effective headline.

Boastfulness is one of the less-endearing qualities of human beings. It is no more desirable in advertisers. Now and then a hornblowing headline represents a part of a carefully worked out plan that fits well into marketing and sales strategy. In other cases it represents the failure to discover a better way to accomplish your objectives. Therefore, before writing such a headline, you should ask yourself: "Would another headline approach be better?" If you can answer "no," then go ahead. Otherwise, keep working.

Slogan, Label, and Logotype

Sometimes your goal in an advertising campaign is to obtain high recognition for the company name, the product name, or the advertiser's slogan. Many times, of course, this objective is achieved through an illustration of a product's package or container that shouts the name in big type, or might even carry the slogan, too. Other times the headline may offer the best way to get the recognition and sometimes *both* the headline and illustration carry out this objective.

When copywriters use the slogan-label-logotype approach, they do so with one of two ideas in mind. They feel that the name of the product or company is, in itself, their most important attention-attracter, *or* they are willing to sacrifice a potentially more intensive reading to pound home a name or an idea.

Name emphasis has been the goal of many famous and successful advertising campaigns. As a copywriter working for such accounts, your headline-writing chore is easy. You may, as a couple of advertisers have, simply head your advertisements:

I. Magnin

or

The Burberry Look

or, if the product is a perfume, you simply write:

No. 5 Chanel Perfume

Then again, as the copywriter for a car or well-known store, your respective headlines consist of nothing more than:

Dodge Ram Wagon

or

Bonwit Teller

Just about as simple is the *label* headline used for a wine that reads:

Collector's Items

Although name emphasis and label headlines can be effective, and are often seen, most copywriters would look for some other type of work if there were no more challenge to their creativity than the writing of such headlines.

What about the *slogan* headline? It can be effective for a long campaign if it is a *strong* slogan. Perhaps it began as a slogan placed at the bottom of the advertisement, but its strength became so apparent that it was upgraded to headline status, and there it stayed, possibly permanently. In other cases, a good headline has been used briefly and then became a permanent slogan, used in every advertisement.

Sometimes the slogan headline is adaptable to products promoted through reminder advertising such as Coca-Cola, Pepsi-Cola, candy bars, gum, cigarettes, and other items selling in volume across the counter and for low cost. Such products frequently have no demonstrable superiority over their competitors.

In other cases this lack of competitive advantage may not be true, yet the slogan headline is used. Examples:

Lord & Taylor
The American Store

The Bold Look of Kohler

Long-time campaigns using a slogan as a headline are exemplified by:

A title on the door . . .
rates a BIGELOW on the floor
(advertisement for carpeting)

When you care enough to send the very best

A truly strong slogan is used not only in all print advertising as a headline but also as a theme line in the broadcast media. One use reinforces the other.

As a beginning copywriter you probably will not on your own decide the use of slogan-label-logotype headlines. That decision may have been made long before you entered the scene. You simply carry out policy in most cases when such headlines are used.

You'll Enjoy Writing Some Headlines; Others Are Harder to Do

As you mature in copywriting, you find that certain types of headlines are easier for you to write than others. You may never be a good creator of offbeat headlines because you just don't think that way.

Don't be discouraged. Many competent copywriters don't think that way either, but they may have strong talent for writing other types of headlines—powerful news presentations, for instance, or they may have an unerring feeling for emotional headlines that will reach out to the reader.

Although many headlines are of the straight news or direct benefit type that do not call for the offbeat type of thinking, you will go farther in this business if you can add the little twist, or the touch of cleverness, to such headlines to make them stand out on the page.

Otherwise, the world of copy would start to become a bit dull with every copywriter churning out straight headlines that had nothing to distinguish them from all the other straight headlines.

As a copywriter you'd be pleased with yourself if you wrote a headline for a clock that reads:

Give her a clock like this and she'll have
the time of her life.

It's hard work to get the twist, the touch of cleverness, or the different approach in a headline. Sometimes you simply turn a familiar phrase around as in the following headline written for a luxurious resort hotel:

Every view comes with a beautiful room

And then sometimes you jar the readers out of their apathy with a headline for a *New Yorker* advertisement for high-priced aluminum cookware:

If the price doesn't shock you, it could
mean you're either very rich or
very serious about cooking

There is a well-bred breeziness about the foregoing headline that is admirably suited to the readers of the *New Yorker.*

Or, if you work extra hard, you might create a headline that uses a humorous twist in headline and illustration that will evoke a smile (and attention) from every reader. Here's such a headline:

Can a chair this beautiful also be comfortable?
Would a sleeping dog lie?
(The illustration for this advertisement shows a small dog sleeping comfortably in the chair.)

Despite the fact that creativity in headline writing is a quality admired and rewarded in advertising, such creativity isn't always allied with "cleverness." Straight thinking, clear writing, and a deep knowledge of what moves consumers—these are all important, too.

Questions and Answers about Headlines

Get a group of young copywriters, or potential copywriters, together. They'll usually get around to questions on the headline because headlines are more spectacular than most body copy. Furthermore, every advertising writer has been fed figures relating to the astounding percentage of readers who read nothing but headlines.

Here are some of the questions that beginners so often ask about headlines, and the answers to them. Remember as you read the answers that no rules are given as inflexible—it is a matter of fitting the answer to the situation, and in the offbeat headline, anything goes. You may consider the answers as observations rather than rules.

Should the Question Headline Be Avoided?

No. The question headline is very useful. It can get directly to the point that is in the reader's mind. In such cases it serves as a lively opening into the discussion that answers the question.

Perhaps the suitability of the question headline hinges

upon the ability of the question to draw the reader into the body copy for the answer. If the reader can answer the question without further reference to the advertisement, you'd better look your question over. Be especially careful with direct questions. This warning is doubly emphasized in radio and television commercials.

All of us have, at one time or another, sassed announcers when they asked directly, "Wouldn't you like to double your income?" Despite the fact that all of us do want to double our income, it is hard to resist saying "No" when the question is asked.

Keep that in mind when you write your question headline. Also, the question headline is often overused by beginning copywriters. Make sure that the question headline is the best device for putting over your copy message, and be sure to shape your question to get the answer you want.

One of the more annoying traits of good salespeople is that the questions they ask are phrased in such a way that you, as the prospect, must answer as they wish you to answer. A smart salesman won't ask: "Wouldn't you like some of these?" because such a question invites an interview terminating "No!"

In advertising, follow the salesman's example. Avoid the direct question that elicits a "No" answer or, in some cases a "Yes" answer. For example, suppose a woman were asked:

Have you had a lab test to see if you were pregnant?

Whether she answers "Yes" or "No," you may be in trouble. Either answer might kill further interest in the advertisement. To avoid such a situation, provide the answer quickly, usually in a subhead placed in conjunction with the main head. Here's how the technique was handled in the headline just mentioned:

Have you had a lab test to see if you were pregnant?
With E.P.T. you use an identical test method at home.

Other direct questions, followed by quick answers:

Like luscious brownies?
Try Kwik-Bake tonight.

Got something you can't glue?
Hold-Tite does the job in seconds.

Most copywriters avoid the direct question. For example, an interesting example is the following:

How smart is the new G.D. 2500 dishwasher?
Just ask it.

or

Hay fever plus a headache?
Now there's a special Allerest just for you.

A well-designed question headline doesn't *have* to be answered with a subhead. Handled correctly, a good question headline is hard to resist, impelling the reader to read the copy for the answer. The following examples demonstrate:

What does Lipton Noodles & Sauce do for simple, everyday dishes?

How would he feel if you looked younger?

What's an easy way to make lunches something scrumptious?

If you were in their place, what would you do?

Summing up. Go ahead. Use question headlines but, in general, avoid the direct question unless you provide the answer quickly. Also, don't overuse question headlines at the beginning of your copywriting career; such overuse is too often the mark of the beginner.

Is It Better to Make Headlines Brief?

A few years ago this question would have been called silly. The answer would have been: "Of course it is." That's because early advertising people felt that long headlines told too much of the story and, in doing so, discouraged readers from going over the body copy. There are still people in advertising who believe that the headline should say just enough to entice the reader into the following copy, and no more.

Evidence seems to be piling up, however, that long headlines often sell better than short ones. Following are a number of lengthy headlines that would have shocked the advertising experts of yesteryear. If you happen to be more comfortable with the short-headline philosophy, would you say that *these* headlines are wrong?

Not Rolls Royce. Not Mercedes.
No other luxury sedan.
Only the all new Chrysler New Yorker protects the entire car for 5 years or 50,000 miles.
Just take care of normal upkeep.
We cover the rest. No deductibles.
No ifs, ands or buts.

"There are hundreds of homes better than mine but I love this one.
I like big wonderful rooms with a lot of wall space.
Art is important to me.
I like mobiles and I like movement.
It brings a room to life."

**We don't know
how to solve every
problem in
the community,
but we know
the people who do.**

Just remember this, if you begin to worry about the rule "Headlines must be brief"—your prospects are assaulted by so much advertising that only those advertisements with big, informative, catchy headlines and illustrations may have enough attention-getting quality to make readers pause and partly sell them. Today's headlines do more preselling of the reader than was true in the past days when headlines had completed their mission if they had attracted the reader's attention.

Despite all the defense in this section of the long headline, it is desirable normally to write short, interesting headlines that say much in a few words. Certainly if you wish to use large type in the headline, you are forced to keep it brief unless you have a big-space advertisement.

There is a certain drama in the punchy one- or two-word headline—a memorable quality that is lacking in the very long headline. Volkswagen advertisements over the years specialized in such headlines, achieving an impact that caused them to be discussed, admired, and imitated.

Must You Always Use a Verb in a Headline?

Hardly anything must *always* be done in copywriting. That is true of the use of verbs in headlines. Almost every authority in copywriting will tell you that it is usually better to use a verb in a headline. Others declare that every headline should have a verb, or an implied one. While there is no question that it is desirable to use verbs in headlines, many fine heads are verbless. Some of these good heads don't even imply a verb. For instance, consider this headline that was written for a fine bone china to emphasize its timeless quality:

Yesterday, today, and tomorrow

Sometimes the verb is clearly implied such as in this head:

**Lagerfield
A Fragrance For Men**

On the contrary, the headline "Catamarans & Caviar" (for a luxury beach hotel in the Bahamas) tells its story graphically without even implying a verb and, because it is such a short head, the type size is attention getting. The same graphic quality is true of the following:

**7 miles at sea . . . an island of pleasure
Martha's Vineyard**

or the following:

**Out of the pages of history into the
hearts of collectors**

Verbs impart vigor. The verbless headlines just listed create atmosphere and describe well but do not impart movement. That is their negative trait, although sometimes if you must choose between action and a particular suitability to the subject or situation you may select a verbless headline.

Passivity is a characteristic of a headline such as "News about Polaroid." Compare that to "Polaroid makes news," "Here's news about Polaroid," or "Polaroid *is* news."

Still, because of its appropriateness with the illustration, the verbless headline often has its place but, if you follow expert opinion when writing headlines, you'll *use a verb as often as you can.*

Can Directive Headlines Cause Reader Rebellion?

From early childhood through adulthood we're told to do this or do that. In the main we accept such orders

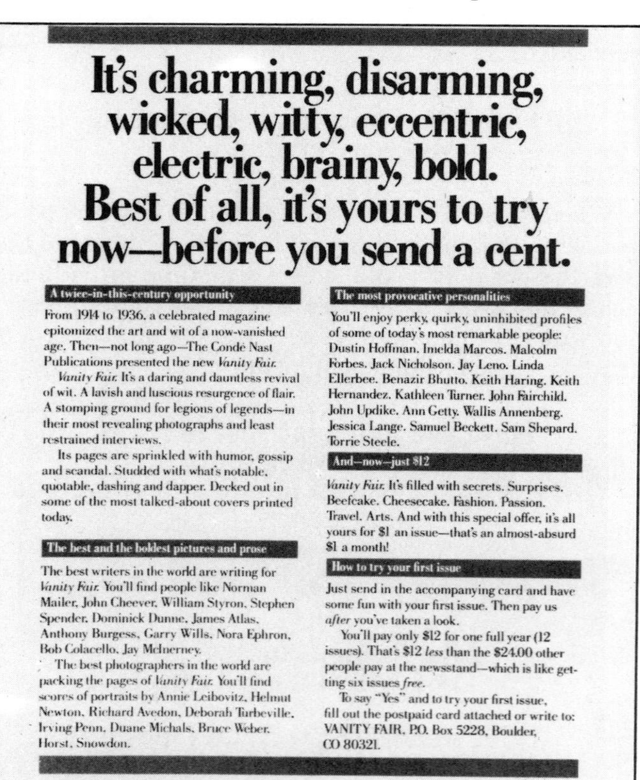

Figure 6–4. Long headline. An interesting headline that uses unusual words, and is set in big, bold type, develops strong impact, as this 22-word headline demonstrates. Despite the absence of an illustration, this all-type advertisement succeeds. Credit the success to well-written copy and a powerful headline. In an advertisement such as this, the headline *is,* in a sense, the illustration.

Courtesy of *Vanity Fair* magazine. Copy by Judy Weiss. Art by Marty Davidson.

without thinking much about them. Added to the orders received in your personal lives are thousands of printed advertisements and radio/television commercials ordering, suggesting, and directing us to:

- Don't ever be late to work again.
- Watch your diet for better health.
- Get top mileage from your motor oil.

Orders get under anyone's skin after a while. On the other hand, the average reader is inclined to move only after prodding. What do the copywriters do when they consider that readers may resent an order but won't make a buying move unless they are given some sort of push? The answer is that the copywriter must pitch the headline in the right "tone."

All through life you have probably found that one person asks you to do something and you do it willingly, whereas another person may ask you to do exactly the same thing and you resent his or her doing so. Perhaps it was the latter's tone of voice—the *way* of asking—that caused your resentment. It is your way of phrasing that causes success or failure in your directive headlines.

Usually you'll do better to suggest than to command. The words "stop" or "don't" often sound unpleasant to the reader. From childhood to the grave someone is using those words. If you start your headline with them, the reader may react instinctively against your product.

Also, be careful not to offend him by assuming in your directive headline that he is doing something foolish. Headlines of this type would be "Don't waste your money," or "Don't be careless with your child's health."

Is There Any Reason *Not* to Use Quotation Headlines?

The quotation headline is often a pleasant variant of the straight headline. When you remember that dialogue enlivens almost any book, you can see how quotation headlines can be useful in advertisements.

A headline using a quotation has human interest. It often enables the advertiser to make a product claim more believable; a quotation headline has an element of storytelling about it. Most of us like a story, so when we read—

"We took a few steps into this dark cave, and then it happened . . ."

this headline for a flashlight is pretty hard to resist. What *happened* in the cave? Any normal reader will want to find out. The quotation headline is especially suitable for creating suspense and curiosity.

"Testimonial" copy is, of course, the most logical vehicle for the quotation headline. Too many of the persons pictured in advertisements seem unreal. The quotation headline can humanize them.

In view of the foregoing, what possible objection can be made to a quotation headline? When it is used by experienced copywriters, there will usually be no objections because they will probably use it with discretion.

The beginning copywriters, on the contrary, will be inclined to overuse such headlines. Not being able to write effective straight headlines easily, they constantly make people in advertisements do the talking. Because the quotation headline is especially desirable as a change from the conventional headline, the copywriter robs it of its freshness by using it too often.

It has been observed in college classes in copywriting that, left to their own devices, the young copywriters would rarely write anything but question or quotation headlines. Such headlines are easy to write and that's that.

Sometimes a quotation headline is followed by body copy that continues quoting the person delivering the headline. Perhaps all the body copy is a quotation, or just the opening paragraph, or all but the last paragraph.

You will read some quotation headlines in the following. The first three use a quotation only in the headline, not the body copy. The other headlines continue the quotation wholly or partly in the body copy.

Quotation headlines, not followed by quotation in body copy:

"The earth abounds with luxuries but precious few are musts."

"I had this throbbing right on top of my head. Then I took Anacin."

"They told me not to drink the water. I think I'm going to need The Specialist."

Quotation headlines followed by quoted body copy:

"I stay here because of Otto and Teleplan."

"Switching to Hershey's Cocoa made my devil's food cake richer and more chocolaty."
(The paragraph that followed continued the quotation.)

"At Gulf we're working on a way to light lights, cook meals, and heat homes with energy stored in water."
(The long body copy that followed continued the quotation except for a closing paragraph.)

How about it? Is it desirable to continue the quotation in the headline into the body copy? In general, it is better to let the quotation headline suffice. That is, do not have the person delivering the headline also deliver the whole copy message. Occasionally, such a technique works very well but, on the whole, it is difficult to keep such advertisements believable. A single, short statement, as expressed in a quotation headline, is about all you can expect a person to say about a product or service. When such a person also provides copy for an entire advertisement, he or she tends to sound like a copywriter. The message sounds contrived and phony.

Why Should "Hanging" Headlines Be Shunned?

First, to make clear what is meant by a hanging headline. It is the type of headline that is not complete unless the reader reads the first words in the body text. An example would be:

Headline: What company . . .

Body text: . . . makes the solar-powered electric shaver?

When you examine the example, you see that the headline doesn't make sense unless the reader immediately reads the first words in the body copy. Neither does the body text beginning mean too much if the reader hasn't read the headline.

Now the inconvenient part of all this is that readers fail to follow neat paths in their reading. Some will start with the headline and skip to the logotype. Others will start with the first line of body text, look at the illustration, and then glance at the bottom of the advertisement. It is difficult to predict just how the reader will read your advertisement.

If you have used a hanging headline, therefore, you may lose much force in your advertisement. Headline readers may look at the meaningless fragments you have written and not bother to find the first line of body text to complete the headline's meaning. They may be irritated if they start the body text and find that they must backtrack to the headline to find out what you're talking about.

Even if you lay out your advertisement scientifically, using every possible device to lure the reader from the headline to the first line of body text, you will often fail to do so. This situation is made even worse in layouts that separate the head and body text widely by illustrations and other elements.

Generally, therefore, it is sounder practice to avoid hanging headlines. Unless your headline and body copy are completely independent of each other for meaning, and unless each will make sense by itself, you will be treating the readers more kindly if you avoid hanging headlines.

All this advice about hanging headlines is aimed directly at the beginning copywriter because the experienced writer simply isn't going to use the technique. If you examine hundreds of advertisements, you may not find one example of a hanging headline. Yet, initial advertisements turned in by beginners will almost always include one or two hanging headlines.

Is There a Place for Cleverness in Headline Writing?

A problem with cleverness is that the clever headline is often obscure. In addition to being difficult for the reader to interpret, it may have no sell and an absence of direct benefit.

Yet, there is need for cleverness in advertising, a quality that might make your headline stand out from others. A clever headline may draw better attention to your advertisement. Let's say that we're not necessarily talking about real cleverness but of a headline that is different, so different that it piques curiosity.

What can you do to use that clever and/or different headline and still make the headline a selling vehicle? One answer is to put the clever (or different) words in big type to draw immediate attention to the advertisement. Then, in order to do the selling, use a main subhead that gets specific and sells directly.

An example of the foregoing technique is demonstrated in the following:

BAFFLE THE BURGLE

Our Shur-Alert alarm system stops thieves cold

"Baffle the Burgle" has little meaning to the reader and no discernible benefit but the phrase is a good attention-getter. In combination with the strong subhead it becomes a strong headline.

Of course, you can be clever with one-liners such as the headline:

Our China tour will have you climbing the wall.

or the head for a bargain-priced dictionary that read:

The price of looking it up just went down.

Cleverness, as long as it is relevant, is almost always desirable in advertising.

Okay, You've Written the Headline. Now, Here Are Some Other Points to Consider

1. If in doubt, use a strong news headline with an appealing benefit. This is an all-powerful combination. Look for the news value in your product and find its most appealing benefit. Join them in a strong headline that can still, if you're clever, provide a twist that sets it apart from other headlines. But remember. News and benefits. They're always good and always in style.
2. See that the headline is important *looking*. This is a matter of type size and/or type style. Check with your art colleagues on this point. Make your wishes known, or you may end up with an anemic-looking headline.
3. Be sure your *clever* headline is truly clever and not baffling. Cleverness defeats itself if you, or a tight little group of insiders, are the only ones who understand your headline. Prefer clarity to

cleverness unless, of course, you can devise a clever head that's also clear.

4. Try to write a headline in such a way that the readers know at a glance what your big point is, what benefit you're offering, or simply what you're advertising. In short, hook them quickly. Sometimes this can be done simply by being specific. Instead of "fast," say "in less than 2 minutes."
5. Be sure your headline appeals to the reader's self-interest more than your own. Too many headlines are company or product oriented—not reader oriented.
6. Decide whether you should include the name of the product or the name of the advertiser in the headline. There's no rule that says you must do either, but often you'll get better product or advertiser identification if you do. Do not, however, force the name into a headline that may be clever or forceful in its own right (and might be more effective without the inclusion of the product or advertiser name).
7. Consider giving your headline an editorial look instead of an advertising look. This "look" may result from the kind of type that is used, as well as the content of the headline.
8. If you have a particular segment of your market in mind, aim the headline directly at this segment if the segment is large enough to be worth promoting. It may be young mothers, the Geritol set, or the macho group. If you know your target, let them know from your headline that you're talking directly to them.
9. Question the overuse of capital letters in headlines such as:

   MILDER THAN SOAP

   or

   Milder Than Soap

   Readers favor printed messages that give them what they're used to seeing. Accordingly, why not write the foregoing heading like this:

   Milder than soap

   If you do, you're following the advice of the readability experts, who frown on capitals, italics, and other artificial forms.

Even after considering these nine points, there is one more action to take. Ask yourself (and answer honestly) in a loud voice:

IS THIS THE MOST INTERESTING HEADLINE I CAN POSSIBLY WRITE?

If you can't say "Yes" to both questions, try again. Too many writers are lazy. They settle for what comes easily. Most good writing comes hard.

Okay, you've answered "No" to both questions. Next step: Scratch out that headline you were willing to use and try once more. And, if necessary, again, and again, and again.

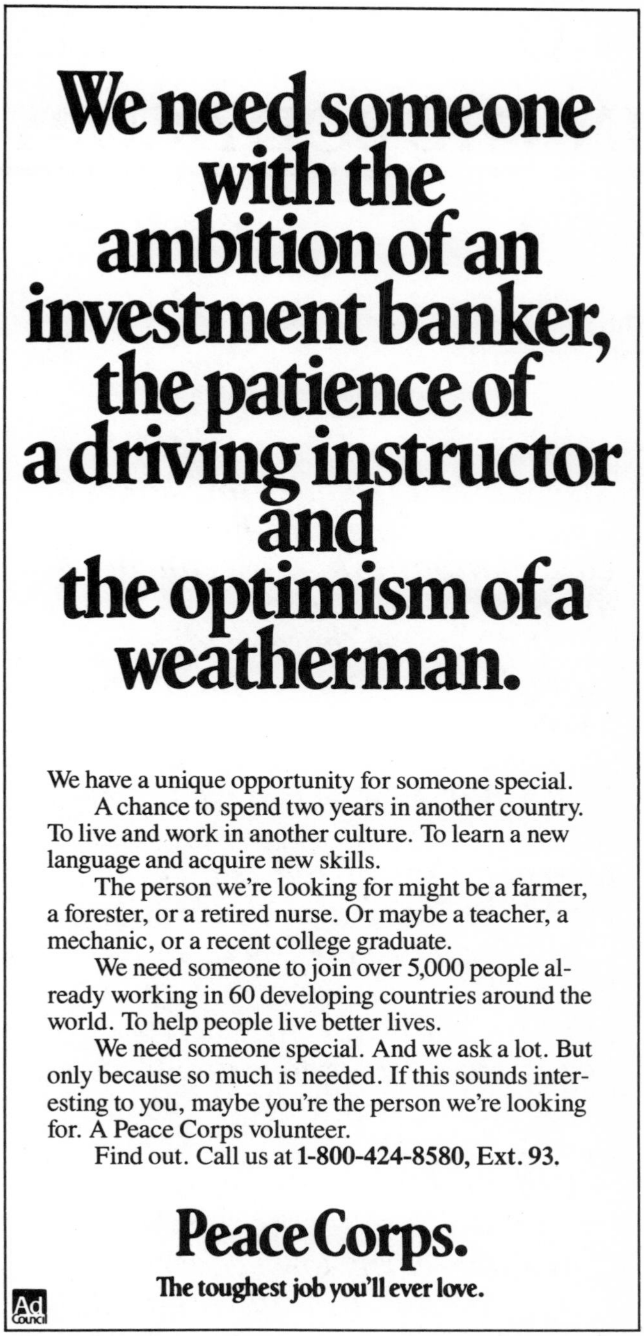

We need someone with the ambition of an investment banker, the patience of a driving instructor and the optimism of a weatherman.

We have a unique opportunity for someone special.

A chance to spend two years in another country. To live and work in another culture. To learn a new language and acquire new skills.

The person we're looking for might be a farmer, a forester, or a retired nurse. Or maybe a teacher, a mechanic, or a recent college graduate.

We need someone to join over 5,000 people already working in 60 developing countries around the world. To help people live better lives.

We need someone special. And we ask a lot. But only because so much is needed. If this sounds interesting to you, maybe you're the person we're looking for. A Peace Corps volunteer.

Find out. Call us at **1-800-424-8580, Ext. 93.**

Peace Corps.

The toughest job you'll ever love.

Ad Council

Figure 6–5. Long headline. As this headline demonstrates, it isn't the length of the headline that matters but how it is written. In this one there are interesting, challenging words that will engage reader attention. Because the headline is so interesting and dominant, it substitutes for the usual illustration.
Courtesy of the Advertising Council.

7

YOU DO YOUR SELLING IN THE BODY COPY

Part A

"Body copy, who needs it?" Bill Siegle asked the question somewhat despairingly of his luncheon companion, Jo Conroe, another copywriter.

"Did you see those readership scores? Two percent for men. Three percent for women."

Jo gave Bill a sympathetic look. "Bill, I know just what you mean. All that effort for that kind of readership of the body copy while the head and illustration combo grabbed a 45-percent figure. Makes you wonder why we bother. Why not just write a head, put in a logo, supply an illustration—and let it go at that?"

Bill and Jo were right and wrong. Right in saying that body copy often earns low readership scores. Wrong, in implying that it isn't worth a copywriter's time to put strong effort into writing the body copy.

Look upon the headline as the piquant sauce whose enticing aroma arouses your salivary glands. Now you're interested in the meat and potatoes that follow. Body copy is the main course of the copywriting meal. Headlines, illustrations, subheads, captions, slogans, and logotypes are important elements in the meal. Your sales-clinching argument, however, must be done in the body copy. It is here that you present your facts or your reasons-why-to-buy material.

In some advertisements, it is true, the chief objective is merely to identify. Where this is the case, headlines, illustrations, and logotypes carry the advertising burden. Advertising for perfumes, soft drinks, sugar, and salt usually falls in this category. Body copy plays a minor role, as a rule, in promoting these products.

Should selling be required, however, body copy assumes a major role. Although an illustration of a new car model can certainly interest prospective buyers, they usually need more than an attractive picture to get them into the dealer's showroom. They need to know what is under the hood, what improvements have been made, what kind of mileage to expect, whether power steering is offered, and on and on.

Your body copy does the same sort of persuasive work for a host of other products. In a television commercial, "body copy" is normally a powerful combination of video and audio, although sometimes all of the selling can be done by video, or by video with a minor contribution by audio.

Your Body Copy Direction Is Dictated by Your Headline and Illustration

Copy direction and the type of copy will be set by the direction of the headline and illustration. Once you have decided upon a good headline and illustrative device, the selection of the body copy style will not require much planning. For example, if you use a direct selling, factual headline, your body text will usually be most effective if it, too, is factual. Make it back up your headline claims *immediately.*

As an example, read the following headline and opening body copy:

How to enhance your exterior environment

Send for our Small Building Catalog and discover easy-to-assemble garden houses, storage spaces, cabanas, and much more. There's an architect-designed small building for every use.

Likewise, if you employ an offbeat or a curiosity element in your headline and/or illustration, your body copy should explain the connection before you can get into your selling arguments.

Setting the direction of your body copy requires common sense. Logic will show you that effective body copy must, in the main, follow the pattern established by the headline and illustration.

Avoid Being a Specialist. Be Able to Write Any Type of Copy

You are going to discover—if you are like most copywriters—that you write one or more types of copy better than you do others. The question then arises: Should you attempt to make yourself a specialist? Should you try to limit your writing to those types of copy you do best? The answer is "No."

No matter what kind of copywriting you get into—agency, retail, mail order, direct mail—you will find that your daily routine may call for all types of copy. The products you will be asked to sell will not lend themselves to one specific style of copy or headline-illustration-copy treatment.

If you try to specialize, you may have more fun writing what you do write, but you'll soon be writing strictly for fun and no longer for cash. There are few places for a "one-shot" copywriter in the nation's big advertising operations today.

To be more sure of your future, you should be versatile. Naturally the advertisements decorating your sample book will demonstrate the type of copy you write best. Your seniors in the business will certainly recognize your skill in handling certain types of work and will make that recognition evident in the assignments they give you. Just the same, become proficient in writing keyed to all the various categories.

Above All, Be Believable

One of the most common errors made by copy people is that of overselling. When you create an advertisement, you have two objectives: one, to wrest the attention of your readers from whatever else they may be thinking about, and two, to persuade them into some sort of action or belief.

Your job is highly competitive, since you are bidding not only for a sale of your product against the editorial material of the magazine or newspaper, but also against the ingenuity and skill of other trained and imaginative copywriters. In this competitive situation, it is easy for copywriters to be foolishly enthusiastic in making claims which simply cannot stand up. They are often encouraged in such extravagances by clients, who may take a somewhat inflated view of their own product's attributes.

In almost every one of the major copy categories, you can find examples of flagrant violations of good taste and sound selling principles. Copy that is intended to represent the endorsement of someone, real or imaginary, is a particular offender.

However, claims for a product seem somewhat less bombastic if they appear to be made by a user of the product rather than by its manufacturer. Thus, a testimonial often seems more believable and sincere than a straight claim of a manufacturer, but when overselling occurs in a testimonial it is more noticeable than when it occurs in the straight claim of a manufacturer. The cry of "phony" rings out in such cases. Regardless of the technique, overselling must be shunned.

A Product Should Live Up to Your Claims

If you are writing advertisements for a soft drink, for example, be certain that what you say about that soft drink is recognizable to people when they try it. Straight-line copy simply cannot promise more than the product offers. It must do more than produce a consumer. It must produce a satisfied consumer, or it fails to accomplish the job for which it was intended. If you say of your soft drink—

Once you taste the completely new and different flavor of Gulpo, all other drinks will seem flat and insipid.

—you are guilty of the worst kind of overselling. Your own experience, common sense, and practical analysis of what's in that beverage will tell you that the public will not get that kind of reaction from a bottle of Gulpo, or any other drink. If they have been led to suppose that Gulpo has some magical qualities of life and sparkle that other beverages don't have, the disappointment will be sharp when they find that Gulpo is just another soft drink.

You will make your first sale, but you will have left the people with the feeling of having been deceived—thus your repeat sales will suffer. You have sacrificed the good attributes your product has to offer for an extravagant claim that can't be backed up. A more modest claim might have led the way to repeat business.

Real Talk versus "Advertising" Talk

Because advertising writers are so prone to exaggeration, hyperbole, and unbelievable statements, you have a special problem in writing strong copy that *will* be believed.

To illustrate the kind of unbelievable, exaggerated statements that cause the general public to say too often "That's just 'advertising' talk," here are a few lines culled from national and local advertising. This list could have been expanded by hundreds of examples, but the point is made clearly after you read but a few examples:

The only way to get anywhere is with a new (*name of car*).

Victory employees are the most courteous anywhere.

The purchase of a mobile home at Oakridge is the smartest investment a couple can make.

***(Name of car)* makes any trip more fun.**

Every meal's a feast when you serve 7-Up.

Biggest little treat in all the land.

This beer is the most enjoyable companion for any time and any occasion.

Chewing Doublemint gum doubles the pleasure of everything you do.

Nothing tastes as good as a cold Ballantine beer.

Quality takes a back seat these days unless you shop at Acme.

Not one of those statements stands close inspection. Not one is illegal but not one is credible to any thinking person. When advertisement after advertisement uses such flagrantly unbelievable, unprovable assertions, it is no wonder that so many of the public look upon advertising practitioners as a bunch of glib "con" artists. Occasionally, you would do well to look over this list of statements to remind yourself to keep *your* copy believable.

Beware the "Alka-Seltzer Complex"

Many copywriters suffer from what is called the "Alka-Seltzer complex." That is, they are sometimes inclined to project "immediacy" into their copy that the product cannot substantiate. Alka-Seltzer or any of the effervescent salts can be sold on the basis of the immediacy with which they act to help relieve unpleasant ailments, such as headaches of certain types, gas on the stomach, indigestion, and others.

To use the same sort of appeal for bacon, cigarettes, beer, or ballpoint pens would seem to make little sense, yet a glance through any magazine will bring to light plenty of examples in which copywriters have tried to do so.

At the first captivating taste you'll recognize this beer as tops in master brewing.

Even the aroma of this marvelous bacon convinces you instantly of its quality.

Just a few words written with this precision instrument will prove to you that it's the *peak of pen craftsmanship.*

Are any of those statements true, do you think? You may fancy yourself as an expert on beer, but could you recognize any beer as "tops in master brewing" with one taste? Of course not, so why lead your consumers to think they're going to get a beer so outstandingly different that they'll be able to do so?

Anyone who happened to be in the market for a new pen might be impressed with "precision instrument" and "peak of pen craftsmanship," but do you believe that these abstract boasts could be proved by a few scrawled words on a piece of paper? Hasn't the pen's leakproof quality, or its shape, or its appearance, or its capacity anything to do with such claims?

Don't be a "baloney artist," as copywriters many times are called. Far too many copywriters have already sacrificed believability and sincerity for the one unit sale that exaggerated selling can and will bring—men and women who have turned their typewriters into tripewriters.

When you write copy, make sure that it is straight in *honesty* and in *presentation of product points.* Your job is to build a sales curve of steady customers and the only way to do that is to advertise your product for its merits alone.

Believable copy is not difficult to write if you keep straight-line "selling" in mind. "Sell," with the words you choose, in exactly the same, direct, uncomplicated, and sincere manner you would use if you were selling in person.

Naturally, you should use care in the selection of the right phraseology—observe the rules you learned long ago that make writing smooth flowing and smooth sounding—but remember, in all good copy the overall aim is simplicity.

Bad Grammar: There's Too Much of It in Advertising Copy

English teachers have not been noteworthy for their praise of advertising copywriting's observance of the rules of grammar. Some of their criticism has been justified because not all copywriters are good writers and a big number certainly are not grammarians.

People in advertising are among the severest critics of the bad grammar of copywriters. In the trade press they complain constantly about such advertising phrases as:

Nobody doesn't like Sara Lee

You never smiled so good

We better be better

I could care less

When you gotta have one, you gotta have one *(Baby Ruth bar)*

Me and my R.C.

We're giving away free gifts

" 'cause they make me look like I'm not wearin' nothin'." *(model talking about her pantyhose)*

I only smoke Facts

Because of often deliberate misuse of the language, the advertising business is on the defensive. Critics from many segments of our society deplore the liberties that are taken in printed and broadcast advertising messages.

A common defense is that the offending words and phrases are used, not because the writers are ignorant but because this kind of writing will be more effective and more memorable. Others in advertising assert that English is a flexible, everchanging language and that advertising writing reflects those changes more quickly than other forms of writing. Furthermore, they say, the object of advertising is to communicate quickly with a vast audience; and if unorthodox words and phrases can accomplish this goal, they should be used.

A strong argument is that advertising is written as people talk but critics counter that, even granting that this is true, the advertising writers shouldn't write as if their audience were composed mostly of dropouts. For instance, even a copywriter employing "talk" language should not write "less calories" instead of "fewer calories."

Probably no one has summed up the write-as-you-talk point so well as T. S. Eliot in his observation: "If we spoke as we write, we should find no one to listen, and if we wrote as we speak, we should find no one to read."

The fact is that printed advertising simply creates the *illusion* of spoken communication. To test this, listen carefully to people when they talk. Such speech, put into print, will be a mish-mash of single words, chopped-up phrases, and incomplete sentences. There will be no form, grace, logic, and continuity.

No one will deny that a thorough knowledge of the fundamentals of grammar and sentence structure is helpful to a copywriter. Yet you will find that sometimes a piece of copy will sound better and more sincere if it does not *quite* meet the standards of perfect prose.

Remember that most of the people reading your advertisements, who will eventually buy the products you are selling, do not sport Phi Beta Kappa keys. Give them simple talk, not fancy language. But one caution is needed here—usually you should not violate good grammatical usage. Your readers will soon see through your attempt to write "on their level."

"Usually" was used two sentences ago because occasionally an outstandingly successful advertisement has resulted from the deliberate breaking of a grammatical rule, such as: "It ain't hard to speak good English."

Despite these successful violations, most copywriters observe the rules of writing and grammar without being pedantic. Most good copywriting has a conversational tone. Although such easy, informal writing might offend the purists and the authors of social science textbooks, it is admirably suited to advertising that communicates with a mass audience composed of people who vary greatly in educational background.

Your writing style in advertising should be interesting, yet simple. It should be straightforward, yet subtle. You should abhor dull writing above all else.

Effective Writing Style

One writer had these words about achieving interest through observance of a number of writing niceties. His hard-boiled, commonsense suggestions should be read very carefully.

> What do I mean by writing style?
>
> Just this. The simple sentence starts with a subject. Then the simple sentence has a verb. Then the simple sentence has an object. The simple sentence ends with a period. The simple sentence gets boring as hell after you've read three or four of them. And you just did!
>
> Let's try again. By hanging a phrase out in front of the subject, you can add extra thought, and more interest to a sentence. And by starting sentences with a "non-th" word, ("th" words are the, then, there, etc.) you make your copy flow more smoothly . . . read more easily. Of course, ending a sentence with a question mark helps, too, doesn't it? Exclamation points are even better!
>
> If you're the copy-writer, become the copy-reader. Read what you write with a red pencil in your hand. Be brutal. Cut out meaningless words and useless phrases. Combine some sentences and eliminate others. Give the reader a long flowing sentence that combines several thoughts and presents facts which are of average importance. Then use a shorter sentence to quicken the pace for the reader.
>
> And then . . . hit him in the eye! Shock him. It's amazing how short sentences can catch people. They stir the imagination. They create desire. And produce positive action.
>
> Of course, there's more to good writing than varying the length of your sentence. Vary the length of your paragraphs, too.

Headline: As a hostess, you want to be *sure* the meat is tender.

Subhead: Tender-ite, the electronic tenderizer makes it happen—and in only five minutes.

Copy: What a blow at your dinner party to find that the gorgeous roast you're serving is tough. If you had popped it in Tender-ite's pressure pan, you'd be smiling instead of worrying.

Tender-ite makes the toughest meat tender and does it every time. One less item for a fastidious hostess to worry about. Here's how Tender-ite works. (Etc.)

Figure 7–1a. Straight line copy. The main headline is followed directly by the opening copy. Notice that the main headline is written chiefly to get attention. It does not mention the product, nor is it selling directly. Thus, the burden of selling and product identification is carried by the subhead.

Headline: We PROMISE . . .

Subhead: If you get one of our PRESSURE-PAN electronic meat tenderizers, no one in your home will ever be served a tough piece of meat.

Copy: You'll admit that's quite a promise when you think how tough meat can be at times. But PRESSURE-PAN can make the toughest meat tender in five minutes. That's for uncooked meat. If you find that meat you've cooked is still tough, PRESSURE-PAN will make it tender in even less time.

How is this possible? It's really very simple. (Etc.)

Figure 7–1b. Example of straight line copy that follows up the headline directly. This is retail copy. The illustration showed the product in full detail.

Like this.

Simple, isn't it?[1]

Free-flowing, easy-to-read copy will be more effective than will writing that is self-consciously stiff and precise—whether you're selling cologne or corn plasters—or even a book on English grammar.

Types of Body Copy

Once again, a list is given to you, this time of body copy types. It's a short list because body copy can be categorized rather well in six types. Each has its own advantages and difficulties. You decide which will do best in helping you reach your sales objectives and copy platform objectives.

- **Straight-line copy,** in which the body text begins immediately to develop the headline and/or illustration idea in direct selling of the product, using its sales points in the order of their importance
- **Narrative copy,** the establishment of a story or specific situation which, by its nature, will logically lead into a discussion of a product's selling points
- **"Institutional" advertising,** in which the copy sells an idea, point of view, service, or company instead of presenting the selling features
- **Dialogue and monologue copy,** in which the characters illustrated in your advertisement do the selling in their own words (testimonials, quasi testimonials, comic strip, and continuity panel)
- **Picture-and-caption copy,** in which your story is told by a series of illustrations and captions rather than by use of a copy block alone
- **Offbeat copy,** unclassified effects in which the selling power depends upon humor, poetry, foreign words, great exaggeration, gags, and other devices

1. *Copy Service Newsletter,* International Newspaper Promotion Association, February 1973, p. 7.

In many advertisements you will be able to discover more than one type of copy. Pictures and captions, for instance, very often are used as an amplification of the selling ideas, although the main block of copy is straight line and factual. The same is true of all other classifications.

Although occasionally you may find some advertisement that defies classification, almost always the six preceding listings can be used for classification purposes. To check this out, all advertisements in a copy of *Family Circle* (published at the time this new edition was being prepared) were examined carefully. Each advertisement was classified.

The classifications were as follows:

Straight line	100
Narrative	0
Institutional	1
Dialogue/monologue	1
Picture/caption	1
Offbeat	4
Combination	1
	108

Notice the great dominance of the straight-line copy style. It would be surprising *not* to find such dominance. Every examination of an entire issue of a publication reveals the same utilization of straight-line copy but this will vary somewhat from magazine to magazine. The *New Yorker,* for example, while being dominated by straight-line advertisements will have more narrative, dialogue, and institutional advertisements than will women's service magazines such as *Woman's Day* and *Family Circle.*

For Consistent Results Use Straight-Line Copy

Straight-line or factual copy is copy that proceeds in a straight and orderly manner from beginning to end. It does not waste words, but starts immediately to sell the product on its own merits, and directly following the headline. Such copy is naturally the most used type because, in a majority of cases, magazine or newspaper space is bought for just one purpose—*to tell people about something for sale.* That space costs money—a lot of money.

From the standpoint of getting satisfaction for your advertising dollar, straight-line copy is like a white shirt—correct for any affair—whereas testimonial copy, picture-and-caption copy, and the other forms of copy are not always suitable for every purpose. This does not mean that straight-line copy is ideal for all advertisements—simply that it can be used for any approach, whereas the other types have more specialized functions.

Especially good if your product has an advantage. The style or type of copy you write for advertisements must follow the pattern and pace established by your headline and illustration which are, in turn, paced by the theme idea of your campaign. If you are selling a product that has certain competitive advantages over other similar products, or lends itself to interesting uses, or does something unusual (glows in the dark, for instance!), the chances are that your theme idea will capitalize upon those facts in its plan. Your headline will flag the reader's attention with the most appealing and interesting facts.

The body copy of your advertisement must *maintain the momentum already established.*

All copy—all body copy—regardless of product medium, or market, must be written to keep alive the interest that the headline and illustration have created. Nowhere is this of more immediate importance than in the straight-line type of copy. Straight-line copy will almost always follow a headline and possibly a subhead which has used a product feature to gain the reader's attention.

It must not fail to maintain the interest, and yet it cannot logically confine itself to one feature, if the product has more than one. This type of copy must be a rapid-fire form of selling—starting with one idea or one sales point and quickly putting others across. The most important fact to remember in writing straight-line copy is this: *Most often, if you have something to say to your readers that you have reason to believe will interest them, it pays to say it at once.*

Notice in the following example how quickly and directly the advertiser's body copy carries out the benefit described in the overline and headline.

Overline: Shocked by new furniture prices?
We'll help you recover!

Headline: REUPHOLSTERY

Opening copy: For a lot less than it costs to buy new furniture, you can restore the furniture you already own to its original, beautiful condition. Or give it a new look. Custom upholstery can save you 25%–50% off the cost of comparable new furniture—which can mean hundreds of dollars in savings.

The foregoing example of straight-line copy shows how an advertiser with a strong product advantage stresses that advantage immediately. There is no wind-up. There is no attempt to be cute, different, or clever.

The advertiser knows that nothing will engage the attention of the reader more firmly than to show the product in the illustration and then use the body copy to let the readers know what they are seeing.

Picture-and-Caption Copy

In an earlier chapter, *caption* was defined as being a small unit of type employed descriptively in connection with illustrations and other parts of an advertisement. When such captions are the principal means of telling a copy story, the advertisement is said to be a picture-and-caption advertisement. Reference is made here only to advertisements in which the captions are the sole selling copy.

No rule will tell you precisely when to plan advertisements of a picture-and-caption style. That can depend on the type of product you are advertising, the type of sales features the product has to offer, and the physical space for the story, as well as other factors.

One point to remember is that picture-and-caption advertisements lend themselves much better to sizable space than to small space. Magazine quarter-pages usually don't allow enough room to produce top-quality illustrations in series, together with headline, subhead, caption, and logotype.

Even in half-pages, the problem may be difficult unless your captions are so brief as to be almost classified as subheads. You will find that if you try to put more than one or two illustrations in the space of one-half page or less (still speaking of magazines), you will tend to be cramped for room to give adequate display to your copy or to say all the things you wish to say. In addition, unless you plan to illustrate something very simple, the illustrations will suffer by being reduced too much.

As a generalization, caption copy goes best in advertisements where you have a page or more to tell your story. Like all generalizations, this statement can be challenged by advertisers who go ahead and defy the principle by using less than page units for picture-and-caption advertisements. Despite this, you would probably do better to plan most of your picture-and-caption advertisements in page sizes—it will be less strain on the ingenuity of your layout people.

The type of product you are advertising may influence your use of caption copy. If you are working out a campaign for an automobile, for example, you'll agree that the reader is likely to be more interested in the looks of the car and more attracted to your advertisement if the predominant portion of it is given over to a large illustration showing the beauty of the car, than if you show a series of illustrations and captions concerning its brakes, mileage, upholstery, and driveshaft.

Shoes provide another good example of products that do not lend themselves particularly well to picture-and-

Figure 7–2a. All-type advertisement in straight-line format. Occasionally, circumstances are favorable for the elimination of an illustration. Here, for example, the ingenious picture-frame border, along with an interesting headline set in a highly readable type, draws attention. Furthermore, the subject matter that is conveyed in well-written copy will appeal to the high-level readers of the *New Yorker* magazine in which the advertisement appeared.

Courtesy of Ellen Wulfman, president Signature Advertising, and Marcia L. Vose.

Figure 7–2b. All-type advertisement in straight-line format. Notice how campaign continuity is achieved in the headline's repetition of key words: "Why" and "Yet." (See Figure 7–2a.) Also, although the copy style is straight-line, it is also narrative in execution providing a combination of the two styles.

Courtesy of Ellen Wulfman, president Signature Advertising, and Marcia L. Vose.

caption advertising. The points of interest to the reader in shoe advertising are primarily style, price, and name. Because illustrations of these features would be dull, the use of picture-and-caption copy is eliminated.

Use interesting material. Before you plan to break down the selling points of your product into pictures and captions, be very sure (a) that those selling points will be of personal interest, pictorially, to most of your readers; and (b) that the captions you write for the illustrations back up the promise of the illustrations.

Some time ago the manufacturers of a new-type automotive lubricant inaugurated a series of picture-and-caption advertisements in which the features of this lubricant were highlighted. Illustrations, dramatic and interesting, pictured what happened inside your car when the product went to work. Captions backed up the illustrations with hard-selling copy.

The public response to this campaign was sluggish and disappointing. Finally aid was asked from one of the nation's top advertising people. He had no quarrel with the pictures and thought the copy was well written and strong. "But," he said, "people just aren't interested in the mechanics of what goes on inside their cars."

The reason for this, of course, is that the average person doesn't know enough about motors to understand anything even vaguely technical. The advertising expert wrote a headline which stated "Cuts Your Repair Costs in Half!" used a big block of straight-line copy telling how, and the lubricant immediately became a sensational seller.

If you are going to use pictures and captions, be positive that the pictures reflect the self-interest of the readers or your finest copy in the captions will not sell.

Research people will tell you that, generally speaking, advertisements of a picture-and-caption style will get more thorough reading of the copy than will advertisements that contain a big block of body text. This may be true, because people are interested in pictures and will read short captions.

It is, however, true only if the advertisements you are comparing are both good advertisements. A good headline and all-type advertisement, for instance, will usually get better reading than a picture-and-caption advertisement with a poor headline and dull, unimaginative pictures.

Easier to write captions than straight-line copy. You will find it easier, usually, to write captions for picture-and-caption advertisements than to write straight-line copy. The reason is clear. In straight-line copy, you must develop your story in a strong, orderly progression of

Figure 7–2c. All-type advertisement in straight-line format. Like the other two ads in the campaign (see Figures 7–2a, b), this one combines the narrative style with straight-line copy. The format of the layout is certain to register the campaign in the minds of *New Yorker* magazine readers. To accomplish such registration it is necessary to follow the same format in advertisement after advertisement.

Courtesy of Ellen Wulfman, president Signature Advertising, and Marcia L. Vose.

ideas, one leading smoothly to the other, but you have no such problem with caption copy. Once you have selected the specific sales points to be illustrated, your job is to sell each point by itself. You do not have the "transitional" type of writing which carries you easily from one point to another as in straight-line copy.

One of the great weaknesses of beginning writers is that their copy lacks flow and transition. They fail to make their ideas and sentences connect.

If the pictures in picture-and-caption copy have been arranged in a logical sequence, the transition is assured. The writer merely writes the captions independently, as dictated by the pictures.

An example would be a versatile garden and lawn tool that performs many tasks. Supposing in analyzing its functions you discover that it does the following:

Trims hedges	Shapes bushes
Edges walks	Mulches leaves
Prunes trees	Destroys crabgrass
Cuts grass	Cuts branches
Mows weeds	

Now, you devise a headline that stresses the versatility of the unit and points out that it can do nine lawn and garden tasks. You then call for illustrations that will demonstrate each of these nine functions. You arrange the illustrations in a sensible order and write each caption without any reference to the preceding and following caption.

Your advertisement is tied together by the headline that tells of the overall function of the unit—to perform many lawn and garden tasks. From then on, if you have arranged the pictures logically, your advertisement will be a smooth, flowing production.

Major and minor captions. In planning picture-and-caption advertisements, evaluate first the nature of the claims you want to make in selling your product. If you discover a single particularly outstanding feature that distinguishes your product from the competition and you are sure that this feature will be important to prospects, discard the picture-and-caption idea in favor of a smashing presentation of that certain feature. (You can always illustrate other features in minor roles, with captions, but a good strong block of straight-line body copy can do the best job of selling *one* specific feature.)

Picture-and-caption technique is best adapted to products with multiple sales features, no one of which is outstandingly potent.

It is possible, of course, to use picture-and-caption copy and still gain major emphasis on one point in a series of product advantages. The emphasis is gained by displaying the major illustration in larger size than the other illustrations and by running the lead caption in larger size type.

Such treatment may be considered as almost a combination of straight-line copy if it does not confine itself to selling the one feature involved in the picture, and if it presents a complete story. It must be considered a caption, regardless of the length of copy and what size type it appears in, if it does not stand by itself as a complete and all-inclusive sales story.

Avoid covering too many ideas in captions. If you are using a picture-and-caption technique, be sure that your caption completely covers the illustration to which it is keyed and does not wander off into selling other features that have no bearing upon what is illustrated.

Every extra idea that you insert in your individual captions should have a direct relationship to the main point you're trying to get across in that specific caption. Also, each idea maintains the connection with the main selling ideas written in the headline. Use this technique to prevent your advertisements from being disconnected and incoherent.

If you have hooked the prospects into reading each caption solely on the basis of what they see in the picture, don't lose them by failing to give them a direct and powerful sell on what they are interested in in the first place (through the overall theme set by the headline).

Lead-in lines and headings. If you had enough space to work with, every caption would have a headline that highlighted what it was going to say. Rarely can you afford, however, to give that much space to minor headlines. Copywriters, therefore, use three means of gaining

Figure 7–3. Straight-line copy. An intriguing headline is followed immediately with words that tie in with the headline and illustration—one more example of an advertisement that makes all three parts work together for sales effectiveness. Because of the nature of the prestige product, this is not a hard-sell advertisement; it will, however, appeal strongly to the type of buyer it seeks.

immediate attention to key words and phrases. One of these techniques should be used in the writing of every caption.

- You may display a word or two as lead-in, running it in heavier, slightly larger type.
- You may simply have the first few words of your caption set in boldface type, or color, if color is used.
- You may number captions to help greatly in increasing readership.

All these devices help the advertisement from two standpoints. They serve to gain just that much more sell, in case the reader looks at the illustration but fails to go on to the copy; and they help dress up the page, mechanically speaking.

When you write your captions, keep this lead-in idea in mind. Put down your most interesting words first, thus giving them the added strength of the extra weight or color.

Narrative Copy

Your job becomes much broader when you are following a format that requires narrative copy. Your writing problem is no longer one that can be solved with a clear, straightforward, well-organized summary of your product's sales features. You must also create a "preface," a prologue to your selling story, and one which is not only calculated to select the proper reading audience, but which fits into the overall sales plans of the product you're selling.

Take, for example, an advertisement for a $500 wristwatch designed especially for men. Copywriters may reason that $500 watches are not very often sold by simply pointing out how pretty they are or how well they run. They also know that few people who would be reading their advertisements in a popular weekly magazine would actually be live prospects for such an expensive watch, regardless of what superlatives they could think of.

Neither do they consider as prospects the women who want to give a watch to their husbands or sweethearts. Straight-line copy, accordingly, is out. So is testimonial copy, because while Mr. America possibly will wear jeans because a theatrical figure does, he will not be likely to spend $500 for a watch because anybody does.

No, the problem here is to write an advertisement which will hand-pick those men and women from the millions who read it who could afford a $500 watch and to offer them a subtle enough sales message to make them wish to do so.

The entire selling power of this copy lies in its ability to cause a small group of people to act. By adroit writing alone, this copywriter appeals to the good taste of the successful executive, the ego of the semi-successful executive, the wishful thinking of the newly rich, and the desire of many people to make an impression upon others.

Narrative copy in product selling does not, however, require such unusual products as $500 watches. You will find that narrative structure, although it may be used effectively for almost any kind of product, is best adapted to products that can be sold on a highly emotional basis. Insurance, deodorants, toothpaste, jewelry, cosmetics, clothing, antiseptics, and similar articles or services may be described in their most appealing light when you can dramatize the results they produce.

Narrative copy is usually not short. If you are writing an advertisement in straight-line style, be as brief as possible while still giving adequate emphasis to all the sales points you wish to make. If you have only one thing to say and you can say it in three words, then three words is all the copy you should write.

If you are preparing a piece of narrative copy, on the contrary, you can't very well confine it to a few words or sentences, although your copy may be every bit as or even more powerful from a sales angle than a terse, telegraphed message.

Don't waste time worrying about whether copy should be long or short. When you have convinced yourself and your associates that the approach is right, tailor the copy to do the job, regardless of the number of words you use.

You can have fun writing narrative copy. Product selling, narrative style, is usually more fun for copywriters than any other type of copywriting because it allows a freedom from rules and regulations that sometimes will inhibit copywriters in doing straight selling copy. Few people will argue, for instance, that insurance cannot best be sold to a person who is "in the mood" to buy insurance. You can scarcely get a person in the mood to take on another policy by reciting a series of facts and figures, unless they are sensationally interesting.

You may, however, start someone thinking about insurance needs by painting a word-picture of some of the unpleasant events that could happen if that person did not have enough insurance.

By using (a) an illustration of sufficient strength and human interest that he can easily associate it with himself or his own family, and (b) a poignant story that also could well be his own, you can precondition someone to listen to your offer much more receptively than you could if you started in by saying, "Look, I have an insurance policy here that, etc., etc."

It's fun to let your imagination wander into such writing, away from the fetters of product features, laboratory reports, scientific tests, advertisers' do's and don'ts, and other qualifying factors which regulate much of a copywriter's daily work. Narrative copy gives you a chance to write a "story."

Have fun, but don't forget to sell. Narrative copy, then, is fun for copywriters to write. It is a challenge to creative imagination. It is a fine way to establish a good selling situation—sometimes.

Watch out for this—be very sure that the story you tell in your narrative has a quick and easy transition to your selling message, and be sure your selling message *sells hard.* Don't waste space to tell a story that does not give a powerful springboard into the sales arguments that you wish your reader to hear. Once you make that transition, leave the characters of your playlet to themselves. Do as the veteran copywriter does. Turn your guns on the reader. Get back on the straight line to show how your product is needed to overcome the problems you have presented.

The place of emotion in narrative copy. Because narrative copy doesn't utilize a straight recital of facts, there is a chance for the copywriter to employ emotion to draw people to the advertising message. To do so is to answer those critics (within the advertising field) who say that print advertisements and commercials stressing product attributes simply bore the audience. As one agency creative head said at an American Advertising Federation national convention: "Through emotion you reach inside people. You reach them more effectively than the most ambitiously financed beating about the eyes and ears can possibly accomplish."[2]

Emotion is too often discarded by noncreative advertising people—product managers and/or account executives—who feel safer with strictly factual and formula writing. Yet, everyone knows that many, possibly most, buyer decisions are made wholly or partly for emotional reasons.

Advertisers of motorcycles, for instance, have made purchasers feel that buyers of motorcycles are buying not just a piece of machinery, but a way of life, an unharnessing of the free, adventuresome spirit.

Eastman Kodak sells the emotional rewards of recording baby's first step and then the following of that baby through the growing-up years.

The telephone company, likewise, stresses an emotional theme: the joys of keeping in touch with family members through long-distance telephone calls.

A good aspect for the writer who uses emotion is that so much variety is possible because there are so many emotions to draw upon—sorrow, pathos, melancholy, pride, joy, anger, satisfaction, humor.

A bad aspect is that many writers can't execute emotional writing. Instead of sadness, they produce mawkishness. Instead of justified indignation, they express waspishness. Instead of humor, they produce silliness. Humor, especially, is an emotional tool that only the rare writer should attempt, and yet the attempts continue because successful use of humor in broadcast and print pays enormous dividends in attention and sales.

Emotion is especially useful when a product or service offers no distinct advantage. Thus, the skillful use of emotion will create your point of difference because your product or service cannot.

One prominent creative person has listed the times when it is useful to incorporate emotion into copy. They are:

- When I have absolutely nothing of importance to say
- To add importance to something of relative insignificance
- To add interest when there is nothing new to say
- To heighten the drama and importance of significant messages
- To create a difference when our benefit is generic
- To create a common denominator in appealing to a diverse audience
- To suggest superiority when it cannot be proved
- To provide continuity between diverse messages
- To help preserve and improve a client's image while at the same time selling his product[3]

---

2. A.A.F. Meeting, Washington, D.C., June 1981. Speaker: Don Esensteiner.

3. Hal Riney, "Emotion in Advertising," *Viewpoint* (New York: Ogilvy & Mather, 1981) Vol. 1. (Booklet)

Figure 7–4. Emotional approach. A quick, sympathetic response is evoked by the words and illustration in this advertisement aimed at curbing child abuse.

Emotion isn't always used. Don't get the idea that all product-selling narrative copy is, or should be, filled with pathos or fear or one of the other great emotional appeals. The only factor that makes narrative copy "narrative" is its requirement for telling a story before selling the product. It doesn't need to establish fear or uncertainty in the minds of its readers. Yet it does maintain a very definite air of self-association for most people. It sets up a situation of normal, everyday nature—notably, self-criticism.

Product selling in narrative copy is best adapted to products of a certain type. This, you will probably agree, makes sense, because most such narrative copy is based upon emotionalism. Even the narrative copy for the $500 watch was emotional.

8

YOU DO YOUR SELLING IN THE BODY COPY

Part B

> *"I believe about half of what I see in the ads—maybe not that much."*
>
> *"Those man or woman on-the-street TV interview commercials give me a big laugh. What a put-up job! You know darned well they're paid to say those good things about the product."*
>
> *"Just about 99 percent of products I see advertised say they're the best.*
> *That's bunk. They can't all be the best."*

You've probably made comments such as these, or you've heard others make them. The "believability" of advertising is low. Much of the disbelief stems from what are purportedly unrehearsed interviews with product users in print or broadcast.

An example of the kind of testimonial that occasions incredulity is the quasi testimonial (described on pages 84–86) for More cigarettes. The illustration shows a glamorous-looking young woman reclining in a chair. She is holding a package of More cigarettes in one hand and a cigarette in the other. The headline reads:

More Never settle for less.

Underneath there is a quote from the young woman:

> "Me and My MORE.
> We've turned a few heads, I admit.
> My MORE is longer. Smoother.
> And we both have such great taste.
> I guess it shows."

Contrast this statement with the two following that were overheard as this book was being written. The speakers were people who didn't know that their words were being jotted down:

> "Ever use that Fantastik? You just put it on smudges or fingerprints. It's terrific. It's one of the few products that lives up to its advertising claims. It does exactly what it says it's going to do."

In another instance:

> Person A: "This floor *does* look better."
> Person B: "Yeah! It's *shining*."

When an advertisement features a person who is talking about a product—usually praising it and telling how it worked—you may have a smashing success, or you may arouse cynical disbelief.

In the successful advertisement, you will undoubtedly have a strong, *believable* statement delivered by a person whose credibility is unquestioned.

In the advertisement greeted by disbelief, you may have (a) a statement that doesn't ring true because it makes a salesperson out of the person delivering it; or (b) a statement delivered in artificial or unnatural language (where a homemaker talks like a Ph.D. in chemistry about a personal product such as cleansing cream, a household detergent, or a cold remedy).

Monologue and Dialogue Copy

Included in monologue and dialogue copy are true testimonials, quasi testimonials, comic strip, and continuity panels. This is copy in which you let others do your selling for you—real people, imaginary people, cartoon characters. It can be down-to-earth or whimsical.

Testimonials, when judiciously handled, have proved their ability to produce outstanding results. The trick is to write testimonial headlines so that the message retains its selling power and at the same time is natural sounding when placed in the mouths of human beings. The same problem is of constant concern to copywriters when they carry the testimonial type of advertising into the body copy.

If you use personalized selling in your headline, whether the statement of a real person or that of an unidentified person, it does not mean that your copy must also *continue* with personalized selling. Very often you will want to use a testimonial headline from some well-known person as a means of attracting attention, and then develop your own sales message in straight-line copy, captions, or other copy approaches.

Often, however, you will wish to make more monologue or dialogue copy than is possible to put into a headline. You may do this by letting your featured character do the complete selling job clear through the advertisement (a dangerous procedure), or by including additional endorsing remarks in captions.

You will be called upon to write three different types of copy for personalized advertisements: (a) true testimonials, in which you prepare statements for real people to "say"; (b) quasi testimonials, in which you illustrate, by photography or artwork, supposedly real persons but do not identify them by name; and (c) comic strip and continuity panel advertisements, copy for blurbs, or balloons where the testimonial-givers are obviously fictitious.

True Testimonials

The longer the statement, the more danger of incredulity—this assertion is almost axiomatic in testimonial writing. You start off fast in testimonials because in the first exposure to the advertisement your audience is influenced by the name and picture of the celebrity. In fact, the stopping value of a celebrity testimonial is in the person's name, not necessarily in what he or she says.

After the first statement is cleared, however, and the reader settles down to what purports to be sincere talk about the product by the testimonial-giver, *plain talk is necessary.* Movie stars, lion tamers, baseball heroes, or ballerinas shouldn't be presented as experts on nutrition, engineering, or economics. At least you cannot expect the public to believe they are.

It is possible that thousands of American readers will buy a certain product because a famous person says he or she likes it. Readers can also be urged—in straight-line copy—to use the product on the reasonable assumption that it will help them (ingredients and other factors that make it a quality product may be discussed, for instance.). The moment, however, that you attempt to put such selling into the mouth of a celebrity you are injecting a phony note into something that might other-

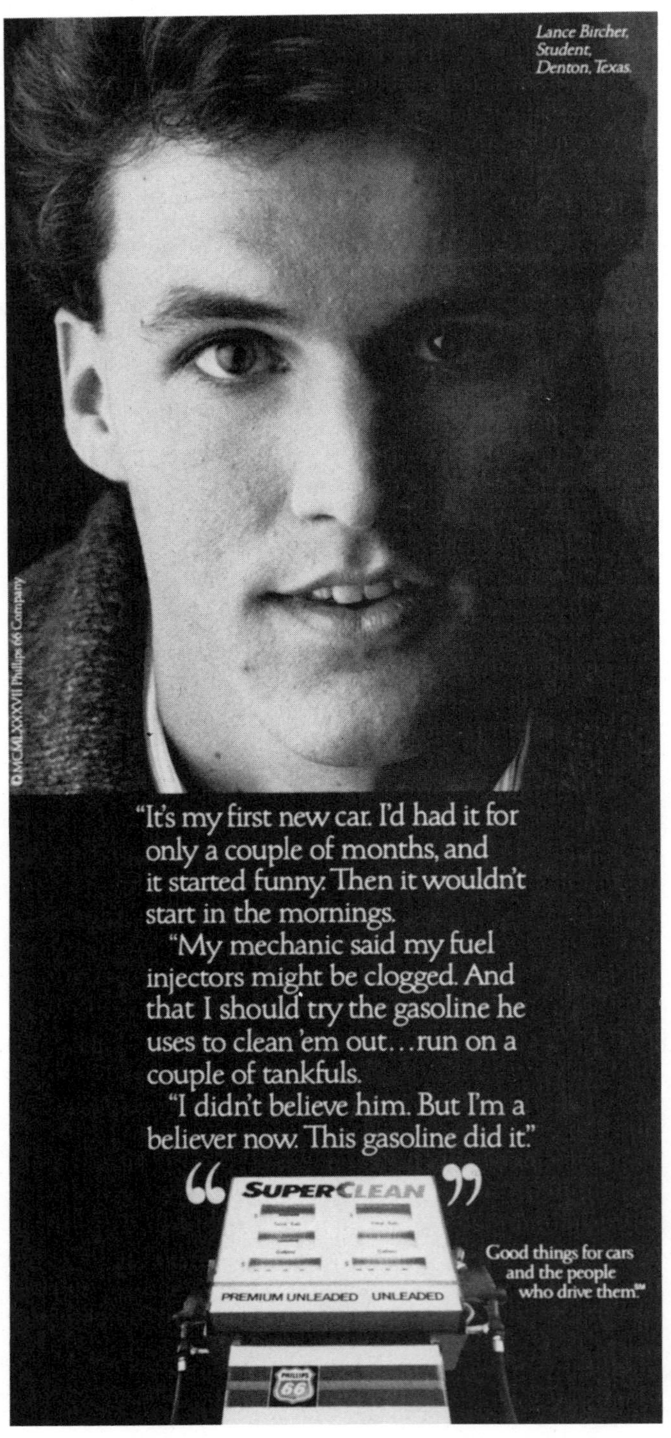

Figure 8–1. Testimonial copy. One of the strongest devices for attention and readership is the testimonial. Several cautions must be observed, however. (a) Keep the first-person copy short. (b) Unless the testimonial-giver is an expert, don't make her/him an expert. (c) Make it natural. Don't use the testimonial if it sounds as if it were written by an advertising copywriter.

wise be easily believable and salable. There is a huge difference between the following two statements when you are asked to believe that a screen personality said them spontaneously about a well-known soap:

> I think Blank soap is just *wonderful!* It seems to leave my skin extra soft and smooth. I never use any other brand but Blank soap.

That is believable, but who could seriously believe that a person would normally speak in the words of this testimonial:

> Blank soap is the perfect soap. That cottonseed oil in it keeps my skin soft and smooth. None of us in Hollywood would think of using any other soap.

Now notice the difference in those testimonials. In one, the person speaking does not make any claims other than having a very strong liking for a brand of soap and giving her own personal reactions to using it. That is enough to gain power from the name of the celebrity as far as influencing the public is concerned. In the second statement, however, the testimonial attempts to take in a lot more territory.

The endorser—in this case, a woman—is claiming more than she could possibly be expected to know. She says, "It's the perfect soap." She asserts that the "cottonseed oil in it" is what keeps her skin smooth and soft, yet so far as the public is concerned, she would have no understanding of the action or effect of any of the ingredients, even assuming she knew what they were.

After all she's a name star, not a dermatologist. Furthermore, she makes a completely unbelievable claim concerning the soap-using habits of her Hollywood colleagues. There is a big difference between saying that you prefer a certain product and crediting everyone else with the same sentiments.

If you are writing a testimonial for use in cereal advertising, it is logical to have your endorser say that the product has "finer flavor" or is "crisper" or "stays fresh longer," or even to make a general claim about its being "good for you."

It is not logical to have the endorser refer to the actual nutritive qualities of the cereal, such as claiming that its wholesomeness comes from "niacin and Vitamin B_1" or that children will thrive on it because it has a high protein content.

Testimonials for candy can indicate a natural preference for its "delicious goodness," its "nutty, crispy, crunchy, chocolaty, chewy, delicate, or otherwise luscious flavor," but they are on thin ice if they present normal citizens talking about "dextrose" or "rich in food energy."

A testimonial for a whiskey advertiser demonstrates the folly of putting "expert" words in the mouth of the endorser:

> "I tried it and it's true."
>
> "*(Product name)* true bourbon taste comes from the finest grains, long, lazy years of aging in charred oak barrels and the priceless know-how of *(name of distiller)*. It's a true value."

It is very easy to let yourself drift into such errors in writing testimonial copy because you know more about the products you are advertising than does the general public. If you are responsible for writing advertisements for men's clothing, for example, you know how those clothes are made, what percentage of wool they contain, how they are styled and tailored, and other features that only someone close to the operation could know.

If one of your friends asked you, "What's so good about these clothes?" you would undoubtedly answer with a rundown of the features that most impress you. If the same question were asked of a man who had been wearing one of the suits, he would probably reply in the simple but enthusiastic way in which American men talk: "It fits well," "I get lots of compliments," "I like the style and the price."

This kind of simple, believable talk is used in the following headline and copy for a washer. The illustration is of a pleasant-looking mother with her husband and two children:

> **Headline:** "A working mother's best friend is her Maytag," writes Mrs. Lang.
>
> **Subhead:** Between her family and her job, who has the time to wait around for repairmen?

Figure 8–2. True testimonial. A famous performer endorses the product. Notice that the brief testimonial is given to be followed by straight-line copy. In most testimonial advertisements it is best not to have the testimonial-giver deliver too long a tribute. Also, as in this case, the giver should be qualified to speak of the product.

Opening copy: "Thank you for making a washer a working housewife and mother can count on," writes Mrs. Nancy Lang, Hampton Bays, New York.

"Eleven years ago, I purchased a Maytag. It wasn't till just this past spring that it needed its first repair."

Simple, short, and believable. Keep those words in mind for testimonial copy such as the conversation overheard of a man talking to his wife about a new type of cracker: "These things stay crisp. They don't seem to lose their crispness no matter what the humidity is." That's "real people" talk, not the nonsense that causes so much disbelief in advertising.

Here are a couple of suggestions to help you avoid causing your endorsers to talk too expansively and/or technically in testimonial copy:

1. Associate the copy you are writing with some real person whom you know well and ask yourself what he or she would say about the product if giving an endorsement. Remember that the person with whom you identify the product does not know much about it beyond having a high regard for its qualities in general. If you can easily imagine your friend saying what you'd like to have the advertisement say, then the chances are you have created a good, believable testimonial statement.

   If you can have this friend actually make a statement to you, or read aloud what you have written, you'll be aided even more.
2. Test your copy on somebody not in the advertising business, preferably a person who already uses the product you are advertising. Let this person read the statement and tell you whether he or she would make such a remark. Only in one or both of these two tests can you be sure you are not, because of your knowledge of your product, putting words into the mouths of real people—words that sound strained, insincere, or too expert.

Be sure testimonials are honest. Testimonials should be used to gain the name of some prominent person *only if that person actually uses the product regularly and he or she subscribes wholeheartedly to the feeling about it you wish to get across.*

The Federal Trade Commission, the various advertising organizations, and other groups interested in better advertising frown upon the practice of writing testimonial statements without regard for the identity of the endorser and then paying someone a large sum of money for the use of the name and for signing the statement.

You may look foolish and dishonest if one of these operations backfires, as they often have, and it is learned that your prize endorser actually uses some rival product. Know your endorsers. Talk to them, if possible, and get their own honest appraisal of your product before you write anything. You'll come up with better-selling copy and you'll save yourself embarrassment.

You will be responsible, usually, for the writing of the testimonial statements your endorsers sign. Usually they won't care much, and you will be expected to do the writing for them. Just remember, make all testimonial statements sound like normal people talking. On rare occasions, endorsers insist upon making their own claims and refuse to sign anything else.

Quasi Testimonials: Why Use Them?

In planning an advertising campaign you and your associates may decide that the story may be told most effectively in the first person, testimonial style. Yet for one of many reasons you may not wish to use the statements of actual personalities. The increased costs of paying for testimonials may be one reason. Availability of well-known people who might be interested in endorsing the particular product may be another. The most common reason for discarding the true testimonial approach is simply that the product does not lend itself particularly well to the endorsement of a celebrity.

In this case, you may decide to use the "quasi testimonial." In the quasi testimonial you have a copy approach, and also the sort of product (or service) that might be sold by an unidentified person, as well as by an identified person.

You might have what appears to be an endorsement of a certain type of retirement insurance and an insurance company by a man of late middle age and average appearance. The headline and practically all the body copy are of testimonial character, with the selling story handled in the first person singular.

Yet nowhere is this man identified. He is used solely as a *type* with whom every man of fifty-five can conceivably associate himself. It would be worthless to use the endorsement of a well-known person here, since most readers would not believe that any celebrity could or would "retire" on the modest retirement income mentioned.

Secondly, most people who have retired would be reluctant to publish the facts concerning their income from an annuity or elsewhere. To gain, therefore, the added human interest of the personalized copy, those responsible for this advertisement decided to go ahead and write it just as if this were to be a signed testimonial but to use a photograph of a professional model rather than that of a real endorser.

An interesting slant to this advertisement is that the headline is written with a "you" approach to capture the personal interest of every reader, while the body text is entirely within the testimonial pattern.

If the copywriter had used a headline, "How I retired at 55," he would have sacrificed readership from those men who might automatically say to themselves, "Well, maybe he could do it, but I'll never be able to retire." The "you" approach flags interest; the testimonial technique provides believability.

This type of copy is one of the most frequently used

and most successful tools of copywriters. Just remember, though, that you must keep such copy material simple, believable, in print or broadcast copy.

An example of a quasi testimonial approach is offered in an advertisement showing a very masculine man holding up a partially eaten drumstick and wearing a chef's hat. He is saying:

> "The only thing ZIPLOC can't protect food from is me."

In the following copy he talks about the many virtues of ZIPLOC® brand storage bags.

Quite often you might wish to use a whimsical type of quasi testimonial wherein the lines are delivered by an animal—a bird, a fish, or some other creature. An example is an advertisement for Kitty Litter® brand showing a cat in the illustration supposedly saying the words (in headline form):

> "Doesn't anyone care about the odor in my cat box?"

Another example of an unnatural type of quasi testimonial is demonstrated in an advertisement featuring a sultry-looking young woman who says:

> "I'm absolutely bare. My face doesn't have a stitch on.
>
> And it looks and feels better than ever.
>
> Because before I put anything on, I clean and moisturize with nothing but (*product name*). And (*product name*) nothing is really something.
>
> Hypo-allergenic and fragrance free.
>
> Then I dress up my face with (*product name*) fresh, natural-looking foundation.
>
> (*Product name*). Everything you want. And nothing you don't."

Make quasi testimonials natural and factually correct. You will have more latitude in writing statements for imaginary people to "say" than for real ones. In the first place, you eliminate all worry that the endorsers might not really believe what they say and actually are not boosters of your product.

Secondly, and this is especially true when the illustration of the "endorser" is shown in a painting or a drawing rather than in a photograph, the public has become familiar enough with the quasi testimonial treatment to understand its motives.

People will not be so critical of the statements of imaginary characters in advertising as they are of those supposed to be said by real ones. However, don't let this comment lead you astray. The difference is very, very slight, and you will be wise to treat the copy in quasi testimonial advertisements exactly as you would if you were writing for a quotation by a real individual. Keep it natural. Keep it simple. Don't try to sell.

In the following example of a quasi testimonial the illustration showed a glamorous, curvaceous model drinking a nonalcoholic beverage through a straw. The headline and copy were:

Headline: (*Product name*) has got the taste that keeps me lookin' good."

Copy: (*Product name*) Mix, you keep me lookin' good. 'Cause there are only 2 slender calories in every glass. I just add water and stir up something delicious. Because (*Company name*) blends choice teas with natural lemon flavor, then presweetens to taste . . . M-m-m-m. (*Product name*) Mix, you've got the taste that keeps me lookin' good . . . from top to bottom."

It is highly unlikely that any real person would deliver such a perfect sales pitch and in language that is obviously that of a copywriter, not that of a typical product user. Thus, the credibility of the copy message is low. Even the headline sounds contrived. The fault isn't with the quasi testimonial technique but the way it has been handled. Again, be *natural.*

Personalized copy can sometimes get so far afield that the foregoing rules don't apply. If you are preparing advertisements for a dog food, you may want to show a talking dog and let him do your selling for you. You may use an illustration of a baby for a soap or talcum advertisement, putting grownups' words in the baby's mouth.

If you look through magazines and newspapers long enough, you can find examples of almost every conceivable kind of object brought to life for advertising purposes—railroad trains, cats, clocks, fish and fowl, vacuum cleaners, and hundreds of others.

These advertisements represent an imaginative use of personalized copy, in which the copywriter is working more for the humorous and attention-getting value of the unusual.

There are some advantages to using nonpeople spokesmen: (a) They are memorable. (b) They don't die, get old, or get into situations that result in bad publicity, and they don't ask for more money. (c) They are less likely to wear out their welcome than a person. (d) They can be used in print and broadcast copy (as can people, for that matter). (e) They create a "fun" feeling that extends to the company using them.

As a possible disadvantage, it is incongruous to have a humorous, fun-type character delivering an earnest, factual copy message. Real people can do better in this respect.

Morris the Cat and Charlie the Tuna have become famous spokesmen for their brands. Because of the humorous way they do their selling, full attention will be given the sales message in contrast to the half attention that is, unfortunately, given to so many commercials.

Despite the fun-and-games approach used in commercials delivered by nonhumans, copywriters must remember that they cannot have a cat or a tuna making claims that aren't literally true even though they may be delivered in an unrealistic atmosphere, such as Charlie's statements coming from the bottom of the sea. In short, as a consumer you don't have to believe that the message is coming from the ocean depths, but you have every right to believe that whatever Charlie says about a product is as true as what the president of the company might say.

To sum up this particular point, when writing for human beings, make their statements and language realistic. When writing for cats, dogs, fish, and so on, don't worry about realism but *do* make certain that product claims are wholly true. Also, don't get *too* cute in your writing.

Institutional (Corporate) Advertising

Even more common than narrative copy is the type of copy you have probably heard called "institutional." In many cases, institutional copy is narrative in style, because under normal conditions you are not trying to sell a specific product or service.

At one time, defining institutional advertising as "all advertising that attempts to sell the company instead of its product or service" seemed to satisfy advertising people. In recent years, however, the definition has seemed too narrow.

Thus we now have "idea" advertising, "corporate" advertising, "public relations" advertising, and "management" advertising. While each of these designations has merit, the term "institutional advertising" is still the term most commonly used to describe advertising that does not sell goods or services of a corporation.

One criticism of the term, of course, is that a considerable amount of advertising that is called institutional advertising is conducted in behalf of hotels, hospitals, and other organizations that fall under the heading "institutions." In this chapter we are *not* referring to this type of advertising.

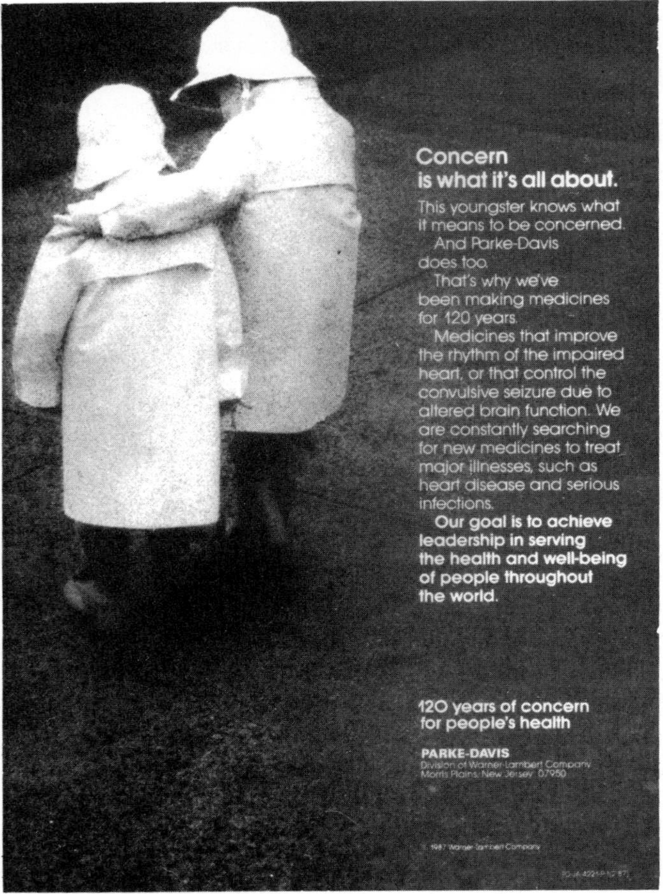

Figure 8–3. Professional advertisement of the institutional type.

Why use institutional advertising? Before copywriters begin to write an institutional advertisement, they must have a clear idea of what it is trying to accomplish. In the usual product advertisement their objective is relatively clear and simple; they are trying to sell the product. Objectives in institutional advertising are not so clear-cut and often are quite subtle. Ordinarily, however, those objectives will fall into one of the three following:

1. To create confidence in the company that will help sell its products and to make the company's stock appealing to investors. This confidence may be required because:
   a. The company makes so many products that the institutional campaign serves as a sort of umbrella. Thus if confidence is engendered, it is not so vital that the public remember individual selling points for each of the products.

      Instead, if the institutional campaign has done its job, public reaction will be: "I don't know much about this product, but if it's made by the ABC Company, it must be good." Such thinking is especially valuable when quick buying decisions must be made by supermarket or drug store shoppers.
   b. The company makes the kind of product that will never be bought if the consumer doesn't have strong faith in the reliability, integrity, and skill of the maker. Pharmaceuticals, such as remedies and medicines, require consumer belief. Squibb, Lederle, and Eli Lilly are advertisers whose great growth has largely developed because of the public trust they have enjoyed through the years.
2. To explain the company management's stand about such pressing matters as a labor dispute, a bad product, or a drastic price rise. Such advertisements have a public relations flavor and very often are tied in with news releases published at the same time. Sometimes they are signed by top officials of the company, although they have been written by the copywriter.

   Exceeding care must be exercised in the writing of such "policy" advertisements because they are scrutinized closely not only by the company's advertising department but also by top management, by the company's public relations agency, and by the corporation lawyers.

3. To express the company's philosophy about government, politics, or other aspects of society. Enlightened management executives in a corporation feel keenly the need to speak out on the pressing issues of the day—ecology, the drug problem, education, slaughter on the highways. Advertisements are often used to give voice to these feelings. Once again, critics will be looking over your work to be certain that it expresses accurately what management intends to convey.

What has probably driven more companies into institutional advertising has been the increasing difficulty of impressing advertising messages for individual products on the minds of prospective buyers. The profusion of brands, coupled with the similar profusion of advertising messages, has made it increasingly difficult for advertisers to register their selling points. Research of print and broadcast advertising has revealed a dismaying lack of product-point registration and, equally as alarming, poor identification of the advertisers paying for the advertising.

Interesting institutional advertising, not designed to sell but to do one thing only—to create a favorable feeling for the advertisers and hence any product they promote—has been viewed as a possible way out of the "too many products, too many advertising messages" impasse. Copywriters writing institutional advertising, accordingly, face a stern challenge in their writing task.

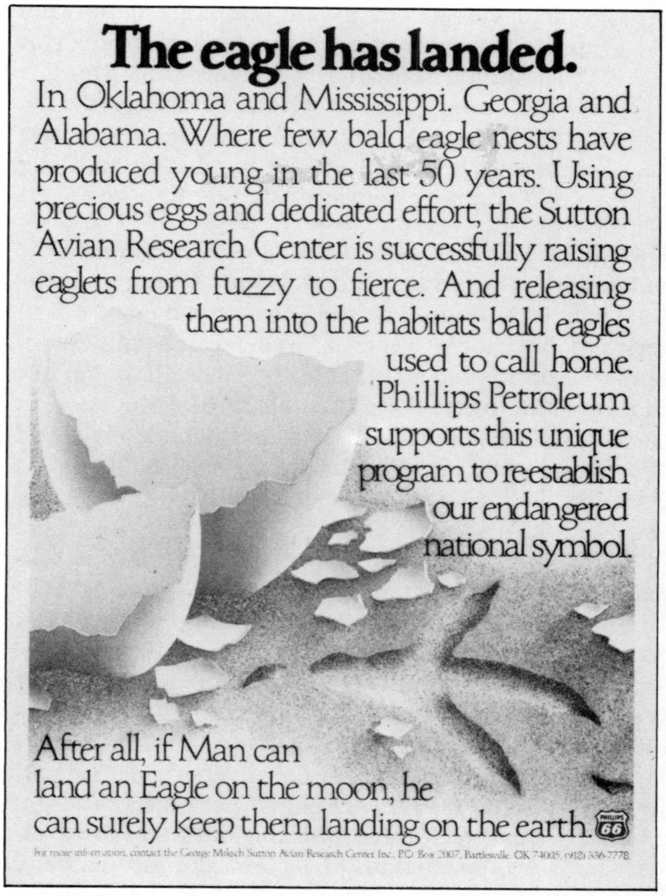

Figure 8–4. Corporate public service advertisement. This advertisement can also be called an institutional advertisement with a public service slant. There is no sell for the advertiser in this advertisement but it is hoped that goodwill will be generated. Institutional campaigns typically run a long time, many for years. Eventually, if such campaigns are successful, the favorable opinion created by the advertisements will extend to all the advertiser's products or services.

Be extra careful with your facts. Give extra long and careful study to the subject about which you are to write. If you are going to sell your firm to the public on the basis of its ability to help develop a jet engine, be very sure that what you write about that jet engine makes sense, not only to people you think don't know, but to jet experts. If you are going after readership with the story of an antibiotic, get your information from unimpeachable sources.

There is no room for extravagant claims in institutional advertising. If you lose believability, you lose everything. Be sure of what you're writing before you start to write, and check it after you've finished with the same unimpeachable sources.

In this type of copy, again, the nature of the firm or product you are advertising has a lot to do with the selection of the style of the format, and, therefore, the body copy style. Institutional copy is used mainly by four kinds of advertisers:

1. By organizations such as drug firms that serve the public's vital needs. It lends itself very well to building goodwill and prestige.
2. By companies whose products require precise engineering or research, the oil companies, or the automotive industry. Thus an advertisement based on "creative imagination" sells General Motors' ability and ingenuity rather than the separate merits of the individual G.M. cars. These, of course, are advertised in other campaigns planned individually for each car.
3. By advertisers (discussed earlier) who either because they make a great many products themselves, or because they are discouraged by the difficulty of fighting for recognition against the myriad of advertising products, decide to strive for company-name registration as a form of advertising umbrella.
4. By "association" advertising or advertising paid for by a group of independent operators in the same industry. Thus the fruit growers of California advertise Sunkist rather than their own names. The Washington State Apple Association advertises the merits of the big red beauties grown in Washington. And the National Association of Life Insurance Underwriters uses copy that sells "life insurance," not that of any particular insurance company.

This category of institutional copy many times promotes sales of a certain type of product. A beer advertisement run by the U.S. Brewer's Foundation, even though it cannot describe the good features of any brand of beer in competitive beer selling, can sell beer in straight-line copy and sell it competitively against other beverages.

Downplay the "we"—stress the "you." Beware of the outstanding peril of institutional copy. That peril is the tendency to write in terms of the company and not in terms of the readers' interests. Writers, especially beginners, get so wrapped up in the traditions of the company, in its astounding (to them) manufacturing processes, in the details of its operations, that they completely forget the reader. The copy becomes chestpounding in its boasting, and the "you" approach is entirely replaced by the "we."

Such copy often results from the urging of a self-satisfied executive of the advertiser's company who finds it difficult to believe that the success story can fail to be as fascinating to the readers of the advertisements as it is to him. Remember then—keep in mind your reader's interest and never let your reader become subordinated by the urge to stress "us" and "our" and "we."

A poem, deriding institutional advertising, appeared in the magazine *Advertising & Selling* some years ago. This irreverent verse, after pointing out that the advertiser may be interested in the factory and the company history but that no one else is, ended with the following almost bitter admonition:

> So tell me quick and tell me true
> (Or else, my love, to hell with you!)
> Less—How this product came to be!
> More—What the damn thing does for me!

Memorize these words and they may keep you from going the way of a good many copywriters when they tap out institutional copy on their typewriters or word processors.

It's how interesting you make your copy that determines whether an institutional advertisement will be read. Picture some typical readers of an institutional advertisement. They turn the page, and there is your creation. It has no product that will make their lives easier or more pleasant or more profitable. There are no prices to arouse their interest or selling features to compare with other products.

In short, your advertisement is likely to be viewed as a big fat nothing that offers not one reason for their taking the time to read it. If it follows the lead of too many institutional advertisements, it is likely to be dull, self-centered, stuffy, overly long, and full of "we" and "our" and the board-of-directors language.

You have a vital obligation to be interesting because you won't be read if you're not. Institutional advertising is characteristically at the bottom in readership figures.

To get readership, pull out all the stops. Entertain, shock, amuse, fascinate, be unusual and even bizarre. Grab attention with your headline and reinforce it with a different, exciting illustration.

Except for unusual situations, forget dignified prose. Be human. Write relaxed, conversational copy. Concentrate on the "people" approach. Reduce the awesome corporation to a person—possibly a person who works for it, or a person it serves. The telephone company has done this for years. AT&T is a monstrous corporation in size but the advertising for this company has consistently over the years focused on people, and usually each advertisement spotlights one person. The corporation is thus reduced to dimensions to which the readers or viewers can relate, and which they can understand.

From the writing standpoint, to repeat because it's so important, your most vital single job is to be *interesting.* Then, and only then, will you force readership of your institutional advertisement—an advertisement most readers would rather "not read" than "read."

Offbeat Copy: A Creative Grab Bag

If the discussion on offbeat headlines is not fresh in your mind, it might be well to review it briefly, since the term "offbeat" is used also for body copy for which it is difficult to find a better term. Any copy not falling into one or another of the foregoing categories may be termed "offbeat" copy. You are familiar with advertisements written as limericks or jingles or formal poems. Those are offbeat. So are advertisements in which the copy is set to music or written in pig Latin or set upside down and sideways.

They are rare because, despite the type of headline treatment you use or the unusual or bizarre illustration you and your associates may plan, the body copy is usually a place for sober selling. And you can't get much selling out of an advertisement written backwards.

Offbeat copy is used where you have no need for telling a straight, hard-selling story and you wish to gain added attention and continued interest in an already interesting situation. You aren't shown any fundamentals of writing offbeat copy because there aren't any. It's a case of the person with the first idea having the best one—or the worst. At any rate, you won't have many occasions to worry about it.

Other Thoughts on Writing Body Copy

Before getting into additional aspects of body copy, ponder once again the importance of simplicity, honesty, and sincerity in all the copy you write. Then remember that if you have the ability to write well, the desire to write, and have a full knowledge of your product or service, you'll need to do little thinking about which copy type to use.

The style of your copy will be the style that will appeal to the greatest number of prospects and that will cause them to act. This style can be any one of the types described in the two chapters on body copy.

Involve reader through word pictures. Too much copy is impersonal because there is no use of the "suffering points" mentioned earlier. Body copy should involve readers by picturing situations they have encountered. Consider the breakable thermos. Anyone who has used one has heard that dread tinkle when the thermos falls off a table, rolls off a bench, falls out of the car, drops from a picnic table, or is knocked over on a table. In your copy, bring in those happenings if you happen to be selling an *unbreakable* thermos. Don't just talk about the steel construction. Show what that steel construction means in terms of solving everyday problems.

Let's say that you're selling a cordless, battery-powered lawn mower. Now, what pictures are evoked? There's the tangle of the cord on the conventional electric lawn mower that catches on every bush and wraps itself in a snakelike fashion around the feet of the user.

Another picture comes to mind if you're selling against the gasoline-powered mower—the glares of the neighbors disturbed by the racket made by the mower. A contrast could be, of course, the serenity of a Sunday morning that remains unshattered because the homeowner is using an electric lawn mower.

Think in everyday pictures as you spin out your body copy because through such pictures you create empathy, involvement, and sales.

The following "picture" copy gives the reader a picture in the headline, illustration, and body copy.

Headline: How can a man only 5′ 7″ clean the snow off his roof?

Subhead: He can use our 19′ Sno-Go snow puller—that's how.

Copy: Each blizzard piles snow on your roof-line. And then a thaw, followed by a freeze, builds ice. After this, water backs up under the shingles. Result? Ruined ceilings and wallpaper spotted and wrinkled by seeping water.

If you have a Sno-Go puller, you can stand on the *ground* and clean off the snow before it turns to ice. You see, Sno-Go has a lightweight 19′ pole that lets you reach way up on the roof with the toboggan-shaped shovel. It beats doing the job from a slippery, swaying ladder.

Another reason for clearing off that snow is to avoid the hazard of ice sliding off the roof—ice that can injure people and wreck shrubs, shutters, and outside lighting fixtures.

But, you might ask, what do I do with a 19′ pole when spring arrives? That's easy. Sno-Go comes in three sections. In a minute you can take the unit apart and store it. By the way, the poles and shovel are rustproof as well as durable.

Better look into this handy item before the first big snowfall. Only $16.95.

Illustration: Short man using Sno-Go snow puller to remove snow from roof-line of a two-story house. Snow is deep on the roof.

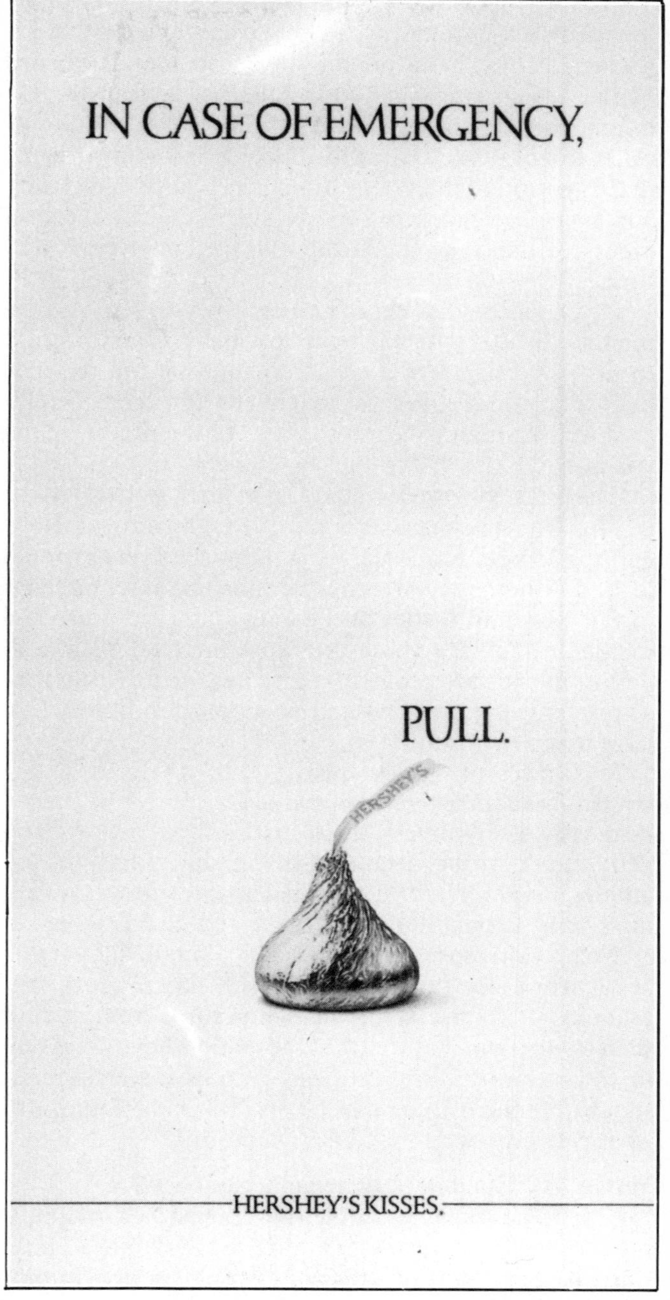

Figure 8–5. Offbeat advertisement. As this example demonstrates, cleverness is often more important for the success of an advertisement than the writing of reams of copy. Four words of copy and an illustration of the product result in a memorable advertisement. The trick is to pick the right words. *Offbeat* here refers to the unusual and unconventional. Such an approach does not fall into the standard classifications of copy.

The *Hershey's Kisses* chocolate advertisement is reprinted by permission of the copyright owner, Hershey Foods Corporation, Hershey, Pennsylvania, U.S.A. The conical configuration, the attached plume device, and the words *Hershey's Kisses* are registered trademarks of Hershey Foods Corporation and are used with permission.

Tips on writing public service advertising. Public service advertising promotes causes such as the ones that are the subject of so many notable advertisements furnished by the Advertising Council in behalf of education, participation in politics, conservation, and innumerable other topics related to public benefit. Such advertising, in this period of public protest and consumer advocacy, has been seen more and more, even though advertisements of this type touch the average copywriter very little.

If you do have a chance to fashion such advertisements, consider yourself lucky. You have an opportunity to use advertising as a useful social tool and to write body copy that gives you a chance for more intelligent writing than you find in much of the product copy you do.

There is no formula writing here. Usually, you will be writing from the heart, although if your advertisement is concerned with economic issues it must be very rational indeed. Your copy will center around the reader's sense of fair play and justice and goodwill toward those less fortunate. You may wish to arouse the reader's awareness of the need to protect—those less fortunate, the environment, the political and economic traditions that have made us strong.

Such advertising, like institutional advertising, answers no selfish interests of the reader. It can be passed over very easily unless, as in institutional advertising, you: (a) use strong, attention-getting headlines; (b) use ample, but not overly long body copy; (c) are, above all, *interesting* in headline, body copy, and illustration.

Last, avoid reproving the readers too much. Don't be accusatory. Refrain from making the readers feel ashamed of themselves. It's easy to cause resentment in such campaigns. Assume that the readers have done well in their contributions to causes. Your advertisement should lift them to new levels in their contribution to whatever worthy cause you're promoting.

Watch out! Humorous advertising can backfire. Some very good advertising people find themselves in opposing corners about the use of humor in advertising. Those who like it point to the attention-getting power of humor and the fact that if humor is well done, it provides the basis for a long campaign.

On the contrary, the sales message *can* get lost in humorous copy. It's easy to become so involved in the humorous story line that the product is subordinated to the humor, and poor sales and/or poor identification may result.

Furthermore, humor can kill you in the marketplace if it is poorly done. If it is, it has a short life and an ability to irritate enormously, to the detriment of goodwill toward the company and its product. A poorly done humorous campaign is less likely to enrage the print audience than the radio and television audience. The wear-out factor is especially quick in the latter.

Yet, there have been numerous successes chalked up for humor on television (also radio), especially with the under-35 market that has been reared on television. And these successful campaigns using humor, such as Maytag and Star-Kist, go on for years entertaining and selling millions.

Television has an advantage over print in the use of humor because of its ability to convey humor through voice intonations, bodily movements, and changing facial expressions. Gag humor, however, is less successful than humor based on human interest situations to which people can relate.

The biggest problems in the use of humor, apart from trying to judge how long to use it before you've worn out your welcome, is to judge how many people will like and respond to your particular type of humor. What makes one person laugh may disgust another person.

The moral here is that a humorous approach should be tried out on many persons before the campaign is launched. Two objectives should be sought: (a) to determine how well the sales message, or product identification, comes through; (b) to determine how well the mass audience is likely to respond to the humor.

Humor is great if it works. It can be a disaster if it doesn't. So use it with caution.

No U.S.P.? Here's what to do. Applicants for copywriting jobs are sometimes asked to write advertisements for products with no product advantage. The reasoning is that building copy around a unique selling proposition (U.S.P.) is relatively easy but that true creativity comes hard when you must achieve an interesting and selling approach for a product that doesn't stand out from the crowd. In today's crowded marketplace, products with a U.S.P. or strong product difference are becoming fewer.

It is a fact that many products simply do not have a U.S.P. and are greatly similar to others in the market—soaps, coffees, soft drinks, cigarettes, gasolines, and many other products have become indistinguishable in the public's mind. If you are writing for such a product, your challenge is to make your product stand out by the way you promote it.

An advertising agency that has been unusually successful in achieving such recognition is Leo Burnett, which has produced memorable and long-lasting campaigns for Star-Kist Tuna (Charlie the Tuna), Marlboro, Virginia Slims, Maytag, United Airlines, Green Giant, Pillsbury, and Keebler.

Let's examine some of them to see how the agency's creative teams made the product or service a prominent part of the American scene:

- A real-life spokesman is used. (the lonely Maytag man)
- A trademark character is invented. (the Pillsbury Doughboy)
- Memorable music is applied. (United Airlines)
- A symbol is used (the Marlboro Man, the Merrill-Lynch bull)
- A lovable animated character carries the message.

(Charlie the Tuna, the Keebler elves, the Jolly Green Giant and his lovable companion, the Sprout)

These are just a few of the ways to create recognition for products. Creativity is the ability to sit there in front of your typewriter or word processor and let ideas evolve to make that just-one-of-a-mob product stand out like a beacon light.

Sometimes your success will be the evolving of something so outlandish as Mr. Whipple and "Don't squeeze the Charmin." It helps, of course, to have your success assured because of the sheer weight of advertising put behind the product, as in the case of Charmin. The Mr. Whipple character may have annoyed a portion of the television audience, but as a whole, the campaign sold the product in a very competitive field and against products quite similar to Charmin. This is another instance of selling a product that has no scintillating advantage.

Selling products without an advantage? Rise to the challenge. How you do so will help peg you as a real prize or as just another ordinary creative person.

Think first: Then write copy. Unfortunately, some writers write first and think afterwards. A good writer organizes first. A careful review of the selling points is made for straight-line advertisements or, for products without selling points or specific advantages, the general theme is carefully worked out.

You have probably already gone through much of this operation in the original planning of your advertisement. You have selected the most outstanding feature your product has to offer and have worked out a clear, forceful headline built around that feature. Your opening copy should now be aimed at the feature also. *Immediate follow-through on the headline* is nearly always vital to top-notch copy. Whether your copy actually fulfills its function and maintains interest and selling power largely depends upon how you carry on from there.

Practicing copywriters have various methods of organizing their thinking before writing, depending upon their temperament and manner of working. Some simply close the office door and think. They keep the different angles of their sales story in mind until they develop a clear picture of how it should unfold. Others write a preliminary piece of copy with little attention to sequence, point of order, or emphasis and then, when they decide what they want, they rewrite in order to obtain sufficient continuity and strength in the sections lacking those qualities.

Neither of these methods is ideal for producing the best in copy. One places too much burden on the copywriter's memory; the other often causes a stilted style of writing. Nothing seems to work so well as a simple checklist of selling points. To see how you may compile such a list, look at an actual advertisement and see what steps the copywriter might have taken in writing it.

Notice that the advertisement will usually follow a list of the points of importance. As a result, it has continuity and a simplicity that makes it easy to read and understand. It gives primary emphasis to the sales ideas the copywriter wished to feature, yet one point leads to another in logical progression.

Making a list of what you want to tell the reader before you write a word of copy seems like a great deal of extra work, but it will result in clarity and continuity. After you have worked out your campaign and written a number of advertisements within its pattern, the list-making will of course be less important, since experience with a given product and a given sales approach will so familiarize you with what you have to say that reminders won't always be needed. In most cases, once you have established your list, you need never change it unless:

- Product is improved.
- Audience aim is changed. You might have started out with a homeowner campaign and then decided to advertise to carpenters through business papers.
- You decide upon an entirely different approach.

Especially for your first attempts at *straight-line* copy, close reference to your checklist is an excellent means of keeping your copy on a straight line. It is a system used successfully and continuously by some of the nation's most experienced men and women copywriters.

Looking for ideas? You might try brainstorming. Occasionally, a group can do what an individual cannot in generating ideas. This is the time for brainstorming, a process in which a few persons sitting in a room spark each other by supplying ideas in rapid succession.

The participants may sit in a circle. Each member supplies an idea in regular turns. There is no criticism of the ideas offered, in order to encourage a free flow. Thus, many of the ideas may be wild and wholly unusable, but sometimes the wildest idea might spark a brilliant, usable idea.

Often an idea will appear that seems to have merit, so the group may supply ideas that build up this idea until the group leader halts the buildup. Usually, a brainstorming session will be limited to an hour. Above all, no negative thinking is permitted. Otherwise, participants will be inhibited and idea generation is slowed. Criticism takes place *after* the brainstorming session.

Before the session, the participants should determine what the problem is and, if they are sparking ideas for selling a product, they should be thoroughly knowledgeable about the product.

Although brainstorming can result in some good ideas, most of the ideas so produced are usually worthless. Furthermore, to go over the ideas (usually taped) is time consuming, especially when so little usable material may result. Still, the procedure occasionally provides a campaign idea when ordinary methods have failed. Also, there is a creative excitement engendered by such a group effort that is stimulating and enjoyable for jaded creative people.

Suggestions if you write "editorial" copy. Occasionally, you'll notice advertisements that look like the surrounding editorial material. As an unsuspecting reader, you may have begun reading some of these advertisements and then realized suddenly that you were *not* reading an *article* in the newspaper or magazine. To help you differentiate between articles and advertisements that look like articles, publishers put "Advertisement Advertisement Advertisement" at the top of such advertisements or sometimes put a small "Adv." at the bottom.

Despite the warnings, such advertisements obtain good readership because they have the editorial look. The secret is to be consistent. Be editorial throughout—in headline, body copy, and illustration. Avoid the hybrid—part editorial and part advertising. Usually, the one departure from the wholly editorial approach is the use of the logo. Even this can be sacrificed on rare occasions.

Sometimes you eliminate the illustration. If the "advertorial" advertisement is small, for example, there is little point in jamming an illustration into the space, especially if by so doing you destroy the editorial look.

In other cases, you may cut the illustration because you're announcing an important new product breakthrough or a new service to be offered. The use of the usual illustration will detract from the news-article feeling.

Your writing should have the news flavor throughout. In making your important announcement, write like a newsperson instead of like an advertising copywriter.

For instance, because "editorial" style advertisements are often lengthy, break up your copy with punchy subheads and make your main headline bold in size and newsy in flavor. The total advertisement should look important.

One last suggestion—if the magazine will permit such a technique. Some of these "Advertisement Advertisement Advertisement" types of advertisements can adopt the makeup of the magazine in the type style, kind of headlines, and writing style in the body copy.

In short, the reader can hardly detect the difference between your advertisement and the magazine's editorial material. This makes it imperative that your advertising material is so interesting and important that readers won't feel tricked when they realize that they're reading an advertisement rather than one of the publication's features.

Comic Strip and Continuity-Panel Copy

Although there is little chance that you will write comic strip or continuity-panel copy, the practice of making advertisements resemble comic strips or editorial cartoons is widespread and successful. Researchers have provided considerable evidence that such formats for advertisements often gain greater attention from readers, especially in newspapers, than those designed in a more conventional format.

There is not much variation between the comic strip and the continuity-panel advertisement. Both are normally planned to tell a story that stresses the selling features of a product. Both usually involve a character or group of characters whose actions present a problem to be solved. The problem is then solved through the purchase of the product being advertised.

Both types feature copy displayed in blurbs or balloons, and in many cases this copy accomplishes the entire job of telling the story, reaching the happy ending, and selling the product. Often, however, either a straight-line copy block or selling caption under each panel is used in addition to the balloons.

Newspaper comic strip advertisements should be designed to resemble, as closely as conditions permit, an editorial comic strip. They should be of the same size and horizontal shape, if possible, and carry a heading and title just as regular comic strips do.

Continuity-panel advertisements may use a horizontal or vertical arrangement of panels that tell a type of story similar to that of the comic strips, but they often carry a headline, a large illustration, and a logotype.

In many advertisements you will see a series of comic strip and continuity-panel advertisements of various kinds. Note that there is no set pattern for their construction. Some use the last panel for a display of the product and a straight-line copy story, while others depend on the payoff of the blurb continuity to carry all the sell.

All these points about this style of advertising are mentioned because in both comic strip and continuity advertisements your job requires a greater amount of creative ingenuity than is needed in many other forms of advertisement writing.

Since success of panel advertisements depends upon a logical, believable story, you must plan the illustrations and the action before you write your copy. In creating most other advertisements you can often count on plenty of help from your art associates to get a good illustrative device, and your main task will be the writing of headlines, subheads, and body copy. In the strip or continuity-panel advertisement, you'll have to go way beyond that. Your job here can almost be likened to that of a movie scenario writer rather than a copywriter, although it is actually a twofold proposition, since in addition to artistic creation you are, of course, trying to sell something.

The Newspaper Advertising Bureau, Inc., has made these suggestions to copywriters interested in improving their copy for comic strip advertisements. The following is a discussion and enlargement of some of their suggestions:

- *Follow editorial style.* If you are writing a comic-strip advertisement, make it look as much as possible like a real comic strip. Do not include panels that look like little advertisements. Do not vary the size of the panels. Remember that you are trying to hook readership on the basis of public familiarity with and liking for comic strips. You will not obtain this bonus readership if your advertisement doesn't look like a comic strip.

- *Keep your first panel interesting—humorous or action-packed.* By doing so you gain impetus in leading your reader along into the next panel and through to the conclusion. Sometimes you will see examples of comic strip advertisements that beg for further reading and that do not offer enough excitement about what is coming to lure maximum readership.
- *Change focus.* Comic strip artists and writers have discovered that it attracts attention to mix up long and short shots of characters in the strip. The same technique is true of comic strip advertisements.
- *Keep blurb copy short.* If you can't set up your situation, develop it and sell the product in short, natural-sounding blurbs; don't try to use the comic strip style. You will repel the reader if you jam your blurbs with long, involved copy in order to establish your story. Your characters are supposed to be speaking, and the things they say must be things anyone would say in similar circumstances. If they aren't, you will lose selling power even though all the other directions have been carefully followed.

Most of the foregoing comment on comic strip copy is also applicable to continuity-panel copy, except, of course, for the requirements of staying within the physical confines of the actual comic strip format. Continuity panels are used when it is felt that the comic strip technique is desirable, but for one reason or another—usually space limitations—the true size and shape of the comic strip cannot be followed.

Continuity panels, for instance, will be used in magazines, rather than the familiar comic strip, since readers of magazines are not accustomed to seeing comics in them; and, too, magazines do not sell space the size and shape required for comic strips. The continuity panel is also often used in newspapers when a space larger than the standard comic strip is considered necessary.

Both of these types of advertising depend, for their maximum effectiveness, upon their ability to lure readership rather than to compel it. The closer they can be designed and written to resemble the editorial features after which they are patterned, the better chance they have of succeeding.

Today's Copywriter Writes with Consumerism in Mind

In today's consumerist climate it isn't enough merely to write copy that is legal; it must also be socially responsible. Corporations and the advertising they issue are being held accountable by aggressive consumers and by the numerous federal and state consumer bureaus. Your copy had better recognize the responsibilities of business in today's changing and contentious world or you and your client may find that you have become targets.

What are the consumer attitudes toward business and hence toward advertising that affect how you write your copy? Some of these attitudes are expressed in the anti-business gripes that follow. These were written at a time when all our institutions (especially business) were under fire. They are still pertinent because large segments of our society continue to distrust business.

The Major Anti-Business Gripes

1. Business provides materialistic quality in American life but does not necessarily advance the quality of life.

Figure 8–6. Cartoon-type advertisement. Such newspaper advertisements appearing in the familiar cartoon format draw reader attention. For best results they are often placed in the sports section or in, or near, the comic page.

2. Business appears too impersonal and selfish, and "humanity" is sacrificed to efficiency in the pursuit of profits.
3. Business too often fails to meet the basic needs of poor markets, as in the ghetto areas, or charges exorbitant prices to these essentially captive markets.
4. The market mechanism is restricted in some cases where the danger to consumers is open to speculation (e.g., marijuana, pornography), but is allowed to function without restraint for many products that do affect the safety of others (e.g., guns and overly powerful cars).
5. The value added by marketing is difficult to justify, both in terms of high markups on many goods and in exorbitant prices.
6. Marketing misallocates resources by encouraging the consumption of "non-necessities."
7. Marketing breeds contentment with mediocrity (it offers nothing "higher") and does not serve markets (e.g., ballet, symphony, chamber music, etc.) if they are not directly profitable.
8. Marketing, through restyling and poor quality in production, encourages and engages in planned obsolescence.
9. Many products in an individual product category are not very different, if at all. An excess of products in one product category represents a misallocation of resources and also breeds consumer bewilderment.
10. Consumer recourse for defective products is sadly lacking.
11. Advertising creates false needs and manipulates the consumer.
12. Advertising and other promotion efforts, including packaging and labeling, are often deceptive, false, and misleading. Many products are not as distinctive or as differentiated as the promotion implies. Many advertising claims are voided by obsolescence (advertisements induce dissatisfaction with past purchases).
13. Producers foul public resources for private profit. Lumber companies destroy beautiful forests. Firms pollute once beautiful rivers. Neon signs and outdoor advertisements blight once pleasant thoroughfares.[1]

Obviously, if you're a socially attuned copywriter, you'll be conscious of these consumer sensitivities when you write about certain products or services. You will do well to keep in mind the following comments by Donald Jugenheimer:

> Although the consumer movement may already have peaked, it certainly is far from being on the wane. Consumers now know what they can and should expect from marketers. Consumers know that advertising can help them become better buyers by using the information contained in the advertisements to help them buy more efficiently and more economically.
>
> Some advertising spokesmen have suggested resisting this consumer trend; they want advertising to stand up for its "rights." What these people seem to be missing is the point that advertising is as much of a servant of the consumer—the buyer—as it is of the seller.
>
> Why should the seller of a product or service be the only one to benefit from the huge amounts of time, energy, and money which go into advertising? If a product or service really meets a want or a need on the part of consumers, why can't the advertising for those items point out these benefits?
>
> One key to successful advertising is to find a suitable benefit and to present it as an appropriate appeal to the consumer. Why, then, go only halfway and talk only about the benefits of the products and services? If they are to provide consumer benefits, why shouldn't the advertising which supports them also provide consumer benefits?
>
> In the future, advertising must realize that there are two ends to the communications channel, and that the other end, the consumer's end, has much more economic power than the advertiser's end. Consumerism can help advertising to do a better job of serving both the advertiser and the consumer, but the advertising industry is going to have to recognize this opportunity first.[2]

There's Trouble Ahead If You Ignore Group Sensitivities

In the 1960s, Volkswagen ran an advertisement that showed a "Beetle" with a dented fender. The headline copy and opening were:

> **Headline:** Sooner or later your wife will drive home one of the best reasons for owning a Volkswagen
>
> **Opening copy:** Women are soft and gentle, but they hit things.

The rest of the copy continued the theme of feminine driving incompetence but pointed out that, because Volkswagens were inexpensive to repair, husbands could be tolerant of their wives' errant driving habits.

This sort of condescending advertisement run today would result in a storm of complaints from women who, justifiably, resent being portrayed as helpless or incompetent as a group.

Allied with consumerism is the heightened sensitivity of so many groups in the United States these days. Copywriters careless with words will sooner or later offend one of these groups. Women, especially, have developed a new advocacy and are quick to resent words or situations that seem to demean them or their status.

While it is impossible to put down here all the words and phrases that might be described as sexist, a common charge, here are a few that seem particularly offensive to women who read advertising:

---

1. Y. Hugh Furuhashi and E. Jerome McCarthy, *Social Issues of Marketing in the American Economy* (Columbus, Ohio: Grid, Inc., 1971), p. 9.

2. Ronald D. Michman and Donald W. Jugenheimer, *Strategic Advertising Decisions: Selected Readings* (Columbus, Ohio: Grid, Inc., 1976), p. 413.

- Lady, instead of woman. The former is considered by some feminists as connoting affected, artificial, overly nice persons. Girls, instead of women, spurs similar wrath. Gals is even worse.
- "Man-sized job" seems to imply a task beyond feminine abilities.
- Chairman, instead of chairperson.
- Housewife, instead of homemaker.
- Salesman, instead of salesperson.

Women are annoyed by advertising that implies that the chief concern of all women is running a home while failing to recognize the importance of women in industry, politics, and other facets of American life. Depicting women as being wholly dependent upon men is another sore point.

Although women now make up 50 percent of the work force, too many copywriters are writing as if stay-at-home housewives were the majority group. These same writers too often fail to show the working women in responsible, executive roles (although there has been a slight improvement in this respect). An oft-voiced complaint is that copy and illustrations in advertisements and commercials depict women as sex objects, household drudges, or mental lightweights. A critical assessment of advertising for household products provides justification for the complaints.

Male or female copywriters will find that it is not easy to write without offending the special-interest audience. Constant awareness of the problem is the only answer. This period of social activism is a perilous time for advertisers who must in their advertising be very much aware of minority groups, environmentalists, and all the others who are asserting their rights and who seem constantly to find new words, phrases, and situations that cause offense.

In innocence, copywriters may use such words or phrases in their copy and learn to regret it. You must, therefore, as a copywriter in this pugnacious world, have a keen knowledge of the social currents and cross currents. Your lack of knowledge and vigilance can cost your clients goodwill and sales.

Consumerism's Effect on Advertising Copy Has Been Helpful and Harmful

Despite the cries of persecution from some advertising writers, as a copywriter you should be grateful for the critical, skeptical looks given copy these days. Writing copy in today's climate is more than writing copy that is pure in a legal sense.

In addition, you must be credible. You avoid the careless statement, the almost dishonest claim, or the claim not backed by proof, even though the claim is technically correct. In the category of the careless statement was the claim of milk producers using a slogan "everybody needs milk." The slogan was changed when doctors protested, saying that some people are allergic to milk. Legal objections were not raised to the slogan, but it was changed nonetheless because of the concern of the medical profession.

Watchful for the consumerist's baleful glance, you try to eliminate simplistic portrayals of your product as the answer to all domestic problems. You're conscious of the need for copy that is not offensive but is in good taste as well as defensible legally. You try to write copy that is useful because it helps the consumer arrive at a rational buying decision.

With all this good stemming from consumerism, how can the movement be bad for copy? The answer is simple enough. Rather than take a chance with strong claims and aggressive advertising, the copywriter may play it safe with innocuous copy, or often downright silly copy. Humor is substituted for information and possibly challengeable claims. Copy becomes bland and boring, or if not boring, it relies on cleverness for cleverness' sake.

Sometimes it is easier to go institutional in advertisements rather than to dig up hard facts about the product. Accordingly, with an eye out for the consumerists, we find as a substitute for "selling" advertisements, a myriad of campaigns that boast of the advertiser's contributions to the solving of world problems—anything from environmental concerns, to economic panaceas, to population control. These are "safe" campaigns, though unfortunately even they must be executed with exceeding care or the consumerists may attack them for oversimplifying complex issues.

Summing up, the demands of consumerism are not outrageous. You are asked merely to write about your products in a way that you would approve if you were a consumer instead of a copywriter. With this in mind you should approach each copy assignment with two viewpoints, the copywriter's and the consumer's. You will omit the latter at your peril.

Comparative Advertising: The Case for and against

When you buy a product in a retail store, you're accustomed to having the salesperson show you competing brands. If you buy a toaster, for example, you check such points as the pop-up feature, controls for light/medium/dark, the appearance of the unit, and so on. Or, if you're interested in a General Electric refrigerator, for example, the salesperson will tell you what features this brand offers that make it superior to the Amana, the Coldspot, Westinghouse, and other brands. You take such comparisons for granted when you buy any item in a store. Indeed, you would not feel very intelligent if you did not insist on these comparisons.

Despite the acceptance of product comparisons in the shopping situation, the use of comparative advertising has become one of the most talked-about and controversial issues in the field of marketing. On one side, it is considered a beneficial development by many in the consumerism movement and the FTC looks indulgently upon it. So long as there is no clear-cut deception or unfairness and advertisers can substantiate their claims, the FTC is not likely to take action because of the Commission's feeling that product comparisons serve a useful consumer function.

Within the field, however, advertising people revile it or praise it. As for consumers, some don't know what to think, although many feel that it isn't cricket to name competitors in an advertisement. Furthermore, as comparative advertising is used increasingly, consumers seem to find it more difficult to make judgments when they are assailed by so many contradictory claims.

Looking at comparative advertising from the researcher's point of view, the president of Gallup & Robinson pointed out in a television workshop that a study of ninety-seven brand contrasts showed that such advertising produced a 22 percent premium in recall among viewers and that the technique performed significantly better among men than women.[3]

Warning that comparative advertising does not guarantee success, the researcher recommended that comparative advertising should emphasize product benefits and attributes rather than just price alone.

Despite this testimony for comparative advertising as used on television, the Ogilvy & Mather advertising agency measured the effectiveness of the advertising of six packaged goods brands, each represented by both a non-comparative and a comparative commercial. Their conclusions[4]:

- Comparative television advertising does not offer any advantage to the packaged goods advertiser.
- It does not increase brand identification.
- It makes consumers more aware of competitors.
- It results in lower belief in claims.
- It results in increased miscommunication and confusion.
- It is not more persuasive.

Others echo the Ogilvy & Mather findings and say that you simply can't make valid product comparisons in 30-second commercials. At least, they say, use print advertising if you must use comparative advertising. In print, it is asserted, the consumer has time to weigh the facts, the claims, and counterclaims.

Thus it goes. As a copywriter, you may or may not be asked to write comparative advertising. Also, you may believe, as many do, that comparative advertising reduces advertising's credibililty, or you may believe with many consumerists that its use is giving buyers solid information that enables them to make buying decisions based on something other than entertainment, jingles, and factless advertisements.

Whether you feel pro or con, comparative advertising is riding high just now. Thus if you write such copy, you should see that it is done sensibly and honestly. To aid you in that objective you would do well to follow the guidelines of the American Association of Advertising Agencies. Should you follow these guidelines, there is a reasonable chance your copy should gain the approval of consumerists, lawyers, and even most present critics of comparative advertising. The following guidelines have been widely printed in the advertising press:

Guidelines for Using Comparative Advertising

1. The intent and connotation of the ad should be to inform and never to discredit or unfairly attack competitors, or competing products or services.
2. When a competitive product is named, it should be one that exists in the marketplace as significant competition.
3. The competition should be fairly and properly identified but never in a manner or tone of voice that degrades the competitive product or service.
4. The advertising should compare related or similar properties or ingredients of the product, dimension to dimension, feature to feature.
5. The identification should be for honest comparison purposes and not simply to upgrade by association.
6. If a competitive test is conducted, it should be done by an objective testing source, preferably an independent one, so that there will be no doubt as to the veracity of the test.
7. In all cases the test should be supportive of all claims made in the advertising that are based on the test.
8. The advertising should never use partial results or stress insignificant differences to cause the consumer to draw an improper conclusion.
9. The property being compared should be significant in terms of value or usefulness of the product to the consumer.
10. Comparatives delivered through the use of testimonials should not imply that the testimonial is more than one individual's thought unless that individual represents a sample of the majority viewpoint.

NBC has placed particular emphasis on the need for care in price comparisons, an issue that worries many in marketing.

1. Comparisons of retail pricing may raise special problems that would tend to mislead rather than enlighten viewers. For certain classifications of products, retail prices may be extremely volatile, may be fixed by the retailer rather than the product advertiser, and may not only differ from outlet to outlet, but from week to week within the same outlet.

   Where these circumstances might apply, NBC will accept commercials containing price com-

3. The 1976 meeting of the Association of National Advertisers.

4. In 1980, Ogilvy & Mather followed up with another study of comparative advertising and found, contrary to the 1976 study, that under certain circumstances comparative advertising can be useful and productive as a short-term tactical weapon.

parisons only on a clear showing that the comparative claims accurately, fairly, and substantially reflect the actual price differentials at retail outlets throughout the broadcast area, and that these price differentials are not likely to change during the period the commercial is broadcast.

2. When a commercial claim involves market relationships, other than price, which are subject to fluctuation (such as, but not limited to, sales position or exclusivity), the substantiation for the claim will be considered valid only as long as the market conditions on which the claim is based continue to prevail.
3. Whenever necessary, NBC may require substantiation to be updated from time to time.

Magazine and Newspaper Advertising Copy Quite Similar

You will not find separate chapters in this book on the writing of newspaper and magazine advertisements because the material on appeals, headlines, and body copy applies fundamentally to both. Newspaper and magazine readers respond to the same basic appeals. As for writing approach, many advertisers use similar adver-

Figure 8–7a. Picture-caption advertisement (in which the captions are not the principal means of telling the copy story). In this instance, the illustrations simply show what the advertiser is offering but the selling is done in the straight-line body copy that follows. Many picture-caption advertisements place the entire selling burden on the captions.

Figure 8–7b. Picture-caption advertisement. Here is a one-third page version of the advertisement shown in Figure 8–7a.

tisements in newspapers and magazines and certainly utilize the same campaign approach in each.

If, however, you make certain assumptions about the magazine reader, you may in the light of those assumptions write copy somewhat differently for magazines and newspapers.

Assumptions: That magazine readers tend to be somewhat better educated and of a higher income level. That they read magazines in a more leisurely fashion over a longer period, and that during this period they will pick up and put down the magazine a number of times. (This is in contrast with newspaper readers who read quickly and tend to finish their reading at one sitting.)

What implications are there for you in these assumptions? One, of course, is that the language level in newspaper copy may sometimes be a trifle lower than for magazines, especially selective magazines aimed at an obviously upper-level audience.

Headlines can be more direct and localized, and the following body copy should likewise be direct and localized. The body copy may tend to be brisker and more telegraphic than magazine copy. Because newspaper readers go through the publication so speedily, it is well, if the copy is at all long, to break it up with subheads in order to hold their attention.

Once more, however, copywriters usually do not need to make a sharp distinction between the way they write for newspapers or magazines. The rules for writing headlines and body copy apply by and large to both. This is especially true of mass circulation magazines and newspapers. Differences will become pronounced only when the advertisements are to be placed in publications appealing to high-level audiences.

Writing Body Copy? Some Last Suggestions for You

Here are a few suggestions that you can use when you're at the typewriter or word processor, some more important than others. They are concerned more with actual writing than with strategy and with bigger issues of body copy.

- Start with the reader, not the advertiser or product. Beginning writers tend to become so full of facts about the advertiser and the product that they neglect the reader. If you've begun your copy with the product, rewrite it. Talk to the reader first.
- Use the singular you. Avoid the "all you ladies" approach. Talk to the individual in order to achieve a personal, intimate style.
- Write transitionally. A mark of the professional writer is the way the copy hangs together. You achieve this by connecting ideas, sentences, and paragraphs. Learn to use bridging words for writing flow and cohesion. What are bridging words (or phrases)? Here are a few: Moreover. Furthermore. Too. Also. In addition. To continue. And. But. Otherwise. Of course. As for. If, however. Thus. Above all. While. Although. Accordingly. Or. Lastly. To start. Another. Then.
- Use an occasional underline. An underlined word can sometimes convey powerful emphasis such as: "This is the <u>only</u> product that gives you . . ." Don't overuse the underline but employ it when it gives force to your writing.
- Use contractions freely. Advertising copy is usually informal and creates a conversational feeling. Contractions are used constantly in conversation. Thus, if you want your copy to have a conversational quality, you'll write "won't," not "will not," and "don't," not "do not."
- Go easy on "so" endings. Beginning writers tend to end most print advertisements and practically all commercials with "so" phrases such as "So don't forget," "So be sure to see this product," "So next time you're shopping." The use of "so" in such instances isn't a major offense but it *is* grossly overused. Furthermore, when the reader or listener hears "so" he knows the advertiser is winding up the message and tends to tune out what follows the word.
- End almost all advertising copy with an urge to action. By urging action you supply a climax to what you have written and perhaps move the viewer or reader to do something. Don't just let your copy trail off without making a suggestion of some kind—"buy," "try," "see," "look at," "drop in," "find out," "don't wait," "do it today," "learn," "discover," "examine." Too often copywriters end their copy with vapid, cute phrases instead of using a positive, action ending.

One Last Point

Advertising's highest awards go to writers who consistently create fresh writing that stands out from conventional approaches. Few writers are capable of such sustained freshness. Even fewer can spark campaign ideas that can be used year after year.

Keep these two objectives in mind: (a) Write fresh, different copy. (b) Write copy that will, in the words of the Leo Burnett advertising agency, incorporate the "power of the enduring idea" for longtime campaigns.

9

WRITING COPY FOR PUBLICITY, PACKAGING, AND OTHER EXTRAS OF A COPYWRITER'S JOB

"Mr. Lund? Isn't a bit boring to do nothing day after day but write print ads and commercials?"

Asking the question was a young woman attending a careers conference at a local hotel.

Jerry Lund, copy chief of an agency across the street from the hotel, smiled: "First of all, I'm not bored turning out ads. But even so, there's much more to my job than that. Let me tell you about some of the other things I do. . . ."

Just the day before, Jerry recalled, after a hard day of writing those ads the young lady referred to, he had received a memo marked RUSH. It read:

"Calthorp Industries is not satisfied with any of the names suggested for their new product. By Monday, therefore, we'd like to give them some new, interesting names to choose from.

"Please contribute a list of names by Monday at 9 A.M. Furnish all the names you can think of. Keep in mind the unique attributes of this product. Try for a fresh approach."

You become aware once more that there's much more to your copy job than merely writing commercials, body copy, and headlines. There are many odd byways into which your title "copywriter" will lead you. Some of these will take little of your time; others may swallow many of your working hours. Most copywriters learn very quickly that these "odd jobs" of copywriting can sometimes be the most important in a day's work.

Copywriters turning out a client publicity story, for example, may discover that sometimes clients may be more impressed by a five-inch publicity story in the newspaper than by a full-page advertisement running in the same issue. They may learn to their chagrin that the same clients will overlook the truly excellent creative work in an advertisement if something about the company's signature displeases them. Thus, these "little jobs" that a copywriter does, or supervises, are very frequently "big" when viewed through the eyes of a critical client.

Let's look over some of these miscellaneous activities that you, as a copywriter, may do but which may not be mentioned as part of your regular duties in a formal job description.

- Providing the dialogue for executives taking part in a closed-circuit sales meeting.
- Writing the copy for window or interior displays for stores.
- Preparing a feature magazine article about a client's business that will appear in a national magazine and will be signed by a top executive of the client company.
- Writing copy for a company's bulletin board.
- Preparing speeches for various client executives or for the members of the advertising staff.
- Organizing and writing a taped interview in which the client will take part, or possibly someone in the advertising agency such as the agency president.

- Helping out the account executive by writing a presentation to be given at a client meeting. This will describe creative, media, and marketing plans for the forthcoming six months or a year.
- Writing copy for sales portfolios. Contained in these may be sales talks, examples of advertising and display aids, and a boost for the advertising support.
- Putting together comments, talks, or remarks to be made by agency or client personnel at regional or national sales or dealer meetings.
- Inspiring dealers or salespeople with pep letters, urgent bulletins, or telegrams.
- Writing the sales portion of package copy (the legal material will be furnished by lawyers).
- Preparing booklets, or even short books, that concern the client's products, history, or personnel.
- Turning out promotional pieces for the advertising agency that can be left with prospective clients.
- Writing a client's company newsletter, or preparing articles for it, or acting as its editor.

Publicity Writing: It Might Be an Important Part of Your Work

Publicity is of increasing importance as an adjunct of advertising. You may well, from time to time, be called upon to write publicity stories to be released to newspapers, magazines, and trade papers. Publicity stories are run free by publications, but only if they are newsworthy and if the editor happens to have some space to spare at the time.

Because publicity releases will not be published unless they meet accepted editorial standards, you must write them as straight news stories, avoiding the jargon of the advertising business and any attempt at high-pressure selling. Don't, above all, attempt to make publicity stories thinly disguised advertisements.

What kind of situations produce publicity stories of real news value? Here are some:

- An executive of a company makes a speech of some importance.
- A company builds a new plant or wins a safety award.
- An executive is promoted.
- An employee of long standing retires.
- An employee wins a big national contest.
- A company makes an important change in a product that is well-known nationally, regionally, or locally.
- A company announces the introduction of a product totally different from anything on the market.
- An employee wins a big suggestion-box award.

All these are legitimate news stories. Don't lose sight of that word "legitimate" because any publicity story without real news value is doomed to end in the editorial waste basket. Do you really know what "news" is? Editors may disagree with you in defining the word. They may, in the way of editors, refuse to run an item you think is the story of the century.

Xerox Corporation

FOR IMMEDIATE RELEASE Contact: Gina Greer-Whitley (212) 704-7221

XEROX

XEROX INTRODUCING NEW CORPORATE AD CAMPAIGN SATURDAY

NEW YORK, July 16 -- Worldwide leadership in document processing in the office is the theme of a new, multi-million dollar corporate advertising campaign Xerox Corporation will launch Saturday, July 18.

The campaign, produced by Ted Bates Advertising, focuses on what Xerox feels is its greatest technological and marketplace strength. The campaign theme is: "Xerox. We Document the World."

Michael E.G. Kirby, director of Xerox corporate advertising and promotion, said, "We believe this new advertising successfully communicates to our audiences that Xerox products provide more efficient ways to process documents in the office."

He pointed out that in document processing -- the creation, reproduction, distribution and filing of ideas, both electronically and on paper -- "Xerox has traditionally been in a class by itself."

-more-

XEROX INTRODUCES NEW CORPORATE ADVERTISING
Page 2 of 3

The introductory 45-second commercial called "World" will debut Saturday on the British Open golf tournament on ABC. It illustrates, through a series of familiar office scenes, that Xerox means more than superior copiers. It shows the company's broad range of business communications products, including electronic typewriters, laser printers, desktop publishing systems and facsimile machines.

The commercials will air on network primetime television programs, including 60 Minutes on CBS, ABC Sunday Movie, and St. Elsewhere and L.A. Law on NBC. The media plan also features such sports programming as the U.S. Open tennis and PGA golf tournaments.

Gerard Hameline of Gerard Hameline Productions/New York directed the commercials.

A four-page, four-color insert in the July 27 issue of U.S. News & World Report (on sale July 20) and a four-page spread in the July 21 Wall Street Journal are scheduled for the print ad launch.

-more-

XEROX INTRODUCES NEW CORPORATE ADVERTISING CAMPAIGN
Page 3 of 3

Four-page inserts, followed by four-color spreads, will appear in newsweeklies and business/trade publications such as TIME, Newsweek, Business Week, Forbes and Fortune (see separate media schedule).

Additionally, the campaign will be supported by 60-second radio spots premiering July 20 in 15 major markets, including New York, Philadelphia, Boston, Washington D.C., Chicago, Los Angeles and San Francisco.

Kirby said the new Xerox corporate campaign will cover established company products and new products in the United States and in international markets.

The international campaign will include airport dioramas in Europe and Canada. Print advertising is scheduled for a September debut in major English language newspapers and business publications in Europe, Canada, Asia and Latin America.

Xerox has been a client of Ted Bates Advertising since June 1986. The agency recently announced its plans to merge with Backer & Spielvogel to form Backer Spielvogel Bates Worldwide, Inc. It will have estimated billings of $2.7 billion.

# # # #

Figure 9–1. Publicity release. In some instances, part of a copywriter's duties might include writing releases such as this. Usually, the writer will have had journalistic training in order to write in this style. Notice the comprehensiveness of the campaign described.

Courtesy of the Xerox Corporation.

What is important to you, or to your client, may be wholly unimportant to editors because they feel your "news" will not interest enough of their readers. A newspaper editor will refuse a story that a trade magazine editor will accept and vice versa. Each story, then, must contain news of consequence to the readers of the publication in which you'd like your story to run.

Knowing just what constitutes news is the whole crux of successful placement of publicity material. One test, of course, is to ask yourself this question: Would I (or anyone) have any interest in this story if I didn't already have a personal stake in it?

The writing of publicity copy, sometimes disparagingly called "puff" copy, requires a sound knowledge of news procedure. After you have determined that your story has real news value, you must prepare it in accepted news style. It should be ready to insert in the news columns as you have written it.

If it is a general release going to a great many newspapers, you may send out one version of the story, since in most cases there will be no duplicate readership. The papers may or may not rewrite your copy; it makes little difference here. Say, however, that you are sending a story of interest to the grocery trade and that you send the same version of the story to three magazines.

All these magazines may have high duplication of readership. If the readers read the same story in the same words in all the magazines, they will be bored and disgusted. Furthermore, the editors will be resentful when they discover that you were too lazy to write the story differently for each of the publications.

To be able to write the same story in three different versions and make each version interesting will test your ability in news writing. If you have done some reporting, you won't have much trouble. If you haven't, a publicity release may cause you some anxious moments. Principal things to keep in mind:

- Follow the usual news style of putting essential facts high in the story in all but out-and-out feature stories. One way to accomplish this is to use the well-known 5-Ws approach; that is, tell who—what—when—where—why early in your story.
- Remember that because of makeup requirements a story may be cut to fit a space; the space won't be stretched to fit the story. Write your copy so that it can be cut at the end of any paragraph and still make sense (all the more reason for getting important material high in the story!).
- Make paragraphs, sentences, and words short, and write so that it will be easy for the copy desk to dig out a headline for the story. In other words, say something significant and say it quickly.
- Don't worry too much about style rules, but if in doubt, use a "down" style for newspaper stories since most newspapers are inclined toward that style. A "down" style uses a minimum of capitals; an "up" style newspaper capitalizes heavily. The *Associated Press Stylebook* offers a handy guide for style rules to follow.
- If possible, get a picture to send along with the story and write a snappy caption for the picture (8 × 10 glossy prints are best!).
- Avoid too many references to your company or client. If you can put over your idea without any direct mention of your product name or company, all the better. If not, tread very easily. Many editors will throw a story out as soon as company or product is mentioned.
- If your story has an interest for a special section of the newspaper, send it to the editor of that section, such as financial editor or automotive editor.
- Be accurate—if your facts aren't correct, your first story will be your last. Don't kill your chance for future publicity.

Here's an extra note about the 5-Ws approach previously mentioned. If you're wondering what elements might properly go under each of the Ws for a publicity release, here are a few ideas for you. These are, of course, but a few of the many points you might consider.

- WHO are the people involved in the story?
  Names
  Titles
  Departments
  Interesting history or accomplishments
  Newcomers or old-timers
  Quotes from important people involved
- WHAT has happened?
  Is this the first time?
  Is it a major event in the field?
  Is there anything different about it?
  Does what happened fill a long-felt need?
- WHEN did it happen?
  Has it already happened?
  Is it taking place over a period of time?
  (How long a period?)
  Is it yet to happen?
  Exact date (and time, if necessary)?
- WHERE did it happen?
  At the workplace?
  Is it local, or did it happen at a number of places simultaneously?
- WHY is it happening?
  What is the story behind the event?

Publicity Writing of Another Type: The Feature Article

The foregoing material has stressed the writing of straight news-publicity material. You may, however, be asked occasionally to write a feature story. Normally, this will be a longer piece suitable for publication in a newspaper or magazine. If the latter, very often you will write it for the signature of an executive in your client's company, possibly the president.

When doing a feature style, you forget the 5-Ws approach for the lead. In fact, whether for a newspaper or a magazine, the feature story resembles magazine articles in writing style and general structure.

Especially important and distinctive is the feature lead. This may stress human interest, an oddity, an historical event—anything that is interesting enough to capture quick attention.

Throughout the feature story, you maintain this magazine style but manage to incorporate enough hard news value that the editor will approve what you have done. Quite often, if the piece you are writing is a magazine feature, it may be quite acceptable to refer frequently to your company, personnel, and products because your feature is being sent to a publication that serves the client's field.

Thus, if your client is a bank, the article could discuss in *Banking* magazine the inner workings of your client's bank. There is no need, as in the straight news release, to hold back the references to the client.

It is especially desirable when placing feature stories to accompany the material with good photos and lively captions. In fact, the magazine will often request photographs or illustrative material.

As a copywriter in a small or medium-sized agency or in a company advertising department, you may be expected to do both news and feature publicity stories. If, however, you work for an agency or company big enough to have a separate public relations department, such work will normally be assigned to that department.

What Happens When Publicity Is Bad?

In recent years our increasingly litigious society has produced a new challenge for those who write publicity. This is the need to write good publicity to counteract bad publicity. Some years ago, as an example, Rely Tampons were blamed for the deaths of some users. Inevitably, lawsuits ensued with the attendant unfavorable publicity.

The question then arises: Should the product company combat this with advertising or with publicity? Both have been used and both have worked.

Sometimes a product can become an innocent victim. Tylenol suffered sales drops when poison had been put into product containers by some demented person. Through adroit use of advertising and publicity, the makers eventually overcame lowered sales and adverse reaction, but not before considerable financial and emotional trauma.

Another interesting instance was the widespread whispering campaign that associated Procter & Gamble with Satanic symbolism because of its man-in-the-moon trademark. At first, because the accusation was so patently absurd, the company ignored it. Eventually, however, with thousands of letters pouring in and the subject being taken up in television shows, the company acted vigorously through advertising, publicity and legal action to answer its tormentors.

Often, of course, these parlous situations are more than the ordinary copywriter can handle and require the services of skilled public relations practitioners and upper-echelon advertising people. Somewhere along the route, however, the copywriter may become involved.

Promoting Premium Offers—a Big Boost to Sales

Some years ago a well-known advertising agency executive was given the title, by his admiring colleagues, of "Box Top King." This was a tribute to his skill in selecting resultful premiums and then planning promotions utilizing them.

While you may not select premiums, you may be asked frequently to write advertisements containing premium offers. In particularly competitive periods such advertising is an important part of total marketing. Billions may be spent on premiums, and more billions on advertising that centers around them.

A premium is an item that product buyers get at a greatly reduced price for sending in some evidence of purchase and a specified amount of cash. Evidence of purchase is usually in the form of a label or box top, but a purchase receipt might be used, too.

An example of a recent premium offer run in the summer (premiums are often seasonal) is a Wheat Thins offer of a picnic basket. "This $25 basket can be obtained by sending in $9.95 plus proof of purchase." Like most premium offers, a bargain for the purchaser.

Sometimes a premium is related to the product being sold, such as the premium offer of a serving tray with the purchase of a Butterball turkey. Many times, however, there is no close relationship between product and premium.

While you will probably be more concerned with the writing of premium advertising for newspapers and magazines, you may also write package copy featuring premium offers because packages are important vehicles for premium promotions, especially for very youthful prospects.

When your advertisement contains a premium offer, a decision must be made: should you feature the premium totally, to some extent, or not at all? Rarely will the third choice be made, but one or the other of the first two will be found frequently. The decision rests in the attractiveness and bargain represented by the premium, especially if the product has little real advertising appeal, such as a soft drink, cigarettes, or some other routine product. In such a case, the advertisement may be dominated by the premium offer.

Here are some suggestions for premium offers:

- If the premium is physically attractive or interesting-looking, give it a good illustration.
- Highlight the cash retail value of the premium if it is sufficiently high or there is a substantial gap between the amount to be sent in and the actual value of the item.
- Sell the premium. Dramatize it. Make it appealing. If you don't, the advertiser may end up with a warehouse of unwanted premiums, so you and your col-

leagues will then have an unhappy advertiser to deal with.

- Include a statement of a time limit for the offer.
- Urge readers to take up the offer quickly. It's vital that they act at once; if they delay, you may lose them.

When you design a premium advertisement, a danger is that in order to achieve excitement you end up with a cluttered mishmash sort of advertisement. The layout is messy and the headlines too black. Keep the layout clean. Above all, make the illustration of the offer appealing and attention-getting. Use color judiciously.

When you are looking for a heavy return of box tops, about two thirds of the advertisement should concentrate on the selling of the premium. For fullest effectiveness this copy should be situated at the top of the advertisement.

Another Shot in the Arm for Sales: Sweepstakes and Contests

Sweepstakes in which sometimes almost fabulous prizes are awarded in exchange for a box top can be tremendously effective sales stimulators. Many advertisers run such sweepstakes year after year. (Although the more commonly used sweepstakes are stressed here, the points given apply equally to contests.)

If you should ever be assigned to write a sweepstakes advertisement, there are several points you will want to know. For instance, there are two schools of thought on the subject of such advertising. One believes that a fair part of the advertisement should be devoted to the regular copy story on the product itself. The second is convinced the entire advertisement should be used to sell the sweepstakes—the sweepstakes being the "product," in such an instance.

The first school reasons that because every reader isn't going to enter the sweepstakes, you should make an effort to sell such readers the product on its own merits. Straight product copy is necessary, then, to sell that "undecided" segment of the audience. The people who question their chances of winning must be persuaded that they have nothing to lose by entering, that they will get their full money's worth for what they spend in buying the product even though they don't happen to win a prize.

The second school reasons that more entries (and thus more purchases) are obtained when the entire space is given over to selling the sweepstakes. The inclusion of straight product copy, they feel, divides the reader's interest because it presents two separate thoughts to be considered, as if advertising two different products in the same advertisement.

Regardless of which of the two foregoing patterns your sweepstakes advertisements take, here are some copy points worth remembering:

- Most readers think in terms of winning the first prize, so play up your major prize; stress it. Use a big headline to do so.
- Generally speaking, a long list of secondary prizes has been found more effective than a small group, even though the total cash value in each case is the same. If you have an impressive list of such prizes, don't merely say "50 prizes." Instead, give that fact extra appeal by saying "50 chances to win!"
- Spotlight total retail cash value of all prizes if this is an impressive sum.
- "Win" is a magic word, so headline it.
- In a subhead, drive home how easy it is to win.
- In your copy, get over in a hurry how easy it is to enter the sweepstakes.
- Give examples of jingles, sentences, and puzzle solutions that might be typical of prizewinning entries, if you are writing contest copy.

Figure 9–2. **Sweepstakes advertisement.** This advertisement meets the first requirement of a sweepstakes advertisement—it is exciting. This excitement results from the action-filled illustration, the big-type headline, and the stress on prizes. The inclusion of a "free" offer adds even more sales power.

Reprinted with permission of the Del Monte Corporation.

Figure 9–3. Advertisement with strong package identification.

- List rules simply and clearly, leaving unanswered no question that might come to a reader's mind. Always include the specific date on which the sweepstakes entries close.
- Be sure to tell readers they may enter as often as they wish if this is the case.
- Urge readers to enter "NOW."
- Warn that offers are void where prohibited by law.
- Make clear that all prizes will be awarded.

Package Copy: A Last-Minute Reminder

No layman can possibly imagine the effort devoted to packaging by every packaged-goods manufacturer, but *you* will if you are assigned to write package copy. Every bit of package space is taken up with illustrations, directions for use, legal requirements, ingredients—*and* selling copy. The latter is your chief responsibility, but you may be involved with the other factors, too.

Writing package copy is no easy job, especially since you can count on everyone looking over your shoulder to criticize, to make suggestions, and to reject what you've done. Your critics will be anyone from brand managers to account executives, lawyers, creative people, and the sales staff.

Because copy on product packages is infrequently changed, this, again, is an assignment you will be given only on rare occasions.

Following is a checklist of some of the more important elements of package copy. Some are "musts" for all packages, while others are included only under certain conditions.

- *Brand name.* This, obviously, is a "must." It's the headline of your copy.
- *Nature of product.* Let buyer know what the product is, whether coffee, cheese, or a mattress.
- *Specific nature of product.* If product is tea, give the exact type—whether green tea, black tea, Ceylon tea, or India tea. If coffee, tell what kind of grind—drip or regular. If aspirin, indicate how many grains are contained in each tablet.
- *Uses of product.* If use of the product isn't obvious, give its use clearly. For example, although you might presume that everyone would know that Betty Crocker is used for cake mix, the manufacturer doesn't take this for granted. In letters almost as big and bold as the product name itself, you'll find the words "cake mix."

  If the product has multiple uses, give these other uses. The Cascade package, as an example, points out that Cascade can be used for washing dishes, aluminum, and silver. A package containing a food product ordinarily consumed as a result of further preparation will often carry recipes.

  Your purpose in listing multiple uses or recipes is, of course, to induce the consumer to "run through" a package of the product quickly, thus hastening the repeat purchase.
- *Sales claims.* If the product has some definite sales point, highlight it. To illustrate, Comet "bleaches out stains." It's Crest toothpaste "with Tartar Control." Beautiflor wax "cleans as it waxes."
- *Directions.* If special directions must be given for use of product, state them clearly and simply, avoiding all scientific or technical terms, or any words that might not be immediately understood by a person of limited education.
- *"Family" products.* If the manufacturer makes other allied products, call the buyer's attention to them. For example, every box of Kellogg's corn flakes mentions that Kellogg also makes other cereals.
- *Premium offers.* If premiums or contests are being offered by the manufacturer of the product—and this policy will continue long enough to justify its mention on the package—it's sound strategy to do so, provided the package offers you enough space.
- *Ingredients.* Food and drug products are required by law to state their composition on the package. Copy of this nature, however, is usually prepared by a lawyer so is of but passing interest to you.

- *Nutrition information per serving.* This information is another legal requirement that doesn't require any creative work from you. It is sufficient that you know that such information must appear on food packages and cans because of regulations established by the U.S. Food and Drug Administration.

Probably the best advice anyone can give you regarding package copy is to "make your package a good advertisement." That's what it is or should be. Don't clutter it with words at the sacrifice of good design, but don't keep your product's good points a secret either. When a person picks up a can of peas to inspect it, *sell* with the copy you've written.

Many supermarkets offer "Storecasting," which, in conjunction with packaging, gives shoppers one more last-minute nudge. The intercom "storecast" mentions the product and then the shopper sees the package—a powerful combination of sight and sound.

Brand Names and Trademarks, a Challenge for Your Skill

Work long enough in copywriting and eventually you'll be asked to supply a list of proposed new names for a product or service. As you can surmise, this is not a frequent assignment but it's a refreshing change from the usual work, albeit somewhat discouraging. As you will discover, many good names are already being used and are protected by law. Thus your initial list of 200 names may not have any winners. Furthermore, when you compare your list with those supplied by your fellow workers, it's deflating to see how many names are duplicated. It's hard to come up with different, original names.

Product names are commonly known in business as "brand names" or "trademarks." The terms can be synonymous.

Brand names, as we shall refer to them, are not necessarily registered as trademarks. They may become so, however, once they have been used on goods shipped in interstate or foreign commerce, and provided they violate no governmental restrictions applying to trademarks. Pictorial representations may also be registered as trademarks.

Because a new product obviously must be highly developed prior to its introduction into retail channels, its naming is an assignment met more often by those copywriters who work in agencies or for a manufacturer than by writers in the retail field. It is only an occasional assignment at most, but one whose importance cannot be overemphasized.

On the brand name rests much responsibility for distinguishing one product or family of products from any and all others; of making a given product (or line) stand out above the mass of competitive goods or services. In the soap field, for instance, any new name must compete with Ivory, Dial, and the numerous other soaps now being manufactured.

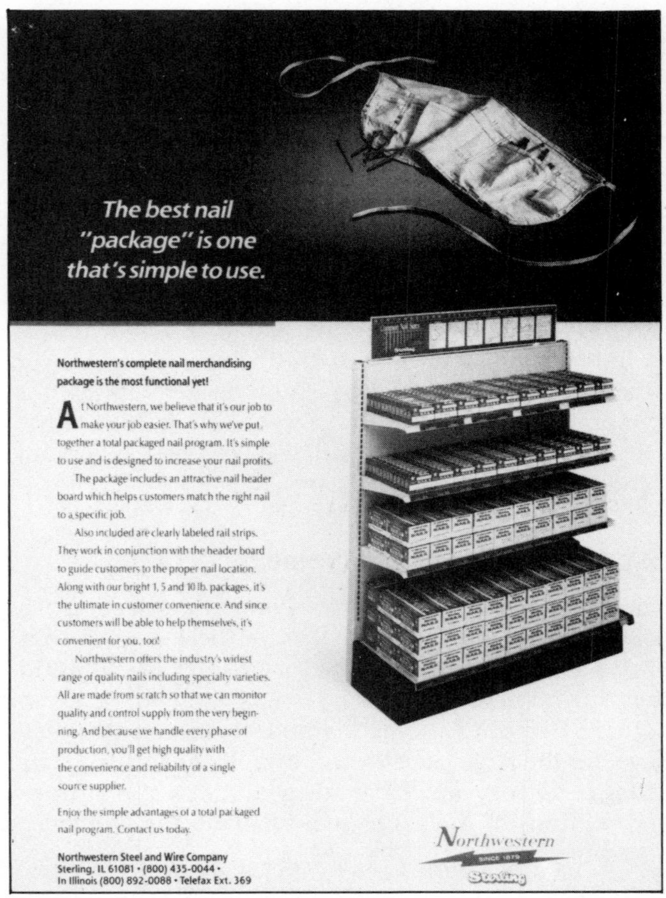

Figure 9–4. Trade advertisement emphasizing the importance of packaging.

Usually, you will not be charged with the full responsibility of creating a new brand name. You will be asked to get up a list of as many suitable names as you can think of. Other people in your organization will be asked to do the same thing.

The advertiser's employees, as well as those of the agency—from top brass to office clerks—may contribute ideas. Sometimes, as an incentive, a bonus rewards the person who offers the name finally selected. The selection of a brand name is so important that getting a good one is worth almost any effort.

Brand Names Should Have a Long-lasting Appeal

Even products and services of exceptional merit have little chance of survival, much less marked success, if they are burdened with unappealing, inappropriate, or hard-to-pronounce brand names.

Remember that changing a brand name once a product has been put on the market and advertised is a costly and involved procedure. It necessitates writing off as a loss the advertising expenditures made prior to such a change. Satisfied users, accustomed to calling for the product under the abandoned name, must be made aware of the change. Thus if you start with a name, you must usually continue with it.

The firm establishment of a distinctive brand name protects the consumer and producer alike. In the "cracker barrel" days great-grandmother had to ask for products in terms applicable to all merchandise of similar nature—the good as well as the bad. (Many types of meats, fruits, cheeses, and vegetables must still be called for by their generic names.)

When great-grandmother needed oatmeal, she could ask for "oatmeal" only by that name and *hope* that it would be satisfactory—not full of chaff, vermin, or other foreign matter. Today grandmother can ask for Quaker Oats and *know* that the quality is high—that every subsequent purchase will meet the same high standard. Such repeat purchases are vital.

Suggestions for Brand Name Selection

There are many guideposts to follow in the selection of a good brand name. There are, nevertheless, numerous brand names now known in every corner of the world that violate many of the suggestions you will be given here. As exceptions come to mind, remember that they have, for the large part, been constantly advertised over a long period of years. It has taken millions of repetitions and millions of dollars to win for them the eminence they enjoy today.

Make it distinctive. Since a brand name's first function is to *identify* one product from others, it should be above all things, distinctive. It should be different, preferably different from all other products, but certainly entirely different from the brand name of any product which might be considered even remotely competitive.

To be distinctive does not necessarily mean that a brand name must be clever or tricky. The name Perdue is simple and ungarnished. Yet, because it is an uncommon surname, it is distinctive. Many other family names, on the other hand, lack such distinction.

Be careful, when submitting suggestions for brand names, to avoid names similar to those of established products. In the early days of brand names, some brand names almost identical to established ones were intentionally chosen. The purpose, of course, was to attempt to capitalize on the established product's reputation: to try to capture a portion of a competitor's sales by confusing the public.

Actually, such sharp practice has almost invariably harmed rather than helped the imitator. The similarity in names, in fact, usually confused the public so much that upon reading the newcomer's advertising, people assumed these advertisements were boosting the established product rather than the new one. Purchases were thus made automatically for the well-known brand, defeating the imitator's purpose and causing the advertising to lose a large degree of its effectiveness.

Not only is it dishonest and poor business to trade on an established leader's name, but costly lawsuits for infringement are almost certain to be instituted. Every possible precaution should be taken to learn whether a proposed brand name has been previously registered by someone else as a trademark. Such preliminary checks may be made by contacting any one of the various trademark services found in many large cities.

One possibility is the Trademark Bureau of the Diamond International Corporation, New York. This company, for a small fee, will check files to see if your proposed trademark has been used before. The file is the largest independently owned collection in the country.

It must be noted that, while such organizations make fairly comprehensive searches, their findings are not an absolute guarantee that the name is not already in use. This can be officially determined only after the U.S. Patent and Trademark Office has passed on the application for trademark; and even a federal registration is subject to challenge by someone who has made prior use of the mark. The files of the trademark search organizations, however, include U.S. Patent and Trademark Office trademarks almost as soon as they are recorded by that agency.

Make it easy to remember. A brand name should be easy to remember. If the name is not memorable, winning widespread public recognition will take longer and be more expensive. Models of brand names that are extremely easy to remember are Duz, Seven-Up, and Jif, among many others.

The ease with which a person can remember a brand name is of great importance. To illustrate, let us say that a person goes into a drug store for a hair tonic. The night before, he had read about a certain brand and was impressed by the benefits it promised him, but now that he is in the store, he can't quite recall the product's name. "It's right on the tip of his tongue," but he can't remember it. As a result, Vitalis or Wildroot gets the sale, a sale actually created by a competitor's advertising.

It's unfortunate, but true, that if people have to think to recall the name of your product, they will buy a competitive brand bearing a name that comes to mind automatically.

Make it pronounceable. Still another very important consideration regarding brand names is that they should be easy to pronounce by consumers and by announcers in the broadcast media. As the makers of Baume Bengué Analgesique (now simply Ben-Gay) learned, the general public is reluctant, to say the least, to ask for a product whose name it finds difficult to pronounce.

There is a very sound psychological reason for this. All of us fear ridicule. Consequently, we resist putting ourselves in a position where we might appear ridiculous, even in front of a completely impersonal clerk whom we may never again see.

A customer might well hesitate to ask a druggist for Hexylresorcinol. It's a name only a scientist might be expected to pronounce with any facility. Recognizing this, the makers of this product wisely gave it an additional name—S. T. 37—which a child could easily remember.

If you had never heard the name Sal Hepatica pronounced, there's a possibility that you might have trouble pronouncing it. Constant advertising, however, has familiarized a huge section of the population with its correct pronunciation. Still, Sal Hepatica may well be losing sales it could make if its name were easier for all people to pronounce.

A somewhat similar example is Campho Phenique, easy enough to handle if you have heard it, but think of the trouble it might give the poorly educated or those who speak English as a second language.

An exception to this rule about ease of pronunciation is the naming of perfumes, such as Yves Saint Laurent, cosmetics, high fashion clothing, and a number of luxury items such as Cristal d'arques. Many advertisers of such products feel that the use of foreign, scientific, or other difficult words provides a certain aura that enhances the names. Difficult names such as these are sometimes provided with pronunciation instructions.

Despite some successes for products with difficult names, it is best to use simple names. Selling products is hard enough. You simply add to your problems by providing names that the public cannot pronounce or remember. Remember, too, that a product may be advertised in the broadcast media. The name may be hard to visualize or hard for the announcers to handle.

See that it has pleasant associations. The fourth "must" in the selection of a good brand name is associations. Unpleasant associations should be avoided. The initials DT might, to illustrate, seem an acceptable name for a coffee made by a man named Daniel Thompson. Here is something short, distinctive, easy to remember, and easy to pronounce.

In seeing the name of the product in print, or in hearing it mentioned on the air, however, many would instantly think of drunkenness, not coffee. Others might possibly think of DDT, the insecticide. In either instance, unappetizing mental pictures would be created, instead of the pleasant thoughts which should be associated with the product.

"Balloon" would obviously be a very poor name for a girdle, for another example, even though it might be made of balloon silk.

Avoid dating your brand name. Unless you are trying purposely to establish a product as being of old-fashioned vintage—obviously the case in the selection of Old Spice as a name for a line of toiletries—brand names that too closely ally a product with a certain era are best avoided. For instance, although "23 Skiddoo" might have been a "stopper" as name for a mosquito repellent in grandmother's day, the term is now almost meaningless because it is out of vogue.

If a catfood named "Hepcat" had been introduced in the 1940s, it might have enjoyed success for some time, but as jitterbugging went the way of the bunny-hop and the Charleston, the term would have lost its meaning. The danger of becoming passé is always present in any name adopted to take advantage of a current craze. When the craze is over, your name then becomes unintelligible, or old hat.

Types of Brand Names

One of the most frequent objectives in the creation of brand names today is to make the name suggestive of some property or benefit of the product. An example is Plax. You can surmise, also, from the name Filter Queen that this vacuum cleaner filters the air. It is a benefit in which you can easily see the merit, and its name blares forth the virtue. Mum and Ban are two other examples of suggestive names.

Suggestive names are of special advantage during that period when a new product is fighting to win wide recognition. This is particularly true if the product is one that is entirely new or one that has definite properties or benefits exclusively its own.

Once the product has become firmly established, however, the full significance of its name is often lost. Illustrative of this is the fact that when you refer to the brand name Frigidaire, you aren't actively conscious of the fact that you are, in essence, saying "air that is frigid." At least you aren't if you are like most people. The same principle is true with other such well-known brand names as Beautyrest, Kissproof, and Eveready.

Numbers and initials. Many famous brand names are built on numbers or initials, or both. For example, 3-in-1, S.T. 37, PM, ABC, and ZBT. These are easy to pronounce, and, because of their brevity, allow for a proportionately larger logotype, both in advertisements and on the packages itself, than do brand names that are longer. But again, they are often difficult to obtain as one's own exclusive property.

Geographical or patriotic names. Columbia, Liberty, American, Hartford, Waltham, and Palm Beach are foremost examples of brand names in this group. Such names have been popular in the past, but, because they lack true distinctiveness in most instances and are not subject to exclusive proprietorship, they are not considered among the best for new products.

Coined names. Another rich source of brand names is tapped through coining words. Coined brand names may be divided into three types:

1. Those devised by uniting various components of the company name to form a single word. Exemplifying this are Nabisco (*Na*tional *Bis*cuit *Co.*), Alcoa (*Al*uminum *Co*rporation of *A*merica), Duco (*Du* Pont *Co.*) Such contractions or abbreviations, if easy to spell, pronounce, and remember, often make excellent brand names that have the added advantage of calling to mind the full name of the producer. Armco (*A*merican *R*olling *M*ill *Co.*) and Texaco (The *Texa*s *Co.*) are con-

tractions that proved so successful the companies eventually changed their corporate titles and now are known legally by what once were just their brand names.

2. Those such as Tenderleaf, Treet, Perma-Lift, Holeproof, Palmolive, and Rem. These are created in several ways:
   a. They may be shortened versions of common words, as is Rem (for "remedy").
   b. They may be phonetic spellings, such as Kool and Duz.
   c. They may be created by combining two or more words, or parts thereof, employing either orthodox spelling or simplified variations. For example, Spam (from "spiced ham"), Pepsodent, Car-Nu, and Noxzema. Among these are many of those brand names which spotlight some benefit or property of the product. No-fade and Pye-Quick promise definite benefits, while Bromo-Seltzer and Pepto-Bismol are semiscientific descriptions of properties of the products.
3. Those brand names that are out-and-out inventions, such as Keds, Kodak, Dic-a-Doo, and Drax.

Coined names are today among the most popular brand names. Good ones have numerous advantages. They are distinctive. They have high recognition value, are easy to pronounce, easy to remember, and timeless in their durability. Full legal protection may usually be obtained for them, making them the exclusive property of a single company or individual.

Some names such as Cellophane, Linoleum, Aspirin, Kerosene, and Shredded Wheat have become so firmly associated with a product that they have become generic—that is, part of the language. When this happens, the company loses the exclusive right to the name. Call it the penalty for having a really excellent name. The only protection is constant watchfulness by the advertiser.

One of the most determined corporations in the protecting of its trademark is the Coca-Cola Company. This organization reminds others constantly that when they refer to Coca-Cola in its abbreviated form they will keep the meaning "clear" if the shorter version "Coke" is spelled with a capital C. This, the company explains in its advertising, will help protect a "valuable trademark." The Coca-Cola Company recognizes the peril confronting its trademarked abbreviation; editors and others are constantly reminded that the word *Coke* is the trademarked property of the Coca-Cola Company and not merely a convenient and generic term for a general class of soft drink.

Even though the true meaning of suggestive names may after a time no longer consciously register in the minds of customers, their value in the initial stages of a product's development can be considerable. So long as the benefit or promise contained in the brand name is both important and believable, it is difficult to see how it can be other than an asset in promoting sales.

General designation of quality. Excel, Royal, Ideal, Perfection, Acme, Hi-Grade, Apex, Superior, A-1, and so forth, are included among those brand names which may be said to give a general designation of the quality of the product. These are not the best of names. They are not distinctive.

Actually among the many brands emblazoned with the name Acme, to name but a few, we find Acme pencils, Acme paint, Acme oil burners, carbon paper, card cases, fire extinguishers, snap fasteners, shower curtains, scissors, wire, stepladders, thermostats, tables, chair seats, and gasoline. And that list could be enlarged with ease.

Another point against such general descriptions is that constant usage has caused the average person to become oblivious to their literal definitions. Third, the claims to superiority implied by such names are so lofty as to lack credibility. In addition, being common words of the public domain, it is almost impossible to protect such names adequately.

Family names. More numerous perhaps than those in any other one classification are products named after the founder or owner of the company marketing them. Among those most advertised currently are Parker, Heinz, Borden, Westinghouse, Pabst, and Remington.

There are three reasons why it is often well to avoid family names. (a) Often a family name lacks distinctiveness. (b) The name may be difficult to spell or pronounce, such as is Ghirardelli, the name of a large West Coast chocolate producer. (c) Family names are hard to protect. Any person of the same name can enter business in direct competition with you and use the name you both possess. Sometimes if another person's so doing will obviously cause damage to your business, the courts will rule against this practice. In the past, however, a number of unscrupulous firms have deliberately hired people having the same names as leading competitors. Giving these people the title (in name only) of head of the firm, they were thus able to use their competitor's name as their own brand name and still argue that they were technically within the law.

Fictional, historical, or heroic names. Robert Burns, Chesterfield, Victor, Admiral, De Soto, Pontiac, Maxwell House, Aunt Jemima, and Bo Peep all fall into this category. There is nothing wrong with such names so long as they fulfill the requirements of distinctiveness (which Admiral certainly lacks), ease of recall, ease of pronunciation, and pleasant associations. They are, however, difficult to protect.

Care must be taken when you choose such a name to make your selection from those characters, events, or places whose durability has been firmly established. If you select the name of some person, place, or event of recent prominence, you may find in the years to come that such fame will have passed.

Group sensitivities, previously discussed, must be considered also in such names. An example is furnished by the Sambo food establishments, which ran into trouble with the nation's blacks who felt the name was demeaning. This name, of course, stemmed back to the character Little Black Sambo. Still another example is the name "Helpee Selfee" laundry franchise that was termed insulting to the Chinese.

Animals, minerals, vegetables. Among the first examples of brand names in this classification that come to mind are Camel, Caterpillar, Blue Boar, Walnut, White Owl, and Swansdown. Again, some such names lack distinction and in some cases are difficult to spell, pronounce, or protect. One virtue, however, is that they usually have more pictorial interest—much more so, for instance, than are brand names based on the name of the company founder.

Familiar objects. Names based on common objects generally are not so distinctive as some others. In that respect they are like brand names in group number one—Hi-Grade, Acme, Ideal. For example, in addition to Arrow shirts, we have Arrow mucilage, Arrow shovels, Arrow desks, Arrow golf balls, and Arrow needles, to mention but a handful.

Such names as Diamond, Anchor, Star, and so forth are similarly duplicated on products of almost every conceivable variety. These names usually do, however, have the advantage, like the animal/mineral/vegetable group, of being translated easily into a pictorial form that increases the recognition value of the name. Nevertheless, they are best avoided.

Figure 9–5. Name-change advertisement. Changing an established name is a major undertaking. It is done here with humor in the copy and a memorable illustration that should register the change forcefully. Name changes are never done nonchalantly because the process is costly and sometimes upsetting to customers, who tend to resist change of any kind.

Trade Characters and Pictorial Trademarks

Such trade personalities or symbols as Aunt Jemima, the Pontiac Indian head, and the Fisher Body coach are often employed to give an extra and continuous recognition value to a company's advertising. When such characters or symbols are also affixed to the product or package (as are all of those just mentioned), the advertising and the product itself become closely identified. Application to the product or package, where practicable, helps to create instantaneous recognition in the minds of consumers the moment their eyes alight on the product on the shelf of a store, on the hood of an automobile, or on a gasoline pump in a service station.

Many products are actually called for, moreover, by description of the pictorial trademark on the package rather than by name. That is, a customer might ask for "the cocoa with the lady on it" instead of saying "Baker's Cocoa."

The actual designing of suitable trade characters or symbols is plainly a job that requires the talents of an artist. But more often than not, these illustrative devices are based on ideas sparked by copywriters. Here are a few do's and don'ts for you to remember should you ever be confronted with an assignment of this nature.

Review the requisites of brand names that are also applicable to things pictorial. That is, an illustrated trademark should be: (a) simple, yet distinctive; (b) easy to remember; (c) subject to legal protection.

You should *avoid* unpleasant associations and current fashions (which might appear ludicrous ten years hence).

If the subject is something the passage of time might make obsolete, it should be avoided. An example is the use of the radiator design of an automobile. Because these designs are changed periodically, any trademark showing one would necessarily also have to be changed from time to time, appreciably reducing its recognition value.

Trademark and Copyright Symbols

As a copywriter you may wonder at times about when to use certain symbols in connection with your brand name or trademark. These symbols ®,™,℠,© appear in countless advertisements, and the best advice is not to use them unless the lawyers insist on your doing so. Consumers are confused enough by all the various abbreviations encountered in daily life, without having to wade through more clutter in advertisements.

Still, you should know what the symbols represent and when they might be used. An ® included in your advertisement means that the trademark is registered in the U.S. Patent and Trademark Office and a certificate has been issued by the Commissioner. You can own a brand name without using the ®, but it can help warn off others who might wish to use it, perhaps not realizing its proprietary nature.

The ™ is used for a trademark that has not yet been registered; an application may be pending. A similar situation is encountered with the use of ℠, which stands for service mark. The symbol ™ is for merchandise of any kind, while ℠, which is seen very little, is for services, such as insurance, transportation, broadcasting, and so on.

The symbol © stands for copyright, but this symbol has no legal meaning when used by itself. If you are going through the process of copyrighting, which means you're trying to protect the entire content of your advertisement, you will have to use a notice that includes the © and the name of the copyright owner as well as the year the advertisement was first published.

The best advice is to use these symbols as little as legally possible. They simply get in the way of easy reading by the consumer. However, be *sure* to use them if the advertiser insists, because there are many situations in which they can be vitally important.

Important? Yes. But Slogan Writing Is an Infrequent Assignment

You may *never* be asked to write a slogan. Long before you began working, your client may have been using a slogan that will continue to be used. A good slogan, once established, has the permanence of a national monument. An example is "99 and-$^{44}/_{100}$% pure." Occasionally, however, you may be asked to write a slogan for a new product.

Many slogans are accidents. They start out as headlines and then become slogans. Others begin as campaign themes such as:

Promise her anything but give her Arpège.

Sometimes you'll write a deft phrase that pops out of the middle of your copy and begs for recognition as a slogan. You weren't deliberately writing a slogan; it just happened. If you think that you have a good slogan, see if it meets these criteria:

Does it make a specific claim or promise a believable benefit? Such a slogan is

"Dove doesn't dry like soap/because Dove isn't soap"

This specific promise for people who suffer from dry skin is a powerful sales tool when repeated. A direct promise of this type is more potent than mere cleverness, an attribute most people associate with slogans.

Strong promise is contained in this slogan aimed at arthritis sufferers.

Bufferin: For the pain and inflammation of arthritis.

No cleverness there but lots of sales power. And another slogan for a charge card says:

VISA: It's everywhere you want to be

These few words express a strong benefit in easy-to-remember words, as does:

"All the appeal of a homemade meal" . . . (for a dog food).

Does it contain a command to action, a direct appeal to buy? This type of slogan has merit because it has vitality. Likewise, it involves the reader directly in the action. Placed at the bottom of the advertisement, it ends the advertisement with an urge to action, always a desirable technique. Examples:

Get back into life with Depend

American Express: Don't leave home without it.

EconoLodge: Spend a night, not a fortune.

Does it create a favorable identification or image for your product, service, or company? Some slogans that answer this third question:

Bayer: The wonder drug that works wonders.

Mercury. The shape you want to be in.

AT&T The right choice.

America's favorite store K-Mart. The saving place.

Certain writing attributes of slogans appear in the examples that have been offered here. For instance, most have a strong sense of the vernacular, of a conversational style that is breezy, informal, and offhand. A slogan talks "people" language. It is rarely literary in tone and it almost never uses a word that will make anyone reach for a dictionary.

It is rare, too, to find a long slogan. To be memorable a slogan must almost always be brief. A world of copy strength can be packed into a few words, as "It's toasted" and "It floats" will testify.

A further aid to memorability is the use of rhyme and alliteration. "Be sure with Pure" is more likely to be remembered than "Be certain with Pure," although the meaning is the same for both. If you used alliteration by writing "Pick Planters Peanuts," you'd achieve more memorability than if you wrote "Choose Planters Peanuts."

If your proposed slogan doesn't meet these requirements, see if you can't come up with a phrase that does, such as the one for a local appliance dealer whose print and broadcast advertising suggested:

For heating advice,
call Amos Rice

Once more, about cleverness. There *are* clever slogans. It's highly desirable to inject cleverness into a slogan if you can retain sales power while doing so. Yet, thousands of slogans have been effective without cleverness, just as millions of advertisements have been effective without slogans. Furthermore, effective slogans often are rather ordinary examples of writing; they're effective simply because of heavy use, not because they have any notable literary quality.

Want to Help Your Advertisements Stand Out? Use a Distinctive Logotype

When an advertisement does not carry the company's name, its "signature" is usually the product name. (With such family names as Campbell and Heinz, the product name is actually part of the company name. That is, the brand name, Heinz, is derived from the full firm name, H. J. Heinz, Co.)

The style of type or lettering in which the name of a given company's product is displayed sometimes varies from one advertisement to another. Most often though it is given a distinctive design, and almost without exception it is used in this particular style in every advertisement and in all other promotional material, including the actual product label.

When the product's name is thus treated, it is referred to formally as a "logotype" and informally as a "logo." Excellent specimens of such logotypes are those for Sunkist, Palmolive, Larvex, Coca-Cola, Van Heusen, and Valvoline, to cite but a few.

Under most circumstances, it is preferable to use one consistent design in the logotypes. This makes for far greater recall value than when the style of type or lettering is frequently changed.

Creation of a logotype, being primarily a matter of design, is not the direct responsibility of the copywriter; nevertheless, you will often make suggestions and offer criticism of logotypes. A little knowledge of logotypes will enable you to tell whether the finished logotype is sufficiently simple, easy to read, and distinctive.

Since the logotype is of a distinctive style and ordinarily unlike the type in which the body text is set, it is rarely included within the actual copy block. Although you will not design the logotype or the signature, as the copywriter you may insist, for instance, that they be displayed in type that is big enough to be seen easily by readers.

Readership studies consistently show that many readers of print advertisements are unable to recall the name of the advertiser or the product. Quite often this is due to a silly delicacy on the part of advertisers about displaying their names in a type size that they think is vulgar.

Possibly the delicacy traces back to an art department that is more concerned with artistic integrity than with such mundane considerations as registering company or product names.

Naturally, judgment must be used. An advertisement for Tiffany's, for example, will use restraint in the kind and size of type used for the logotype. For most advertisers and products, however, it is better to be conspicuous than to be delicate and unseen.

As the copywriter you have a stake in this matter. You have the right to question the inconspicuous logotype or signature. Make your voice heard or that low readership figure will be blamed on your copy and not on that diminutive logotype or signature.

10

LOCAL ADVERTISING FOR QUICK, STEADY RESULTS

Although there's an early-morning freshness in the air, people are already bustling along downtown's Central Avenue and five miles east in the shopping mall.

Downtown, Jack Levinson is standing on the sidewalk planning changes for the big window of his fur salon.

A few doors down, Jackie Kriebel is writing buyer's copy to send up to the seventh floor advertising department for a new shipment of Swedish crystal.

Out at the mall, Judy Slattery is already busy with a salesman. She must decide whether to increase the size of an order for her line of prestige women's shoes. She can visualize the attractive advertising she'll build around them.

So it goes all over the area. It's like a humming beehive as planning and movement go on in banks, hardware stores, sports shops, dress shops, restaurants, auto dealerships, newspapers, radio stations, television stations, and all the other enterprises engaged in local advertising.

This is where the action is; where you meet face to face with your customers who are there before the doors open to pick up those bargains featured in last night's newspaper.

To Be Accurate, It's Better to Say Local Advertising Than Retail Advertising

You're in local advertising, often inaccurately called "retail" advertising, a term not broad enough to embrace advertising for such businesses as health clubs, auto repair shops, hotels, racquetball clubs, warehouses, and others. Local advertising is an all-inclusive term; retail advertising is not.

Whatever term is used, this advertising is fast-paced, at the point of sale, and significant in the numbers of people and dollars. Workers in such advertising have satisfactions denied the writer of national advertising.

One, to see an advertisement prepared on Wednesday in print on Thursday. Two, to learn on Thursday how successful their Wednesday creative efforts have been. No other phase of advertising permits the writers to deal so directly with their merchandise and their customers, and to learn firsthand how effective their approach and methods have been.

In this chapter the emphasis is on department store advertising because it provides the most diversified picture of such copywriting. Most of the principles can be applied to other forms of local selling, too.

Retail copywriters usually turn out more copy at a faster pace than do the usual agency copywriters working on national advertisements. Furthermore, the power of their copy is checked immediately by sales results, whereas the copy written by national copywriters is seldom measured by the sales results obtained by one advertisement.

When local copywriters type out selling copy for a $350 microwave oven, or cross-country skis at $99.50, they know just how many units were sold by the advertisement. If many, they have quick gratification. If few, they're depressed despite the fact that some other factors may be responsible for the poor sales figures. Thus local copywriting is exhilarating, demanding, satisfying, and exhausting. Above all, it's exciting because it's where the action is, at the consumer buying level.

Unfortunately, much local advertising is poorly done. An examination of advertisements in newspapers (with the exception of first-class establishments in big cities) reveals a depressing picture. Too often the copy is prepared by persons in the establishments who have had no training in advertising, or by newspaper space salespeople who do the copy because they are expected to write copy as part of their overall selling duties. It is obvious from their copy that many space salespeople should concentrate on their selling and leave the writing to better qualified persons.

The result of the inexpert approach in advertising on the local level that has these common faults:

1. Telegraphic copy that has no flow or character.
2. Label headlines that don't lure readers into reading the body copy.
3. Impersonal writing that doesn't reach out and involve the reader.
4. Little, or no, use of suffering points to give solid reasons for buying.
5. Product-oriented copy instead of people-oriented copy.
6. Too much mere listing of product or sales points.
7. No localization of the copy that takes advantage of the shared experiences of the advertiser and the customers.
8. Overall dullness of the copy—a lack of sparkle, imagination, and use of colorful, persuasive words.

The principles of good copywriting for department stores can be applied by these advertisers and, in the case of banks, are often applied exceedingly well. This excellence is largely due to the fact that most bank advertising is prepared by advertising agency copywriters. This is likely to be true, also, of large dairies, hotels and car dealers, and some other local enterprises that invest substantially in advertising. Still, as said, there is much local advertising that is not done well.

In the material immediately following, you'll find suggestions for the actual writing of local advertising. Before the writing begins, however, there are many people involved in the advertising, buying, and selling process with whom copywriters must work, or who influence their work. The fairly complicated superstructure into which the copywriter fits is taken up in the conclusion of the chapter.

Before You Write, Ask These Questions

Who Is My Customer for This Merchandise?

Obviously, if it's a very high-priced pair of shoes, you appeal first to the person who can afford to pay that price. That consideration is going to govern your entire approach. Your advertisement is dignified. Your appeal must be to pride and a desire to wear the best of everything.

If the shoe is a moderately priced item, you know it will have general appeal to all people. If it's a sale item, you know again that it will have general appeal, but now you concentrate on the price feature. You will be determining meanwhile whether it's the type of shoe worn by young college students or dignified bankers. Perhaps your market is the rugged outdoor type, or possibly the shoe is the type fashion-conscious people wear.

What Benefits Does This Merchandise Offer?

This is part of, yet different from, the actual description of the merchandise qualities. The shoe is described as "soft and pliable." These are qualities, but you must translate these words into copy that is meaningful to the people who wear the shoes.

Saying "soft and pliable" doesn't mean so much to Mr. Smith as saying that the shoes will allow his feet to bend properly, thus easing foot fatigue. Saying that the leather is durable is not the same as reminding the prospective customer that the shoes will take all sorts of rough treatment and bad weather, and that they will last a long time.

Saying that the shoes are handsome is not so strong as saying that they're the latest thing out of *Gentlemen's Quarterly* or that they'll really make his wardrobe stylishly complete.

The idea of benefits is tied up with the idea of knowing who your customers are and what they expect to get out of the merchandise you want them to buy. Translate the buyer's cold facts into personal benefits that your reader wants—foot comfort, value for money, prestige, and admiration.

How Shall I Attract the Reader's Attention?

This is most vital, particularly in a newspaper where your advertisement—whether it's a full page, or two columns by six inches—is competing vigorously for the attention of the man or woman who paid money to read the news stories in the paper.

Remember, most of your readers did not pay their money to read advertisements, although a considerable number may have. Since many people are interested in news, not advertisements, your advertisement itself must be news if you want to interest such readers.

You must get those factual benefits up where they can be seen. You stop readers with benefits and you can stop them with advertising headlines—just as news headlines catch the readers' eyes and cause them to stop.

Layout and illustration will stop them, too—but merely stopping the readers is not enough. Well-chosen words in the body copy, captions, or subheads must instantly tell them the story of your merchandise and get them to recognize that this merchandise is what they've been looking for; that this merchandise fills a need they have; that this merchandise is what they're going to buy.

Your headline, in this instance, has stopped the readers and has caused them to read in the body text why they should buy these particular shoes—but that's not enough. Your shoes are for sale at one place and one place alone as far as you're concerned. You must convince the customers not only that they should buy these shoes but also that they should buy them at *your* store.

How Shall I Identify the Store?

Some stores merely put the sig or store name logotype at the top of the advertisement and let it go at that. You will

Figure 10–1. Dealer-manufacturer advertisement. In this institutional advertisement there is no overt selling—just a statement of leadership.

usually make your advertisement more effective if you mention the store also in a subhead or lead-in line, and then refer to the store as often as you can in your body copy.

In all local advertising this matter of identification is vital because in this day of "famous brands," competitors on every street in town may be carrying the same brands. Without proper identification of your store as the place to buy, you're often merely running an advertisement to help your competitor sell his merchandise.

Your main points then are:

1. Determine who your prospective customer is.
2. Present the appeals of your merchandise in the form of direct benefits.
3. Present those appeals to attract and hold the reader's attention.
4. Identify the store so that it will be linked immediately with the benefits to be obtained.

The urge to buy the product advertised must be the ultimate end of your copy—to stimulate the reader into coming to your store to buy your goods.

Three Big Differences between Local Copy and National Copy

Although no one will deny that all copy—national, local, radio, direct mail, newspaper, and magazine—has certain basic similarities, it is also true that local copy has some characteristics that set it apart. A local copywriter, especially one who has been familiar with the national field, should be aware of these characteristics along with the beginner who has had no experience. You will find the characteristics in varying degrees in copy for small, medium, or large stores.

Imagine that you have had some experience with other types of copywriting but that you have decided to try local copywriting. At the moment you are seated across the desk from the advertising manager of the department store for which you are going to work.

Knowing your background in other types of copy, the manager is discussing local advertising. You realize that he is very diplomatically indicating to you that although you were competent in other forms of copywriting, it doesn't follow that you can automatically write local copy. He is giving you the same briefing he would give anybody else entering copywriting.

It isn't your writing the advertising manager is concerned about; he's aware that you're a good technician. Rather, he's anxious for you to understand the basic concepts of the local approach—some of the important differences between the writing you have been doing and the kind you'll do in local business.

A methodical person, the advertising manager ticks off points for you. He says, "We're glad to have you with us. Also, I'm glad that we have a few minutes now to talk about this local business. I'm well aware of your background. I know you can write so we'll forget that.

"What I do want to make sure of is that you get something of the local picture before you type a word of copy. Some of the things I'm going to tell you may be obvious, but they bear repeating because their very obviousness often causes them to be overlooked, even by us who have grown up in local advertising.

"First of all, and I'm not sure that I wouldn't list this as the one and only point I'll make: *a store is part of the community.* A big part. You people who write the copy share the same community with your readers. You swelter in the same heat and get nipped by the same frost. You enjoy the same football team, and the current crime wave is a mutual worry.

"The financial ups and downs of your city and county are of acute concern to all of you. The business is, except in the case of some very large stores, 100 percent local. This fact you will feel in all the copy you write. Let's see how this affects your thinking."

The advertising manager then makes the following points. He tells you that in local advertising three facts must be recognized:

Urge to "Buy Now" Is Stronger

There is immediacy in most local copy. Stores depend upon turnover of stock. The best kind of stock is the kind that is "here today and gone tomorrow." Local copy, for the most part, should be slightly breathless and urgent. You should push generally for the quick sale.

In local advertising you expect a quick response to your copy and you must get it. Thus your copy should ever be prodding the customer, sometimes subtly, and sometimes with all the subtlety of a meat-ax. Get the readers to come to the store; get them to telephone; get them to put their money down for a quick purchase.

Phrases such as "Come in today," "Buy while they last," "See them today," or "Get yours now while quantities last" are important in local advertising. Sometimes you push people more delicately, but almost always there is some sort of urge to action—*immediate* action. This urge is much more pointed than in national advertising, which usually doesn't expect or need such immediacy of purchase on the part of the reader.

Readers Are More Price Conscious

People who read local advertising want to know the price of merchandise. They have become accustomed in national advertising to price-less copy, but in much of local copy, price is all important. Consciousness of cost creeps into all your copy. It weaves a web around the customers until they ask themselves, "Can I afford not to spend my money?" When you think of price in local copy, you don't think of price figures. Instead, you look upon your entire advertisement as building justification for the moment when the customers dig into their pockets and say, "I'll take that."

There are very few stores that aren't price-conscious down to the last word in the last line of copy. Big stores, little stores, exclusive stores, and bargain stores—all of them use prices as the wedge for sales.

You should get in the habit when you finish a piece of local copy of looking it over and asking yourself whether your words would make you buy if you were the ordinary reader—to whom dollars are keenly important. You have few chances in local copy to forget that all the words you write simply act as background music for that all-important tag line, which reads, "Only $00.00 while they last."

Developing of Store Personality Is a Must

Taken as a whole, you probably don't look much different from the people around you. You have the usual number of limbs, eyes, and ears. Compare yourself with the next-door neighbor. Based upon appearance, there isn't much to choose between you, yet you may have many more friends. Credit your personality.

Likewise, you can credit successful stores with personality. Development of the personality of your store is a constant copywriting job. The ability to write "personality" copy is something you acquire on the job. You don't learn it the first day. It comes after you have studied your store's advertising; after you have got the feel of the place; after you have talked to other store employees; after you have been around a while.

Those saucy Bloomingdale's advertisements, those dignified productions of Lord & Taylor's, those slambang sales-producers of Macy's—they reflect personality. *Personality in your advertising is what makes people come in to see your merchandise instead of going to your competitor's store to see the same merchandise.*

The basis of store personality is found in many things—friendliness, bargain prices, service, dependability, long establishment in the community, size of operation, or perhaps a combination of some, or all, of these. Remember that most stores can match goods with their competitors these days. If all you have to offer is merchandise, you may fall back of competitors who have found a personality and let it shine through their advertisements.

Personality marks you as different from your competitor. Downtown streets are lined with famous stores, each striving to be different from its neighbor. Saks is different from Bonwit Teller. Bergdorf Goodman differs from B. Altman's and Neiman-Marcus is different from Bloomingdale's; and no one would mistake a Lord & Taylor advertisement as one from Ohrbach's. Each store works hard to be different, especially from its closest rival. A celebrated rivalry exists between Marshall Field's and Carson Pirie Scott & Company in Chicago. Although both stores use effective selling copy, many little differences exist which enable the reader to recognize a Field's advertisement from one out of the Carson copy department.

Personality comes also from the creative technique—from the borders you use, the twist on words, the art treatment, the typography, the repetition of certain copy points or phrases such as the well-known "It's Smart To Be Thrifty" of Macy's.

Companies engaged in national advertising develop personality in their campaign themes, but they are not usually forced into doing so, as are retail stores. The normal store has certain natural rivals who sell the same kind of goods at the same prices to the same type of customer.

Rivalry between these stores is very personal. It is a matter of frantic interest to them that the stores themselves and their advertising reflect an individual personality which makes the customer differentiate one store from the other.

When you work in a store, you may find that your toughest assignment is to capture your store's special personality in your copy. It's tough, because the personality is made up of so many little things. Be sensitive to those little things and be observant, and one day you'll find that you have pinned down the elusive spirit that spells your store to the customers. If you don't capture this spirit, you'd better move on.

Use Specific Words in Local Copy

Your language in a local advertisement walks a tightrope. Normally, local copy goes out after the sale. Yet this hard-smacking sales copy must be clothed in friendly, good-neighbor talk because of the personal relationship of the store to its customers.

The specific words are the ones that sell. If you're selling moderately priced items like hats, then "Prices cut in half" punches harder than "Huge savings." Perhaps the lines "Save $5 to $10" may sell the best of the three because it gets even more specific.

A salesperson is specific in talking to a customer—you can be, too. Naturally there is some difference between printed sales messages and those spoken by the person behind the counter. The clerk can be more specific, more pointed, and more down to earth because the clerk is not held down by space limitations of a newspaper page.

Just the same, a better sale will usually be made if you talk in your copy in the specific language of the salesperson, and not in the words of a copywriter reaching for the well turned phrase and the empty adjective.

Write Enough to Make the Sale. Not Too Much. Not Too Little

You'll be faced in local copy, as in other types of copy, with the problem of how much copy to write. As in other copy, your solution is obvious: write enough copy to do the sales job. For instance, suppose you are writing an advertisement that is describing several items.

You have decided to use a main copy block and several subsidiary copy blocks which will serve as captions for the multiple items being advertised. You'll defeat your advertisement if you try to jam too much copy into the main copy block, trying to describe in detail all the sales points for all the items in the advertisement.

In short, here is a case where you would be writing too much copy. You would do a better sales job if you made one overall sales point covering all the items in an interesting way, thus luring the reader into the specific selling copy in the captions. In such a case, the main copy block might be more effective if it had six lines of copy than if it had twenty.

Judging the right amount of copy is the mark of the skilled, experienced copywriter. As the young copywriter soon finds out, it is often easier to write a page advertisement than a one-column, three-inch advertisement. Most people have more trouble "compressing" than "expressing."

You may find it particularly hard, at times, to keep from writing too much copy. Suppose, for example, you have a really sensational promotion—really "hot" merchandise. The natural tendency is to write your head off. You and your buyers get excited. You load yourself with so many interesting facts that you could write a campaign for the product.

Sadly, however, you realize that all these facts and all this enthusiasm are going to be earthbound by the fact that you have just one advertisement in which to do your sales job.

In such a case, don't lose your momentum. Go ahead and write your head off, then start the sifting process. Get rid of the fluff. Get rid of the long-winded explanations that attempt to make clear this remarkable value. Tell the story straight, like a newspaper reporter.

Knowing when to stop in the writing of copy is especially difficult in the writing of institutional copy. Such copy, in which you explain store policy, pricing, service, and other facets of store operation, can easily become too long. You can get so wrapped up in the store that you forget the customer. Institutional copy can be fascinating copy, but if you write too much, it can easily be the dullest copy for readers because you may take many words to talk about something in which they are not basically interested.

Find Out What Results Were Earned by That Copy You Wrote

A good copywriter rarely can sit in an office and write about merchandise two floors below and not have personal contact with the merchandise. That's why you should school yourself to follow the entire process from start to finish—from the buying of the merchandise, if possible, to the investigation of the effectiveness of the advertisement you wrote.

If you can possibly find the time, you should get to the selling department after your advertisement has run. Find out the reaction. If a crowd of shoppers flocks in at the opening bell and rushes to the department using your advertisement, you have a good idea that your copy was effective.

Later, again granting that you have time, check with the buyer and the salespeople to find out what they've sold. At the end of the day, ask again and keep a record of the dollar volume and the advertised items sold off your advertisement. Some stores will actually require that you attach a form listing these results to a tearsheet of the advertisement. You then turn this in to the advertising manager.

Whether or not your boss requires it, make it your business to keep in touch with your advertisements all the way through. If an advertisement doesn't click, find out why. If you ask the buyers, they'll more than likely tell you why it was a poor advertisement.

Buyers might tell you, for instance, that the item is one that is usually bought by the husband and wife together. They might show you rather pointedly that your advertisement is slanted too much to one side—that you failed to recognize that both parties share in buying responsibility.

Perhaps you'll say the merchandise wasn't salable. Puzzle out the trouble. You might even rewrite the copy. Some copywriters have actually rewritten advertisements, asked that they be run again with the new slant, and hit the jackpot on the second running.

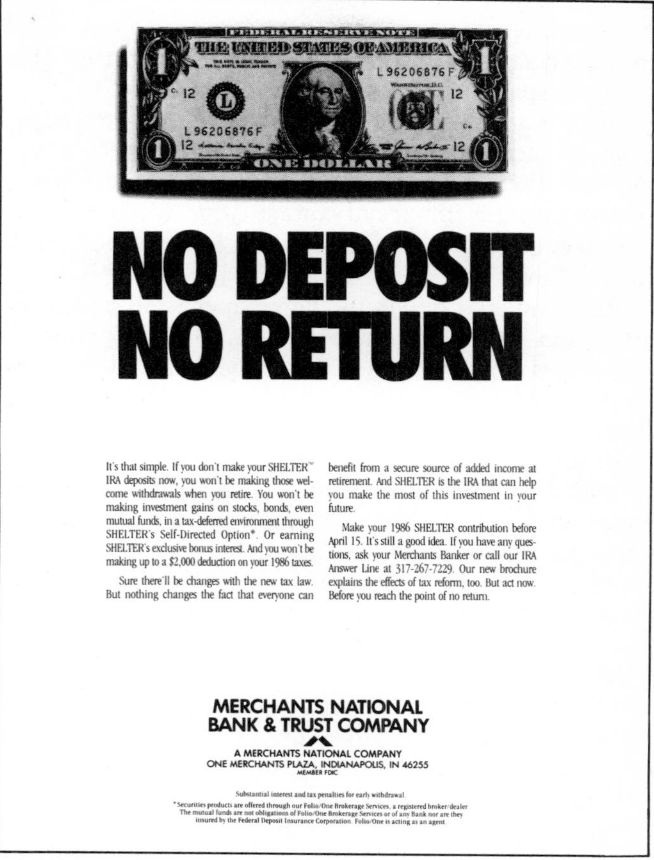

Figure 10–2. Local advertising for a bank. A clever headline with a twist attracts attention for this advertisement. Notice how the opening copy ties in with the headline.

You'll Get a Lot of Outside Help

Copywriters in a local organization do not have to depend on their brains alone for ideas. In small stores, especially, where the copywriter may be a person with a thousand jobs, outside material may be a lifesaver. In big stores or small stores, however, be careful that you don't use so much material from your merchandise sources—often called "resources"—that you forget how to turn out advertising on your own.

Agencies, manufacturers' advertising departments, newspapers, magazines—everybody wants your store to work cooperatively in promoting their products. Magazines will give you tie-in promotional material complete with copy and illustrations for use in your newspaper advertisement. Agencies and company advertising departments will send you brochures full of information, glossy prints, TV scripts and tapes, radio spots, copy ideas—and they're all yours to use or discard.

How much you will use depends upon several factors. The most important factor is the soundness of the ideas offered to you. Sometimes these outside sources forget that you are operating in local advertising. They seemingly overlook the fact that on the local level, when you talk with your chin right up against your customer's, you must be direct and careful in your use of ideas; often even more careful than in national advertising.

For instance, a national campaign on girdles and "designer" shoes may be built around the distinctiveness of a certain brand—the exclusiveness of its makers. Played up in color, in fine art treatment, such a story may be interesting and effective, and may do much to keep the firm's name connected with prestige and dignity.

On the local level, your customer is primarily interested in how those shoes will go with other outfits, and what that girdle will do for her particular figure. Out go the fancy words and tricky, cute expressions, and vague references. Your language is direct. Chances are that in all the material provided you'll find something to hang your "direct" advertisement on—something about the variety of sizes, prices, shapes, and so on and that will be your springboard.

You May Write Direct Response Advertising

You'll find that most local organizations think largely in terms of newspaper advertising. Buyers will talk about a "spread" in their favorite evening paper. Most of the store's budget will be spent in newspapers because the store can see what it's doing and can depend on reaching a healthy circulation guaranteed by the newspaper. Because it's a proved medium, you'll find that most of your time will be spent writing newspaper advertisements.

In larger stores, you'll find much use of direct response advertising. Some stores have had great success with this. Many have built big orders with simple postcards or bill inserts sent out to inform charge customers that a certain item will be offered. With no other advertising of certain items, some stores have found selling departments jammed with customers who responded to mailing pieces. Stores have also enjoyed great success in response to mailers that invited the customers to phone or mail in coupon orders.

You should understand the basic differences between

direct response and newspaper copy. Though the selling purpose may be the same, your direct response piéce may necessarily lack the forcefulness of illustration that your newspaper advertisement could command.

Size alone can make a big difference. A full newspaper page, for instance, has the wallop of a pile driver—a wallop that direct response can hardly match. Since newspapers have this impact advantage, your words, whether in letters, postcards, or inserts, must be even more carefully chosen.

Remember, although the newspaper itself had some attraction for the customer (in its news value), your insert comes entirely uninvited into the home—the letterhead or store name itself may be enough to cause it to be thrown away without being read.

Be just as specific as you can. Avoid being cute. Make your letter friendly, newsy, interesting. Get out what you have to say as quickly as you can, catching the reader's eye and imagination with a fact that is of personal interest to him. Avoid printing letters upside down or employing other such tricks. Devices of that sort only irritate and confuse.

Much material can be obtained from the manufacturer of the goods you advertise—a fact of great value to the small store, especially. Almost all companies produce mailing inserts for the use of their local outlets.

Some are given to the store free, while others can be bought on a cooperative basis. Be sure the store name is imprinted on any mailing piece you buy from a national source, and avoid mailing pieces that lack a local, personal flavor. After all, your purpose is not so much to sell the national brand, but to sell the national brand in your store.

Direct response for stores may require you to write much in addition to letters. You may do copy for postcards, illustrated invitations to fashion shows, announcements, and college booklets. You'll find an interesting variety usually.

Suggestions for Writing Local Radio Commercials

Writing for local radio is so similar to writing for national radio that there is no need to detail how to write radio copy for a store. The suggestions found in the radio chapter will apply to local radio writing.

One caution might be observed, however. You might remember that, as in the case of local newspaper advertising, you will do well to capture the local flavor in your radio commercials. You can be a shade friendlier and more intimate. The very fact that you are mentioning a local store in your copy immediately establishes a rapport difficult for the national advertiser to match.

Notice how the following radio commercial stresses the local advantages such as the strong emphasis on price, the reputation of the advertiser, and the push on "act now." Also, the writing style is more chatty and breezy than the usual national commercial.

Preston Safeway
"Double Coupon" : 60 Radio

ANNCR: OK, it's time to do the weekly grocery shopping. Time to read five or six circulars, find out what's on special where, who's got double coupons this week and who doesn't, drive all over, and hope the frozen food doesn't melt before you get home. Right? Wrong. It's time to shop Preston Safeway. Where you know you get absolute minimum prices everyday. And now, because we're absolutely committed to saving you time and money, Preston Safeway is where you can do something you can't do anywhere else. Double the value of absolutely every manufacturer's coupon—absolutely everyday. That's every manufacturer's coupon up to 50¢ in value—not just a few—but absolutely every one you use. Everyday. Not every once in a while. Double coupons with absolutely no restrictions on how many you use, absolutely everyday. Only at Preston Safeway. An absolutely better supermarket, absolutely close to home.

Figure 10–3. Straight radio commercial delivered by an announcer for a supermarket.

Wow! Here's an offer from Johnson's Jewelers that'll knock your hat off or, better yet, get you to visit Johnson's today to take advantage of a tremendous bargain. You see, Johnson's is starting its *remount* days today. This means that you can bring in your old diamond jewelry and then, while you watch, one of Johnson's experts will reset the stones in 14K yellow, or white gold, settings. The price for this includes sizing, setting, polishing, and ultrasonic cleaning. All this for prices starting as low as forty dollars. Now, you know Johnson's reputation in this area for quick, reliable work and for unexcelled low prices. Get in on this latest chance to save money. And hear this—Johnson's will *give* you a genuine diamond worth twenty-five dollars just for keeping your appointment. Phone for your appointment now at 677-8888. That's 677-8888. Remember, this is a once-a-year opportunity from Johnson's. Grab it!

Another local radio commercial is given here. Note how the writer begins with the stress on locality and ends the same way. Once more, too, price—the big local advantage—is emphasized throughout as well as a strong push for action.

People in Greene County have become used to great savings from the Vision Center in the Greene County Mall, but wait'll you hear this. Vision Center will pay you *ten dollars* to wear Bausch and Lomb Softlens contact lenses. That's right. You'll get a ten dollar rebate for wearing Bausch and Lomb Softlens contact lenses for thirty days. Here's how it works. Come in for our complete eye care package. This includes a thorough eye examination, fitting fees, the B & L lenses, followup care, and a complete care kit. Then, if you wear your Softlens contact lenses for thirty days, we'll give you a ten dollar rebate off the $99.95 price. You get the whole eye care package for the astoundingly low price of $89.95. Come see us today—right opposite the fountain in the beautiful Greene

Preston Safeway
"Photo Department Radio"

Announcer (RR) is friendly, trying to make conversation. Photographer is distracted, impatient, totally absorbed in the shoot. Shutter clicks under throughout.

SFX:	(Shutter click.)
RR:	Nice shot!
PHOTOG:	Yeah-yeah . . .
RR:	Where'll you get these developed?
PHOTOG:	just—a little more this way.
RR:	Somewhere clear across town?
PHOTOG:	Not that far. (Click.)
RR:	A store that makes you buy two prints . . .
PHOTOG:	No, no. . . .
RR:	when all you want is one?
PHOTOG:	Loosen up.
RR:	One where you wait in line to drop your film,
PHOTOG:	Okay-don't-move. . . .
RR:	then wait a week to get your prints?
PHOTOG:	Hoooo-oold-it.
RR:	Or someplace that charges a fortune for what's *supposed* to be great developing?
PHOTOG:	This is no good. (Yelling off-mike.) Can we get some makeup over here?
RR:	Why not go to Presto Photo at Preston Safeway?
PHOTOG:	H-mmmmm.
RR:	Presto Photo at Preston Safeway.
PHOTOG:	That's better.
RR:	At Preston Safeway's Presto Photo, you never wait in line.
	(Click-click-click-click-click.)
RR:	You get top quality Kodak Colorwatch processing . . .
PHOTOG:	Big smile!
RR:	and *your choice* of single, double or super four-inch prints.
PHOTOG:	Okay, just give me a lot of different looks, real fast.
RR:	And Presto Photo gets your prints back in two days or less.
PHOTOG:	One more. . .
RR:	Presto Photo at Preston Safeway gives you *absolute minimum prices* on processing,
PHOTOG:	That's good, that's good!
RR:	*and* on film.
PHOTOG:	Let's shoot another roll.
RR:	Presto Photo at Preston Safeway. An absolutely *better* photo store, absolutely close to home.
	(Click!)

Figure 10–4. Two-voice radio commercial for a supermarket.

> County Mall. That's the Vision Center where we care for your eyes *and* your budget.

If a department store is a heavy user of local radio, it may air numerous spots. Short commercials will be mixed in with regular-length commercials, especially when some special event is being featured. The following short commercial is typical:

> Dress up that porch or patio, and do it at bargain prices during Steuart's summer clearance sale. Prices that were $120 to $450 are now $59 to $219. Select from wrought iron or aluminum in chairs, loveseats, cocktail and end tables. Limited quantities means you'd better come to Steuart's *today* to take your pick of summer furniture bargains. Nine to five every day in Steuart's second floor furniture department.

Even though short, such a commercial should include item descriptions, prices, store hours, and the department in which the item is sold.

Local commercials are usually quite enthusiastic and fairly hard-driving. How much pressure is exerted depends upon the nature of the account and the kind of radio station airing the material. A used-car dealer, a price-cutting supermarket, or a discount house are usually pushy in their approach. The talk may be fast and the selling quite forceful, especially if the commercials are aired on a rock station that features super-glib announcers who maintain a mad pace all day long.

On the other hand, hotels, banks, and insurance agents are normally low key. You'll slow the pace and avoid any sense of pressure. This doesn't mean that you won't incorporate the urge to act or that you won't write enthusiastic copy. How you judge the dividing line between high pressure and permissible enthusiasm is something you'll learn with experience. Sometimes, the advertiser you're writing for will tell you when you've stepped over the line.

Still another factor that influences how you write local radio commercials is the announcer. Sometimes, of course, you don't know who will be announcing what you write. If you do, you should write for the style of that announcer. Some are better at hard-sell commercials with fast-paced deliveries. Others are sincere, slower-talking persons. Some will deliver humor deftly; others have a heavy touch unsuited for humor.

In a local market you soon become acquainted with all local announcers. Study them. Capitalize on their strengths; avoid their weaknesses. If you supervise taping sessions where announcers are doing commercials you've written, talk to the announcers. Find out what they like and don't like. Get their suggestions. You'll discover that they have strong opinions about writers of the commercials they deliver. As professionals, announcers have much to tell you that will make you a better radio writer.

What's the likelihood of your writing local radio commercials? If you're working for an advertising agency handling local accounts such as banks or department stores, you may do a lot because banks and department stores hire agencies for such writing. Conversely, if you're working for the bank or the department store, you'll usually have no chance to write radio commercials.

If you're working for smaller organizations such as hardware stores, shoe stores, or independent drug stores, you'll find that such writing is often handled by the radio stations that have copywriters for the small budget advertisers. Copywriters in these stations crank out volumes of commercials, often of unimpressive quality.

Limited Budgets for Local Television Commercials

Naturally, every local enterprise is fascinated by the thought of using television advertising, but the majority of such enterprises simply cannot afford to be on the air frequently enough, or long enough, to make an impression on the market.

Unless they're in a big-city market, those who can afford the medium rarely use the expensive commercials that are customary with national advertisers. No fancy animation. No expensive live-action commercials using big name stars and exotic location shots.

Local copywriters create television within the framework of a limited production budget. Occasionally, they may call for live studio shots, or open-end syndicated materials. Also, co-op commercials may be supplied by the advertisers. These supply information about advertisers' products but allow cut-ins for local identification.

You'll depend upon your local television stations' production facilities for talent and mechanical equipment. You may draw upon their stock shot collection and their musical library and, of course, if you happen to shoot any live-action studio material, you may use station announcers.

Great improvements continue in videotape, however, with the present use of smaller, more versatile and flexible cameras; and stations of almost any size are prepared to offer videotape facilities. Such facilities bring down costs, thus making possible more use of local television advertising. Furthermore, optical effects, now possible with videotape, are available to local advertisers.

On the local level, in bank advertising especially, the copywriter may make heavy use of bank personnel as presenters. Presidents, tellers, vice-presidents, and other personnel may appear before the camera, as well as customers or well-known local personalities who speak in behalf of the bank. If these presenters are not amateurish, they can be effective. Their use ensures a local flavor that is desirable. Videotape with its instant playback gives the production people a chance to go over the announcement enough times with the amateur talent to ultimately come out with a commercial that looks reasonably professional.

In the case of big-budget banks and department stores, the advertising money allowed for television may be sufficient to permit the use of a first class production house. Accordingly, if you're writing for such an advertiser, you can call for the sort of production used by national advertisers. Normally, however, you'll be using creative procedures that hold down costs, which are always very much on the mind of local television users.

Here are some suggestions for the writer of modestly priced local commercials:

- A commercial should star the product or service, use the camera skillfully, and avoid the use of high-priced on-camera talent.
- Use a good voice—male or female—for voiceover presentation, even though the general rule is that on-camera voice is more effective.
- Develop a distinctive logo.
- If several commercials are to be used, produce them all at one session to cut production costs.
- Use music in public domain.
- Shoot in 16mm instead of 35mm.
- Hold down editing or use no editing in videotaped commercials.
- Use actual advertisements for artwork, as is often done on local shows in which commercials are presented live by station announcers.
- Sometimes call for suitable stock shots such as crowd scenes, historical moments, personalities, nature scenes.

What you have read in the material under the heading of local television advertising has been slanted toward the cost-cutting aspect of television commercial writing. This section is quite brief because later in this book there are two chapters on television advertising that cover most of what you need to know. While those chapters zero in on national advertising, most of the principles apply to local television commercial writing, also.

The big difference, however, is that you are severely restricted when writing for local advertisers by how much your commercials will cost. While budget and cost is a factor on the national level, the national advertiser is thinking in tens of thousands of dollars while you (or the local advertiser) may be thinking in hundreds of dollars. This has quite an influence on your approach.

Here's What You'll Do before and during the Writing of a Local Advertisement

Now to get down to the actual procedure of writing an advertisement. Suppose the buyer of women's shoes has an advertisement on her schedule and that she's supposed to have her "buyer's copy" up to you by a certain date (you usually will work anywhere from six to fourteen days ahead of publication date).

Ultimately, after the buyer has sent her material through her own merchandise manager and then through the advertising manager, you and the other staff members will discuss this advertisement along with others when you confer about advertisements about to be put into work.

Some stores may have such discussions for each advertisement. Others may simply determine general treatment for a group or series of advertisements and leave it up to the copywriter to develop copy for individual advertisements according to this overall plan. General copy meetings in such stores may be called only for special promotions.

During your meeting, suggestions for treatment may come from any of the copywriters, from the advertising manager, from the art director, from the production manager—from any advertising person at the copy meeting. Perhaps it may be decided that the advertisement is to be hard selling, that it will emphasize the variety of styles.

You and the art director will discuss the tie-in of illustration and copy. You'll agree that the illustration should feature many shoe styles. You are to write captions for the numerous shoes pictured. After much discussion, you leave the meeting with a rough idea of the copy and art approach. You're ready to go to work.

Talk to the Art Department

One of your most important jobs at this point is telling the art department what sort of layout treatment the advertisement requires. You discuss the merchandise being advertised, suggest the type and the number of sketches, tell what your headlines and subheads will be—even prepare a rough layout or thumbnail sketch of the advertisement. This last item will be even more vital in a smaller store where the copywriter may be called on to turn in a complete "visual" of the advertisement.

The instructions to the art department are not the final word, of course, since the layout must be approved by the advertising manager before any finished art can be started.

The ideal way to tell the art department exactly what you have in mind is to write every word that you want to have in the advertisement. The layout person then knows how much of a copy block you need, how many and how long the display lines must be, how many items you will have in a listing of merchandise, how many figures must be illustrated, and so on.

Your providing the actual copy assures you that the layout you get from the art department will be much closer to your wishes than if you had merely turned in some vague directions about "large copy block required," or "big display head," or "generous copy space."

If you were the artist, what would "generous" mean to you? Just as you need complete information from your buyer in order to describe the merchandise, the layout people need complete information in order to turn out the right layout for the merchandise.

Remember, however, that many stores do their artwork first and then the copywriter goes to work. In such stores you would write copy that would fit the character of the artwork, and that would fit into the space that wasn't taken up by illustration. As a copywriter, it is much more satisfactory to work in the situation where you, rather than the illustrator, will be controlling the makeup of the advertisement.

Unfortunately, there are probably more stores in which the art treatment comes first. You might as well realize this right now and be prepared to adjust yourself to playing second fiddle to the art department if you happen to land in a store that gives the art people principal authority in the construction of advertisement.

All right: the layout's made and approved, and the art is to be prepared. In this case the shoes were photographed in the photographer's studio after the buyer had delivered them to the studio. In the case of big items, such as furniture, the photograph will usually be taken after hours in the department involved. If you can, it's desirable for you to be around when your merchandise is being photographed or sketched. You might be able to make useful suggestions.

You Write—and Perhaps You Rewrite

While all this art activity is going on, you're supposed to be writing the copy. In large departments you'll be given a copy of the layout as it was actually approved, and the headlines will be represented properly along with copy space and listings.

Perhaps you may have some simple adjustments to make. You may need to cut your copy slightly or change your headline somewhat. The important thing is that this layout is no stranger to you. Most of your planned thinking has been done.

Sometimes, of course, your original ideas may be thrown out completely and you will have to start from scratch when you receive the final layout. Now assume that this is the case with the advertisement in question. You had what you thought was a fine idea but someone along the line—the advertising manager, or sectional manager, or perhaps both—caused your fine idea to be dropped into the wastebasket. Now you see the fresh layout in front of you. You're really starting all over again because a new slant has been thrown at you.

Go Over Your Buyer's Copy Again

Pick up the buyer's copy—the sheets containing all the information that the shoe buyer had to offer. First ask yourself: What am I selling? No, the answer isn't shoes alone, because everybody sells shoes. What's the idea behind this advertisement? What's the story behind all the illegible writing on the buyer's sheet?

Dig down into the buyer's copy. Digest what was given to you. Call her up or go see her. Ask to see the shoes. Ask to see any manufacturer's data on the product or any promotional material. Why does she want to advertise these shoes? How does she happen to have this merchandise? Is it a new brand, a special price, a new idea? *Get all the facts before you sit down to write.*

At Last! You're Ready to Write the Final Copy

Although you may have all the information you need, you might, as a newly minted copywriter, want to make a checklist that will put down those facts in order of importance and in the order you will present them. Then, when you write, you can refer to the list to keep yourself on track. Such a checklist is useful for broadcast copy, direct mail, or newspaper copy.

Obviously, if you're under great pressure, you'll be in too much of a hurry to operate with a checklist. You'll simply start writing. But if you have time, try the checklist. After you've had some experience, you'll be so adept you'll scorn checklists, but if you're a beginner, they can help you.

When you take all the preliminary steps discussed—the talk with the art department, the talk with the buyer, the rechecking of product facts, and the making of a checklist, you'll find that the copy will usually not cause you much trouble because you've prepared so well. Good copy is harder to achieve when you dash into it.

There's been no discussion of headlines, because most stores seem to be content to write label headlines that simply identify the merchandise. Creative headline writing is not common for most retail advertisements, but if you can persuade your superiors to let you try creative, selling headlines, both you and the store will profit.

So How Do You Handle an Advertisement That Offers More Than One Item or Many Items?

Up to this point the stress has been on how to write single-item advertisements, but a department store with many items to sell frequently features a number of items in one advertisement.

For clarity, the multi-item advertisement is described here as an advertisement containing three or four strongly related products. The omnibus advertisement, taking up a larger space of possibly a page or two pages, will include numerous items, far more than the multi-item advertisement.

When you write a *multi-item,* follow certain procedures for top results: (a) Write a strong selling headline that expresses the commonality of the products, and you might use a strong main subhead immediately under the main headline. (b) Write an opening copy block that sells the items as a whole and sets the tone for the entire advertisement. (c) Write strong selling subheads for each of the copy blocks that sell the individual items. These subheads will carry the reader through the advertisement. (d) Write the copy blocks and, in them, sell the big points for each item. Each copy block will contain information about the department selling the item.

Layout is important in the multi-item advertisement. Work with the artist in the judicious placing of elements—prices, product labels, and others.

As for the *omnibus* advertisement, supply a headline that ties the advertisement together. Unlike the multi-item headline, this one won't have a close relationship to every product because you'll usually have a hodge-podge of product types in an omnibus advertisement.

If time and space permit, write selling subheads for each product section. Try to avoid the impersonal, telegraphic writing so often characteristic of item copy in omnibus advertisements.

Possibly some of the items can be related to other products, as in the case of ski equipment, golf equipment, men's apparel, and others. Make the connection in such cases.

Perhaps your omnibus advertisement carries the headline WINTER CLEARANCE SALE. In such a case all the products will be cold-weather-related, even if they're not closely related to each other. Thus, you'll have a common theme of cold weather and low prices, even with greatly different products.

You Can Be Important in the Department Store Structure

You're a vital part of the selling process in a big department store, but you may sometimes feel insignificant as you contemplate that big superstructure over you—all those buyers, managers, and others who see, supervise, and criticize your work.

A department store is a subtle, vital organism, composed of many parts. You find immediately that you must learn those parts and how to fit your skills and efforts into this complicated structure of which you've become one of the smaller parts. Always, however, you have the ultimate comfort.

Your words are going to be visible on those newspaper pages or in the direct response pieces. If they're clever, bouncy, persuasive, elegant, *selling* words, they'll be noticed. And if you turn them out day after day, you can be assured that, no matter how massive the retail structure, you're going to get recognition and an escape from anonymity.

Marshall Field's

CREATIVE FIELD'S
ADVERTISING FACT SHEET

SERIAL NO. 143928
AD NO. 3MAG5
JOB NO.

- PLEASE TYPE OR BLOCK PRINT ALL INFORMATION AND DELIVER COMPLETED FORM WITH MERCHANDISE SAMPLES, LOAN BILL AND VENDOR DEBIT TO *CREATIVE FIELD'S*, NINTH FLOOR, STATE STREET.
- FAILURE TO COMPLY WITH ALL OF THE ABOVE WILL RESULT IN A POSTPONEMENT OF THIS AD.

AD DATE March '87	MEDIUM "M" magazine	AD SIZE full page	☐ BLACK/WHITE ☒ COLOR
AIR DATE IF BROADCAST	DEPT. NAME Men's Casual Outerwear		SEC. NO. 464
BUYER'S NAME N. F. Newport		TELEPHONE EXT. 3949	CAMPAIGN OR FORMAT magazine
VENDOR NAME Davidsson		MERCHANDISE DESCRIPTION Men's Casual Outerwear	

CHIEF SELLING POINT OR CUSTOMER BENEFIT (ARE ADDITIONAL DESCRIPTION PAGES ATTACHED ☐ YES ☐ NO)

--From Iceland--Davidson outerwear
--Created by designer Jan Davidsson
--Crinkle nylon fabric resists wind and water
--Oversized silhouettes provide freedom of movement
** Show on models with white T-shirts and Timberland boots and boot socks

IS THIS A PRICE STORY ☐ YES ☐ NO IF YES, EMPHASIZE ☐ % OFF ☐ PRICE POINT ☐ PERMANENT MARKDOWN ☐ TEMPORARY MARKDOWN ☐ POINT OF SALE ☐ SPECIAL PURCHASE INDICATE PRINCIPAL SELLING POINTS IN ORDER OF IMPORTANCE:
1.
2.
3.
4.

PLEASE CHECK TARGET CUSTOMER

	OPENING	MODERATE	BETTER	BEST
TRADITIONAL/CLASSIC				
UPDATE		XX		
CONTEMPORARY				
JUNIOR				

SPECIFIC VENDOR REQUIREMENTS (I.E. TRADEMARKS, HEADLINES, ETC.)

ITEM Crinkle nylon jacket 3-tone -- 100% nylon	ITEM Crinkle nylon pant --solid-- 100% nylon
STOCK # W/CHECK DIGIT # 2004 / TOTAL UNITS / PREP	STOCK # W/CHECK DIGIT # 2016 / TOTAL UNITS / PREP
CLASS # W/CHECK DIGIT # / COMPARATIVE PRICE $ INDICATE COMPARATIVE: ☐ REG. ☐ ORIG. ☐ OTHER 115.00	CLASS # W/CHECK DIGIT # / COMPARATIVE PRICE $ INDICATE COMPARATIVE: ☐ REG. ☐ ORIG. ☐ OTHER 50.00
HOUSE # W/CHECK DIGIT # / PROMOTIONAL PRICE $ ___ % REDUCTION ___%	HOUSE # W/CHECK DIGIT # / PROMOTIONAL PRICE $ ___ % REDUCTION ___%
SIZE S-XL COLORS Ass't / $ PREP 84.4	SIZE M-XL COLORS Ass't. / $ PREP 17.3
COUNTRY MATERIALS ARE FROM Italy / COUNTRY MATERIALS ARE ASSEMBLED IN Iceland	COUNTRY MATERIALS ARE FROM Italy / COUNTRY MATERIALS ARE ASSEMBLED IN Iceland
IS MERCHANDISE EXCLUSIVE WITH US IN ☐ ILLINOIS ☐ TEXAS ☐ WISC ☐ USA	IS MERCHANDISE EXCLUSIVE WITH US IN ☐ ILLINOIS ☐ TEXAS ☐ WISC ☐ USA
ITEM Crinkle nylon pullover jacket 3 tone--100% nylon	ITEM Crinkle nylon short--2 tone--100% nylon
STOCK # W/CHECK DIGIT # 2006 / TOTAL UNITS / PREP	STOCK # W/CHECK DIGIT # 2018 / TOTAL UNITS / PREP
CLASS # W/CHECK DIGIT # / COMPARATIVE PRICE $ INDICATE COMPARATIVE: ☐ REG. ☐ ORIG. ☐ OTHER 105.00	CLASS # W/CHECK DIGIT # / COMPARATIVE PRICE $ INDICATE COMPARATIVE: ☐ REG. ☐ ORIG. ☐ OTHER 40.00
HOUSE # W/CHECK DIGIT # / PROMOTIONAL PRICE $ ___ % REDUCTION ___%	HOUSE # W/CHECK DIGIT # / PROMOTIONAL PRICE $ ___ % REDUCTION ___%
SIZE S-XL COLORS Ass't. / $ PREP 46.2	SIZE M-XL COLORS Ass't. / $ PREP 18.7
COUNTRY MATERIALS ARE FROM Italy / COUNTRY MATERIALS ARE ASSEMBLED IN Iceland	COUNTRY MATERIALS ARE FROM Italy / COUNTRY MATERIALS ARE ASSEMBLED IN Iceland
IS MERCHANDISE EXCLUSIVE WITH US IN ☐ ILLINOIS ☐ TEXAS ☐ WISC ☐ USA	IS MERCHANDISE EXCLUSIVE WITH US IN ☐ ILLINOIS ☐ TEXAS ☐ WISC ☐ USA

IS THERE AN EVENT TIE IN? YES ___ NO ___ | NEWSPAPER LOAN BILL NO. 31758 | TELEVISION LOAN BILL NO.
IF SO, WHAT? | OLD ART (ATTACHED COPY OF TEAR SHEET) PICK-UP DATE | MEDIUM | DATE SELLING BEGINS | DATE SELLING ENDS

WHICH OF THE FOLLOWING SHOULD BE INCLUDED IN THE AD ☐ CLUB PLAN ☐ BRIDAL REGISTRY ☐ FIELD'S FASHION SERVICE ☐ CARRIAGE TRADE ☐ HOME PLAN ☐ MAIL ORDER BLANK ☐ PERSONAL SHOPPING SERVICE ☐ ___

MERCHANDISE AVAILABLE AT

STORE										TOTAL UNIT PREP
ILLINOIS	☒ SS	☒ OR	☒ OA	☒ WT	☒ WF	☒ RO	☒ HC	☒ FX	☒ OL	TOTAL $ PREP 166.6 ORDER #
	☒ BD	☒ CV	☒ PF	☒ SM	☒ JL	☒ LF	☐	☐	☐	BASIC STOCK
WISCONSIN	☒ M	☒ GA	☒ SR	☒ NR	☒ AP	☒ HD	☐	☐	☐	
TEXAS	☒ TG	☒ DG	☒ TW	☒ SA	☐	☐	☐	☐	☐	ON HAND ___ OTHER ___

SUBURBAN AD PICK-UP

STORE	DATE	MEDIUM	UNITS	$ PREP	SIZE	VENDOR DOLLARS	AD NO.	STORE	DATE	MEDIUM	UNITS	$ PREP	SIZE	VENDOR DOLLARS	AD NO.
☐ RO								☐ AP							
☐ SM								☐ HD							
☐ CV								☐ TG/TW							
☐ LJ								☐ DG							
☐ MIL								☐ SA							

I HEREBY CERTIFY THAT ALL THE STATEMENTS ON THE ADVERTISING FACT SHEET ARE TRUE. I FURTHER CERTIFY THAT I HAVE NOT OMITTED ANY FACT WHICH AFFECTS THE TRUTH OF THE ADVERTISEMENT. I ALSO CERTIFY THAT THE FABRIC CONTENT AND COUNTRY OF ORIGIN ARE CORRECT.

BUYER'S SIGNATURE NF Newport DATE 11/21/86
DMM SIGNATURE DATE
GROSS / VENDOR / NET

43-01 F12A 10/86

ACCOUNT EXECUTIVE

Figure 10–5. Filled-out buyer's fact sheet (also called buyer's copy). A department store's buyer fills this out and sends it on to advertising where the copywriter looks it over and then starts writing. If the buyer has been conscientious in supplying full information, the copywriter may need no more help. If, however, as sometimes happens, the buyer has provided only sketchy information, the copywriter may need to speak personally with the buyer and/or check out the merchandise in person. Teamwork between the buyer and the copywriter is important for a smooth operation.

You have three bosses. You have three bosses in retail advertising—your advertising boss, the buyer who buys the merchandise, and the salesperson who stands behind the counter selling the goods you're writing about. If the salesperson works on a bonus or percentage basis, his or her very living may depend upon the skill with which you do your job—that increases your importance, too. Local copy can't be written without a close relationship between the copywriter and the store personnel inside and outside the advertising department.

You will find in the following material a description of some of the activity going on about you in a typical department store. You will find more details of the work of those people who are so important to you, such as the advertising manager, the buyer, and the comparison shopper.

Key Persons in the Department Store Structure

Examine the organization of a large department store to get an idea of the extent of your copywriting duties. Keep in mind, too, that despite differences stemming from the type and size of the store, the advertising budget, and the size of the advertising department, the situation is basically the same in all local establishments.

Advertising managers. Advertising managers oversee the entire advertising operation and plan future campaigns on a top-management level. In direct contact with the store manager, in most cases, they translate management's wishes into actual printed or spoken advertising. Many times they are "yes-men" to management. Other times they may come up with fine ideas which they sell to management.

Advertising managers usually make up the entire month's advertising schedule in advance—or they might even plan two or three months ahead. All advertising goes through their hands for final approval, whether it's a newspaper advertisement, a television or radio commercial, or a mailing insert. They control all personnel in the advertising department, including you.

Section chiefs. Large department stores often employ section chiefs or divisional advertising managers to head the various copy sections such as homewares, men's furnishings, downstairs store, fashions, and others. These people are responsible for actual planning within their divisions. They work with buyers and their merchandise managers, check advertisements as they are written by copywriters, consult with the art department on layout suggestions and art treatment. In effect, they are the advertising managers for a group of "clients" within a division of the store.

Merchandise managers. Each major division within the store has a merchandise manager who may control as many as thirty buyers. Such managers are responsible for buyers' buying plans and their spending and sales figures. In an advertising sense, the merchandise manager's job is to allocate money from a monthly budget to the various departments in his or her division. Merchandise managers also turn in a tentative monthly schedule to the advertising manager that is used to make up the entire store's schedule for the coming period.

Merchandise managers pass on individual advertisements for their departments and see that buyers provide full information to the copywriters preparing the advertising.

Buyers. These men and women go into the market to buy the goods you write about. Some of them gladly cooperate with the writers who must turn out selling copy about their goods. They provide "buyer's copy" to tell the writer about merchandise.

The buyers can give the copywriter every chance to see, feel, try, and test the goods. They are, in a sense, the copywriter's clients. You will respect their wishes as long as they result in good advertising.

Regrettably, a good many buyers give copywriters the poorest kind of cooperation. They must be begged for information. Not seeming to care about the copywriter's side, they give information only about the obvious things such as colors, sizes, and prices.

Your job will require you to dig for more than these bare facts. Desperately you may hound the buyers for more help than the scanty facts they give you in their buyer's copy. Though some buyers will be a real help to you, rely on your own effort and ingenuity to get facts for writing your copy.

Buyers have their own problems to worry about and copywriting is not among them. If they give you complete information—fine. If they don't, you get it yourself.

Comparison shoppers. Almost all large stores maintain a comparison shopping department to check the truthfulness of statements made in the store's advertisements, to determine whether quantities of merchandise on hand warrant advertising, to act as liaison between the buyer and the advertising department, and to shop in other stores in the community for comparable values and comparative store activity. "Comparison" usually has the final word on all advertising, especially on descriptions that may go counter to policies of the store and trade principles as laid down by the Better Business Bureau.

In addition to being in contact with the buyers, section managers, and the others mentioned during the advertising day, you will also work closely with the *art director,* who is responsible for layouts, finished art, and photographs; the *production manager,* who marks the type, handles the proofs, enters corrections, and sends all material to the newspapers; the *clerk,* who controls the flow of merchandise that is sent up for sketching or photography.

As you can see, a great many people contribute to the preparation of every advertisement, from the warehouseperson who hauled furniture for a camera shot to the clerk who checked copy for accuracy. The combined activity is slanted toward one end—to create advertisements that produce—advertisements that sell!

You May Be Busy-Busy-Busy If You Work for a Small Store

An advertising major, having been graduated from college, began work with a small store as a copywriter. Eventually, though somewhat dazed, she reported that, sure enough, she *did* write copy, but also she did all the layouts, planned the monthly advertising schedules, gave the space orders to the newspapers, and worked with the store manager in determining the advertising budget.

And this "copywriter" also filled in as a salesclerk at busy times, put up window displays and, when time was heavy on her hands, talked on fashion trends to local women's groups.

Although all small or medium-sized stores might not expect so much from their young copywriters, you may well find, if you work for a small establishment, that writing copy is just one of your activities.

Be prepared to be a copywriter, advertising manager, production chief, media buyer, and display manager rolled up into one very busy person. Often in such a position you will not write much original copy. A good portion of your writing will consist of revising, shortening, or lengthening the "canned" copy that accompanies the material from the manufacturer of the goods you are advertising.

Many small stores depend upon art services and proof books to provide them with layout and copy ideas. Very often, also, small stores let their newspapers do copy-layout work for them. If you land in a store like that, you won't find much challenge to your copywriting ability. In other stores, however, you may write much copy, since you will wish to key your advertisements to the local situation. You may use outside material, but just as an occasional help.

One thing you can almost be certain of: in a small store you will usually find that there is not enough copywriting to fill all your working hours. This means you will fill out the rest of the time doing practically anything that comes along.

11

THE MARVELOUS, ZANY, CHANGING WORLD OF FASHION ADVERTISING

Dorothea Chandler had always wanted to write fashion advertising. As she said, when she applied for a copy job in a smart, Fifth Avenue shop: "I've always been crazy about clothes—what's new, what's going to happen this year and next year. I want to be a part of this business of leading the fashion parade. Maybe that's what I like most of all, a chance to influence new trends."

Early in her study of fashion advertising Dorothea realized the subtlety of the field, so different from the hard reality of selling a garbage disposal, a dishwasher, or a clothes dryer. Copy for fashion items evokes images, a state of mind, an emotional response even if the subject of the copy is something so mundane as a winter coat, dress shoes, or a sweater.

There's a magic in the terms and names you and the Dorothea Chandlers meet in the world of high fashion. It may be famous designers such as Bill Blass, Dior, Halston, Calvin Klein, Pierre Cardin, and Ralph Lauren. It may be famous fashion centers: B. Altman, Saks, Bergdorf Goodman, Bonwit Teller, Givenchy, J.G. Hook. It may be the magazines that carry the exotic names and styles of fashion: *Vogue, Town & Country, Harper's Bazaar, Glamour, Mademoiselle.*

Even the language is different in this world. Writers of fashion advertising and poets have much in common. Both can twist the language into marvelous, often zany, shapes. Their use of imagery and mood sets them apart from ordinary mortals whose writing is earthbound. A poet's departure from conventional paths can be viewed indulgently. "Poetic license" excuses much. A similar tolerance is extended to the fashion copywriter.

Most men and women do not understand much of the language of fashion advertising. Comprehension of the oftentimes stilted, haughty phrases is, however, not required. What cannot be understood may be felt, which is often more important than literal understanding.

If you have worked up a comfortable set of rules to guide you in copywriting, you'd better drop them in the bottom drawer of the file before you begin writing fashion copy. Good creative techniques for fashion promotion can be radically different from acceptable techniques for selling ordinary goods and services. You are entering a new creative world when you begin a fashion-copy career.

Full of Fancy, Full of Facts, Too. How Can This Be?

Anyone who enters fashion advertising thinking, however, that it consists of nothing more than creating mood and a series of airy, somewhat silly phrases will soon be disabused of this notion. True, fashion advertising writing can use a flip, mode (or mod) language, but the moment of truth arrives when facts must be given and the fashion writer then employs tough, resultful, reason-why copy. The writer knows that the reader can't base a buying decision on fluff.

For example, what other copywriting world inspires such prose as the following from one of the fashion magazines?

> Night hybrid in bloom,
> botanically inspired.
> A bejeweled bud
> gathers double ripples
> of this yellow chiffon
> jersey struck with
> shimmering dew drops.

Such copywriting isn't learned in school, nor by writers for more prosaic products. It derives from a long exposure to and deep love of fashion and from a knowledge of words that trigger response.

Most fashion copy, however, is not so totally fanciful as the example just given. Most is written partly in the language expected of fashion advertising and partly in practical, reasons-to-buy language, as shown in the following:

> You're going to love "The Fuzz." It just might be the world's softest tunic. Also could be the world's most comfortable fashion-thing. You'll believe it when you touch it. Feels like whipped cream. Soft because of the blend: lambswool, angora, and nylon. Soft because of the cut: full, flowy sleeves, shirt-tail bottom, seven-button neckline you can open as wide as you want to. Soft because of the color: foamy heather gray. You'll wear it at the office, on country weekends, maybe even (with a bright sash and slim pants) to dinner parties. In other words, you shouldn't try to live without this tip-top tunic by Vesna Bricelj for Overture.

Added power is given to the foregoing copy in its very pronounced involvement of the reader by picturing the various uses for the product.

Here's another example of the skillful fashion writer's ability to combine almost poetic fantasy with the practical. While the opening lines are almost pure fantasy, notice the weaving in of practical details in the last few lines.

> Let Halston light up your nights with his new dazzler, "Firefly." Fiery red sparklers, catching light, reflecting light, surrounding you with high-voltage, electric-bright excitement. These glimmering bugle beads are stitched (by hand, of course) on a soft little body-contoured cardigan of midnight black silk chiffon. Underneath, an understatement of slim pants and surplice halter, both in pure black crepe of rayon and acetate. All, sizes 6 to 14.

Added strength is given to this copy by the featuring of a famous designer.

Learn What Fashion Is before You Write Fashion Copy

What is fashion copywriting, and how can you learn to write it successfully? Like all other types of copy, it has its tricks. You must learn those tricks. Also, before you can learn to write fashion copy, you must first learn what fashion is. At the outset, then, you will pursue the elusive fashion.

Perhaps you'd better start by thinking of fashion (a) as exemplified in high fashion periodicals and in advertisements for exclusive stores, and (b) as exemplified in volume selling in department and moderate-price stores. When you have thought about these two divisions of fashion, you will be ready to absorb a few do's and don'ts of fashion writing.

You probably have surmised already that fashion is a capricious commodity. What is and what is not fashion almost defies analysis. Every few years some scholar comes out of research activities to write a new and learned treatise proving that fashions stem from wars and the general economy of a country.

In the broad, overall view she's probably right. However, in view of fashion's inherent ephemeral quality and because the motives and causes underlying changes in fashion are as subject to change as the fashions themselves, it is of no great importance to pin it down, dissect it, and catalog its component parts.

Consider what happened to fashion after World Wars I and II. When women began bobbing their hair after the first war, it was supposedly to assert equality with men by looking more boyish. It was even argued that since women had shared the hardships of war as Red Cross workers, nurses, and so forth, they intended to share the rewards.

Ostensibly, the generalization to be drawn from this example is that women express their emancipation after a war through more masculine fashions, but this analysis does not work out. Many thousands of women also served in World War II. Again, when the war was over, they swarmed to have their hair cut shorter. This time the motive was changed. They clipped it off not to look more boyish but to achieve a fluffy, feminine look.

The war had made fashion static, imposed regulations, prescribed tailored suits, demanded practical, mannish clothes. The outburst of the new, the curved, the longer skirted silhouette, as well as of the short coiffures, was an expression not for equality, but against the deadly regimentation of war.

More recently has been the feminism movement, the era of the working woman, of the woman who lives alone and likes it, of independence and great gains of women in politics, business, and science, of the seating of a woman on the U.S. Supreme Court. Such dynamism affects and influences fashion.

A Woman Has an Advantage in Selling Fashion

The approach in fashion is so personal that many feel that it takes a female copywriter to sell another woman. A man can understand how important it is to a woman to wear a skirt three inches longer (or three inches shorter) than last season, but he's at a distinct disadvantage in having to guess how she *feels* in it. A woman knows. She sells the feel of fashion, of low waists or high waists, flared skirts or straight skirts, or whatever, almost before she sells the specific merchandise.

Fashion moves in cycles. If you're an aspirant for a

Figure 11–1. Fashion advertisement for men. In this instance, the copy and illustration aim at men on the move—in business or the professions. Quietly and richly conservative describes the tone of the advertisement.

top job in fashion copy, you'll need to read as much as possible about the clothes of all periods. While you're at it, you'll profit also from exposure to the humanities, history, literature, and the economics of the world. Writing fashion advertising is less inspiration than it is a comprehensive knowledge of what made the world turn in Cleopatra's time and what keeps it spinning today.

Fashion is emotion. You must live with it. It is your job to begin where the photograph or illustration leaves off. Your work is good when you give the reader the feel of fashion, when you make a coming event inviting by letting your reader know how it will feel to appear in an original by Yves Saint Laurent.

There's Fun (and Pain) in Keeping Up with Fashion

Keeping up with fashion is your joy and despair. One moment it's the peasant look, at prices far beyond the "peasant's" ability to pay. Gone is the tunic over pants and the graceful drape of chiffon. Suddenly, the sumptuous look takes over in place of the simple chiffon or jersey dress. "Importance" has become the word.

Because the dress must look important, the swing may be to velour fabrics. For originals, the price is important, too, at $950 (less, of course, in copies). So understated elegance is out, and the change can occur at a dizzying pace. For example, one high fashion store, less than two weeks after a Paris showing by a renowned designer, presented the new style in New York. Eight dresses at $500 were sold the first day and the store continued to sell the new fashion at the same brisk pace.

Positive fashion images can be created by important events, such as a change in the White House or a royal wedding in England, two events that caused one designer to declare that the future fashion image would be rich, warm, and gala. Looking ahead, the designer saw clothes as young, sometimes very sophisticated, and rather stately.

At the same time, other designers were envisioning clothes as more softly feminine than in recent years, with flowing skirts, ruffled dresses, and an opulent theme. But who really knows what can happen two years ahead? Fashion runs from season to season with dramatic changes possible between seasons.

Unless your antennae are quivering ceaselessly, significant changes may catch you unawares. When they occur, you need to call upon new words and to evoke new moods. Meanwhile, amidst all the newly coined elegance, you may still be selling designer jeans with a fashion flair and at prices unmistakably in the fashion range.

For Fashion, the Word is Mercurial

Nothing demonstrates the mercurial nature of the fashion cycle better than the lightning adoption in 1987 of daring new styles that featured, above all, knee-revealing short skirts. Seemingly, there was almost a rebellion against the "success" look, the conservative approach to dressing adopted by women intent on career advancement.

Suddenly, women's fashions were more feminine, sometimes outrageously so, with skirts high above the knees, bubble dresses, flounced and ruffled styles. At the time, surprised suppliers made such statements as: "It swept the country overnight" and "It was a change." That's what fashion is all about: change.

Even *within* change there is change, as demonstrated by the combination of stretch fabrics and short skirt lengths. One designer, for example, alternated short skirts with snug, long pants making it hard for the observer to judge whether a woman was in trousers or a miniskirt.

Experimentation is what fashion change is all about. When radical new styles appear, it is the result of experimenting both by the designers and the women who wear the styles. These are the bolder spirits. Still, as in the 1987 switch to shorter skirts, there are many who will not change so the writer of fashion advertising will be writing to a considerable number of women who simply don't want to expose their knees and who know that because of maturity or body build, or both, they would look ridiculous in the extreme new styles. Then, too, what might be worn socially is rejected for office wear. Above-the-knee skirts find little acceptance by the working woman.

Sooner, or later, the fashion pendulum will swing the other way again. With this change there will be a change in fashion writing once more. Volatility is the very essence of fashion. As a fashion writer you anticipate change, welcome it, and adjust to it. These dizzy swings to and fro make your job ever-interesting, ever-challenging.

So much for fashion in general. Now, to point up the distinctions between high fashion advertising and volume-fashion copy.

Formal or Informal? Either Can Set the Fashion

High-style fashion writing can be fairly formal, as on the pages of *Vogue* or *Harper's Bazaar,* or as it is in the advertisements of Marshall Field's. Or informal, as in *Mademoiselle.* Or formal or informal, as in the top fashion advertisements of Lord & Taylor. Whichever it is, this copy is authoritative; it sets the fashion.

From these editorial pages and advertisements spring the words and phrases that articulate the fashion. Through the years, the words associated with fashion have been as essential to the fashions themselves as the very fabrics from which they are cut. For instance, the Gibson Girl shirt, the hobble skirt, the swing skirt, the D'Orsay pump.

High fashion copy is designed primarily *to sell the idea of the coat of the moment, rather than a specific coat in stock.* The importance of this objective must not be underestimated. Writing for this type of advertisement is an exacting job.

Newspapers and magazines from time to time carry striking examples of superb advertisements. Quite a number, by their originality and daring, have started whole new circles of advertising thought. In New York, for example, such establishments as Lord & Taylor and Bloomingdale's run newspaper advertisements written by copywriters who have distinguished themselves by being able to put down on paper just a few really thought-through words. These writers are masters of the art of saying a lot by writing little. It isn't easy. Years of apprenticeship and hard work are necessary before a writer can hope to achieve this skill.

Nothing has been said here about the fashion artists as important members of the creative team. In many eyes they are more important than you in inducing sales. Fruitless and unending arguments can be held on this point since words and illustration must ultimately work together. Each can enhance the other.

Make no mistake, however. Recognize that illustration, as important as it is in other forms of advertising, is still more important in fashion advertising in conveying mood and authenticity. Fashion artists are usually superior artists. Such artists will provide you with a strong creative challenge—to do as well with words as they do with art. The test is whether the art embellishes the copy, or vice versa; or does each match the other perfectly?

A study of high fashion advertisements will reveal these characteristics:

- They are directed toward people who set the pace.
- Their appeal is prestige.
- They speak with authority (usually written in third person).
- They strive toward mood and illusion.
- Their concern with details, if any, is secondary.
- They contrive to make the readers feel they are influencing fashion, rather then being influenced by it.
- The copy is usually brief and always enhanced by dramatic artwork and distinctive typefaces.
- The words themselves are fresh as an April leaf, highly dramatic and descriptive.

Notwithstanding the fact that good high fashion advertising has these characteristics, there is a regrettable amount of high fashion advertising appearing in magazines and newspapers that does not measure up. One criticism is the sameness in the sleek illustrations and the copy's artificial sheen—the bright, insincere patter that has confused shallowness with sophistication.

There is the tendency, too, for fashion advertisers to fall in love with prettiness. Advertisements are judged as pretty or not pretty—whether or not they have ideas or selling arguments. The advertisements—copy and art—show and talk about merchandise but make no real attempt to sell it.

Selling in Volume but Keeping the Fashion Mood

Whereas high fashion advertising is designed to set the pace, volume-fashion advertising is directed to selling the people who must keep the pace. The student looking forward to a career in advertising will very likely start here. This does not mean that volume-fashion advertising is easy, nor does it imply that the techniques involved are less exacting.

It does mean that there are more opportunities in this phase of advertising because this is the category into which most advertising falls. The stores and agencies engaged in promotional work to move stocks of merchandise are in the thousands. In contrast, the smart shops and periodicals whose concern is high fashion are relatively few.

You must realize that a flair for writing is not enough for writing fashion advertising that sells. You need to understand selling techniques, adaptations of style, human nature, and above all, you must have an intimate knowledge of the people who buy and wear the clothes you are writing about—the people who do the volume buying upon which all stores depend.

In one sense, your knowledge of people's buying habits, their whims, and their enthusiasms is more important than your writing skill. If you don't have the former, you're just another writer spinning out glib, bright patter that fails to convince and thus fails to sell.

Although there are vast differences in the markets and in the writing techniques used, a fashion writer and an industrial writer have a lot in common. Each must have an intense personal interest in his specialized field and must be able to turn out copy precisely geared to that field.

As mentioned earlier, you must, above all, be breathlessly intrigued with fashion change and fashion detail. In the illustrative part of your advertisement, it must be important to you how a glove stops at the wrist and where the flower is pinned on the dress. It is easy to be wrong in these details. Likewise, it is exceedingly difficult to recover the confidence of the reader who looks over your advertisement and finds that you, seemingly, have less interest in these details than he or she does.

This sense of fashion leadership is demonstrated in the following copy that stresses the offering of a fashion exclusive originated by a famous designer:

> *Another* Lord & Taylor *exclusive*
>
> Andrea Pfister's
>
> black satin Pierrot pump
> glistens with enchantment.
>
> Ours alone, dazzled by a golden sequined orb in a gilt-edged Pierrot cocarde, the evening pump is transformed into pure magic. On the little Louis heel we love. $220.00

The writer engaged in volume-fashion advertising must correlate three factors: selling techniques, human nature, and forceful style.

Effective volume selling, like other forms of selling, is based on six rather commonly accepted objectives: to attract attention, to hold interest, to create desire, to overcome obstacles, to stir to action, and to give satisfaction and pleasant reaction for money spent.

Figure 11–2. Volume fashion advertisement.

You Must Understand Human Nature

Although the precepts of effective selling can be learned in Psychology 201 or in basic courses on salesmanship, human nature cannot be so conveniently catalogued. Textbooks can give you general knowledge about the man or woman consumer. All people want recognition, want response, work for security, and yearn for new experience. But—the person you are trying to reach considers himself or herself less a member of a particular group as an individual who is different and has different problems. You must know and understand this person in particular. Recognize his or her problems. If you want your copy to sell, you must show this reader how to dress attractively, but you must be aware, too, of the concern with a budget, and the determination to keep healthy.

Your job is to sell this person fashions. Dozens of considerations and economies are pulling against you. Hundreds of commodities are competing with your dress jacket for this reader's attention and, to make your selling job tougher, a dozen stores are competing with you to sell that same $45 dress.

If your advertisement is successful, you will attract that reader, persuade him or her, and bring that person into your store to buy the dress jacket you describe. You will have found a way to say it better. You will have convinced your reader.

A successful advertisement, you see, is good writing plus a point of view that enables your copy to begin where the reader is.

Tips for Writing Volume-Fashion Advertising

Significantly, the appeals in volume-fashion advertising are quite different from the specialized appeals in high fashion advertising. In the case of women's fashions, the message is toward the woman who must keep the pace. A volume advertisement:

- Helps a woman to feel she is buying and wearing the new, the smart, that she is *keeping* pace.
- Assures her that she is well dressed. (Note: not because she is imitating, but because she has the good judgment to recognize "smart fashion.")
- Recognizes that she may be a working woman whose attire must be appropriate for her personal and her professional life.
- Emphasizes what is new about the dress you are advertising and shows her why it will be becoming to her.
- Indicates that her standard of dressing is parallel to "best dressed" through the merchandising or designing abilities of your store—her store. (Note: it's always a good idea to sell the store or the label in addition to the merchandise. In the long run, if the merchandise is good, it will add to sales by making the manufacturer's line, or that store, a habit with the woman.
- Connotes fashion in terms of her activities.
- Answers her implied questions on wearing qualities, washability, and so forth.
- Tells more of the details—width of seams, fabric, colors, sizes. A woman may be looking for a dress or coat in pink wool. She reads carefully. Nothing is said about color—nor about the fabric. Remember, by supplying information about the color and fabric of the merchandise you do not necessarily detract from the atmosphere of "style."
- Gives more stress to price. While you should certainly be aware that price gains more prominence as it drops lower and lower, watch out for basing fashion copy wholly on an economy appeal. "Now—a woolen suit for $59.98" probably will not appeal. Women prefer not to identify themselves with $59.98 even if that's all they have to spend.

Although interesting style is pretty much a personal matter, there are, nevertheless, some precepts and rules that cannot be ignored. Since copywriting is a craft—like building a bench or cobbling a shoe—you should think in very clear terms of problem solution. Every block of copy, whether it pertains to mink or walking shoes, has a message to convey. You decide what is to be said and why, and you must say it exactly the way it should be said.

You must do justice to the fashion in terms suitable to your reader audience, its age, its tastes, its way of life. The medium and the audience set the slant for the copy. An advertisement scheduled for *Seventeen* must be written to dovetail with its readers' way of speaking or thinking. This is not the way of speaking or thinking of a woman who reads *Vogue* or *Harper's Bazaar.* The fashion writer knows to whom the eyes peering at the page belong.

You must have facility with words, a sharp ear attuned to the turn of a phrase, and the perception to recognize gestures and attitudes of readers. If you're good, you visualize the reader before you attempt to reach her with your copy.

Stress Designer Names

Because of the importance of fresh, striking design in fashion items, designers are given almost Godlike reverence in fashion salons and boutiques. Their pronouncements on fashion are quoted respectfully. Thus, fashion advertisements feature designer names as the following copy demonstrates:

> IT'S A MAUD, MAUD,
> MAUD, MAUD WORLD
>
> Maud Frizon, how do you do it?
> You've outdone outrageous.
> Masterfully mixed style and sculpture,
> carving rich black suede into sinuous
> curves, defining the curves with a
> molten stroke of gold. Maud, your
> shoes and boots and bags are stories
> unto themselves. Full of passion and
> humor and eloquence.
> All we can say is tell us more, Maud.
> Tell us more!

Writing Style: Dos and Don'ts

Here are some dos and don'ts on interesting writing style. You will do well to remember them.

- *Do* . . . make your caption sound smooth and unstilted.
- *Do* . . . whenever possible, use an active verb for description instead of a descriptive adjective. Verbs make a caption stronger, give it movement. NOT: The black skirt has circular bands around it. BUT: Black ribbon bands encircle the skirt.
- *Do* . . . keep your sentences simple, whether long or short. Be careful that your modifiers fall as close as possible to what they modify.
- *Do* . . . avoid the phrase that's crushingly last year's. Catch phrases of the day can be effective, but bear in mind whether you are writing for a daily newspaper or a periodical. The smart phrase that's on everyone's lips now is likely to become completely passé in the long interim between writing and publication of a periodical.
- *Do* . . . be light and gay and humorous, if you can be. Don't try to be if you can't.
- *Do* . . . digest thoroughly all information on merchandise (study the photograph or layout intensively if you can't see the merchandise yourself) before you put your pencil on paper. You can't write interestingly if you don't write knowingly.
- *Don't* . . . use a tired simile. It's even more soporific than the tired adjective. Don't say "crisp as lettuce, sleek as a seal, striped liked Joseph's coat." Say "bright, like a fire-engine; fresh as a four-year-old's cheeks; gala as the evening that starts with an orchid."
- *Don't* . . . rely on a clutter of lush adjectives. When you do use adjectives, make them as specific and fresh as possible. Embellishments "pretty, marvelous, charming, wonderful, divine" don't really accomplish anything. Paillette floral designs; dropped-torso bodice; supple, glove-tanned cowhide; pin of patinated brass—these all give you a definite picture and a definite association. These adjectives have feeling.
- *Don't* . . . imitate someone else's style. Read other people's advertisements for the ideas they contain, but when you have an advertisement to write on the same dress, write in your own way. Be fresh.

By this point in the chapter you have come to realize that the fashion copywriter must be as subtle as a glance behind a veil, and as direct as a salesclerk in Macy's basement; as factual as a catalog sheet, and as imaginative as a mystery writer.

Fashion writers must have a strong love for fashion and for glittering, human, persuasive words—and most of all for ideas around which they wrap the words with precision and that mysterious quality called "flair." Possessed of all these qualities they may survive, and even thrive, in the demanding, volatile field that is fashion copywriting.

Men's Fashions: Another Area for the Fashion Writer

At one time men smiled indulgently at women's concern with fashion, cosmetics, and other feminine enthusiasms. The woman's world was far from the world of clean-shaven males who wore dark suits, sober ties, and short, neatly clipped hair.

In the last decade, however, men have burst into the fashion scene. We shrug as they daub themselves with colognes and perfumes and apply makeup. Clothing and personal grooming ideas are dictated by *Playboy, Esquire,* and *Gentlemen's Quarterly* and the many men's magazines that have caused much of the departure from male conservatism in dress and personal habits.

How can you, fashion writer, create advertising for this newly emerged male butterfly? First, you must understand that you are addressing three markets.

One is the *still* conservative, young-man-on-the-move market. Your target is the young executive whose clothes have a quiet distinction suitable for the appearance of the investment broker in the boardroom, for the account executive who must present a campaign at a client meeting, for the young lawyer in a prestigious Boston law firm. This man's well-groomed hair may be slightly longer than in the past, but he is much the same in dress as he always has been.

Copy for this market is subdued and deferential. It recognizes the importance of the impression that the reader's attire must make on his associates. The stress is not so much on what is new as what is appropriate. This man doesn't want to be innovative in dress so much as quietly—and possibly expensively—correct.

Two is the swinging market. This is the machismo male who glories in his virility and attractiveness to females. Copy directed at him, whether for musk oil scents or contoured slacks, has sexual overtones. Sometimes, the copy can poke fun at the image. Fun or not, this male target is moved by self-gratification and a desire to impress the women he meets. He has a self-image that is largely created by the clothes he wears, the hairstyling he adopts, and the cologne he splashes on himself. The *Playboy* reader, typical of this market, is highly conscious of styles, is innovative, eager to try the new, and blanches if described as not in the know.

In writing to this market of males, you pull out all the stops. Your words are bolder and more colorful to match the styles, and you cater to the fantasies and self-image of these men who have broken the shackles that inhibited men's styles for so many years.

Three is the casual market. Here we have men who dress to please themselves, not others. Clothes selection is easygoing with the accent on comfort: open collars, sport shirts, denims, slacks with sport coats, slacks with sweaters or denim jackets, loafers.

This market is more complex than it seems. For instance, allied with the casual look is the "country" look that embraces a number of fashion permutations such as the pairing of rustic Harris tweeds with country tartans, or suede elbow patches on a plaid sports jacket.

Likewise, the "preppy" look has been a part of the casual scene for some time, a self-consciously youthful look. And then, of course, there once emerged "leisure" suits, so carefully tailored that they began to appear at dressy affairs. Warm-up suits for jogging and other sports are now part of the casual look and worn quite often at nonathletic times by men and women.

Copy matches the mood of the casual man. You recognize his easygoing lifestyle, his interest in sports, and his desire to be individual in his dress. He likes to put combinations together to suit himself. You "suggest" to this person. You don't tell him that he *must* dress according to a fixed or prescribed mode.

Outside Influences

To these other types, we might add the avant garde male clothing purchasers who welcome the European look. Thus, we have the tweedy look of the British designers and the bold colors from France that sometimes deliberately match the colors of sports coats with the striking colors of the sports cars so loved by the millions of Formula One racing fans.

Italian men's fashions, in contrast to the French boldness, tend toward simplicity expressed in toned-down, quiet elegance—elegance for which the fashionably dressed male pays handsomely.

Despite the invasion by the purveyors of men's fashions from the Common Market, the three men's groupings previously listed still hold true. In European styles, however, the distinctions tend to blur with a subtle crossing-over of styles; for instance, the casual with the business and the swinging with the casual.

Fashion swings in men's clothes, as shown in advertising, are less likely to gyrate so wildly as in women's fashions. Still, the writer for men's fashions, as in women's fashions, must keep an eye on fashions around the world as well as on those in the United States.

Current Events Cause Fashion Swings, Too

Big news events that center around national figures—Presidents, heroes, rock stars, television celebrities—affect what men will wear and thus affect fashion writing.

An illustration of this was shown by what happened when President-elect Carter announced that he would be wearing jeans at the White House.

The story was headlined in all print media and given full treatment in broadcast media. Denim manufacturers, already worked to capacity, anticipated an avalanche of additional sales once the White House became the locale of scores of photographers snapping pictures of a denim-clad President of the United States.

Denim, already a phenomenon for its acceptance by both sexes and its use for all occasions, was thus given a further boost up the ladder of total acceptability.

Then along came a U.S.A. Olympic team garbed in Western style, followed by Ronald Reagan, a horseback-riding President who popularized jelly beans and a Western clothing look. Cowboy hats appeared everywhere and numbers of urban males looked as if they had just ridden in from the Bar-X ranch, complete with sombreros, high-heeled boots, and other items of Western living. Meanwhile, back at the White House ranch, Nancy Reagan was encouraging a dressier mood for women than had been seen during the Carters' White House occupancy.

Still later, Lt. Col. Oliver North burst on the television scene in 1987. Immediately, there was a national rush for "Ollie" T-shirts and "Ollie" haircuts. Had he been wearing a civilian suit, instead of a Marine uniform, the men of the nation would soon have been dressed the same way—another example of the exasperating, yet fascinating, capriciousness of the fashion scene, male or female.

12

Advertising for Direct Response through Mail or Telephone Orders

Part A

At 8:05 A.M., Stewart Price saw in the latest L. L. Bean catalog just what he had been looking for, a new type of rugged hiking shoe. Ripping out the order blank, he began writing.

That afternoon, June Ritter, a working mother with two children, gazed raptly at the issue of Woman's Day *she had picked up at the supermarket checkout counter. Tearing out a page, she filled in a coupon for a booklet on a new type of coated window that could keep her home warmer in the winter and cooler in the summer.*

At 9:15 P.M., Jack Shonnard, age 71 and a confirmed TV watcher, jotted down the 800 number given urgently by the announcer for an insurance policy that would pay medical costs not covered by Medicare.

At different times of the day and night these three persons are doing what millions of others are doing: responding to the fastest-growing segment of advertising—direct response advertising, also referred to as mail-order or direct marketing.

Our three respondents will look hopefully for the arrival of their orders. They are taking advantage of this popular alternative to shopping in stores.

Thousands of other hopeful people, running small businesses, seek sales through direct response for a staggering variety of goods. Sadly, many do not succeed. Perhaps their products are not right for the market or the times. Often their advertising has no magic pulling power because the writers simply don't know how to do an entire selling job through advertising.

To balance these failures there are many successes. Currently, direct response buying is reaching new peaks. There are many reasons for this. Costs for transportation and for fuel continue to rise, making trips to stores more expensive. More and more women are working and have less time to shop. Last, buying by direct response has achieved a general acceptance and this acceptance becomes even greater as the variety of purchases through direct response widens.

In addition to a complete range of conventional goods, direct response business now includes many luxury items and even food, including meats, poultry, and gourmet items that are mailed packed in dry ice.

If *you* write copy for any of these items, you must do the complete sales job through words and illustrations alone. This means that those words capture interest, spur want or desire, overcome objections, and persuade the prospect to sign the order. In such selling you have no alternative. There is no sales force to carry the burden. *You* are the sales force. If you don't create sales, you're a failure and your business fails; or, if you're working for someone, that person goes out of business.

This direct responsibility for results is not necessarily the curse it may seem to be since such selling produces such a prompt reaction—or lack of it—that you have an almost instant measure both of the effectiveness of your idea and of the success of your message. If they've proved "pretty good," you may be able to inject into your next message just the right touch needed to make it produce excellent results.

If your first message obviously has proved "not so hot," you know at least that you'd better try another version of your idea or even a new idea. You may then, through analysis of the results of the first message, be able to spot the exact flaw.

Of course, you won't ignore the possibility that a poor reaction to a piece of direct response selling and the accuracy of any analysis you may make of that reaction may depend somewhat on two other factors not basically a part of the advertising sales effort: "product" and "prospects." If the product is poor or if the prospects are not reasonably well defined (and therefore not reached), reaction is fairly certain to be discouraging.

The single most important factor in success is the product. You *must* have a product people want. A poor product will hurt you more than poor copy in attaining results. Superb copy, on the other hand, can't sell a poor product.

Although only a genius, or a very lucky person, can be right all the time in picking products that will be successful sellers, here are a few questions to ask yourself to determine a product's potential:

- Does it have an exciting newness?
- Is there a real need for the product?
- Will *most* of your prospects find the product appealing?
- Is the product right for the market in terms of price, market's general taste, and way of living?

Direct Response Sells Services, Too

Because of the nature of the selling method, the product offered is usually some item of merchandise. A service may, however, be sold by the direct response method. Examples: a personal income-tax computing service, a manuscript criticism/correction service for amateur writers, and—yes—a direct response copywriting service (on a fee basis) for small businesses that have no advertising agency or creative personnel of their own. Normally, such a small percentage of direct response selling is of services—and so much is of tangible goods—that throughout this discussion the terms "product," "item," "merchandise," and the like will be used to designate anything sold by direct response.

Media Factors in Direct Response Advertising

As in all advertising, in addition to knowing everything possible about product and prospects, you need the answer to one other major question before beginning to write your direct response sales message: "How—through what medium—am I going to tell my prospects about my product?" The medium used affects not only the physical requirements of your message—its length, its layout, its illustration, its space for and location of headline, and so forth—but also the handling of your message.

This handling may include the approach your copy takes, the use of attention-getting words and copy devices, the relative emphasis of appeals, and the inclusion (or exclusion) of other copy elements. You can see that you must ask, "What medium am I writing for?"

Although television has become a significant factor in direct response selling, along with the telephone, the average person often equates the term with catalogs, especially such monster productions as that of Sears, Roebuck.

After that, this person has become conscious of a following host of other catalogs that offer almost any item or service the human mind can conceive. Some of these catalogs have achieved steadily increasing recognition and clientele, such as L. L. Bean, Norm Thompson, Carroll Reed, and, for unusual and/or luxury items, the Horchow Collection and Hammacher Schlemmer.

Direct Response Pulls Orders in Newspapers and Magazines

In the magazine field, typical publications in which appropriate items are successfully offered for sale include many that on first thought might not be considered good direct response media at all, including upwardly-targeted consumer specialty magazines in the home furnishings and fashion fields. *Town & Country, Better Homes and Gardens, Vogue,* and *Glamour* customarily devote special shopping sections to advertisements, for instance. The advertising columns of general magazines occasionally carry successful direct response offerings, usually in small-space advertisements because of the high rates of wide circulation publications.

Somewhat more commonly associated, perhaps, with the direct response selling of specialty types of merchandise are those magazines appealing to certain classifiable economic, occupational, avocational, and/or social segments of the population. Typical examples of these might be:

- The pulp groups of movies, romance, adventure, and detective magazines appealing mostly to the people of modest education and income.
- The farming and livestock publications such as *Farm Journal.*
- Comics, and the children's and youth magazines.

Figure 12–1. Direct response magazine advertisement. An attention-getting illustration, tell-all copy, and a sensible coupon invite ordering from readers.

- Sports and body-building publications and outdoors periodicals.
- Hobby publications such as home mechanics, amateur photography, arts, and antiques.
- The lower income and/or small town and rural magazines such as *Grit.*
- Publications appealing to specific racial groups such as *Ebony.*
- Magazines whose paid advertising columns are composed largely of direct response offers—and whose readers over the years have come to regard them as "marketing places."

In addition to their prestige and selectivity, magazines offer color to enhance direct response items. A writer, however, used to the long-copy possibilities of direct response brochures, leaflets, and booklets, will find that writing must be tighter in magazine advertising.

At one time direct response advertisers shunned newspapers because color either was not offered or was poor. Now, with newspapers jammed with inserts printed on good paper stock and offering excellent color, business has picked up. Thus, despite the handicap of a comparatively short life, newspapers offer many opportunities for successful direct response advertising, especially in comic sections, Sunday magazine pages, and Sunday supplements. Comic page advertisements have been important in reaching the youth market with box top premium offers, whereas Sunday magazines such as that in the *New York Times* appeal to a wide audience with a variety of products and services offered.

A Natural for Use in Direct Response—Direct Mail

A third general category in the field of direct response media is that of mailing pieces, which usually make from one to several offers (a larger number, of course, would become a small catalog). Here is where the two branches of "remote control" advertising meet, and in fact are synonymous. This is direct mail selling.

Direct mail pieces may take many forms, some of the more common ones being leaflets, circulars, return post cards (today usually with postage payment guaranteed by the vendor), letters, broadsides, booklets, brochures, envelope stuffers, and the like, or combinations of any two or more of these forms.

These may be sent in reply to a paid (or unpaid) response to some other advertising. Often they go out as individual mailings. At other times they are grouped with similar pieces making other offers and are sent out to mailing lists either maintained by the merchandiser, or rented or bought from a mailing list service or another advertiser. Often, too, they are used as enclosures, perhaps with a department store's monthly statements to its charge account customers, or possibly enclosed with other purchases being sent from the store or from a firm such as Sears.

Dear Business Person:

At first you tell yourself, "One phone's as dependable as the next. Besides, look at the money I'll save." But when you catch your phone deceiving you call after call, when you're forced to resort to a phone booth . . .

That's when you need good, old reliable AT&T -- and the **MERLIN®** Communications System. The **MERLIN** System is a perfect combination of old-fashioned service and sophisticated technology. And it's designed expressly for a small business like yours.

Consider a system so dependable it memorizes your most important numbers for fast one-touch dialing, redials your last busy number, sets up conference calls, provides an intercom, pages -- even grows as your business grows.

And a system so flexible it can be customized to meet the needs of each employee -- with the flick of a switch.

Above all, think of the peace of mind you'll have with a system from AT&T. One that offers everything from a neighborhood office to a support staff of specialists ready to help in any way, at any time.

Plus, the **MERLIN** System is more affordable than you think -- with payment plans to meet your budget -- including low monthly rental rates, low purchase prices and financing options.

Come back to phones you can trust. Come back to AT&T. You'll wonder why you ever left.

For more information on how the **MERLIN** System can help you run your business better, complete and send the enclosed reply card or call our Small Business Specialists today.

Sincerely,

Susan Stoll

Susan Stoll
Sales Manager

P.S. Send for your free brochure today and find out how the **MERLIN** System can help your small business.

Figure 12–2. Direct response letter. Such letters develop a strong selling message and then end with a call for quick action. Two other examples of direct response material for this company are included in this chapter. (See Figures 12–3, 12–4.)

TV: A Direct Response Powerhouse

Any steady television viewer cannot be unaware that commercials with direct response offers have been increasing, almost annoyingly so, because of the high-pressure character of many such commercials. Television offers the almost-perfect medium for the direct response advertiser because viewers can see the product, can watch it demonstrated in action, can hear the product (such as an album), can be persuaded by the enthusiastic voice of the announcer. And, very importantly, a vast audience may be exposed to all these qualities of the television commercial.

On the negative side there is the cost, so high that disaster looms if the product and the advertising aren't appealing enough to draw heavy response. Little wonder that so much pressure is applied in writing commercials. Also, in contrast to print media, the message, once given, is gone; no page to read and reread and no coupon to study and to fill out.

If you write direct response advertising, you find out quickly that the usual offer simply cannot be made in television's standard unit, the 30-second commercial. In fact, you're hard put to do an offer justice in a 60-second commercial. Thus, you may find yourself working with

Figure 12–3. Direct response mailing piece. This unit gives full buying information on one side, and on the other side is a reply card that is obtained by cutting around the dotted lines.

120-second units. Very often these units are not available, another handicap for the direct response advertiser and, of course, such a long commercial is discouragingly expensive.

To be able to justify the cost of a 120-second commercial, the item *must* be timely; of wide, certain appeal; and it should be announced by a trusted figure, such as a famous football player whose sincerity and character were admirably suited for promoting insurance plans in a series of commercials.

A writer of television direct response commercials should, before writing, understand what objectives are sought by the advertiser paying for these commercials. Obviously, many such commercials seek quick, direct sales. Other commercials are more long-range. Some, as in the case of insurance plans and policies previously cited, try to build up a prospect list by getting viewers to send or phone for more information. Other commercials simply support advertising appearing in other media such as magazines, newspapers, and direct mail.

Home shopping by television gives the direct response advertiser a huge audience for his messages. More than a half-dozen cable channels now sell, nonstop, a limitless array of goods. Presenters demonstrate the goods forcefully, as anyone who has watched the Home Shopping Network will testify. Considerable pressure is exerted through a push on "buy now," "this offer won't be repeated," and similar phrases. To lure viewers, these channels offer attractive discounts on the merchandise they push.

Radio: Some Good Points, but . . .

Radio advertising has produced good, and sometimes outstanding, direct response success stories because of the persuasiveness of good announcers, especially of local announcers known and trusted by radio listeners. Listener loyalty is a significant factor in local advertising.

Radio has other pleasing qualities for the direct response advertiser. It is low in cost. It can be produced easily, far more simply than almost any other medium. It can be produced quickly, an important factor to the advertiser with a hot, timely item that should be put before prospects while the appeal is the greatest. And radio can give the advertiser same-day delivery.

It takes little perception, however, to see that radio has serious direct response advertising handicaps. Among these are no visualization of the product, no coupon, and the transitory character of the message.

By the time an announcer has tried to describe in words what the product or service is and has then attempted precise and repeated ordering instructions, time will have run out. Thus, except for cost, radio direct response advertising suffers from the same handicaps as television advertising and adds some handicaps of its own.

Keep in Mind Media Audiences When You Write

If the same product were to be advertised in magazines as different as *Town and Country* and *Grit,* your copy would differ not only because your prospects were of a different economic and social status, but also because your advertising, to be effective in the medium in which it appears, must conform to the makeup of that type of medium. An advertisement planned, designed, and written for *Grit* will frequently look out of place if used in the *New Yorker* and vice versa. With few exceptions, an advertisement that is out of its element will not produce successful results.

Assume, similarly, that the same product was being sold by radio or television direct response to different groups of prospects in the same general area. Not only would your programs differ but possibly your time of broadcast and the stations you use. Your copy, likewise, would probably be geared to each group despite the fact that the basic appeal to each group might be almost the same.

Assume for the moment that you are writing commercials for a large retailer of tapes, records, and CDs located in a medium-size midwestern city. The retailer handles a complete line of records, tapes, and disks of all the major recording companies, and does a large direct response business, but sells at regular retail prices (including postage, however).

It has been decided to push three types of records—classical music, jazz, and country/western. This means three distinct markets must be reached, perhaps at three different times of the day or week. Depending upon the coverage and listening patterns of your local radio stations, you may use more than one of them to reach your markets.

Yet your programs will be similar in that all of them feature recordings (naturally!). So, too, will your commercials be similar, and yet they will vary widely. Your basic appeal to all three markets is almost certain to hinge on one idea: the convenience of getting any recordings you want without the bother of going to a store. Yet, just as you will vary your programs—though all will be music—to appeal to lovers of symphony, to youthful addicts of popular tunes, and to bluegrass devotees, so must you vary the appeal in your commercials to suit the varying situations of your audiences:

- *To the rural audience:* "Shop from your fireside; no need for a special trip to town. And avoid disappointment; our stocks are always complete."
- *To the teenagers:* "Just drop us a note (or fill in an order blank) between classes or in the evening; don't miss that important class meeting, play rehearsal, or basketball game just to come downtown (or into town).
- *To the serious listener:* "A new concert's just as near as your desk (or your phone—if charge accounts are permitted or C.O.D. deliveries encouraged); avoid a long bus ride, traffic jam, and parking worries downtown."

To everyone, of course, goes the general story of "same-day" service, of quality products at standard prices including packing and mailing costs, of satisfaction or your money back—and perhaps some sort of a premium with each order of so many dollars.

Most likely you will write even such "standard" parts of the commercials in a different style and in different words for each audience. If you do, then you've adapted your copy to your media; and, other factors being favorable, you should have a set of successful direct response commercials.

Writing for Direct Response Advertising: General Suggestions

Assume, now, that your product is one that can be sold to your prospects, and that the medium selected is an effective one for reaching the prospects at low cost. The next question is how to induce those prospects to make purchases. What are you going to do that will make the potential customer order? The results depend on how effectively you present the merchandise.

Think like a Retail Merchant

Since you are the salesperson, compare your job with the selling process of the owner of a small specialty shop. The shop owner first of all creates an inviting window display to attract the casual shopper or passerby into the store. Assume that he does go in. The shop owner gives the shopper a closeup view of the merchandise—opens it up or takes it apart, giving a sales talk point by point. He answers the customer's questions and meets all objections. Finally, as the customer is about convinced to buy, he presents his final sales point—the clincher—an irresistible reason for not postponing the purchase. Then, ideally, the customer says, "I'll take it," and lays the cash on the counter.

That's the ideal sale. It's exactly what you hope to do with your direct response offering. Your show window that stops your prospect is your display (in type and illustration) or the opening words of your commercial. Your copy (and detailed views, if any) comprise your closeup of the product and your salestalk.

Next, because you're not face-to-face with the prospect, you have to anticipate what his questions and objections are most likely to be and work the answers into your sales talk (keeping them in a positive vein, of course) as you write.

Then you weave in your clincher—*why it's important or necessary to order now*—frequently a matter of limited supply, a special price for a short time, or perhaps a premium for promptness. So far you've pretty well paralleled the retail sales procedure.

At this point your retail customer would say, "Wrap it up" and dig into his wallet. You'd take his money and hand him the change and his parcel. It's not that simple in direct selling since the customer—the prospect—still has one more step to take on his own. He has to make out his order (perhaps getting out paper, envelope, and a stamp), probably write a check (or quite possibly go to a bank or post office to buy a money order), and then mail the order to your firm.

Not only do you have to make these extra steps simple and easy as possible, but you must also make your whole offer seem so attractive that the customer doesn't mind the extra work.

The extra attraction you must weave into your copy is difficult to define but might be explained by saying that you write in a somewhat "higher key" so that your copy reads or is heard at a higher pitch. Perhaps some of this is the result of your urge to immediate action. This feeling, nevertheless, is often an integral part of the entire advertisement. Perhaps a careful look at each element of the direct sale will show what's required to give the entire advertisement its high pitch. Begin with the headline.

Your Headlines Are Show Windows

Headlines are the "show windows"—attention-getters—of your shop. Windows pull prospects in from the sidewalk to the shop's inside. Headlines pull prospects into the copy. Your headline material in this instance may be described as any display-size type wherever it appears in the advertisement.

Considered alone, this physical handling (layout) of the headline material imparts a large measure of its high pitch—its aura of urgency. Direct headlines are frequently written in a more exciting style than for usual consumer advertising. They may be *exhortative*:

Save on Farm Income Taxes before April 15th

Look Taller Instantly

Make Beaded SEQUIN Lapel Pins—Easy at Home

Now! Be Stunning in a Rainstorm

Remove Any Stump

Treasure Your Baby's Tooth

Each one is a command to action as well as an appeal to some need or desire.

Others, by brevity alone—a sort of terse *index* quality—impart a feeling of urgency:

Delphinium

New Miracle Wall Cleaner

Feet Hurt?

Gardenia Plants

Orchard Fresh Holly *(for Christmas)*

Wristwatch—Military Style

A third headline type, somewhere between exhortative and index for forcefulness, is the *exclamatory* headline. This is an excited, enthusiastic headline well suited to direct response advertising that creates a sense of urgency and merchandising excitement. Some examples:

Dazzling duo in solid brass. $19.95 for 2!

Gift of the year. Only $12.95.

World famous tomato sauce now available after 76 years

Not every direct response headline *must* fall into the exhortative, index, or exclamatory types. There *are* other types, and combinations of types, but these are the most common. Some index headings include a selling word or two; others none, except possibly by inference. Display lines in other advertisements rely for their excitement primarily on exclamatory sentences or phrases:

Two Bushels of Ripe Tomatoes from One Vine

3 Crochet Beauties Easy to Make

Lifetime Knife Cuts Anything

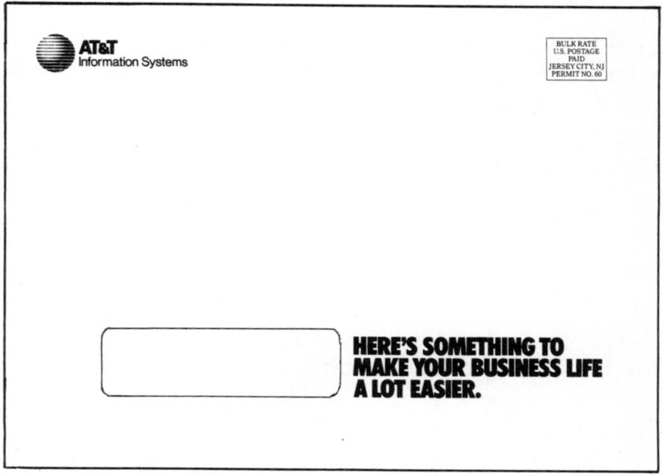

Figure 12–4. Direct response envelope with outside message. Such messages on the envelope build curiosity to see what's inside. In advertising parlance such message carrying envelopes are sometimes called "flashes."

The Oriental Symbol of Power

At Home, Your Own Manufacturing Business

Price Pulls Prospects

Because the majority of people who shop by direct response do so for a real, or imagined, price advantage, a quoted price in the headline is usually your chief attention-getter. Price, as you can see in the following headlines, is a powerful element in the exhortative approach.

Develop your Kodak film for 39¢.

Bathe your body in pure silk. Le Tee $21.

Put an alarm, a stopwatch, and a calculator on your wrist for just $89.

Try our $16 alternative to the $24 button-down.

Remove hair permanently. $19.95.

Even index headlines, not considered so forceful as exhortative headlines, develop much more power when combined, as they often are, with price. Here are some examples:

4 new craft catalogs 25¢.

Pecans! Only $19.95 delivered.

Homemaker's garbage disposal wrench $7.99.

Solid brass piano lamp. Only $24.95.

Religious collection 30¢.

Like the exhortative and index headlines, the exclamatory headline can use or not use price, and like the others, it's a stronger headline when it *can* use price. Some examples:

You'll never get a better offer. 5 pieces, $9.95.

Each magnificent panel is only $3.00.

Imagine this handsome crystal pendant for only $1.50!

You Can Imply Price

Giving an attractive price directly in a headline is always attention-getting, but occasionally you may want to suggest that the prospect is getting a good price but not do so directly because of some marketing reason. If so, you imply a good price or a good saving. Examples:

The quality alternative to high-cost inflatables.

Sew it together and *save!*

Shoes! At direct-from-the-factory-to-you prices!

In these examples you see the pattern of price-implying in the direct-from-the-factory point, the do-it-yourself-and-save appeal, and the appeal of a lower-cost alternative.

Catalogs and Direct Mail: Readers Are Interested

Most of the examples you've read of direct response advertising have been from publication advertising, but just about all of them would be suitable for direct-mail pieces or catalogs. These latter two have an advantage, however. In the case of the direct-mail pieces, readers are not dividing their attention, as they do in reading publications, between many competing advertisements and editorial matter. In the case of catalogs, interest is already assumed or the readers wouldn't be opening the catalog in the first place.

In such cases, unless price, or perhaps something essentially emotional, is your basic appeal, you will probably use material for your major display that either tells some pertinent fact about your product or else identifies it categorically, and perhaps includes at least a mention of one or two of its features.

If you do copy for catalogs issued by the smaller organizations, you'll probably find yourself writing exhortative and exclamatory headlines that are just as forceful as any used in publication direct response advertising. This approach is effective for the prospects of these catalogs as the long usage indicates.

There has been a trend in recent years for catalog copy to take a quieter tone, especially in the catalogs published by the giant mail-order houses. Index headings have increased. Where they are not used, the headlines resemble the kind of writing used in newspaper advertisements by national advertisers. Here are some catalog headlines that demonstrate the more subdued, clipped style:

Top carrier saves space; more comfort inside your car.

Flexible shafts—many tools in one.

Wash your window while you drive.

Much warmer—double-woven wool fleece overcoats.

Fine bags *can* be low priced.

The Steinway Inspiration.

The guidance and dedication of a good piano teacher can never be underestimated in a student's musical education.

But the instrument itself can also be an important influence, and a Steinway brings special qualities to a student's early confrontation with scales and practice.

This is the time at which musical values are being formed.

At a Steinway the student encounters standards of tone and performance which will influence the musical judgments of a lifetime.

If all he were learning was the mechanical task of fingering the keys, the quick response of the Steinway keyboard would be reason enough to start learning there.

But he is also learning to appreciate music. And only at a Steinway can he fully come to learn the range and subtlety, the promise and the possibilities which the piano holds for him and which makes it unique among musical instruments.

At the start, the student may not seem to get the most out of a Steinway... but in the long run, a Steinway will get the most out of the student.

Figure 12–5. Catalog institutional advertisement with human interest appeal. One of the best ways to obtain readership for institutional advertisements is to focus on one person, in this case an appealing boy in a football jersey. Anyone who has taken piano lessons as a child can relate to the illustration and copy.

How to become a

SUCCESSFUL CONSULTANT

in your own field.

Have you ever wished you could quit your job and start working for yourself?

Well, maybe you can! Many people are amazed when they discover the tremendous amount of professional experience and specialized knowledge they've accumulated — experience and knowledge that others will gladly pay for. Literally thousands of people who made that discovery are now prospering as **independent consultants.**

The way to begin is by reading *How to Become a Successful Consultant in Your Own Field*, by Hubert Bermont.

Clear, straightforward, packed with solid information and advice, this authoritative manual tells you everything you need to know to establish your own independent consulting practice. Here's a sampling of the contents:

- What does it take to be a successful consultant? (See Chapter 1.)
- How to get started. (See Chapter 3.)
- How to operate your business — a collection of "tricks of the trade." (See Chapter 5.)
- What to charge your clients — plus five helpful rules on fees. (See Chapter 6.)
- Why you should **never** work on a contingency (speculative) basis. (See Chapter 7.)
- Ingenious ways to promote yourself — and make people want your services. (See Chapter 9.)
- Contracts: why you should **avoid** them at all costs. (See Chapter 10.)
- Just what do consultants do all day? (See Chapter 11.)
- How to market your ideas. (See Chapter 11.)
- Why you'll never have to worry about competition. (See Chapter 13.)
- And much more!

Perhaps no one is better qualified to have written this book than Hubert Bermont. He has served as consultant to more than 70 major corporations and trade associations, including the U.S. Chamber of Commerce, McGraw-Hill, the Electronic Industries Association, Evelyn Wood Reading Dynamics and the Smithsonian Institution. Yet he made the decision to become a consultant only after being fired from an executive position at the age of 43. You'll learn first-hand how he did it — and how **you** can do it, too!

How to Become a Successful Consultant in Your Own Field is just $20 (tax-deductible if you use it for business purposes), and you're fully protected by this **unconditional money-back guarantee:** Keep the book for three weeks. If you're dissatisfied with it for any reason whatever, simply return it and **every penny of your $20 will be promptly refunded** — no questions asked!

How many times have you told yourself that you're not getting anywhere — that it's time to think seriously about a major change in your career? **Don't put it off another day!** Clip and mail the coupon now!

How To Become A Successful Consultant In Your Own Field

Enclosed is my check or money order for $20. Rush me, postpaid, *How to Become a Successful Consultant in Your Own Field*, by Hubert Bermont. I understand that I have the right to return the book within three weeks for a complete refund if I'm in any way unhappy with it.

Name ______

Address ______

SAMPLE

City ______ State ______ Zip ______

BERMONT BOOKS

Dept. , 815 Fifteenth St. N.W., Washington, D.C. 20005

Figure 12–6. Successful mail-order advertisement for a book. Many sales were made for this $20 book from this advertisement that incorporates such techniques as a personal style, a strong "How to" headline, and vigorous appeals for reader action.

Copy by Don Hauptman, New York City.

You Can Assume Catalog Readers Are Definitely Prospects

Although you work hard to attract the attention of catalog readers, you can assume that they are more truly prospects than the casual readers of magazine advertisements. Catalog readers may already be customers, or they may want to be. Evidence is in the fact that they are reading the catalog.

Furthermore, they are usually in a buying mood—at least for a certain type of product. When they turn to that item, then what you've said in your display headings about the product focuses their attention more sharply on it or its features. But if your display fails to interest them, they may turn to your competitor's catalog or decide to go to a store to shop.

Although lacking competition for attention, you still have competition for the order. What you say in your headlines (or in major subheads if the main heading is essentially the index type) and in your other display lines may well affect the prospect's interest and so, in turn, influence his decision to purchase from you.

Direct Approach Is Usually Best in Direct Response Advertising

Almost all direct response display copy is direct and to the point. Whether you say,

> Develop a torso the girls will admire!
>
> Quick-drying, one-coat flat oil paint—one coat looks like two!

you tell something immediately about the product or the results of its use or application. You do essentially the same thing if you are just a little less direct and write, instead,

> The girls never even used to look twice at me on the beach
>
> You wouldn't think one coat of paint could make such a difference in a room!

You'd scarcely, however, write a headline for a direct response muscle-building course that says, "I'd Rather Stay Home with a Book," or for one-coat wall paint, "I Never Enjoyed Entertaining the Smiths until Tonight." No, you certainly wouldn't use these as major display lines for direct response selling. They *aren't* direct response selling. They may represent a technique suitable for a campaign in which you hope to build up an impression over a period of time, but a direct response sale, nine times out of ten, is an *immediate sale*—often even an impulse sale.

The first caption you write, as you rough out, experimentally, your first draft of copy, may be just as indirect as the last two examples. If so, you'll find yourself hastening almost automatically to add a second display line that tells something much more meaty about your product or the *direct* advantages of its use. Next you discover that you can either eliminate the first line entirely or at least incorporate its basic idea merely as a minor lead-in element of the second line. It will then be likely that you've written a display line that's a real stopper; you've set up a "show window" that brings the prospect right into your "store."

Radio Direct Response Has Show Windows, Too

If your commercial's used on a very distinctive program, you have a sort of built-in show window. But many commercials are not written for any particular program, and certainly not for a distinctive program. You must, accordingly, *create* a show window. Sometimes this can be done with music and sound effects or an unusual voice. Most of the time, however, you'll create your own show window with attention-getting, arresting words and phrases. You may use the direct approach previously mentioned as effective in catalog advertising. Examples of the direct approach:

> Joggers—here's a tip for better performance.
>
> Gardeners—now you can haul big loads without effort.
>
> Collectors—learn how to spot genuine values every time.

For a less direct approach, there are many phrases that can be used:

> Here's good news . . .
>
> At last, there's an answer to . . .
>
> Everyone's a winner when he . . .
>
> If you want a new experience, try . . .
>
> Getting in a rut? Here's how to get out.
>
> There's a surefire way to . . .

The first words in a radio message are important because the average radio listeners are giving half-attention, or no attention, to the commercials. You need to pull them out of their indifference. Jar them to wakefulness with a statement that makes it clear that it might be profitable to listen to what the announcer is saying.

Keep Your Listeners Listening

As in print, you want the show window of your commercial to do more than merely arouse attention. You want it to inspire interest as well—listener interest sufficient to hold that attention throughout your message. So you write into your next sentence or sentences, immediately following your stopper phrase or device, some idea or thought that will be of interest to the largest group of prospects among your listeners.

This opening thought is the "display" of your commercial. See how these sample opening lines, all of them from successful direct response commercials, are written to hold the attention of the greatest number of potential prospects for the offers which follow:

> Friends, the record you just heard, and *any others* you hear on the ______ *(an evening-long program with several co-sponsors),* can be bought from ______'s Records-by-Mail. It's the new, easy way for you to buy the records you want . . ."

> Ladies . . . Here's how you can easily win a complete five-piece bedroom set, a portable electric Singer Sewing Machine, and 101 additional valuable prizes . . . *(quilt-patch bundle offer; a contest entry blank accompanying each bundle ordered)*

> Folks, due to a very special purchase, the makers of the nationally advertised ______ combination cigarette case and lighter . . . for a limited time only . . . will send you a remarkable three-dollar-ninety-five-cent value . . . at the rock bottom bargain price of only *one*-dollar-ninety-eight!

> Wouldn't you be thrilled to win a new Ford station wagon or equivalent in cash, just by taking part in a simple, interesting game? . . . *(contest sponsored by rural magazine; each contest entry to be accompanied by $1 for magazine subscription order)*

> Say, what musical instrument do you think is the easiest and quickest to learn to play? *(harmonica offer)*

An extra display line may be inserted occasionally in the middle of your commercial—an additional attention-getter—just in case interest in your message lags a bit after the first excitement has subsided. This is akin to a prominent subhead or second display line. About a third of the way through the commercial for the cigarette case/lighter combination, for example, we find, "But that's just the *first* half of this sensational offer! Second, you will receive the world's smallest ballpoint pen, complete with key chain!" Here the advertiser has reserved part of his offering for use as a mid-way "headline."

You'll write headlines and subheads into your radio direct response selling for almost identically the same purpose that you'd decorate the show window of your specialty shop. And you'd set up supplementary displays inside to attract and hold your prospect's attention and interest until he hears your complete message and decides to make the purchase.

These are not passive headlines and subheads. They're active, vigorous messages that inform, excite, move to action, and literally pull the listeners along. The subhead comes into its own in mail-order and direct mail.

Unlike so much of non-direct response magazine and newspaper advertising that uses no subheads, the direct response advertisement—no matter what the medium—uses subheads generously. Long copy will never put your prospect to sleep if it's broken up with lively subheads.

Ending Direct Response Radio Copy: It's a Challenge

Asking for action is an axiom in advertising and selling. Unless you *do* ask, your advertisement lacks the final push. In most media the request for action is a simple suggestion that something be done.

In writing direct response radio commercials, however, a whole new dimension is added. You must give ordering instructions. These must be clear and full. If they're not, you've wasted your time and that of the listener.

Naturally, the problem is that all of this must be done with words; no illustration or television picture will help you. Furthermore, you must watch your word count as you give these instructions.

Because you have just so much time to work with in a radio commercial, this means that you must cut down some of the product sell and description in order to get in the urge to action and the ordering instructions. Also, to help that listener you will, of course, have to repeat key parts of the instructions. Such repetition uses up more of that precious time. As you can see, the time factor is one of the serious challenges of direct response radio commercial writing. If you can meet it, congratulations!

13

Advertising for Direct Response Through Mail or Telephone Orders

Part B

Nick Pittard and Curt Blanchard were college chums who had majored in business. Now, Nick was working as a catalog copywriter. Curt wrote agency copy.

"I wouldn't trade jobs with you agency types," Nick replied when Curt asked if he wouldn't like to switch to agency work.

Stung by Curt's skeptical look, Nick said even more forcefully, "Look. Most agency copy is mere come-on stuff. You set the stage for someone else to make the sale.

"When I write catalog copy, I do the whole job. I sell them, pal; I don't just tease them. If I've done my job right, there aren't any unanswered questions. I've made a sale. That's what I call job satisfaction."

Catalog writing is serious business. About 10,000 catalogs—for everything from needles to his-and-hers airplanes—flood the mails. In addition to the millions of Sears catalogs, many more millions are added by Christmas catalogs alone, of such big retailers as Bloomingdale's, Neiman Marcus, Bergdorf Goodman, and Marshall Field's. Even such a sedate organization as the Metropolitan Museum of Art issues more than a million catalogs yearly.

Just as in advertising in other media, your appeal in catalog copy is based on the product's ability to satisfy the desires of your prospects. One difference, however, is that you use "tell-all" copy. This means that first you imagine all the ways your item can answer the wants or desires of your prospects. Then you include as many of these ways as possible in your message. Your hope is that you will thus interest the majority of your potential customers.

Few advertisements in general media such as newspapers or magazines offer an opportunity for tell-all copy, but then such advertisements are not expected to do the entire selling task. Tell-all copy requires space; it relies on a willingness on the part of readers to read a long copy message. Catalog readers have that willingness. Furthermore, they will read a message in print much smaller than that used in the usual general media advertisement.

How to Write Catalog Copy (in General)

Before the specifics, here are some general observations. First, hard-sell is the norm in catalog copy. Soft-sell is rare. Those pages, or those square inches of space, are expected to produce sales. Woe to you if they don't.

Second, there are vast differences in catalog copy, from the somewhat unemotional copy of Sears Roebuck and Hammacher Schlemmer to the bouncy, irrepressible copy of Norm Thompson, and then back again to the sober, tell-it-as-it-is style of L. L. Bean. Thus, you might be a sensation when writing for one type of catalog and a failure when writing for another.

Third, the word "clarity" assumes a new meaning when you write catalog copy. Because your reader is going to make a buying decision based on your writing, you must write words that simply cannot be misinterpreted. When you deal with people in large numbers, you learn that they have a sort of twisted genius in their ability to misread what seems to be clear writing. Your task is to reduce those misinterpretations significantly; you'll never eliminate them totally.

Your Writing Style Should Be Right for the Catalog's Prospects

Tell-all copy can be dull if you simply give every product fact without embellishment. You've been told that direct response copy is *complete* copy. This is true no matter who your prospects are. But the style in which you convey all those product points makes the difference between sparkle and dullness. Just what *is* style? It's the mood, impression, or character of the copy that varies from company to company and from writer to writer.

One way for you to understand this matter of fitting style to prospects, and hence to the advertiser, is for you to examine closely examples of catalog advertising as executed by two outstanding catalog advertisers: L. L. Bean and Norm Thompson. What makes these examples especially valuable for your analysis is that the styles are radically different, yet each is highly effective.

In the following example from the L. L. Bean catalog you see sincere, straightforward copy—the direct, uncomplicated talk of one outdoorsman to another. As you read, you may ask: "But where's the excitement? Those are index headlines. What about highlighting major selling points? And what about those small pictures?"

The answer is that this copy is written for a specialty catalog for hunters and outdoor-types. Here's one case, admittedly a rather exceptional one, where because of the limited appeal of the class of merchandise, the field of prospects is limited, too. Almost everyone reading this catalog reads nearly every listing on practically every page. Because this catalog enjoys this unique advantage, its manner of obtaining attention and maintaining interest in itself and in its offerings is not so apparent as in other publications.

How I earned my label at Lands' End.

LANDS' END

(A brief tale by one of our Sportshirts.)

Earning a Lands' End label isn't something any sportshirt can do.

In fact, the Quality Assurance testing program here makes basic training in the Army seem like a piece of cake!

The "big five" fabric tests.

First, my fabric had to be right. So the Quality Assurance people at Lands' End put me through the paces in their lab.

As I entered the lab, my heart pounded with fear. I was surrounded by an impersonal array of gleaming stainless steel machines, many with dials and gauges on them. Was I strong enough to withstand the five trials I had to face?

First, they put the clamps on.

The giant tensile machine (I had heard stories about this one...) loomed over me. Big clamps held me in place as I was stretched to the breaking point. But was I tough! Took 60 pounds of force without breaking, though a good 30 would have passed me.

Then they sewed a seam in me and put me on that blasted machine again, and I took that without slipping, too. All so you won't get a sportshirt that gives out on you!

Crocking, "running" and other trials.

Next came the crocking test. (Yes, it is a strange word, but that's the way they talk in the QA Department.) I was put on a machine that rubbed me back and forth across a piece of white fabric to see if my color came off—so you won't have to worry about wearing a red shirt that comes off on your slacks. I passed with flying (and intact) colors.

Then they threw me in a washing machine with five other pieces of fabric—stuff that would end up in your washing machine, like wool and nylon and cotton. Fortunately for my self esteem, I didn't "run" on any of the other pieces. And who would want me if I did?

Then they tested me for shrinkage. Tumbled me around in that darn washer and dryer again, over and over, just like you would at your house. To my relief, every time they measured me—and it was a lot—, I hadn't shrunk much. (I had heard that if I did shrink more than 3% or so, I'd be out on my ear!)

After the fabric, the "make".

When I said this was like basic training, I wasn't kidding. They even use military guidelines for pulling inspection samples at Lands' End. And it was just my luck to be yanked for a thorough going-over of my construction, too.

Quality Assurance got out my specification sheets and their trusty rulers again. Measured me all over the place—my collar spread, chest, even my sleeve placket, to see if I matched their guidelines.

They scrutinized my stitching. Counted the number of stitches per inch—14 to 16.

Eyeballed my color. Even put me on a light box to check my shading.

Fit—the final test.

I was supposed to be a size 15½, but who would know it just by looking at me?

So they called in their 15½—not a manikin but a real guy. And lo and behold, I was a great fit!

Only the strong survive to wear this label.

Now that I've passed my trials, I'm suitable (and proud) to wear my Lands' End label.

And when you see that label on me and all of my companions in the catalog—pants, skirts, dresses, ties, jackets or whatever—you can rest assured we've all passed equally arduous tests. All in the interest of bringing you the best-made, greatest-fitting, longest-lasting clothing around.

Figure 13–1. Catalog direct response advertisement. In this engaging catalog page we have a talking shirt. Through this device the advertiser delivers a message that is wholly readable while giving a wealth of facts about the product. The long message is made easy to read because it is broken up with strong subheads. Here is an example of how a "quality" story can be made interesting.

Figure 13–2. Page from famous mail-order catalog. The name L. L. Bean has become synonymous with integrity in the mail-order world. Although the firm has broadened its line, it still caters primarily to the person seeking the best in outdoor equipment, especially those persons interested in hunting and fishing gear. As you can see, the copy style is simple but persuasive. Headlines are of the index type. Such is the reputation of L. L. Bean products that it is sufficient simply to present an item and tell what it is. This is part of the homespun character. L. L. Bean devotees don't need hard-selling headlines and jazzy illustrations.

Another advantage which eliminates the need for any specifically stated claims of quality or value is the reputation of the firm and the integrity behind the name L. L. Bean, which has become synonymous over a period of years with a good buy at a fair price.

These are things not easy to acquire, and lucky is the catalog copywriter in such a situation. Of course, it should also be noted that this firm does not seem to be overly anxious to expand its list of prospects greatly. Therein, perhaps, lies part of the reason for the seeming lack of more aggressive selling usually considered normal for any merchandising house.

Despite its nonflamboyant style, the copy sells hard. There is a simple directness that is persuasive and disarming.

Notice, too, the clear-cut, simple explanations that tell all. There is conviction in these words—much more than most "hard-hitting" copy could achieve in pages of superlatives. This is intelligent copy. Much of it has been written by people who have tried most of the products in the fields and woods. For these specialized products, offered through this unique medium, to this definite group of prospects, this copy is appropriate.

An oddity of the L. L. Bean copy is that it seems to appeal equally to the backwoodsman and the sophisticated city-dweller who escapes to the woods for weekends. In fact, the L. L. Bean company has been the subject of many admiring comments in the *New Yorker* magazine and runs advertising steadily in that urbane publication; advertising written in the same simple style found in the company's catalogs.

Now, to demonstrate a contrast to the L. L. Bean style, there is the Norm Thompson copy. Examine the examples closely. This Portland, Oregon, organization writes advertisements that carry out the principles for successful catalog copy.

Elements of Direct Response Copy as Shown in Norm Thompson's Catalogs

- Tell-all copy that answers every question a prospect might have.
- Challenging, different, benefit-filled main headlines.
- Strong main subheads to amplify the main headline (not used in *every* advertisement).
- Strong minor subheads throughout. They break up the copy and lead the reader from the start of the copy to the bottom.
- Personal writing that reaches out in a warm, friendly manner.
- Vivid, interesting writing that is never humdrum and is always *enthusiastic.*
- Vigorous endings that urge the reader to order *now.* Each advertisement included in the catalog ends on a positive note.

Now that you've seen these contrasting styles, you may be puzzled. Do the index, or label, headlines of L. L.

Figure 13–3a. Page from well-known catalog. Interesting, hard-selling headlines and an informal, story-telling style in the copy characterize the advertising of this organization.
Courtesy of Norm Thompson, Inc.

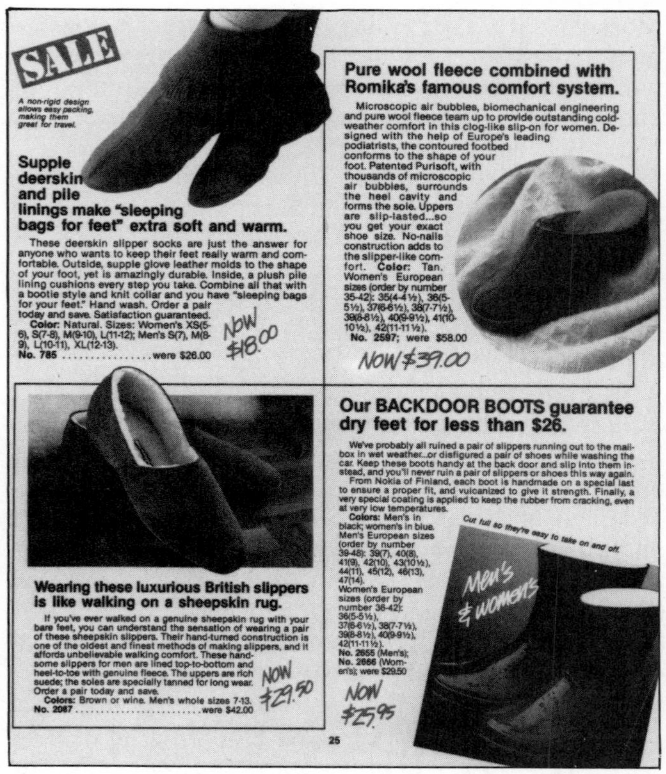

Figure 13–3b. Catalog page. Notice how the advertiser has combined a number of elements to achieve a compelling sales message: (a) Unusual headlines that create "pictures" for the readers ("is like walking on a sheepskin rug"). (b) Informal, personal, easy-to-read copy. (c) Full details that provide all the information needed to make a buying decision.
Courtesy of Norm Thompson, Inc.

Bean contrast unfavorably with the power-packed, more interesting headlines of Norm Thompson?

Many catalog authorities would say they do, but once more we get back to the advice: fit your style to the catalog's prospects. L. L. Bean's customers like and respond to the index headlines, just as they respond to the less colorful copy underneath those headlines.

In both cases, however, the writers pack the beginning and middle of the copy with the most important facts and information and then follow with material that could be cut, if necessary. This technique is somewhat reminiscent of the newswriter who puts the who-what-when-where-why in the lead and writes the rest of his story so that it can be cut at any point without making the story an incomplete unit.

Last, as is the case with all successful catalog advertisers, both companies have made the writing of ordering instructions a precise art. These instructions, given in a separate section of the catalog, are detailed, clear, and reassuring to persons inexperienced in direct response advertising.

Figure 13–4. Direct response magazine advertisement. All the elements for success are present here—an interesting headline and illustration; clear, personal copy broken up by hard-selling subheads; and a coupon that is wholly usable (unlike many coupons that provide no room to write).

Copyright Lands' End, Inc. Reprinted courtesy of Lands' End catalog.

How to Write Direct Response Copy for Magazines

Most of what has been said about writing for catalogs applies to magazines. Obviously, the tell-all principle cannot be applied so literally because of space limitations and the fact that type size in magazine advertisements is bigger than in catalog advertisements.

Once more, the copy is written to appeal to as many prospects as possible without scattering the message so broadly that it hits no one. Unless the publication itself is limited in circulation pretty much to one class of people, your display will have to do the job of attracting the attention and arousing the interest of the particular field of prospects to whom you are writing.

Despite your having been given a warning that tell-all copy is not quite so comprehensive in magazines as it is in catalogs, don't be afraid to write long copy when doing a magazine advertisement.

Long-copy direct response advertisements very often outpull short-copy advertisements, but follow these suggestions if you want your long copy to be successful: (a) Use facts and figures. (b) Avoid general statements. (c) Write interestingly. (d) Break up long copy passages with strong, selling subheads. (Persons writing magazine advertising too often forget to insert those subheads.)

Next we come to *proof.* Even more than in catalog copy it is necessary to provide proof of your claims to convince readers and to get them to act. A catalog can offer introductory pages to build its stature and its reliability, and thus the reader's confidence in the products it describes. Furthermore, after the catalog has been issued for a number of years, it achieves such a reputation for integrity that people know that the products advertised in the catalog will live up to claims that are made. Proof is still supplied, but in catalog advertising it is, in a sense, simply added insurance.

Your magazine advertisement, in contrast, must supply proof of claims as a vital ingredient, especially if the advertiser is not well known or the product is new, unusual, expensive, or complicated. Here's how to present that proof.

Eight Ways to Support Claims in Magazine Advertising

1. *Testimonials, or favorable statements.* A straightforward testimonial delivered by a credible user in a credible way is fine proof. The more specific, the better. Even if you don't have a testimonial but simply a favorable statement, you'll convince the doubters. If you have the space, you might include several such statements from users.

2. *Performance of product under demanding (seemingly impossible) conditions.* Let's say your product is a steel storage box that safeguards valuable documents in the home. Two pictures, perhaps three, show the results of a home fire that consumed everything but the box. The box is opened after the fire. Behold, the contents are unscathed. You don't need many words if you have such pictures. Without the pictures, a strongly worded account can *still* supply proof of your fireproofing claims.

3. *Performance of product under controlled conditions.* Although laboratory tests are sometimes viewed with cynicism, they still convince many persons if the tests are genuine and the laboratory is respected. Certainly, if the laboratory test is honest, it constitutes genuine proof.

4. *Figures and facts given by authorities.* Authorities are everywhere. Doctors and dentists in the professions. Scientists and engineers in the technical world. Athletes and coaches in the sports field. Your copy should make it clear that they are voicing opinions as experts, but most importantly as *disinterested* experts who have nothing to gain from their opinions. Such opinions are enough proof for many of your readers.

5. *Official recognition.* Your company's hybrid seed corn or animal feed won the gold medal at the state fair, or your flour won the bake-off at a home crafts show. Because the product won out over many rival products, you have proof of its superior qualities.

6. *Details of materials, ingredients, workmanship, or design.* Unless you're careful, this approach can be boring. If written interestingly and enthusiastically, you may be supplying all the proof needed. A sportsman will devour details of the workmanship in a deep-sea fishing reel. A homemaker reads with interest the information about the design of a new food processor that prepares vegetables or meat delectably. Many products cannot be sold without giving details—from clothes to garden carts, or stopwatches to reducing remedies.

7. *History, reputation, or background of supplier.* You're almost forced to supply this information at least occasionally. Although many will already be acquainted with the firm, there are always new prospects who must learn.

   Sometimes, the history is the history of the founder of the firm, especially in the case of a picturesque individual such as L. L. Bean who, at the beginning of his operation, was said to have personally tried out every outdoor item offered by the firm.

   Whatever route you take, individual or impersonal, at some point you will build up the supplier as proof that the goods you describe have an honorable heritage.

8. *Money-back guarantee.* Although this has been abused, and sometimes mocked, it is still regarded as proof that the advertiser has confidence in the product offered.

   Some companies have not made it very easy to "get your money back if not completely satisfied," but nevertheless most buyers are comforted by the presence of the phrase.

   When a firm achieves a towering reputation, it may not be so necessary for you to hammer this money-back assurance, but always use it for a little-known firm, especially if the product is the type about which readers might be skeptical.

Ask for the Order and Make It Urgent

You've read elsewhere in this book (and you'll read it again and again) how important it is to ask for the order. The super salesperson is the one who is a good "closer," the kind of person who, with vigor and persuasiveness, gets the prospect to sign the order or to say: "Yes, I'll take it."

Be a "closer" in all your direct response advertising. In magazine advertisements there are certain procedures you can follow. Asking for the order is handled more forcefully in direct response copy than in most other advertising (where you merely ask for some future action, perhaps no more than inviting the reader to visit a store to see the advertised product).

In direct response advertising you're actually asking for action *now* or *today.* You're asking the reader to get out a checkbook, to phone an order, to give a credit card number. You're asking for buying action that very minute. Usually, your action suggestion is at, or near, the bottom of the copy, but you can be making action suggestions throughout the text material with the biggest push to come at the end.

Ways to Get Ordering Action in Direct Response Advertising[1]

Describe special nature of offer If the offer *is* special, that fact should be made clear immediately. Normally, the special nature of the offer will be associated closely with the bargain the product or service represents. An example:

Our burglar-proof system, used by thousands of businesses, has just been modi-

1. Obviously, some of these suggestions can be used in other media, too.

fied for home use. This means that you can now enjoy complete protection in your home—*professional* protection at a price you didn't think was possible.

Caution that price will go up or show savings because price has come down

A canny direct response person never forgets that the overwhelming reason for such shopping is to get a good product at a money-saving price. This can work two ways. (a) You do the prospect a favor by giving a warning of an imminent price hike. (b) You reverse this by offering a reduced price because the firm made a good deal in its buying and is now passing on the saving, one that may never occur again. Some examples:

Warning of price hike:

- 14K gold chains $10 until Aug. 31.
- You'll never see such a low price again.
- This low price good only until May 1.
- Order today before the price goes up.
- This bargain price is going-going-GONE by Sept. 30.

Offering of reduced price:

You may wonder why we offer these religious artifacts at even lower prices than last year. The reason is simple. Two months ago our buyer located a veritable treasurehouse of these artifacts. He bought the lot at huge savings which we can now pass on to you. Savings such as you'll never see again.

Warn that there's a limit to time or supply

Prospective purchasers can get almost panicky when they learn that only a limited supply of a product is available, or that they might miss out on a bargain by not acting quickly. This "limited time" or "limited supply" approach is one of your most powerful weapons in direct response copy. It's especially suitable to magazines because catalog copy seldom talks of limited supply. That's not the way catalog houses do business. Some examples:

- Offer expires Oct. 31.
- Limit 1 per customer.
- Limited time only!
- Limited one to a family.
- Offer good while they last.

Use action-inducing words

From the beginning to the end of direct response copy, strong, exciting, moving words should be used. This is not calm, reflective prose. You must cause people to act who find it easier *not* to act. Some examples.

- Rush name and address.
- Order this exciting new catalog now.
- Don't delay. Why miss out on even one day's fun?
- Act *now!*

Stress benefit *of acting quickly*

Delay is fatal. A prospect who puts off an ordering decision is too often a lost prospect. Give this person a reward for quick action and you may turn that word "prospect" into "customer." Some examples:

- Order now and save $2.
- Orders received by Oct. 1 earn this low $15 price.
- Earn a bonus for answering before May 31.

Offer money-back guarantee

Just as the money-back guarantee is proof of your confidence in your product, so it is the final convincing argument for quick action on the part of the prospect. It can erase the last, lingering doubt. Sometimes the guarantee is headlined, but normally it's placed at the bottom of the copy. An example:

- You be the judge. If this unit isn't what you expected it to be in your 30-day trial period, return it undamaged for a no-questions-asked refund.

Use a coupon and urge reader to act upon it

Every readership study shows that coupons increase advertising readership. They also increase the number of sales and inquiries that you may expect. Unless you're very tight for space you should stress the coupon in the copy, usually in the vicinity of the coupon. In the coupon itself you should make the offer sound exciting and the filling out of the coupon quickly as an absolute-must action. Some examples:

- For your peace of mind, fill out and mail this coupon today.
- Rush coupon now while this great offer lasts.
- To be sure to receive you free catalog, mail coupon now. It will open a new, exciting world.

Writing Copy for Small Space

You may feel a bit deflated if your first direct response copy assignment is the writing of a one-inch or two-inch advertisement. Don't be upset. You'll find it a challenge. You'll learn quickly that it's an art to describe, persuade, and ask for the order in about thirty words, or less. Each word is important, so you learn not to write useless words. You cut, compress, and cut again.

You agonize over the headline which, because of space limitations, must be short. Many times you'll use an index headline, but if you have room you might try an exclamatory headline, or even an exhortative type.

Opening the copy fast with your most important benefit or appeal is more important than ever because your space is so small that there's not much left when you've written the opening. What *is* left will usually consist of a vigorous push for action, again brief.

Notice the admirable compression in the following one-inch advertisement that, despite its brevity, avoids the dull, telegraphic style that characterizes the writing of many small advertisements.

> **Vibrant Violet Bouquet.** Plant a little blooming color in your kitchen when you hang this POTHOLDER by the stove! Also, Daffodil, Zinnia, Pansies, Hyacinth, Daisy, Perfect Pinks, and a crochet basket to hold them all in! Patterns, $2 ea. All 8, $7.98. Kits, $5.98 ea. All 8, $39.95. All ppd. Annie's Attic, F138 Rte. 2, Box 212b, Big Sandy, TX 75755.
>
> (Illustration of the POTHOLDER just above the copy)

Direct Response Copy for Department Stores

Once more, if you write copy that is aimed at persuading department store customers to order by mail or phone, you'll find yourself providing full information. Bill enclosures are a common vehicle for such copy. Here are two examples:

> Outstanding Value . . .
> Wonderful Wool Sweaters for men $50 each
> Two-ply French zephyr worsted . . . that's tops in wool! These handsome sweaters are firmly knit, and sized generously. Knit tapes at neck and shoulders reinforce the seams they allow to stretch. Lightweight, warm, in colors for fall: tan, maize, blue, gray, or green. Small (38), medium (42), and large (46).
>
> Blue, pink, or white wool for your little lamb! baby blankets $19.95 each
> Keep baby warm in his transfers from bath to bed with this soft blanket. It's made in a lovely weave that is exclusive with our baby-pampering department! It has a deep fringe that actually will not tangle, thanks to an entirely new finish. Big enough for a crib . . . 40 by 48 inches.

Notice how many more factual details are included in these pieces of selling copy than would normally appear in a department store's newspaper advertisement for the same merchandise. Yet the facts are not just listed. Their importance is emphasized and their meaning expanded by an occasional, well-chosen word or phrase that doesn't merely tell the reader something—it sells him on the merits of the item. The sweater is not "all wool," it's "worsted," and "Two-ply French zephyr worsted" at that.

Yet the copy doesn't leave it to your knowledge or imagination to make even this categorized description of the material suffice. It doesn't dare, because the store knows that among its many customers are some who aren't acquainted with this type of wool, or who may not get the full implication of its quality by merely reading even this impressive description. It says in so many words that two-ply French zephyr worsted is "tops in wool!"

What's more, it recognizes that two common faults of sweaters often, paradoxically, are unwanted snugness and a tendency to stretch out of shape, especially around the neck and across the shoulders. Thus, beside the size listings at the end of the copy, it tells you that these sweaters are "sized generously," yet "firmly knit" and "knit tapes at neck and shoulders reinforce the seams they allow to stretch." Now these are some good, positive, product selling points specifically included to answer possible questions and objections by the store's prospects.

So, too, with the baby blanket. The copywriter knows that some of the more experienced shoppers among the prospects may shy away—and justifiably!—from a fringed baby blanket. The necessarily frequent launderings may do things to fringe that make it unattractive, but this blanket definitely has fringe, as the illustrations show.

Does the copy ignore that possible objection? It does not. It turns the objection into an advantage: "deep fringe that actually will not tangle, thanks to an entirely new finish." The fringe becomes another selling point.

Ordering Instructions for Printed Direct Response Advertising

Magazine, newspaper, catalog, and department store advertisers all face the problem of making ordering instructions so clear and simple that the prospect overcomes a natural reluctance to bother with the inconvenience of ordering by mail. To many persons, any mail communication is a dreaded chore. Following are some of the specifics you'll need to know about setting up the ordering process for mail response.[2]

How do you make ordering simple, easy, or even inviting? There is no single way applicable to all direct re-

2. Use of 800 toll-free numbers is discussed separately.

A safe and effective way to rid clothing of ugly pills.

Sometimes clothes look old before their time because of the accumulation of fuzz and pills. Our compact Garment Groom safely and easily removes them to give your clothes new life. It works wonders on fine knits and woven fabrics... including sweaters, the collars of dress shirts and the inseams of slacks.

Rid collars, inseams and sweaters of pills.

This cordless device glides over fabric, clipping off fuzz without pulling or tearing. Pills are collected in a see-through bin that can be easily removed for cleaning. Our Garment Groom was developed by a facial-shaver manufacturer, so it utilizes the same high-tech innovations as the newest shavers on the market. Requires one C battery (not included). **$13.95 ppd.**

Dept. 02-129, P.O. Box 3999, Portland, OR 97208

Garment Groom **No. 9397F** Qty_____ Total $_____
☐ Check ☐ VISA ☐ M.Card ☐ Am.Express ☐ Diners/C.B.

Card # _____ Exp. _____

Sig. X_____ Phone _____

Name _____

Address _____

City_____

State _____ Zip _____

Order toll free 1-800-547-1160
☐ **Send FREE "ESCAPE from the ordinary"® catalog.**

Norm Thompson

Figure 13–5. **Direct response magazine advertisement.** Notice how the writer of this copy started out by stating a "suffering" point and then proceeded to show how the product answers the suffering point. A strong headline leads the reader into the copy by stressing a benefit. Despite the small size of the coupon, it supplies the needed information for ordering, and, happily, provides room to write.

Figure 13–6. **Direct response advertisement.** The company selling this product has had much success in selling leisure-type products. In this instance, the advertisement ran in *Architectural Digest,* a publication reaching an affluent and responsive market. One fault, which the advertiser has since corrected, is that there is far too little space in the coupon for the city name and address.

sponse selling, so first look at the three principal methods of encouraging or inviting the order by mail:

- An order blank (perhaps with an addressed postage-guaranteed envelope)
- A return postcard (always self-addressed and usually, today, with postage guaranteed) and coupons
- Advertisements without coupons; contain mere statements of ordering requirements and mailing address

Obviously, the first two are definitely *ordering aids.* They remove some of the burden imposed upon the purchaser by the fact that he can't just hand you his money and carry off his purchase. The third relieves the purchaser of none of the effort required to place an order. Which method should you use? The major consideration is your medium. Catalogs, for example, usually include an order blank, perhaps several, to encourage frequent ordering. Direct mail-order offerings frequently have a return postcard enclosed. The coupon is commonly part of a direct response advertisement in a publication. Ordering information alone is usually used either in printed advertisements too small to accommodate coupons or in radio commercials. Now to discuss each of these methods.

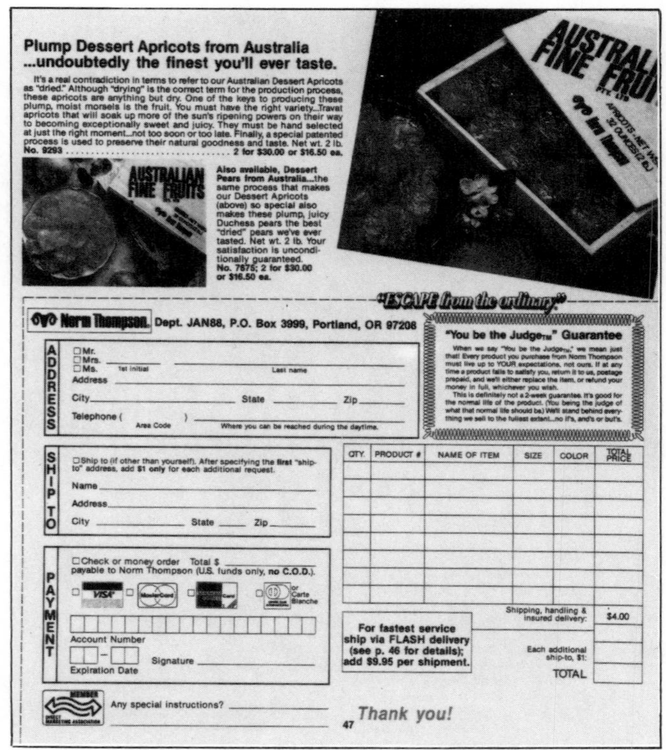

Plump Dessert Apricots from Australia ...undoubtedly the finest you'll ever taste.

It's a real contradiction in terms to refer to our Australian Dessert Apricots as "dried." Although "drying" is the correct term for the production process, these apricots are anything but dry. One of the keys to producing these plump, moist morsels is the fruit. You must have the right variety...Travat apricots that will soak up more of the sun's ripening powers on their way to becoming exceptionally sweet and juicy. They must be hand selected at just the right moment...not too soon or too late. Finally, a special patented process is used to preserve their natural goodness and taste. Net wt. 2 lb. No. 9293 .... 2 for $30.00 or $16.50 ea.

Also available, Dessert Pears from Australia...the same process that makes our Dessert Apricots (above) so special also makes these plump, juicy Duchess pears the best "dried" pears we've ever tasted. Net wt. 2 lb. Your satisfaction is unconditionally guaranteed. No. 7675; 2 for $30.00 or $16.50 ea.

"ESCAPE from the ordinary"

Norm Thompson. Dept. JAN88, P.O. Box 3999, Portland, OR 97208

"You be the Judge™" Guarantee

When we say "You be the Judge™," we mean just that! Every product you purchase from Norm Thompson must live up to YOUR expectations, not ours. If at any time a product fails to satisfy you, return it to us, postage prepaid, and we'll either replace the item, or refund your money in full, whichever you wish.

This is definitely not a 2-week guarantee. It's good for the normal life of the product. (You being the judge of what that normal life should be.) We'll stand behind everything we sell to the fullest extent...no if's, and's or but's.

ADDRESS
☐ Mr. ☐ Mrs. ☐ Ms. ____ 1st initial ____ Last name
Address ____
City ____ State ____ Zip ____
Telephone (Area Code) ____ Where you can be reached during the daytime.

SHIP TO
☐ Ship to (if other than yourself). After specifying the first "ship-to" address, add $1 only for each additional request.
Name ____
Address ____
City ____ State ____ Zip ____

PAYMENT
☐ Check or money order Total $ ____ payable to Norm Thompson (U.S. funds only, no C.O.D.).
☐ VISA ☐ MasterCard ☐ ☐ or Carte Blanche
Account Number
Expiration Date Signature ____

QTY.	PRODUCT #	NAME OF ITEM	SIZE	COLOR	TOTAL PRICE

Shipping, handling & insured delivery: $4.00
Each additional ship-to, $1:
TOTAL

For fastest service ship via FLASH delivery (see p. 46 for details); add $9.95 per shipment.

Any special instructions? ____

47 Thank you!

Figure 13–7. Order blank for catalog. Simple and well-organized, this order blank can serve as a model.

Order Blanks

Order blanks usually are the most elaborate of the methods to invite orders. Because they normally accompany catalogs, more than one type of item may be—and usually is—ordered on one blank. This means that often different kinds of information may be required for each item: color, pattern, finish, initials (for monograms), width, length, size, model, price each, per pair, or per set, and so on.

General merchandise houses have many regular customers ordering several times a season or year; thus, they must keep up-to-date information on customers' addresses, past and current.

Because they sell on several different sets of terms—cash, time-payment accounts, open accounts, and credit cards are the most common—the payment method must be recorded on the order blank. Spaces are provided for such details.

A choice of shipment methods must be provided on the blank. Then allowance must be made for catalog numbers, quantity ordered, name and shipping weight of each item, and then totals on the weights, prices, postage, and taxes, as required.

Coupons and Return Postcards

Coupons and postcards are similar to each other, although the customary difference in their sizes may at first mask the resemblance. A study of their mutual requirements will show their similarity.

Very frequently both return postcards and coupons include some inducement for prompt reply, often in addition to any such urge previously incorporated into the accompanying mailing piece of advertisement. One of the most common is some variation of the magic word "free":

Free Examination Postcard

Free 10-Day Trial Coupon!

Free Sample

Free Catalog

Don't Wait—Send Coupon Today for Approval Offer

Good for Both Free

As a rule these are in some sort of display type—quite often in a "reverse" panel—but sometimes they may be set in relatively small type, especially in small coupons. Other typical incentives for ordering include such inducements as variations of the common one, "Mail This Coupon Today!" and others a little more original, like:

Clip This Coupon—Mail Today

Order with This Handy Coupon

We Accept Your Invitation

Mail This Card to Secure Your Copy

Complete Crochet Library—Only 10¢ a Book

Get the Facts by Mail

Mail Opportunity Coupon for Quick Action

Phone—Wire—Use Coupon

This Certificate Saves You $3

All of these, of course, besides urging prompt action, call attention to the coupon (or card). To accomplish a similar purpose, an arrow or some similar eye-directing device is sometimes incorporated into the advertising layout, although nowadays many layout artists tend to scorn such "corny" treatment.

They prefer to accomplish the same result more subtly by designing the entire piece to lead the eye "naturally" through the steps of the selling process, ending logically with the final step: the action-inducing coupon.

Another feature that most return postcards and advertisement coupons share is the inclusion of some sort of statement to make them more personal, as if the purchaser had written them himself. The one you are most familiar with undoubtedly is "Please send me . . .," or any of its close relatives, followed by a brief restatement of the offer made in the mailing piece or advertisement, again usually phrased in the first person, supposedly the sender's words.

Offer a Choice of Ways to Pay

Common also to both return postcard and coupon order forms is not merely a restatement of the price but a provision for stating the method of payment chosen. Even where no choice is offered, this is included as a precaution against any misunderstanding by the purchaser.

The following illustrations of typical wordings (most of them self-explanatory as to the terms offered) will show you how such statements may be handled:

☐ Charge My Account; ☐ Find Check or M.O. Enclosed. Please include 3% sales tax on orders in *(state).*

☐ Money Order or Check; ☐ Charge My Account. (Please do not send currency or stamps.)

Check for ________ enclosed. No C.O.D.'s
Check ☐ I am enclosing $________. Ship Postpaid.
One ☐ Ship C.O.D. I'll pay postman $________ plus postage.

Please send me the books checked, at 25¢ each. I enclose ________ .

Mail *(Title of book set)* on 7 days' free trial. If O.K. I will remit $1 in 7 days and $1 monthly until $6 is paid. Otherwise I will return them. No obligation unless I am satisfied.

Within ten days I will either return the books and owe nothing, or send you $1.50 and the $2.00 a month for three months until the special price of $7.50, plus postage, is paid.

☐ Check here if you send the full price of $7.50 with this card. We will pay the postage. Same return privilege and refund if you're not satisfied.

Enclosed is 25¢ (in coin) and the top of a package or sack of your ________. Please send me one of ________.

Total enclosed	Or please charge to my account
$ ________	• Visa
Bank # ____ ____ ____	• MasterCard
Account No. ________	Expiration date ________

Many cards and coupons offer return privileges "without obligation," or perhaps a "free trial" offer, restated in the body of the card or coupon, to make sure the purchaser understands that his signature does not obligate him finally and irrevocably to buy.

Other Details, Such As Keying and Addressing

All return postcards and coupons include the name and address of the seller. The cards, of course, always have them printed on the address side of the card and some-

Figure 13–8. Direct response advertisement. Look carefully at this advertisement. It sold more than 5,000 of the item in a 6-week period. In that time it ran several times in the *Wall Street Journal, New York Times,* and *USA Today.*

times repeated on the order side for the prestige they may lend the offer. The coupons include them primarily to ensure that the purchaser has an accurate address for use on the envelope in which he sends the coupon.

One other use is to test the response to the publication in which an advertisement appears, or the returns on each of several mailing lists the seller may be renting. This may be done by "keying" the address. Frequently this key is a fictitious "department" designation.

For instance, suppose you are running the same advertisement in the magazines *Farm Journal* and *Successful Farming* and want to test their relative effectiveness as order-getters. Like the rest of the advertisement, you make the coupon the same in both publications except for the department in the address, which you would most likely designate as "Dept. FJ," "Dept. SF," respectively.

As for the customer's name and address, illegibility is such a problem that you'll probably use the common request, "Please print." The form and space you provide for the purchaser's address may vary with the classes or groups of people who are expected to respond.

If they are city folks, for example, you'll most likely ask for *street and number* (and perhaps *apartment number*), *city, state, and zip.* In addition, you may want other information about the purchaser:

- Is "he" Mr., Mrs., Miss, Ms.? (one to circle)
- What is his date of birth?
- Does he own a car? What make? What model? What year?
- Is he a homeowner or does he rent?
- Does he carry insurance? On himself? On his house? On his car? Other?

Perhaps you need credit references—a bank, names of two business houses where he has established credit, or names of two businesspeople who know him. In any case, your card or coupon will have to provide space for any of these additional pieces of information which you require.

One word of caution: *give your purchaser enough space to fill in the information most important to you*—usually name and address. You'll find it wiser and more profitable to forego some information in order to give the respondent room in which to write out name and address. If a customer's name and address is "Humphrey Stanislavski, Oklahoma City, OK," but you have provided barely enough space for a customer to write: "Ned Hay, Erie, PA," then you'll get no reply. Give *plenty* of room for the city name.

Finally, your "miniature order blank" may have to provide spaces for information essential to proper filling of the order, if any choice is involved, or if alternate selections are offered.

Advertisements without Coupons: What to Do

What about the advertisement that doesn't have enough room for a coupon?

You might as well make up your mind that you aren't usually going to get so many replies from couponless advertisements, as compared to those in which you include coupons. You may say, "I don't have room for a coupon, and I don't have enough money to increase the size of my advertisement sufficiently to include a coupon, but I still have to run an advertisement for my mail-order offering. What do I do then?"

First, you can include adequate ordering information as a part of your advertisement's copy so that it brings in a profitable number of orders. Second, you can state the ordering requirements simply. Third, be certain that the requirements are reduced to the basic necessities; that only truly essential elements are included. Fourth, you can sometimes use the page margin as a place to put ordering information.

¡Speak Spanish like a diplomat!®

What sort of people need to learn a foreign language as quickly and effectively as possible? *Foreign service personnel,* that's who. Members of America's diplomatic corps are assigned to U.S. embassies abroad, where they must be able to converse fluently in every situation.

Now you can learn to speak Spanish just as these diplomatic personnel do—with the Foreign Service Institute's Programmatic Spanish Course. You'll learn Latin American Spanish recorded by native speakers.

The U.S. Department of State has spent thousands of dollars developing this course. It's by far *the most effective way* to learn Spanish at your own convenience and at your own pace.

The course consists of a series of cassettes and accompanying textbook. Simply follow the spoken and written instructions, listening and repeating. By the end of the course, you'll be learning and speaking entirely in Spanish!

This course turns your cassette player into a "teaching machine." With its unique "programmatic" learning method, you set your own pace—testing yourself, correcting errors, reinforcing accurate responses.

The FSI's Programmatic Spanish Course comes in two volumes, each shipped in a handsome library binder. Order either, or save 10% by ordering both:

☐ **Volume I: Basic.** 12 cassettes (17 hr.), manual, and 464-p. text, **$135.**

☐ **Volume II: Intermediate.** 8 cassettes (12 hr.), manual, and 614-p. text, **$120.** (CT residents add sales tax.)

TO ORDER BY PHONE, PLEASE CALL TOLL-FREE NUMBER: **1-800-243-1234.**

To order by mail, clip this ad and send with your name and address, and a check or money order, or charge to your credit card (VISA, MasterCard, AmEx, Diners) by enclosing card number, expiration date, and your signature.

The Foreign Service Institute's Spanish course is unconditionally guaranteed. Try it for three weeks. If you're not convinced it's the fastest, easiest, most painless way to learn Spanish, return it and we'll refund every penny you paid. Order today!

130 courses in 46 other languages also available. Write us for free catalog. Our 15th year.

Spanish

AUDIO·FORUM®

Audio-Forum
Room K200
On-The-Green,
Guilford, CT 06437
(203) 453-9794

Figure 13–9. Direct-response magazine advertisement. This very successful, hard-selling advertisement served as an illustration in the fifth edition of *Advertising Copywriting.* Since that time, it has been updated but the basic copy, and approach, remain unchanged. The "Tell-All" principle is admirably demonstrated in the copy. By the time the reader reaches the bottom of the advertisement all needed information has been given. A measure of success of the advertisement is shown in the low rate of product returned, only 5.2%. This is evidence that those ordering the item have found that it lives up to the words describing it. Although this is a long-copy advertisement (especially for its size), when a product is good, interesting, and needed, and the copy is first-rate, people will read the long copy to the last word.

Courtesy of Jeffrey Norton and Don Hauptman.

If There's No Coupon, How Do You Ask for Payment?

If you read carefully the quotations from postcards and coupons a few paragraphs back, you'll recall that even with these ordering devices some merchandisers have avoided the need for a remittance with the order. Of course, this is relatively simple for a department store selling either to its charge account customers or making C.O.D. sales locally where its truck drivers can collect for the merchandise at the time of delivery. But the requirement for cash, money order, or check with the order is being omitted by more and more nonlocal advertisers who have neither charge customers nor any delivery system of their own.

Credit card purchases through such reputable issuers as VISA, MasterCard, Diners Club, or American Express are welcomed more and more by mail-order advertisers who use, or don't use, coupons. The credit card holder is asked to give the card number and the expiration date. This request can fit easily into the coupon-less advertisement.

Along with the invitation to buy through the credit card is the invitation to phone in the order through a toll-free 800 number. Usually, you'll ask the prospect to give his credit card number when the call is made, or you may warn that *only* prospects with credit cards should use the 800 number.

Once popular with advertisers, the C.O.D. payment is almost invisible these days. In fact, many firms include the phrase: "No C.O.D.'s, please." Credit cards have done much to replace the C.O.D. method of payment, which was used chiefly for bigger purchasers.

"Bill me later" is a phrase found in some advertisements, especially when the advertiser is pushing hard for the sale and is willing to chance a number of nonpayments. Book clubs and record clubs also use time-payment plans wherein the purchaser pays each time a book or record selection is received.

If you're typical you'll probably agree that cleaning silver is one of the most dreaded household tasks. Still, if you want to show off that fine silver of yours you have to *clean* it, so what's the answer? Here it is—the Ezy-Kleen magnesium silver-cleaning tray. Now, at *last*, you can clean silver without all that hand-rubbing and those messy cleaning solutions. Here's how the Ezy-Kleen tray method works. Put tarnished silver in the tray, cover with hot water and detergent, and let it soak for twenty minutes. Take it out, rinse and dry. You'll find your silver sparkling clean. You see, while it's in the tray the detergent working with the magnesium coating of the tray cleans silver gently but with such effectiveness that it shines like new when you take it out of the water. No wonder Ezy-Kleen carries the Good Housekeeping Seal and is endorsed by leading silver manufacturers. But this tray, that lasts a lifetime, does more than just clean flatware. It's big enough to hold and clean bowls, platters and other sizable silver items. You've seen Ezy-Kleen advertised in *Woman's Day, Good Housekeeping* and other top women's magazines and now, while supplies last, you can buy it only at Barkliss Brothers in our downtown store. To get *your* Ezy-Kleen send $22.50 to our silverware department, or phone 338-9999. That's 338-9999. This is being offered only to our radio listeners. Get your order in now for Ezy-Kleen, the magnesium silver-cleaning tray—*only* at Barkliss.

Figure 13–10. Direct response radio commercial (tell-all type). In this instance the advertiser wanted to test the pulling power of radio. Thus, the offer for this very special item was made only on radio. In order to do a complete selling job the advertiser bought a 90-second commercial. Even then the announcer was instructed to read fast and with enthusiasm. Because the commercial was repeated several times, it was felt that any facts missed in the first airing would be absorbed in other broadcasts. The department store is so well-known in the listening area that ordering directions were simplified.

Can You Use Tell-All in a Radio Commercial?

The answer is that you don't. Even a person buying an item in a retail store would seldom have each feature pointed out before deciding to make the purchase. In radio, too, although you include important details, you won't include *every* point. Suppose, for example, that you were writing the commercial to follow the interest-arousing lead-in for the silver-cleaning tray (Figure 13–10). How best can you (in one minute, or sometimes less) tell your prospects the features most likely to induce them to purchase? What would they want to know about the product? First, forget you're a copywriter. Instead, you're all the listeners to the station carrying the tray offer. You're attracted by and interested in the announcer's opening lines, but even so, you may be overwhelmed by all the details.

Radio is not the ideal tell-all medium. Instead, it's used most effectively to put across one point emphatically. Listeners simply cannot absorb a number of points made over the air, even though they give the commercial full attention.

Despite the fact that it seemed that the tray commercial was jammed with selling points, one big point was made and repeated—that the listeners owning the tray could clean silver easily.

Sometimes you may make an offer on radio that consists of many points, no one of which you expect to register strongly with your listeners. Your purpose is simply to make prospects aware that your product or service has an amazing number of fine attributes for the money you're asking.

Although such a technique will work, it is still best to write radio commercials that register one idea overwhelmingly. If this means you don't use tell-all in your radio commercials, so be it.

You Show Them in Television; It's Better Than Just Telling

Television, of course, can go beyond radio in its ability to show merchandise as well as talk about it—and often even more important—to *demonstrate* it. Your selling principles for copywriting are not changed by television, merely enhanced.

Possibilities of television go beyond even illustrations in print, for the product can be shown in actual use, including all views of it and demonstrations of its performance. Different models, patterns, or styles available may be shown—and color selections, too. In fact, the scope of direct response selling by air is unlimited when the possibilities of showing products being modeled or otherwise in use, a full range of styles or patterns—and colors, too—are considered.

Direct response selling will merely be adapted to suit the medium and the selling advantages it offers, but direct response selling principles will not—cannot—be eliminated. Nor will their fundamental sales psychology be altered. Television's biggest asset as a sales-maker lies in its illustrative advantages, its ability to enhance verbal description, not replace it.

Added Tips for Direct Response Television

Believability, of course, is a goal of all advertising, no matter what medium is being used. If you have been used to writing print direct response, you may be shocked on occasion by what happens to believability in television commercials. That's because the announcer's style and manner of delivery can make such a difference. What is desirable enthusiasm in print can become pitchman pressure in television. Repetition that is acceptable in print copy can, if not handled well in television commercials, become inexpressibly boring and/or irritating.

If your announcer comes on too strong in your commercial, believability suffers. Believability in television is based on two elements: (a) Believable words and claims. These are *your* contribution. (b) Believable delivery of those words and claims. This is out of your control unless you can persuade your bosses to let you participate in the choice of announcers and contribute your ideas of interpretation at taping sessions. No one knows better than you how you want your lines delivered. But if you don't get the chance to express your opinions, an insincere, glib, con-man type of delivery can turn off your audience. So do everything you can to be a part of the production sessions.

Uncomplicated commercials, whether for radio or television, should be your goal. What is uncomplicated? A commercial that holds down the number of ideas and speaks in language understandable by all levels of your audience. A commercial with a message that can be picked up even by the inattentive viewer (and you can count on most of your viewers to be inattentive).

Use *supers* freely. Supers (for superimposition) are printed words appearing on the screen that repeat an important point being made at the same time in the audio. When your audience reads a message at the same time it's hearing it, you put the point over strongly.

Ask for *orders* positively and don't hesitate to be repetitive. Ordering directions should be given at least twice. And the closing panel in which appear all the instructions for ordering—such as telephone number to call, method of payment, and description of the offer—should remain on-screen long enough to give the viewer a chance to write down what is needed to order.

Joe and Sally Fiske are sitting in the living room watching television. Suddenly, a friendly sounding voice is trying to sell a product on the screen. Now, as a writer, how do you keep Fiske Senior from instantly pressing the "mute" button on the remote control? You'd better be sure you've made that "friendly sounding voice" forceful enough to hold their attention for the message.

Above all, you want to persuade Joe or Sally to pick up a pencil in order to write down the 800 number. Otherwise, zap goes the commercial.

As said earlier, your announcer must avoid being too aggressive but must, nonetheless, create a sense of urgency so the Fiskes will pick up that pencil.

To create that urgency you fill your copy with action words and then hope that the announcer knows how to deliver them forcefully, but bearably. Your good copy can be enhanced by such factors as the announcer's tone of voice, emphasis, and rate of delivery.

14

DIRECT MAIL

When You Really Want to Get Personal

It was just another day along the 400 block of Frederick Avenue as three persons opened first-class letters delivered a few minutes earlier.

Jim Orton sighed. Another letter from his college asking for a contribution to the building fund, along with a description of the wonders of the school's educational program.

Jane Milne, on the other hand, read with interest a letter urging her to add to her set of collector's-item plates that seemed to appreciate in value each year.

Carl Brock, like Jane, liked what he read about the opening of a local travel agency. A frequent traveler, Carl put the letter to one side for future reference.

Each of this trio had to handle the communication—to feel it, see it, think about it. It was a personal experience, an individual experience. It was different in these respects from other media contacts.

For instance, you may have in your typewriter a copy sheet on which you've written several ideas for a television commercial that will be seen on the network by millions of people. On your desk is a version of the same campaign that will appear in big-circulation magazines. Despite your progress, you're dissatisfied. You've found it hard to invest your copy with any personal quality. How do you get personal with millions of people?

One way is to forget you're writing to a faceless mass of viewers or readers. Instead, you visualize one person in that mass. You write to him or her. Possibly this will work. Perhaps it won't. Lucky you, if you're writing direct-mail copy, because there's no need to pretend. You *are* writing to one person. Herein lies the great advantage of the medium.

This personal quality is one reason why direct mail has become almost a universal medium. Of thousands of businesses, only relatively few advertise on the air, in national magazines, or in any medium but their local newspapers. Almost every firm, however, uses direct-mail advertising, even though it uses other media as well.

You Pick Your Targets in Direct Mail

Direct-mail advertising gets your message in print personally and individually to a selected group of prospects or customers with whom you want to do business or whose goodwill you want to establish or maintain. This is a truly "direct" medium, usually conveyed entirely by "mail," as opposed to direct response, which may use radio, television, and publication advertising in soliciting mail business.

Some direct-mail pieces are also distributed in other ways. A folder, for example, devised primarily as a mailing piece to accompany a department store's monthly charge account statements, may also be used as a pickup piece in a suitable spot in the store—probably in the department whose merchandise or service it publicizes.

This kind of promotion is sometimes called direct advertising and is considered the same as direct-mail advertising. In this discussion it will be assumed, however, that you are writing to relatively sharply defined groups—in other words, you are creating direct-mail advertising.

Why Use Direct Mail?

At one time the Direct Mail Advertising Association issued a list of forty-nine ways direct-mail advertising could be used as a part of modern merchandising methods. Although many variations in these applications have been made, a listing of some of the most common basic uses will give you an idea of the scope of this medium and how greatly you would have to vary your writing to meet the requirements of some of these uses:

- To sell goods or services by mail. (Although this use does not necessarily anticipate return orders by mail, its purpose is primarily the same as "direct mail-order," covered in the last chapter.)
- To reach all customers regularly with merchandise offers, thereby keeping accounts active.
- To support salespeople, pave the way for them, thus backing their selling efforts and economizing on their time (and on the prospects' time and patience) when actually making sales calls.
- To bring in orders between salespeople's calls or from territories not covered by salespeople (or, in consumer selling, areas not serviced through retail outlets), or to open up new territories.
- To broadcast mailings to and request inquiries from a large group of prospects. Names thus obtained are passed on to dealers, jobbers, or salespeople for solicitation, or are further contacted by additional direct mail. Getting names this way saves the expense of indiscriminate distribution of catalogs since requests are from definite prospects.
- To provide news and information about the firm or its products. This might include "education" of stockholders on company products, services, and policies—either from a public relations point of view, or as encouragement of their patronage, or perhaps of their word-of-mouth advertising.
- To tie-in with trade or consumer publication advertising or to sell dealers on trade paper or consumer advertising programs. Such selling stimulates their cooperative efforts.
- To stimulate dealer sales by consumer mailings—perhaps by suggesting a visit to the prospect's "nearest dealer." Jobber sales may also be spurred by mailing to dealers.
- To induce a dealer's own customers or prospects to visit his store—or a manufacturer's customers his showroom—to see some special goods described or illustrated.
- To overcome competition threatening the established customer or adverse market tendencies. The quick publicizing of a revised price list might fall into this class.
- To pretest on a limited scale contemplated offers or presentations against each other, using different lists or splitting a single list.
- To stimulate sales or to increase acceptance of the firm's merchandise or services through enclosures in all outgoing envelopes (with dividend checks or financial statements to stockholders, for example).
- To request information from prospects to determine their needs. The information will be used as a basis for further mailings or salesperson's solicitation. The items will be specifically suited to prospects' requirements.

In this incomplete list, you have a range of jobs that call for many different types of copy treatment. Yet they offer you one advantage—that of knowing the needs and wants of the prospects to whom you are writing. Because of the selective nature of direct mail, you write more surely to the prospect's interest than in general media such as newspapers, radio, and TV.

One prestige retail clothing chain, for example, mails advance announcements of its seasonal traveling merchandise displays to charge customers and former cash customers. Because this is a very well-defined group of prospects already aware of the company's reputation, styles, and values, the headline of one announcement reads merely

> (*Company name*) Clothes for Spring and Summer

almost a pure index-type headline, with institutional and prestige overtones. Contrast this with another—this one of a nonmail-order catalog cover of a chain of retail auto supply stores, based primarily on price appeal (but including some reassurance of quality):

> SAVE 25% to 50% from List Price on GUARANTEED REPLACEMENT AUTO PARTS

Here is a headline aimed unmistakably at a large—almost universal—but yet quite definite class of prospects (automobile owners) to induce them to visit their local store of the chain where the products listed may be purchased.

Normally, You Don't Complete the Sale in Direct-Mail Advertising

Unlike mail-order selling, direct-mail advertising does not attempt to do the entire selling job, right down to and including asking for the order except, of course, in the case of direct mail-order selling. Rather, any one piece of direct-mail advertising generally is intended to accomplish only one step in completion of the sale.

Referring to the list of common uses of direct mail, you will find that, while it usually suggests some sort of action—perhaps only passively as in showing willingness to listen to a salesman when he calls—it may actually be used merely to implant a certain idea in the mind of the recipient which calls for no action (for the present, at least) by him. Because direct-mail advertising usually is intended to further the sale and because it is not intended to complete the sale by itself, the copy you write must be keyed to the purpose for which the mailing is intended—but *must not go beyond it.*

There is another reason, however, for not telling all in

many direct-mail pieces, even though they may not be one of a series or campaign, but merely a single mailing. Imagine that you are writing a "one-shot" direct-mail piece for the women's better-coat department of a retail store. You are announcing to your store's charge customers, in advance of your general newspaper advertisement, the arrival of a special group of luxuriously fur-trimmed cloth coats, and you are urging the customers' advance inspection of these models for a complete selection.

Your purpose is to get customers into the department. Do you tell them, then, all about the coat? Do you list all the colors available? Every kind of fur in the group? Do you illustrate every style? You do not! If you list certain specific styles, you're sure to cause some prospects to shun your copy because they have other styles in mind.

Of course, there are some things you will want to tell your prospects. Sizes, for example. There's no point in making the size 12 or size 44 customer angry at you for wasting the time it takes to come downtown when your size range begins with 14 and ends at 40. In most cases, you'll list the range of prices, too, for much the same reason. If your buyer is a smart merchandiser, there should be included at least one model in the group that can be priced at a comparatively low figure, perhaps because of a lesser amount of fur used (although probably not a cheaper fur) on a coat which, because of its styling or material, seems otherwise to "belong" with the more expensive models.

Thus, instead of having to admit to a limited price range, say of $375 to $449.50, you may be able to claim that "these exclusive creations begin at the tiny price of $225, while you'll hardly believe we could sell the most luxurious models for their modest price of only $449.50."

Tell Just Enough to Keep Prospect Interested

In all direct-mail advertising that contemplates an eventual sale, tell enough to interest the prospect—and to keep him interested until you have the opportunity to complete the sale. But don't tell "your all" or you may never have the chance to make that sale. This strategy applies as well to a series of related, progressive-step mailings as it does to a single one. Don't weaken your next mailing by telling its story before the strategic time. It applies even when your anticipated sale, following a direct-mail campaign, will be requested by mail as well—a direct-mail order.

When you don't follow this strategy—when you rob your following mailings of their impact by anticipating their parts of the sales story early in the campaign—your prospects either become confused by the size and scope of the early bombardment or become tired and bored with the succession of old stuff which comes in subsequent mailings. In either case you have almost certainly lost the sale.

One caution you should remember, however, in applying this strategy: In any direct-mail campaign—despite the fact that one major impression is all you can expect to get across in any one mailing—each mailing should be complete in itself. It should not be dependent either upon earlier pieces or pieces yet to come. Even though you cannot, of course, tell all of a multipart story in a single mailing, you must stress adequately the feature chosen for emphasis in that mailing. Know exactly what purpose you want each piece to accomplish, then write your copy to achieve that purpose—and nothing more.

Writing the Copy

As in any other type of copy you're concerned with: (a) Start out powerfully. (b) Continue in the body of your writing (letters or folders or mailers) the momentum generated by the opening. (c) End positively.

To break down these three steps:

Start out powerfully by:

- Offering a benefit in the first paragraph and/or headline.
- Playing up this benefit in the following paragraph to emphasize its importance.

Continue the momentum by:

- Explaining in detail the attributes of the products, or service, and how these attributes will be of value to the prospect. This explanation must be preceded by your learning everything about the product, especially what makes it different or superior to rival products.
- Offering proof that the product is what you say it is, and will do what you say it will. Proof can be in the form of performance tests, laboratory findings, surveys, endorsements, testimonials, or a report that shows how well the product is selling.
- Building the stature of the advertiser for integrity, reliability, and longtime contributions.
- Using, in folders and other long-copy vehicles, attention-getting, strong-selling subheads. Make them so strong and so clear that the prospect will know broadly what you want him to know if he reads nothing but the main head and subheads.

End positively by:

- Repeating what benefit the prospect will derive if he gets the product or service and pointing out the melancholy consequences of not getting it.
- Urging immediate action, namely buying, trying, inquiring, seeing, or some other sort of follow-up.

Techniques to Utilize

Remember the previous stress placed on the personal character of direct mail? In general, use a simple, personal, conversational writing style. No fancy words and sentences. (You may wish to ignore the very simple, very personal style for certain audiences that are used to technical language and suspicious of excessive familiarity. Such audiences might be composed of doctors, engineers, and other professionals.)

For direct mail, don't be afraid to repeat the name of the product. Repeat it enough to drive it home. You'll be surprised how often you can repeat the name without offense; that is, if you're clever enough.

In folders and other long-copy pieces you'll probably use a number of illustrations. Accompany each of these with strong, interesting captions. Write these captions so that the quick-glance reader will be given a quick, clear explanation of the illustration.

Your Material Should Be Physically Inviting to Read

Certainly, what you say is important. Unfortunately, if your material is physically unattractive, your prospects may never read what you say. Make your letter or folder so attractive and make it look so easy to read that you won't lose your prospects before they find out what you have to offer. Much material received in the mails *looks* so difficult that a prospect's initial glance is the *only* glance given it.

Because direct mail appears in so many forms, it is not possible to discuss them all. Thus, only two of the more common forms will be covered here: the letter and the folder. Following are some ways to make them more physically attractive and, by doing so, to make more certain that they will be given more than one quick glance:

Letters

There are general rules applying to sales letters. There are many variations possible but what you read here, if applied, can help you avoid some of the great faults of direct-mail letters, physically speaking—and quite apart from writing technique. For this discussion, we will assume that we are talking about one-page letters and that we are using block form in which the type is flush left with no indentations for paragraphs.

Short opening paragraph. Don't smother your reader with the first paragraph. Limit it to a maximum of four lines and it can be shorter.

No paragraph longer than eight lines. When a paragraph is longer than eight lines, the sales points tend to become buried. Furthermore, the sight of long paragraphs has a depressing effect on readers—the kind of feeling that they had when they were faced with long, laborious paragraphs in school textbooks. A textbook writer can get away with this because the student has to read a textbook; a prospect does not have to read a sales letter.

Paragraph length varied. A letter with all paragraphs the same length looks dull and monotonous. This observation applies whether the paragraphs are all long or all short. It is easy to vary paragraph length. Do it. Occasionally, you might want to use a paragraph of a single line or just several words. This will make your letter more interesting.

Type masses broken up. Why daunt the reader with a whole page of solid, unbroken type? One way to open up the letter invitingly is to use the occasional one-line paragraph already mentioned. Another effective method is to set off important material by indenting it and giving it space above and below. As an example, suppose you want to give a name and address in the letter. The preceding line might read:

When you're in Parkersburg be sure to visit:

John G. Smelzer
Smelzer Pottery Company
18 W. Elizabeth Street

The centering of the name and address creates a pleasing open effect in the letter and focuses the reader's attention on the information.

George S. Gratote
1118 N. Palmetto Drive
Wiscasete, Florida 32118

Dear Mr. Gratote:

Your name was given to me with a notation that you might be a prospect for membership in our club. This is good news indeed. You will find information about our facility in the enclosed brochure.

Some of the highlights of the Wiscasete Athletic Club as described in the brochure:

- An Olympic size 6-lane swimming pool.
- A 3-lane indoor track for walkers, joggers and runners.
- A whirlpool adjacent to the pool.
- Six courts for racquetball and handball.
- Two completely equipped exercise rooms.
- Two full-sized basketball courts.

As you can see, there's something for everyone at the WAC. This has been our guiding principle at the Club--to provide a wide variety of activities for all age groups and for all levels of athletic ability. You can be as vigorous as you wish, or you can exercise enough to achieve a feeling of well-being without any attendant strain.

A special program is available for young mothers. While these mothers take part in group or individual activities they can leave their children in the care of an attendant in the large, attractive nursery.

A full-time staff guides athletic programs with much attention given to individual instruction in sports or in fitness exercises. A physical education specialist will chart out a program for you that is geared to your degree of physical fitness. This will be done after our Fitness Center has first determined your blood pressure, heart and lung condition, and other points relating to your overall fitness.

Our hours make it possible for you to enjoy your Club whenever you wish--seven days a week from 6 a.m. until 10 p.m. And you'll be comfortable whenever you come in because we're completely air-conditioned.

Notice that a schedule of rates and classes of memberships appears on the back page of the brochure. When you've looked this over please call me if you have any questions or, better yet, let me know when you'd like to join our club.

Cordially,

J. R. Minifield
Membership Secretary
Wiscasete Athletic Club

Figure 14–1. Sales letter. The writer has made the letter physically inviting by using:

- A short opening paragraph
- Indented material to break up the type mass
- Paragraphs of different lengths
- No paragraph that is more than eight lines
- A short closing paragraph that asks for action

You can use the same technique to call attention to several selling points. Suppose you are selling a typewriter. You'll use an introductory line and then center the points and list them in this manner:

Among the features you'll like about this typewriter are that it:

1. Operates electrically or manually.
2. Has a feather touch.
3. Can be carried easily—very portable.
4. Makes switching ribbons simple.
5. Includes all features of a standard office typewriter.

By centering material in this way and giving it space at top and bottom you spotlight your important materials for sure reader attention. Furthermore, you open up the letter with white space.

Short closing paragraph. You've said what you had to say, so end quickly. Three or four lines should be sufficient to end any letter.

Folders

One of the most frequently used mailing pieces is the four- or six-page folder that fits as an insert into a No. 10 envelope. It is used also as a counter piece in establishments from hardware stores, drug stores, and plumbing shops, to banks. Considering the folder page by page, here are some suggestions for physical attractiveness.

Page 1. Use a strong headline physically to catch the reader's attention. An attractive illustration is desirable accompanied by a short copy block. Save the long copy for the inside pages. In many cases, it is desirable to use some technique to create enough curiosity to impel the reader to turn to the inside pages. Your headline might do this as:

> See the 10 ways this superb tool can save you time and money.

You may wish quite frequently to use curiosity-developing words at the bottom of page 1 that make the reader want to see the contents of pages 2 and 3. For instance, your bottom line might say:

> See inside if you want a more carefree, more colorful home . . .

Sometimes you may wish to use an arrow at the bottom. The arrow, pointing to the inside, could follow the line that says:

> Turn the page to learn how you can cut your fuel bills.

Also, three dots (. . .) can serve as a pointer. In short, literally force readers to turn from page 1 to pages 2 and 3.

Here are some more examples of copy lines used on the cover pages of folders that almost force the reader to turn the page because they build up curiosity about the benefits to be obtained if the reader looks inside the folder:

> Here's an
> important device
> that can lower
> your heating and air
> conditioning bills
> substantially!

> How to get the most out of your painting effort.

> If you don't know beans about boilers but you think your heating system needs a new one . . .

> Now . . . the incredible watch—
> so incredibly water tight
> it actually comes to you
> packed in water!
> And that's only one of the
> extra features of this
> amazing watch.

> See how this planning guide can assure you a better financial future.

> How to give the most for
> your money this year.

> How to enjoy a marvelous vacation
> and save money too . . .

> Because we care, here is an
> important message to you, one
> of our many valuable shareholders.
> Please take your time and
> read it carefully . . .

Pages 2 and 3. Treat these pages as one. By so doing, you can use a strong headline that spreads across the two pages and you can use a big, dominant illustration that takes up part of each page. This combination of strong head and illustration will draw the reader's gaze and create a vitality that would be missing if each page were treated separately.

In order to create excitement for these pages, use selling subheads liberally over the copy blocks. If small illustrations are used, along with the dominant illustration, give each a caption. Use these techniques to carry the reader through the pages and infuse the section with vigor.

Page 4 (back page). Sometimes advertisers leave this space blank. This is a grievous mistake since the back page of folders receives good readership. Treat the back page pretty much as you do the front page with an omission, of course, of any urging to turn the page.

Sometimes the back page is a good place to put a guarantee, a special offer, a listing of important points. Make it just as attractive as the front page since often readers look first at the first page, flip the folder over to the back page and then, if sufficiently interested, turn to the inside pages. Make the back page worth looking at.

By all means, include the usual elements on your back page such as a headline, possibly subheads, and an illustration. In short, make it a *working* page.

Jay R. Bearley
2810 N. Garden Street
South Haven, Michigan 49090

Dear Mr. Bearley:

Thank you very much for your letter of June 3 in which you ask for a leaflet and the name of a local dealer for Kwik-Aire, our portable electric air compressor. You will find the leaflet enclosed. Your dealer is:

Donald S. Ashcraft
Ashcraft Auto Supply Store
811 Fairfax Avenue Phone: 342-8791
South Haven

As you will notice when you read the leaflet, our Kwik-Aire compressor works from the cigarette lighter of your car. Just plug it in, attach to the valve of your tire and in seconds the tire will be inflated without effort on your part. It works equally well on tires for cars, trucks, campers, and bicycles.

You'll find Kwik-Aire handy for items other than tires too. For instance, use it to inflate beach balls, basketballs, air mattresses and inflatable furniture. This compact unit that fits snugly into your car trunk can be used around the car, home, cabin, the beach, or recreational vehicles.

It's important to keep tires inflated properly to make them last. Kwik-Aire is ready to use day or night. No need to depend upon service stations being open.

Your complete Kwik-Aire kit includes:

. Air compressor unit.
. 10 feet of electric cord.
. Nozzle adapter for inflatable objects.
. 3 feet of neoprene hose.
. Plastic carrying case.

After you've considered these facts and have looked over the leaflet, we'd suggest that you see Mr. Ashcraft to see a Kwik-Aire first hand. Mr. Ashcraft, who has handled our products for 10 years, has a supply of Kwik-Aires in stock. He'll be glad to demonstrate one of the units and to answer any questions.

With summer driving about to get into full swing, be prepared. Get a versatile Kwik-Aire. It can help you in many ways.

Yours very truly,

Joseph L. Beveridge
Sales Department

JB/a
Enc.

Figure 14–2. Follow-up to lead generated by advertising. One of the shameful areas of American industry is the lack of follow-up to inquiries generated by advertisements. What happens too often is that companies fail to answer such inquiries or delay so long that the prospect loses interest or has bought some other product. Each inquiry should be handled quickly by a letter that resells the product and tells the prospect where the product may be purchased.

In such letters the most important task is to get the prospect and dealer together. Thus, as shown, the dealer's name leads off the letter, and at the end of the letter the prospect is urged to see the dealer.

The center of the letter sells the product by calling attention to important sales points that appear in the leaflet enclosed with the letter. With this sales talk, added to the leaflet and the advertisement that prompted the inquiry, the prospect should be very much aware of the advantages of the product.

Follow-up letters of this type may very well be form letters that are reproduced to look personal. In such a case certain elements are "dropped in" such as the dealer name and address at the top.

Donald S. Ashcraft
Ashcraft Auto Supply Store
811 Fairfax Avenue
South Haven, Michigan 49090

Dear Mr. Ashcraft:

A South Haven resident is interested in our Kwik-Aire portable electric air compressor that you handle. He is:

Jay R. Bearley
2810 N. Garden Street

Mr. Bearley, seeing our May advertisement for Kwik-Aire in Popular Mechanics, wrote for a leaflet and asked for the name of a local dealer. He now has the leaflet and has been given your name as a reliable Kwik-Aire dealer.

This inquiry from South Bend demonstrates that our massive advertising in behalf of Kwik-Aire is paying off. Inquiries such as Mr. Bearley's are pouring in from all over the country. And no wonder! First of all, millions are seeing strong, colorful advertisements in such influential publications as Reader's Digest, Sports Illustrated, Parade, Newsweek, Field & Stream, Popular Mechanics, Four Wheeler, and Car & Driver.

On top of this great national advertising push we're bringing Kwik-Aire down to the local level with generous co-op support in newspapers and radio. In addition, we'll supply you with point of sale materials and display units either free or at cost.

Why such massive advertising support?

There's a simple answer. Kwik-Aire's a product with enormous customer appeal. It's versatile, reasonably priced and useful in many, many ways. For instance, your customers can use it to inflate tires, beach balls, basketballs, air mattresses, and inflatable furniture--all without any effort. Plug that "without any effort" point. We're certainly hitting it hard.

Other Kwik-Aire dealers are pushing a use-it-anywhere theme, stressing its use for the:

. Car.
. Home.
. Cabin.
. Beach.
. Recreational vehicles.

A phone call, or a note, to Mr. Bearley might turn him from a prospect into a customer. Better go after him now while Kwik-Aire's fresh in his mind.

Cordially,

JB/a

Joseph L. Beveridge
Sales Department

Figure 14–3. Sales letter to dealer urging follow-up of a lead generated by advertising. Another weak spot in the advertising-selling chain is the lack of follow-up by dealers who have been sent sales leads. It is up to the advertiser to push dealers into follow-up action.

In the letter shown here the company leads off with the most important news—that a person in his area is a prospect for the product he handles. Any good dealer should be delighted to get such a lead but, unfortunately, many dealers are apathetic, lazy, or too busy to go after these prospects.

The letter has three functions: (1) To give the lead. (2) To sell the dealer on the company's advertising and promotion that generated the lead and may well generate more leads. (3) To resell the product.

On point 2, it is important to remind dealers of the advertising support behind a product. In this instance, the support is so impressive that the dealer will be assured that it will be a help in making sales.

While it may seem odd to resell a dealer on the product he is handling, keep in mind that he handles hundreds of other items. He needs reminding of your product. Furthermore, what you tell him in such a sales letter can form the basis of his own sales talk for your product. You're putting sales ideas and sales phrases in his mind.

Note that in this letter and the one to the prospect there is a strong urge to action. Also, both letters are set up physically to make them easy to read.

Follow-up Letters Are Vital

One of the greatest tragedies of American industry is the lack of follow-up. A prospect writes to a company about a product or sends in a coupon. No answer is received. Or the answer arrives so long after the inquiry that the prospect is no longer interested or has bought a competing product.

Not only do many companies fail to follow up consumer inquiries adequately but also they fail to follow such sales leads with their dealers as they should. If a sales lead has been derived from advertising, it should be given to the dealer immediately. He should be made aware of the advertising backing that produced the lead because dealers need constant reminding of the power of advertising supplied by their manufacturing sources.

Often, too, the follow-up letter provides the manufacturer-supplier with a chance to resell his product and to provide the dealer with selling words and phrases that he can use on prospects who come into his store. This reselling is often needed because the dealers, carrying many, many lines, can't possibly be knowledgeable in depth of all those lines.

This sales letter to the dealer is very much like an advertisement he will see in his trade magazine because it emphasizes the 3-P's of product-promotion-profit. Its chief object is to get the dealer and the prospect together so that a sale can be made. Its secondary object is to resell the advertising backing and the product.

Figures 14–3 illustrates a letter that follows a sales lead, sells the dealer, and strongly urges action that may result in a personal sales talk. Without such follow-up the company has wasted money in conducting an expensive advertising campaign.

Messages on Envelopes Increase Readership of Letters

Many a letter would be tossed unopened and unread into the waste basket were it not for an irresistible message on the envelope, a fact that alert direct mailers have recognized. The message, or invitation, on the envelope has become standard procedure these days. Thus, prospects are invited to "Look inside for the greatest bargain you've ever seen."

To make the message on the envelope even more exciting and curiosity provoking, many of today's envelopes have windows—round, square, rectangular—that let you take a peek at the treasures within. An example of a selling envelope is one used by a chemical company. Within a box on the front of the big envelope is the following message:

> Would you like
> to use only one
> herbicide for all
> your crops?
>
> See inside . . .

Another front-of-the-envelope message from an oil company is:

> An important announcement to all Shell credit card holders.

Still another development in envelope messages (called "flashes" in direct-mail parlance) is the use of the *back* of the envelope. Sears, Roebuck has made good use of such space as the following demonstrate.

Envelope 1:

Illustration: Dramatic display of jewelry.

Copy: Elegance
and Sophistication
Stunning union of diamond and
gold can be yours . . . for far less
than you expect.
You can count on Sears

Envelope 2:

Illustration: Woman sitting by a lamp. Nearby is product.

Copy: *Overline:*
Unique conversation
piece . . . practical,
complete weather
information
Headline:
Enjoy both with the
SEARS TALKING
WEATHER STATION
Captions:
"No rain expected tonight"
"Clear and mild tomorrow"
Subhead:
Talks . . . because it's a radio too!

Still more information is given on the inside of the envelope. In short, every part of the envelope is working for the advertiser, a good point to remember whenever you prepare direct-mail material.

Three Ways to Resultful Direct-Mail Advertising

Entire books have been written on direct-mail advertising techniques. In this chapter you have read some of the highlights. To sum up matters, three basic suggestions will follow—suggestions that apply to all direct-mail users.

Use the YOU Point of View

Look at any magazine or newspaper, listen to an evening of television commercials—with the eye and ear of the consumer, the prospect. Which advertisements or commercials have the most appeal? Ten-to-one they're those that say "you."

In mail-order selling using the "you" viewpoint is vital because it is your only contact with the prospect, your only chance to present your product so that he will want to make a purchase.

How best to inspire that favorable thought? By shouting I—me—mine—we—us—our . . . the biggest—the best—the oldest—the newest? Or simply by saying or implying "you" and "your"?

It is not important to tell your prospect that your firm is, for example, the oldest or the largest in your field. Your firm's age or size might give your prospect confidence in either the integrity of your house or the dependability of your other selling claims. But even such a claim can be phrased in "you" language: "Your assurance of a quality product is ________ Company's fifty-three years of building Dinguses for over 81 percent of the Whatsis Industry." That's written from the reader's—not the seller's—point of view . . . a requisite of good selling copy.

Be Truthful and Believable

You may think it superfluous to stress "truth in advertising" any more in the creation of direct-mail selling than in that of other types of advertising. You need only to think of the success of the great mail-order merchandising houses, such as Sears, as ample proof of the fact that truthfulness pays, and pays well. A close relative of truth is believability. Some mail offers seem actually to ignore both these qualities, depending for both their attention value and selling impact upon startling, even fantastic, claims. These may trap the gullible once, perhaps twice, but no business lasts long when its sales depend upon such a weak foundation.

Not infrequently you may be able to make an advertising claim in all truth, but lacking in believability. If so, don't make it, for your prospects will believe you are not telling the truth anyway. Don't make it, that is, unless, as soon as you do, you back it up with proof, believable proof, that can remove any taint of even suspected untruth.

This is particularly true of a new product and its advertising, which the buying public always examines with critical suspicion if not outright distrust. Particularly in selling by mail, then, must you create an aura of truthfulness and believability, for oftentimes to your potential customers your product is a new one, because they've never had the chance to see it before.

Some firms even follow the practice—and successfully too—of underselling their products on the proved theory that the customer who finds his purchase superior to its claims will be an eager repeat customer, the ideal situation for any merchandiser who plans to stay in business. At any rate, avoid exaggeration.

Statements needn't be weak or unenthusiastic—you can state a simple fact in a way that comes out strong. Stick to the truth, avoid exaggeration, and make your claims believable.

Keep Old Customers Sold

One of the most important of these pointers is to remember that the backbone of any permanent success in selling is the retention of the goodwill and the business of old customers. Much of the responsibility for keeping old customers as satisfied current customers is not the province of the advertising copywriter, but rather that of direct salespeople, sales and credit correspondents, and others. At the same time, nevertheless, the firm's advertising also has a share of the job to do in being so planned and written that the needs and wants of the old customers are not sacrificed in the attempt to win new customers as well.

Laurence P. Grailing, Jr.
929 Mt. Piskor Drive
Tacoma, Washington 98422

Dear Mr. Grailing:

In a world where fulfilling obligations is often not done you are to be congratulated for the conscientious way you have paid off your mortgage loan. We deeply appreciate your consistent observance of due dates. In the 15 years we have held the mortgage there has not been <u>one</u> missed date.

Naturally, your credit rating with Peoples National is at the highest level.

Too often people such as yourself obtain no recognition for quietly and steadily paying off a debt. We'd like to extend such recognition by inviting you to utilize any of the various services this bank can offer. Because of the credit rating I spoke of above, you are automatically qualified for any type of loan, such as:

Home improvement loans.
Boat loans.
Mortgage loans(should you ever require another one)
Personal loans.
Consolidation loans(where we lend you money to pay off all debts so that you have just one loan to settle).
Auto loans(our rates are lower than those of the finance companies).

Should you require any such loans please let us know. Our loan officers will be delighted to talk to you and to give you speedy no-nonsense service devoid of red tape. After all, you <u>are</u> a very special customer of ours.

I hope, too, that you'll avail yourself of many of the other services of a full service bank including our various types of checking and savings plans as well as the expert guidance of our trust department.

In your next visit to the bank I <u>do</u> hope that you come see me in order that I may personally congratulate you for the honorable and businesslike way you have fulfilled your mortgage loan requirements. My desk is immediately to the left as you enter. It will be a pleasure to meet you.

Sincerely,

L. L. Linveil
Mortgage Loan Officer
Western Bank & Trust Company

LLL/r

Figure 14–4. Letter to present customer. Present customers are often a company's *best* customers. A pat-on-the-back type of letter such as this will help an advertiser hold on to a customer and sell him additional services. An alert advertiser will be on the lookout for such opportunities.

Advertising also frequently plays a big part in the maintenance of friendly relations between seller and customer. During periods of raw material shortages, transportation delays, and other difficulties—even labor troubles—advertising of every sort, including both mail order and direct mail, can and does help out in the big job of explaining the situation to customers and retaining their business.

Many firms, both retail and industrial, have adopted the sending of purely goodwill direct-mail letters to their entire list of customers periodically. These are sent annually at the New Year or at other appropriate intervals and times, thanking each customer for his business, hoping for uninterrupted "friendship," possibly pledging increased service and improved products, and perhaps requesting ideas for still better fulfillment of the customer's needs.

And sometimes just such a simple mailing will make a customer realize that here indeed is a firm interested in him and worthy of his continued business.

Gadgets: Often Silly and Often Effective

Although you may tend with some justification to think of gadgets as fripperies, as frivolous, undignified devices to get attention, you may have to work with them sometime if you're connected with the creating of direct-mail material. A gadget, by definition, is an item or device included in a direct mailing to rivet the recipient's attention long enough to halt his tendency to rid himself of the mailing before reading it.

Your part in the use of gadgets is to write tie-in copy which relates the gadget to the idea you wish to put across. Suppose, for example, a tiny bugle is attached to the mailing. You might write something painfully obvious such as "We don't want to blow our horn, but . . ." Don't groan. Gadgets *do* work.

Chosen and used with imagination, the gadget can often help dramatize your message and get your point across quickly and effectively. Frequently, a gadget is a small copy of a larger, familiar item, but it can be any life-sized item—a candy mint wafer, a vitamin pill, a burnt match (never send inflammables through the mails), a golf tee, a pair of dice, a bobby pin, a button, a nail, a nut and bolt, or a bottle cork. Samples or pieces of the actual item or product being advertised may also be used as direct-mail gadgets (not, in this case, as samples or swatches to facilitate direct-mail orders). Such gadgets may be a piece of wool yarn used in the nap of a rug, perhaps a swatch of the carpeting itself, a sample of printing paper, a page from a new dictionary, or a patented combination washer and lock-nut.

Gadgets generally are attached in some manner to the leaflet, letter, or circular to avoid their dropping out when the envelope is opened. Seldom are they merely loose enclosures. Yet, if the gadget itself contains any part of the message, and if it does fall to the floor when the envelope is opened, the recipient's curiosity might be piqued and his interest increased by the part of the message he reads on the gadget as he picks it up. Usually, however, you'll find the gadget fastened on the outside of a folder or near the top of a letter—tied into the copy by a provocative headline or by the lead-off paragraph in a letter.

Sometimes these headline tie-ins are forced to the point of absurdity. This oldie actually used—a miniature axe with the headline "Do you mind if we axe you a few simple questions?"—is not recommended as a shining example of the catchy tie-in, yet some continue to be written that are even more insulting to the prospect's intelligence and sense of humor.

But, like a famous series of direct-mail letters—one of which, with two small dice attached, opened "The luckiest buy I ever made in my life"—most tie-ins attempt to build a natural bridge from the gadget to the message. Here are a few of the other headlines in the same series used successfully on a cooperative basis with the dealers. The dealer's name was used twice in the letterhead and as the signature:

Gadget	Lead Copy or Headline
Small spoon	You don't have to be born with a silver *(spoon)* in your mouth to be able to afford the comfort and luxury of one of our Bench Made Suits.
Full-size pocket comb	We have combed the country for the best coat value we could find.
Blue poker chip	Here's a suit that's a "blue chip" when it comes to luxury and tailoring. Yet you don't have to pay a "blue chip" price for its custom quality!

Sometimes a gadget can be so very clever that it defeats its own purpose—the prospects remember the campaign so well that they forget the advertiser's identity—or confuse it with a competitor's.

Here are some cautions in the use of gadgets:

- Don't expect a gadget to sell a product that can't be sold on its own merits. A gadget is merely an attention-getter.
- Be sure the gadget fits your message and doesn't resort to bad gags or dubious humor.
- Avoid the too-clever gadget that pushes your name and product out of the prospect's mind.
- Look for possible ways your gadget may antagonize or insult your prospects.
- Avoid anything dangerous—matches, sharp objects such as glass, inadequately protected knives, razor blades.
- Don't rely entirely on your own personal like or dislike for a particular gadget or for gadgets in general.

15

BUSINESS, PROFESSIONAL, AND AGRICULTURAL ADVERTISING

Part A

For some time, Tim Prentice and Al Herridge have been laying out plans for a spring introduction of a new line of garden tools. Tim is advertising manager of Garden World, Inc., which is introducing the line. Al is a partner in the Herridge Advertising Agency.

"Then we're agreed, Tim, that we should have a pretty good backup campaign in the trade books?"

"Right, Al. My inclination is to hit the garden supply magazines and the hardware publications."

"For the hardware push, how about DIY Retailing *and* Hardware Age*? They'll hit most of the independent hardware outlets as well as True Value, Ace, and the wholesalers."*

"Okay with me, but what kind of schedule do you have in mind?"

"I'd like about six issues. Maybe every other month, or maybe DIY *one month, and* Age *the next. Either way, we'll break before our national consumer campaign. A hot new product and a big advertising push—with all that going for us, we'll lay the groundwork for your salespeople. Our ad support alone should soften up the dealers."*

"Al, how about getting in a plug in each ad for new dealers? This has been a tough year; we've lost quite a few."

"Sure thing. I'd suggest running plugs in the ads that are scheduled before the consumer ads. Then more plugs in ads running during the campaign. We'll get 'em coming and going."

Few persons in the general public are aware of the trade advertising discussed by Tim and Al. Consumer advertising in television and big circulation magazines, the public knows. Yet, there are far more business magazines than consumer magazines.

Certainly, consumer advertising that sells furniture, jewelry, gasoline, loan companies, milk, perfume, airline trips, and a myriad of other personal products and services is a vital concern of many copywriters. Business advertising, however, is the chief and often only concern of great numbers of copywriters, especially copywriters in advertising agencies and in the advertising departments of large manufacturing firms. Furthermore, many copypeople write both consumer and business advertising.

Business advertising is often called "business paper" advertising. This is too narrow a term because business advertising includes trade, industrial, and professional advertising. Don't look for such advertising in general magazines, newspapers, outdoor posters, radio, or television. Almost exclusively it appears in business publications, a term to be preferred to "business paper."

Almost every field of enterprise has one or more publications serving it, a magazine or newspaper that is published periodically and contains news and information of special interest to those in the industry represented.

Thus *Bakery Production and Marketing* is an expertly managed and edited magazine, circulated to those concerned with the baking industry. Bakers large and small, millers, wholesale and retail grocers, and others are familiar with its interesting articles, stories, news items, and advertising, as they are with those of other business publications servicing the bakery industry.

Iron Age Metal Producer is a famous magazine of the industrial type for the steel industry; *Progressive Grocer* is one of the many magazines of the trade type that serves the grocery field. *WWD* goes to the clothing industry, and *American Funeral Director* is read by most of the country's morticians.

Classes of Business Advertising Are Markedly Different

Because you can write acceptable copy for one class of business-publication advertising doesn't mean that you can do so for another class. For instance, you may be comfortable writing to physicians about a new pharmaceutical product, but you may be decidedly *uncomfortable* if you're told to write about a capacitor that will be featured in a magazine advertisement read by electrical engineers.

What you learn very quickly is that business advertising embraces a vast array of products and services and that much of it is exceedingly technical and complex. What will give you a sense of quick humility is knowing that the people reading your copy are, in the main, experts, specialists in their fields, and quite ready to find flaws in what you have written.

As you read the following brief descriptions of three of the chief types of business advertising, you may be struck by two points: (a) How different they are from each other and (b) How odd it is to call advertising addressed to professional people such as doctors and dentists "business advertising." This is not so odd when you realize that such advertising generates much business in surgical equipment, pharmaceuticals, dental equipment, and numerous other products. Thus, it is professional advertising and business advertising at the same time.

Trade advertising. The advertisements in business publications of the trade type are designed to gain the selling and merchandising support of the dealers who offer your product for resale.

When you write this kind of copy, remember to follow the 3-P's formula: product, promotion, profit. Emphasis on one, two, or all three of these elements is characteristic of all trade advertising.

Industrial advertising. Advertisements appearing in business magazines of the industrial type enable one industry to advertise to another industry, usually about items such as a punch press, that can be used for helping production. In contrast to trade advertising, industrial advertising is not concerned with the factor of resale.

Professional advertising. The third classification, professional advertising, which appears in such publications as *Journal of the American Medical Association, Dentist,* and *Journal of Dental Research* is aimed at professional people who can do two things for you: They can use your product and they can recommend the use of your product.

In addition to doctors and dentists, professional advertising is addressed to other professionals, such as architects, lawyers, and teachers.

To avoid confusion, consider the term "business advertising" as referring only to that kind of advertising that appears in business publications—trade, industrial, or professional. Direct response house organs, films, specialized presentations—all aimed at the trade—will be eliminated in this discussion.

For the time being, so will "collateral"—all the display or point-of-sale materials, training manuals, merchandising presentations, and portfolios that copywriters are called upon to produce and that usually come under the heading of "trade."

Business Advertising Is a Supplementary Aid

Business advertising is essentially a supplementary selling force that strengthens and meshes with the merchandising and selling program of the advertiser.

Here are some facts to remember about business advertising.

- Business-publication space rates are low compared with consumer media. Thus many copywriters don't consider business advertising important. Some agencies don't consider it worthwhile to hire competent writers skilled in business copy because space commissions aren't high enough. Yet there are notable exceptions to this. One large agency, for example, has a vice president in charge of their business-publication operation.
- Some advertisers and agencies feel that consumer advertisements alone can do the job—that specially

designed advertising to trade or industry is not necessary. Such thinking can lead to unsound and wasteful advertising, especially in trade advertising.

Retailers can switch customers from one product to another. They can favor one product by displaying it at eye-level on the shelves and putting others down low where people have to stoop to get them. Consumer advertising can and should be supported with a good, heavy program for the trade in most cases.

Consumer and Trade Advertising Are Sometimes Alike

Sometimes trade advertising and consumer advertising aren't much different. In *Progressive Grocer,* for example, you will find many advertisements offering products used by the dealers themselves, such as paper bags, twine, and business machines. This, of course, is consumer advertising even though it appears in trade publications. Its primary interest to them, however, is in its offering a product or service as a source of profit because these people are in business to make money—to earn a livelihood.

The beautiful new color of a transparent comb, for example, may be advertised in the *Ladies' Home Journal* in terms of its vividness, glowing good looks, and newness. Advertising of the same comb in the trade papers that reach drug and department stores would also tell of the new color idea, but would interpret it in terms of why more people will want and buy the comb; how well it is advertised to create a demand; and how store tests showed sales went up quickly when it was displayed—and increased all other comb sales, as well.

And the advertisement might end, "If you haven't seen them . . . if your salesperson hasn't been around and told you the mighty pretty profit story we've got to tell, let us know—but quick. Better write or call right now."

No fancy writing there. Just a straight appeal for action. But don't misunderstand. Trade advertisements can be dramatic and interesting—and you can employ all the basic essentials of effective copywriting already mentioned in previous chapters.

Trade advertising, as previously said, is generally confined to products or services handled by wholesalers or retailers for resale. Some exceptions might be the advertising of flour and baker's supplies in bakery trade publications read by wholesale and retail bakers. Another exception is the advertising of certain equipment such as meat cases, frozen food cases, and paper bags in grocery and meat trade papers. These products, while not purchased for resale, can very properly be advertised in trade papers as a type of consumer advertising.

Products advertised to the trade are often nationally advertised through magazines, newspapers, radio, and TV. When this is true, you may often be called upon to tell the trade the story of these consumer advertising programs, so dealers will know and appreciate the pro-

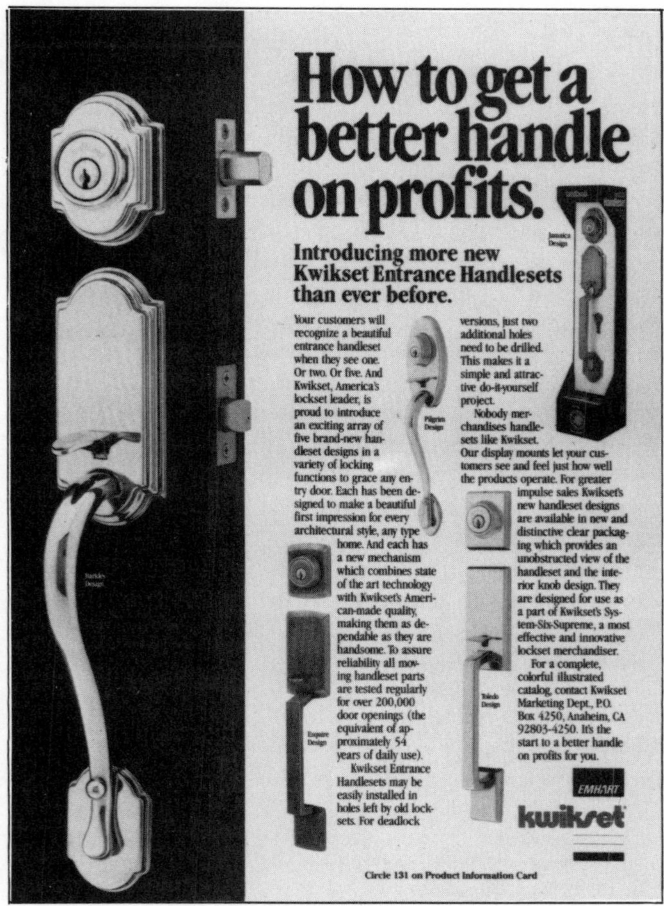

Figure 15–1. Trade advertisement putting stress on profits to be made.

Reprinted with permission of Kwikset Corporation.

motional help the manufacturer is giving through the national consumer campaign.

Specific, Enthusiastic Copy Needed in Trade Magazine Advertising

"Clever" slogans or gimmicks alone in small space will rarely pay off as trade advertising techniques. Such thoughts as "Beans by Glick Always Click," run time after time in trade advertisements with the assumption that "we're doing a job with the trade," do not offer retailers any reason for featuring Glick's beans.

Tell the trade how it can make money with Glick's beans—how repeat sales steadily grow—or how to display the product more successfully. Tell the retailers that store tests have revealed above-normal turnover and shelf velocity. Isn't that what good sharp salespersons would ordinarily tell dealers? They certainly wouldn't come in time after time just chanting "Beans by Glick Always Click."

Use as much space as possible. Only then can you give a certain amount of prestige and importance to the product. You need that space for fair readership and for a complete sales talk.

Many advertisers and agencies will turn out poorly produced business advertisements on the grounds that "the budget won't stand better stuff." This is faulty thinking when you have something important enough to say—or when the time is critical (such as during the announcement of a new product, a price slash, and so forth). Get in there and pitch for more color, better art, or more space in your business advertising.

Trade advertisements will usually require more copy than consumer advertisements since you will be much more concerned with explanatory material. Also, your profit-minded readers are more willing to read long technical material if they see value in what you say.

Enthusiasm is a priceless element of trade advertising—the enthusiasm any good salesperson feels and expresses when talking to a prospect. Such enthusiasm should be evident in every line of your copy because it carries conviction. Your enthusiastic ideas are expressed in a language level that will generally be lower than that used in industrial or professional advertising but likewise will usually be expressed more forcefully and more colorfully.

What to Include in a Trade Advertisement

> Your whole week's wash done in
> 30 minutes . . . while you shop!

Obviously, that's a headline for an automatic washer. Assume that it is the headline of an advertisement in a campaign ready to break in national consumer publications. Support for this consumer advertising will be provided through a special campaign to reach the trade. Electric appliance stores, department stores, and a few special outlets will be the trade in this case.

The people who run these stores handle automatic washers for resale. To them the only value of the claim "Your whole week's wash done in 30 minutes . . . while you shop" lies in the fact that this is a powerful weapon to use in their sales talks. It helps them sell more "X" washers.

Consider the foregoing heading. The thought expressed in it will probably be the basis for other consumer advertisements and will be used to merchandise that advertising to the trade. The people who handle the "X" washer—and prospective new dealers—will thus be informed that a comprehensive and effective national advertising campaign is starting; that it will reach people and prospects in every locality; and that, naturally, it will stimulate interest in the washer and bring people into your store for more information or a demonstration.

National Advertising Backing— Hit It Strongly

Orthodox treatment might start out this way. First advertisement is a double spread, uses some color, and the type of news headline mentioned in the chapter on headlines.

> Most powerful consumer advertising ever . . . To help you ring up record sales on "X" washers
>
> **Subhead:** New, surefire, full-page color advertisements run in 5 leading magazines—aimed to reach more than 65% of prospects in your own neighborhood!
>
> **Second subhead:** All through the year, these advertisements will appear in *Ladies' Home Journal, Family Circle, Better Homes & Gardens.*

Illustrations might show a few typical advertisements, as large as possible; small covers of the magazines mentioned; and possibly a small chart illustrating how 65 percent (figure used only for example) of prospects are reached by this advertising, for the average dealer.

Copy would explain why the consumer advertisements should be effective, why people are interested in saving time, being able to shop, do housework, etc., while clothes are being washed. All copy would be written from the dealer's side—how all this advertising is aimed to work for him; how it brings people into the store; how it actually pays off at his cash register. Such an advertisement might logically ask for action at the end, like this:

> Continuous advertising support in your own neighborhood is only one reason why the "X" franchise is such a money-maker for dealers. A franchise might be available for you. A special Profit Table that shows sales and profit potentials for your own locality is yours on request. Get yours—and other facts and figures you should have. Better do it now . . . before your competitor's request arrives first.

Here's some comment on this advertisement. The headlines are quite long. The headlines and the subheads, however, certainly tell the story, and that's good practice because two kinds of readers see trade advertisements: (a) Quick readers who seldom read more than the heads and subheads and (b) Thorough readers (a small group) who will read anything and everything having to do with their business. If, in view of the foregoing, you can get your fairly complete story into your headings, chances are you'll get high readership from both classes of readers.

The headlines contain some "you" element and mention the name of the product. The whole tone of the advertisement is on the "you"—directed straight to the dealer—and that is an essential in trade advertising, because the writer simply must explain everything the advertiser does, in terms of benefits, profits, help, and so forth, which the dealer-reader can expect from the product or service being advertised.

Stress Impact of National Advertising on Dealer's Local Customers

Assuming that the national advertising is the most important message the "X" company has for dealers, the next trade advertisement in the series could well treat the "local" effect of all the advertising the "X" company does—including the new campaign. The heading for such an advertisement might be:

New "X" washer advertising "talks to"
nearly 7 out of every 10 people
Right in your neighborhood.

The whole advertisement might use the "believe it or not" technique, and with several illustrations and little copy for each, show how the advertising works for every dealer in his own area. This "local advertising" versus "national advertising" question is important since the local readership of national advertising is the only interest any dealer has in it. Boasting that yours is the biggest national advertising campaign ever to hit the magazines just leaves the dealers cold unless you can show them the effect this campaign will have on their own customers. The question in any alert dealer's mind is, "What does this advertising do for me?"

The next several advertisements in the trade series could dramatize store tests and store experiences of progressive dealers with the "X" washers. Advertisements would explain how the consumer advertising brought in prospects to find out how a whole week's wash could be done in 30 minutes, and how, with a few little display ideas of the dealer, sales of the "X" washer rose to a new high level. The purpose here, of course, is to persuade dealers reading about these experiences to think that they can do as well.

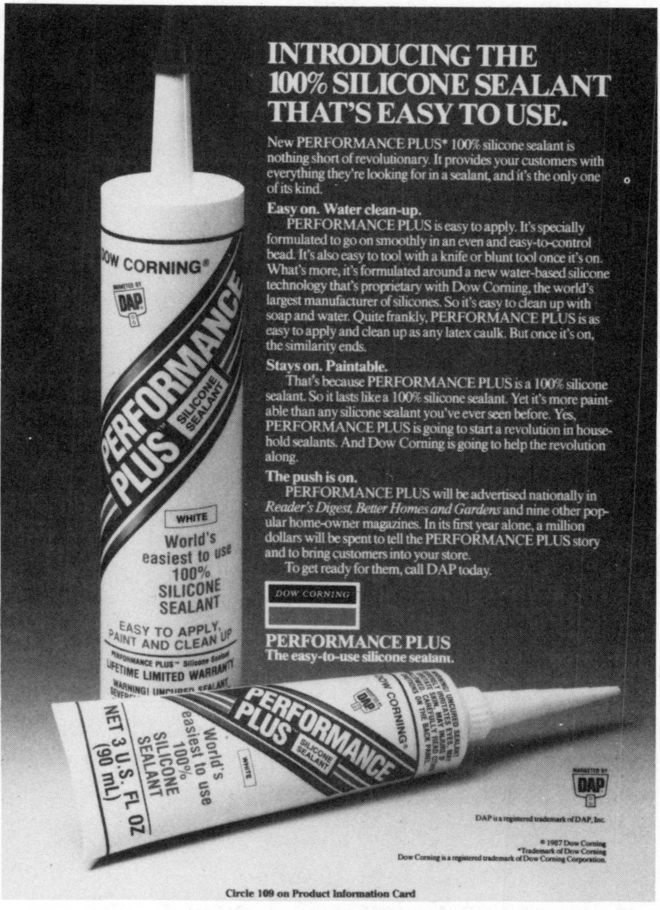

Figure 15–2. Trade advertisement stressing the two P's of product and promotion. Note the specific nature of the copy on the promotional backing.

Supply Proof If You're Offering Something New

Time of the year, specific problems that arise at times, and new company policies—all these and more affect trade advertising. What these special conditions are often dictates what the advertisements will say. A few of them will be shown with special situations; the headlines of advertisements show how the situation might be met.

Suppose, for instance, users had experienced considerable difficulty with the Swirler—a patented clothes agitator of the "X" machine. Dealers were getting too many complaints; machines were returned; sales dropped ominously. One effective solution would be elimination of the Swirler and introduction of a new agitator of proven trouble-free operation. Wouldn't it be big and important news for the trade to know:

Revolutionary new clothes agitator of
"X" washer eliminates service headaches!

Copy would explain how a "torture treatment," equal to five years' normal use, was set up in an independent laboratory, and that five machines out of every one hundred going through the factory were put through this test. Attention would be focused on the "trouble-free new agitator" that would certainly overcome most of the previous difficulty. The same theme would be used by salespeople making their calls.

Suppose the washer action of the "X" washer is "oscillatory." Other washers use the "reciprocating" action. If it could be proved in unbiased tests that oscillatory were far superior, tests could be set up in noted laboratories, and results of these tests would make the basis of a series of advertisements. Here's one such headline:

Oscillatory action of "X" washer
Outperforms reciprocating 3 to 1
in actual tests

You'd have to be prepared for controversy and you'd need to be very sure of your facts, but if the advertiser were strong enough, he could settle the argument positively. He might possibly devise an action that combined the advantages of both—if they were equal to varying respects—and, so to speak, work both ends. The heading in such a case might be:

Advantages of both oscillatory and reciprocating
actions
Combined in radical new oscil-rep action of "X"
washer

To the trade that's big news. And as mentioned before, you've got to know the trade, what's going on, what interests dealers.

You Write a "Package" of Advertising and Promotion

Building around the theme line . . .

> Your whole week's wash done in
> 30 minutes . . . while you shop!

. . . you will create a package or a packaged promotion which will include point-of-display pieces, gimmicks, results of store tests, direct mail, and newspaper art for dealers' use. Also, you'll include a portfolio for the salespeople who call on dealers. The portfolio explains the whole deal. Added to the foregoing, you will also promote the package to the trade through regular trade publications.

Assume the Swirler is an ingenious and exclusive agitator of the "X" machine and is the main reason why clothes wash so quickly and so clean. Also, the Swirler is one important part of the automatic operation which permits people to leave the machine while it goes on with its washing. You'll then dramatize the Swirler in every way, bring it into all your promotion and advertising, and introduce a catchy theme that will be the core of your promotion. It is your U.S.P.

You may decide to use the traffic light idea, which is quite suitable for this example. The slogan or keynote will be

> *Stop* Washing
> *Go* Swirling

In the consumer advertising, headlines would continue on the timesaving and leisure theme, as exemplified by the headline "Your whole week's wash done in 30 minutes." Copy would explain how this was possible, heavily promoting the Swirler.

Somewhere in the main illustration or in an illustration of the washer or Swirler, you might show a gaily waving banner with traffic light effects and the theme words, "*Stop* Washing . . . *Go* Swirling." Already you can see how this device can be carried through all promotion and advertising—magazines, outdoor, newspapers, direct response, display material, trade—even radio, where sound tricks would take the place of the signal lights.

Here's the promotional material you could logically include in your package and which you will promote in your trade advertising (to be explained later on).

- A series of newspaper ads and radio and TV commercials for the dealer's use, built on the "stop and go" idea.
- A series of three to six direct-mail pieces for dealers to send to selected prospects, built on same idea.
- Several large display pieces using the red "stop" and green "go" traffic light idea, possibly plus one life-size cut-out figure of a traffic policeman with a red and green light above him (flashing on and off alternately) for use in store window or inside store, next to "X" washer or washers on display.
- A series of "how to display the 'X' washer" suggestions. This would consist of several illustrations of putting washer on elevated floor platform, placing certain display material around it, casting colored light from a baby spotlight on it in store or window, and other similar ideas.

Figure 15–3. Trade advertisement that points up the product's number one selling position and the advertising support behind the product.

Then using the same red and green traffic light technique, all this material or pictures of it will be arranged in logical order in a salesperson's portfolio, titled

> Stop Washing . . .
> Go Swirling

Next: A Campaign of Trade Magazine Advertisements

Next the trade advertising. With all this material ready to help the dealers and with the attention-getting red and green traffic light treatment, we now have:

- A packaged promotion—complete and available for the dealers, to help them capitalize more effectively on the power of the consumer advertising.
- A gimmick—in the red and green lights and the slogan, which will provide immediate identity in all collateral and trade advertising.

First, the trade advertising could well announce the big consumer campaign already mentioned—bringing in the slogan and the traffic light idea in a subordinate way. In every trade advertisement—sometimes large, sometimes small—this plug would always be made: "*Stop* Washing . . . *Go* Swirling." Use of this phrase would provide a note of recognition when the salesperson called with the same device and wording on the front of his portfolio.

The second advertisement in the trade series might be a big play on the central theme of "*Stop* Washing . . . *Go* Swirling" and explain how this catchy little selling phrase will work and work on the minds of people, wearing down sales resistance and exciting curiosity. Copy would still devote some words to the big advertising support.

The following advertisements might run in this order:

1. Big splash on all the material available to help dealers sell more "X" machines.
2. Reproductions of telegrams from dealers telling how well the new advertising is working for them.
3. Straight appeal to dealers to "see what's in the big black book the 'X' salesperson has ready to show you." This refers to the portfolio, and copy would hint of the "money magic" that the book brings to readers.
4. Series of advertisements built on store tests, showing how successful dealers used all the material available on "X" machines and how well sales are going. In other words, success stories.

Sell Dealers and Salespeople on Value of Advertising and Promotion

You've probably noticed that the store tests are mentioned many times. Unbiased store tests are convincing to dealers. First, no dealer can overlook such data when they have to do with his bread and butter. Second, not many advertisers are willing to go to the expense and trouble of making the tests (and results may not be suitable for publication). When such test results do appear, they constitute material that is far from common.

All the advertisements mentioned as suitable for this series—whether based on store tests or not—would, of course, always end with a strong urge to the dealer to "write, or telephone us to get the full facts," or something along that line.

It should be mentioned that when the entire campaign was approved and when the first samples of all the advertisements and material were finally available, everything was timed in order that the whole plan could be presented to the sales organization at its convention, so the salespeople could sally forth into their respective territories filled with the fire and fervor of their cause. It's just as important that the sales force be sold on your advertising and promotion as the dealers or "the trade."

Institutional Copy May Be Used If Company Makes Many Products

Most trade advertising tries to sell a product or service in a very direct way. Some advertisers, however, cannot always do this. Consider Hotpoint. They market many products sold through the appliance trade.

If every Hotpoint product division decided to use an aggressive advertising campaign in trade magazines, a competitive free-for-all would ensue. In the case of such multiproduct advertisers, it is sensible to use an institutional theme. Here, for example, the name "Hotpoint" is promoted and each product is introduced as a member of the Hotpoint family of quality appliances and the selling-theme idea may be expressed as the "quality of Hotpoint."

Merchandising the national advertising and selling the dealer on promotional assistance and institutional advertising are not, of course, the only means of using trade-paper space. Hundreds of different ideas, plans, deals, promotions, and "packages" are offered to the retailers through trade campaigns. The subject matter of your trade advertising will be dependent upon what is the most important message to get across to the trade who will resell your product.

Thus if you are marketing a brand new product through a company with no national prestige or name perhaps the most important single thing for you to accomplish in trade advertising is to build confidence among the dealers in your company and in its financial

Figure 15–4. Trade advertisement putting emphasis on product and advertising support. The engaging illustration made the advertisement stand out in the trade magazine in which it appeared.

Figure 15–5. **Trade advertisement putting stress on advertising support behind the product.**

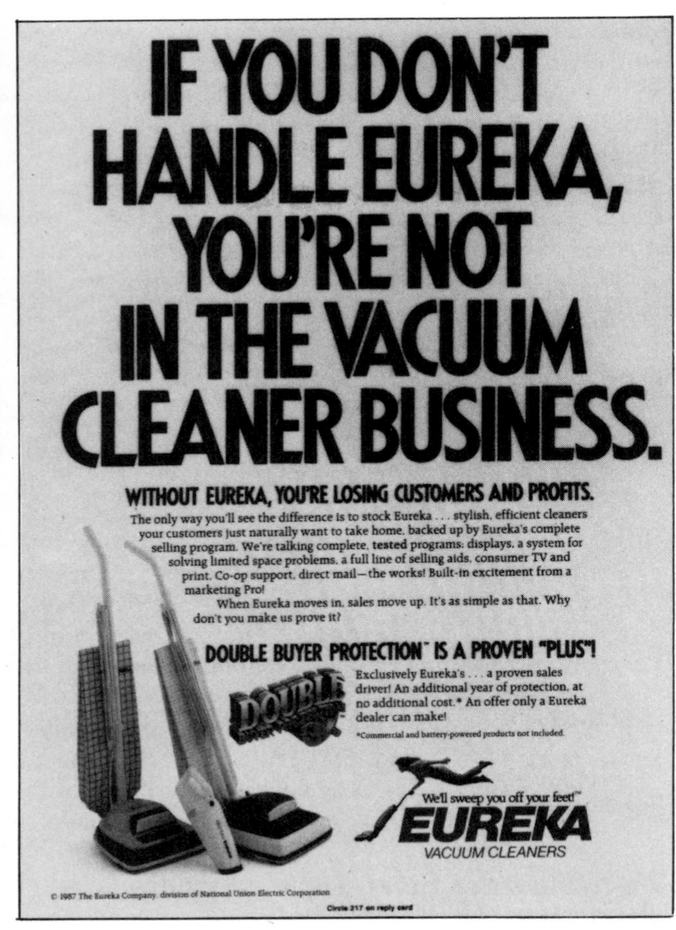

Figure 15–6. **Trade advertisement featuring the importance of the product.**

background. If you are introducing a new automobile, you may wish to inspire such confidence and backing by running trade advertising on your personnel, their experience in manufacturing, designing, and selling cars.

Trade advertising, as you have examined it here, is good for one major result: to gain the selling support of retail merchants. In order to do this, your trade campaigns must offer something to the dealers that will make them want to feature and sell your product.

Underlying everything, of course, is their desire to make a profit.

Still other advertisements will put the stress on the handsome display units offered to dealers. These units provide an attractive means of displaying the manufacturer's line, a very important consideration to dealers who have limited space and a pride in the appearance of their stores. Accordingly, you will find many trade advertisements that stress display opportunities or that feature packaging.

Product or Advertising: Which to Stress?

Copywriters are so product-oriented that they almost automatically think in terms of product first, and yet this can be a mistake in some trade advertisements.

Let's assume that you are selling a product without any special distinction and that there is no new product feature to exploit in the advertising. Still, the product is a steady seller in retail outlets and must be advertised to maintain its competitive position. Assume, too, that the product has an outstanding promotion behind it: big-circulation consumer magazines, television, radio, newspapers.

Clearly, the promotional backing should be headlined and the bulk of the copy should concern the support the dealer can expect. The product can simply be mentioned at the top of the advertisement, but the promotion is what you dwell on.

Consider another situation: a new product with appealing sales features and a strong promotional support behind it. In this case, the headline and possibly an opening subhead can stress the product *and* the excellent advertising support. The first impression the dealer gets is that the company is offering a hot new product and is backing it with equally hot advertising. You can then follow the headline by talking first about the product, or you can start with the promotion. Either is suitable.

Another situation: General Electric is introducing a new microwave oven, a proven seller. When the adver-

Figure 15–7. Trade advertisement stressing importance of profit and display.

tiser has a name as powerful as General Electric, any product it introduces is big news in itself. In this case, stress the product and then bring in the advertising support strongly.

As you can see, there are various ways to handle this question of product or promotion. The point is that promotion can be as important to stress as the product and sometimes should be stressed first and harder than the product.

Advertising backing should be sold specifically, enthusiastically, and with conviction. Dealers too often aren't aware of the extent of the support; they should be told. Furthermore, because many dealers resent the amount their suppliers spend on national advertising, trade advertising should make it clear to them just how much such advertising can help them. Dealers must be sold over and over again on the value of promotion and even company salespeople need such reminding because they, too, frequently fail to realize the power of a good advertising campaign.

Following is a suggested checklist that you can use after you have written an advertisement to appear in a trade magazine. See if your layout and copy embody most of these points:

Layout

Overall impression of excitement, liveliness, and vitality.
Liberal use of subheads.
Strong illustration of product in sufficient size to sell it.
Big, bold head, physically speaking.

Copy

Strong, exciting headline. Has specific benefit and/or promise.
Strong sell for product with sufficient details supplied.
Strong sell of promotional backing with sufficient details supplied.
Use of dealer language.
Use of material that will appeal to dealer, such as reference to display qualities of product, turnover, experience of other dealers, profit to be made, customer appeal.
Use of strong selling subheads to lead reader through advertisement.
Overall employment of the 3 P's (profit, product, promotion).
Overall feeling of excitement and enthusiasm.
Copy about advertising backing brings advertising down to local level.
Copy *sells*—doesn't just *tell.*

An Important Backup: Trade Collateral

Closely associated with trade advertising is the writing and production of what is called "collateral." Under this term are included all the special pieces of advertising used in product selling, either by the advertiser's own sales force or by the retail merchant.

Such things as special mailing pieces addressed to the trade, portfolios containing promotional aids for the sales force, store display material, and other miscellaneous advertising are called "collateral." Their creation represents an important and voluminous part of almost every copywriter's duties.

Much material is normally supplied to the product manufacturer's salespeople to aid them in soliciting business from the trade. If you are an agency copywriter, you prepare a considerable amount of this material on behalf of your clients. If you are writing copy for an advertiser in the advertising department, preparation of such items will occupy an even greater part of your time.

Sales Portfolio Performs a Three-way Function

Perhaps the most usable collateral piece regularly supplied to a sales force is the "salesperson's portfolio," or "sales manual."

These portfolios do a threefold job:

1. They show the dealers that advertising is being put behind the product, both nationally and locally, what display material is available to dealers for their stores, and how the combination works in preselling the product for the dealers.
2. They arouse enthusiasm for the product and its potentialities in the dealer's mind and the same emotions among the salespeople for their own advertising and merchandising promotion.
3. They offer the salesperson a complete graphic checklist to follow in giving the dealer a salestalk.

There are two important points to remember in writing a sales portfolio:

One is to *write simply.* A lot of the value that the sales force will derive from your portfolio will come while they are in routine conversations with their retailer customers. If you can write interesting, punchy, and informal copy in the portfolios you prepare, the salespeople will often find themselves picking up these expressions and using them in their daily calls. Use the kind of talk that salespeople would be likely to use.

To give yourself a working background in this trade talk, you ought to spend some time on the road with a salesperson, go on calls, and listen to what is said to the dealers. If you are working in the advertising department of a manufacturing house, you will find that such trips are considered standard procedure.

If you are a copywriter with an advertising agency, you may find trips more difficult to arrange, since the agency will want to keep you busy writing. Advertising executives, though, will recognize the value of such extracurricular experience for copywriters, so you can get out if you try hard enough.

A second point in writing sales portfolios is to *keep them brief.* Imagine yourself as a busy, impatient dealer who reluctantly agrees to take the time to look over the portfolio. Also, imagine yourself as the harried sales representative who goes over the portfolio with the dealer. Most dealers must be persuaded to give sales representatives time to put on a presentation of the advertising and display plans described in a portfolio. Prepare your material so that it can be read and understood in glance-reading.

Here's What Goes into a Sales Portfolio

A lot of consultation will occur between agency, company, and the copywriter about the portfolio's content. It can vary from portfolio to portfolio. Changes in marketing and advertising strategies can affect it. Still, there are certain basics and certain materials standard to most portfolios. Here are some of the inclusions:

- A cover, with an illustration of interest, that tells what the portfolio is all about. If you are giving salespeople a manual covering their firm's spring and summer advertising, say so. Headlines of general interest to dealers and salespeople may be used if desired, but they are not necessary to the effectiveness of good sales portfolios. Usually, however, a breezy headline such as "Even MORE Sales Power for YOU This Spring!" is a common device to get interest in the ensuing material.

- A section devoted to the advertiser's advertising-to-come. In this part of your portfolio you will show either reprints of the advertisement, which may be slipped into a "pocket" or flap in the pages, printed right on the pages themselves, or "tipped in"—glued along one edge and inserted in the manual.

  Normally you will discover that the pocket method is best for advertisers who have a heavy and complete schedule of advertisements, since it enables the salesperson to carry more advertisements conveniently. It is also much less expensive than printing or tipping.

  In addition to showing the advertisements in your portfolio, you will want to give a complete schedule of where and when those advertisements will appear and how many readers they will reach. You will also want to point out to the dealers, if the campaign you show is national, that much of the national circulation is right in their town, even in their own neighborhood, so that the advertisements actually function partly as local advertising.

  If the operation is of a type that supplies complimentary advertising to dealers for their own local use, you will include a page or two in your portfolio to show reprints and tell how to get them.

  The same is true of all phases of the advertising program. Show the whole business: posters, car cards, TV and radio programs, spot announcements, and any other national or local advertising effort that is being put behind the product.
- A section devoted to merchandising. In this part of your manual you will illustrate all the various store and window display material that is made available to the dealer and tell how to order it. You will point out how this material is designed to "tie in" with the national advertising theme, to provide recognition and recall value, and to give the final impetus to the buyer at the point of purchase.
- A windup page or pages where you can ask for the dealers' support, emphasizing that it means more sales for the dealers to feature your product and is evidence of their sound business judgment.

Store Display Material: Your Part in It

Many copywriters make a mistake in giving too little attention to the creation of store display material. Because much of such creation is an art problem—simply adapting advertisements or parts of advertisements and simplifying them to different proportions—you can easily take the attitude that it does not require much thought on your part. Many sales are lost daily because copywriters did not understand the nature of the display piece they were building and made an error that caused their work to be wasted.

Figure 15–8. Trade advertisement that features heavy advertising support backing the company's products.

For example, suppose you are copywriter on a chocolate pudding account. You do a good job of writing and directing an advertising campaign based upon the simple idea of large heads of happy, cute children just about to take a bite of Yummy chocolate pudding. A headline may tell the special good things it has to offer. Following is more short copy and, at the bottom, a picture of the package and a logotype displaying the brand name. The campaign is fine. Everyone likes it. In the magazines or newspapers, it's sure to get lots of attention.

Now the pudding manufacturer wants you to make up a counter display card for grocery stores.

You whip up a counter card, perhaps 12 inches by 14 inches which is almost an exact duplicate of your advertisement. That makes good sense, you say to yourself. Cute kid eating the product. That's sure-fire for mothers shopping.

Well, the big hope for counter cards is that they are used together with a counter display of the product: card in the middle, packages around it. But big hopes are rarely attained. Where is the product identification on your counter card when this happens? *Yes,* that's right—down at the bottom of the card, completely obscured by other merchandise. It's still a cute picture—still has that important appeal to mothers—but nobody has any idea what you are advertising.

That sort of mistake stems from a too hasty examination of what kind of collateral material you are asked to prepare and an inadequate study of how it is to be used.

When you've devised an effective display, you've helped the salesperson where it counts the most: at the point of sale. If your display piece is faulty, you make the sales job more difficult. Help the salesperson with consistently good displays.

Other Ways You'll Help Company Salespeople

In addition to portfolios and displays, you will be called upon to write items designed to aid salespeople in making their rounds. Circulars, merchandising folders, sales letters, and postcards are among the types of material referred to. All these items will usually contain highlights of one or more of the basic elements of your sales portfolio—advertising or merchandising.

Their function is to arouse interest among the dealers to give display prominence to the product you are advertising, to push it because they are convinced that your advertising is helping them do business.

You will also probably write items to help the salespeople directly, such as sound slide films, skits, and other dramatic presentations to be used in sales meetings and sales rallies, showing these people how to sell. By associating with the staff of the sales department, by cultivating their friendship and understanding, you can build information on sales problems that will help you throughout your career.

Friendship with the sales department is important to copywriters in agencies or advertising departments or even in retail stores. If the salespeople don't function correctly, no matter how good your advertising may be, it doesn't look good. On the other hand, if you don't function correctly, you may make the sales department look bad. The whole business is, or at least should be, a matter of the utmost cooperation.

16

BUSINESS, PROFESSIONAL, AND AGRICULTURAL ADVERTISING

Part B

"Ye gods! How's a guy who majored in English Lit ever going to make it in this business?"

The question came from Jon Krasfelt, newly minted copywriter for Creative Group, a small agency specializing in pharmaceutical and medical supply accounts.

His boss, Mary Ensminger, smiled. "Jon, it would have helped if you had majored in biology and chemistry, but all of us in this agency have had to struggle with the language and terms no matter what we majored in—and we still have problems at times.

"You're going to have to go to school on the job, as it were. Study the professional journals, talk to doctors, and don't hesitate to ask questions when you talk to our clients."

She paused. "We hired you because you're a good writer and a quick learner. Now it's up to you to apply those qualities to a specialized form of writing. It's not easy, but you can do it."

Professional-Advertising Suggestions

Many activities, such as those of architects, lawyers, teachers, and others, may be classified as *professional* but the emphasis in this section is on advertising to the medical profession. Many of the observations can be applied to dental advertising, too.

Copywriters assigned to agricultural or industrial accounts can, if they are observant and industrious, learn the problems and language of these fields; it is more difficult to achieve similar success in the medical field. Yet, there are nonmedical copywriters who write medical or dental copy. Just as industrial writers profit from having a technical bent, so the medical writer profits from a scientific bent. An especially good prospect for such work would be a person who took pre-med in college or who dropped out of medical school. Here is some advice for copywriters in the professional field (especially in the writing of copy for advertising appearing in medical magazines):

Medical Advertising

Use the specialized language of the medical profession. Look over this excerpt from a medical magazine advertisement.

> Most patients with sustained hypertension have normal cardiac output and an elevated total peripheral vascular

Figure 16–1. Professional advertisement. In this advertisement addressed to medical doctors, the language is wholly professional. A copywriter working on such advertisements must learn that language and use it correctly.

> resistance. Reducing cardiac output, as beta blockers do, lowers blood pressure but does not seem to correct the primary abnormality—increased peripheral resistance.

This example is relatively simple compared to the writing in many medical advertisements, but it demonstrates the language level expected of medical writers. Readers of medical magazines have learned a different vocabulary; it is your obligation to learn it and to use it until it becomes your language, too.

Advertising of pharmaceuticals is especially demanding of the writer without thorough grounding in chemistry and biology, as the following excerpt demonstrates:

> Warnings: BEFORE CEPHALEXIN THERAPY IS INSTITUTED, CAREFUL INQUIRY SHOULD BE MADE CONCERNING PREVIOUS HYPERSENSITIVITY REACTIONS TO CEPHALOSPORINS AND PENICILLIN. CEPHALOSPORIN C DERIVATIVES SHOULD BE GIVEN CAUTIOUSLY TO PENICILLIN-SENSITIVE PATIENTS.
>
> SERIOUS ACUTE HYPERSENSITIVITY REACTIONS MAY REQUIRE EPINEPHRINE AND OTHER EMERGENCY MEASURES.

Avoid overly personal language. As in industrial advertising, the "you" approach should be avoided. When doctors read advertising in medical journals, they expect to be addressed in a professional manner. Don't write like an advertising copywriter. Medical people, whose writings and talks have been twisted out of shape by promoters of products, are distrustful of advertising people. Thus, they dislike "ad-dy" advertising but will accept advertising written in the style of one doctor addressing another.

Although few advertisements in medical magazines use consumer language or consumer approaches, occasionally an advertiser will choose a more "consumerish" approach. If handled well, it will be welcomed by the readers as a change, but it must be viewed as a variation, not as standard procedure. One such departure was used by a respected pharmaceutical company in the following manner:

Illustration: Portraits of Francis Bacon, Oliver Cromwell, Louis XIV, Carolus Linnaeus, and Thomas Gray.

Headline: The touch of Louis XIV, it was said, would cure gout. But he was one of many famous men who had gout.

Opening copy: Gout has had its share of wondrous "cures." In fact, in the early eighteenth century, many French physicians believed that a touch of the hand of Louis XIV would cure gout. Louis, however, was unable to cure his own case of gout. And that must have led to some embarrassing moments at medical meetings of the day!

Use scientific evidence. Persons dealing in matters of life and death eschew the casual approach. They want proof, presented by recognized authorities and backed by careful investigation. Little wonder then that you must constantly draw upon evidence to back any claims you make—and woe to you if the "evidence" is not supported by proven facts.

Because readers of medical journals are not going to accept unsupported statements about results obtained by the advertiser's product, medical advertising is replete with the kind of support supplied in the following:

> Typical of the results obtained against these troublemakers: In a recent study of patients with acute, nonobstructed lower urinary tract infections caused by these organisms, Gantrisin therapy produced sterile urine in 9 out of 10 patients.

This supporting statement was backed by a table from the study and a statement about where the reader could obtain the complete findings of the study.

Scientific evidence is usually in the form of research conducted by doctors and sponsored by reputable pharmaceutical houses such as Bristol Laboratories, Sharp & Dohme, and Eli Lilly. Before a new product is accepted, many research studies may have to be made and the process may take years.

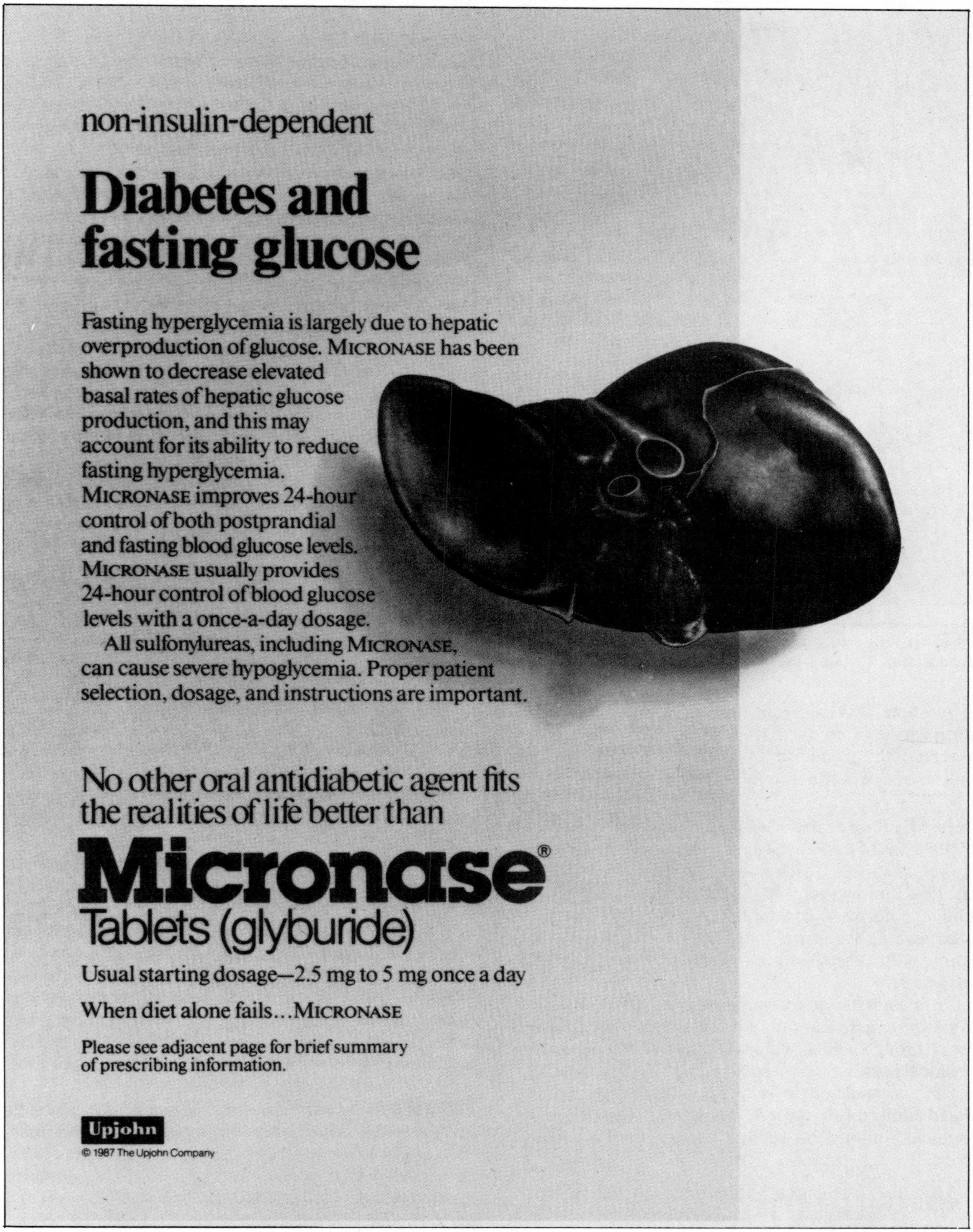

non-insulin-dependent
Diabetes and fasting glucose
Fasting hyperglycemia is largely due to hepatic overproduction of glucose. MICRONASE has been shown to decrease elevated basal rates of hepatic glucose production, and this may account for its ability to reduce fasting hyperglycemia. MICRONASE improves 24-hour control of both postprandial and fasting blood glucose levels. MICRONASE usually provides 24-hour control of blood glucose levels with a once-a-day dosage.
All sulfonylureas, including MICRONASE, can cause severe hypoglycemia. Proper patient selection, dosage, and instructions are important.
No other oral antidiabetic agent fits the realities of life better than
Micronase®
Tablets (glyburide)
Usual starting dosage—2.5 mg to 5 mg once a day
When diet alone fails...MICRONASE
Please see adjacent page for brief summary of prescribing information.
Upjohn
© 1987 The Upjohn Company

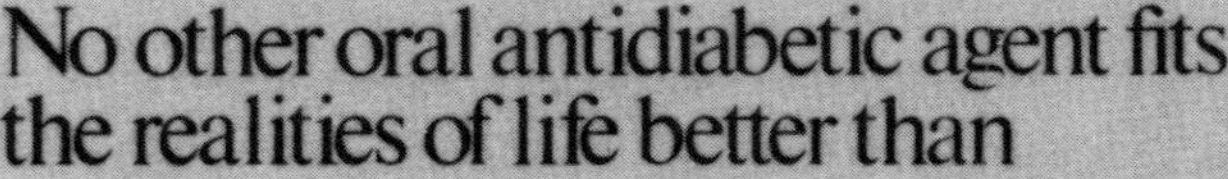

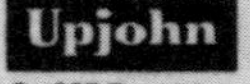

Figure 16–2a. Professional advertisement addressed to medical doctors. See other advertisements in this campaign as shown in this chapter (Figures 16–2b, 2c).

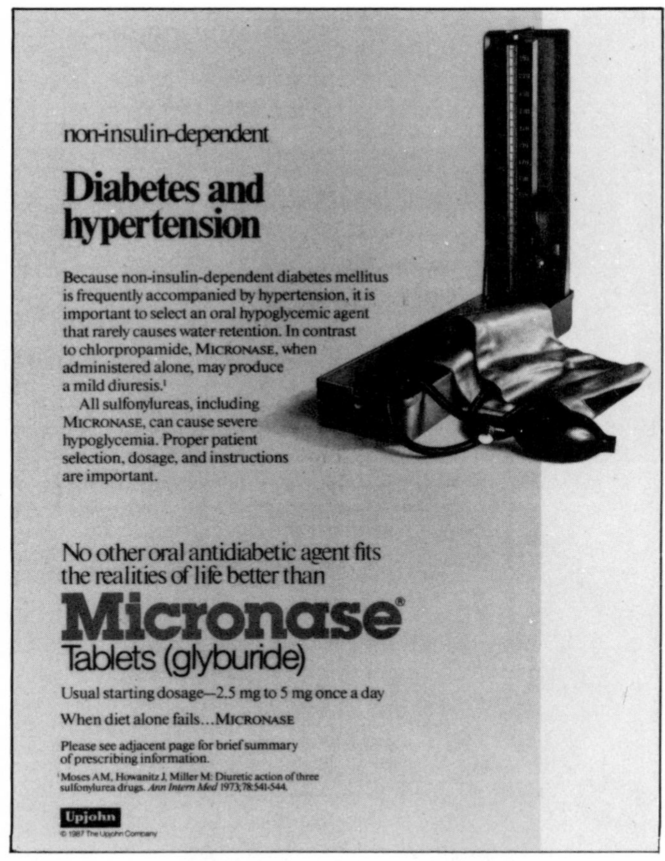

Figure 16–2b. Professional advertisement addressed to medical doctors.

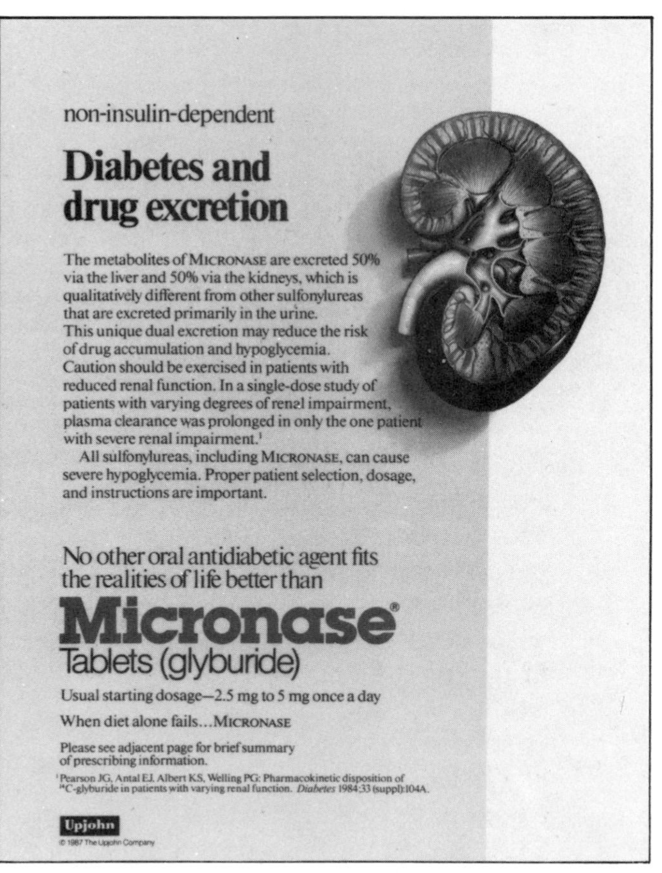

Figure 16–2c. Professional advertisement addressed to medical doctors.

A whole advertisement may be taken up with a description of a study that includes both the positive aspects of the product and—just as important—its limitations, given in the form of warnings about its use.

Recognize their desire to keep up in their profession. One of the trials of the professional person—doctor, dentist, lawyer, architect, teacher—is that new developments occur so rapidly that it is almost impossible to keep up. Thus the doctor is constantly attending medical meetings, reading scientific journals, and exchanging viewpoints with other doctors to keep abreast of the latest advances.

Your copy should recognize this need to be informed. If you have new features, stress them. If yours is a real breakthrough, which will make the reader a better professional person, stress it so that it won't be overlooked.

This compulsion to keep up with changes is illustrated admirably in the following excerpt from an advertisement for medical reports appearing in a medical journal.

Headline: Announcing a stimulating new educational alternative for AAFP members

Subhead: ER Reports gains AAFP approval! Now family physicians can stay up-to-the-minute and earn 30 AAFP prescribed credits a year.

Opening copy: Good news for busy physicians. This year you have a practical and provocative alternative for meeting your CME requirement. Thanks to recent approval by the AAFP's Continuing Education Committee, ER Reports gives you one of the few sources of AAFP prescribed credit in a convenient journal form.

Any conscientious physician never stops learning or educating himself or herself. Medical school graduation is just the first step in a lifetime educational process. You will do well to consider your advertising in that context. Advertising is a part of what the doctor needs to know. He reads the advertising, along with the editorial content of medical journals, to keep his head above the flood of new developments in the field. In short, you are instructing the physicians in something that they may not know about your product.

Recognize the reader as a user or recommender. Doctors and dentists especially, among professional people, may be viewed in two ways: (a) As persons who will use the advertised product, such as a dentist's drill or a surgical instrument, in conducting their profession, or (b) As persons who will recommend the product's use to patients. A drying lotion for acne, elastic stockings for varicose veins, and a mild soap for bathing babies fall into this category. Ivory Soap, as an example, has been adver-

Figure 16–3. Professional advertisement. A combination of a striking headline and illustration commands attention for this advertisement.

tised for many years in medical journals because a doctor's endorsement is so powerful with the new mother anxious to give her baby the best care.

If your chief objective is to give physicians enough information about a product to enable them to recommend its use, your copy will probably include such phrases or headlines as:

> Effective Therapy You Can Safely Recommend
>
> After *your* counseling on the safety issue, she may decide that her best option is the (*name of product*)
>
> Give your patients a break from ordinary antacids

When you write a good medical advertisement you are preparing the way for a call by "detail" men or women. These are highly trained sales representatives who call upon doctors (and dentists) to do just what your advertising attempts. They tell the doctors about new developments and, in a low-key way, suggest the use of the product by the doctor.

If you have written your copy well, the detail person's call will be more resultful because you've already implanted the important product points in the doctor's mind. You will not do your detail person a service, however, if your copy consists of column after column of tightly packed small type that makes your advertisement look like a section from a difficult-to-read medi-

Figure 16–4. Professional advertisement with unusual illustration. This award-winning advertisement has been a great success. It is so different from the usual professional advertisements that it stands out in every medical magazine in which it appears.

cal textbook. Even eager-to-learn doctors are daunted by such advertisements.

You'll pave the way for your detail person more effectively by at least occasionally cutting down the excessive columns of backup laboratory proof in favor of an open-looking advertisement with copy that both the busy doctor and the detail person can read and understand more easily and more quickly.

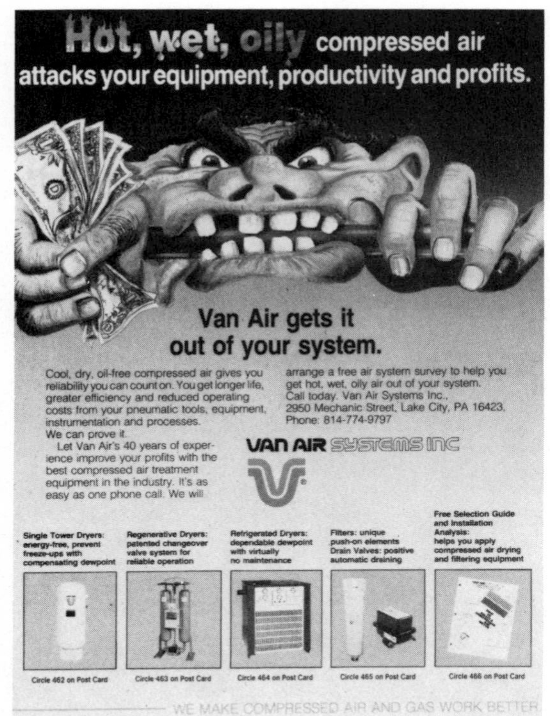

Figure 16–5. Industrial advertisement with unusual, attention-getting illustration. In this case, the copy message is augmented by the picture captions at the bottom of the advertisement.

Figure 16–6. Industrial advertisement with imaginative illustration.

Industrial Advertising

You may have been, or are, a star in writing consumer copy—perhaps for hair preparations, headache remedies, cereals, menswear. But if you switch to industrial copy, you may feel like a beginner again. Lacking the feel for technical copy, you're not at home writing to engineers, technicians, factory managers, chemists, electronics experts, and others who make up the industrial market.

Consider *your* background and abilities. Now read this description of the reading material found in an industrial magazine listed in *Standard Rate & Data Service.* Think you're qualified to write advertisements to the readers of this publication? Do you have the background, or the inclination? (This latter word is very important.)

> Serves those in such fields of experimental mechanics as stress analysis by strain gages, photoelasticity and brittle coatings—fatigue and vibration studies—impact—instrumentation. Feature sections include papers of experimental investigating methods and evaluation of new techniques and instruments, behavior of structures under test and analysis, and solutions to production problems.

Or this publication, edited for:

> Mechanical, electrical, and nuclear engineers in the total power market—utilities, process and manufacturing industries, service complexes, plus the consulting engineering firms working in the power technology; they are responsible for the design, construction, operating, and maintenance of equipment and systems involved in power generation plus the process, control and supply of energy in its many forms—electricity, steam, water, compressed air/gases, and so forth.

Learning How to Write Industrial Advertising Is Not Easy

Good writers learn quickly what they must know in order to write about most consumer products. There is no way, however, that they can learn quickly what they need to know about such products as industrial pumps or giant turbines. They can't bluff. They can't dazzle hydraulic engineers or electrical engineers with cute selling phrases.

Before they write they must study the products, see them operate, and talk to the plant people, the salespeople, and the advertising manager. They must study the specification sheets and engineering catalogs. When they thoroughly know the equipment, its uses, and its applications, *then* they might be prepared to write in the language of their hard-boiled market. No glib consumer approach will work here.

Now and then someone in the advertising field will assert that there's little difference in the writing demands of consumer and industrial advertising. Contrarily, if you talk to people who have written both, you'll hear many times how an industrial advertisement appearing in an industrial publication that charges $6,000 a page took more creative time and downright hard thinking than a consumer advertisement in the *Reader's Digest* that charges about $110,000 for a 4-color page, or a 30-second television commercial that costs $400,000 for time charges and many more thousands for production.

Any writer in the consumer field has, on occasion, rattled off radio commercials or print advertisements in a few minutes, especially if this person has been working on an account for a long time and is thoroughly familiar with the background and general style desired.

In contrast, it's just about impossible to dash off an industrial advertisement. Every word is weighed and every fact is checked for accuracy and acceptability by an extremely critical audience. Furthermore, the vocabulary is usually specialized, extensive, and technical.

Some copywriters *do* work well in both fields, but they are the exception. Most writers concentrate in one or the other. Not very many are switch-hitters. It is more likely that a good industrial writer can adapt well to consumer copy than that a good consumer writer can switch successfully to industrial advertising.

What do you need to make it as an industrial advertising copywriter? Most of all, you should couple a reasonably good writing ability with a liking for technical material or an education in technical or engineering curricula. Engineering school dropouts are often the types who adapt well to industrial advertising. They have the vocabulary and the necessary ease in technical matters.

Figure 16–7. Industrial advertisement with clever head and copy, plus a strikingly different illustration.

How to Write Industrial Advertising

Make your approach much less informal. The "you" approach, so loved by the consumer-product writer, is usually out of place in industrial advertising. You don't cozy up to a vice president of manufacturing, a plant manager, or a safety engineer. They don't use the products you sell; they consider their purchase for use in their plant operations.

Then, if they like what they read, they may ask someone else to "look into it" or to "specify" it. Because there is no personal use involved, you have little or no chance for the "you" approach, or for informal, personal language.

Don't use hard sell. You don't push industrial readers. You don't high-pressure them. You don't urge action as you do with consumers or trade-advertisement readers. The industrial purchase is likely to be large. A committee may be appointed to decide whether your product should be used plantwide. Perhaps the purchase will be in hundreds of thousands of units.

Possibly six months to a year will pass before the purchasing agent is told to put through the order. In that time there may have been competitive bidding, demonstrations, tests, and presentations.

Against this background you would look absurd were you to use consumer-copy exhortations of "order now," "act quickly," "don't delay," or other action phrases, the favorites of writers of consumer and trade advertising. Industrial buyers simply aren't the impulsive types swayed by such urgency.

As a rule, avoid the light touch. Now and then you may invest industrial advertising with humor or a lighthearted, consumer-type approach—but rarely. Your readers aren't poring over industrial advertisements to be amused or entertained. Your product might reduce accidents, increase production, cut down pollution, or improve morale.

These are not lighthearted goals. They are approached in a serious manner and you call upon the vocabulary of the readers to tell them what your product will do for their plant or the products turned out. That vocabulary will be down-to-earth, specialized, and often

Figure 16–8. **Long-copy industrial advertisement.** Readers of industrial publications are willing to read long copy if it provides information needed to make a buying decision. In this instance, it puts stress on costs and long-range savings—two important points with industrial readers.

Figure 16–9. Industrial advertisement stressing "New" in the headline, followed by down-to-earth copy.

difficult. It definitely is not carefree nor (usually) even cheerful. This kind of writing comes hard to consumer-product copywriters who, to this point, have prided themselves on the "easy, conversational touch."

When you're writing to engineers, purchasing agents, and other industrial realists you give facts, not frills. Although businesswriting principles in general apply to industrial-publication copy, some specifics are explained in the following material.

Get into your story quickly. Although interested readers of industrial advertising are willing to read long copy, they are not willing to waste time guessing what the copywriter has in mind. Many of your readers go through mountains of reading matter each day. Although your copy should be complete, it shouldn't be leisurely. Let the reader know immediately through headline, illustration, and the first copy block what you're talking about.

Getting into your story quickly means that your headlines are specific, and research shows conclusively that specific headlines get better readership. Just as an example, here are three headlines for the same product. As the headline becomes more specific, it becomes more effective in attracting and holding readers:

Headline 1: The production boosters

Headline 2: Get more working time out of that router

Headline 3: Three reasons why Superior routers can cut downtime as much as 70% over your yearly production schedule

Push long-range savings more than long-range costs. Your competitor's metal tubing may cost 40 cents a foot but may last only half as long as yours. Your tubing at 60 cents a foot would, consequently, be a better buy. Remember that purchasing agents are buying greater productivity for the firm; that means they are interested in saving manpower and materials. Thus, long-lasting materials and equipment are almost always their first interest.

Connected with the same idea is the industrial buyer's continual interest in machines that will require little maintenance. Little maintenance translates to little cost and, over the years, long-range savings.

Write copy with an individual reader in mind. In many advertisements you'll be writing to management in general. Preferably, however, you should direct your copy with a specific person (called a "Buying Influence" in the industry) in mind: engineer, the plant architect, maintenance supervisor, the head of operations. Point your message at that person's interests. Use the person's language.

Using the "language" means not only the words but the daily concerns of the person. What are the concerns of industrial management, or call them motivations? Here are some that would be appropriate if you were selling a floor absorbent that reduces slipping accidents on factory floors:

- To reduce insurance rates
- To boost worker morale
- To maintain production levels
- To lower accident rates
- To make the plant known as a good place to work

Here's how you apply these ideas in tough factory language:

> "A worker who slips as he walks down a line of melting pots can be in for a bad burn—and you're in for a session on workmen's compensation regulations."

Another example:

> "If your factory had a high accident rate last year because of skids and falls on stained or soaked floors, then you should think about using a floor absorbent as part of your company's regular safety equipment this year. And when you think of floor absorbent, think No-Slip. Better yet, specify it."

Another:

> "Risks belong upstairs—not on the ground floor. Business management necessarily involves calculated risks, but when it comes to slippery floors on the manufacturing line, play it safe."

As for language, use words and terms of the field such as "specify," "man-hours," "downtime," "men on the line," "OSHA regulations," "union stewards." If you don't know the language, learn it and do so before you write your first industrial advertisement.

An example of a down-to-earth industrial headline that achieves the right tone because it uses appropriate language is this quotation headline, supposedly said by a rugged-looking worker sitting astride a steel beam in a building under construction:

> "If the guy who specifies bar grating had to make the field modifications, he'd specify something better!"

Figure 16–10. Industrial advertisement stressing safety. Management people are deeply concerned with safety for many reasons. This advertisement is wholly concentrated on this concern.

Use a strong news slant. Purchasing agents and others who read industrial advertising are constantly asking, "What's new?" Industrial readers are on the prowl for information that will help them or their firm do a better job. Latest developments are their meat—feed them a heavy diet. Your new product, or new use for your product, should be told about in fresh, lively news style.

An example of the news approach in an industrial headline:

> Diablo introduces the first printer that runs on four wheels

Another example:

> **Head:** A bright new engineering achievement moves air management into a new technological age
>
> **Subhead:** Newex. The all-new spun aluminum fan line from Greenheck.

Give complete information. Talk about your servicing facilities, the construction of the item being sold, the lasting qualities, the type of work for which it is best

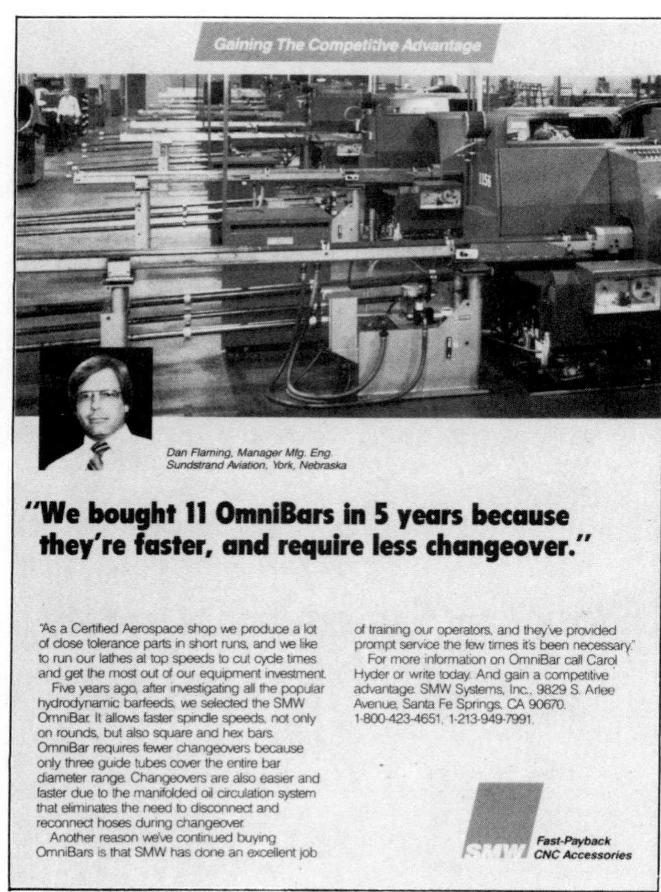

Figure 16–11. Industrial advertisement using testimonial.

suited. Tell why your product gives better performance. Why is the material in your product superior?

Remember this also: Your advertisement may be clipped and filed. It may be dragged out later to be placed next to a competitive advertisement. The copy that does the most complete job may get the sale. Industrial advertising, unlike much consumer advertising, is often referred to long after the advertising has run. Make your copy worth going back to. The typical industrial-paper reader doesn't shy away from long text—so long as it has something to say.

Although industrial copy should be thorough, the reader of such copy is like anyone else in not liking dull, lifeless catalog-type copy. If your material is better suited to a specifications sheet or parts catalog, save it for those uses.

Recognize a problem—then show how your product can help solve it. The readers of industrial advertising are beset with problems: abrasives don't hold up; V-belts break; the accident rate is too high; perhaps production is falling. If your advertisement suggests a way out of their troubles, they'll read it like a novel.

An example of the problem-solving approach is afforded by the following headlines and a portion of the body copy of an industrial advertisement:

Headline: Pittsburgh Paints
Solves Downtime Problems

Subhead: PROBLEM:

Avoid costly
production interruptions
when repainting

Subhead: SOLUTION:

PPG Fast Dry Alkyd
Industrial Enamels

Copy: PPG Fast Dry Alkyd Industrial Enamels have a tough, brilliant, high-gloss finish that's dry to the touch in about 15 minutes and to handle in 30 minutes. This compares to normal alkyd paint drying time of 6 to 8 hours. . . .

Catch interest with case histories. The usual industrial buyer moves cautiously. Industrial advertising is largely directed to those who buy in big quantities. Successful use of your product by another business makes absorbing reading for the person going over your advertisement. Perhaps, in addition to selling him, you are helping sell management on buying your product. Your case history of successful use of your product may often be the only sales argument that carries weight.

One difficulty with the case-history approach is that the "history" used may be so narrow in application that many of your readers won't find what you say applicable to their situation. This problem isn't acute if you are using a vertical magazine (one that concentrates on a single industry, such as a magazine directed toward manufacturers and users of industrial pumps). In such a case, almost anything that can be said about industrial pumps will interest the majority of the readers.

On the other hand, if your advertisement appears in a horizontal magazine aimed at a wide cross section of industries, your case history may be of limited interest unless in your writing you make it clear that the kind of technical expertness applied in your case history would be useful in other applications, too.

An example of the case-history approach written in such a way that readers will interpret the results broadly is shown in this excerpt from the body copy of an advertisement for an energy-saving ventilation system. This well-illustrated advertisement supplies *two* short case histories for added effectiveness.

No. 1

It's bad enough that the cost of energy is going through the roof, but the Chelo Brothers of Rhode Island discovered that their energy itself was going up the exhaust flue and through the roof. They installed a Seco Wash Ventilation System. The energy they're saving will pay for the system in about 3 years.

No. 2

In a United Airlines Flight Kitchen where as many as 20,000 meals per day will be prepared, both energy efficiency and almost nonstop operation are key requirements. With A Seco Wash Ventilation System they not only save thousands of dollars on energy but countless man-hours, too.

THE HEADACHES OF EXCESSIVE INVENTORY GOT YOU DOWN?

WE'VE GOT THE CURE!

The foundation of 64 years of Value Added service to industry has been based on helping our customers cut their on-hand inventories. Carrying inventory adds 20-30% to your costs. With Bearings, Inc. as your bearing and power transmission supplier, you can reduce your back-up stock, or eliminate it completely. You won't buy product till you need it.

Bearings, Inc.
Dixie Bearings, Inc.
Bruening Bearings, Inc.

INTEGRITY IN DISTRIBUTION

World Corporate Headquarters
3600 Euclid Avenue
Cleveland, Ohio
U.S.A. 44115-2515
216-881-2838

Figure 16–12. Industrial advertisement stressing cutting of costs. A striking illustration makes this advertisement stand out.

Use important-looking, reader-interest headlines. Industrial advertising deals with heavy industry and with big purchases. It is addressed to hard-driving decision makers engaged in important work. Make your headlines reflect the character of the industrial people and their jobs—in typography (no delicate script types) and in what you write.

Hit hard and specifically in attention-commanding headlines. A good example is the following headline that offers a benefit sure to appeal to step-saving, cost-cutting industrial-magazine readers. Not only is this headline very long (but specific enough to arouse quick interest), but it also uses a price figure. Price mention is rare in industrial copy, especially in headlines. If, however, it is possible to mention price, it will increase readership.

Main Headline: MicRIcon Rewrites
the law of
Cost and Effect

Subhead: It's a complete 3-mode process control system with automatic or on-demand printout logging for under $5,000!

Two more long headlines follow. Both are admirably direct, unlike many industrial advertisement headlines.

Microcomputer Hero

Intel's new 8051 packs more processing ingredients onto a single chip than ever before. And serves it up with total development support.

Designing a control system with 15 relays or more?

Specify this rugged General Numeric programmable controller that speeds up system design and gives you more flexibility for less money.

Think of readers' interests when selecting illustrations for industrial advertisements. Often you won't be the one to determine the nature of an illustration to be used but, if you are, ask that the product be shown in use, if possible. Much of industrial advertising is concerned with equipment and machinery that often look dull when not in action. "Action" in such cases normally means that you will show a person, or persons, using the equipment or operating the machinery.

There are, on the other hand, occasions when a person shown in an industrial advertisement is a distraction. Unless the presence of a machine operator contributes to the understanding of the working of the machine, the industrial reader may prefer to look over the details of the equipment minus any human element. The operator is superfluous.

Big-space, dominant-illustration advertisements pull good readership from industrial readers. Because of their technical bent, however, not all of these illustrations are interesting in the consumer sense of the word. An engineer will find strong interest in a cross section of a machine, in a schematic drawing, in a blueprint. Graphs and charts are a form of industrial language easily understood by industrial readers. They sometimes pull better than so-called interesting illustrations.

In calling for illustrations, always remember that the industrial-magazine reader is most often technically oriented. This reader's taste in illustration material is, accordingly, different from that of readers of consumer advertisements. Occasionally, successful industrial illustrations will have a consumer flavor, but most such illustrations are suited to the vocational bent of the industrial reader.

Coupons play a prominent role in industrial layouts. When you prepare such a coupon, you will ask for a respondent's name and company affiliation. Too often, however, the person's title is not requested. This causes trouble because coupons come back to the advertiser's sales department and are then distributed to salespeople according to sales territories.

Such salespeople customarily find that only a few buying influences in any given plant are accessible to them. By asking for the title of a coupon respondent, you may provide a sales representative with a big list of buying influences to call upon. Unless the title is given in the coupon, the sales department won't know whether the respondent is a purchasing agent, a company president, or an engineer, and will not, accordingly, know just how to follow up the lead generated by the coupon. To repeat—*always* ask for the title of any respondent to a coupon.

Summing Up Industrial Copywriting

Never forget you're writing to a management person, often engineering-trained. Well-educated in business as well as in technical matters, ambitious and mature, this person is likely to be skeptical of advertising claims yet reads advertising for news of products and techniques.

This person has pride in running a tight shop. Part of this pride is in rising production curves and with safety as it affects production. What are management concerns? A few include union relations, insurance costs, problems with OSHA (Occupational Safety and Health Act), worker morale, and the perception by even higher management that the manager is doing a good job.

If an industrial copywriter wants to catch interest, he uses terms that people in industrial plants use. He may refer to dust, fumes, mists, hot metal, flying particles, harsh light, or dangerous heat levels. Reference to familiar equipment will catch attention, too: for example, bench grinders, metal shavers, lathes, saws, and high-speed drills.

You begin to see from what has been said in this summing up that you get very specific in industrial copy. Fancy writing is out. Direct, almost hard-boiled, writing is in. Think of yourself as being on the factory floor and casting your experienced management eye on what is going on around you. You see a problem. Now, as the copywriter, you write copy that points out how that problem can be solved with your product or service. If you do your job well, you're going to help the management reader do a better job—the big goal in industrial advertising.

Figure 16–13. Institutional advertisement aimed at agricultural field. This ran in a farm publication.

Agricultural Advertising (or Agribusiness or Agrimarketing Advertising)

Unless you've lived or worked on a farm, you face a handicap in writing farm copy—not an *impossible* handicap but a severe one. And even if you *have* an agricultural background, you still have some handicaps to overcome. Your experiences as a hog raiser in Iowa, for example, mean little when you're communicating with a Southern cotton grower. Even those working the same crops, corn growers, for instance, have their differences, as a Minnesota farmer and an Arkansas farmer can tell you. Individual farmers know their soil and climatic conditions better than anyone else. Because of this, they are most responsive to advertising that seems to be aware of their particular problems.

Apart from the actual business of writing to the farmer, what are some aspects of agricultural life you should know?

How farmers get information. Advertising is only one way of communicating with the farmer, an assiduous information seeker. Much of what a farmer needs to know about new products, methods, and equipment is obtained from state fairs, farm shows, agricultural schools, and word of mouth with other farmers, county agents, company salesmen, and farm dealers. It is especially important to farm marketers to get the farmers to talk to their dealers.

As for advertising media, farm magazines and farm radio are generally rated as the most important in communicating with the farm market. Approximately 50 percent of the farm advertising budget is invested in farm magazines. Following these two are outdoor advertising, television, and direct mail. Direct mail is becoming more important because farmers with specialized crops sometimes are so few in number that it is unprofitable to publish a magazine to reach them.

The farm market is sharply segmented. The extent of segmentation in agriculture is evident in the more than 200 farm magazines and in the many regional and specialized editions published in the field. Some magazines, catering to the regional and agricultural differences, offer as many as 300 different versions of their publications to meet the needs of readers.

To serve the segmented markets, many of the magazines are vertical, such as *Guernsey Breeders' Journal, Grass & Grain, The Sunflower,* and *The Sugar Producer.* In addition to segmentation by agricultural interest, there is segmentation by geographical region, as illustrated by *New England Farmer* or *Tennessee Farmer.*

To cover general farming news and developments, there are a number of strong horizontal publications, such as *Successful Farming, Farm Journal,* and *Progressive Farmer.* These publications are useful to farmers who shift from crop to crop as prices vary, or to those such as hog raisers, who must also raise grain to feed their hogs. A horizontal magazine can also appeal to the dairy farmer, who puts the herd out on part of his acreage and then raises corn, wheat, dry beans, oats, barley, and hay on the remainder of the acreage. Such readers are well served by the broad scope of the horizontal publication.

"Helpful" is a key word. Farmers help each other. They share with each other. They tell neighbors about products that work for them. Word-of-mouth communication is important for fertilizers, seeds, and tractors. Such help, when it is needed, has been called "country manners." Companies serving agriculture such as John Deere for tractors, Pioneer for seeds, Monsanto for pesticides and herbicides, and Ford for trucks are compared in terms of their helpfulness.

A majority of the nation's farms and ranches are run by individuals who, in the main, do not have full-time help. This means that products and machines do the work once supplied by full-time help. Thus, farmers need all the help they can get from whatever source.

LYRIC: Say, what do you know, they're talking corn,
It's the corn-talk time of year,
And mostly when you're talking corn,
You're talking Pioneer.
MAN A: I'll tell you, I have a great deal of loyalty to one certain brand of seed corn.
MAN B: Oh? Which one?
MAN A: The one that yields best on my farm.
MAN B: Pioneer?
MAN A: Yeah, mostly.
LYRIC: Mostly when you're talking corn, you're talking Pioneer.
MAN C: I try to spread my risks by planting three or four different Pioneer hybrids.
MAN D: UmHmm. Pioneer calls that genetic diversity.
MAN C: I call it common sense.
LYRIC: Yeah, mostly when you're talking corn, you're talking Pioneer.
MAN E: You sure hear a lot of folks comparing their yields to Pioneer yields.
MAN F: (Never thought of it that way.) Y'know, that's right.
MAN E: 'Course I figure if those Pioneer numbers are the ones to beat . . .
MAN F: Yeah?
MAN E: They must be the ones to plant.
LYRIC: It's best to go with what you know,
You hear it loud and clear:
Living and learning
And planting Pioneer.

Figure 16–14a. Farm radio commercial with straight sell for product.

LYRIC: Well I chose to go the Treflan way,
It's the path most growers take;
But life doesn't always hand us
Choices that easy to make.
MAN: Well, did you get the carpet picked out?
WIFE: I just couldn't decide on the color.
MAN: (Amused) A whole store full of carpet and you couldn't decide.
WIFE: Well, at first I thought I liked the beige . . .
MAN: Beige would be good.
WIFE: But now I think maybe bright red.
MAN: Bright red carpet? For the whole house?
WIFE: Not carpet. I was thinking of that big red tractor you've had your eye on.
MAN: Wha . . .
WIFE: The carpet money would be a partial down-payment.
MAN: But what about the carpet?
WIFE: Well, there's always next year.
REX: On the farm, it seems like there's just one decision after another. And farm people know that the results they get depend on the choices they make. For good weed control, most growers choose Treflan . . . because they know they'll get good results.
MAN: This new tractor is gonna save us a lotta time this spring. . . . Quite a view from up here.
WIFE: Yeah . . . nice carpet, too.
LYRIC: Of all the right choices you make,
Treflan's only one.

Figure 16–14b. Farm radio commercial with humorous approach.

Understanding the farmer. Farmers are individualists who are still strongly dependent upon others, whether the "others" are the banks that carry their loans, the farm machinery companies that defer payments, or the government that subsidizes them. Despite such help, they feel isolated, put upon by nature, the government, and the unrelenting laws of supply and demand that determine the prices they can obtain for what they produce.

You must realize the wide gulf between the agribusinessmen farmers, whose acreage is vast and equipment investment enormous, and the small farmer eking out a bare living from a few acres. These considerations affect the nature of your advertising.

Compare the medium-size farmer in the Midwest with a modest number of feedlot cattle to the big-scale Western rancher with 5,000 grazing cattle. For the first, you'd probably show the familiar red barn and nearby corn field in your illustration. For the latter, you'd show open plains and many cattle grazing.

Problems vary markedly from farm to farm. Dairymen have little in common with citrus growers. A truck farmer faces a different situation than the Dakota wheat grower. Yet, all are classed as farmers.

Understanding the farmer calls for an understanding of the role of women on the farm, too. As farms have become more businesslike, women farmers have taken an increasingly important role in farm management and financial decisions. Women farmers are now, very often, owners or partners in a complex operation.

Specific Tips in Writing to the Agricultural Field

Despite all the differences in those who make a living from agriculture, there are some general principles you can observe in writing to them. Here are several:

Watch your language. Today's farmers have, to a large degree, received specialized instruction in agricultural school. Even those who haven't, have learned about antibiotics, animal husbandry, and the fine points of difference in hybrid seed corn on the job. You can use a level of language, therefore, that is much above that used some years ago. Be careful, however, that you don't write like a city person trying to talk to a farmer.

Use farm language and don't slip. If you do, your copy will be discredited. Remember, too, that although the farmer can be addressed in language more sophisticated than was once advisable, there are farmers who are not college-educated. Avoid literary flavor and too much urbanity.

As an example of down-to-earth language, here is the headline for a chain saw:

> "Three busted saws in the barn aren't worth a lick when I've got fence to build."

Not elegant language, but expressive, and it conveys a sense of realistic earthiness. In contrast is the following section of copy that also conveys a sense of on-the-farm language, aimed at a somewhat higher level:

30- and 60-second Radio Commercials

ANNCR: Is it too early to be thinking about NA-CHURS Liquid Fertilizer for next spring? Not when you figure that by acting early, you can save up to sixteen percent . . . almost like getting every sixth gallon of your NA-CHURS free. You earn the discounts by early ordering, delivery and payment. The sooner you act, the more you save. Call your NA-CHURS representative. NA-CHURS. Helping you make the most of the fields you know best.
(:05 local tag)

ANNCR: Is it too early to be thinking about the NA-CHURS Liquid Fertilizer your fields will be needing next spring? Not when you start adding up all of the money you can save by acting early . . . acting now. Because a growing schedule of discounts can save you up to sixteen percent off the cost of your NA-CHURS . . . almost like getting every sixth gallon free. You earn the discounts by following a timetable this fall for ordering your NA-CHURS, taking delivery, and making payments. The earlier you act, the more you save. There's something else you'll get, too: a soil test with an agronomist's report that'll help you plan a total field-by-field fertilizer program. Call your NA-CHURS representative. He's the man not too far from you who's got the nation's number one liquid fertilizer—NA-CHURS—and the facts on how you can save up to sixteen percent. From NA-CHURS. Helping you make the most of the fields you know best.
(:10 local tag)

Figure 16–15. Farm radio commercials. Radio is a powerful medium in the farm field. Notice in this instance that each commercial leaves room at the end for the local dealer to identify himself.

> Gives instant, on-the-spot moisture readings so you can zero in on the optimum level of moisture for ensiling and harvesting. (Monitor moisture levels of forages and grains every hour if need be.)

To demonstrate how far the modern farmer is from his relatively unsophisticated predecessor of some years ago, here are a few phrases from an advertisement addressed to hog raisers. They demonstrate the technical and scientific bent of today's agriculturalist:

- Confinement research
- Artificial insemination
- Liquid feeding
- Feeder pig specifications

Give them proof. Agricultural people have traditionally been skeptical. Alone much of the time and given to introspective thinking, they are cynical about salespeople and their claims. That is true of their attitude about advertising, too.

Testimonials and case histories, accordingly, are useful in agricultural copy if: (a) they relate to the reader's particular interest—hogs, corn, soybeans, dairy herd management, and so forth—or (b) they pertain to the reader's geographic area.

Research has become a buzzword in agriculture, as in so many other forms of endeavor, as this excerpt from a seed corn advertisement shows:

> Results: In this area, this field-tested yield and standability performer averaged $45.30 more profit per acre than 3780; $17.40 more than 3901.
>
> It was no accident. No one has a stronger commitment to seed corn research than we do.

With some agricultural operations becoming so big that they should properly be called "agribusinesses," your copy should stress information, facts, and research. Consider for instance a feed company in North Carolina that raises and markets 60 million broilers yearly. This organization owns three farms in Indiana simply to keep the broilers supplied with corn. In addition, the company owns breeder flocks, hatcheries, and processing plants. It even has a substantial interest in a supermarket chain to provide an outlet for the sale of the broilers.

The management of such an organization consists of businessmen-agriculturalists. They want proof that whatever it is you are selling will help them in the operation of their big business.

In general, proof can also be supplied by certain methods. You can show a product in use. If a fertilizer, for example, have the farmer put the fertilizer in a hopper or spread it on a field. You can also show the results of using the product. Perhaps this could be a lush corn field for which a fertilizer or seed or herbicide is responsible. Or you can tell, or demonstrate. Either can be used to convey how to cut labor costs and increase production or yield. Illustrations of equipment might do this, or possibly charts, graphs, or tables.

Instill a management feel (in some instances). This suggestion is made if your product or service is designed for the truly big agricultural establishment where the top people are business managers as much as agricultural people. They are buying big-ticket items in combines, tractors, silos, and other equipment, not to mention fertilizer, seed, and less spectacular but still expensive items. Talk to them like management executives.

Obviously, because there are still many small farms, you must pick your situations and products when using management approaches. Nevertheless, the word "management" comes up constantly in agricultural advertising: herd management, crop management, breeding management. A headline for the latter, for instance, reads:

> Your veterinarian's total breeding management program can help ensure successful results with Lutalyse.

Suffer with them. With some justification, farmers feel that the forces of nature, government, and economics are against them. Let them know that you're on their side and that you know their problems. This can be done subtly, of course.

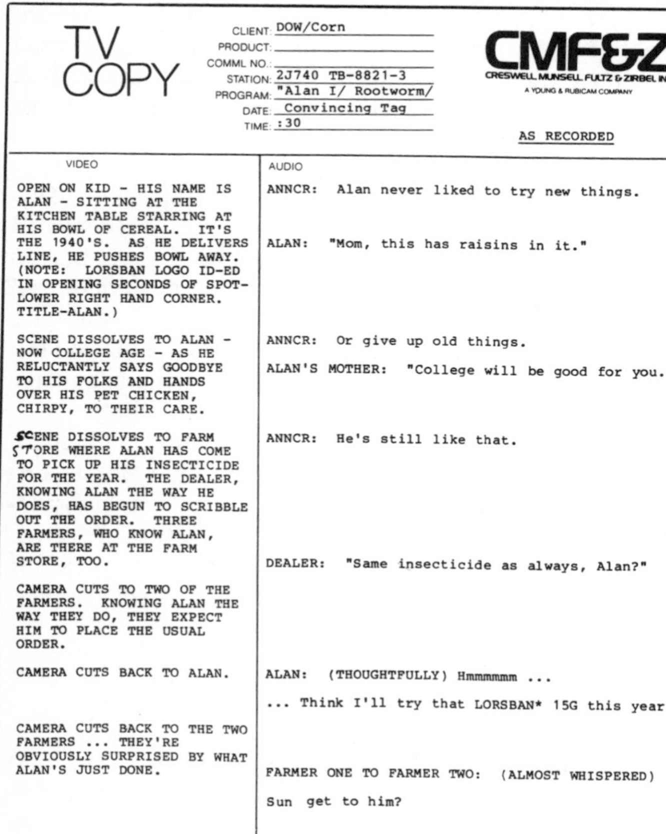

TV COPY

CLIENT: DOW/Corn
PRODUCT:
COMML NO.:
STATION: 2J740 TB-8821-3
PROGRAM: "Alan I/ Rootworm/
DATE: Convincing Tag
TIME: :30

CMF&Z
CRESWELL, MUNSELL, FULTZ & ZIRBEL INC.
A YOUNG & RUBICAM COMPANY

AS RECORDED

VIDEO	AUDIO
OPEN ON KID - HIS NAME IS ALAN - SITTING AT THE KITCHEN TABLE STARRING AT HIS BOWL OF CEREAL. IT'S THE 1940'S. AS HE DELIVERS LINE, HE PUSHES BOWL AWAY. (NOTE: LORSBAN LOGO ID-ED IN OPENING SECONDS OF SPOT-LOWER RIGHT HAND CORNER. TITLE-ALAN.)	ANNCR: Alan never liked to try new things. ALAN: "Mom, this has raisins in it."
SCENE DISSOLVES TO ALAN - NOW COLLEGE AGE - AS HE RELUCTANTLY SAYS GOODBYE TO HIS FOLKS AND HANDS OVER HIS PET CHICKEN, CHIRPY, TO THEIR CARE.	ANNCR: Or give up old things. ALAN'S MOTHER: "College will be good for you."
SCENE DISSOLVES TO FARM STORE WHERE ALAN HAS COME TO PICK UP HIS INSECTICIDE FOR THE YEAR. THE DEALER, KNOWING ALAN THE WAY HE DOES, HAS BEGUN TO SCRIBBLE OUT THE ORDER. THREE FARMERS, WHO KNOW ALAN, ARE THERE AT THE FARM STORE, TOO.	ANNCR: He's still like that. DEALER: "Same insecticide as always, Alan?"
CAMERA CUTS TO TWO OF THE FARMERS. KNOWING ALAN THE WAY THEY DO, THEY EXPECT HIM TO PLACE THE USUAL ORDER.	
CAMERA CUTS BACK TO ALAN.	ALAN: (THOUGHTFULLY) Hmmmmmm ... ... Think I'll try that LORSBAN* 15G this year.
CAMERA CUTS BACK TO THE TWO FARMERS ... THEY'RE OBVIOUSLY SURPRISED BY WHAT ALAN'S JUST DONE.	FARMER ONE TO FARMER TWO: (ALMOST WHISPERED) Sun get to him?

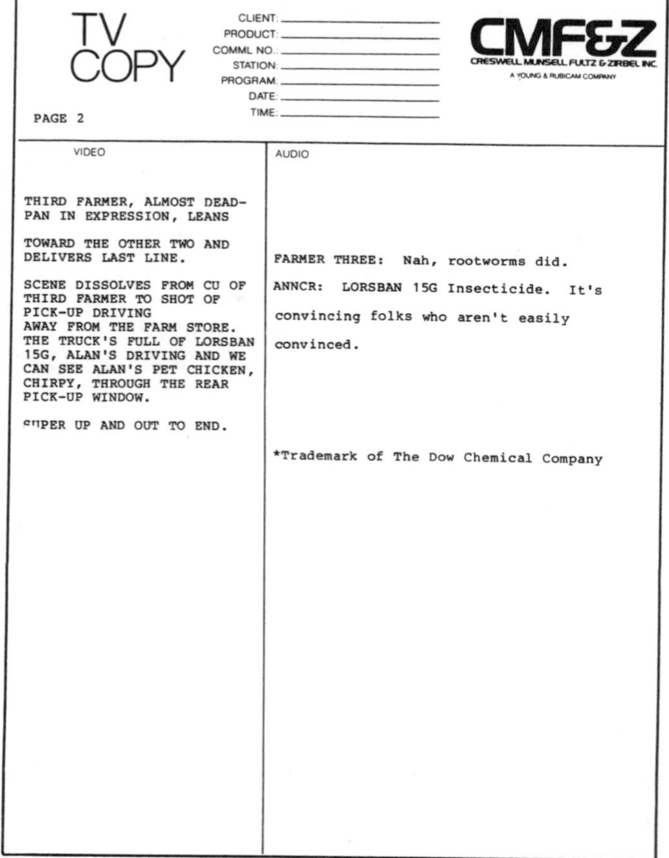

TV COPY

CLIENT:
PRODUCT:
COMML NO.:
STATION:
PROGRAM:
DATE:
TIME:

CMF&Z
CRESWELL, MUNSELL, FULTZ & ZIRBEL INC.
A YOUNG & RUBICAM COMPANY

PAGE 2

VIDEO	AUDIO
THIRD FARMER, ALMOST DEAD-PAN IN EXPRESSION, LEANS TOWARD THE OTHER TWO AND DELIVERS LAST LINE.	FARMER THREE: Nah, rootworms did.
SCENE DISSOLVES FROM CU OF THIRD FARMER TO SHOT OF PICK-UP DRIVING AWAY FROM THE FARM STORE. THE TRUCK'S FULL OF LORSBAN 15G, ALAN'S DRIVING AND WE CAN SEE ALAN'S PET CHICKEN, CHIRPY, THROUGH THE REAR PICK-UP WINDOW.	ANNCR: LORSBAN 15G Insecticide. It's convincing folks who aren't easily convinced.
SUPER UP AND OUT TO END.	*Trademark of The Dow Chemical Company

Figure 16–16a. Farm television commercial with strong human interest feeling.

TV COPY

CMF&Z
CRESWELL MUNSELL FULTZ & ZIRBEL INC.
A YOUNG & RUBICAM COMPANY

CLIENT: DOW/Corn
PRODUCT:
COMML NO.:
STATION: 2J740 TB-8821-1
PROGRAM: "Roscoe/Rootworm"
DATE: (Convincing Tag)
TIME: :30

AS RECORDED

VIDEO	AUDIO
OPEN ON 5,6 OR 7 YEAR OLD KID. LIKE MANY KIDS HIS AGE, HE HAS AN IMAGINARY FRIEND. HIS IS NAMED ROSCOE. THE BOY'S FATHER OBVIOUSLY ENJOYS HIS SON. LIKE ALL FATHERS OF YOUNG CHILDREN, HE KNOWS HIS SON IS ALWAYS WATCHING AND LISTENING & REPEATING SOME OF THE DARNEST THINGS FROM COMMERCIALS & GROWNUPS ... AND EVEN OTHER KIDS. SO HE'S NEVER REALLY TOTALLY SURPRISED BY WHAT HIS SON COMES UP WITH. OFTEN HE FINDS HIMSELF PLAYING ALONG TO HIS SON'S DELIGHT. SCENE OPENS AT THE FAMILY'S PORCH WHERE THE LITTLE BOY IS SITTING. FATHER JOINS HIS SON AS THEIR PLAYFUL CONVERSATION BEGINS: (NOTE: LORSBAN LOGO ID-ED IN OPENING SECONDS OF SPOT -- LOWER RIGHT HAND CORNER. TITLE-ROSCOE)	DAD: Say, what 'cha doing? BOY: Talking to Roscoe.
CUT TO DAD	
CUT TO BOY	BOY: He's a worm. DAD: Oh. What's he eat? BOY: Corn
CUT BACK TO DAD AND BOY	DAD: Where's he eat this corn? BOY: He used to eat it over at Uncle Bob's, then he moved.
CUT TO DAD	DAD: Didn't like it over there?
CUT TO BOY	BOY: (SHAKING IS HEAD) uh-huh.

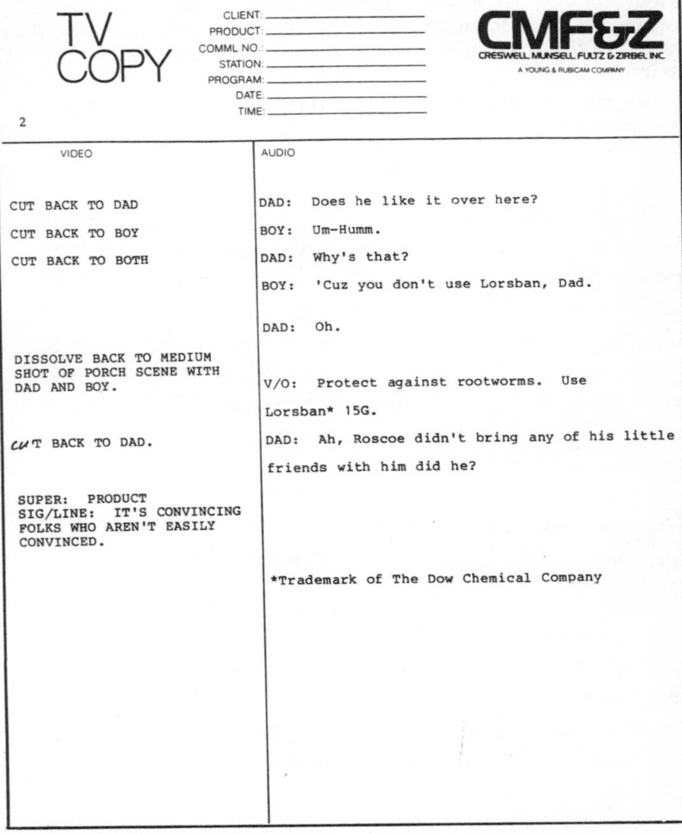

TV COPY

CMF&Z
CRESWELL MUNSELL FULTZ & ZIRBEL INC.
A YOUNG & RUBICAM COMPANY

CLIENT:
PRODUCT:
COMML NO.:
STATION:
PROGRAM:
DATE:
TIME:

2

VIDEO	AUDIO
CUT BACK TO DAD	DAD: Does he like it over here?
CUT BACK TO BOY	BOY: Um-Humm.
CUT BACK TO BOTH	DAD: Why's that? BOY: 'Cuz you don't use Lorsban, Dad. DAD: Oh.
DISSOLVE BACK TO MEDIUM SHOT OF PORCH SCENE WITH DAD AND BOY.	V/O: Protect against rootworms. Use Lorsban* 15G.
CUT BACK TO DAD.	DAD: Ah, Roscoe didn't bring any of his little friends with him did he?
SUPER: PRODUCT SIG/LINE: IT'S CONVINCING FOLKS WHO AREN'T EASILY CONVINCED.	
	*Trademark of The Dow Chemical Company

Figure 16–16b. Farm television commercial. Although much farm advertising is serious and down-to-earth, farmers will respond to family-oriented advertising with a light touch—if such advertising is well done, as in this example.

The Martin Agency

COPY CLIENT Mobil Chemical DATE December 20 REVISION# 2
JOB# MOC 2226-2 "Insects" :60 Radio

(ANNOUNCER:)

If you could hear the insects that eat your corn, you'd start using Mocap nematicide-insecticide as soon as possible. If you could hear rootworms (SFX: ROARING) ...wireworms (SFX: SCREECHING) ...nematodes (SFX: HISSING) ...and black cutworms (SFX: CRUNCHING). If you could hear the worms robbing you of 40 bushels of corn or more per acre... If you could hear the cutworms cutting your good, healthy stalks off at the base... (SFX: TIMBER FALLING) ...If only you could hear it... (SILENCE). But you can't. So you may be sitting back using no insecticide at all. Hoping the worms don't do too much damage this year. Or maybe you're using an insecticide that doesn't protect against all four of these deadly pests. We repeat: if you could hear the rootworms, wireworms, nematodes and black cutworms, you'd be using Mocap--the only insecticide in America that protects against all four. Because you're in business to save corn. And so is Mocap. Mocap. Get it. (ROAR) And save the corn.

THE MARTIN AGENCY INC. ADVERTISING. 500 NORTH ALLEN AVENUE. RICHMOND, VIRGINIA 23220. TELEPHONE (804) 254-3400
WASHINGTON D.C. (202) 484-1986 / VIRGINIA BEACH (804) 425-6179. MEMBER AMERICAN ASSOCIATION OF ADVERTISING AGENCIES

Figure 16–17. Clio-winning radio commercial. High drama is created here through outstanding sound effects that will rivet the attention of the farmer-listener—or that of any other listener.

Writer: Mike Hughes. Agency: Martin Agency, Richmond, Virginia.

Figure 16–18. Management advertisement aimed at those in the executive suite.

In an earlier chapter you were advised to use the suffering-points principle in writing copy—to tell how the use of your product would answer a problem. Farmers have a multitude of problems: among them how to dry hay in a hurry; how to hold down bugs and weeds; how to get seeds to germinate even in a cold, wet spring; and how to combat diseases in farm animals. Make the farmer ever conscious that you understand such problems and give him solutions.

Suggestions for Writing Executive-Management Advertising

Products and services appearing in executive-management publications reflect the broad responsibilities of the readers, embracing such widely varying items as computers and calculators, financial services, security guard protection, high-speed building elevators, business insurance, corporate jets, and export banking.

We're concerned here especially with the high-level readers of business publications such as *Fortune, Wall Street Journal, U.S. News, Business Week,* and the business section of the *New York Times.* Included in this readership are the readers of institutional magazines in the hotel or hospital fields, or readers of industrial magazines aimed at management in heavy industry—magazines addressing themselves to management.

Horizontal publications such as *Fortune* include a substantial number of personal products in their advertising pages. Mostly, these are luxury products such as high-priced automobiles, watches, liquor, cameras, and other accompaniments of good living.

Gear your advertising to the executive suite. High-level, urbane language is much more evident in executive-management magazines than in any other business magazines. The men or women in the executive suite are likely to be sophisticated, well-educated, and cosmopolitan. Today, they are likely to be global in their thinking. They may be in Japan one week and in Yugoslavia for a trade fair the following week.

Recognition of this multinational character of the readers of executive-management publications is quite evident in this small section of copy:

> The American International Group of companies has more pins in more parts of the world with more people of-

Figure 16–19. Advertisement aimed at management people with international interests.

Figure 16–20. Management advertisement that points up the importance of research in company operations.

fering more kinds of insurance than practically any other commercial insurance organization.

So if your company has a lot of branches around the world, you have to go to a lot of insurance companies around the world to cover each one of them.

As for "urbanity," the writing in many management publications, like so many of the readers of such publications, is relaxed, polished, and very much at ease, as in this fragment of copy from an advertisement for a Swiss bank:

Incredibly Swiss

If we were to have a national animal, it would very likely be a St. Bernard. We just simply cannot think of another beast so incredibly *Swiss.*

Originally bred by monks in the 17th century on the summits of the Great and Little St. Bernard passes, the quiet, friendly, and dependable animal became famous for rescuing lost travelers.

It's not that all Swiss are quiet and friendly, but most of us have a thing about being *dependable.*

And we're quite Swiss in this respect at Credit Suisse. For us *dependability* is one of the most basic requirements in business today.

Dullness is the unforgivable sin in the writing of management copy. Although the readers engage in important work, they have a tolerant attitude toward whimsy in the advertising, so long as that whimsy is accompanied by material useful to decision makers. For instance, there is this headline by a computer manufacturer:

Bugs, Burps, Glitches, and Other Computer Demons

And then there is this headline that is not whimsical but is certainly not dull in the way it addresses itself to management:

You can't control
labor costs.
You can't control
material costs.
You can't control
fuel costs.
But you can control
your bottom line.

Recognition of the exalted lifestyle lived by the upper echelon of corporate management is ever present in horizontal business publications. There is a deference and subtle flattery of those beings who tread the thick carpeting in quiet executive suites. Advertisements for corporate jets that whisk two or three executives swiftly from New York to London and luxurious foreign hotels that invite their business provide a vision of a life only a relatively few persons may experience. The copy must achieve the right tone, respectful but not fawning. The following headline for a corporate jet embodies this vision:

With the amount of fuel it takes to fly the aircraft on the left from New York to London, you can fly the aircraft on the right from New York to London. Then Amsterdam, Brussels, Frankfort, and Munich.

While management people are concerned with ecology and the impact of industry on the environment, they are also concerned with such less broad-gauge management matters as profit-and-loss statements, plant safety, and what the stockholders are thinking. Thus, they are always receptive to advertising that tells them crisply, and sometimes entertainingly, about products and services that will result in a better-run business.

Aim your language level at people who appreciate the nuances of good writing. The discussion to this point has centered around the very top management, but you might, in the case of many products and services, be aiming at ambitious middle-management people who have heavy responsibilities but not the final word in very top-level decision making.

If you are consciously aiming at the middle-management executives, your copy may tend to include more facts and figures that the readers may use to arrive at a decision. Advertisements intended for the very top management may, in contrast, be broader and less detailed. The purpose may be to interest the occupants of the executive suites enough to cause them to send a memo down a couple of floors asking a lesser executive "to look into this."

A headline can make it quite unmistakable whether you are aiming at middle or upper management. The following, for example, is clearly a middle-management type:

> Introducing the Xerox 820. You tell us what you do, we'll tell you what it is.

Another:

> The 30-minute file fiasco vs. the 30-second file find

In contrast, here is a head unmistakably top-management in direction:

> Why shouldn't boards of directors expect something more from accounting firms?

Business Advertising—a Summing Up

As you have noticed, the knowledge required for the various forms of business advertising is so diverse that no one can come prepared to write copy for all the fields represented unless, of course, he or she is a triple-distilled genius.

Still, through diligent study and immersing oneself in the language and subject matter, it is surprising how well a good writer (and intelligent person) can adapt to the varying demands. In many ways, because of the incessant challenge, business advertising is more personally satisfying than consumer-advertising writing. Monetary rewards may be less, but career satisfaction and enjoyment may well be higher.

17

OUTDOOR AND TRANSIT ADVERTISING MAKE YOU CHOOSE YOUR WORDS WITH CARE

"You're about to become a man of few words," said Ozzie Thorne jovially to Walt Larsen, copywriter in the agency where Ozzie was creative director.

"That look in your eyes makes me think I'm not going to like what I'm going to hear, Ozzie."

"My boy, relax. All I'm asking is that you condense that two-page ad you wrote for the garden tractor to a max of seven words, maybe fewer."

"You've gotta be kidding!"

"I never kid when it comes to being brief in outdoor copy. And that's what I'm giving you, an assignment to write a dynamite set of six posters for the tractor. For a theme, draw upon the print campaign. Your poster copy will make a great backup."

"But, Ozzie. Seven words?"

"You've got it, Walt. Seven words or fewer. And make 'em count."

What Walt was discovering is that a poet and a writer of good outdoor advertising share some common abilities. Each is able to convey a powerful message in the fewest possible words. Each, likewise, will utilize emotion with telling effect upon the reader.

You may never discover these truths because the average copywriter has few, if any, requests to write outdoor copy. If that chance comes your way, welcome it because there is little in advertising that offers such a creative challenge. This is true of both outdoor and transit copy if the writer, not content with mediocre copy, tries for a creative twist that will make the copy effective, memorable, and different.

In recent times, outdoor and transit advertising have had problems: the former with environmentalists and many limiting laws, the latter because of the reduced use of inside cards on many transit systems. Yet, each survives because each offers a way to reach out-of-home prospects as they travel to buying centers. Each, while seldom a principal medium, serves as a powerful backup to major campaigns in print and broadcast. Then, on the local level, outdoor advertising may be the only medium usable by the motel, hotel, or eating place that wishes to sell itself to persons traveling through the area.

Outdoor Advertising

Posters and Painted Bulletins

If you're assigned to outdoor advertising, you'll write copy mostly for 36-sheet, 30-sheet, 24-sheet, or 8-sheet posters. These sheets are heavy paper stock and are printed by lithography or silk screen. Posters are in standardized sizes. They are called billboards by the general public but not by those in the outdoor business.

You may also write copy occasionally for painted bulletins. Painted bulletins, usually larger and more expensive than posters, are now generally standardized around the country and are becoming much more popular than in the past. They are bought and produced in individual units, unlike posters. Usually they are left unchanged for longer periods than posters, which are most often changed monthly. The copy message and illustration are painted directly on a metal surface. The reproduction quality is less consistent than that of posters. In a number of larger markets, painted bulletins are rotated to different locations to vary the advertising message in various sections of the market area.

Painted bulletins have never had the quality of outdoor posters that use lithographed sheets. A new development, however, is a vinyl-coated fabric introduced by Gannett Outdoor Group that can be computer-painted. Called Superflex, the new fabric makes possible painted bulletins that have magazine-quality reproduction that will not fade for two years. Because most painted bulletins are customarily repainted two or three times a year, the long life offered by Superflex has strong appeal.

"Outdoor advertising," as the term is ordinarily used in the advertising business, is intended to apply only—solely and exclusively—to those companies[1] engaged in standard outdoor advertising; that is, the companies represented by the standard, well-maintained poster boards, the neat, regularly painted bulletins and "well-groomed" units—not the torn and tattered circus, theatrical, and election posters that continue to proclaim their wares months after their advertising usefulness has passed or the rusty metal signs and crude homemade signs still seen decorating fences, buildings, and roadside pastures.

Why Use Outdoor Advertising?

People, generally, like to read outdoor advertising because it *relieves the tedium of the long journey* or the daily commuting trip. This, of course, does not mean that people see and read every sign they pass, nor does it mean that the same results would be obtained everywhere. It does, however, indicate that outdoor offers you a huge potential audience for your message—if you make it appealing enough to arouse the public's interest.

Outdoor advertising *offers continuity.* Your message will remain on the same location for a full thirty-day period and may be backing up a copy idea your magazine or other advertisements have established. Since most people travel and retravel the same route every day on their way to and from their work or shopping, you are able to hammer home your message to the same group of people day after day after day.

You can *obtain repetition* because an outdoor poster showing will usually be displayed simultaneously on a number of boards along major traffic arteries. As people travel down such roads, they will often see (and read) the same poster several times before reaching their destinations. This constant repetition has a cumulative effect much like that which makes a song a hit. When a tune is introduced, it usually elicits little response; but as you hear it played again and again, you find yourself unconsciously humming or whistling it as you go through the day. The repetition, not the song alone, has made a deep impression; so it is with the frequent viewing of the same outdoor posters.

Outdoor advertising *permits you to use color* at relatively low cost. Because newspapers and magazines will not accept color advertisements except in large-size space, many publication advertisers who would like to use color cannot afford to do so. An outdoor advertiser, on the other hand, can easily afford to use color, even though the total advertising may consist of but a single painted wall sign.

Outdoor showings of any magnitude *greatly impress dealers* stocking the advertised product. Day after day they are constantly reminded of the advertising the manufacturer is putting behind the product in order to help dealers sell more of it.

Outdoor advertising is *often the only medium that can successfully reach an advertiser's best prospects.* The hotel signs a person sees when approaching almost every city in an automobile are a good example. They are the only economical and effective means the hotel has for reaching motorists who plan to spend the night in the city.

Simple Posters Are Best

What you put on that poster must rivet the attention of pedestrians ambling down the street, drivers tooling along in their cars or trucks, and bus passengers peering out of the windows. To get that attention, your posters must offer a good idea, preferably a *striking* idea. Also, preferably, the idea should be clever, although, admittedly, great numbers of posters are devoid of any spark. They are ordinary and even dull.

Let's assume you succeed in supplying a clever and/or

Figure 17–1. Outdoor poster with play on words.

1. Known in the trade as "plant owners."

Figure 17–2. Humorous outdoor poster.

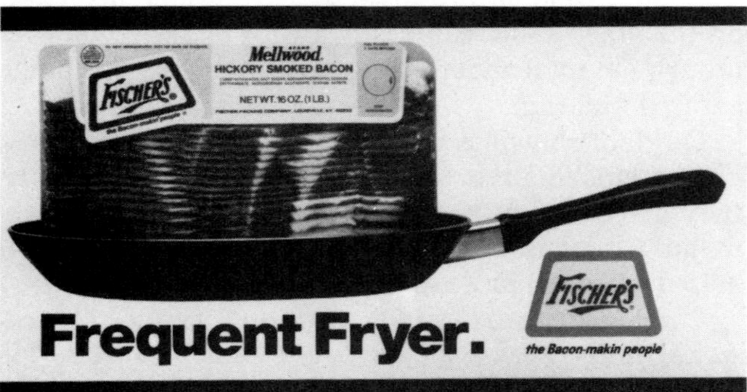

Figure 17–3. Outdoor poster with clever play on words. In addition to cleverness, the poster also offers strong sensory appeal and good identification of the product and advertiser.

striking idea. Your poster will still be a failure if you don't keep it *simple*—simple in execution and simple for the reader to grasp quickly.

Simplicity is very evident whenever effective posters are studied to determine why they are effective. You will find simplicity mentioned often as an important attribute of effective posters. There are, however, some situations in which it is possible to be more subtle in your copy situation—for instance, in a sign on a crowded city street. Such a sign could be read by walkers or slow-moving drivers. Where reading must be done more quickly, however, it is best to use a simple message.

Unfortunately, there is no set formula to follow that will enable you to hit on prizewinning poster ideas regularly. Such ideas are elusive to even the best of creative people.

A pair of quotations might be helpful here as the first guides for your poster-winning efforts. Both are from the pen of the famous nineteenth-century editor and theologian Tryon Edwards:

> Have something to say; say it, and stop when you're done.
>
> Never be so brief as to be obscure.

Or, as another man of note once said:

> "The surest way to be dull is to try to say it all."

Having achieved your selling idea, it is important in glance-read poster copy to concentrate attention on your one idea. Don't try to make two, three, or four copy points. Be satisfied to slam one point at the readers. If it's tires, it may be safety; gasoline, mileage; bread, taste; soft drinks, refreshment; automobiles, beauty.

Each of the foregoing products has other appeals, but don't use them in combination. *Stick to one idea.*

Short Copy—Almost Always

Remember, your message must be telegraphic—so concise, yet so clear, that people will get it the instant their eyes hit the board. You have *five seconds* to register if the panel is visible at 250 feet and the motorist is going thirty-five miles an hour.

One study of poster advertising examined 500 posters to see how many words of copy were to be found in each. Here is the way the analysis broke down:

Number of Posters	Percent
Without words	3.5
With one word	3.1
With two words	9.8
With three words	16.5
With four words	21.2
With five words	16.1
With six words	11.3

Such brevity is admirably illustrated by a Volkswagen poster that used a simple illustration of the automobile and four words of copy. Those four words were:

> Buy low. Sell high.

Like everything else in copy, however, the length of poster copy is not to be established through fixed rules. Although it is obvious that keeping your poster copy short normally makes good sense, it is possible to find instances of use of longer messages.

Readability and comprehension should guide you in determining length of poster copy—not inflexible rules that limit your imagination and originality.

Suppose, for example, you know that your poster showing is going to be concentrated in areas of heavy pedestrian traffic. Under such a circumstance, you can certainly exceed the four words used in the Volkswagen poster.

Volkswagen, incidentally, uses a poster technique in its print advertising; namely, a simple illustration, a brief, clever headline, and a minimum of body copy. Volkswagen print advertisements, like posters, put over a clear message with the illustration-headline combination. The body copy is helpful but not absolutely necessary.

The Morton Salt Company, which has had many prize winning posters, used a short, simple, but hard-selling line for an extended period:

> If it's worth its salt, it's worth Morton's.

It was illustrated by luscious vegetables, melons, fruits, and other food items commonly improved by the addition of salt.

Figure 17–4. Prize-winning outdoor poster that uses clever humor. Just three words of copy convey a message that will draw a smile and a strong appeal for the would-be traveler looking for escape from the humdrum.

Figure 17–5. Outdoor poster with play on words. Like many examples of outdoor advertising, this one could double as a transit card of the extra-size type.

Figure 17–6. Outdoor poster with clever twist, plus strong appetite appeal. This poster could serve also as an effective transit card. Copywriter and artist have combined their talents admirably in this poster.

Figure 17–7. Clever outdoor poster. As in the other example for this product, the writer and artist have added appetite appeal and strong advertiser-product identification to cleverness. The result is memorable outdoor advertising.

Figure 17–8. Clever outdoor poster.

Standard Oil of Indiana once won a poster competition with a poster which had just one word on it . . . TOPS! It was illustrated only with the cap worn by the Standard filling station operator.

You don't have to be brilliant, but often it helps a great deal to make your poster sing out from a highway lined with less imaginative efforts.

Whether you elect to be cute or whether your product and problem call for straight selling, above all keep your outdoor advertising simple, short, and interesting.

You'll see a number of posters in this chapter's illustrations. Study them. See how in every case the copywriter and art director worked together for a total effect of a fast, memorable impression.

Poster Elements

Although the number of copy and layout elements varies according to the complexity of a poster, the following is a list of the elements normally included. Not all five will be found in every outdoor poster, as in the case of the Volkswagen poster previously described.

- Product name
- Principal illustration

Figure 17–9. Outdoor poster with a play on words.

- Short copy to back illustration
- Package
- Headline (often a clever and/or selling phrase)

Other elements might have been included, but these five are found most often. To keep the list simple, such elements as trademarks, company name, and price were not included.

In many cases the package may well be the principal illustration. A headline may be a slogan or it can constitute the "short copy to back up the illustration." In brief, the elements are juggled around as demanded by the institution, the campaign, or the product itself.

The elements are clear-cut. It is your use of them that results in effective or ineffective posters. Since simplicity is so important to quick reading, attain simplicity by avoiding the mixing of too many elements in one poster.

Because there are five elements listed in the foregoing does not mean you must use them all. Remember—*strive for simplicity by limiting the number of ideas and elements.*

It Takes a Lot of Ideas to Spawn One Good Poster

When you receive a request for "one" outdoor poster design, do not be misled by the use of the singular. In order to create a Grade A poster, you may have to hatch a dozen or more ideas—and have several rough, thumbnail layouts of each sketched out on tissue by an art associate.

After these numerous rough tissue layouts are assembled, you and the other persons working on the account will give them a going-over—discussing and appraising each in detail and eliminating many. The ideas or designs that survive this first session will be revised and polished and again be subjected to the close scrutiny of all concerned.

Posters are usually either (a) direct adaptations of advertisements, using the same headlines and illustrations used in magazines or newspapers; (b) semidirect adaptations, in which the theme idea is followed, but which use specially created headlines and/or illustrations; or (c) presentations that are completely different from the advertiser's publication or radio copy. In the last type, no attempt is made to tie in with the campaign theme. New ideas are used, but usually a certain family resemblance is maintained.

Outdoor is an ideal medium for publicizing tradenames, trade characters, package identifications, slogans, or any idea that may be quickly stated with perfect clarity. Because it permits the use of color at relatively low cost, it affords an excellent means for putting over appetite appeal. A bowl of corn flakes and strawberries looks like wood shavings and licorice drops when reproduced in black and white. But give it color and it will look so tempting as to be almost irresistible.

Although outdoor advertising is a true mass medium, usually aimed at the total public, there are exceptions in which the copy message is aimed at a relatively selective group. A farm feed or hybrid seed poster advertisement along a road traveled by farmers is an example. Another is a motel poster aimed at that portion of motorists who are looking for overnight accommodations. An extreme example of "selective" outdoor advertising is the poster displayed in the Detroit area that read:

O.K. Show it on TV. But sell it in magazines.

This message was aimed at a tiny number of high-ranking executives in Detroit-area auto firms who might have some say in the selection of media for advertising campaigns. Outdoor advertising was used because it was felt that the targets of the campaign were too busy to listen to long media presentations.

No Form of Advertising Requires More Originality

As you have already been told, outstanding outdoor advertising requires a high degree of creativity, largely because you must do so much despite the limited amount of space for words and illustration, the need for terse yet clever copy, and the requirement for product or package identification.

The chief function of poster advertising is to serve as a buying reminder to people who are, or will soon be, in a position to buy. You are often going after what is called the "impulse sale" when you write poster copy. Since you haven't the time or space to persuade people to buy your product, you have to assume that they have already been sold by some other form of advertising; your job is to remind them of your brand in a bright, memorable, and attention-compelling way.

Products such as beer, soft drinks, gasoline, cigarettes, and candy are naturals for poster advertising. Your prospects are in an automobile. They are going to stop within minutes. Chances are good that they will purchase one or more of these items, or similar ones, when they do.

It must be equally obvious to you why hotels advertise so extensively on outdoor signs—also, restaurants, taverns, and other public services. They want to remind the immediate prospect of what they have to offer.

It is often said that the outdoor poster which advertises a grocery store product is a giant point-of-sale display. Food retailers know that a poster placed on a main traffic location near their store will serve as a quick reminder to shoppers who may very well be on their way to

Figure 17–10. Outdoor poster with sensory appeal.

buy from them. These locations, near shopping centers and village business sections, are considered ideal by advertisers whose products sell through food stores.

You'll see much automobile advertising on outdoor boards. While an automobile is neither an impulse purchase nor an immediate-action type of product, remember that a large percentage of the people who see a car displayed on an outdoor poster are driving cars a year old or more. They cannot help being influenced by a sales message showing a beautiful new car. These impressions will multiply to help make the eventual sale. What better time to sell the product than when it is actually being used by the prospective customers?

Combine Selling and Entertainment

Provided you adhere to the number one rule of simplicity, both in illustration and message, you can use cuteness, or cleverness, and the more of either the better. If you're bright enough to make your poster tell an entertaining story, while it punches home a copy message and product identification, you have probably succeeded in creating a good poster. Remember, however, that you have to get the whole story told in five seconds or less.

One of the most famous outdoor posters of all time was one old-timers may remember now that convertibles have made a comeback. It read:

The only convertible that outsells Ford!

The illustration was a baby buggy.

The copywriter who did this poster had a perfect combination of influences. It's simple—just five words besides the name of the product. It gives a selling point of importance—more people buy Ford convertibles than any other, and it says so in a very clever, warmly human, memorable way.

Another great Ford poster from the past violated every rule in the copywriter's book. That was the one which showed a little boy looking longingly into a Ford dealer's window at a new model, and the only brand identification shown was the Ford name on the dealer's window, which was *backward.*

Emotion Pulls in Outdoor Advertising

Because the poster message must be read and understood so quickly, the use of emotional appeals—especially humor and pathos—is especially effective in outdoor advertising. Emotional copy elicits what might be called a "gut" reaction—a quick response that requires no considered thought or pondering.

Figure 17–11. Outdoor poster with striking illustration.

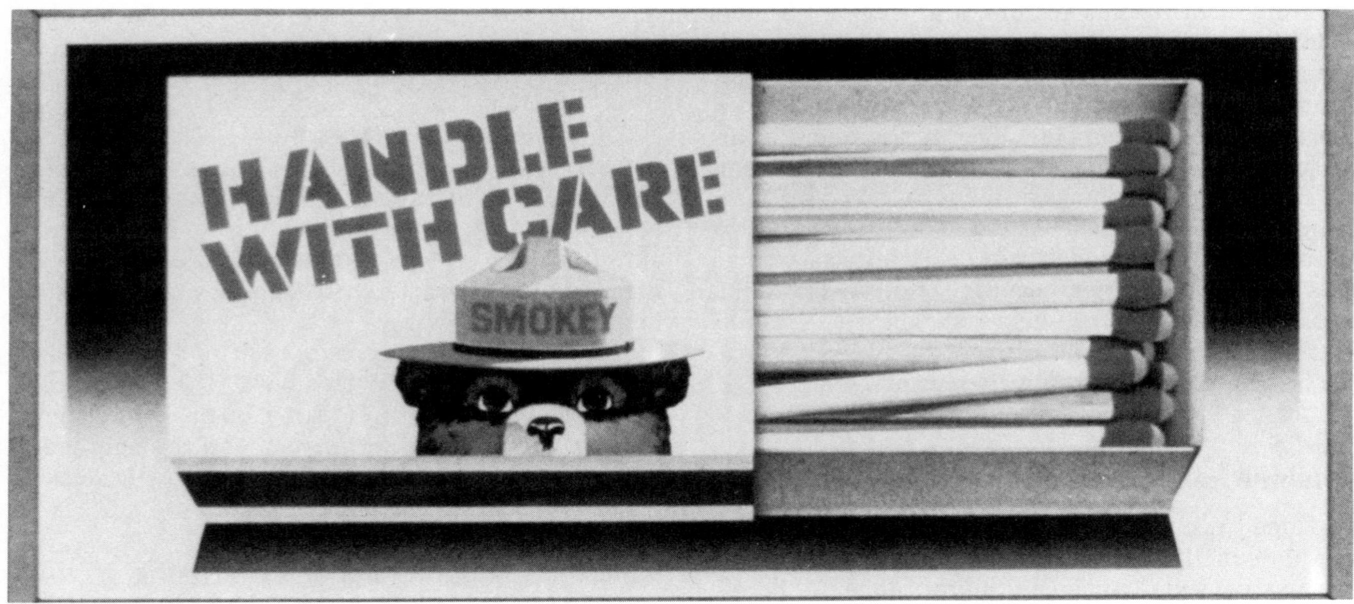

Figure 17–12. Public service outdoor poster.

Well-done humor is superb in getting viewer reaction and instant response, such as the outdoor poster for Fischer Hams that showed a very nervous turkey looking appealingly at the outdoor audience and imploring viewers to serve Fischer hams for Thanksgiving.

Cleverness and humor were also combined in a memorable campaign for a West Coast exterminator company which put the following startling message on a 48-foot outdoor structure:

> There are no termites in Spokane.

One week later a huge chunk had been taken out of the sign as if a giant termite had bitten it off. A few days later another chunk was gone. The procedure continued until, at the end of four months, only the advertiser's name was left.

Pathos and indignation also score well in outdoor advertising, especially for public service campaigns devised by the Advertising Council in such campaigns as those against racial prejudice, drunk driving, or child abuse.

Writing Points to Remember

To sum up, you might keep the following in mind when you write and design posters:

1. Be satisfied generally to put over one idea in a poster.
2. Use as few elements as possible and make those elements count.
3. Be brief, but don't be brief for brevity's sake. If your copy needs to be more than ordinarily long in order to do the job more effectively, then make it longer.
4. Don't be subtle in most posters. Make your poster simple—easy to understand in glance-reading.
5. If you're promoting a packaged product, you can increase package recognition by featuring the package on your posters.
6. Use positive suggestion—although you won't use this technique in all posters, many posters will be stronger if you suggest something the reader can act upon.
7. Above all, try for a twist—a clever, attention-getting (often humorous) phrase that ties in with an equally clever, attention-getting illustration idea. Actually, the phrase and the illustration are one. Your object is to make the viewer react quickly—smile, frown, get angry, feel pity, make a resolution. Force the viewer to single out your message from all the competing influences around the poster. Use of emotion might help you get the attention you want.

Transit Advertising

Inside Cards

Inside transit cards come in different sizes and shapes, although most are proportioned about the same as 30-sheet or 24-sheet outdoor posters. The greater number of cards are in the side positions. Popular sizes in these positions are 11 × 28 in. and 11×14 in., although much longer cards are often used. You might also prepare copy for cards placed at either end of a transit vehicle. In this discussion, however, emphasis is on the side cards.

Some copywriters prepare all transit cards exactly as they do outdoor posters. This is a mistake. If they would but compare transit cards and outdoor posters, they would see that, except for their shape, there is little similarity. Thinking of transit cards as "baby billboards" has caused many copywriters to write poor transit cards. They are not posters and should not be treated as such.

It is often mistakenly thought that it is necessary for an inside transit card, like a poster, to get its message over in the flickering of an eyelid. The thought is not sound. Your transit card is traveling right along with your audience, whereas the poster must be read quickly as the automobile whizzes by. The transit card and the reader are relatively stationary. The people you are interested in reaching don't rush by your transit card at a gallop. They sit or stand near it, for a long time, twenty-seven minutes per one-way trip on the average. Readers can thus linger over your copy, if you have caught their eye and if you have interested them sufficiently to make them want to do so. You don't, accordingly, have to limit your copy to five or six words. Or fifty or sixty for that matter. One important restraining element on the number of words is the requirement that the message be readable three seats ahead of or behind the card.

Transit cards can be designed to be real "traveling salespeople"—selling advertisements that can, by themselves, put over a sale instead of being mere reminders.

As you write a transit card, recall that you are not expecting to reach everyone in the car at one time. Passengers aren't going to stretch, and crane, and twist to read your copy. The only people you will usually reach at any single moment are those passengers standing or sitting close to where the card is posted. This is why it is not essential to keep copy brief, nor type kingsize. If a person can read your poster from six to eight feet away, readability is all right. A good way to test readability quickly is to place the poster on the ground at your feet. If you can read it easily, the card will probably be readable for riders in vehicles carrying transit cards.

Another point to remember about transit cards is that sometimes they curve. Also, the bottom of the card, rather than the top, is closer to the reader's eyes and is, therefore, usually easier to read. That's why you find some transit card headlines at the bottom. Because of curvature, the upper inch or so of the card often is practically flat against the roof of the car or bus. If you put any of your copy story in this top area, make it a subordinate line, not your real selling message.

Regarding inside transit cards, remember—you may make them "miniature posters" if you will thus more effectively get over your message, but do not consider such practice as standard. These days the poster often takes one technique and the transit card another.

Figure 17–13. Package identification outdoor poster.

Figure 17–14. Inside transit card. This end position card capitalizes on well-known sporting figures, as well as the famous Hathaway eyepatch. A sure attention-getter, it was used on rail systems in New York City, Chicago, San Francisco, and Washington, D.C. Such retailers as Marshall Field's in Chicago and B. Altman, in New York City, tied in with it.

Outside Cards

In recent years there has been a falling off of the use of inside transit cards and a veritable stampede to the outside cards displayed on the ends and sides of buses. Advertisers using the outside cards obtain readership from pedestrians, motorists, and even from homes as people see the buses going by their windows.

Figure 17–15. Transit traveling display. This poster on the side of a bus is attention-getting with its striking illustration and clever one-word message. This was award-winning advertising.

Figure 17–16. Traveling display on side of bus. Using a play on words, this big transit card carries its message throughout the city. It is like an outdoor poster on wheels.

In a sense, the outside cards are a form of traveling outdoor advertising that carries the advertiser's message into all parts of the town. For the copywriter, the outside cards constitute a strong creative challenge since the length of the sales message must be severely limited. Truly, in the case of outside transit cards, the copywriter must consider them closer to outdoor advertising than to the transit advertising represented by inside transit cards.

To write the copy for such cards, the copywriter should, therefore, follow exactly the same suggestions that were made for writing outdoor advertising. Brevity. A single compelling idea. Few elements. Simplicity.

An example of this is the traveling display on the side

of a city bus that showed three luscious ice cream sundaes with the message:

> Ice cream
> makes everyday
> a Sundae

Another form of outside card is the station poster that greets subway and train riders before they step inside the cars. These are treated like outdoor posters except that they are vertical instead of horizontal. Somewhat more copy may be written for these posters than for 24-sheet posters because reading time is longer both by people standing on platforms and by people reading the posters when the transit vehicle is discharging and picking up passengers.

Suggestions for Writing Transit Advertising

Although it has been pointed out that inside transit cards are not small posters, you should consider that there are some techniques that might transfer from one to the other.

1. As in posters, transit cards will usually be more effective if one sales point is made. An attempt to make more than one point usually will dilute your message.
2. Although reading time is greater for your copy in transit cards, like posters they should not have too many elements if they are to be efficient and readable.
3. A transit card can use more copy than a poster, but don't go wild. Brevity is still desirable for most cards. The use of a little white space will be helpful sometimes in giving your card a favorable contrast to the crowded cards next to yours.
4. Simplicity is another quality shared by posters and transit cards. Because of your being able to use more copy, you may indulge in more subtlety in transit cards, but don't overplay it. The average rider is usually better sold by a simple message.
5. The featuring of the package, of course, is desirable in transit cards as well as posters—especially so since your card may be the last advertising contact with someone who is about to start a shopping tour.
6. Positive suggestion is a part of transit card copy, too. As in poster copy, it is not used in every advertisement, but in the right advertisements it becomes a forceful, selling technique.

Thus, in summarizing the essential differences in handling the two—posters and cards—you find that:

- Unorthodox layout tricks are often used in transit card designing—placing of the headline at the bottom of the advertisement, for instance, and allowing for the curved surface.
- More latitude is possible in writing transit card copy since average reading time of transit cards is about twenty-seven minutes, contrasted with five to ten seconds for posters. The end result is longer copy and an opportunity for more subtle copy.

Both outdoor posters and inside and outside transit cards offer you more chances to be clever in one-liners than any other advertising medium. If you have the kind of mind that is original and capable of putting a fresh twist into your writing and illustration ideas, here are two areas of advertising where cleverness and originality pay off handsomely.

Also, to attain success in these media, just being skillful with words is not enough. You must likewise excel in layout ideas because almost all outstanding posters or transit cards demonstrate a happy marriage of the visual with the verbal.

A Final Word on Brevity

It seems fitting in a chapter where so much emphasis has been placed on the need for calculated brevity to draw upon powerful outside sources to stress the point.

Shakespeare, for example, wrote that

> Men of few words are the best men

and

> Brevity is the soul of wit.

And then, of course, the oft-quoted proverb:

> One picture is worth more than ten thousand words.

While the proverbist didn't have outdoor advertising in mind, your outdoor illustration *is* powerful, and accompanied by a *few* carefully chosen words, can be even more powerful.

Lastly, we have pertinent advice from Ecclesiastes: "Therefore, let thy words be few."

18

Radio Advertising

It Reaches Prospects Wherever They Are

Promoting itself as "The radio station with music for every taste," WKTU reaches into all corners of its listening area, day and night. As a small sampling, consider:

- *Harry Yeager, 62-year-old night watchman, taps his feet to the beat of "Golden Oldies" in between making his rounds at the factory.*
- *Alice Hufford, hair stylist in a unisex shop, listens to a new British rock group while passing time between customers.*
- *Igor Porozelski, tending bar at a downtown watering spot, has little to do at 11 A.M. before the noon rush, so absentmindedly he listens to the news while polishing glasses. His favorite listening, however, is the weekly polka hour emceed by a Polish-speaking announcer.*

To understand how to write radio advertising, think of yourself and others as radio listeners. You have probably listened to radio in kitchens, bathrooms, bedrooms, basements, automobiles, boats, restaurants, on the beach, in banks, service stations, airline terminals, and doctors' offices. And while you listened to radio you may have been milking a cow, ironing, knitting, cooking, studying, working under a car, writing a letter, eating, driving a tractor, operating a payloader or a truck, cleaning house, painting the siding, doing woodworking, playing bridge, dusting, fishing, sitting in a ski lodge, or passing time in a hospital bed.

Radio has become the medium that reaches people while they are doing something (other than purposefully listening to radio). Radio, as the industry reminds advertisers, reaches the audience anywhere and everywhere, no matter what that audience is doing.

Awareness that the radio audience is not immobile and attentive has caused radio writers to change their writing formats. Where once the typical radio listeners tuned in to program after program and listened carefully to all of them, they are now restless, dial-changing listeners to whom radio is a background to other activities. Their attention must be captured and every device must be used to hold that attention.

Because of the flighty, inattentive listeners, radio commercials have become increasingly entertaining. In the effort to entertain, much humor is used. The hope, often vain, is that the humorous approach will hold the audience as effectively as the surrounding program material. Also, music is used to capture attention or to create moods.

Yet, despite the increased use of various attention-getting and mood-creating techniques, radio commercials have become simpler. Good radio writers know that in this era of half-listening radio audiences it is vital to give the listener just one principal idea to carry away. They know, too, that details should be kept to a minimum.

Make Listeners "See" What You're Talking about

Although many commercials do not call for descriptive writing, the ones that do will make you realize that the greatest handicap you face in selling by the spoken word is the inability to illustrate your product. This difficulty overshadows the restrictions of writing against time and the dependence upon the imaginations of your listeners. The lack of illustrative possibilities makes commercial writing a confining form of sales writing. You must be like the storytellers of ancient times who, through ballads and skillfully told tales, made their listeners see the wonders of other lands and other peoples.

Many times you'll envy the fashion copywriter who can call for a gorgeous illustration, tag a short line of copy to the art, and be off to the next assignment. If you wrote a radio commercial for the same garment, you would describe the style, the cut, and you'd use all your cunning to make the listener imagine how she would look in the dress, or hat, or coat.

The need for visualization in radio influences greatly your commercial writing, since you must choose selling points that can be described readily and convincingly to listeners. No longer can you depend upon artwork or photographs to help you capture and hold the attention and interest of your prospects. If, for instance, you are describing on the air the sales features of a ham, you are missing your most potent sales howitzer—the strongest, most compelling attraction of any ham advertising—a colorful photograph of a big, ready-to-eat, luscious ham. Your job is to make those listening to your commercial see that ham through your words alone—make them smell it, taste it, want it.

If you are asked to prepare radio commercials for an automobile, you can't refer to the sleek, new compact parked alongside your copy in the magazine pages. You don't have that help. You must, solely by the deft use of description, put your audience in the driver's seat of that car—make them feel its lively response, its ease of handling—make them see its handsome lines.

Description is vital in many radio commercials. Perhaps you aren't an agency writer concerned with cars and hams and nationally advertised brands. Maybe your job is to turn out radio announcements by the hundreds for use on local stations to bring people into your department store—bring them in to buy shoes, clothes, radios, washing machines, and toys.

To those listening as they bustle about their homes, you must do more than offer generalities about the service offered by your store, its charming decor, or pleasant salespeople. To stir their interest enough to get them out of the home and into the shopping center or downtown area, you must create desire for the articles you're selling. You must make those articles appealing. And you must do it completely with words. Unlike print advertising, you can't depend upon the artist to do your selling job—possibly 75 percent of the selling. In your copy, you can't write: "As you can see from the illustration, this carpeting will fit nicely into any background." In radio you draw your own illustration—with words.

1.

EDNA:	Hi, Sally. What are you doing?
SALLY:	Making ice cream with my new Ezy-Mix ice-cream maker I got at Kitchenaire's store adjacent to Hawkeye Center.
EDNA:	Making ice cream? That's hard work.
SALLY:	Not with my new Ezy-Mix ice-cream maker. A few turns of the handle and I have a quart of flavorsome ice cream. And I can make it without using electricity, ice, or salt.
EDNA:	The Ezy-Mix ice-cream maker must cost a fortune.
SALLY:	That's the best part. It's only $39.95 at Kitchenaire's friendly store.

2.

SMALL BOY:	Let's see now. Mom said this Ezy-Mix ice-cream maker can make super ice cream. She said it's not like the old days when it was hard to make homemade ice cream. All I have to do is turn this little handle a few times and I get all kinds of ice cream and any flavor I want. Mom says it's better than the old days because the Ezy-Mix doesn't use electricity, salt, or ice. And she says it's easy to clean, too. Mom's always talking about how hard things are to clean like my sweatsocks. But she says Ezy-Mix cleans like a whiz. When I grow up, I'm going to have my very own Ezy-Mix.

Figure 18–1. Commercial 1 demonstrates the straight man-stooge approach wherein Edna is a stooge who asks the right questions and supplies the right reactions. Sally plays it straight and ends up sounding like a salesperson instead of the real-life person she's supposed to be.

Commercial 2 makes the little boy unbelievably precocious. How many little boys of your acquaintance can deliver such a sales spiel? Give such a character a sentence or two and then let someone else do the selling presentation.

Artwork Is Better, but Descriptive Words Can Come Close

Even good sound effects and music, as effective as they can be in enhancing a commercial, cannot substitute for even ordinary artwork. The real picture beats the word-picture for putting over product detail quickly and surely. Still, the good radio writer tries to come close to art in the use of descriptive words. It's a difficult challenge because writing good description isn't easy, whether in the writing of books, articles, or radio commercials.

Following is a radio commercial for a paint company. Paint is a colorful product. It must be seen. Television and colorful magazine advertisements are powerful media for selling any product so visual as paint. Yet notice how the radio writer can, through descriptive words, help the reader "see" the different colors of paint.

> It's fall. It's beautiful. It's colorful. It's also time to paint your home before winter comes. At Every-Hue Paint Company we'll give you colors to fit the fall season and your moods. Reds like the scarlet maple leaves. Blues like soft October skies. Brilliant yellows like goldenrod waving in windswept fields. If your mood is gloomy in anticipation of the winter ahead, we have blacks as deep as cold, starless fall nights. But, why be gloomy? Every-Hue has

(SFX background noises of court scene under speaking)

(Judicial-sounding voice): And I hereby sentence you to make the ice cream.

(Utterly distraught voice): Oh, no Judge. Not *that*!

ANNCR (Amused tone): True enough, making ice cream has been the equivalent of a sentence to hard labor, but now we have Kwik-Freeze, the ice-cream maker that turns out a quart of ice cream with a few easy turns of a crank—and doesn't require salt, ice, or electricity. Now, anyone in your family can make ice cream. Pick up a Kwik-Freeze ice cream maker today at Kitchenaire, next to Hawkeye Center. Only 39.95.

Figure 18–2. Humorous commercial that sets the stage with two voices and then has the announcer come in to do the selling.

> whites to lift your spirits—chaste whites as pure and unspoiled as the snows to come. Paint to suit your mood, your home, and the season—paint with Every-Hue paints.

Obviously, *all* radio commercials don't require great descriptive powers. Neither do all of them demand writing perfection. The appearance of some products does not need description. Why describe an aspirin tablet? Or a cigarette? Or a tube of toothpaste?

Many radio commercials belong to the "see-how-many-times-you-can-get-the-public-to-listen-to-it" school, where the main object is to pound away with your product's name and perhaps one sale idea or buying reminder. Others, such as those for cosmetics and food products, require explanations of what the product can do for you. A third huge category, especially in department-store radio advertising and other local operations, stresses price.

Rule Number One: Read Out Loud What You've Written

The one most important rule to learn about writing for radio, whether for commercials or continuity, is that every single word you set down on paper for use over the air *must be read aloud by you before you give it your personal approval.*

You may not have a private office in which to work. It makes no difference. Even if you have to adjourn to the coatroom for privacy, find yourself an unoccupied corner and play announcer. You see, every writer always relies on seeing in print the words that are written. What looks readable may not sound the least bit so.

Embarrassing fluffs by announcers rarely will occur if commercials have been given an advance "out-loud" test. Such a test would have prevented the following tongue twisters that appeared in two commercials. In both instances, the announcer faltered, started again, faltered, and finally gave up, passing over the incident with a quip. The writer had succeeded in making the announcer laugh, but advertisers have a very unsympathetic view of the kind of humor that may cost them product sales.

One of the phrases causing the most trouble was "... prepared for *welcoming me in as a....*" Try out that phrase on an unsuspecting friend to see what trouble it can cause when read out loud rapidly without rehearsal. The other phrase was "... fresh, flavorful, fragrant coffee." Alliteration, as you will read later, is a real troublemaker. It was in this instance, and yet a quick reading aloud in advance of broadcast could have resulted in a correction.

To go a step beyond reading your own commercials, you should listen to the announcer as he delivers them. The announcer is someone reading the commercials who has nothing to do with producing them. He is not acquainted with the thinking behind them. His reading of your commercials may reveal additional pitfalls not discovered in your own reading. Notice the announcer's mistakes and remember to avoid copy that prompts those mistakes in your next set of commercials.

By keeping a few rules in mind as you approach writing for radio, you can give yourself a head start on those who walk gaily into commercial writing with the attitude that it's no different from any other kind of writing.

As you read your commercials aloud, get into the spirit of things. *Be* an announcer in your inflections, pauses, and most importantly, your pace. Deliver your words at the pace you'll want an announcer to deliver them in order to get the timing right—not too short and not too long.

Whether or not you observe the various admonitions listed, keep in mind one point. Once more this advice will be emphasized, since it's all important—*Read 'em aloud!*

How to Make Your Words Easy to Say and to Hear

In many respects you'll throw away the rulebook when you write radio commercials. In the following section are suggestions that are, in general, aimed specifically at radio writing, although some may be applied to the audio portion of television commercials and some also can be used in print writing. All of them are useful, however, when you write for reception by the ear.

Use Short Words, Short Sentences, and Contractions

Short words are usually the best radio words. Regardless of their pronunciation or ease of understanding, words that contain more than three or four syllables should be used only when absolutely necessary. Thus, "a great car" is better than "an exceptional car," "lovely" preferable to "beautiful," "good" to "outstanding," and so forth. Similarly, short sentences are usually easier for the announcer than long ones.

Sometimes, however, awkward sentence structure can make even short sentences poor radio. Short sentences aren't always the final answer. A skillfully written sentence that is moderately long but well phrased can often make better listening than a poorly written short sentence.

When you make an effort to break up your radio copy into short, easy-to-read-aloud sentences, you will discover another fact about commercial writing—certain conventional writing practices do not apply. Well-written prose has few sentences starting with the words "And" or "But." Yet these two words are standard openers in radio sentences because they preserve the flowing, conversational quality of the announcer's delivery. Likewise, they stop him enough to keep him from crowding his words and from going too fast or too breathlessly.

You will find that sentence fragments will sometimes serve better than full sentences in radio. Listen to a conversation between two or more persons. Count how many times sentences are not completed. Yet the conversationalists understand each other perfectly. Utilize this conversational tendency in commercials, but use it carefully or you may end up writing gibberish.

The frequent use of contractions is another characteristic of radio writing. In printed prose, contractions may make writing appear overly informal and undignified. In radio copy they often enhance the sincere and conversational qualities of the commercial. If you read, "Do not miss this chance to . . . " or "You have not tasted candy until . . . ," you wouldn't criticize the writer for faulty technique. The writing seems natural.

When these phrases are said aloud, however, they sound stilted. They are not phrases that you, the announcer, or the listener would use. You would say, "Don't miss the chance . . ." and "You haven't tasted candy. . . ."

Give conscious attention to contractions. They are a definite part of American speaking idiom, and that means they are particularly good for radio use. As one caution, however, remember that occasionally you will want to emphasize a point, and the use of a contraction might weaken your sentence. Suppose, for instance, you are writing copy for a nonskid tire with a claim of "You can*not* skid." Where a negative element needs emphasis, then you might prefer to avoid the contraction. But in most cases the contraction is desirable.

Punctuate Intelligently to Help the Announcer

Closely associated with sentence length in radio is the use of punctuation. Punctuation, if anything, is more important in radio writing than in writing for print because bad punctuation can mislead the announcer and cause him to make a disastrous mistake over the air. To the radio writer all punctuation marks are important, but especially important are the underline, the double dash, and the hyphen.

Underline. The underline should be used sparingly and with purpose. Usually the announcer will know through experience what words to punch, but here and there you may have a word you wish to stress because of company policy or some other reason. In such cases, underline the word but—and this is important—just the *one* word. Almost never is it advisable to underline two words or a whole phrase. It is nearly impossible for the announcer to put true stress on more than one word. Similarly, avoid scattering underlined words throughout a commercial because, by so doing, you overemphasize your message and you make the announcer's job more difficult.

Double dash. A useful punctuation device is the double dash (--), which gives a conversational flow to your writing. It gives a dramatic pause that is less abrupt than the full stop created by a period. Used correctly, the double dash gives a graceful ease to radio writing and aids the announcer in his delivery. An example from a commercial for a savings bank reads, "But a savings balance--that's something else again." Notice not only how the double dash contributes a natural pause in the delivery, but also that the underline gives vigor to the whole sentence. Note, too, that all that is needed here is one word underlined. It would have been a mistake to underline "savings balance," since this emphasis would be awkward for the announcer.

MUSIC:	(TV news theme under)
LARRY:	Hi, I'm Larry Simpleton . . .
JUDY:	And I'm Judy Bimbo, with some quick facts about TV news. Larry, why is our reporting so superficial?
LARRY:	Well, Judy, we figure the audience is pretty stupid, and we're none too bright ourselves.
JUDY:	That's exactly right, Larry, and since we don't have much hard news, we have to spend a lot of time agreeing. . .
LARRY:	You bet we do!
JUDY:	. . . and congratulating each other on terrific reporting.
LARRY:	Terrific reporting, Judy. Maybe you could also explain why we have to look like models.
JUDY:	I'd be happy to, Larry. TV news isn't about ideas . . . it's about mascara and high cheekbones. That's why we get these huge salaries.
LARRY:	Hmm!
JUDY:	Back to you, Lare.
LARRY:	Well, I'd just like to add that we're smug and condescending because we have these jobs and you don't.
JUDY:	Too true. Thank you for joining us. I'm Judy Bimbo . . .
LARRY:	And I'm Larry Simpleton. Goodnight from all of us at TV news.
JUDY:	(Privately to Larry) Good newscast, Lare.
LARRY:	Nice dress, Jude.
ANNCR:	Tired of the inane babble of TV news? The *San Francisco Examiner* is a better way to spend your time. To get two months for the price of one, call 800-345-EXAM. That's 800-345-EXAM.

Figure 18–3. Award-winning radio commercial.
Created by Goodby, Berlin & Silverstein Advertising Agency.

Many writers use the three-dot (. . .) punctuation device in radio and print copy. Once a writer has contracted the three-dot habit, he finds it difficult to write complete sentences. Avoid this habit. If you wish to make a pause for effect, use the double dash, but do not overdo that, either.

Hyphen. When you wish to join two words in order that they may modify a third word, you can use a hyphen (-). Sometimes your announcer must be guided by the hyphenated words or there will be a mistake in the reading. In the bank commercial previously referred to, the writer used a hyphen in this manner: "Open a dividend-paying savings account. . . ." If the hyphen had not been used here, the announcer might have read the passage as "Open a dividend." In using hyphens, however, avoid the precious, cute, and artificial combining of words that have given advertising writing a bad name in many writing quarters. Phrases such as "bunny-soft," "cozy-warm," and "baby-cute" illustrate the point.

Use Easy-to-Say and Easy-to-Understand Words

Avoid words that are hard to pronounce, even if they are easily understood words. "Indisputable" is a word that everyone would understand, but it could be a stumbling block for a radio announcer. "Applicable," "particularly," "demonstrably," and "detectably" would be correctly defined by most high school students, yet any of them could cause an announcer to hesitate a split second, thus disturbing the natural flow of the words.

Sometimes very innocent-looking words that are simple to pronounce by themselves can become nightmares for the announcer when they are combined with certain other innocent-looking words. A good example is a sentence actually used on the air which very effectively tied the announcer in knots—"A government order of twenty-two stainless steel twin-screw cruisers." Also, if you put "in," "an," or "un" next to a word beginning with any of these three sounds, you will give almost any announcer a moment of pronunciation juggling. For example, say "in an unenviable position" fast, and notice the mumble that results. To attempt to memorize all such sound and word combinations that might cause you trouble would be pointless. Experience will teach you some of the troublemakers, and reading aloud should take care of the rest.

Beware of adverbs. The suffix "-ly" is a tough one for radio people to pronounce with consistent precision. If you can twist your sentence to gain the same thought without the "-ly," you will usually have a better commercial. It is not as good radio to say:

> The shoes that men are increasingly favoring.

as it is to say:

> The shoes that more men are favoring every day.

And you might wish to say of a cereal product:

> Nutritionally, too, it's the buy for you.

But in radio, much better to say:

> For nutrition, too, it's the buy for you.

You don't sacrifice the swing of both, or the rhyme of one—both attributes of good radio commercials—yet you have constructed a sentence that will be easy for the announcers to read without much chance of stumbling.

One fault you must guard against is permitting words to creep into your commercials which are similar, in sound, to other words with different meanings. One of these, for instance, is the word "chief." If you are writing a commercial about air travel, you might wish to say, "It has many advantages over all other forms of travel, the *chief* one being. . . ."

Now *you* know that word is "chief." You might have used "main" or "outstanding" or some other synonym, but "chief" looks all right to you, and it sounds fine as you read it. Now consider your *listener.* First of all, he's not hanging on your announcer's every phrase. Second, he hears the word "chief" only one time as it slips past, and he doesn't know, as you do, what comes next. It would be very easy for him to think the announcer said "cheap." You'll admit that the difference in meaning between the two words is great enough to warrant care in their use, whether you're selling air travel or aspirin.

"Breath" and "breadth"; "smell," "swell," and "spell"; "prize" and "price" are other examples of words which might be misinterpreted or given a wrong meaning by the listener. It's just as easy to use a simple synonym and take no chances.

Remember—Alliteration Alienates Announcers

The print writer's use of alliteration in radio can cause trouble. Visually, the phrase "Prize-winners in perfectly proportioned peach halves" *seems* harmless. If you saw it in an advertisement, even if you are one of those who reads everything with your lips, you might view it as a nicely turned phrase. Say, however, that you have been assigned to write some radio commercials for X peaches and you hit upon that sentence—which looks fine as it leaves the typewriter or word processor. Perhaps it also looks fine to those with whom you must clear your copy. It gets an okay and is released to the radio station. Just how do you think it is going to look to the radio announcer who is scanning the copy ten minutes before broadcast time? The way to find out how he'll like it is to stand up and read it just as you want him to read it. Do that to the peach halves atrocity right now. Read it aloud. How does it sound? Doesn't it sound a little bit like a person about to lose an upper plate?

A little bit of alliteration is certainly acceptable in radio writing. In fact, wisely used, it often helps to spark up copy. But alliteration is like dynamite—a little too much is going to blow your commercial apart. Use alliteration if you wish, but be very careful not to overdo it. Your own sense of hearing will be your safety valve. If it doesn't sound good to you when you read it aloud, change it.

Watch Out for "S" and "K" Sounds

Another thing you may discover, as you stand up and announce your first try-'em-out-loud commercials, is that you have given your copy too many hissing sounds. Radio announcers hate the "double-ess" ending and dislike it even in the middle of words because it is hard to say clearly and with force. The word "sensational"—almost a routine part of many copywriters' daily vocabularies—causes announcers to wince. Your commercials would probably sound better if you could manage to write them without ever using the letter "s," "z," or the soft "c."

For example, while reading the last two sentences you are not likely to have experienced a difficulty or an unpleasant reaction from the words used. Yet several times in those two sentences, you can find the soft "c" or the "s" sounds. They would not have been pleasant sounding on the air. Were this page to be read for radio, some rewriting would have to be done. Remember, too, that the particularly harsh sounds in the English language do not broadcast well. The sounds "ark" and "ack," "eesh" and "ash," "app" and "amm" should seldom be used.

As you enunciate your copy, listen to your voice and try to sift out the sounds that grate on your ear. Assume that the sounds that grate on your ear as you hear them in the solitude of an office or room will sound much worse with even the minimum distortion produced by modern transmission.

As in Print Copy, Make Your Writing Flow

You were strongly advised to write transitionally in print copy. "Bridging" words and phrases were suggested, some of which you'll find repeated here. That same use of transition and "bridges" should be part of your radio writing, too. Transitional writing should be as natural as breathing, whether you're working in print or radio.

A radio commercial should be a unified presentation whether it's 30 seconds or 60 seconds. Each sentence should connect with and flow from the preceding sentence. Your points should be bridged by connecting words and phrases. Instead, inexperienced radio writers tend to run together a series of unrelated points. The result is a jerky, clumsy commercial that even a very good announcer will find difficult. "Difficult" here, means that the announcer cannot achieve the smoothness of presentation that a well-written commercial encourages.

To create a natural flow, incorporate conversational bridges. Sometimes the bridge may be a single word that indicates continuity, a carrying over of a thought from one sentence to another. "And" and "but" are such words, as are "furthermore," "so," and "also."

ANNCR: The people who blended the original wine cooler would like to share their recipe for a good party. The first essential ingredient is an authentic wine cooler—made with white wine and real fruit—like California Cooler. The second ingredient is music. ("Louie Louie" up and out) Of course, if you're planning a soiree with your California Cooler, you might want something a little more elegant. (Harp and soprano version of "Louie Louie") Or jazzy. (Tenor sax and scat singer version of "Louie Louie") Or maybe you want something festive. (Mariachi band and singer's version of "Louie Louie") So you see, with a little planning and a lot of California Cooler, just about anything will sound good at a party. (Cheesy roller rink music under) Well, almost anything. California Cooler. The real stuff. California Cooler, Stockton, California.

Figure 18–4. Award-winning radio commercial.

Sometimes you'll use a phrase to achieve transition. Examples include:

But that's only the start.

Listen to this.

In addition,

Remember, ask for

Here's something else you'll like.

If you've been needing help, think of this.

Following is a commercial that demonstrates how you can achieve unity through transitional writing:

If you live in the Midland area, you can make sure you have a great Christmas next year and get a fine gift for doing it. Here's how. Just come in before Saturday to Midland Trust to open a Christmas Club for next year, a Club that pays interest, by the way. That's right. Unlike many Christmas Clubs, this one pays regular interest. And here's another plus. When you open your Club you get a handsome, decorative hurricane lamp that'll brighten whatever spot you put it in. Just think, a valuable gift simply for opening a money-making Christmas Club. Even without the gift it makes good sense to open a Christmas Club. Bet you'll think so next year at this time when you have plenty of cash to spend in the holiday season. Better make a note right now to open a Midland Trust Christmas Club and to get your hurricane lamp—a yuletide duo from Midland's leading bank.

Notice all the bridging words and phrases:

Here's how

Just come in

That's right

And here's another plus

Just think

Bet you'll think so

Better make a note right now

Notice two more important aspects of this commercial. One is the strong action ending. Two is the repetition of the offer at the end of the commercial. Repetition of the main selling point is one of the attributes of good radio-commercial writing.

Be Selective in the Slang You Use

When you are urged to "be conversational" in radio commercials, you are being given good counsel, but counsel that might possibly lead you astray—the conversation of a large percentage of Americans would be unsuitable for radio usage. You will have to use your judgment in deciding what is conversational and what slips into the area of poor taste.

The inclusion of a certain amount of slang, informal phraseology, and current jargon will often lend a naturalness and spontaneity that greatly increase the believability and selling power of commercials. Whether to use such devices in your writing, and how much to use them, will depend pretty much on what you are trying to sell and, more than that, to whom you are selling.

For example, on a sports program assumed to interest a young male audience, the most logical types of products to be sold would be such items as men's clothing, beer, shaving products, or automotive services. If you were assigned to write commercials for such a show, it would probably be perfectly good technique to use occasional phrases such as "a rock-solid deal," "lets 'em know who you are," "top-gun precision," and similar masculine-like phrasings. Such writing will help make your audience feel that the commercial is part of the show, written for them alone, and hence will be more likely to take effect. Needless to say, that kind of talk would not sound very appropriate to a person listening to a soap opera.

Similarly, a children's program should be liberally sprinkled with words currently being used by children. If you are asked to write the commercials for such a show, you would be very wise to do some on-the-spot investigating and pick up the phrases and slang of the moment. Be quite sure, when you do, that you are not writing expressions that mean something only in one locality—one neighborhood—or, if your show is national or your spot announcements are for wide distribution, one section of the country.

Steer clear of slang words that might alienate large groups of your audience, even though at first thought they might seem all right. A good example of such a word is "darn." Now you may have used that expression since you were two years old, heard your mother, sister, and even your minister say it often. Yet to many people the word "darn" is simply another way of saying "damn," and even though many listeners may use the word themselves, you might offend one of them by putting it in your commercial. There is no need to take chances with words or expressions that have the slightest chance of producing a negative effect even on a few people. Those few might otherwise be easily sold on your product.

"Scram," "blow," "nuts," "oh, yeah," "so what," "screwy," "lousy," "stink," "jerk," "baloney," and other such words should not be included in your radio-writing vocabulary. They do not represent the slang that makes acceptable, picturesque American talk for radio.

Before using the lighter words and phrases in your commercials, try them out on some of your more pedantic friends. If you get a lot of voluntary suggestions to do away with a word or an expression, it's probably wise to do so.

Work Hard to Get and *Hold* Attention

Mrs. Jones is stirring cream sauce while she eyes the roast in the oven and the cauliflower boiling in a pan on the stove. Little Freddy is noisily playing games with his friend Billy in an adjacent room.

Now, the magic moment. Your commercial sounds from the kitchen set. What will win? Your commercial, or Mrs. Jones's cooking and other distractions?

What is done in the opening seconds of the commercial determines the answer. What have you done to *force* listenership? Are you using music, sound effects, or an unusual opening statement by the announcer? Surely you have done *something* to jar Mrs. Jones into attention? If you haven't, check off another commercial that lost the attention battle.

Perhaps you've used that reliable device, the humorous man-on-the-street interview, or another old reliable, a conversation between unlikely types, such as the award-winning commercial that featured a pair of voracious, talking termites. After you've captured the listener's ear, of course, you pull out all the stops to *hold* attention. Some down-to-earth suggestions for keeping attention are given here by a veteran radio writer.

Sixteen Ways to Capture and Hold Attention for Radio Commercials

1. *Product-in-action sound effects.* Coffee comes to life in the percolator. Similarly, there are sounds relevant to just about every product, just waiting to be employed as creative tools. Beyond the sound itself, how it's used can also make a big difference.
2. *Mix 'em up.* Experiment with various combinations of jingle, dialogue, straight announcement, sound effects, music, and so forth, all in one commercial. Presented with this kind of variety, the listener is likely to be attentive, wondering what's coming next. The commercial can be a miniature show.
3. *Symbolic character.* Have a distinctive voice represent your product. If it's indigenous to a foreign country, such as spaghetti and macaroni, the voice can hold listener attention by speaking with an accent typical of that country.
4. *Tie in with stations' features.* Integrate your commercials with the weather reports, time checks, musical styles, or even the call letters.

Any way you can sound less like an interruption to regular programming helps.

5. *Call on comedy stars.* For truly entertaining spots, you can use the guys whose job it is to be funny. But don't let it fall flat; get real comedy material, either from the performer—if he writes, or from his writers.
6. *Variations on a theme.* Once you hit on the magic jingle, don't be content to present it at one tempo, over and over. See that it gets every treatment, from cool jazz to old-fashioned waltz.
7. *Tie in with current events.* What's going on in the world that has everyone interested? Is there a world heavyweight championship fight in the works? Sign one of the fighters for your commercials—assuming the product lends itself to endorsement by a name from the world of sports.
8. *Ad libs.* For the height of realism, why not let your spokespeople call it the way they see it? Foreign actors are most articulate and convincing, given the freedom to speak of their country's advantages for radio airing.
9. *Speed ups—slow downs.* Often you can capture attention by tampering with the speed of sounds in radio commercials. Caution: take care that important words don't get garbled in the process.
10. *Real-life interviews.* Questioning the man or woman in the street about your product can turn up the kind of praise which, captured on tape, can serve to activate the listening audience. Inclusion of actual street noises in the sound track helps to heighten the realism.
11. *Orchestrate sound effects.* For greater appeal to the listeners' imagination, let music simulate the sounds you're after in a commercial. You can establish the real sound, and follow with the musical treatment. The tempo of the product sound can be effectively translated to music.
12. *Use real kids.* Where dialogue from youngsters is indicated, you may reach the heights of realism—and charm—by giving the part to actual children rather than character actors. With editing, the little scene stealers have been known to come up with topnotch copy through ad lib.
13. *Publicity-hungry stars.* No need to spend a fortune to enlist big names in your radio commercial cause. Check into which show business luminaries are a little short on work and anxious to get back into the limelight. Chances are you can work out a satisfactory arrangement.
14. *Authoritative voice.* Radio listeners are accustomed to accepting the word of the commentators who bring them the news. That same voice—and the authority that goes with it—may be available for delivery of your sales message. Local and regional personalities may be of use.
15. *Use a popular or standard tune.* If you can get the rights to a familiar tune, you've taken a giant step toward bridging the gap between entertainment and the commercial.
16. *Character switch.* Play a trick or two on the listeners now and then to perk up their attention. Try introducing one type of character, say a gentle housewife, and have her enter screaming at her husband; or have a prize fighter talk like Casper Milquetoast.

ANNCR:	(In hushed voice as if he doesn't want to be overheard) It's the year 1520 in Florence, Italy, and we're listening to a conversation between Michelangelo, the famous painter and sculptor, and his friend Tony. Both speak in very Italian accents.
TONY:	Hi, Mike. What are ya working on?
MIKE:	Lessee. My next job's the Sistine Chapel. Gotta paint the ceiling.
TONY:	*Forget* it. Here's an *important* job—a new pizza-baker. Right down your alley.
ANNCR:	Michelangelo never got around to the new pizza-baker but Pizza-World *did* and it's ready for you right now. And you're gonna love it. Here's how it works.

Figure 18–5. Humorous opening for a two-voice commercial. Notice that the two characters merely set the stage for the announcer. Having caught audience attention, the copywriter now brings in the announcer to do the actual selling.

VOICE:	"If you haven't given yet, it's time for you to give."
ANNCR:	In 1985, a Tulsa television station broadcast a story on a multimillion dollar charity. It showed that charitable claims were greatly exaggerated—that donated-funds were used to buy a Rolls Royce, a Florida condo, an airplane and more: for the private use of the charity chairman and his family. It triggered federal investigations—investigations that wouldn't have occurred, if a couple of television reporters hadn't been looking for a story. It's an example of how individual rights can be protected when the public is kept informed. It's an example of how a free press works in a free society—and what can go on without it! Because if the press didn't tell us, who would? To learn more about the role of a free press, call the First Amendment Center at 1-800-542-1600. A public service message of the Ad Council and Sigma Delta Chi Foundation.

Figure 18–6. Straight commercial. Although straight commercials are sometimes thought of as routine or even dull, they don't have to be. In this one, a high degree of interest is maintained because of the use of a story-telling technique.

SFX:	(Sitar)
WISE MAN:	A perplexing problem has puzzled young people since the beginning of time. How to get a job without experience? How to get experience without a job?
ANNCR:	The answer is co-operative education. A nation-wide program that helps college students get real jobs for real pay, while they're getting an education. Write Co-op Ed., Box 999, Boston, Massachusetts 02115.
WISE MAN:	I knew that.
ANNCR:	A public service from the National Commission for Cooperative Education.
WISE MAN:	And the Ad Council.

Figure 18–7. Dialogue commercial.

SINGERS:	(Music under) To write the words and make the plans that bring the future in sight.
SAM:	They changed the deadline again, Harry?
HARRY:	What else is new?
SINGERS:	To take those dreams and set them down, set them in a whole new light.
SAM:	They want to revise the marketing strategy, update the graphics. . . .
HARRY:	Some things never change.
SAM:	And they need it by the end of the week.
HARRY:	End of the week? I'll have it by the end of the day.
ANNCR:	Xerox document processing. Machines and systems that create, copy, distribute, and file ideas. On paper and on a computer screen, what you see is what we do.
SINGERS:	To share it all so all the world can see a new tomorrow.
SAM:	You're brilliant, Harry.
HARRY:	What else is new?
ANNCR:	Document processing. From Team Xerox.
SINGERS:	We document the world.

Figure 18–8. Two-voice radio commercial.

Types of Commercials

If you are to produce commercials for a radio program—either network or local—there are a number of different techniques upon which you may draw. These techniques are discussed in the sections that follow.

Straight Commercial

The straight commercial is a straight-selling message devoted to the merits of your product, service, or institutional story. It might be compared with a piece of straight-line body copy and is delivered by a commercial announcer with no outside means of attracting or holding attention.

Many advertisers now look critically at this type of commercial since they feel that inattentive, uninterested listeners will not wait out the announcer for the full period of the commercial. Still, on thousands of radio stations the selling messages are delivered straight and they are still selling goods and services, even though artistically they are not so satisfying to creative people as other commercial types.

Dialogue Commercial

By "dialogue" we mean a conversation between two or more persons. Such a conversation can be conducted by: (a) An announcer and others. (b) Two or more characters who deliver all of the commercial without any participation by an announcer.

In (a) the announcer may talk with users of a product, with product experts such as dealers or the actual maker of the product, or—in the case of a bank, say—with personnel from tellers to the president. Sales features of a product or service are worked into these commercials. Such commercials can be convincing if the announcer and the people spoken with are natural. One danger is that participation by actual users, or actual company personnel, can result in an amateurish commercial because nonprofessional talent frequently sound unnatural and forced.

In (b) you have a real problem, even if your speaking characters *are* professional actors or actresses. Making the dialogue believable and natural is exceedingly difficult. This type of commercial generally reduces credibility of advertising because radio listeners dismiss it as phony. It simply isn't a part of a daily routine for two persons to spend 60 seconds talking about a product. Still, the two-voice commercial is used, so you'd better learn how to handle it for maximum believability.

Ways to Make Two-Voice Commercials Believable, or at Least Acceptable

If a commercial is being delivered by two supposedly real-life people such as two wives, two husbands, a husband and a wife, or two children, it is almost impossible to deliver a number of product points without making salespeople out of the characters. Generally, such commercials make a stooge out of one of the characters. Thus, one, possibly a housewife, will say to the other, "But Kleen-O must cost a lot." The other then replies, "Not at all, Jane. Due to a new manufacturing process, Kleen-O has been able to reduce its price to the low, low price of 78 cents. And that's not *all* they've done either. Listen to this . . . ."

The easiest way out of the artificiality of such two-voice commercials is to let the characters set the stage by posing a mutual problem. After an exchange of two or three lines, the announcer comes in to do the selling. This is natural because announcers are supposed to be salespeople.

But suppose you want to use the real-life characters for the whole commercial. Can you do so successfully? "Successful" here means that you maintain naturalness and believability at the same time that you put across enough product selling points to sell the product to the listening audience.

Following are many ways to so "succeed."

- One character reads copy from the package to the other character. By reading the copy, the character avoids being a "salesperson."
- One character reads copy from a product advertisement to the other character.
- Character talks to a store salesperson. The character asks questions and the salesperson replies by giving a sales talk for the product.
- Character talks to a knowledgeable repair- or serviceperson, such as a plumber, electrician, and so forth. The latter points out why the unit works so well, lasts so long, is so easy to repair, or needs repair so infrequently.
- Character reads directions on the item itself, especially when those directions indicate the ease of operation.
- Character phones someone qualified to talk about the product—a factory employee, a dealer, a serviceperson. (In television, the split-screen technique can be used for the two characters.)
- Two salespeople talk about the product, mentioning salesworthy points.
- Sales manager conducts session with novice salesperson, demonstrating the perfect sales talk. This would well be humorously exaggerated.
- Copywriter gets reactions from his wife about sales points he's putting in his advertisement. She makes pertinent suggestions that give the woman's viewpoint that he has overlooked.
- Earnest student type is telling teacher what she's found out about the product assigned as a class study.
- Same technique as in preceding example except that professor is telling class and answering questions. Again, possibility for exaggerated humor exists here.
- Two computers talk to each other. Each discusses product facts in mechanical sounding voices associated with computers or mechanical person.
- Someone presses button of computer, or of a mechanical person, and gets flood of information to each question asked.
- If product is intended for a dog, such as a dog food, two dogs talk to each other about it. Or it could be two cats, two birds, or some other creatures.

Of course with the above points "success" demands more than technique. The techniques must be implemented creatively and well.

Dramatized Commercial

The dramatized commercial is an often-used type that may be compared with the narrative-copy approach. A situation is dramatized in a brief playlet, in which the product is introduced as the solution of a problem. Thus, in the first 15 seconds or so, a boy is horrified to

ANNCR:	If your car's engine were to stop . . .
SFX:	(Car engine. Not starting up. Continue under:)
ANNCR:	. . . you'd probably know what to do to get it started again. The sad fact is, more people know how to jump-start a car than know how to save a life.
SFX:	(Car starts. Heartbeat starts and continues under:)
ANNCR:	Learn how to jump-start a life. Learn Red Cross CPR.

Figure 18–9. Dramatized commercial. Effective use of sound effects creates attention and drama in this 30-second radio commercial.
Courtesy of the Advertising Council.

learn that he has bad breath. Then he hears about a new kind of toothpaste, and in a twinkling you discover he wins love and romance. Finally, in normal routine, the regular announcer closes with a straight product sell and a plea to buy. Dramatized commercials usually require the hiring of a professional cast and may range all the way from a few simple, uninvolved lines of script to full-scale production with music, sound effects, and lengthy rehearsals.

Like the dialogue commercial, the dramatized commercial often becomes artificial and unbelievable. Frequently the action is humorously exaggerated to the point where the advertiser spoofs his product and audience. It can be a very effective technique if enough episodes are presented to avoid boring the radio audience. The same story presented day after day, however, can soon increase the number of tune-outs.

Musical Commercial

Sometimes a singing commercial can deliver all or part of the sales message by song. Whether singing or instrumental music is used in whole or in part, the musical commercial has become an increasingly common form of radio technique. This growth has occurred despite cries from the public against singing commercials.

"Jingles," as they are so often called, are hated when bad, but among the best-liked commercials when done well. Two cautions for creators of musical commercials:

- Be sure the music is good. Especially try to use music that can be committed to memory—outstanding commercial music that will please listeners indefinitely.
- In singing commercials, make certain that the words can be understood. Otherwise, you provide the audience with a pleasant musical experience but no incentive to buy. Make the lyric as well as the music memorable; if you do, you will have a strong selling vehicle for your product or service.

Musical commercials take many forms. For example, such a commercial might have a musical introduction

(Music: The Olympic theme which transforms into the Xerox "We Document the World" theme.)

SFX: (Olympic crowds cheering.)

AVO: Behind the brilliant performance of the athletes in the fifteenth Olympic Winter Games, . . .

SFX: (More cheering crowds.)

AVO: . . . there is another brilliant Olympic performance you don't see, . . .

SFX: (Machines and general office hubbub)

AVO: . . . the processing of the millions of documents that make the Olympics happen.

SFX: (More machines.)

AVO: From the first invitation . . .

SFX: (More machines.)

AVO: . . . to the last result sheet of the last event . . . the Olympics runs on documents. Some 25 million documents by the end of the last event. Documents created, printed, copied and distributed electronically and on paper.

(Music up)

Xerox is proud to be a key player on this unseen but most vital Olympic team.

(Music)

Team Xerox. Official supplier of copiers, duplicators and facsimile transceivers. Official Sponsor of the Fifteenth Olympic Winter Games. A world leader in document processing.

(Sung: "We Document the World.")

Figure 18–10. Sixty-second radio commercial that makes liberal use of music and sound effects.

(intro) of 10 seconds and a musical close of the same length. The intro and the close may be furnished by a "jingle house," an organization that writes music and lyrics on order. As a creative person, you may be required to supply the jingle house with information about the product or service, marketing objectives, and just what you want this particular commercial to accomplish.

If the material submitted by the jingle house is satisfactory, then you write 40 seconds of script to complete the commercial. Local accounts may use musical intros and closes indefinitely. Thus, as a copywriter you'll learn to live with the writing of the 40-second inner portion of the commercial. Such use of music is one way to relieve the alleged tedium of the straight 60-second commercial.

Sometimes music will be heard in the background throughout the entire commercial, very often coming up louder at the end. Except for unusual circumstances it is not desirable to have music under the entire commercial. It is distracting and may make the spoken words harder to hear.

Although you will not be expected, unless you're a musician, to write the music for musical commercials, it is helpful if you have a wide-ranging knowledge of popular and classical music. If so, you know what is appropriate and you will be able to specify music that will be suitable for the audience, the product, and the station. Very importantly, you should be able to judge whether the music will wear well. If it's pleasing, there is almost no limit to the time it can be used; it can be a sort of trademark for the advertiser. If it is *not* pleasing, you can turn off your audience after very few airings of the commercial.

Knowing the musical tastes of those who enjoy musical commercials is not easy given the bewildering variety of popular music today. Once a few musical styles predominated, such as Dixieland, swing, romantic ballads, and New Orleans jazz. Young and middle-aged listeners today break into sizable units that like pop-rock, hard rock, country rock, punk rock, Southern rock, mellow rock. Add to these rock choices funk, punk-funk, soul, gospel, and country; currently, there are nearly two dozen different types of country music alone, including country western, country swing, bluegrass, and Tex-Mex.

If you are responsible for guiding the choice of music for musical commercials, you'll need to know your audience, the latest trends in popular music, and how much of a following each style commands. This is no easy task.

Use the Right Number of Words; Not Too Many, Not Too Few

If you are writing 60-second announcements and you plan them to be straight announcements delivered by an announcer, be sure that each one can be completed within one minute. An average announcer takes about 60 seconds to read 160–170 words. But don't rely on that. Some commercials are easy to read, some hard. The hard ones move at a slower rate. Often you will want your message to be given slowly with exaggerated emphasis. Other times you'll want the announcer to read it fast. Do not rely upon a rule of thumb. Read your announcements to yourself; time yourself to be sure.

Most straight commercials can be delivered understandably and sincerely at a rate of 160–170 words per minute. Some announcers, however, may be comfortable with a slower or faster rate than this. If you know what announcer will deliver your commercial, pace it to the announcer's style.

Type of Commercial Affects Word Count

The character of the offer being made might affect your word count. For instance, an announcement for a sweepstakes is usually charged with excitement. To maintain the excitement the announcer will speed up his delivery, and thus you may elect to put considerably more than 170 words in such a commercial. You do so knowing that the listeners' playback of the commercial message will suffer in terms of individual points registered. Still, if you have made the listeners aware of the sweepstakes and its prizes, you will have accomplished your objective. You have made them want to enter. They can get full details later from entry blanks in stores or from magazine or newspaper advertisements.

(Music intro)

ANNCR: (In slow southern drawl) The other night, me and my two friends was watching the muskeeters fry on the bug zapper, when clear out of the blue, Billy Ray asked me where I got my New York accent from. I said to him, you know, I love the South, and I do. But ever so often I like to go up North. So I hop on New York Air and fly to Philadelphia, Boston, Hartford (speeding up his speech) Cleveland, Rochester, Newark or any one of four New York airports. Why, I can talk real fast to people named Salvatore and Irving, instead of Jimmy Bob and Sally Sue. Or I can say things like, ask your mudder and I dunno. And instead of having New York style pizza, I can have pizza in New York. Then when I've had my fill of the North, I hop on New York Air and fly (slows speech to southern drawl) right back down to the South, because I just love it here. Well, I do. New York Air.

(SFX of airplane)

Figure 18–11. Award-winning radio commercial.

A similar principle is at work in the frenetic two-voice commercials often heard for local firms, such as tire shops. The two-person announcer team announces the message at a tremendous clip without any hope that many points will be recalled, but with a very real expectation that listeners will realize that the company is offering something very special in the way of price, a variety of choice, or a dazzling new product.

Two-voice commercials may, on the other hand, be used for supposed real-life conversations between two friends, a husband and wife, a sales clerk and customer, and any number of combinations. In such simulated situations, slow down the word count. Make the conversation natural. People in real life don't bark out words with machine-gun speed, so write fewer than the 160–170 words employed in straight commercials, and far fewer than for the two-voice commercials delivered by a team of two station announcers.

Two Ways to Get Your Word Count Right

If you want to be sure of your timing, count your words *and* use a stopwatch. Most writers are content merely to use a stopwatch, but a person reading a commercial sometimes tends to speed up the reading pace to make the commercial fit the time. The practice of counting the words will help keep you honest. On the other hand, just counting words and not using a stopwatch may cause trouble, since a commercial with a fairly low word count may read long because of the use of many polysyllabic words. The stopwatch helps correct for this.

When you become adept in writing for broadcast, you may let the number of lines of copy help determine whether you're writing within your time limitations—but this is only a rough guide. You'll always be right if you double-check yourself with the stopwatch and by counting the words. For example, you might be fooled by a commercial that uses several numbers and consequently is short on lines. Each numeral, however, counts as one word. If you give a telephone number and repeat it, you may be devoting as many as twenty-five words just for this part of the commercial.

From an advertising standpoint, it is far better to limit your message to the words that can be read with sincerity and selling strength, than to take liberties with the time and length of your announcement. If you force the announcer to race through your selling message, you lose effectiveness and power.

If you call for sound effects (SFX) in your commercial, figure the number of seconds taken up by the effects and allow for that in your word count. For example, if you're writing at a rate of 160 words for a 60-second commercial, each second of a sound effect should be figured at two- and two-thirds words in your word count. Naturally, the same observation will apply to music. When you call for sound effects, it's helpful to take two precautions:

1. Indicate the number of seconds to be consumed by the sound effects.
2. Don't ask for a sound effect that the audience will not understand or that is impossible to convey without explanation. To illustrate, suppose you call for the sound of an eggbeater. Many sounds can resemble an eggbeater at work. Because, unlike in television, the radio audience cannot see the eggbeater, they will have trouble identifying what they are hearing. To get around this difficulty, explain in words what is causing the sound. In the case of the eggbeater, simply write: "When you're beating eggs, etc." In short, except for something very clear, like the ringing of a telephone, don't expect your audience to figure out the sound effect you've called for. Tell them what they're hearing.

Guide for Character-Count Method

Although few copywriters will use the character-count method of timing commercials, it is included here in Figure 18–12 for those who do. It gets around the difficulty in timing commercials that have many long, or many short, words. (Note that the material in Figure 18–12, if read aloud at the suggested 16 characters per second, will time out at 60 seconds. It meets word-count requirements, too, because it contains 166 words.)

Live or Taped Commercials?

Customarily, especially in writing radio commercials for broadcast in local markets, the writer will ask: "Live or taped?" The answer will influence how you write the commercial—whether you'll ask for music, sound effects, or a special style of announcing.

Announcements are broadcast in two ways. An example will illustrate these methods.

```
Here's your guide:

1234567890123456  1234567890123456  1234567890123456  1234567890123456  1234567890123456

An embarrassing moment for a broadcast writer occurs if it is discovered at a
recording session that the writer's commercial exceeds the 20 seconds, or the
60 seconds planned for the commercial.  On-the-spot rewriting must then be done
while high-priced talent sits around.  The careful writers read their commercials
aloud and use a stopwatch to time them.  As an extra precaution they may count
words also.  It has been found that one hundred sixty to one hundred seventy words
per minute for a straight commercial is comfortable reading time for most radio
announcers.  Such a rate allows for a sincere, easy-to-understand delivery but the
pace is brisk enough to make the commercial lively.  A writer who counts words,
reads aloud, and uses a stopwatch is almost certain to turn out commercials that
time right.  Another safeguard is to use the character-count method described
here on this page.  The important point is that every commercial should fit within
the allotted time.
```

Figure 18–12. Character-count method for timing broadcast commercials. Timing commercials becomes easier if you'll remember that 16 typewritten characters will equal one second when read aloud. When you type your commercial, don't worry about typing each line exactly 80 characters as shown in the example. Just come close. Another suggestion. Don't hyphenate words at the end of the line. Type them out on the following line if necessary. Sometimes, if you're typing an 80-character line, as shown here, the line will be longer or shorter. It will still be close enough so that the line should take 5 seconds to read. This estimate is based on the average rate of delivery.

Assume you are the manufacturer of a product for general consumption, but being relatively new in the business you do not yet enjoy complete national distribution of your product. You must proceed in your marketing strategy by opening up different markets individually, until each market has good distribution.

You select a new city into which you wish to introduce your product and you allocate money to advertise it there. You decide that newspaper advertisements plus a series of spot announcements make the best combination of local advertising media available for your purposes, and you buy a schedule of spot time on the local radio station. You purchase minute spots, to be extended over a period of six weeks.

- You can simply have those commercials typed, along with instructions as to how they should be read, and send them to the radio station, instructing the station representative on which days to read which announcements. Then a local announcer will be assigned to your account and will deliver the spots as you have written them.[1]
- You can hire an announcer whose voice you like and whose delivery you can control through rehearsals, tape all the announcements—one after the other, and send that tape to the radio station in your new market. They will then play the designated tape at the times you request, instead of having one of their own announcers read the material.

1. Often, however, the station may tape the commercials delivered by its announcers.

Need a Change of Voice: Use Tape

This procedure may also be used if you have purely local accounts, such as a bank or an insurance company. In a local market, the announcers' voices, names, and personalities become well known to listeners. If, as so often happens, the announcers are competent and trusted, this audience familiarity is desirable. Occasionally, however, you'll want a change, especially if you're starting a new campaign. You may, accordingly, go to another town to tape commercials delivered by an announcer whose voice is not known to your local listeners.

This change of voice has another plus. Let's say that in the past your bank commercials were delivered daily each morning by a well-known local announcer. Before the day is over that same announcer may have delivered commercials for two other banks also. The audience can understandably wonder how the announcer (who sounds very, very sincere in his delivery) can truly be sincerely enthusiastic about all three banks. Inevitably, there is some loss of credibility for the announcer, or for the message. Hence the taping of commercials delivered by a nonlocal announcer.

So, live or taped? Each has its advantages. If your messages are simple, straightforward, and do not require a highly dramatic or specialized type of voice, the first way is generally preferred, since it is less expensive. If you wish to control the manner of delivery, in regard to emphasis and pace, the tape is your answer.

Of course, the first technique, that of sending the station the script for your announcements, is workable only when you have a straight commercial handled by an announcer only. When you wish your spots to be dramatic, or to contain music or gimmicks, they necessarily must be taped. The local radio station could hardly afford to charge you the little they do for a spot announcement of a few seconds and also stage a musical production for you.

Another situation that will become familiar to you is the writing of a commercial that will be taped for a 50-second segment (written by an advertising agency for a national advertiser). The last 10 seconds will be delivered live by a station announcer, but sometimes will be taped by the local announcer if it is going to be used frequently. You will write the 10-second tag. In the tag you will localize, giving the name, address, and possibly the phone number of the local outlet.

As mentioned previously in the section about musical commercials, you may be writing around a musical introduction and ending, both of which are taped before you begin writing the words to go between the music portions.

Help for the Writer of Local Commercials

If you're working with local advertisers, there are a number of helps available to you. For one, there are the area radio stations. Many have extensive libraries of music and sound effects upon which you can draw. It's up to you to find out what's available. Keep a list in your desk and use every opportunity to draw upon the station resources to make your commercials lively and different. One trouble is that too many copywriters aren't energetic enough in finding out the availability of these helps. Another is that most stations don't volunteer the information. You must dig it out yourself. Once you get your music or sound effects list, however, it can be an immense help in creating commercials that are out of the ordinary.

When you need musical help, you also can call upon the "jingle" houses mentioned in the section on musical commercials. These organizations can whip up, with amazing speed, music and lyrics to be used by local advertisers. The companies have on-call gifted writers and musicians who provide music and lyrics for any type of product, often at a surprisingly low cost.

Just give them the necessary background help (product facts, advertising objectives, and possibly some past copy) and let them give you what you need, whether it's a complete singing commercial or simply supplemental music.

Utilize every such help you can find. Although the straight commercial is still a powerful sales agent, try for the variety of music and sound effects—whether you obtain them from your local stations or from an out-of-town jingle house.

ANNCR: Clint Eastwood is a little upset.

EASTWOOD: It seems some misguided people out there have been abusing our public lands and that really bothers me. Vandalizing parks, robbing historic sites, or overrunning wild areas. These are ours and we have to save them. As I see it, these clowns can either clean up their act, or they can get out of town.

ANNCR: A public service message from the U.S. Department of the Interior and the Ad Council.

Figure 18–13. Celebrity spokesperson commercial.

LYRIC: Anywhere farmers get together
You'll learn a lot about crops and weather;
And when they talk about corn, the name you'll hear,
Will more than likely be Pioneer.

(Music open—The opening SFX need to establish a grain elevator on a busy day. All noises and muffled conversations should be off mike and in the background, but we should definitely hear a phone ring and a man answer, "Co-op Elevator, Frank speaking.")

PETE: (Still slightly off mike) I gotta get home. See you guys later.

(SFX: Door opens)

PAUL: (Right on mike) Hi, Pete. Selling your corn today?

PETE: No, just talking corn.

PAUL: Did you learn anything?

PETE: (Really thinking about it) Well, yeah, I did.

PAUL: You did?

PETE: Um Hmm.

PAUL: What?

PETE: Well, a lot of the guys who came in here, when they're talking about their corn yields?

PAUL: Um Hmm.

PETE: They keep comparing the hybrids they planted to Pioneer hybrids.

PAUL: So . . . what's that prove?

PETE: Well I figure, if Pioneer hybrids are the ones to beat . . .

PAUL: Yeah?

PETE: Well . . . they must be the ones to plant.
(Both men laugh)

LYRIC: Livin' and learnin' and plantin' Pioneer.

Figure 18–14. Farm radio commercial. Farmers listen to radio programs and depend on radio commercials for information about products from seeds and herbicides to tractors and animal feeds.

End with Urge for Action

Books, plays, and motion pictures come to a climax at the end. So should radio commercials. Your climax is when you ask your listener to do something, or when you make a suggestion. There is hardly a radio commercial that should not ask for action. Examples:

> See this bargain today.
>
> Drop in. Learn for yourself.
>
> Find out why National Bank is called the "Friendly" bank.
>
> Let our experienced investment counselors help you.
>
> Remember, give your family *extra* nourishment on these chilly days—give them steaming, delicious Seaside Chowder.
>
> Come in *today.* We'll show you how easily you can play a Tune-Time Organ.
>
> Try this new corn-popper now. It's a family-pleaser.
>
> Why delay? Enjoy your home now. Get a quickly arranged home improvement loan.
>
> Think it over, and then see us about terms.

Calling for action doesn't mean that you actually expect instantaneous obedience from the listener. A request for action does, however, give vitality to the ending. Without the unmistakable call for action, your commercial ending lacks punch. Furthermore, people usually need prodding. Who knows how many tires have been bought because an announcer said, "Don't drive another mile on those worn-out tires. It's illegal and it's unsafe. See your tire dealer *today!*"

As any salesperson can tell you, it's easier for sales prospects *not* to act than to act. Your action words at the end of the commercial provide a psychological boost to your listeners who need the extra nudge you provide.

Try These Radio-writing Fundamentals

Writing copy by formula is not a recommendation you'll find in this book, but there *are* useful guides. In this chapter on radio-commercial writing, a number of such guides have been suggested. They are included here in the summary, along with some additional points. Observe these fundamentals and review them periodically. They can help you write successful radio commercials if you add that extra spark of innate creative ability that no set of guides, and no book, can give you.

1. Keep copy points to a minimum in deference to:
   a. The human mind's incapacity to absorb very much solely through the ear.
   b. The fact that your average radio listener is usually only a half-listener and will have difficulty enough catching one idea, let alone two or three.
2. Identify your band or advertiser quickly. If you wait too long to do so, your listener may have left the room, turned the set off, or stopped listening.
3. Make pictures with words. You are not writing for television. If that package you're pushing has blue stripes, suggest to your listener that he look for the blue-striped package. If it's a round container, call it a "round container."
4. Repeat important benefits, words, elements, and names. Remember the inattentive listener. The first time he barely hears you, but the second time he may have that pencil ready to take down what you're saying.

   Repetition is especially important if you're giving a telephone number. As a general principle, don't bother giving a telephone number unless you plan to repeat it. Ninety-nine out of 100 persons will never catch the number the first time the announcer gives it, but there's an outside chance that the number will be remembered, or jotted down, if it is repeated. The same advice applies to the giving of addresses.

   As for the repetition of product names or the advertiser's name, there is no fixed rule but many writers automatically try to get a name in near the beginning, the middle, and the end.
5. Get attention at the very start. You don't have to scream to get attention at the start, but you should come over "big" in some way to distract listeners from what they are doing at the moment—whether washing dishes, polishing the family car, or putting furniture in order. How can you be "big"? Achieve bigness through music, unusual voices, the kinds of words you use, the sound effects you achieve.
6. Persuade, don't scream. While a number of success stories—especially in local advertising—have been built by the "screamers," you'll do better in the long run to lead listeners to your way of thinking rather than to lash them with shrieking messages.
7. Avoid the overworked superlatives and the trite, insincere, glib radio patter. Any comedian working for a laugh can always get it by imitating radio commercials because so many sound ridiculous, even without parodying. Does yours?
8. Make dialogue believable and unforced. Again, as in point 7, even mediocre comedians can slay audiences with takeoffs on TV or radio copy. The finest target is the two-voice commercial with two supposed housewives, or with a husband-wife combination. It's almost impossible to deliver a believable, serious commercial with the entire message handled by two actors. Set your stage, if you will, with the characters from "life," but leave them quickly and let the announcer do the selling. Exceptions to this rule are frankly humorous commercials in which obvious spoofing occurs.
9. Never forget you're writing for the ear. This point, of course, sums up everything previously said about short words, alliteration, unpleasant sounds. Radio writing is not print copy, not television copy. It borrows from both but has its

ANNCR: Think about this. If every one of us gave just five hours a week to the causes we care about, it would be like mobilizing more than 20 million full-time volunteers. Think what we could do about drug abuse. Juvenile crime. Illiteracy. All those things we keep hoping will go away. Just five hours a week. It has to start with somebody. So, give five. What you get back is immeasurable. A public service of Independent Sector and the Ad Council.

Figure 18–15. Straight commercial.

own unique areas. Above all, radio copy is conversational because the ear is attuned to the sound, flow, and nuances of conversation.

10. Watch your word count. Pace your commercial for understandability and sincerity. To be certain that you're not too far above or below your time limitations, count your words and use a stopwatch. You look like an amateur each time your commercial runs over the time. Be right!
11. In almost all commercials make your endings strong, positive, and action suggesting. Naturally, in institutional approaches and certain humorous commercials, the big push at the end is inappropriate, but in the let's-move-merchandise-from-the-shelves type of commercial, ask for the order.

Following are two commercials that demonstrate much of what has been suggested throughout the chapter and in the foregoing summary. You will see how the guides can be used in a straight commercial, and in a multivoice commercial.

Straight Commercial for Electric Food Liquidizer

(SFX for 3 seconds of the liquidizer working at its highest speed) What you've just heard is a Liqui-Speed electric food liquidizer that performs so many food preparation jobs you can substitute it for a blender, a food processor, and an egg beater—not to mention a chopper, a shaver, and a grinder. It'll let you dispense with some other kitchen implements, too, thus saving cupboard space. More important, you can use your Liqui-Speed for an almost limitless range of tasks. For instance—to name a few—it purees baby foods, makes peanut butter, grates cheese, and chops nuts. Result? Tempting meals from soup to dessert, a gourmet touch you've wanted, and a handsome addition to your kitchen with its contemporary design in gleaming chrome and stainless steel. Furthermore, its Swedish steel blades will *last* and *last*. Another happy note—Liqui-Speed is self-cleaning. See a guaranteed, moderately priced Liqui-Speed today at your nearest hardware or department store for an introduction to exciting new ways to prepare meals.

Features of Foregoing Commercial

- Written within time frame: 155 words, plus SFX amounting to seven words for total of 162.
- Opening explains the SFX immediately so listener knows what it was.
- Transitional writing throughout with word bridges such as "too," "More important," "for instance," "Result?," "Furthermore," "Another happy note."
- An action ending that suggests action by listener and tells where the item may be bought.
- Use of contractions such as "you've" and "it'll."
- Personal writing with liberal use of "you," and references to points important to user such as saving cupboard space, cutting down need for so many kitchen implements, product's contribution to better meals.
- Putting over of one big point—the versatility of the unit. This point is carried from the opening lines to the last lines.
- Brand name mentioned four times.

Dramatized, Multivoiced Commercial for Electric Food Liquidizer

(SFX for 3 seconds of background noises—many voices and miscellaneous sounds)

ANNCR: Here we are at the National Retail Hardware Show. Let's hear what hardware retailers are saying about a hot new item—the Liqui-Speed electric food liquidizer.

MALE VOICE 1: This thing's so versatile I can sell it as a substitute for blenders, food processors, and other types of mixers. Might give me more shelf space.

MALE VOICE 2: I like the *price*. Ought to move *fast*.

MALE VOICE 3: Good-looking unit, too. All that chrome and stainless steel. It'll display well.

ANNCR: And there it is—the Liqui-Speed liquidizer—moderately priced, good-looking, and, above all, *versatile*.

MALE VOICE 1: My customers'll go for an item that does so *many* things. According to this display card it chops, grates, purees, liquefies, grinds, and on and on.

ANNCR: His customers—and that's *you*—will like some *other* features of Liqui-Speed, too. For instance, it's self-cleaning, it's guaranteed, and it has durable Swedish steel blades. For greater variety in meal preparation, start using a Liqui-Speed liquidizer. See one at your nearest hardware or department store *today*.

Features of Foregoing Commercial

- Written within time frame: 162 words, plus SFX amounting to seven words for total of 169.
- Opening explains the SFX immediately so listener knows what it is.

- People, other than announcer, are qualified to deliver product sales points believably.
- Product is mentioned four times.
- Big point—versatility mentioned in beginning, middle, and end.
- Voices other than announcer deliver their lines naturally.
- Action ending that tells prospect where to buy the unit.

A Final Note

You'll like radio writing for its relative simplicity. Eliminated are the complications of artwork and mechanical production of print advertisements. Neither do you, as in television, have the problems of camera work and the critical details of casting.

If you're writing a straight radio commercial on a familiar subject, you can finish the commercial in minutes. Furthermore, there's a satisfying immediacy. Should a sudden need arise, you can whip out your commercial swiftly and hear it on the air right away.

Lastly, there's an easy, friendly, and personal quality to radio writing that makes it actually fun to do—a lot less strain than in most other forms of advertising selling.

19

TELEVISION—ADVERTISING'S POWERHOUSE

Part A

Dan and his wife Sheila switched off the television set and sat for a moment enjoying the post-Super Bowl quiet.

Sheila finally broke the silence. "Great game, but I can't remember when I've seen so many commercials, and a lot of good ones, too."

"They'd better be good when you consider the megabucks they're paying for just 30 seconds, or maybe for just 15."

"Seems to me that with so many commercials coming one right after the other, they'd cancel each other out."

"I know what you mean, Sheila, but those are all blue-chip advertisers. They must be getting their dollar's worth. Otherwise, why would they spend that kind of money?"

"Probably because there are so many Super Bowl nuts like us who sit glued to the set for hours, commercials and all."

If you're typical, you'd *like* to be a good writer of print copy; but you *yearn* to write television copy because the mere idea fascinates you. Its scope, influence, and sales power make television the exciting medium. "Here at last," you may say, "is what advertising creativity is all about."

Because of television's demands, a new breed of writers has evolved since television's first commercial was telecast. Today's television-commercial writers not only have the selling instinct needed by any copywriter but also have a whole range of talents not required by other advertising writers.

To practice their craft intelligently, they must understand the problems and techniques of the producers and cameramen. This is a whole complicated world in itself. Ideally, they should know staging, acting, and the theater. If they are involved in animated television commercials, they also should possess knowledge of the complicated art of putting such commercials together.

To work in animation it is imperative to have an above-average imagination, often tinged with a touch of zaniness because humdrum writers have no part in the humorous and sometimes mad world of animated creation. The copywriters may deal with the producers of animation, an enormously creative group. And without knowing enough about their craft, the copywriters cannot command the producers' respect.

In print advertising a copywriter has a fairly realistic idea of what the finished advertisement will be like when the copy and the rough layout have been made. In contrast, the television-commercial writer has made only the barest start when the script is done.

Television is a visual medium. Most TV writers team up with an art director in the conceptual stage of a commercial. Together they discuss the strategy, then create a commercial which communicates that strategy in a memorable and effective way.

The creative team presents their storyboarded idea through a chain of approvals at both the agency and the client. Once they get a "go," the team is augmented by a producer, and these three carry the project through completion.

The responsibilities of each member of the team are roughly as follows:

- *Copywriter* is responsible for the audio portion of the commercial. This means auditioning and casting the voice talent or announcer and directing them in recording sessions. The writer also has primary responsibility in choosing a music production house and working with the music producer on jingles, post-scoring, and sound effects.
- *Art director* is responsible for the look of the commercial. This includes art design, color coordination, package retouching, and prop selection.
- *Producer* is responsible for the logistics of the commercial production—bidding, directors, maintaining budgets, acting as liaison between the director and the agency, and overseeing every facet of the commercial production to make sure things run smoothly. After the shoot, the producer works closely with the film editor in cutting the film.

As a team works together project after project, these areas of responsibilities mesh. Each member relies on the other for thoughts and opinions, so to make their commercials everything they hoped they would be.

Contrast all this uncertainty and complication with the delightful simplicity of the average radio commercial or print advertisement. A print writer does the headline, body copy, gets a rough layout from the artist, and the finished advertisement is simply a refinement of what has already been done. At a similar stage in the television commercial script, the copywriter has only just begun, and by the end of the production process the commercial could be a flop.

Big Rewards for the "Creative Spark"

Not all television commercials depend upon zany imagination. Many commercials of the demonstration type are clear-cut from the beginning and may be likened to the straight-line copy described in the listing of body copy types. Probably there are more routine television commercials than highly creative commercials, and writers can make a good living turning out adequate, if undistinguished, television commercials. If writers have that creative spark, however, that enables them to come up with the creative point of difference, the rewards for such writing can be enormous. One such idea that made a fantastic difference in the marketplace was the "Don't squeeze the Charmin" campaign of Procter & Gamble.

With various creative and technical production factors combining to make the television commercial more complex than any other current form of advertising, there is a critical need for trained, competent television personnel.

Audio or Video? Which Is More Important?

Television is a visual medium. Ideally, your television copy theme should be one that simply puts into words a piece of action seen on the screen. The best television copy does not call attention to itself. In writing it, you are less concerned with words than either the radio or print copywriter. You are after significant action and ways of bringing it about. You are on your way to achieving these ends if, after writing a final script, you can evaluate it in this manner: block off the audio portion and read through the video to see if it makes an interesting, logical, fluid series of pictures. If you can grasp a basic, solid message from the video alone, you have fully utilized the visual power of television.

Print writers can use heads, subheads, and an illustration to convey the sales story. In television you must sustain interest and sell with a series of quickly vanishing visual impressions. No one scene can dominate as does a powerful print illustration. Also, because of the rapidly changing scenes and the brief time, you cannot deliver the number of sales points possible in a big-space print advertisement.

Even more difficult are the problems of radio writers moving into television, bringing with them the practice of writing for the ear exclusively. The ear is much slower than the eye. For radio, each thought transition must be gradual; word pictures must be drawn carefully with clear definition, and verbal overemphasis is often required to drive home a point.

But television neither needs nor wants these standard radio techniques. In radio, words have always done the job. To relinquish this to the camera is one of the hardest and most essential things for the radio writer to learn about television. As a television copywriter, you will do well to heed the admonition, "Don't tell me—show me."

This is not to say that words are wholly unimportant. In fact, as people have become more accustomed to television, they tend to turn sets on just to have sound in the house. Also, while the sets are on (somewhat as in radio but to a lesser degree), people do more than simply watch the screen—they knit, cook, read, or even write. Thus, because viewers are not watching the screen every moment, the audio message becomes more important in that they can hear the sales message even while not watching the video action. Nevertheless, the visual presentation remains the most important element—though possibly not quite so important as when viewers never lifted their eyes from television screens.

Most helpful to you in creating effective television commercials will be an imaginative visual sense, in order to develop and exploit to its fullest the potential of television for imagery and product demonstration.

"Originality," however, can be dangerous, according to Rosser Reeves, once board chairman of Ted Bates & Co., a New York agency with a huge percentage of its billings in television. In his book *Reality in Advertising,* Reeves raised warning signals about the preoccupation with originality that can lead writers to absurd extremes.

In searching after the different, the clever, and the un-

02-BW-R201-30

H&M

Handley & Miller, Inc.
Advertising·Marketing·Public Relations
1712 N. Meridian St. Indianapolis, Ind. 46202

COPY/CONTINUITY

FOR AMAX COAL COMPANY

MEDIA :30 TV

DATE OF ISSUE

DATE TYPED 10/29/ JOB NO. 2827A

AS PRODUCED

VIDEO	AUDIO
Businesswoman at desk. Using calculator. Print-outs beside calculator.	ANNCR: It takes a lot of coal to run this company.
Woman reacts. Looks at calculator tape. Keeps adding.	WOMAN: This is an office, not a factory. All our business machines are electric.
	ANNCR: And it takes coal to produce that electricity.
Woman tears tape off calculator.	WOMAN: Never thought of that.
Coal dumped into frame beside calculator.	SFX: ("Musical" coal in chute)
Cut to woman putting disk into computer on credenza behind desk. Screen comes on: graphics. Woman operates computer.	ANNCR: Coal generates more than half the electricity in the United States. It takes coal to make your computer compute...
Coal dumps into frame beside computer.	SFX: ("Musical" coal in chute)
Cut to woman at copy machine.	ANNCR: the copier copy...
Coal dumped into frame on copy machine.	SFX: ("Musical" coal in chute)
Cut to woman at electric typewriter.	ANNCR: The typewriter type.
Coal dumped into frame beside typewriter.	SFX: ("Musical" coal in chute)
Cut to printer printing out sheets.	ANNCR: In fact, on the average, every American uses three tons of coal each year.

H&M

Handley & Miller, Inc.
Advertising·Marketing·Public Relations
1712 N. Meridian St. Indianapolis, Ind. 46202

COPY/CONTINUITY

FOR AMAX COAL COMPANY

MEDIA :30 TV

DATE OF ISSUE

DATE TYPED 10/29/ JOB NO. 2827A

Page 2

VIDEO	AUDIO
Coal dumped into frame beside printer.	SFX: ("Musical" coal in chute)
Woman operating slide projector. Coal dumped into frame beside it.	SFX: ("Musical" coal in chute each time coal appears)
Cut to postage meter. Coal dumped into frame beside it.	
Cut to woman's hand turning on "accountant's" light on her desk. Coal begins filling the screen.	SFX: ("Musical" coal continues through end.)
Build to screen full of coal --- moving continuously. AMAX logo comes forward.	ANNCR: AMAX Coal Company
"Powering your world" lights up on screen.	SFX: (Chain turning on light)
	ANNCR: Powering your world.

Figure 19–1a. Script for television campaign commercial. In this commercial, the video action is tied in dramatically with what is being said on the audio side.

usual, or in attempting to imitate some truly original approach, writers can forget that an advertising campaign is not designed to express their individual egos or talents for entertaining. Rather, it is a functional tool whose purpose is to fully bring the basic claim to life with ideas, information, and specific visual interpretations that speak convincingly about why your product is better.

Avoid Offending Viewers with Tasteless Commercials

A strength and yet a weakness of television advertising is its intrusiveness. It bulls its way into living rooms, bedrooms, and other rooms uninvited. It can drive a Super Bowl watcher to a homicidal madness if it interrupts during a crucial play. Your message had better be worthwhile enough to partially overcome the resentment you have created.

Even more important is to write commercials in good taste, because television advertising is so embarrassingly intimate in its probing invasion into our methods of dress and hygiene. Such poking about into our habits in the bathroom, bedroom, and closets causes emotions ranging from annoyance to downright revulsion and outrage. You'd better develop a considerate, sensitive touch in writing commercials in a period when viewers are assailed by messages for bras, pantyhose, feminine hygiene, deodorants, toilet-bowl cleaners, toilet papers, breath-sweeteners, foot-smell remedies, dandruff-removers, pimple cures, and nasal-drip relief.

Nothing seems too intimate for exploitation by television commercials, and great is the resulting outcry from a sizable portion of viewers. Are you going to contribute to the assault upon good taste, or will your commercials establish a proper tone yet sell your product? Here's a challenge you must meet.

In today's better educated, more cynical, and quick-to-resent society, the television commercial is too often viewed as *insulting* and demeaning. Unfortunately, the charge is true of many commercials that portray men and women as mindless idiots who react to advertised products (or talk about them) like subnormal children, or who are portrayed in silly little dramas that totally lack any semblance to real life.

What is your goal—to perpetuate this attack on the good sense of the viewer, or to lift the quality of television commercial writing to the point where it will be acceptable among people of intelligence, sensitivity, and good taste? It had better be the latter because the voices are loud in the land against today's television commercials.

02-MS-R202-30

H&M

Handley & Miller, Inc.
Advertising·Marketing·Public Relations
1712 N. Meridian St. Indianapolis. Ind. 46202

COPY/CONTINUITY

FOR AMAX COAL COMPANY

MEDIA :30 TV

DATE OF ISSUE

DATE TYPED 10/29/ JOB NO. 2327A

AS PRODUCED

VIDEO	AUDIO
Man shaving, looking in mirror. Electric razor.	ANNCR: (CLEARS THROAT) You're shaving with coal.
Man looks at his razor.	MAN: I'm shaving with my electric razor.
Man continues shaving.	ANNCR: And it takes coal to produce that electricity.
Man puts razor down on counter.	MAN: Never thought of it like that.
Coal dumped into frame beside razor.	SFX: ("Musical" coal in chute)
Cut to man pouring coffee from electric coffee pot.	ANNCR: Coal generates more than half the electricity in the United States.
Coal dumped into frame beside coffee pot and cup.	SFX: ("Musical" coal in chute)
Cut to man putting toast into toaster.	ANNCR: It takes coal to fix your breakfast...
Toast pops up; coal is dumped into frame beside toaster.	SFX: ("Musical" coal in chute)
Cut to man's hand turning on portable television set.	ANNCR: tune in...
Coal is dumped into frame beside television set.	SFX: ("Musical" coal in chute)
Cut to man loading, closing and turning on dishwasher.	ANNCR: and turn on.

H&M

Handley & Miller, Inc.
Advertising·Marketing·Public Relations
1712 N. Meridian St. Indianapolis. Ind. 46202

COPY/CONTINUITY

FOR AMAX COAL COMPANY

MEDIA :30 TV

DATE OF ISSUE

DATE TYPED 10/29/ JOB NO. 2327A

Page 2

VIDEO	AUDIO
Coal dumped into frame above dishwasher.	SFX: ("Musical" coal in chute)
Cut to man in workshop using a router.	ANNCR: In fact, on the average, every American uses three tons of coal each year.
Coal dumped into frame beside router.	SFX: ("Musical" coal in chute)
Cut to man adjusting thermostat. Coal dumped into frame beside it.	SFX: ("Musical" coal in chute each time coal appears.)
Cut to man inserting tape into tape deck. Coal dumped into frame beside it.	
Cut to man turning on light with chain. Coal begins filling the screen.	SFX: ("Musical" coal continues through end.)
Build to screen full of coal --- moving continuously. AMAX logo comes forward.	ANNCR: AMAX Coal Company
"Powering your world" lights up on screen.	SFX: (Chain turning on light) ANNCR: Powering your world.

Figure 19–1b. Script for television campaign commercial. Another version of the campaign approach shown in Figure 19–1a.

See That Your Commercial Has B.R.N.—Believability, Respect, Naturalness

Above all else, there is *believability.*

This should be present in claims for and demonstrations of products. There should be the honest promise of a believable benefit expressed in understandable language. Useful information should replace the extravagant, unsubstantiated claim. Change your captive audience to a captivated audience by giving them commercials they can believe, unlike so many of the paid—or so-called unrehearsed—testimonials that stretch credibility. Cynically, the audience has come to believe that anyone—stars or people on the street—will say what the advertiser wants said provided the money is sufficient. So move away from "bombast, brag, and boast" to "simple, useful, and believable."

Then, too, there is *respect.*

Women, the target of so many television commercials, are loud in their resentment of the women portrayed in commercials. You've seen them a thousand times exclaiming over products, discussing trivia as if their entire days were filled with vacuous pursuits and still more vacuous language. Slice-of-life commercials have been special offenders, depicting women whose chief concern in life seems to be ring-around-the-collar or ring-around-the-bathtub. Far too many commercials fail to give women respect for their significant contributions out of, as well as within, the home.

Last, there is *naturalness.*

Natural conversation. Natural situations. Television, more than any other medium, seems to eschew these two. It is not natural for two persons to talk for a full 30 seconds, or 60 seconds, about a product—especially in the high pitched, overly enthusiastic way of the supposedly real-life people shown on the screen. As a viewer, you know that this is so and you reject what is said as unnatural and, hence, as largely unbelievable.

Then there are the wild gyrations of the youthful set as they seem to get high on soft drinks. A succession of quick shots showing youth in high gear driving beach buggies, skydiving, hang-gliding, dashing into the surf, racing down the beach, riding motorcycles, and turning somersaults on the ski slopes depicts an exhilaration no soft drink has ever been known to contribute.

All this is mood stuff, of course, but it is unnatural like so much of television that substitutes mood for more solid material. In the case of soft drinks there is some excuse because there is really very little to write about such products, but still, the frantic pace of such commercials is part of the approach to selling in commercials that causes people to separate advertising talk from real talk and television life from real life.

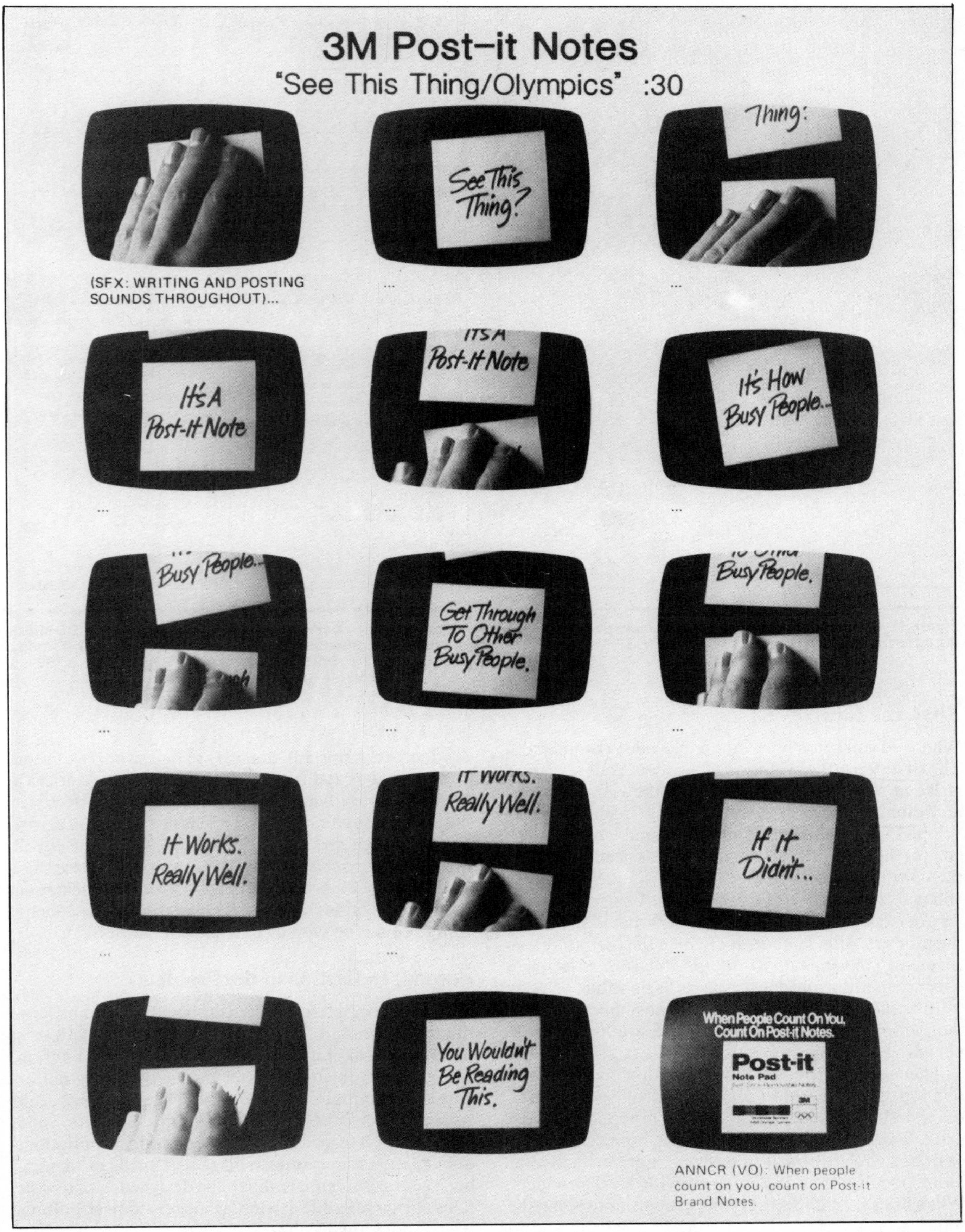
3M Post-it Notes
"See This Thing/Olympics" :30
See This Thing?
(SFX: WRITING AND POSTING SOUNDS THROUGHOUT)...
...
...
It's A Post-It Note
Post-It Note
It's How Busy People...
...
...
...
Busy People...
Get Through To Other Busy People.
Busy People.
...
...
...
It Works. Really Well.
Really Well.
If It Didn't...
...
...
...
You Wouldn't Be Reading This.
When People Count On You, Count On Post-it Notes.
Post-it
Note Pad
3M
...
...
ANNCR (VO): When people count on you, count on Post-it Brand Notes.

Figure 19–2a. Television commercial that sells in a clever and different way.

Figure 19–2b. Print version of the television commercial for the advertiser (Figure 19–1a).

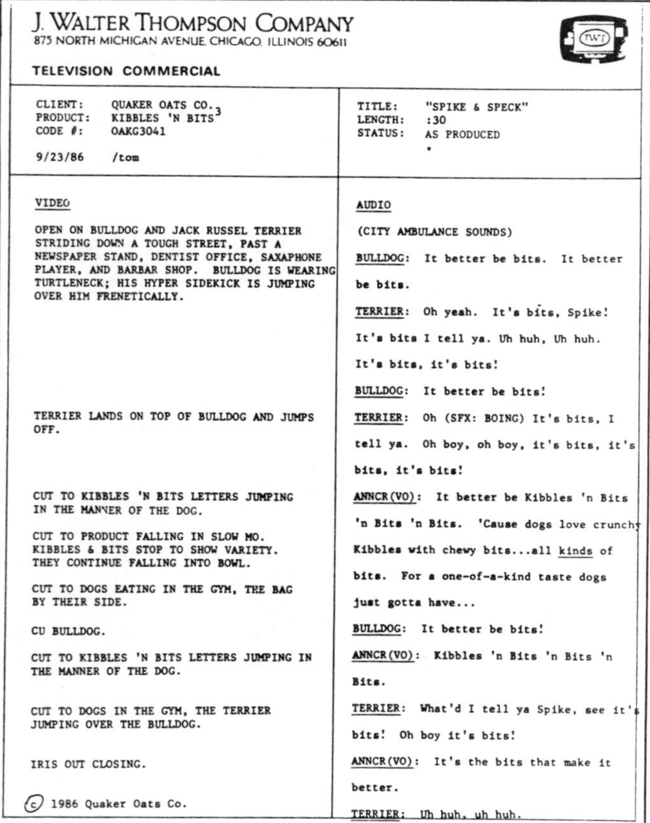

J. WALTER THOMPSON COMPANY
875 NORTH MICHIGAN AVENUE, CHICAGO, ILLINOIS 60611

TELEVISION COMMERCIAL

CLIENT: QUAKER OATS CO.[3] PRODUCT: KIBBLES 'N BITS CODE #: OAKG3041 9/23/86 /tom	TITLE: "SPIKE & SPECK" LENGTH: :30 STATUS: AS PRODUCED

VIDEO	AUDIO
OPEN ON BULLDOG AND JACK RUSSEL TERRIER STRIDING DOWN A TOUGH STREET, PAST A NEWSPAPER STAND, DENTIST OFFICE, SAXAPHONE PLAYER, AND BARBAR SHOP. BULLDOG IS WEARING TURTLENECK; HIS HYPER SIDEKICK IS JUMPING OVER HIM FRENETICALLY.	(CITY AMBULANCE SOUNDS) BULLDOG: It better be bits. It better be bits. TERRIER: Oh yeah. It's bits, Spike! It's bits I tell ya. Uh huh, Uh huh. It's bits, it's bits! BULLDOG: It better be bits!
TERRIER LANDS ON TOP OF BULLDOG AND JUMPS OFF.	TERRIER: Oh (SFX: BOING) It's bits, I tell ya. Oh boy, oh boy, it's bits, it's bits, it's bits!
CUT TO KIBBLES 'N BITS LETTERS JUMPING IN THE MANNER OF THE DOG. CUT TO PRODUCT FALLING IN SLOW MO. KIBBLES & BITS STOP TO SHOW VARIETY. THEY CONTINUE FALLING INTO BOWL. CUT TO DOGS EATING IN THE GYM, THE BAG BY THEIR SIDE.	ANNCR(VO): It better be Kibbles 'n Bits 'n Bits 'n Bits. 'Cause dogs love crunchy Kibbles with chewy bits...all kinds of bits. For a one-of-a-kind taste dogs just gotta have...
CU BULLDOG.	BULLDOG: It better be bits!
CUT TO KIBBLES 'N BITS LETTERS JUMPING IN THE MANNER OF THE DOG.	ANNCR(VO): Kibbles 'n Bits 'n Bits 'n Bits.
CUT TO DOGS IN THE GYM, THE TERRIER JUMPING OVER THE BULLDOG.	TERRIER: What'd I tell ya Spike, see it's bits! Oh boy it's bits!
IRIS OUT CLOSING.	ANNCR(VO): It's the bits that make it better.
© 1986 Quaker Oats Co.	TERRIER: Uh huh, uh huh.

Figure 19–3. Television script. Although there are more words in the audio than in most 30-second commercials, many of the words are short. Notice the name registration achieved through the voicing many times of the word "bits."

First, the Idea

Where do you begin in writing a television commercial? The first step is the evolution of the idea. Your idea must strike at such basic motivations of the viewer as love, ambition, self-preservation, economy. It should be developed with imagination and tempered with a knowledge of the medium and the advertiser's needs, as well as the consumer's desires. By applying simple reasoning, you will find that the product to be advertised contains within itself such sources of ideas as: what is new about the product; what benefits it offers to the user; the experience of consumers with the product; its advantages over competitive products; and its basic value.

In an effective presentation, you must touch the right motivational button and stimulate desire for the product and its benefits.

The greatest "strength of presentation" is in demonstration (or comparison). Demonstrate the new feature, the benefit, the advantage, and—where applicable—the price. Show the product: how it works, how it saves, how easy it is to use, how it makes one more attractive or more popular, how it compares with rival products. When price is an important factor, superimpose it on the screen to make it seem even more of a bargain and to make it that much more memorable.

Another point is simplicity. While advantages of the product are important, don't try to make your television commercial a catalog of all these advantages. If it has a dozen or more advantages, that's great for the advertiser but not for the commercial. Time is needed to put across a point, which means the selling story should be boiled down to one principal point—at most two or three. Just be sure the selling story has enough time to register on the viewer's mind, and that there is time at the conclusion to sum it up with a convincing repetition.

Second, Definition of the Problem

Television commercials vary in length, cost, and production techniques, depending on the specific jobs they are intended to perform. Such variations call for definition of the problem, a matter that may or may not lie within your province as copywriter. The problem deals with such factors as overall sales objectives, location and identification of primary customers, and the limitations of budget. Are you going to hit targets singly or in number? Your commercials should be designed with a basic sales objective in mind: winning new customers, holding regular ones, increasing use per capita, forcing distribution, improving dealer relations, building prestige and good will, or even impressing stockholders.

Program or Spot Use?

Your commercials must also take into account whether they are to be used for program or spot presentation. To present the commercial in the presumed proper environment, an advertiser will often buy (through the advertising agency) a specific type of entertainment or information program, network or local. Often, the advertiser and the product become identified, for better or worse, with the program and/or its star. Commercials used within these programs can be "live" or on film or tape.

Spot television advertising is placed by advertisers on a market-by-market basis originating in the individual market where it is telecast. The advertisement may consist of a hard selling 10-second commercial announcement known as an "ID" (for station identification). It may also be a 15-second, 30-second, 60-second announcement between programs, or within a local program or a network participating program in which a number of advertisers have bought spot time.

Spot commercials are almost always on film or tape. They come at the viewer from all angles and in all forms, and because many of them are irritating, they are the kind of advertising people usually complain about when they point an accusing finger at television commercials.

Factors Affecting Commercial Length

A commercial's length depends upon the theme, approach, and specific product advantages. Different sales stories may vary in their complexity. For example, a good demonstration commercial may require 60 seconds, every second of which will be useful and interesting to the viewer.

A product, in contrast, that has nothing to demonstrate and no high degree of product interest might be a bore as the subject matter of a 60-second commercial. Give it 30 seconds or 15 seconds if the idea of the product can be grasped easily by viewers. As the copywriter you're usually going to be told how long a commercial you're supposed to write. Thus, this is a subject that doesn't concern you much unless you are permitted to participate in precampaign planning sessions.

At one time the 60-second commercial was the standard in television. Because of costs and because research showed that shorter commercials could be equally, if not more, effective, the 30-second commercial became the standard. Only a relatively few commercials are 60 seconds.

The standard commercial length in the future might be 15 seconds. Copywriters with any kind of message to deliver will find such a commercial frustrating. Demonstrations, product comparisons, and interviews cannot be handled efficiently in such a short time span.

"Clutter," the profusion of commercials within and between programs, has reduced the impact of commercials. Clutter became much worse when the 30-second commercial replaced the 60-second as the standard. If 15-second commercials dominate, clutter will be worse still. As a copywriter you have an interest in clutter because attention for your commercial suffers when it is one of a number of commercials presented in rapid sequence between shows.[1]

Repeating Commercials: How Much Is Enough?

Having decided on program as opposed to the spot presentation of your commercial, it is well to keep in mind certain principles about another factor: wear-out. Viewer knowledge increases with repetition up to a certain point, when indifference or psychological deafness and blindness set in. It is difficult, if not impossible, to measure at what point this mental tuning out takes place, but there are four factors that seem to relate specifically to any commercial's life expectancy:

- Frequency of broadcast
- Content as it affects the viewer
- Variety of presentation in a given series
- Techniques used in commercial construction

Many advertisers have been successful with a minimum of well-constructed and oft-repeated messages. Skillfully built and judiciously scheduled, a spot can be used for many months, even years. Another can run its course in a few weeks in a heavy saturation campaign, yet still have been effective and economical. Kellogg's Rice Krispies ran a cartoon jingle fifty times in a row on a children's program and burned it out like a meteor. Yet it served its purpose well, at a low cost per showing.

How acceptable a commercial is refers not to how much a viewer likes it but to its "what's-in-it-for-me" content and how well it entertains, informs, and holds forth a promised benefit. A film series should focus on a central theme for greatest impact throughout the series, but varied repetition is the key here, particularly in the manner in which the commercial begins.

Beer commercials are much the same in any given series, but the variety of ways in which they capture attention at the outset makes for interest. Singing jingles combined with animated cartoons are a combination with long life expectancy, especially if the commercial spot is used intermittently. You cannot, however, expect to repeat too often live action films in which memorable characters or settings are featured, since viewers tend to pick apart your commercial with each repetition.

Station Break Spots

Ten-second station break television spots can best be viewed as the rifle bullets of this medium. Here you encounter the challenge of brevity plus the need for simple, clear-cut selling ideas expressed with visual impact. It may be simpler to write a 5- or 10-minute film script than a 10-second television spot.

1. As a possible ominous note for the future, 7½-second commercials are being tried in France and Japan.

You will be tempted in building spot commercials to crowd too much material into both audio and video presentations, which will only result in a confused and meaningless jumble of words and scenes from which your viewer will derive little. Again, concentrate on the video or visual in your commercial, since this is what must remain with the viewer after your brief message. Remember, however, the sound or audio plays an important role, too, enabling the viewer to hear you even from outside the room.

Ten-second station identification (ID) spots have the advantage over 60-second commercials in their ability to sustain a much stronger sales pitch and the fact that they can be repeated more often than their longer cousin. They are also easier to schedule for more intensive coverage on a number of stations, and thus are effective in coping with local sales problems.

The ID spot, chiefly a "reminder" type of advertising, is on the television screen for a full 10 seconds. It gives you eight seconds of sound. As a commercial form the ID must fight hard for identity and leaves small margin for error. Its brief moments of sound-and-picture glory are almost always preceded by the closing commercial of the preceding program and a chain break. It is immediately followed by the first commercial of the next program. In spite of its physical limitations, the ID can do a fine selling job as both a reminder for impulse type items and as a supporting element for concurrent campaigns for big-ticket advertisers in television and other media.

To detract attention from surrounding commercials, station break commercials often employ cartoons, which are particularly effective because they read well. Since this is primarily reminder advertising, the sponsor's name must be indelibly identified, probably along with a slogan or an important selling point.

It is better not to resort to camera tricks, such as dissolves or wipes, where action on the screen is involved. Stay with a basic setting and be content to move component parts in and out for the sake of fluidity. Hold to the premise, if possible, that the sponsor's signature or logotype should be on-camera for at least half, if not more, of the allotted 10 seconds.

Writing the 15-Second Commercial

Although there can be variations, the basic structure of the "15" calls for a headline or principal "reason why"; once this is set, it is a matter of using it in the audio and dramatizing it in the video. Such commercials are in contrast to those contrived and complicated by local advertisers who seek to make major productions out of the precious seconds allotted. It is enough to succeed in registering one point strongly in even a 60-second or longer commercial, let alone trying to do more in 15 seconds.

In constructing the 15-second commercial, select the dominant sales point and simply polish that point to its finest. Humor is often an effective ingredient for this type of commercial because it evokes the quick reaction needed for such a short presentation.

The success stories of advertisers who have used shorter commercials to advantage are numerous, and many of them have achieved this success with little or no other advertising. One of these, a watch company, used this formula:

> Buy five or six spots a week on a station and hold them for all-year use. Try to reach the entire family by buying spots in prime time (8:30 P.M. to 10:00 P.M.) with adjacencies to good shows, if possible. Buy a volume in spots commensurate with the company's sales in the particular market.

Another advertiser who had done a strong selling job with spots summed up the situation:

> Spots give us more coverage with the flexibility to handle sales problems peculiar to different areas. We can adjust our product commercials according to regional preferences in flavor, for instance.

Storyboards

A storyboard, executed on a sheet of paper, presents a series of small sketches with accompanying description of action, plus audio copy that gives an advertiser an approximate conception of what the commercial will be upon completion. It is a sort of halfway point between the birth of the original idea and the finished film.

In large agencies the copywriter teams up with an art director to come up with the concept. Once they have this germ of an idea, the art director maps out the action with sketches and the copywriter writes the script, indicating how it will fall in relation to the pictures.

Storyboards are preferable to written scripts for a number of reasons. Since the commercial will be presented through a medium in which the visual image is paramount in importance, it facilitates production to think in terms of pictures from the beginning. Furthermore, since a number of people may read and be called upon to approve a script, it is probable that each will have a personal visualization of how the story will appear on the screen.

If a storyboard is prepared, all concerned will think in terms of the pictures shown. Each can check the staging and action as the commercial is actually shot. Also, any errors in visualization from the standpoint of company policy or product value will be apparent and can be corrected before actual production begins.

A properly designed storyboard can also be utilized as a shooting script that suggests camera angles and staging, as a preliminary layout for set designs or backgrounds, and as a guide for the film editor when the film is cut. Closeups, camera moves, and optional effects can all be indicated. The director is also aided by the storyboard when planning the action and staging of the film to obtain the desired dramatic effect.

As in the case of print layouts, the first storyboards may be very rough but the artwork becomes more refined as the storyboard goes through the various levels of persons who must inspect it.

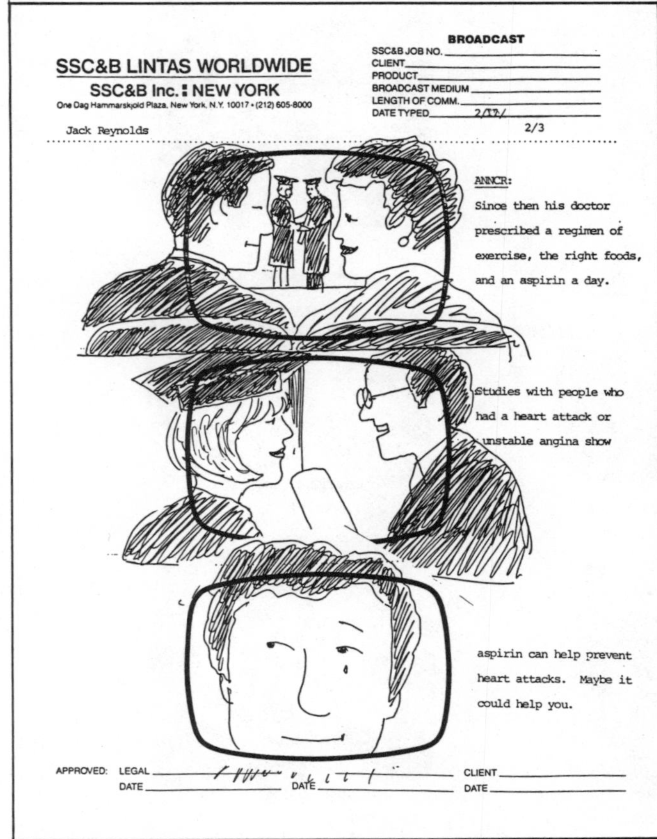

Figure 19–4a. **Television storyboard,** the first step in the long process of going from the idea to the finished production.

Initially, the art director roughs up the sketches. But before the board goes to the client, an illustrator will tighten up the drawings. At the same time the copywriter may try to find music and any visual aids which will enhance the client's understanding of the spot. And creative teams have been known to sing, dance, and pretend to be talking hamburgers in order to bring the commercial to life for a client.

As noted early in this chapter, the copywriter, account executives, client, and production people can tell from a print layout just about what the published advertisement will look like. In contrast, the filmed commercial that is finally produced from a storyboard is usually vastly different from the storyboard.

Thus, it takes a professional with plenty of experience and imagination to judge what is going to result from the incorporating of unusual voices, beguiling characters, superb music, dazzling color, energetic motion, and striking sound effects—none of which is truly conveyed by the storyboard.

Actually, the process works both ways. The storyboard idea may look good and the finished product poor. Or, the storyboard may convey little that gives a clue as to the outstanding commercial that will be developed finally from the idea.

One of the problems in doing a storyboard is that it is necessarily brief compared to the finished film, which is divided into frames that speed through the projector 24 to the second, or 1,440 to the minute.

Sometimes the problem isn't overwhelming, as in the

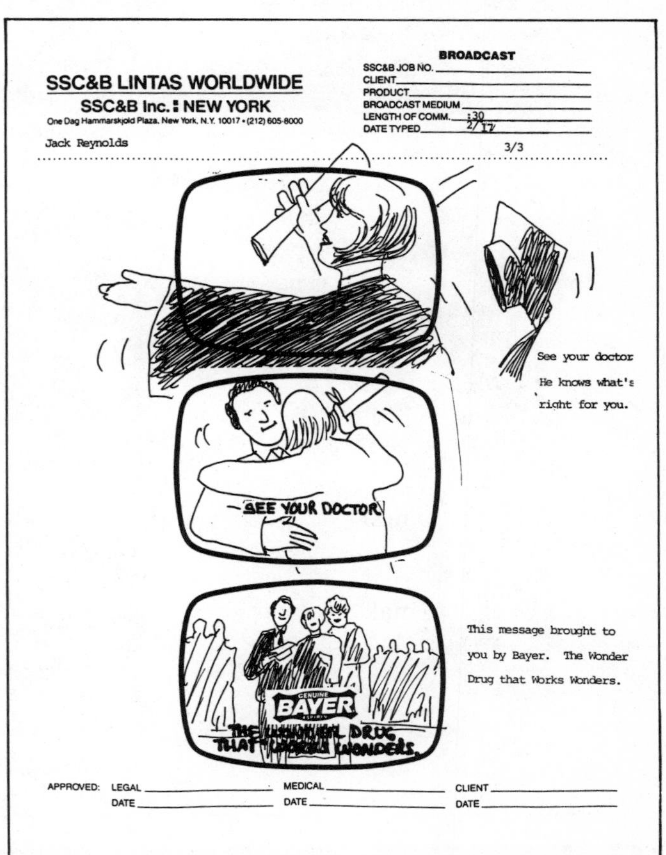

GLENBROOK LABORATORIES

Genuine Bayer Aspirin
"Heart Attack Education" :30

ANNCR.: Dan Miller waited a long time to see this.

He almost

missed it.

Not long ago

Dan had a

heart attack.

Since then his doctor prescribed

a regimen of exercise,

the right foods, and an aspirin a day.

Studies with people who had

a heart attack or unstable angina show aspirin can

help prevent heart attacks.

Maybe it could help you.

See your doctor. He knows what's right for you.

This message brought to you by Bayer. The Wonder Drug That Works Wonders.

Figure 19–4b. Voice-over television commercial. (See Figure 19–4a for storyboard.)

case of a simple demonstration commercial that has only two to five scene changes involving two, or possibly one, performer. On the other hand, a commercial such as the typical Pepsi-Cola or Coca-Cola commercial is difficult to storyboard for full understanding. How can you convey in detail all those quick shots, optical gimmicks, sound effects, numerous people, music, frantic action, and background scenes? You can't. You simply call for enough storyboard frames to serve as a rough guide. You're at the mercy of the production house to bring those few cold pictures to life.

It's especially difficult to plot in advance the exact time each of those frames will require in the finished film. Furthermore, some scenes need more accompanying copy to explain them, and thus more frames. The *exact* time they need is hard to tell in advance. Other scenes convey ideas in a fraction of a second, requiring only a glance of the viewer. They may need no accompanying copy.

Some Directors Need Detailed Storyboards; Others Don't

A word of caution is needed here to point out that the detailed and rigid storyboard is not always the best one. Much depends on who will take over from your storyboard to put the commercial on film. If directors are truly creative, you will be shortchanging your commercial by imposing too exacting directions upon them. They may have ideas about enacting some of your scenes in a manner to make them much more forceful. Or they might have suggestions on how to cut costs by repeating the use of a certain setting or dropping a bit of action that lends only minor support to the story. Such directors can be a tremendous asset, so it is best to give these talented team members a green light with a storyboard that leaves them room for creative contributions.

Before a job is given to the director and production house, the copywriter, art director, and the agency producer usually sit down and compile production notes. These accompany the storyboard and describe the objective, the audience, the tone or mood, the plot, sets, props, casting considerations, and music. This gives the director an idea of what the creative team expects. As the project evolves, these treatments may be revised but the production notes and storyboard offer a detailed blueprint from which to start.

Balancing Audio and Video Is Tricky

A basic problem in writing your television commercial, regardless of its length, is the proper balance of video and audio. Be cautious about pacing the visual side of the commercial too fast and using too many scene changes.

The main trouble, however, lies not with scenes being too long or too short, but with uneven pacing. Long scenes too often are followed by jet-speed, short ones.

This uneven pace stems from approaching the commercial's sales points with words rather than pictures. You may find one point easy to express in a few words, then accord this point a correspondingly short visual. The more involved points get prolonged visuals.

This is working the wrong way. The brief copy point should either not be visualized at all or its audio should be extended sufficiently to cover a visual of comfortable length.

Remember: it is a mistake to pace your audio for television as fast as you would for the typical hard-sell radio commercial. Your audience in television has to follow video as well as audio, which makes it difficult to grasp a television sound track that is paced too fast. This pacing problem is particularly acute in film commercials where the announcer succeeds in getting in the full message only by racing through the script.

These cautions do not apply to the mood commercials mentioned earlier in the chapter. In a soft drink commercial, to illustrate, you are not trying to register product points. Your aim may simply be to associate the drink with youth, good times, and activity. To accomplish this you run scenes in rapid succession with no need to let any of them linger on the screen. Together with equally fast-paced music and offscreen announcing, you create whirlwind action and the mood you're seeking.

An airline might use this technique if it aims to emphasize all the interesting places to which it can take you, rather than to stress any particular feature such as on-time arrivals, safety, the type of aircraft, or the service. Similarly, a hotel could run through a pool, the sauna, the dining rooms, the roof garden, and the nearby ocean beach.

For most commercials, however, don't race—*pace.* Be active but not frantic.

Common Sense Should Guide You in the Number of Words You Put in a Commercial

Most radio announcers read comfortably at 160 to 170 words a minute, and others considerably faster. A governor of Nebraska was once clocked at 487 words a minute in an election campaign speech. Obviously, such verbal speed is well beyond the television viewer's understanding. You will find that 135 words a minute (w.p.m.) will fit into many live-action commercials, although for the most part you will need fewer than that. Recommendations often range from 80 to more than 130 w.p.m., but experience has shown that a rule of thumb of two words per second usually works out consistently well.

Delivery rate is rather hard to define because of pauses and the fact that many commercials use more than one speaker. One study of 350 one-minute commercials by word-count analysis compared these data with effectiveness results for the same commercials. The most effective commercials ranged in word count from 101 to 140, demonstrating that a moderate speaking pace was desired over extremes of too many or too few words per minute.

Figure 19–5a. Television campaign commercial. A number of elements combine to make this campaign outstanding. There is beautiful photography with soft lighting that is complemented by appropriate music. In the case of these three commercials (Figures 19–5a, b, c) the musical theme was based on "Hymne" from the album "Opera Sauvage" by Vangelis. Gallo commercials create a mood through the photography, music, and the distinctive voice of the announcer. Lastly, notice that the story is told with few words. In these commercials the visual dominates. Words become less important.

E. & J. GALLO WINERY
"PROGRESSION"
:60 COMMERCIAL

It started just two decades ago...

The finest varietal grapes were planted

The world's most costly vineyards...

The harvest begins in the Napa/Sonoma growing regions.

The greatest wine making facilities in the world.

Cork, from Portugal...

Oak cellars...

Gallo's first age-dated wines...

Acclaim...

In just twenty short years, the maker of America's most popular wine, has become America's most honored winery...

Today's Gallo...
All the best a wine can be...

Figure 19–5b. Television campaign commercial. See the other two Gallo commercials in this chapter to learn how to create a campaign feeling through consistent use of certain elements.

E. & J. GALLO WINERY "MOST RESPECTED"

:60 Commercial

Chardonnay . . .

Zinfandel . . .

Gewurztraminer . . .

Sauvignon Blanc . . .

Cabernet Sauvignon . . .

The varietal wines of Ernest and Julio Gallo . . .

Among the most respected in the world . . .

Today's Gallo . . .

All the best that a wine can be . . .

1986 Modesto, California

▲ TRI-ADS™ No. Hollywood 91601

Figure 19–5c. Television campaign commercial. A story-telling approach is used in this as in the other two Gallo commercials shown in this chapter.

Having a certain delivery rate, however, is no assurance of successful commercial writing. Some outstanding commercials have used no words; others more than the usual word count. A sensible speaking pace can be a contributing factor, of course, but the important thing is the quality of your words, not their quantity.

Quantity, as it applies to the shorter commercials, would be 20 words for the 10-second spot; 30 words for the 15-second spot; and 60 to 65 words for the 30-second spot. The one-minute commercial will usually take well with 120–135 words; but if the announcer is on camera, give him less to say and, if he must demonstrate, still less than that. The ground rules say that a 15-second sound track cannot run over 13 seconds, nor a one-minute track over 58 seconds. You will be safer aiming for a shorter count, such as 11 or 12 seconds on the short spot, 25 or 26 on the 30, and 55 or 56 seconds in the one-minute version. This will permit an easier pace and more flexibility in your commercials. Remember, too, in production it's much simpler to stretch than to tighten.

Scenes: How Many?

What has been said here about pacing the audio holds true for the video portion of your television commercial. Don't confuse your viewers with too many scenes or those that are too busy and distract from your sales story. You can avoid cutting scenes too short by allowing a minimum of three seconds for viewers to orient themselves to any new scene.

Scenes can also run too long, so keep in mind that after six seconds something had better move, or perhaps the viewer will. Either a different camera angle or some action within the scene can provide movement to prevent a scene from becoming static.

A single scene that is properly plotted out for action and camera angles can sustain interest for 20 or 30 seconds in a commercial. Ordinarily, however, you will want to think in terms of five or six seconds or more per scene. For more important visuals such as establishing a person, demonstrating, or major copy point, you may want to use 10 to 20 seconds or more.

There is no firm rule about the number of scenes in a commercial, but here are a few general measures that will serve to guide you: No more than two to three scenes in a 10-second spot; three to five in a 15-second spot; and 10 in a 30-second spot. Keep in mind that to the viewer a closeup from a previous shot is not considered a new scene.

To show the futility of trying to set up firm guidelines, a study conducted during the writing of this book found that 30-second commercials were averaging 8 to 10 scenes; these were definite scene changes, not merely changes of camera angles or distance.

Customarily, a demonstration commercial will swallow up time and eliminate the need for constant scene changes. A woman demonstrating the use of a new, useful kitchen utensil may stay on camera for a full 30-second commercial without boring her audience. No need for scene changes here although you might wish to change camera distances and angles. Such changes will give a feeling of added action and can improve the value of the demonstration.

Most of all, you keep in mind that television is an *action* medium. You attain action two ways: (a) By having action in the scenes themselves. (b) By changing the scenes (and/or camera angles and distances) to create the feeling of action. Above all, avoid television commercials that are simply a succession of still-life photographs.

As You Write, Ask Yourself: "How Much Will This Cost?"

While your agency's television director will usually control production and costs, this does not give you license to turn out ideas without regard to limitations imposed by a budget. You will learn by experience that it is wiser in building your commercial to avoid costly scenes that will invite price-cutting surgery later, thereby endangering the continuity of the whole script.

The accomplished television copywriter is a many-faceted being—salesperson, psychologist, dramatist, film craftsman, producer, and lyricist. As such, you may take part in planning sessions, production briefings, and the various stages of actual production.

You can make all of these efforts more productive and efficient from the beginning with good writing—the best insurance against faulty interpretation and costly production. If your storyboard calls for five on-camera principal performers, do some rethinking. Could you rewrite and accomplish your goals with four, three, or even two performers? Remember, for videotape commercials an on-camera session fee will run into hundreds of dollars for each person playing a major role, whether the person is called a "player" by SAG (Screen Actors Guild), or a "principal" by AFTRA (American Federation of Television and Radio Artists). This session fee pays for one use of the commercial on the network.

If the commercial is to be used in a major way over the networks, each player (or principal) must be given a reuse, or residual, payment for every time the commercial is shown. Even off-camera announcers and singers are given such payments, although in lesser amounts.

When you call for a person in the commercial to speak, handle, or react to the product, that person becomes a player. Others such as stunt people and specialty dancers are classified as players, too.

Extras are not entitled to residual payments and may be defined as those people seen as hands or backs of heads, for example. They may also be described as extras even if seen in total, but in this case they are well away from the product and they do not react to the product. In a sense, they simply are part of the background.

Because you've called for an unusual number of players (or principals), it may well be that the subsequent reuse payments can cost the client more than the charge for the commercial air time. Assess the value to be

VISA
It's everywhere you want to be.

Client: VISA
Product: CLASSIC VISA CARD

Title: "CALGARY"

Time: 30 SECONDS
Comml. No.: NZVC 1386

VISA

"Just east of the Canadian Rockies,

is a place where people will go faster

and fly farther than ever before.

The place is Calgary, home of the 1988 Winter Olympics

where a lifetime of work will be measured in seconds.

But if you go, bring your camera

and your Visa card,

because the Olympics don't take place all the time,

and this time

they don't take American Express.

VISA
It's everywhere you want to be.

Visa, it's everywhere you want to be."

Figure 19–6. Television advertising campaign. Strong product identification is a noteworthy feature of this campaign along with interesting and action-filled scenes.

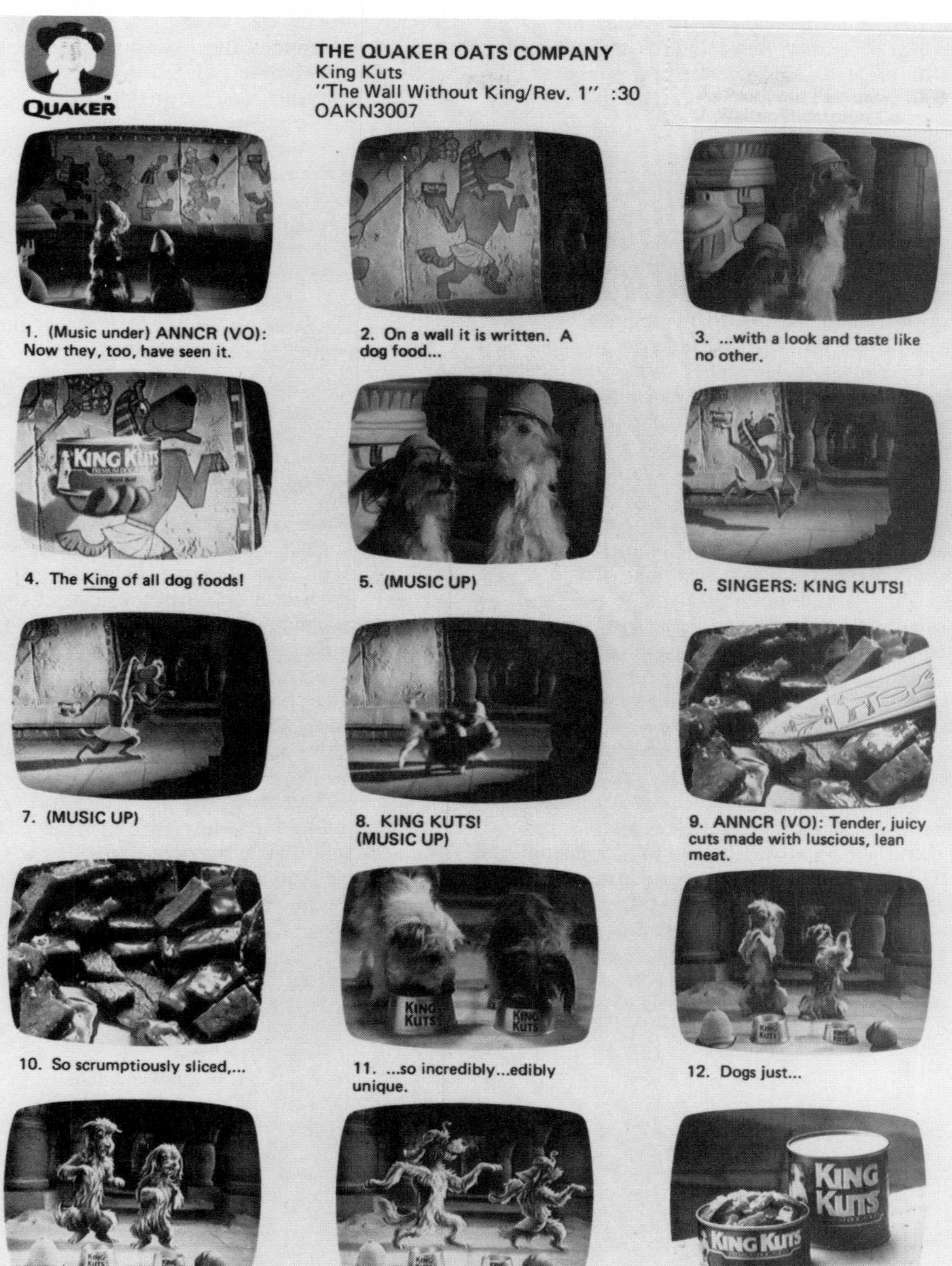

Figure 19–7. Television photoboard using combination of live action and animation.

gained by the lavish use of players against the added cost. Sometimes you may judge that the use of the extra players will result in a more powerful commercial that will better achieve advertising objectives. If not—then cut down.

More Ways to Cut Costs

Sitting at your typewriter it's easy to call for *location* shooting, but it's not so simple to lug all the people, props, cameras, and other equipment to the location—and it can be frightfully expensive. Once again, the question: Is it worth it? Sometimes the answer must be "yes."

If you can't honestly say yes, there are ways around the problem. You could use a stock shot of the location as background; a special crew (without actors) could go to the spot to get such a shot; or you could use stills to establish the location. Actually, *one* shot may be all you need to fix the location in the viewer's mind and to provide the atmosphere you want.

You can also run up costs by asking for effects and shots that are more complicated than they need to be to put over your message. Do you need that view from the helicopter, that fisheye shot, the telephoto shot, the extreme closeups? Some of the most effective television is simple television, and simple television can be less expensive. Think about it.

An example of cutting costs is illustrated by a local bank that couldn't afford to show seven on-camera bank employees demonstrating their various duties. Instead, only their hands were shown. These seven pairs of hands handled papers involved in a typical bank transaction. They were shown in closeup, always desirable, and the viewers could see what was happening to customers' money. It was easier to concentrate on the message than if seven persons had been shown. Also important, shooting time was cut from two days to less than one day.

Such economies are typical of low-cost local commercials in which you may call for public domain music or have the local station videotape material with their personnel. You may elect to shoot in 16mm film or use actual advertisements for artwork. You may lose some polish in the commercials using these techniques, but you can also help make television affordable for local advertisers.

One view of cost in your television commercial is that you may have written it in such a way that it is expensive to produce. Another view of cost is that you may have written it so poorly that it gets little or no attention, or is actually boring. In terms of viewers influenced to buy the advertised product, the advertiser may be spending a huge amount per viewer. It is costly to the advertiser when your commercial registers so poorly that viewers can't remember the product, its name, or its selling points.

Fighting for Attention

Writing for television drains some writers. Messages are so ephemeral. Today's idea is stale tomorrow. New, striking graphics are soon supplanted by even more striking graphics. A celebrity spokesperson of today is soon a has-been. The well-thought-out commercial often loses to a commercial that is inferior, but for some weird reason catches on with the fickle public.

In big advertising agencies the strain on writers is constant. Ideas, ideas, ideas. That's what is wanted and the writer who can't come up with fresh, usable ideas may soon be leaving the agency.

At the bottom of all this is the fight to stand out in the midst of hundreds of commercials crying for attention. With the ability of viewers to remember the commercials they've seen at an all-time low, writers ask themselves: "Will this commercial I've written make even the slightest impression on viewers, let alone sell the product?"

All these doubts and problems make television-commercial writing a job for the stouthearted.

20

TELEVISION—ADVERTISING'S POWERHOUSE

Part B

"My feeling is that a good print writer is better equipped to take up television writing than vice versa. In short, someone who has done nothing but television will find it harder to switch to print."

Monty Sharman, the speaker and a veteran writer of both television commercials and print advertisements, was talking to Jack McInerney, vice president of creative services of a big multinational advertising agency. They were discussing various candidates for a copywriting job that would consist largely of writing television commercials.

"Monty, you may be right, but I still favor June Berkey. She's had a world of solid TV writing. For this job, she's made to order. She should be able to adapt to the occasional print jobs we give her."

Print experience versus television experience. This is the basis of a longtime argument with no definitive answer. One point is certain. June will simply be one of a big team of experts in the task of producing television commercials, as you will be if you write television advertising. Counting all the production people, account executives, client personnel, supervisors, and others, there may be more than fifty persons involved in carrying out *your* idea. *That* makes you important.

It would be pleasant to tell you that as a copywriter you are going to decide just how your television commercials will be reproduced. Not so. Typically, you'll be told to write the commercials, and you'll be told also whether they'll be "live," "film," or "tape." You don't argue. Drawing upon your knowledge of each, you write your commercial to fit the requirements of the technique you've been told will be used.

Film, Tape, or Live?

Film commercials are those shot in a studio, on location outdoors, or wherever there is a suitable site for the desired action. Tape (videotape) is a system that records sound and pictures simultaneously on magnetic tape. Live refers to action seen on the television screen as it takes place right in the studio before the television camera.

Film commercial production is chosen by most national advertisers because it has many advantages over videotape production. Commercials on film have a higher quality look, giving the advertised product a higher quality image. Because film reveals subtle nuances of colors and shadows, it is more realistic than

Advertiser: UPS

Product: Next Day Air Guaranteed

Length: 30 sec

Production: "Nightlife"

Video

1. Open to bright starry night sky. Jet zooms through the sky toward us.
2. Cut to baggage men riding cargo carts out to plane to unload the mail.
3. Cut to TCU of UPS logo on tail fin.
4. MS of train of mail carts with UPS logo on side runs across screen.
5. Cut to baggage men loading another jet for take-off. They close the hatch.
6. Cut to plane slowly moving down runway. Takes off towards us into night sky.
7. Fade out. Fade in logo.

Audio

SFX:	lullaby chimes in background
SFX:	hum of jet approaching, getting louder as jet on screen gets closer
ANNCR:	Every night while you're sleeping, UPS is maintaining its status . . .
ANNCR:	. . . as the only company that delivers overnight to every address coast to coast.
ANNCR:	And now we guarantee it. Introducing UPS Next Day Air Guaranteed.
ANNCR:	And because we're so efficient, we'll still do it for up to half what other companies charge, which is guaranteed to cause our competition some sleepless nights.
SFX:	roar of jet taking off
ANNCR:	UPS. We run the tightest ship in the shipping business.

Figure 20–1a. Straight sales pitch with voiceover.

Advertiser: UPS

Product: Next Day Air Letter

Length: 30 sec

Production: "Super Saver"

Video

1. Fade-in to closeup of large stack of mailing envelopes. Screen is dark, but a light from left of screen slowly falls on stack. Lights up screen.
2. Zoom to top envelope. Closeup on UPS logo on envelope.
3. MCU Envelopes slide off stack. One by one they glide through air across screen into next scene.
4. Cut to envelope gliding rapidly onto series of different desks. Each desk is typical of a different kind of person. (ie., very neat; messy)
5. Cut to last envelope landing on a desk in someone's casual office. "$8.50" flashes onto screen.
6. Cut to UPS logo on screen

Audio

SFX:	abrupt screeching of airplane brakes as it's touching down
SFX:	Band strikes up in background playing a patriotic tune
ANNCR:	American businesses can now save millions . . .
ANNCR:	. . . of dollars every year with the UPS Next Day Air Letter.
SFX:	screeching of brakes each time a letter touches down on each desk
ANNCR:	Unlike other companies which frequently charge up to fourteen dollars . . . UPS, because we're so efficient . . .
ANNCR:	. . . charges only eight fifty. And we guarantee overnight delivery to every city coast to coast. The UPS Next Day Air Letter . . .
ANNCR:	. . . The "Super Saver" of overnight letters.

Figure 20–1b. Straight sales pitch with voiceover.

videotape. This can be particularly important when you are shooting food and want to evoke appetite appeal, or looking for realism in outdoor scenes. Finally, film offers wider creative latitude.

Almost any approach is possible for the writer of film commercials, because production people have ingenious ways to execute the idea through special effects, sets, lighting, and careful editing. For all these reasons, and the fact that a national commercial can run for months or years, film is often a sound choice despite its higher cost.

Tape has been a great boon to local advertising because it makes possible the utilization of local talent and resources in a way not possible with live-studio production, or with film.

At first, tape offered limited special effects. Now, as a writer, you can call for such effects and optical tricks—all at low cost. In fact, compared to film (not live studio), tape costs are lower for shooting and processing. Also, tape can record and store many commercials.

Other Reasons for Favoring Tape Production

- Easier client approval. Before a commercial is finally approved by a major advertiser, it usually goes through numerous hands. Tape makes it possible for many, if not all, of those concerned with passing upon a commercial to be present and to make necessary revisions immediately, thanks to quick playback.
- Alternate versions and testing. Two or more versions of a commercial are easily available with tape. Changes in settings or new approaches suggested on the spot are less costly. Also, with alternate versions, a commercial can be pretested quickly via research before actual telecast to determine the most effective approach. Some larger videotape production houses employ closed-circuit testing facilities for such purposes.
- Man-hour savings. Time schedules in pretape days of live and film television tied down creative and technical people. Now this talent can be utilized more efficiently within the compact time schedules of tape.

Furthermore, tape offers such flexibility that new scenes can be inserted in existing spots in an hour. Sound tracks can be erased and recorded anew in less time than that. Tape thus puts television ahead of newspaper in the all-important area of advertising flexibility.

Live television production offers lower cost for the one-time commercial. It can also be produced, from the written script to the actual production on camera, in less time than film. Live commercials can, of course, be changed in wording or action at the very last minute, a not insignificant advantage to an advertiser—especially in a keenly competitive situation.

On the other side, some of the most deadly commercials are done live in station studios, for low-budget local advertisers. To supply some kind of interest, the writer calls for props to be supplied by the client, the station, or sometimes the advertising agency. These may be mixed in with slides. Also, the announcer may appear at the opening and close. Occasionally, if the station has a good film library, a writer may use stock shots effectively in a live commercial.

Since the development of videotape, live studio or live location shots have been used less and less. If you *must* write live commercials, use every bit of imagination you can in drawing upon the resources of the client and the station. Sometimes, however, if you have a personable announcer with a forceful delivery, it may be advisable to let your announcer make a straight, sincere presentation and use few, if any, props.

Types of Commercials

Like all classifications, this one is arguable. Should you, for example, have a classification for hard sell or soft sell? Should there be an "image" classification? What about "emotional" commercials or "reason-why"? And can you really classify some commercials, such as the ones most commonly seen for soft drinks that feature young people cavorting madly about on beaches, ski slopes, or other locations? Should there be a humor classification?

As you look over the following list, you will see that most commercials will fall into these types. Some will be combinations of types. For those commercials not fitting into a type listed, just make up your own "other" list.

- Straight sell
- Stand-up or celebrity presenter
- Dramatization
- Demonstration
- Testimonial (or endorsement)
- Copy put to music (the jingle)

Straight Sell

This is a very common type of commercial because it affords so much creative freedom. The script is delivered by an offscreen announcer, also referred to as an announcer voiceover. The visuals are limited only by your imagination, focusing on the product or another type of action.

The announcer voiceover can be a man, a woman, a child, or a character voice (for instance, Morris the Cat). The voiceover can give us straight copy points, employ humor, tell a story, affect an accent, or lend great drama to the reading. The treatment is decided and directed by the copywriter and/or producer.

Usually, the straight sales pitch will be delivered in a sincere manner at not too fast a pace. Exceptions are mail-order commercials that use an excited, rapid-fire delivery that comes to a climax with a strong urge to act immediately to take advantage of the offer.

Stand-up or Celebrity Presenter

The stand-up presenter is an announcer who is on-camera for part or all of the commercial explaining product features. Some of the most effective of these are delivered by well-known figures in the sports or entertainment worlds. They become spokespeople for a company's products or services, such as Bill Cosby for Jell-O or George C. Scott for Renault. Such people must be believable, articulate, and forceful.

At times such performers may not work from a rigid, conventional script but, with a minimum of guidance, work from a fact sheet that allows them to develop their video action and audio style in accordance with their entertainment personalities. There should be some guidance, however, for a celebrity presenter may well overshadow the product. The presenter must be at home with the product or service, such as Cosby, whose child-like sense of fun works perfectly with a children's treat. In contrast, George C. Scott's authoritative, no-nonsense air lends credibility to Renault's selling points. Athletes who endorse athletic products achieve the same credibility, but they don't always succeed for products with which they would not naturally be associated.

Other good presenters are second-flight celebrities, such as cooking authorities who tout food products. Sometimes, through heavy exposure, a noncelebrity presenting a product becomes so well-known that he or she becomes a celebrity of sorts, such as Madge for Palmolive or Lee Iacocca for Chrysler.

Your special task in celebrity commercials is to provide audio that is suited to the celebrity. In doing so, the celebrity will appear on the home screen as natural and likable, two qualities absolutely necessary for credibility. For your own peace of mind, you should ascertain whether the celebrity actually uses the product being advertised. The law says he or she should.

Finally, if the celebrity is a comedian and the commercial is humorous, let the humor be at the expense of the performer, not the product. Let the performer make a fool of himself or herself, but don't poke fun at the product.

CLIFF ROBERTSON (VO): We're that neighbor who's always ready to lend a helping hand.

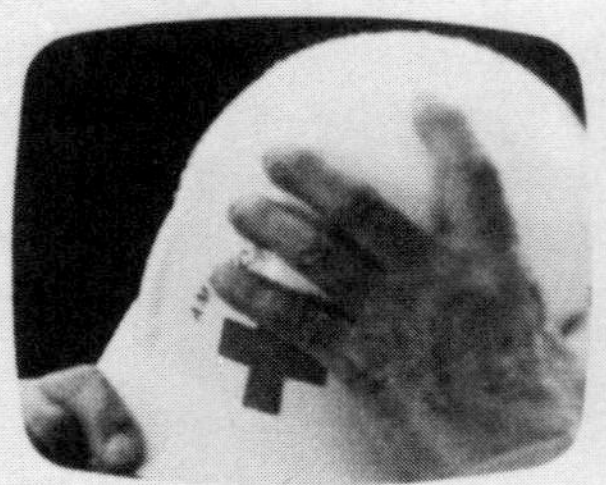

We help when disaster strikes.

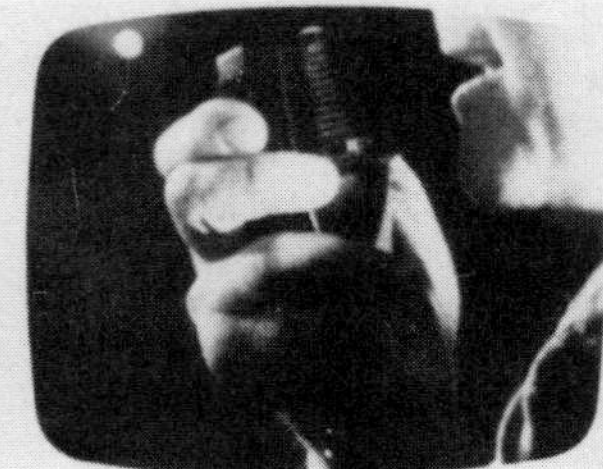

During fires, floods,

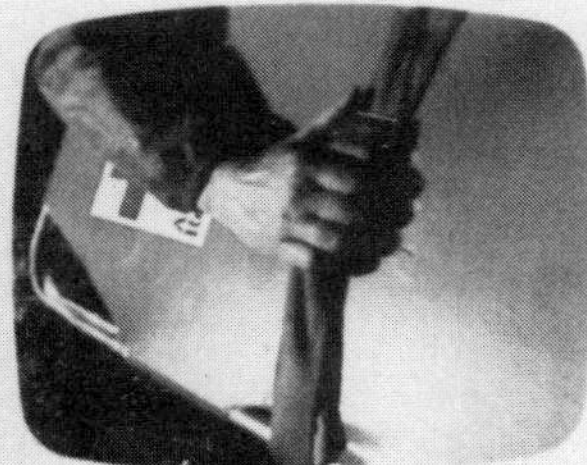

hurricanes and tornadoes.

We help with food, clothing, health care and a place to stay.

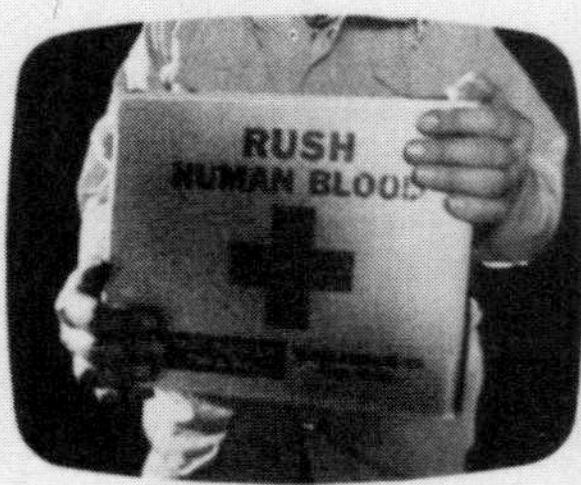

We help when folks need blood.

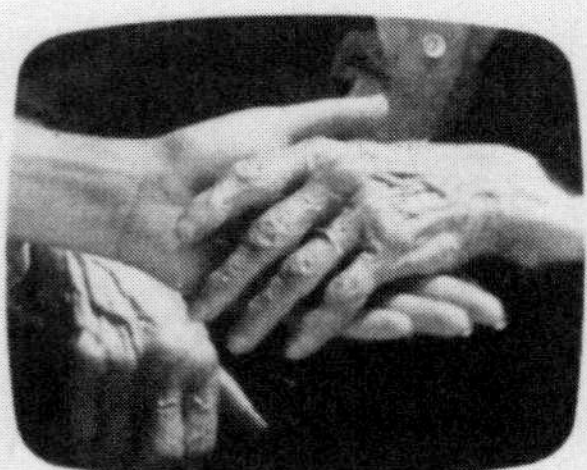

We help the elderly.

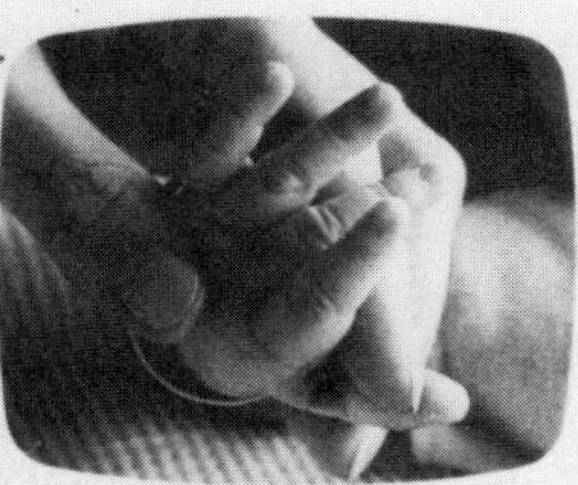

We help expectant parents prepare for their baby.

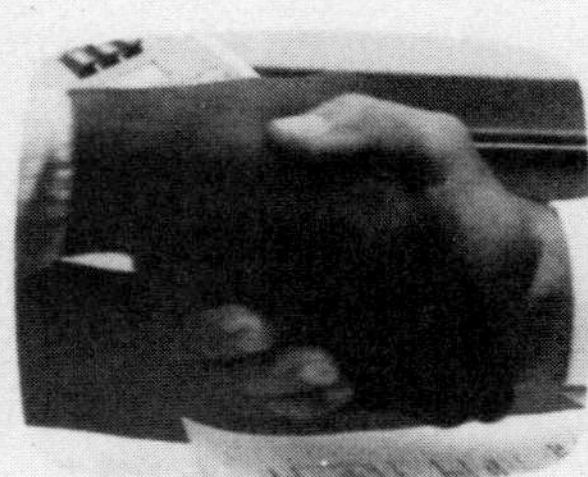

We help veterans get their benefits.

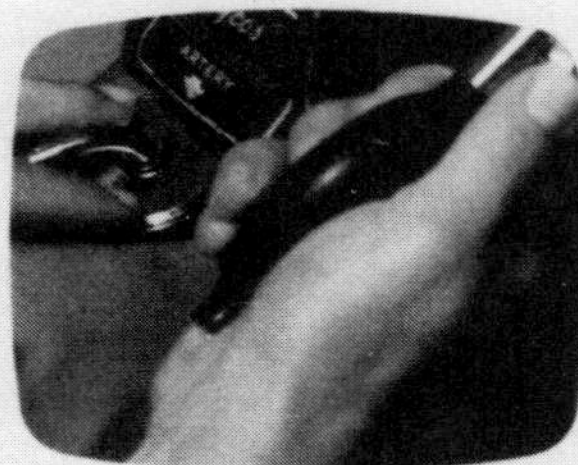

We'll teach you how to check blood pressure.

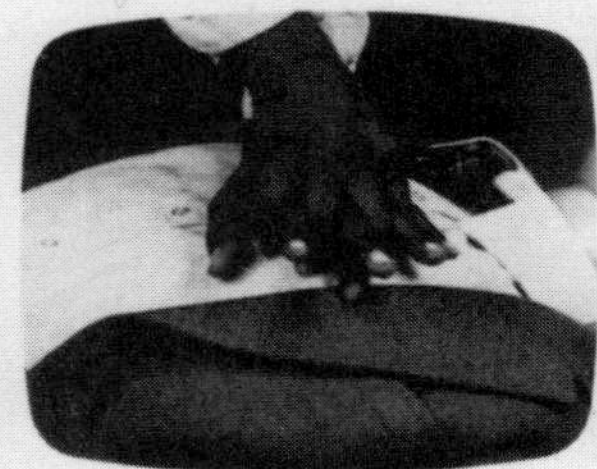

We'll teach you CPR . . . swimming . . .

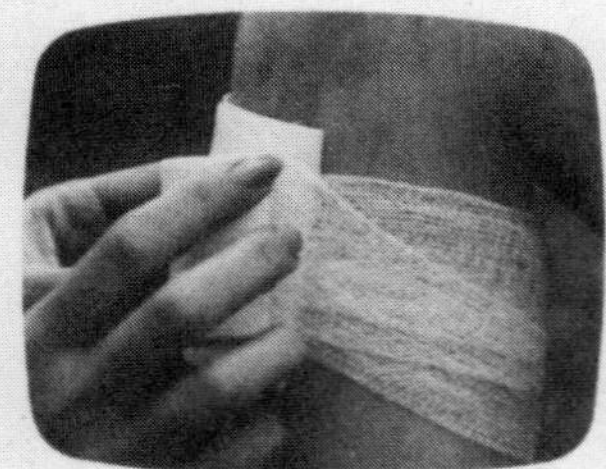

and first aid.

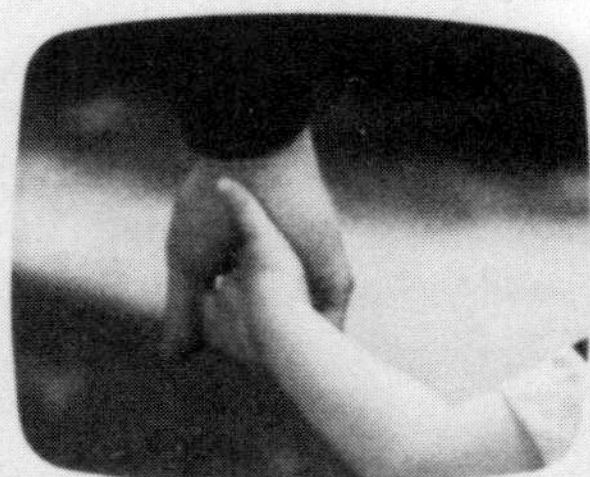

We'll help you learn how to take better care of yourself and your family.

We're the American Red Cross. People, helping people.

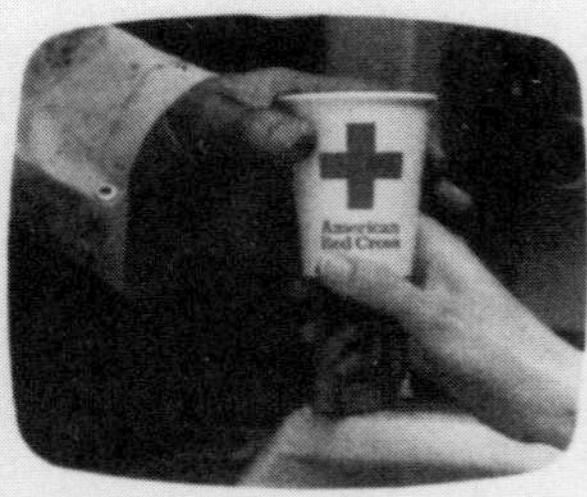

Everyone working together to improve things in your community.

That's what Red Cross exists for. Join Red Cross. We'll help. Will you?

Figure 20–2. Personality salesperson commercial.
Courtesy of the Advertising Council.

Dramatizations

Akin to personality commercials, dramatizations are most often used on comedy, musical, and dramatic programs.

Slice-of-life commercials—those hated, yet effective, presentations—are a form of dramatized commercial. Dramatized commercials can be humorous, serious, complex, or simple. They are distinguished by the fact that participants in the commercial play roles—mothers, fathers, friends, athletes, neighbors. Their value is that they are so wide-ranging that they give you limitless opportunities for promoting your product or service.

As you ponder the different types of commercials presented in this list, you'll soon realize that the dramatized commercial will often be a combination of all the types, with the possible exception of the straight sales pitch—and even that can at times be combined. In short, dramatization is the very essence of television commercials because, in a sense, most commercials are little playlets. That is another reason why some sort of acting or drama background is useful to television commercial writers.

It is easy in dramatized commercials to make characters phony, exaggerated, and wholly unbelievable, especially in the slice-of-life commercials seen on so many daytime serials. Danger lies in the fact that dialogue and facial expressions are artificial. Enthusiasm is *too* enthusiastic and the reactions and audio are too predictable. The world is about ready for conversations about products between two women, or between husbands and wives, that are not filled with bright, silly patter never heard in a normal household. Perhaps you can introduce the new era of "normal" commercials.

Demonstrations

There are several kinds of demonstrations that can be used as part or all of a given commercial:

- *Product versatility,* to acquaint viewers with new and interesting uses.
- *Product in use,* to show how it works, what it does.
- *Before-and-after,* to prove results in use.
- *Extreme example,* to dramatize proof of quality, as in Timex watch commercials that subjected a watch to rugged treatment to prove it "takes a licking and keeps on ticking." Torture tests on proving grounds likewise aim to prove superiority of one make of automobile over another.
- *Competitive tests,* to show superiority over competitor, as in various washing or sudsing tests that seek to show that one brand of soap or detergent produces whiter washes.

Demonstration commercials rely heavily on film-tape production in order to cover periods of time necessary to illustrate points of superiority in use. The full application of a home permanent can be filmed or taped and then simply edited to required length, showing key sales points. Film and tape also permit use of split screens and other optical devices to lend additional impact and drama to before-and-after and competitive-test commercials of the demonstration type.

In recent years, the Federal Trade Commission has insisted that product demonstrations be literally true. In the past, in contrast, glycerine was substituted for ice cream because the latter melted before scenes could be shot. Under the new rules, if the product being advertised is ice cream, then ice cream must be used in the scene, not a nonmelting substitute. This means that the ice cream must be kept cold until the last seconds before shooting, and then rushed on to the set for a quick shot.

Such literalness has greatly increased the cost of shooting many commercials. Copywriters writing for television must keep in mind this requirement of literal honesty in every product demonstration they call for. This is in contrast to television's earlier days, when a maker of glass for auto windows demonstrated the clarity of the product by removing the windows. This supposedly gave the viewer a true idea of just what it was like to be looking through an auto window using the advertiser's glass. The courts, ruling against the advertiser, said that future commercials must use the window glass.

At one time, because of the difficulty of showing many products on television, production shortcuts were taken and given legal approval. Those days are gone. Write accordingly.

Testimonials (or Endorsements)

Commercials in which screen stars, sports heroes, and prominent figures from all walks of life are used as salespeople are a proven type of commercial. The main concern in this type of commercial is to avoid staginess and artificiality. A viewer is all too ready to disbelieve the words of your prominent personality unless you phrase the message in comfortable, conversational language that fits your star salesperson. Keep the testimonial brief, natural, and believable, for even professional actors are not always capable of adjusting to selling roles.

Similar precautions must be observed in testimonials, reactions, or opinions featuring satisfied users or so-called passers-by in the interview type of testimonial commercial. Don't ask these obviously ordinary people to speak complicated and unreal-sounding advertising phrases in praise of your product. It simply will not be swallowed by your viewers.

Exercise care in the casting of these commercials, too, if you have a voice in the matter. Try to use people who are not too beautiful or handsome, but who have faces with character that can quickly win over viewers. In television, there is not always time for viewers to take their eyes off the attractive face and get in step with your message. Use familiar, comfortable settings well within the experience of the viewers, so they do not have to reorient their minds to an unusual setting before grasp-

ANNCR: Trying to please every single taste

with one frozen vegetable

...can be a big waste!

Trying to please

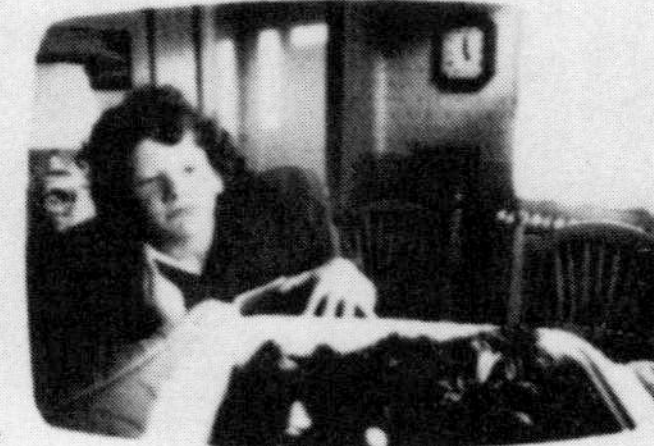
every single

schedule

with one frozen vegetable

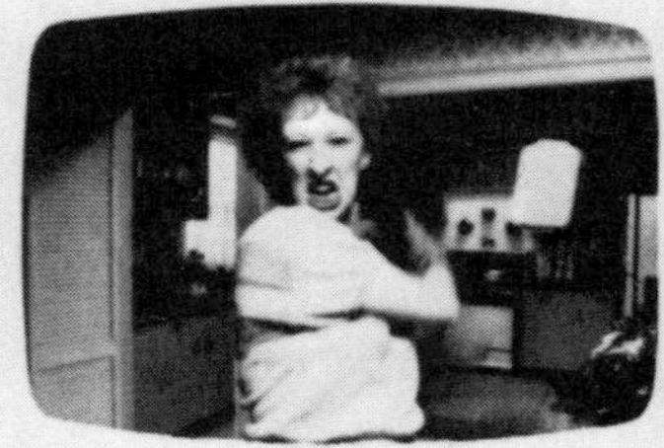
...can be a big waste too!

But new Stokely's Singles®,

14 <u>different</u> single-serve frozen vegetables

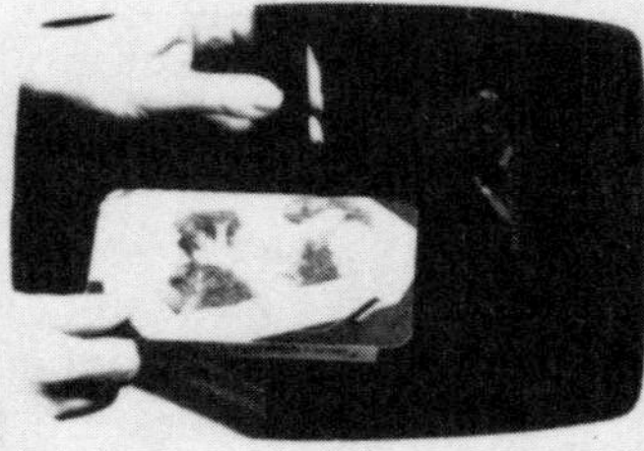
that cook in their own containers

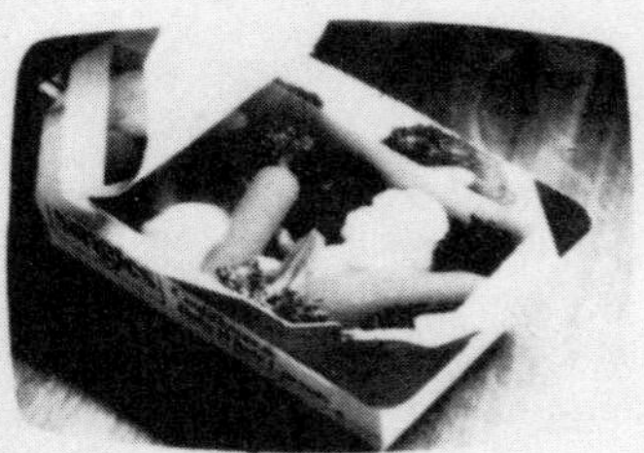
...can be a big help. Without the big waste.

Because with Stokely's Singles®...

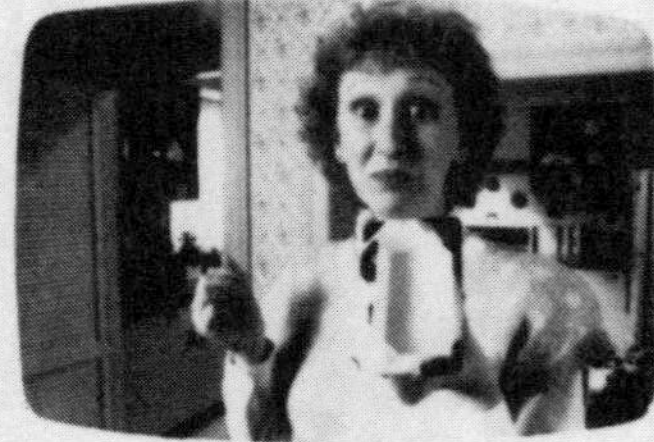
all you throw away is this.

Stokely's Singles® For every single taste, every single time!™

SF-87-9

Figure 20–3. Dramatized television commercial.

YOUNG & RUBICAM NEW YORK

CLIENT: AT&T COMMUNICATIONS
PRODUCT: OUTBOUND RESIDENCE
TITLE: "MY SISTER DELIA"

LENGTH: 30 SECONDS
COMM. NO.: AXOR-7823
DATE: APRIL 10, 1987

ALICE: Last night, my little sister Delia called me from New York and said "Guess what Alice,

hemlines are going up this year!"

Well, I do have the legs for a short skirt, but braving the winters of Toronto wearing a mini is not my idea of a good time.

When Delia calls on Wednesday, I'll tell her she musn't be such a slave to fashion.

V.O.: Only AT&T keeps you this close anywhere in the world.

AT&T International Long Distance.

Figure 20–4. Live action testimonial commercial. In this AT&T international long-distance television commercial, we have successful ingredients: Emotion. A personal quality. Believability.

ing your message. If your commercial is filmed or taped, get enough footage of a particular interview to catch facets of personality and unexpected conversational phrases that no prepared script could ever conjure up for the nonprofessional performer. Subsequent editing can then cull the highlights of the interview for commercial use.

When you prepare a testimonial or endorsement commercial, keep a fearful eye on all the legal bodies ready to pounce if you stray from the legal restrictions—and there are many. Ways to stay out of trouble when writing such commercials are detailed in the legal chapter. Read the advice carefully, because no type of commercial causes more legal difficulty than the testimonial commercial.

Copy Put to Music

This type of commercial lends a new avenue of creativity to the copywriter. Here, copy points are written in a lyric, or rhyming, form and set to music by a music production house. The accompanying visuals are quick vignettes. This type of commercial is usually fun and spirited and seeks to evoke an attractive image for the product, rather than going for a harder sell. It's often used when there isn't a clear-cut product differential.

Copywriters who enjoy poetry and the rhythm of language are best suited to writing lyrics. But anyone can give it a try. To get started, write the words from a melodically memorable popular song. Then use the rhyme scheme and meter as a guide to writing your jingle.

The music house will need an idea of the type of music you have in mind—country, rock, ballad, and so forth—along with information on the visuals and intended audience. These ideas help give the track the personality that you are striving for.

The most notable examples of jingles can be found in the breakfast cereal, automobile, and beverage categories. However, every type of product has used a jingle's warmth and memorability with success.

Animated Commercials

You'd be surprised how many times you'll have to answer "no" to animation as the best possible method for advertising your product.

If you're undecided about using animation as opposed to demonstration, use demonstration if your product has to be demonstrated for full sales effectiveness. Don't substitute cuteness for sales impact. If you decide that animation is the right method for the job, keep the following creative elements of the technique in mind:

Product character or trademark. Animation should fit the trademark or trade character naturally, without being forced. If your character is a Disney-type cartoon—full-animation drawing with rounded lines, full shading, and natural features—it won't fit well with a highly stylized, modern art treatment. Work with your producer to develop animation characters that will save you time and money and that are well suited to the story you want to tell.

Setting and staging. Keep it simple and inexpensive, yet effective, for setting and staging for animation are as important as for live-action films. Your message is on the screen only briefly, so give your cartoon characters and product full attention by eliminating distracting backgrounds. Use simple lines, for instance, to denote cabinets for a kitchen scene. Staging is as important as background, so if your action can take place in one location, don't have characters chasing through many different scenes. If you want special effects such as opticals that make products glow, sparkle, or change, write them into your original storyboards. Extra production charges are added if you want to work them in later.

Movement of characters. Try to keep the movements of animated characters similar to those of a human being in the same situation. Remember that movement in animation should be exaggerated to be appreciated by viewers. Be sure they see that your character's wink is a wink, that a look of surprise is *very* surprised, lest these pieces of action be missed. Allow sufficient time for the movement to be grasped by viewers. Try to plan your animated spots rather loosely so that there is time for little bits of side action that can give your commercial added interest and longer life.

Copy and narration. Consider the soundtrack of your commercial as consisting of two parts: the voice or narrative, and the music and sound effects. The best animated spots are written with a maximum of 40 to 50 words, rather than the 60 to 70 live-action count. This leaves room for the previously mentioned bits of action that can enhance your effort. Give your character time to speak effectively, and write copy to fit the character's intended voice, rather than try to bend a character to fit copy.

Music and sound effects. These lend mood, action, tone, and emphasis that can "make" your animated commercial. If you are using offbeat or stylized art treatment, make the music suitable. Be sure the tempo of the music blends with your type of animation. Sound effects give impact and originality to your spot. If you want them, be sure to leave enough time for them in your script. They seldom fit when you try to squeeze them in later.

Timing the entire spot. It is difficult to time an animated commercial because of the need to consider copy, music, and action. There's no surefire solution, but one of the safest approaches is to act out the commercial in its entirety.

Product package and logotype. With simple handling, animation (and stop-action photography) can do great

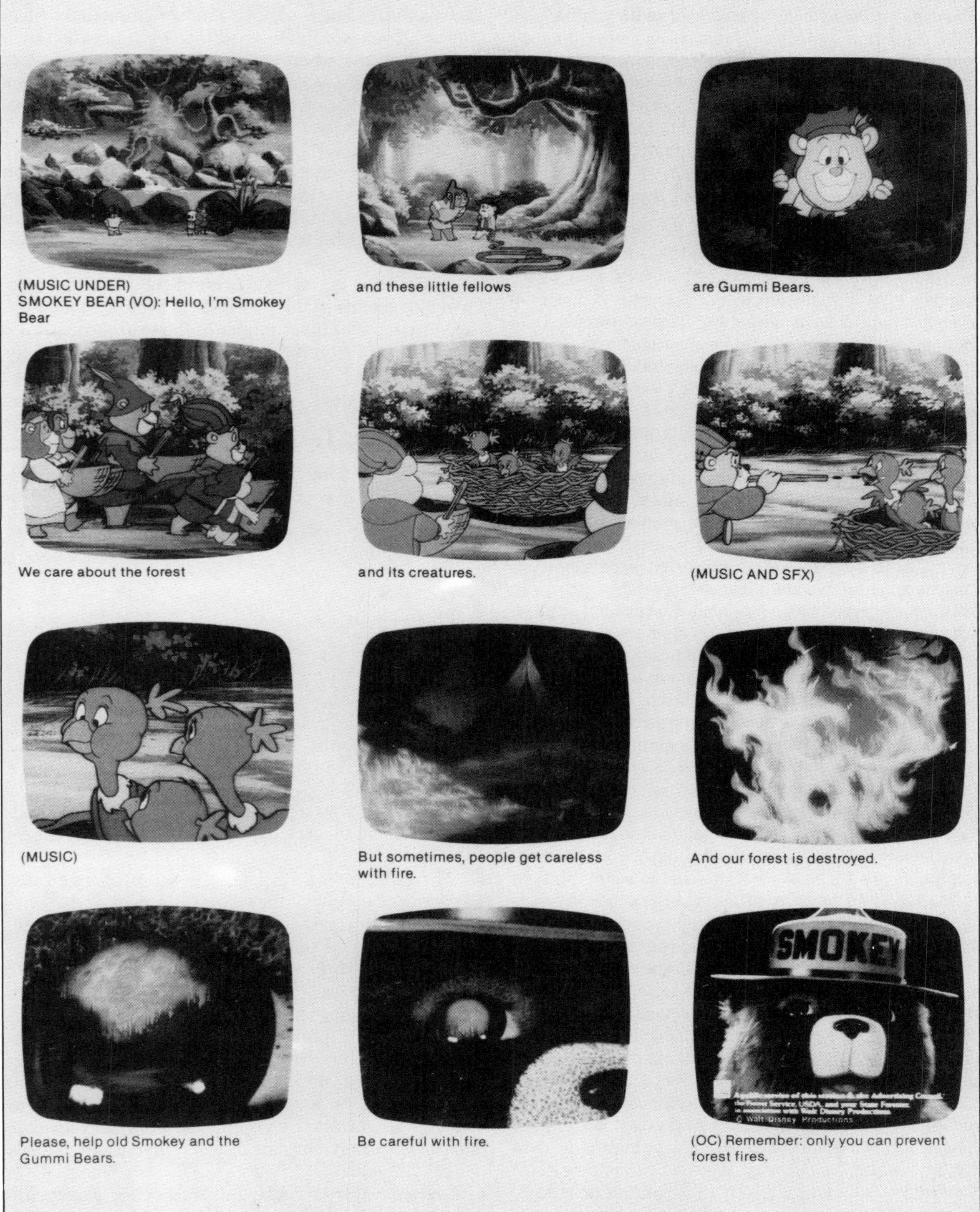

Figure 20–5. Cartoon commercial. By the use of the appealing Smokey the Bear, viewer interest and involvement are more likely than if live action had been used for this forest fire prevention message.

Courtesy of the Advertising Council.

things for your package or product. If your package has illustrations that are not in character with your style of animation, use artwork representation rather than the real package. You can use a matching dissolve from the artwork to the real package or logotype at the end of the spot. Emphasize important features of your package by bringing the elements off the box to full screen, as with a logotype that bounces off the package and then back on.

Animation and Live Action for Best Results

It is the consensus of almost all those who have worked with animation over a long period that the all-cartoon commercial should be approached with caution, for its promise generally outruns its performance. A danger of pure animation is its over-commitment to entertainment at the cost of sacrificing copy ideas. Viewer are beguiled into enjoyment without being sold. Judicious use, however, of *animation in conjunction with live action* has much to recommend it.

There are two basic types of this hybrid commercial: (a) an opening animated segment (often comic or clever but containing the germ of the product story) followed with a live straight sell; and (b) a straightforward sales presentation that moves into animation after a live opening, usually to illustrate a product's "reason-why" story. The first type is best exemplified by commercials that use an animated character with a catchy jingle as an opening, then move into live-action scenes of the product in use. The second hybrid type is exemplified by those commercials for patent remedies that employ diagrammatic views of visceral plumbing to illustrate the nature of their internal action. In either case, the flexibility of the live-plus-animated commercial allows the advertiser to blend exaggerated hyperbole or humor with naturalistic demonstration, thus charming while also selling the viewer.

Combining live action and animation is effective, but it can be expensive. An economical method is to use animated characters over still-photo shots of your product, creating the depth of live action with the adaptability of animation. Another way of reducing expense is to use the same segment of animation to open or close an entire series of film spots. This lets you use your budget for animation of better quality or for more spots.

In trying to determine whether to use "live-on-film" or animated commercials for your particular product, there are some general considerations you'll recognize as helpful. Food products normally lend themselves better to television presentation with live action. Realism, which can be gained by showing real people preparing and enjoying meals, will almost always sell better than the cartoon characters with whom people cannot identify. Sales points of a new car, likewise, can best be demonstrated by actually showing a real person driving it, rather than showing drawings of the car. Cosmetic selling usually needs the realism of beautiful people whose hair, lips, complexion, and overall charm cannot possibly be captured in animation.

On the other hand, many times you will be selling a service instead of a branded product. Sometimes when doing so, you can expect more memorability and attention if you invent an animated character to tell your story. Insurance selling, gasoline advertising, and bank and loan association commercials all lend themselves to the use of animation.

Some relatively new offshoots of animation are pixillation and claymation. Pixillation uses stop-motion photographs—for example, of a live actor; they are shot one frame at a time. The material can be combined with a nonverbal sound track, if desired. The result is an unusual look.

Claymation is clay figures photographed in progressive movements so that when set to film the figures appear lifelike. The most notable example of claymation is the "I heard it through the grapevine" commercial for the California Raisin Board.

Production Techniques

Following are some basic production techniques that may be used if your commercials are to be taped or filmed:

- Live action
- Cartoon
- Stop motion
- Photo animation

Live Action

Similar to human, personal experience, live action is the most believable technique in television commercials. Viewers can identify with the action on the screen and relate your commercial message to their own experience. While cartoons are figments of a fantasy world, and stop-motion and photo animation are products of camera trickery, live action has the quality of genuine reality.

There are two main types of live-action commercials: (a) narrative style with the voices off-screen; and (b) dialogue style with one or more persons speaking on screen, to each other or to the audience.

Narrative style is less expensive, yet it has longer life expectancy because the speaker or speakers are not seen repeating the same story over and over, and thereby suffering loss of credibility. Narrative live action lends itself best to *demonstration,* to display the product in use, with a voice presenting the sales story from off-screen; *exposition,* to set a scene quickly; *human interest,* to show family or other emotional settings; and *appetite appeal,* to exhibit tempting dishes, with the announcer's voice off-screen.

Dialogue has particular advantages for *personality commercials,* in which a name star or well-known announcer does the selling job; *testimonials* by actual users; *key copylines* spoken by an actor as one part of a longer commercial.

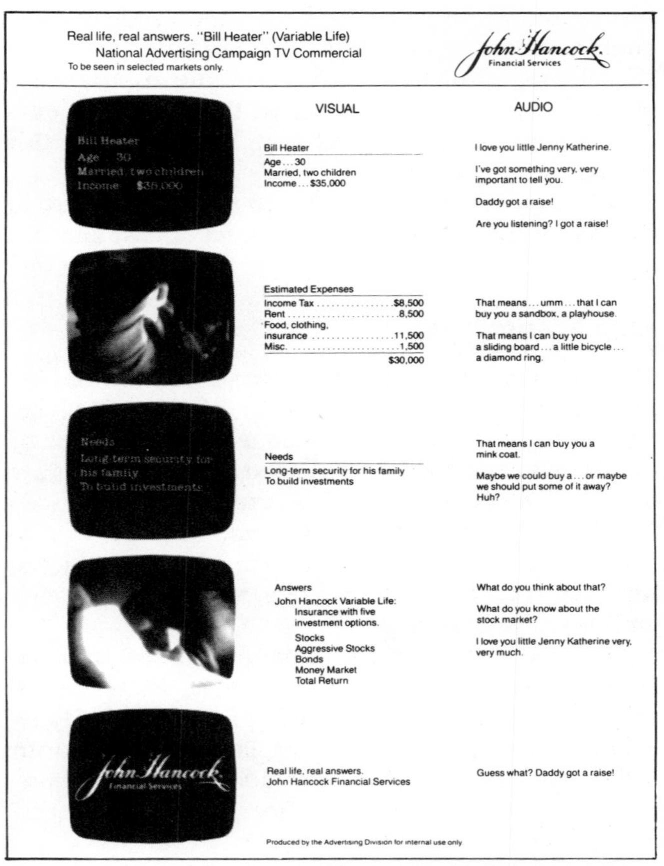

Figure 20–6a. Dramatization commercial using live action. Although there is a strong emotional approach in this commercial, it still contains much information that provides a strong sell for the product. Figure 20–6b is a print version of the same approach—an effective marriage of print and television.

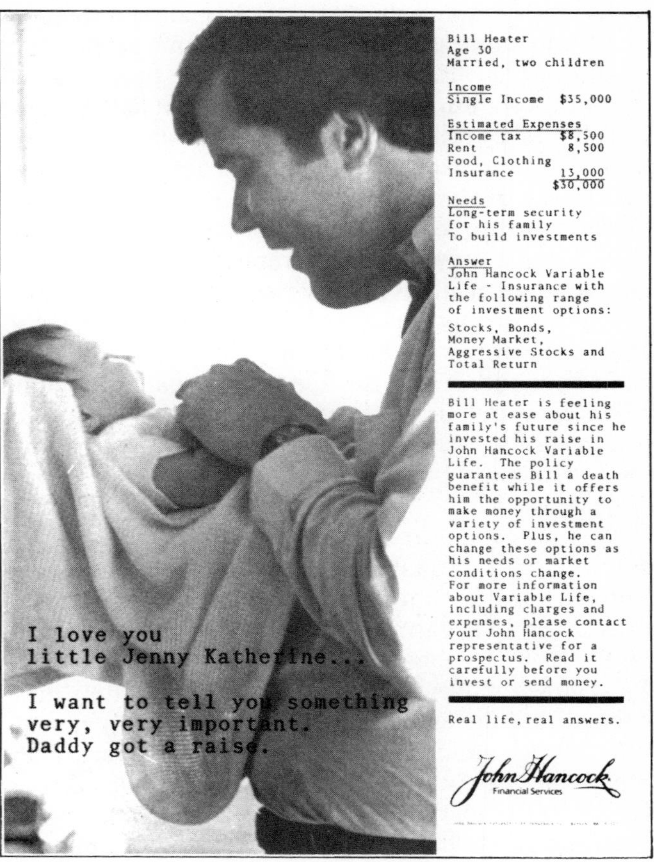

Figure 20–6b. Advertisement with emotional approach. An effective technique is used in this print version of the television commercial shown earlier. One, use emotion in illustration and headline to engage reader interest. Two, having captured interest, follow up in the body copy with a strong, rational story. It is difficult to be emotional throughout an advertisement. The combination of the emotional-rational is a solution.

The cost of live-action films, narrative or dialogue, varies a great deal because of the many factors involved: cast, settings, props, location trips, and so forth. Here again the matter of the SAG code and residual fees to talent used in live-action commercials has tended to switch some advertisers to other techniques. To move away from live action is not always wise, for its basic reality and faculty for reaching out to meet the viewer on common ground makes live action the most useful technique in television commercials.

Cartoon

The cartoon is fun. It is high in viewer interest and it is probably lowest in cost per showing. While it wins interest quickly, it nonetheless lacks depth of penetration because it sacrifices credibility. Because viewers enjoy cartoons but may not be sold or persuaded by them, experienced advertisers will often follow the cartoon segment of their commercials with real people using the product and repeating its benefits.

Cartoons are most effective for *gaining interest* at the opening of a spot by presenting some whimsical or fantastic situation, or an unusual character; *trademark characters,* either the actual company or product trademark or one devised for purposes of a given campaign; *personalizing the product,* whereby a can of wax takes on life and personality with a cartoon face; *fantasy,* which enables just about any character or thing to do just about any type of action—an exercise in exaggeration to stimulate the imagination; *singing jingles,* because bouncy rhythms and cartoons are naturals that comprise one of television's longest-lived types of commercials.

There are three grades among cartoons: full animation, limited animation, and "grow" or "scratch-off" cartoon, in order of decreasing cost and effectiveness. Cost depends largely on what moves in your cartoon, since as many as seven artists may work on each frame of a full-animation cartoon. At 24 frames per second, this means as many as 1,440 drawings may be needed for a one-minute spot. It thus behooves you to use no more characters than absolutely necessary in your commercial and to work closely with your animation director to make maximum use of cycles of the same sequence of pictures wherever possible, especially for backgrounds.

A limited animation, which costs about half as much as full, makes full use of cycles, often shows only extremes of facial expression, and relies heavily on camera movement and lens tricks.

The grow cartoon cuts costs in two again. It works with a single drawing, photographed from the rear as lines are scratched off on successive frames. When projected in the opposite direction, the cartoon seems to grow, or be drawn on the screen.

Cartoons are honest fun and, as such, can do a selling job for impulse-purchase types of products. Where there is substantial reason-why for the purchaser to buy, cartoons need support from live action, as previously discussed.

Making the hundreds of drawings necessary to depict movement in animated commercials has always required a huge amount of expensive art time. Just having a character lift her arm above her head can, for instance, entail many drawings because each drawing depicts only the slightest movement upward. Now computers have stepped into the art and can be used to supply the detailed drawings for certain types of animation. They don't replace artists, but they relieve them of the tedious line-by-line renderings of animated movement.

Cartoon characters don't age so fast as live players. Thus, live-action film commercials are usually given a maximum life of twenty-six weeks, whereas an animated series can run three years or more. Furthermore, while these are used on television, the animated characters can be used in other media such as transit advertising, window displays, and point of purchase.

Animated characters get no residuals, don't get old, don't demand more money, don't strike, don't switch jobs, and don't die. Little wonder that they have appeal to advertisers.

In addition, they can serve so many special purposes and appeal to such a wide range of ages and types. They are preeminent in achieving the light touch, humor, and sell—as in the following audio for a margarine.

FIRST COW:	"Holy cow!"
SECOND COW:	"Gracious sakes!"
THREE COWS:	"Guess what comes from Land O'Lakes! Margarine! Butter folks at Land O'Lakes know the difference flavor makes. Taste Land O'Lakes margarine now! Land O'Lakes margarine on baked potatoes, on any dish . . . moooooo-ie!"

Sometimes cartoon animation solves a problem too difficult for live action, such as animation used by an advertiser to show how a hair groomer works on the hair—a visualization difficulty that was too complex for conventional photography.

Another advertiser, a baking soda manufacturer, resorted to animation to show how the product killed odors arising from kitty litter. Because kitty litter is not visually appealing in photographs, animation was selected over live film. Furthermore, the subject was handled in a lighthearted way by having two cats discuss this special use of baking soda.

Consequently, a subject that could be distasteful in live-action film was presented without offense and in a memorable way.

Stop Motion

The ingenious technique that makes inanimate objects come to life is stop motion. This type of animation is accomplished by using a camera adjusted to move one or two frames at a time. Between exposures the objects are moved slightly or changed. The result is continuous action when projected at normal speed.

Stop action should be confined to inanimate objects, since actors cannot remain in one position long enough for this type of shooting.

The technique provides an impressive way to introduce packaged products. For example, a number of packages shown unevenly spaced on a table suddenly assemble themselves into a neat display. The scene cuts to a closeup, then one package unwraps itself and out hops the product. Automobile doors open and close by themselves, or packages march across the screen.

The advantages offered by stop motion relate to *personalizing the product,* as in the marching packages or other products that are made to fly, dance, walk, zoom, or take themselves apart; *mechanical action,* as in fitting parts of a motor or showing how attachments are used on appliances; and *demonstration,* without human hands, as in a commercial showing a wall oven that opens itself and a roast slides out. In the first of these advantages, stop motion shares with cartoons the ability to personalize a product, while in the last it vies with live action in its faculty for demonstration. It seems advisable here, too, to combine stop motion with a follow-up live action, pairing up the interest-rouser with the realistic demonstration.

Stop motion is expensive because each second of picture requires twenty-four shots. Furthermore, because of this minute movement, it is difficult to know how the footage will flow until a viewing takes place.

An outstanding example of stop-motion production is the television advertising for the Pillsbury Doughboy. This roly-poly character is used in all television commercials and print advertisements for Pillsbury brand refrigerated dough products and flour. So great has been his consumer appeal that he has become a symbol and company spokesman for Pillsbury in the United States, Canada, and Europe.

Photo Animation

The technique that sends bottles spinning and boxes zooming across the televiewer's screen is photo animation. It is the method that the low-budget advertiser can use to excellent advantage to achieve impressive effects, largely through the camera's movement and optical tricks.

It has been called "Fotan" by many producers, and the technique lends itself best to *special announcements*, in which titles and tricks are the main elements, as in coming attractions for movies; *signatures* at the end of most commercials, in which the package, logotype, or slogan pops on to the screen, often in synchronization with voice copy; *retouching products*, as in appliances of chrome and glass, using still photographs which are then reproduced on motion picture film with dissolves or other optical tricks to achieve a dramatic effect; *catalog of products*, where an inclusive line of related items can be presented quickly, clearly, and, again, with startling pop-on effect.

Photo animation is not advisable for use with live action, for it works only with separate still photographs or drawings. To move an inanimate object in a live-action scene involves costly optical treatment.

An example of Fotan at work was shown on behalf of a liquidizer that made tomato juice out of tomatoes, coleslaw out of cabbage, and crushed ice out of ice cubes. Still photos of the original items were shown at top left of the screen. They moved in procession to the center and were whirled downward in the appliance and finally emerged at bottom right as completed dishes. Truly graphic!

Summary of Best Uses of Techniques

Live action (narrative) is best used for demonstration, human interest, and exposition.

Live action (dialogue) is best used for testimonials, personality commercials, dramatic spots, and key copylines.

Cartoon (full animation) is best used for developing trademark characters, personalizing products, exaggeration and fantasy, and singing jingles.

Stop motion is best used for demonstration, mechanical action, and personalizing product.

Photo animation is best used for titles and signatures, retouching products, and cataloging products.

FARM BUREAU LIFE INSURANCE
30 SECOND TV "Not Enough"

My husband Ron died about a year ago.

He left some great memories and a $50,000 life insurance policy.

We figured that would be enough to keep things just about the same as when Ron was working.

We were wrong

Ask your Farm Bureau agent to help you decide how much life insurance is enough for you.

Figure 20–7. Television commercial with a strong message.

Five Ways to Get Better Identification

A dismaying fact for the television advertiser is that a huge portion of the viewing audience cannot remember whose commercials they saw on a show they have watched night after night—this despite the millions poured into television advertising by the advertiser.

Only one viewer in five may be able to identify the sponsor of a show or the product advertised on it. Sometimes the figure goes even lower. Furthermore, in addition to lack of identification, there is *misidentification* wherein the viewer credits a competitor and names his product as the one advertised on a show. Thus, Post cereal may be identified as Kellogg's, or Goodrich as Goodyear.

What with television clutter offering a profusion of 15- and 30-second commercials, billboards, promos, local program break spots, and public service commercials, it's no surprise that the viewer is hazy about who is advertising what product.

As the writer, what can you do to improve the showing for your client? First, of course, you use a strong selling idea in the commercial. In addition, following are some devices and approaches that may help memorability and sponsor or product identification.

- **Avoid themes too much like your competitor's.** This is especially true if your product is not the leader in the field. Any confusion about the identity of the advertiser tends strongly to result in the leader being remembered, not the runnerup.
- **Establish a strong campaign theme.** When you know the theme is good, fight to keep it going. When advertisers change a campaign theme, they risk confusion and throw away the recognition they have built up. With confusion comes lack of identification or misidentification.
- **Use a strong presenter for the product.** A likable, believable presenter can do wonders for product identification if used consistently over a long period of time, especially if the presenter puts on an interesting demonstration of the product.

  After a while, the name of the presenter and your product are automatically linked—a link that becomes even stronger if you use the presenter in print copy, too. A possible danger in using a strong presenter is that the audience will remember the presenter, not the product, because of interest in the presenter. Careful creative work, however, can avoid the problem.
- **Use powerful demonstrations.** There's good memorability in a realistic demonstration, much more so than a mere relating of product facts. Watch out for comparative demonstrations, however, because if your product is being demonstrated against the leader's product, his product may be credited with your product's better performance.

  Comparative advertising is, in fact, a dangerous technique that can turn on you. If your demonstration has great strength in itself, you may not wish to risk a comparative demonstration.
- **Make the product-name registration strong.** Use techniques that enable you to bring in the name emphatically and frequently, not just in the opening and close. Likewise, the more you can keep your product on camera, the better for identification.

  Weaving the product and product name (and package) into commercials is a particular talent of Stan Freberg, whose humorous commercials have sold great quantities of his clients' products. Without diminishing interest or humor, he works in the name of the advertiser's product frequently—as in one commercial that showed a theater of people shouting the name of the product as it was flashed on the screen. No television viewer could fail to know what product was advertised in *that* commercial.

  As part of registering the name, try usually to end with an urge to action. Good planning can make the action ending a natural conclusion, but many writers seem to feel that the urge to do something is a jarring note that upsets the artistic balance of the commercial. Remember, however, from the *advertising* standpoint, the registration of your product name and/or package at the end of the commercial is the most powerful conclusion—much better than merely being cute.

Other Techniques for Emphasis

- Call for close-ups to be more vivid and personal—and do it quickly. If you start with an establishing shot, use it for only a few seconds.
- Develop your video first. If you write the audio before the video, you're simply writing a radio commercial with pictures and thus chancing a loss of the inherent drama in a commercial that emphasizes the visual.
- Use superimposition when you want reinforcement. The "super" should be used sparingly, but when it is, you'll increase the impact by saying in the audio the words flashed on the screen. Limit the number of words on the screen.
- Occasionally use the split screen to hold attention. A two-way split is easier for the viewer to follow, but the four-way split can be an attention-getter.

Questions to Ask about the Commercial You've Written

Before concluding this chapter, it may be profitable to imagine that you have a finished television commercial script in front of you. How can you size up its potential? Its creative worth? Its practicability from a production standpoint? Following are a few telegraphic queries on areas of your commercial that have been discussed in this chapter, and that you'll do well to remember while reading and evaluating the scripts which you may be writing.

You now know that nobody can tell you *exactly* how to write a television commercial. Nobody can tell you exactly what to say or what to show. These are things that can come to you only with time and experience. In this chapter you have been given an idea of what you will be expected to know about television-commercial writing and, to a lesser extent, production.

Remember, however, that as television improves technically and creatively, the scope of your activities in the field will broaden and the challenge to your resources will be greater. Only by increasing its effectiveness can the television commercial pay the ever increasing bill. This will increase your responsibility considerably.

Questions

- Does the video tell the story without audio, and how well?
- Is the video fully graphic (specifying technique, describing staging and camera action)?
- Does the audio "listen" well (language, pacing)?
- Do the audio and video complement each other and are they correctly timed for each other (act it out)?
- Are there too many scenes (can some be omitted)? Do you need *more* scenes?
- Have you identified the product well?
- Does your script win attention quickly and promise an honest benefit?
- Have you "demonstrated"?
- Have you provided a strong visualization of the one major claim that will linger in the viewer's memory?
- Could a competitive brand be substituted easily and fit well? (better not.)
- Is it believable? (*always* ask this.)
- Are you proud to say you wrote it?

Camera Shots

Sooner or later, if you work in television you must learn to distinguish between the various distances represented by the terms "long shot," "closeup," and others. There's no precision in these terms in the sense of their being defined as a definite number of feet. The following guide makes particular reference to the package so often the central object in television commercials:

- **Tight closeup (TCU).** Camera brings viewer so close detail is startling—perhaps a portion of a package, such as the product name, or trademark. Often used for this purpose. Depending upon where you work, might also be called ECU (Extreme closeup) or VCU (Very closeup).
- **Closeup (CU).** Here you zero in on an object, or part of an object. Instead of just the product name, as in the TCU, you get the entire package in the camera's eye. Instead of just the lips of a person, you get the whole face, or possibly head and shoulders. Extraneous details are omitted in the closeup.
- **Medium closeup (MCU).** You draw back from the closeup. You still see the package, but you also see that it's on a table with a mixing bowl and other items. As the viewer, you sense that the package is important, but you see it in relation to other objects.
- **Medium shot (MS).** The package loses some of its importance in this shot in which some details are lost as if the viewer had backed up a few feet from the MCU position. He sees the MCU objects, but now he may see them in relation to people in the spot.
- **Medium long shot (MLS).** You're close enough to recognize characters but far enough back to include items in the setting (such as the package) and to convey some of the background setting.
- **Long shot (LS).** Often this is called an "establishing" shot. It might include barely recognizable people, along with an entire room setting, but the package is now just one of many objects and may not even be noticed. The long shot, used outdoors, may be panoramic in its showing of trees, a portion of a lake, and people who may be discerned as individuals.
- **Extreme long shot (ELS).** As a panoramic shot this can take in a vast expanse of desert, mountains, or a whole lake. People can be detected but not as individuals. Again, like the long shot, this may be an establishing device to introduce dramatically what is to follow. Needless to say, we've lost our package entirely.

Glossary of Terms

Here are some of the terms used in preparing and producing a commercial. As you study them, keep in mind that this is a book about copywriting and not television production. For those interested, there are detailed texts on television production.

Across the board. A program scheduled three, five, or six days a week at the same time.

Ad lib. Impromptu action or speech not written into script; or, in music, to play parts not in the music.

Adjacencies. Shows (on same station) immediately preceding and following the program referred to.

ADR or **"looping."** Automatic dialogue replacement—when an actor re-records his (or another actor's) dialogue while looking at a motion picture projected to match lip movements. It is usually done to replace the defective on-camera sound.

AFM. American Federation of Musicians.

AFTRA. American Federation of Television and Radio Artists.

Angle shot. Camera shot of the subject taken from any position except straight.

Animate. To arrange and film static drawings or objects so that when the photographs are shown cinematographically, they produce the illusion of movement.

Answer print. The first composite print of a commercial. Included are the picture, voice track, music, opticals, etc. Although changes can be made in an answer print, they are costly.

APO or **"action print only."** Used to assess the optical work. There is no sound track on this film at this stage. It is not color-corrected.

ASCAP. American Society of Composers, Authors, and Publishers, which licenses public performances of music of its members and collects royalties.

Background or rear-view projection. Special technique whereby a wanted scene drawn from special photo or stock library is projected on a translucent screen which acts as a background for a studio set.

Back-time. To time a script backwards from end to beginning, with running time indicated every fifteen seconds or less in the margin of the script, to keep the show "on the nose."

Billboard. Announcement at the beginning of show which lists people starred or featured.

Bit. Small appearance or few lines in show. One who plays it is called a "bit player."

Blimp. A soundproof enclosure for a camera. This makes possible the recording of voices without the camera noise intruding.

BMI. Broadcast Music, Inc., competitors of ASCAP.

Boom. Crane-like device for suspending microphone or camera in mid-air and moving it from one position to another.

Bridge. Slide, picture, sound effects, or music used to cover a jump in time or other break in continuity.

Camera or cue light. Red light on front of camera which is lit only when camera is on the air.

Camera right-left. Indication of direction in a setting as viewed from the point of view of the camera or televiewer.

Camera shots. (Referring to people) Head shot, only the head; shoulder shot, shoulders and head; full shot, entire person. (Referring to objects) CU, closeup or narrow-angle picture limited to object or part of it; no background; MCU, medium closeup; TCU, tight closeup; LS, long shot in which figures are smaller than frame and sensation of distance is achieved; FoS, follow shot in which camera follows talent; RevS, reverse shot in which same object already on one camera is picked up from an exactly opposite angle by another camera; DI-DU, dolly in and up; DO-DB, dolly out and back.

Cell. An animation term for a transparent film with the drawing of a single frame. Movement is achieved by running a series of cells.

Clear a number. To get legal permission to use specific musical selection.

Cover shot. Wide-angle television picture to alternate (for contrast) with closeup.

Crane. Camera mount that makes possible camera movements vertically or horizontally.

Cut. Switch directly from one camera picture to another and speed up action for dramatic effect.

Dailies or rushes. All printed takes of a shoot.

D.B. Delayed broadcast of a live show.

Dissolve. Fading out of one picture as another fades in; to denote passage of time and present smooth sequence of shots.

Dolly. Movable fixture or carriage for carrying camera (and cameraman) about during taking of shots.

Double spotting. Also triple spotting. Station practice of placing a second or third commercial right after the first.

Down-and-under. Direction given to a musician or sound effects person to bring down playing level and sneak under dialogue lines that follow.

Dubbing. Mixing several sound tracks and recording them on a single film.

E.T. Electrical transcription, usually 33⅓ rpm's.

Fade. To diminish the brightness of the picture. Also can refer to diminishing of sound. A shot may fade into darkness, as in fade-out, or come from darkness into light—fade-in.

Fanfare. Few bars of music (usually trumpets) to herald start of show or commercial.

15 IPS. ¼″ audio tape recorded at 15 inches per sound (professional equipment).

Film mix. Blending of voice, music and sound effects on a single track.

Fluff. Any mistake, action, word or phrase accidentally included, resulting in an imperfect sound or picture.

Frame count. Counting the specific frames for music cues and supers.

Freeze-frame. A single frame is printed over and over again. This creates an effect of a scene being stopped in motion.

Hiatus. Summer period, usually weeks, during which sponsor may discontinue his program, but thereafter resume his time period until the next hiatus.

Highlight. Emphasizing a subject or scene by special lighting or painting to make it stand out from the rest of the picture.

Hook. Program device used to attract tangible response from the audience; for example, an offer, a contest, etc.

ID. TV station identification or call letters (or 10-second commercial).

Inherited audience. Portion of a program's audience that watched preceding show on same station.

Interlock. Technique of achieving synchronous presentation of picture and matching sound from separate films.

Interpositives (IP). An intermediate film step between original camera negative and the optical negative.

Jump cut. Cutting to the same scene without a change of angle or framing.

KEM. The state-of-the-art editing equipment found at most commercial editorial services.

Kill. To strike out or remove part or all of a scene, set, action, or show.

Lead-in. Words spoken by announcer or narrator at beginning of show or commercial to set a scene or recapitulate some previous action.

Limbo shot. Used in closeups where background is not important. Pictures are taken against a nonrecognized background.

Lip sync. Direct recording of sound from scene that is being filmed; usually refers to film commercials in which actors can be seen with lips moving.

Live. "On-the-spot" television of events or people in contrast to transmission of film, videotape, or kinescope material.

Local. Show or commercial originating in local station as contrasted to network.

Mag track. The magnetic tape in 35mm form used in editing and interlocks.

Make good. An offer to a sponsor of comparable facilities as substitute for TV show or announcement cancelled because of emergency; or offer to repeat a commercial, without charge for time, because of some mistake or faulty transmission.

Matte. Imposing a scene or title over another scene. In such use the background scene does not show through.

Monitoring. To check show or spot content and transmission with on-the-air picture.

Montage. Several separate pictures combined to make a composite picture. Sometimes passage-of-time effects created by running images in rapid succession.

Mortise. An optical effect that places an image on a specific part of a frame.

MOS or **"mit out sound."** A holdover term from decades ago meaning no sound is recorded.

Movieola. Older editing equipment used before the 1970s.

Optical. Trick effect done mechanically, permitting the combining of two or more pictures in one, creating wipes, montages, dissolves, fades, and other effects.

Overcrank. When the film camera shoots more than 24 frames per second, which slows the action (slow motion).

Package. Special show or series of shows bought by an advertiser, which includes all components ready to telecast.

Pad. To add action, sound, or any other material to fill the required on-the-air time.

Pan. Gradual swinging of camera to left or right across a scene to see segments of it as camera moves.

Participating program. A single TV show sponsored by more than one advertiser.

Playback. Reproduction of a sound track in studio during film shooting to enable action or additional sound or both to be synchronized with action; also, playing or recording for audition or reference purposes immediately after spot is made.

Plug. Mention of a name, show, or advertised product; or, loosely speaking, the commercial announcement.

Process shot. Film combining real photography with projected backgrounds or model sets or drawings.

Projectors. Used in TV for still material. They include: Balop, which takes cards or opaques (no transparencies); balop card size is usually 3″ X 4″ or 6″ X 8″. Also, Projectall, which takes both opaque cards and transparencies or slides; card size is 3″ X 4″; slides, 2″ X 2″.

Pull-up. Refers to the silence required at the beginning of a commercial. It is traditionally 1.5 seconds although, with the advent of videotape distribution of commercials, it is frequently .5 to 1.0 seconds.

Punch it. To accent or emphasize an action, sound effect, music, or line of dialogue.

Rating. Percentage of a statistical sample of TV viewers interviewed personally, checked by telephone, or noted in viewing diary, who reported viewing a specific TV show.

Residuals. Payments (required by the Screen Actors Guild) to talent for each broadcast of each film commercial on each network program per thirteen weeks' usage. If same commercial is used in spot markets, payment is additional per quarter.

Ripple dissolve. Optical effect in which scenes appear to ripple during a dissolve.

Rough cut. First assembly of film before completed editing.

SAG. Screen Actors Guild.

Scratch track. To obtain an audio timing guide for shooting or editing, a rough voice recording is made. This is the scratch track.

Segue. (pronounced *seg*-way). Usually the transition from one musical number to another without any break or talk.

Sets-in-use. Percentage of all TV homes in a given locality whose sets are tuned in at a specific time, regardless of the station being viewed.

7½ IPS. ¼″ audio tape recorded at 7½ inches per sound (consumer equipment).

SFX. Abbreviation for sound effects.

Share-of-audience. Percentage of viewers watching a given show or station based on the total sets-in-use.

Slide. Usually refers to still artwork, titles, photographs, or film which are picked up or projected upon camera tube. Slides are of two types: transparent or opaque, their size varying according to station projection method used.

Split screen. Effect obtained when two or more cameras are used and thus two or more scenes are visible at the same time on different parts of the screen.

Sponsor identification. Percentage of viewers of a show or personality who can identify the name of the sponsor or are familiar with specific data about the product advertised on TV.

Spot. A spot is another name for a commercial.

Spot TV. Market-by-market buying of TV time (programs, announcements, participations, station breaks). It affords flexibility in adapting a TV ad campaign to time zone, seasonal variations, special merchandising plans, etc.

Station time. Portion of a station's schedule not normally available for network programs; totals three out of every six clock hours.

Stop motion. Film taken by exposing one frame instead of a number of frames at a time. Objects are usually moved by hand a fraction of an inch for each exposure according to a set pattern.

Super. Superimposing one scene over the other.

Sync sound. When sound is recorded synchronized with the camera. Used primarily with on-camera dialogue.

Take. Single shot picture or scene held by TV camera; also, command to switch directly from one picture or camera to another, as "ready one—take one."

Talent cost. Expense or cost (for music, talent, etc.) of a show or commercial aside from the time charge.

Telefex. Rear-view projection system for special effects, backgrounds, etc.

Teleprompter. Rolling script device for one-takes and celebrity talent. Lines are printed large enough to be read at distance on sheet which revolves, keeping pace with show's action.

Tracking shot. Shot in which camera moves to keep up with the action.

Transcription. Recording of highest quality, usually at 33⅓ rpm, especially made for telecast or broadcast.

Truck. A camera move in which the camera and its mount move parallel to the scene being shot.

24 frames per second. The normal camera speed.

Under. Show that does not use all its allotted time; also, to sustain and subordinate one facet of the drama or situation under another.

Undercrank. Film camera shoots less than twenty-four frames per second, which speeds the action.

Video assist. In order to see what the film camera is recording, a video camera is positioned to enable what is being filmed to be seen on a television monitor.

Videotape. A system that records both sound and pictures simultaneously on magnetic tape; offers great advantage of immediate playback plus exceptionally fine picture fidelity. In one day, commercials can be completed on tape that previously took three weeks in running through film processing.

VO or voiceover. Narration-type recording as opposed to lip sync or live sound; also, voiceover narration where voice talent is not seen.

Wipe. Transition from one scene or image to another in which new scene replaces old one in some gradually increasing geometric pattern; that is, circle (circle in, circle out), square (expanding square), fan, roll, etc.

Word count. Number of words that will fit comfortably into a commercial of a specific length. Rule of thumb for television commercials is two words per second, although count will vary depending on type of commercial. Word count for radio is higher, approximating 170 words per minute spot.

Zip-pan. Effect obtained by swinging camera so quickly around from one point of rest to another that between the two the picture is blurred.

Zoom lens. A lens of variable focal length. Its use achieves in-or-out motion without moving the camera or requiring a change of lens.

Glossary—Who Does What on a Production

Television production involves a great many people. They all have titles and functions. And most of these people are "freelance"—that is, they are hired by the day or by the week and are not on permanent staff. It would be financially impossible for the production companies to employ all the crew members needed for a shoot on a full-time basis. The following is a list of important members of the production crew and what they do.

Assistant cameraman. This person sets up, loads, and unloads the camera for the camera operator. He or she deals with the technical aspects of the camera; also helps execute shots (by operating zoom and focusing).

Assistant director (A.D.). This person runs the set, coordinates the sequence of shooting, and is the "foreman of the crew."

Best boy. The gaffer's assistant (the assistant to the head electrician).

Boom man. The person who operates the microphone on the boom.

Cameraman or camera operator. The person who operates the camera.

Director. The person in charge and responsible for the creative aspects of the shoot.

Director of photography. Designs and composes the lighting and camera moves with the director. This person sometimes operates the camera.

Gaffer. The head electrician on a shoot. The gaffer lights the scene under the direction of the director of photography (D.P.).

Generator man. The person who handles the generation of power when conventional sources are unavailable.

Grip. Moves lighting equipment for the gaffer and handles the dolly.

Key grip. A specialist in designing and building rigging for camera mounts and lighting mounts.

Home economist. The person who prepares food on the shoot day.

Location scout. The person who presents various location choices to the agency and the director (usually Polaroids).

Producer. The person responsible for bringing together all elements.

Production assistant (P.A.). The assistant to the assistant director.

Production manager. The overseer of all production and related financial aspects of a job. Works closely with the director and hires key crew members.

Prop man. The person securing props and responsible for the product during a shoot.

Set designer. The person who works with the agency and the production company to design required sets. Also known as an art director.

Script supervisor. The person responsible for keeping track of what goes on during every take with comments from the director. This person also makes sure each scene is filmed in the correct time.

Sound man. The person who is responsible for recording all sound.

Stylist. The person who creates the esthetic look of a production. Works under the director to obtain required sets, props, and wardrobe.

Teamster. The people who drive the trucks for a production.

VTR man. The person who attaches video equipment to the film camera to allow video monitoring of what the film camera is shooting. Uses videotape to record each scene, too.

Wardrobe attendant. Responsible for the wardrobe before, during, and after a shoot. Supervised by the stylist.

Welfare worker. The required worker (in California) who supervises children on a shoot day.

21

RESEARCH

A Copywriter's Helper

"We're just a small agency; we can't afford research."

"All research does is confirm what common sense has already told us."

"It's silly to guess when research can give you the answers."

"If those Ph.D's in the research department would try writing copy, they wouldn't be so cocky."

"Okay, so we spend a few thousands on research. It's a good investment if it gives us some clues that will guide us in our $20 million campaign."

"Sure, research sometimes comes up with answers, but brilliant copywriters rely more on experience and intuition—and look how many times they're right."

"As a copywriter I don't have any quarrel with research. Frankly, I welcome anything that might help me write better ads because I understand my audience better."

Such comments dominate many advertising and marketing meetings.

Despite the heavy use of research, it is by no means universally used nor always highly regarded. Let's listen to what different workers in advertising have to say about their use of research:

A copywriter in a small advertising agency is talking: "No. We don't use research. Our clients can't afford it, and with our small profit margin, we can't afford to pay for it ourselves. So we get along on experience and common sense."

We hear from a mail-order copywriter: "Research? Of course. There's no guesswork around here. We test by results and that includes every element: headlines, body copy, illustrations, effect of color, coupons, timing, position, nature of the offer, etc., etc."

The big advertising agency copywriter says: "Yes. Our clients are sophisticated advertisers. They budget a healthy sum for research. Much of it is initiated and paid for by their market research division which also gets into copy testing. A lesser amount is paid for out of our funds. As for techniques, we draw upon everything from the simplest types to motivational research and G&R's impact testing. It's a great help, but we still do many ads that simply reflect judgment."

Perhaps you will set up your own homemade research method. Many copywriters do. Retail copypeople, for example, have devised so many individual copy-checking systems that it is impossible to list them all. Some are very good; others are very bad.

Variables Are Vexing

Since the first piece of copy was written, there has never been any real certainty regarding the effect of copy upon the consumer prior to its actual publication. There have been many uncertainties. From the start it was known that consumer reaction to advertisements was variable. An appeal that worked during one year might fail the next year. Even on a day-to-day or week-to-week basis, the success of advertisements is uncertain. There have been attempts to take the uncertainty out of advertising. "Foolproof" systems have been devised to eliminate guesswork in copy. Consumers and their reactions to copy appeals, headlines, and illustrations have been studied as scientists study the beetle and his activities.

It would be pleasant to relate that the research has been completely successful—but it hasn't. There are still uncertainties. As long as people themselves are so uncertain, there will always be a quantity of "by guess and by gosh" in copywriting. The weather, the political picture, the news, epidemics, and a thousand other variables can affect the success of a piece of copy. If any one of the variables is hard at work, the most scientifically conceived job of copywriting can fail.

Most copy researchers admit the variables. They admit that it is difficult to predict the exact degree of success or failure for any single piece of copy. They can merely predict that the copy should be successful or unsuccessful. Copy research is greatly concerned with development of techniques for measuring copy's effectiveness before its appearance in print or in broadcast—and then with analyzing why it failed or succeeded after its appearance.

Some smart advertisers are high-readership advocates. They reason, "If they don't read it, they won't buy it because they don't know about it." Opponents say, "If a thousand persons read but only one buys, high readership means nothing. Advertisements pay off on conviction, not mere readership."

Many advertising people believe in checklists. Others ridicule their use. Some say that only in returns from mail-order advertising can copy effectiveness be measured. Many will refute the assertion by pointing out variables that will affect results even in this situation. There are, therefore, many measuring techniques for copy but certainly no complete agreement on them.

As a copywriter you should know what's going on. You should know the merits and faults of the different testing techniques, but you must be careful to avoid two dangerous traps:

- Don't let yourself become so sold on any one method of copy research that you are blinded to the merits of other types of research. Remember, there is no perfect research method.
- Don't get so bogged down in the mazes of copy research that you forget to write copy that is vigorous, spontaneous, and alive. There is no substitute for the warm, human writing that digs down deep into the consumers' desires and makes them want to buy your product—just because you've produced persuasive copy born out of humanness, intuition, and plain, good writing. You can be *too* scientific in your copy approach and tangle yourself in formulas.

Despite various problems, research has become an important part of advertiser/agency relationships.

From the advertiser's perspective, research can be used to protect and to justify advertising investment to management.

From the agency's perspective, research can strengthen its relationship with the client.

From the creative person's perspective, research makes possible the testing of more ideas to increase the chances of success for the copy. Obviously much money and effort can be saved if you understand proper research techniques.

Before-and-After Testing

Although any research technique can be used in either a pretest or posttest situation, the nature of the interview and the data that is gathered will be influenced by whether the purpose of the research is primarily diagnostic or evaluative.

In a pretest environment, the researcher is more concerned with generating concepts and diagnosing alternatives than with evaluating the expected effectiveness of the actual advertisement.

In a posttest environment, the reverse is more often true, although a good posttest is often a good pretest for the subsequent campaign.

While each study project should be designed to satisfy particular research objectives, some of the more common techniques of copy evaluation are as follows:

Pretest:

- Focus group interviews
- Checklist
- Inquiry or direct response tests
- Split run tests
- Readability tests (Flesch formula)
- Physiological tests
- Motivational research

Posttest:

- Readership study (recognition, identification, recall)
- Impact method
- Communication and Reaction (C&R) tests
- Sales test
- PACT Principles

Focus Group Interviewing

Sometime, if you haven't already done so, you will probably try out some copy on other students, your wife, your secretary, your mother, or strangers. "Just trying to get consumer reaction," you'll explain. The focus group interview is a more elaborate way to do the same thing.

Instead of arbitrarily selecting one person as your guinea pig, you will select a number of persons, perhaps eight or ten. Each will be a typical potential buyer of the product for which you are testing the copy. In addition to being typical, group members must also be interested—that is, "interested in the product." Copy for a product should not be submitted to group members who have not, and never will, use this type of product.

The group's rating of your advertising helps you determine possible reader reaction in advance of publication. If the group members can never be interested in your product, they are not competent to rate your advertisements, since what would appeal to them would not, in many cases, appeal to the regular or potential user.

Often such group sessions are watched by clients and agency personnel through a two-way mirror. Participants in the group know that they are being watched, but researchers maintain that this knowledge does not inhibit responses.

Groups, in addition to being used for opinions on advertising approaches and product testing, may also contribute usefully to concept development, product naming, packaging development, and campaign evaluation. For such participation, group members are usually paid a modest sum.

Order-of-merit ranking. A focus group ranks different advertisements for the same product. Two or more advertisements are presented to the individual members who are asked to indicate, "Which of these advertisements do you like best?" or "Which of these advertisements would be most likely to make you want to buy the product?" All advertisements are thus rated until they are ranked in order of preference. This is sometimes called order-of-merit ranking.

Paired-comparison technique. Another method is the paired-comparison technique, wherein advertisements are judged in pairs. The respondent picks what he thinks is the better advertisement in each pair. Then, through elimination, the best of all the advertisements is selected. Usually this system is used for choosing an approach, format, or theme rather than individual advertisements in one pattern.

Many times different elements of the advertisements are rated. For instance, your advertisements might be identical except for the headlines, which will be rated in comparison with each other. The next rating will compare illustrations, the next copy appeal, and so on.

Focus group interviews do in a group what depth interviews do on an individual basis. A group leader by introducing stimuli (advertisements, parts of advertisements, products, packages) thus stirs an informal discussion among the eight or so persons in the group.

An interesting result of group interviews is the sometimes startling frankness with which group members will discuss subjects that could hardly be approached in the individual depth interview. Likewise, because group members usually try hard to contribute, it will often be found that the group will contribute more points and more talk than will be obtained from the individual interview.

Reasons for Using Focus Group Interviewing

Although the focus group method has been useful for indicating how an advertisement might fare in the final published form, it has faults mixed with its virtues. On the plus side of the focus group method:

Good results. In many instances there has been a satisfactory correlation between group ratings and selling power of the advertisements rated. This correlation has been good enough, despite the faults of the method, to justify its continued use in pretesting copy.

Speed. Once the group has been selected, the job of rating the advertisements can ordinarily be done speedily and easily.

Moderate cost. A few interviewees equipped with copies of comprehensive layouts can do the whole job. A good many advertisements or separate advertising elements can be rated in one session, thus reducing the cost per unit tested.

Consumer viewpoint. You tend to overlook the consumer in some forms of copy research. You think of appeals, copy approach, or the market. The focus group makes you think of the market in terms of persons who view advertisements with like, dislike, or indifference. If you follow the ratings of a focus group, you are being guided by the preferences of a representative segment of your consumer target rather than by your personal, and possibly isolated, judgment. Too, your respondents are classified as to age, work, income, and other aspects.

Some Problems with Focus Group Testing

As in the case of most copy-research methods, it is easier to pick flaws in the group interview than to find virtues. The following list doesn't condemn the method but provides you with some reservations. It should also indicate to you some weaknesses to avoid should you attempt to set up a group.

Respondents. Finding the right person to serve on a consumer group is vital to the success of the method. Determining just what is "typical" and then finding persons who fit that description is likely to be a slow, tedious task. The requirement that such persons be "interested" in a particular product provides a double complication.

Difficult to make conclusions. The questions usually asked of a consumer group fail to obtain a final answer. Examine the two questions again: Which of these advertisements do you like better? Which of these two advertisements would be more likely to make you want to buy the product?

The first question has nothing to do with sales potential. The respondents may like the advertisement because the illustration features a beautiful person. The rest of the layout may please them; they might even read and like the copy. All this, however, might not have the slightest influence in making them buy the spark plugs being advertised. Their favorable answer for a particular advertisement was based upon subjective factors having nothing to do with influencing them to buy.

The second question, although it is aimed more at determining buying behavior, asks respondents to indicate how they might act. There is a great difference between a person's intentions and subsequent actions.

Some copy evaluators have combined the answers to the two questions. The combining is not practical. One question measures liking for an advertisement on a basis entirely removed from buying behavior. The other attempts to measure buying potential. Combining these two unlikes is tricky and conclusions thus derived would be questionable.

Separating elements is dangerous. Although there is some value in dissecting advertising elements and letting the group judge headlines, illustration, and other items individually, the process is somewhat unrealistic. A person thumbing through a magazine is looking at advertisements, not headlines or illustrations. The general rating seems to be more accurate, according to the findings of the Advertising Research Foundation.

Probably the best procedure is to use both methods—individual element rating and general rating. Both should then be analyzed carefully before the findings are accepted. It seems dubious in any event that final judgment of an advertisement should be based on a rating of the separate parts. Remember, some scenery taken feature by feature is not attractive. Assemble the features and you may have a charming vista. An advertisement taken by sections may not be noteworthy. Combine elements and the result is often a persuasive, compelling advertisement.

Group members become copy "experts." Almost everyone feels competent to criticize advertisements. Group members thus frequently forget their consumer function and begin to act like copy chiefs. This tendency causes real trouble, since the group members thus are no longer "typical" consumer prospects. Instead, they have become professional critics. When they no longer view the advertisements with a consumer's eyes, their usefulness as group members has ended.

Hard to compare more than two advertisements. Although many consumer groups are asked to compare more than two advertisements at a time, it is often questionable that more than two should be compared. The fewer the elements to be considered, the more reliable the judgment is likely to be. Thus the paired-comparison method may be preferable to that which gives the respondent the task of giving rank order to six different advertisements.

If he does his job conscientiously, the respondent will probably be confused as he considers all the elements found in six advertisements. It is difficult enough to obtain reliable opinions from consumer groups without complicating the task further by confusing them. The paired-comparison method at least eliminates some of the confusion.

Size of the sample. Although the trend has been toward small samples, the sample size may often have to be varied for different types of products or if the voting is so close on certain advertisements that the advertiser must ask for additional votes.

Impractical for certain items. Some products of infrequent purchase such as figure skates or shortwave transmitters are not suitable for group interviews. Such products call for unusual promotions; ordinary testing procedures are not so suited to them as to ordinary items of everyday purchase like cereals, milk, or coffee.

Prestige factor is operative. Group interviewing, like any procedure requiring decision on the part of respondents, is often inaccurate because of the respondents' pride or vanity. Respondents not wanting to admit that a sexy illustration is appealing will vote against it when under actual reading conditions the same illustration would win delighted attention. Intellectuals might be unwilling to admit that celebrity endorsements attract and convince them. As long as people are subject to vanity, the prestige factor will be at work in situations like those set up by the group copy testing procedure.

Test measures standings—not quality of advertisement. Respondents are asked to rate advertisements on a scale of 1 to 3. This system is followed whether advertisements are good or bad. In some tests all the advertisements might be poor. The rating would simply indicate which was the least objectionable. The highest-rated advertisement might be used because the group voted for it, not because it had merit.

Campaigns are overlooked. Most national advertising is campaign advertising. One advertisement, by itself, might not have the push and appeal that it has as one of a series of advertisements. Yet the consumer group may be asked to judge an individual advertisement, ignoring the cumulative effect of the campaign.

Any one advertisement in the campaign might not have sold this person. Yet the consumer group judges one advertisement in an attempt to answer the question "Which advertisement would be most likely to make you buy the product?" That one advertisement might fit in very poorly with the campaign, and with most national advertisers the campaign is the important consideration. That is why, in many cases, national advertisers will continue to emphasize a campaign even though it is tempting to put all the emphasis on a current prize contest. Long-run considerations, however, are not necessarily a part of a consumer group's thinking.

Conditions are not natural. No matter how skilled the interviewer, or how well the questions are phrased, the conditions under which the consumer group operates are not normal home-reading conditions. The group member cannot help being less casual than in reading in the home. In this test this person is on the alert for faults; the very act of comparing is unrealistic.

Certainly, the usual reader will not match advertisements against each other. Also reading under group conditions allows undivided attention to the individual advertisements. Under more usual conditions, there would be the competition from surrounding advertisements. There would be unfavorable position. In finished printed form, one advertisement might gain over another through better type, use of color, and other mechanical factors.

Checklists

Before you engage in the use of checklists, you had better clarify the meaning of the term. (See the appendix for examples of checklists.)

Practically everyone who has written copy has used a checklist at one time or another. Usually, the list will be a simple little affair—a casual reminder to put in certain important elements such as the slogan, price mention, and selling conditions. Other checklists bring in more elements to watch for. They keep the copywriter on the track without attempting to provide any scientific preevaluation as to the effectiveness of the advertisements.

The checklist, in its ultimate form, goes beyond reminding. It attempts, as in the case of the elaborate systems worked out a number of years ago, to serve as a yardstick for preevaluating the effectiveness of advertising. So confident were the proponents of checklist evaluations that they made assertions such as one man's that through use of his system, you could tell a good advertisement from a bad advertisement before publication in nine minutes flat.

Some of the opponents, however, assert that:

1. Originators of checklist evaluation techniques are engaged in a meaningless battle of points with each such originator simply trying to outdo the other in dreaming up new point lists.
2. Checklist preevaluation methods hamstring originality.
3. Copywriters use points by instinct.
4. Personal judgment is overemphasized in the checklist system.

Checklists—Criticisms

Since sooner or later you will probably be engaged in a discussion of checklists, the four arguments just given are examined here.

Checklists degenerate in a battle of points. True enough. If you use a formal checklist, devised by someone else, you can become a victim of the point battle as you compare the list with someone else's. The best procedure is to avoid long lists because the longer and more complicated the checklist, the less usable it is on a day-to-day basis.

Checklists hamstring originality. "Creative work cannot be written according to a cut-and-dried formula. The checklist provides a mechanical crutch for the copywriter which, if followed, generally would tend to make all advertisements look the same." So go the comments of many copywriters. An illustration of how intensely some advertising people feel about this is provided by the example of one very large agency which threw one of its biggest accounts out of the "shop" when the account insisted on adoption of a checklist system by the agency copywriters working on the account's copy.

Checklist originators deny that their systems choke newness and sparkle in copy. Rather, they say, using a good checklist as a guide, the original writer can produce freely, confident that writing is channeled more effectively for sales-getting. The checklist merely systematizes a job that often has no system.

Copywriters use points by instinct, so checklists are useless. Most copywriters argue that they incorporate the necessary points in their writing without using any "system." They suspect the checklist as an attempt by research people to invade the copywriter's field. "Possibly all right for beginners but not for the experienced person" is a frequent comment about checklists.

The comment is valid in the case of many copywriters who, through long practice, automatically use attention-getting, selling points in everything they turn out. Other writers—beginners and some old hands—might well adopt some system to keep them on the track in their thinking.

The best copywriters in the field might occasionally use a checklist to remind themselves of the fundamentals that sometimes slip away from them as they become more advanced in their jobs. Because checklists contain nothing new, but simply present ever-constant, faithful sales points, they can be a great comfort to the beginner and an occasional aid to skilled copywriters.

Personal judgment is overemphasized. Any checklist, say the critics, is basically a personal judgment on what elements are needed to make an advertisement successful. Any copywriter can, they continue, evolve his own list. Even in using a checklist to evaluate an advertisement, the interpretation is a matter for individual judgment.

That this criticism has some truth is borne out by situations wherein persons using the same checklist evaluating system arrive at radically different results in their ratings of the same advertisement. In short, one person may have more skill in applying the checklist than another, or both may be equally skilled but differ entirely in their use of the system. The method then becomes no better than the ability of the persons who use it.

About the most conclusive thing to say of the checklist is that it's up to you. It's a quick, inexpensive way to evaluate an advertisement—one of the quickest and most expensive. If you use a checklist, be sure that you don't let it make you write like an automaton and that you retain your good judgment.

Inquiry Testing

The idea behind inquiry testing is simple. You run advertisements and you judge their relative effectiveness by the number of inquiries they bring. These inquiries may result from a hidden offer buried in the copy or from a coupon offer, openly made, inviting purchases or inquiries.

The hidden offer rids the advertiser of professional coupon-clippers and inquiries from the curious. It also indicates extent of reading but results in fewer inquiries or sales than does the coupon offer.

In the usual inquiry test, different advertisements are run at different times in the same publication, or at the same time in different publications. Results are then compared.

Split Run Testing

Another version of the inquiry test is the split run test. This test has some of the advantages or disadvantages of the usual inquiry test plus some advantages and disadvantages of its own.

"Split run" refers to the practice of testing advertisements by running two or more versions of the same advertisement on the same press run but on different presses of a newspaper or magazine. Thus, Advertisement A may be exactly like Advertisement B except for the headline. Each advertisement in the case of a newspaper will go out on the same day, in the same position in the paper.

From the response to the advertisement, the advertiser can tell which of the two headlines was more effective. In the case of a magazine, as many as four versions of the same advertisement will go out and each may be distributed in a different area. Response will be judged by the relative readership, by the coupon return, or by the replies to a hidden offer, any one of which may be employed in such tests. Any element of the advertisement may be checked—copy, illustration, headline. In some instances, the advertiser will test four entirely different advertisements.

Figure 21–1a. Advertisement A (Mexico Tourism) tested with the impact method. Study this advertisement. Then study Advertisement B. Which advertisement do you think was more effective? See "Addendum" at the end of the chapter (page 286).

Courtesy of Gallup & Robinson.

Figure 21–1b. Advertisement B (Mexico Tourism) tested with the impact method. See "Addendum" at the end of the chapter (page 286) to learn which advertisement was more effective.

Courtesy of Gallup & Robinson.

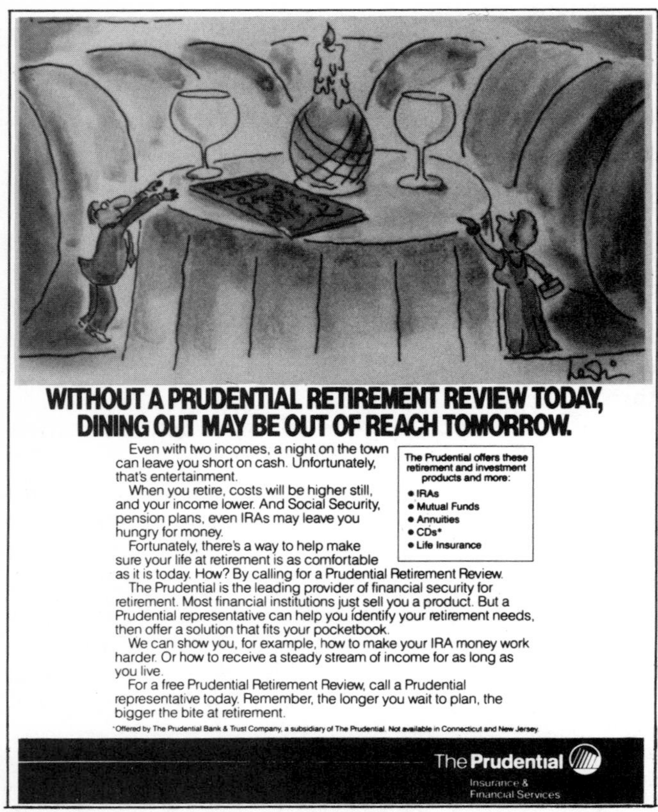

Figure 21–2a. **Advertisement A (Prudential) tested with the impact method.** Study this advertisement. Then study Advertisement B. Which advertisement do you think was more effective? See "Addendum" at the end of the chapter (page 286). Courtesy of Gallup & Robinson.

Figure 21–2b. Advertisement B (Prudential) tested with the impact method. See "Addendum" at the end of the chapter (page 286) to learn which advertisement was more effective. Courtesy of Gallup & Robinson.

You may wonder why this form of testing is not classified with the pretest copy testing techniques instead of the posttest list. Like inquiry, or direct response testing, it could be. It is placed in the pretest group simply because such testing usually precedes general use of the winning advertisement or advertisement elements.

Normally, the advertisements would not have been run before the split run test. In this sense, therefore, the test is a before-publication test. A fact you should realize, too, is that although several hundred newspapers offer split run service only a few magazines offer split run, so such testing is quite limited in its scope for magazines.

Pluses for Split Run

Parallels running conditions. The trouble with so many copy-testing methods is that they are unrealistic. The researchers set up situations which are artificial despite all efforts to make them otherwise. The split run test, on the other hand, gives the advertiser an almost perfect simulation of conditions under which the advertisements will be run.

There will be no tampering with actual reading conditions; there will be no dependence upon the skill of interviewers. Instead, the advertisement readers will read as they always do—right in their homes and unaware that they are taking part in a test. Their response to the advertisements will give an excellent, although not completely reliable, comparison of the effectiveness of the test advertisements.

Test itself produces business. An obvious advantage of split run testing is that the test pulls in business, unlike other tests which produce nothing but information. A split run test may promote the product just as well and bring in just as much business as any other advertising used for the product.

Checks geographical differences. That sections of the country, or even sections of a city, vary in their response to different products, copy appeals, and so forth, is well known. Magazine-reading habits, for example, differ greatly in different cities. One tomato sauce manufacturer found that sales were very good in one city while very poor in another. A TV star who gets a good rating on the West Coast may fare poorly in the South and Midwest but will get a good rating on the East Coast.

This is the sort of thing that will vex you or any other advertising person. A split run test can help you since it provides a means of checking the power of your appeals in four different sections covered by a magazine. Split run provides you with a method of making such a check. As one magazine executive, whose publication offers split run testing facilities, has explained it, split runs make possible:

> Pretesting before general release, eliminating ineffective advertisements; comparison of campaign theme and ideas; development of the presentation; evaluation of different headlines; measuring various illustrative treatments; comparing 4-color to black and white or to black and one color; exploring different layout techniques; comparison of the relative values of various hidden offers.

Problems in Split Run

The coupon or inquiry return from split run advertisements is not necessarily a true measure of the relative effectiveness of the advertisements. Here are some considerations:

- It is difficult to use split run for measuring effectiveness of general advertisements. The method is suited to mail-order advertisements. To make a mail-order advertisement out of a general advertisement for purposes of the test can distort the true picture of reader reaction to a general advertisement run under normal conditions.
- Since most of your readers won't reply to your test advertisements, respondents may not give a fair indication of your readership. Also, you learn nothing in the split run about people who don't send in the coupon.
- Mail returns may not give a true evaluation of potential store sales. People who reply to your coupon or hidden offer often are not typical of the kind of people who come into a store to buy the product. Children and professional "coupon clippers" make a business of replying to advertisements carrying offers despite the fact that they have no real interest in the product. Split run using hidden offers can avoid this difficulty somewhat.
- Unlike some other copy testing methods, the split run reveals nothing about the readers. You know nothing about the way they read the advertisement, their economic or social status, or whether anything in the advertisement actually appealed to them or whether they were just "curious."

Using Split Run on Television

Split run television testing is available through the split cable offered on cable television (CATV). Described simply, the cable station makes it possible to show different commercials in different households simultaneously. Any television commercial can be blanked out and another commercial substituted at any time.

Later, surveys may be made by phone, mail, or personal interviews to get viewers' opinions. The technique is especially good for evaluating a campaign that involves a number of different commercials. Furthermore, by checking viewers after the commercial exposures, the television researcher can learn the personal and demographic characteristics of the respondents—not always possible in testing through print split run.

Other Pretests for Television

In addition to testing procedures that can be used for both print and broadcast, such as group discussion and split run, there are some that are used solely by television researchers. All of these cannot be described here because researchers continue to find many new ways to ascertain viewers' reactions to commercials. One advertising agency, for example, at one time put together a manual that described twenty-four leading methods of television copy-testing. These were just the *leading* methods. There are many more. Included here, however, are four techniques—theater projections, on-the-air tests, masked recognition testing, and animatic testing.

Theater Projections

Many different techniques are used for a theater projection type of testing in which as many as 400 persons may be invited to a theater for the private screening of some "new television material." Usually, the audience will see entertainment programs and television commercials. Later, the audience is asked for their reactions to the commercials, such information as comprehension, brand-name recall, likes/dislikes, interest, and believability. There might even be group discussions to obtain full information. Much television copy continues to be tested in these "laboratory" theaters.

On-the-Air Tests

Under the on-the-air testing method, the respondents do not know they are taking part in a test. A test commercial is aired in one, or a few cities. An advertiser's test commercial may be used on a regular program in one city while the present commercial runs in other cities as usual. Sometimes, the advertiser may buy a new time period in selected cities for a local participation, or a spot.

Following the airing, viewers who saw the new commercial are interviewed (usually by telephone) to find out their brand attitudes, their ability to play back the commercial message, and their brand knowledge. These are compared with those of people who did not see the new commercial but saw the existing commercial.

Most such tests are conducted under an invited-viewing technique. The respondent is invited to view a familiar show into which a test commercial has been inserted.

A re-interview is conducted the next day that asks for commercial recall. In addition, the respondent is checked for attitude toward the advertised brand, ability to play back the commercial message, and knowledge of the brand.

The commercial's communication effectiveness is then evaluated in terms of its ability to command attention (intrusiveness), and for its achieving of a favorable buying attitude (persuasion).

These two factors are then usually compared to the norms of performance for similar products, and/or to control groups. The check of the control groups reveals the attitudes of respondents before they were exposed to the commercial (called pre-post design).

Masked Recognition Testing

This kind of test endeavors to register response to emotion-arousing commercials. The methodology requires that the respondent see a commercial on one day and the same commercial the following day. On the second showing, the product name is absent from audio and video. The respondent is now asked to recall the product name. It is thought that a commercial with strong emotional impact will result in the respondent's recalling the product name.

This same respondent may not, however, explain logically what in the commercial was appealing because the appeal of the commercial was largely emotional and hence less susceptible to explanation. As is evident, this type of test is more useful to determine product-name registration than to evaluate general content.

Animatics (Also Photomatics and Live Action Roughs)

This is a form of television pretesting. Because it is too expensive for an advertiser to produce a number of commercials for testing purposes, animatic testing fills in. This consists of the following steps:

1. An artist draws pictures—often line drawings—that will depict visually the commercial in its various phases.
2. Still photographs are taken of each drawing.
3. A separate sound track is recorded.
4. A film is made of the many drawings.

Out of these steps is derived a limited amount of movement in the video as the film is shown. Accompanying the visual is a voiceover sound track that uses the actual copy intended for the finished commercial.

Such testing helps eliminate poor commercials when shown to a proper sample and provides a basis for selecting the various components for the final commercial. Animatic-tested commercials that achieve a good response in the testing period have frequently shown up as satisfactory final commercials. Also, the animatic method can be used for research of consumer brand awareness and recall.

As is always the case, the method has its critics, who say that it is best-suited to simpler techniques, but that it often is incapable of portraying the big, or dazzlingly different idea. Also, the personal essence of an unusual spokesperson may not be conveyed—the glint in the eye, the subtle shadings of bodily and facial movements, the eloquent use of the hands.

As an alternative to this still-picture technique, such critics suggest the use of real people through videotape and sound against a simulated background of drawings, photographs, or film footage. This technique, while not quite so inexpensive as animatics, is still moderately inexpensive and offers more realism as a testing device.

Communication and Reaction (C & R) Testing

C & R testing is a generic term for several techniques commonly used by advertising agencies. In general, it directs a respondent's attention to a commercial or advertisement.

After the respondent has had an opportunity to look at the commercial or advertisement one or more times, he or she is asked a series of questions to determine what ideas were communicated and what reactions were spurred by the advertising and the ideas. Most larger advertising agencies have their own preferred version of the technique. It is used primarily as an early and economical system for screening advertising alternatives.

For example, tachistoscope testing, described later in this chapter, is one of the techniques used in C & R testing.

Readability Tests

There can be some question that this discussion of readability properly fits into a chapter on testing. A person might ask, "Isn't readability (and the Flesch formula) concerned with writing style and thus more appropriate in another chapter?" Furthermore, isn't the Flesch formula, in particular, concerned more with postpublication analysis than pretesting?

To the first question, it may be said that if a writer examines copy in terms of readability principles—or has a researcher do it—before it is set in print in final form, it is possible to greatly increase its effectiveness. Thus, it seems proper to discuss readability in this research chapter even though there is no denying that readability principles *are* writing principles and can be used as such by the copywriter.

To the second question, it may be said that readability research *can* be used for pretesting or posttesting, but it seems more sensible to apply it in pretesting and thus avoid the use of writing that is less efficient than it should be.

Some years ago, United Press, worried that they were writing "over" their readers, made a thorough study of their wire stories. They found among other things that out of 100 United Press stories going out in a single day, the average sentence length was twenty-nine words, the average length of lead sentences was thirty-three words. Yet comfortable reading for the mass of the population is a sentence length of around twenty words. UP found that although they were averaging around thirty words for their sentences, current magazines ran about as follows:

Magazine	Average Sentence Length
Time	16 words
Reader's Digest	18 words
Atlantic Monthly	24 words

United Press editors found that, in addition to writing long sentences, their writers were also using too many long, complex words. Alarmed by the trend, the wire service began a writing reform within the organization. Sentences were shortened, language was simplified, and readability, according to tests, increased noticeably and quickly.

What was true of United Press has been true of almost every organization writing to the public—magazines, newspapers, advertisers. Sentences have been too long, words too long, and the writing impersonal. The three factors, regrettably, make a good recipe for low readership.

Thanks to readership studies you know that Advertisement A gets 55 percent readership and Advertisement B gets 20 percent. But why? It might have been the headline, illustration, or position in the publication. There are many ways to account for the difference.

One of the most important is this matter of readability. Was the copy a chore to read or did it run off smoothly under your glance? What made the difference in readability between A and B? How do you actually measure readability? At least some of the answers to these questions have been supplied by a former Vienna lawyer, Dr. Rudolph Flesch, whose readability formula you can learn and apply quickly to your copy or anyone else's copy.

Flesch Formula

Basis for the Flesch formula are four elements as they appear in 100-word writing samples:

- Average sentence length
- Average number of syllables
- Percentage of personal words
- Percentage of personal sentences

These are no magic ingredients. Flesch has simply expressed mathematically what writers have always known; short words and short sentences make for easier reading. In sentences, for example, the Flesch table points out that about 88 percent of the population can understand without difficulty sentences that fall in the "Fairly Easy" category. Such sentences average 14 words; their syllable count is 139 per 100 words. "Very Difficult" writing, in contrast, is suitable to only about 4.5 percent of the population. Here the average sentence runs 29 or more words and the syllable count soars to 192.

Personal words. An interesting facet of the Flesch formula is the stress on the use of personal words and personal sentences in order to achieve what is termed a high "interest" factor. Words such as "people, folks" (plus personal names and personal pronouns) are classified as "personal" words. Personal sentences include: spoken sentences set off by quotation marks; questions, commands, and other sentences addressed directly to the reader; exclamations; and incomplete sentences whose meaning must be inferred from the context. A classification of "dull" writing has no personal sentences and contains only two percent or less personal words per 100 words. Typical users of such writing are scientific magazines which, however absorbing to their limited audience, would be found dull by the mass audience. "Highly Interesting" in contrast, has 10 personal words; and 43 percent of personal sentences.

For years, young writers have been told—"write simply—write on the level of your readers." It is not easy to decide what kind of writing is suited to the different levels. Because a folksy advertisement gets a good Flesch rating, and thus can be read by most of the adult readers, does not mean that all advertisements must be written in folksy style.

Certainly if you are selling a mass-appeal item, write in the way that will appeal to the biggest possible portion of that market. However, if you are writing *New Yorker* copy for a very expensive product, you will not be addressing a mass readership. The readers you want to reach probably will be affluent and appreciate precision instruments. They probably will have an educational background that merits a "Difficult" Flesch rating of the advertisement.

By no means should a copywriter write consciously to the Flesch or any other formula. The system is simply a device to tell you whether your writing is geared in readability to the various segments of your readership. That the method has some practicality is evident in its adoption by a number of advertising agencies and publications. The formula is applicable to any kind of writing and, as a matter of fact, has been used widely to determine readability of the editorial content of magazines and newspapers.

The principal danger in the use of the Flesch system is that writers might adopt it too literally. It would be oversimplification to believe that all you must do to write good copy is to write short words, short sentences, and throw in a personal reference now and then. Thought and writing skill must still be used by the copywriter. The Flesch formula does nothing but wave a warning when the copy begins to clank. Because copywriters can read their copy easily, they often forget that others won't have a similarly easy time reading it. The Flesch system acts as a warning that: (a) These sentences are too long. (b) Only half your readers will understand this. (c) Don't forget your readers are human; they like personal references to themselves or other human beings.

Second, be cautioned that the Flesch formula cannot be applied literally to radio or television writing, since a good radio announcer can make material that looks difficult to the eye seem hearable when it is read out loud.

Figure 21–3. Magazine page showing Starch readership scores. All important elements of this advertisement have been checked for readership. This specific advertisement has received high readership throughout—superior to many advertisements.

Courtesy of Starch INRA Hooper, Inc.

Through skillful phrasing and intonation the announcer breaks long sentences into easily assimilated phrases. Even long, unusual words that would daunt the reader of a printed page will "sound easy" when delivered by a good announcer or actor.

In conclusion, don't use the Flesch system as a mold for your writing. Flesch doesn't measure literary excellence or selling effectiveness, but how well you reach your audience. A formula should not be used constantly if you are to maintain elasticity in your writing. Use it occasionally as a sort of checkup on your writing. Employed in this manner, it can help your writing to be more consistently readable—especially if you are writing to a mass market.

Physiological Tests

Pupil dilation, skin moisture, heart rate, voice stress, and brain wave analysis are just some of the fascinating, even exotic, tests based on physiological reactions. Sometimes referred to as "autonomic nervous system measures" these tests have been entered into the list of almost desperate efforts to better understand consumers' attitudes toward, understanding of, and reactions to the advertising messages turned out by copywriters.

Such physiological tests, although widely used and even widely different, have one element in common. All of them measure involuntary response. None depends on what respondents say (so often contradictory to the facts) but on how respondents react involuntarily to various stimuli.

One of these testing devices, the *psychogalvanometer*, has been around for some time. Operating on somewhat the same principle as the well-publicized "lie detector," the psychogalvanometer measures sweat gland activity of persons reading advertisements under controlled conditions.

Another more recent testing procedure measures *brain wave activity.* This testing is rooted in the science of psychobiology, the study of the brain and behavior. In using this the researcher conducts a brain wave test in which the computer analyzes the extent to which the brain registers a piece of information. Proponents of this testing method have declared that they can tell which half of a subject's brain is reacting more strongly to a given stimulus. For example, the assertion is made that if "left-brain" activity dominates, the subject is reacting to words, or logical reasoning, while "right-brain" activity indicates a subjective, emotional reaction.

After initial enthusiasm for brain wave testing, skeptics now say that there has been an oversimplification of the left-brain/right-brain theory and that brain wave testing for advertising shows promise, but much more study is needed to utilize this effectively. There was too much beginning excitement for what has turned out to be a complicated, complex type of research.

One of the initial problems was the difficulty in determining whether a brain reaction indicated a positive or negative impression on the subject's part. Now, most brain researchers believe they can separate positive from negative responses. This, however, is only one small step in the total process of utilizing brain wave activity for advertising research purposes.

Still another testing procedure is based on *voice pitch changes.* Judgments utilizing this method assess the degree of feeling behind a respondent's verbal expression of his or her attitude.

Pupil dilation observation, once considered a viable research technique, has since fallen into disuse. Changes in pupil dilation as subjects looked at advertising were supposed to indicate response to words and illustrations. Contraction of the pupil was interpreted as a negative response; dilation was considered as a positive or favorable response.

Eyes are observed in another testing procedure, *eye camera* testing. This technique, around for many years, has been utilized more than the other techniques described. It is explained in more detail in the following section.

Eye Camera Tests

A film record of the path of the eye over an advertisement is made by the eye camera. Not only does the eye camera indicate eye direction, but it also indicates how long a reader's glance remains on any one section of the advertisement. Although the eye camera is probably more suited to long-range advertisement research than to copy testing individual advertisements, it can be useful in the latter activity.

It can, for example, indicate the relative pulling power of the various advertisement elements. It can answer the question as to whether the subject is merely a headline reader or whether he reads body copy, too. Also, the eye camera may reveal the extent of reading, although under the test conditions necessary for an eye camera test the subject is rather far away from home reading conditions.

Undoubtedly the eye camera can reveal the mechanics of eye flow. The greatest use for the eye camera is in determining the correct mechanical structure of the advertisement. It tells nothing of what the subject thinks about the advertisement, or how he might react to it. It simply indicates how to arrange the advertising elements for the most logical, thorough, and easiest reading.

In this sense it may be considered even more useful as a layout-testing device than as a means for testing copy. It can be argued, however, that interest in copy can be indicated by the length of time the eye rests upon it. As a counterargument, it may be that the subject had to spend much time on a particular section because it was so difficult to understand.

Motivational Research

Researchers know that very often the answer they can obtain from a respondent is not the true answer to the question that was asked. The true answer is hidden in the subconscious. Even the respondent is not aware of it. An advertising researcher, therefore, in probing for reactions about a product or a campaign may, if using ordinary research techniques, obtain a set of answers that will not reveal the real feelings of the respondents.

To dig under the surface, advertising may use motivational research. This form of investigation draws heavily upon psychology—laws underlying thinking, learning, and actions; and sociology, the study of mass behavior.

MR, as it is familiarly called by advertising people, has been used before or after campaigns have been run; thus it fits into postpublication copy research as well as prepublication. Also, it must not merely be thought of as a copy research tool since its findings are used to establish a rationale for the whole marketing process.

Motivational research practitioners usually proceed on the assumption that they do not know what their investigation may uncover, since irrational behavior, drives, impulses, fears, and desires may cause people to act as they do toward the product or situation being studied. Out of a study may come reasons respondents could tell the ordinary researcher but probably will not.

Most motivational research is concerned with the subconscious level. Other thinking levels, of course, include the outer level that those about us can see and the conscious inner level of personality, a sort of private dream world. This, too, is an area for motivational probing.

Although there are many ways to obtain information, a good portion of motivational research depends upon depth interviewing and projective approaches.

Depth interviews. Depth interviews are not the exclusive province of motivational researchers; all types of researchers have conducted depth interviews for years.

Such interviews may last one or two hours, during which time questions are asked that seem, and often are, quite indirect but which, nevertheless, center around the problems investigated. Unsuspected motivations are often unearthed through these interviews.

Projective approaches. Most strongly identified with motivational research are projective approaches. These frequently use the following techniques:

- *Free association.* Typically, respondents are given lists of words, one at a time, and asked to respond with the first word that comes to mind. Judgment is made on the basis of the frequency with which a word may come up, or how long it takes for the word to appear.
- *Sentence completion.* Respondents finish a series of incomplete sentences. A respondent will be guided along a certain direction but, if test is correctly handled, will not know what data is to be obtained.
- *Picture responses.* An illustration is shown to the respondent, who then interprets the illustration or tells its story.

A sort of madness overcame portions of the advertising industry when motivational research first appeared as a tool of advertising researchers. Swiftly people began using motivational research who had no knowledge of its meaning or techniques. In many cases ordinary consumer surveys might have obtained more information for them and at considerably lower cost. Of late, however, the fever has subsided as advertising people have become aware of the limitations of MR.

While much hitherto buried information has been obtained through motivational research, its use brings up questions among the companies, advertising agencies, and the media that employ it. For example, who is going to validate the results among the average businesspeople who pay for the research? How can these businesspeople judge the validity of the work conducted by psychologists?

Too, the businesspeople ask how they are to judge the accuracy of the techniques used when arguments persist among the motivational researchers themselves, not only about the techniques for getting the information but about the interpretation of the results obtained.

Regardless of the doubts and queries and the uneasiness of businesspeople suddenly wading in the esoteric terminology of the psychologist, motivational research, properly conducted, is here to stay. It will remain in some form or other because it helps reduce guesswork in advertising creation by giving copywriters answers to those eternal questions: "What do they *really* like or dislike?" "What do they *really* want?" "What do they *really* think?"

The absorption of creative advertising people with these questions is illustrated by the use during the past few years of such techniques as psychogalvanometer testing and hypnosis.

More Publication Pretest Techniques

The following methods are classed as pretests in the sense that they give advertisers reactions of respondents to advertisements that have been prepared for viewing, but which have not appeared yet in the whole publication run of newspapers or magazines.

This "preview" reaction saves the advertiser the cost of running ineffective advertisements by trying out new approaches in a limited way. As you will see, however, such testing can, in itself, be expensive. The three methods to be discussed briefly here are folio testing, dummy publications, and tip-ins.

Folio Testing

"Folio" here is an abbreviation for portfolio, or a folder of advertisements shown to a cross section of respondents, usually in their homes. A number of methods may be followed in this kind of testing. Advertisements, for example, may be shown to individual respondents and questions asked about each before the next advertisement is shown, or the respondent may look over all the advertisements before questions are asked.

Advertisements are scored one against another, or each against averages. From this, the advertisements are positioned as higher or lower in performance according to each standard of measurement covered by the questionnaire. Usually no more than eight advertisements are shown in one folio interview.

Dummy Publications

The "dummy" publication is a magazine or newspaper that has been prepared especially for test purposes. It contains editorial material and possibly 15 to 20 advertisements. Copies of the publication are given to a cross section of people who are directed to read the publication in a normal fashion.

An interviewer, they are informed, will visit them to question them about what they have read. The questions reveal advertising recall, advertising impact, and a possible increased interest in buying the products advertised. Although this is an expensive testing method, it has been useful in reproducing posttest scores using the same questions asked of those respondents who have read the dummy publications.

Tip-ins

A "tip-in" is a page that is glued to the gutter of a real magazine in such a way that a reader cannot tell it from the regular pages. In newspapers, an insert page may be used. On the page will be a pretest advertisement, plus another advertisement. The tip-in will be inserted in a specified number of copies of a publication—magazine or newspaper—before the publication's release date. These copies are then distributed to enough people to furnish the desired sample size.

Later, the persons who have read the publication with the tip-in page are questioned in a manner similar to that used for the dummy publications previously described. One possible advantage of the tip-in method over dummy publication testing is that the reading situation is more natural because a real publication is used. This may be offset somewhat by the fact that the tip-in copies are planted with readers, not being bought as usual at newsstands or by subscription.

After-Publication Research through Readership Studies

The advertisement has been published. No advertiser can help wanting to know certain things about the advertisement. How many persons read it? How thoroughly did they read? How much advertiser and product identification was created? How well do the readers remember the advertisement? What features of the advertisement obtained the best readership? All these questions and more are answered to a degree by readership studies undertaken after publication of the advertisement.

Arguments have been heard about readership techniques from the time they were first used. You may be sure of one thing, however. You will always have some form of readership study. Like them or not, you will need to know the various methods, and you should determine which one you believe in most firmly. You should learn readership terminology and the mechanical procedures for detecting misleading readership research.

The readership report, like radio and TV ratings, has become an obsession in some circles. The magic percentage figures of readership studies are hypnotic. They lull the advertiser into satisfaction with his advertising or they goad him into anger. With many advertisers a high percentage of readership is the final test of an advertisement's success. "The readership reports say we're on the right track," says the person who produced the advertisement. The advertiser leans back satisfied.

Yet, there are so many variables to consider in readership reports that you will be a very wise copywriter never to accept a readership report at face value. Look behind the figures. Don't let the mesmerizing effect of good readership keep you from setting off on new copy trails. An evil of the reports is that they encourage status quo advertising. "We're going along fine," cries a cautious executive. "The readership reports are good. Why endanger our success with that new technique?" The hesitancy is understandable.

Yet, new ideas are the life of advertising. New ideas are responsible for increased sales and higher manufacturing output. If you rely slavishly on readership reports, you will find a good formula, and you will never leave it. Some advertisers have done well under that system. Most advertising, however, has been flexible. Most advertisers have been willing to try for the greater reward—have been willing to experiment.

Many good advertising ideas would have been lost had satisfied executives refused to experiment. Yet such refusals are frequent when readership figures for present campaigns are good. A bit of the gambler is needed to desert the high-readership campaign for the bold, new idea.

Assume, as you read now about readership study techniques, that there is misinformation in the best of them and some good in most of them. What you find—good or bad—will depend upon your capacity for objective analysis.

Testing by Recognition

"What do you usually read?" "What advertisements did you see in yesterday's paper?" This type of recall questioning was used for years to determine advertisement reading. Opinions were obtained, but not actual behavior. As mentioned before, you will find a big area between what people say they do and what they actually do.

Recognition testing (which is based on presenting published material to find out what has actually been read) ignores opinion. Actual reading behavior is measured.

In magazine readership studies, Daniel Starch & Staff are well known among research organizations using recognition testing. A quick glance at the technique used in a Starch study will show you how newspaper and magazine studies are conducted. Some of the essential differences in analyzing readership of the two media will be uncovered.

Advertisement Readership Service, Daniel Starch & Staff, Inc. Interviewers check respondents on reading of advertisements one-half page or larger in a number of national publications. Respondents are divided equally among men and women. The advertisement as a whole is checked on a three-way basis:

1. *Noted.* Reader has seen the advertisement.
2. *Advertiser-Associated.* Reader has seen or read the advertisement enough to know the product or advertiser.

STARCH READERSHIP SUMMARY REPORT

Reader's Digest — October 1987 — [1A]
Total of 54 1/2 Page or Larger Ads — Men Readers

PAGE	SIZE& COLOR	ADVERTISER	RANK BY ASSOC.	PERCENTAGES NOTED	PERCENTAGES ASSOC-IATED	PERCENTAGES READ MOST	READERSHIP INDEXES NOTED	READERSHIP INDEXES ASSOC-IATED	READERSHIP INDEXES READ MOST
		AUTO ACCESSORIES/EQUIPMENT							
229	1P4B	GM QUALITY SERVICE/PARTS	4	66	65	26-	150	181	289-
247	1P4B	CHRYSLER MOTORS MOPAR PARTS	16	52	45	10	118	125	111
		BANKING/FINANCE							
14	1P4B	U. S. MINT UNITED STATES CONSTITUTION COINS	12	54	50	23	123	139	256
203	1P	1ST NATIONWIDE NETWORK	41	27	25	11	61	69	122
205	1P	1ST NATIONWIDE NETWORK	42	26	24	15-	59	67	167-
		BLDG. EQUIP./FIXTURES/SYSTEMS							
10	1P4B	LENNOX PULSE GAS FURNACE	30	34	32	8	77	89	89
		COMMUNICATION/PUBLIC UTILITY							
12	1S4B	AT&T LONG DISTANCE NETWORK	6	59	57	9	134	158	100
		CONFECTIONERY/SNACKS							
255	1P4B	WRIGLEY'S FREEDENT GUM	19	46	43	6	105	119	67
		COOKING PRODUCTS/SEASONINGS							
214	1P4B	CLAUSSEN PICKLES	32	34	30	9	77	83	100
219	1P4B	PROMISE MARGARINE	37	30	27	2	68	75	22
		DAIRY PRODUCTS							
216	H1/2S4B	KRAFT PHILADELPHIA BRAND CREAM CHEESE	18	46	44	16-	105	122	178-
		FOOD BEVERAGES							
80	1P4B	FOLGERS DECAFFEINATED COFFEE CRYSTALS	12	50	50	12-	114	139	133-
241	1P4B	SANKA GROUND/FREEZE-DRIED & INSTANT DECAFFEINATED COFFEES	8	59	56	19-	134	156	211-
		FRUITS/VEGETABLES							
6	1P4	CALIFORNIA PRUNE BOARD	48	23	20	6	52	56	67
		HOME ELECTRONICS EQUIPMENT							
5	1P4	K MART/GE TELEVISION & RCA STEREO VCR	25	46	38	7	105	106	78
252	1P4B	SYLVANIA SUPERSET TV & VCR HBO AND CINEMAX GIVEAWAY OFFER	11	54	51	20	123	142	222
		HOSIERY							
35	M2/4P4B	HANES FITTING PRETTY SILLY SIGNATURE QUEEN SIZE PANTYHOSE OFFER	52	18	15	*-	41	42	*-

[*] Less than 0.5% [-] Fewer than 50 Words
[**] Not Applicable [=] Fewer than 4 Words
[#] Page/Copy varies

Figure 21–4. Typical page from a Starch Report. All advertisements a half page or larger were researched in an issue of the *Reader's Digest.*
Courtesy of Starch INRA Hooper, Inc.

3. *Read-Most.* Reader has read 50 percent or more of the advertisement's reading matter.

Parts of the advertisement—headline, subheads, text units, illustrations, and logotypes—are also checked for observation and reading.

In addition to determining the percentage of reading for advertisements and their component parts, the Starch service also provides cost ratios of the advertisements and ranks them in terms of dollars spent to obtain readers. These figures are refined to the point where the studies tell the advertiser just how much it costs merely to get the advertisement seen, or seen and associated, or read most. You might get a high cost for the "seen" classification, but your copy may be read so well that a high percentage of those who read the advertisement read most of the copy. Your cost ratio for Read-Most would then be low.

The real value of recognition studies is in cumulative studies. It would be unwise to let one study entirely influence an important decision. You can compare that one study, however, with other studies.

Cumulative figures can show you whether your copy was "on" or "off." The principal strength of readership studies is in the long-trend aspect. As study piles on study, you see certain appeals pulling consistently. Cer-

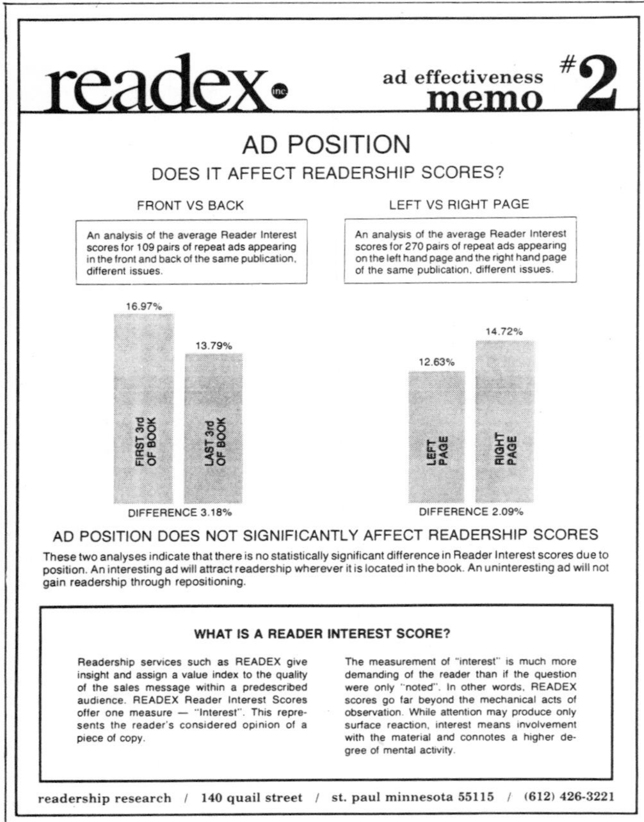

readex inc. ad effectiveness memo #2

AD POSITION

DOES IT AFFECT READERSHIP SCORES?

FRONT VS BACK

An analysis of the average Reader Interest scores for 109 pairs of repeat ads appearing in the front and back of the same publication, different issues.

LEFT VS RIGHT PAGE

An analysis of the average Reader Interest scores for 270 pairs of repeat ads appearing on the left hand page and the right hand page of the same publication, different issues.

AD POSITION DOES NOT SIGNIFICANTLY AFFECT READERSHIP SCORES

These two analyses indicate that there is no statistically significant difference in Reader Interest scores due to position. An interesting ad will attract readership wherever it is located in the book. An uninteresting ad will not gain readership through repositioning.

WHAT IS A READER INTEREST SCORE?

Readership services such as READEX give insight and assign a value index to the quality of the sales message within a predescribed audience. READEX Reader Interest Scores offer one measure — "Interest". This represents the reader's considered opinion of a piece of copy.

The measurement of "interest" is much more demanding of the reader than if the question were only "noted". In other words, READEX scores go far beyond the mechanical acts of observation. While attention may produce only surface reaction, interest means involvement with the material and connotes a higher degree of mental activity.

readership research / 140 quail street / st. paul minnesota 55115 / (612) 426-3221

Figure 21–5. Readex research finding. Various elements in advertising—position, repetition, use of color, etc.—are analyzed and reported in such memos.
Courtesy of Readex, Inc.

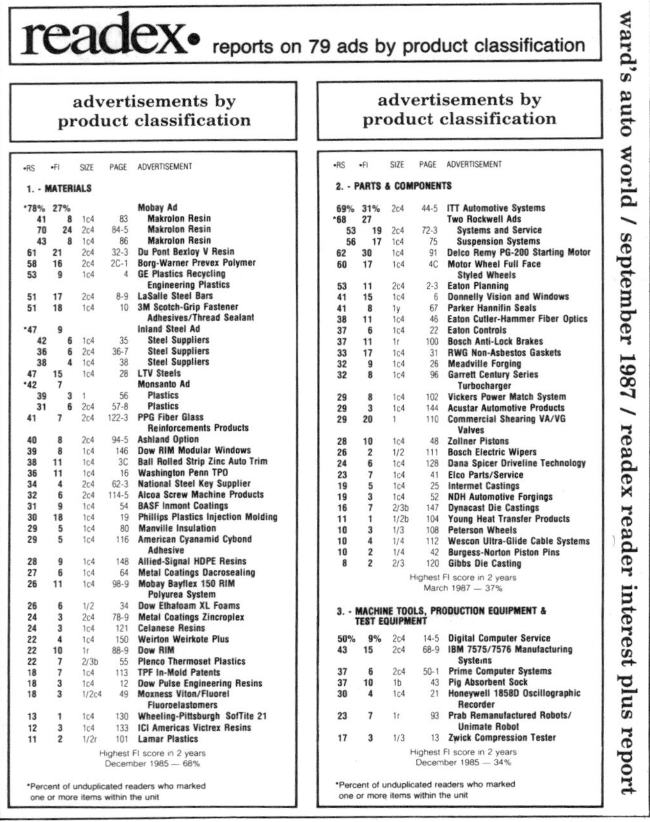

readex• reports on 79 ads by product classification

ward's auto world / september 1987 / readex reader interest plus report

advertisements by product classification

•RS	•FI	SIZE	PAGE	ADVERTISEMENT
1. - MATERIALS				
*78%	27%			Mobay Ad
41	8	1c4	83	Makrolon Resin
70	24	2c4	84-5	Makrolon Resin
43	8	1c4	86	Makrolon Resin
61	21	2c4	32-3	Du Pont Bexloy V Resin
58	16	2c4	2C-1	Borg-Warner Prevex Polymer
53	9	1c4	4	GE Plastics Recycling Engineering Plastics
51	17	2c4	8-9	LaSalle Steel Bars
51	18	1c4	10	3M Scotch-Grip Fastener Adhesives/Thread Sealant
*47	9			Inland Steel Ad
42	6	1c4	35	Steel Suppliers
36	6	2c4	36-7	Steel Suppliers
38	4	1c4	38	Steel Suppliers
47	15	1c4	28	LTV Steels
*42	7			Monsanto Ad
39	3	1	56	Plastics
31	6	2c4	57-8	Plastics
41	7	2c4	122-3	PPG Fiber Glass Reinforcements Products
40	8	2c4	94-5	Ashland Option
39	8	1c4	146	Dow RIM Modular Windows
38	11	1c4	3C	Ball Rolled Strip Zinc Auto Trim
36	11	1c4	16	Washington Penn TPO
34	4	2c4	62-3	National Steel Key Supplier
32	6	2c4	114-5	Alcoa Screw Machine Products
31	9	1c4	54	BASF Inmont Coatings
30	18	1c4	19	Phillips Plastics Injection Molding
29	5	1c4	80	Manville Insulation
29	5	1c4	116	American Cyanamid Cybond Adhesive
28	9	1c4	148	Allied-Signal HDPE Resins
27	6	1c4	64	Metal Coatings Dacrosealing
26	11	1c4	98-9	Mobay Bayflex 150 RIM Polyurea System
26	6	1/2	34	Dow Ethafoam XL Foams
24	3	2c4	78-9	Metal Coatings Zincroplex
24	3	1c4	121	Celanese Resins
22	4	1c4	150	Weirton Weirkote Plus
22	10	1r	88-9	Dow RIM
22	7	2/3b	55	Plenco Thermoset Plastics
18	7	1c4	113	TPF In-Mold Patents
18	3	1c4	12	Dow Pulse Engineering Resins
18	3	1/2c4	49	Moxness Viton/Fluorel Fluoroelastomers
13	1	1c4	130	Wheeling-Pittsburgh SofTite 21
12	3	1c4	133	ICI Americas Victrex Resins
11	2	1/2r	101	Lamar Plastics

Highest FI score in 2 years
December 1985 — 68%

*Percent of unduplicated readers who marked one or more items within the unit

advertisements by product classification

•RS	•FI	SIZE	PAGE	ADVERTISEMENT
2. - PARTS & COMPONENTS				
69%	31%	2c4	44-5	ITT Automotive Systems
*68	27			Two Rockwell Ads
53	19	2c4	72-3	Systems and Service
56	17	1c4	75	Suspension Systems
62	30	1c4	91	Delco Remy PG-200 Starting Motor
60	17	1c4	4C	Motor Wheel Full Face Styled Wheels
53	11	2c4	2-3	Eaton Planning
41	15	1c4	6	Donnelly Vision and Windows
41	8	1y	67	Parker Hannifin Seals
38	11	1c4	46	Eaton Cutler-Hammer Fiber Optics
37	6	1c4	22	Eaton Controls
37	11	1r	100	Bosch Anti-Lock Brakes
33	17	1c4	31	RWG Non-Asbestos Gaskets
32	9	1c4	26	Meadville Forging
32	8	1c4	96	Garrett Century Series Turbocharger
29	8	1c4	102	Vickers Power Match System
29	3	1c4	144	Acustar Automotive Products
29	20	1	110	Commercial Shearing VA/VG Valves
28	10	1c4	48	Zollner Pistons
26	2	1/2	111	Bosch Electric Wipers
24	6	1c4	128	Dana Spicer Driveline Technology
23	7	1c4	41	Elco Parts/Service
19	5	1c4	25	Intermet Castings
19	3	1c4	52	NDH Automotive Forgings
16	7	2/3b	147	Dynacast Die Castings
11	1	1/2b	104	Young Heat Transfer Products
10	3	1/3	108	Peterson Wheels
10	4	1/4	112	Wescon Ultra-Glide Cable Systems
10	2	1/4	42	Burgess-Norton Piston Pins
8	2	2/3	120	Gibbs Die Casting

Highest FI score in 2 years
March 1987 — 37%

•RS	•FI	SIZE	PAGE	ADVERTISEMENT
3. - MACHINE TOOLS, PRODUCTION EQUIPMENT & TEST EQUIPMENT				
50%	9%	2c4	14-5	Digital Computer Service
43	15	2c4	68-9	IBM 7575/7576 Manufacturing Systems
37	6	2c4	50-1	Prime Computer Systems
37	10	1b	43	Pig Absorbent Sock
30	4	1c4	21	Honeywell 1858D Oscillographic Recorder
23	7	1r	93	Prab Remanufactured Robots/ Unimate Robot
17	3	1/3	13	Zwick Compression Tester

Highest FI score in 2 years
December 1985 — 34%

*Percent of unduplicated readers who marked one or more items within the unit

Figure 21–6. Readex report based on analysis of advertisements appearing in a business magazine. In this typical page from a Readex report we have the RS scores (percentage of sample remembering seeing the item) and FI scores (percentage of sample finding the information of interest).
Courtesy of Readex, Inc.

tain ideas pull every time—others fail consistently. The studies attempt to give the "why."

Readex Reader Interest Studies

Readex, an independent research firm, has been designing and implementing readership in print communications since 1947, with a specialization in business publications. In one recent year the firm conducted 225 studies for 107 different publications. It measures "interest" in all editorial and advertising items presented in each case.

"Interest" in advertising is considered by Readex to be a fundamental element of the selling process. The firm says that to sell a product or service (a) a prospective customer must first be made aware of the opportunity and (b) sufficient interest must then be developed to motivate the prospect toward a sale.

When measurement is made of "Reader Interest" in all advertisements and editorial items, one score—the percentage of all respondents indicating interest—is reported for each. Advertisement scores are ranked and grouped by product category.

An additional service is "Reader Interest Plus," which measures both "Reader Interest" and "Remember Seeing" for all advertisements one-half page and larger, plus "Reader Interest" in all editorial items. Advertisement scores are reported by product category.

Readex surveys go anywhere the mail goes, thus including hard-to-reach readers. Results are said to be geographically representative. Because readers complete the surveys at their convenience, Readex samples reflect most personal backgrounds.

A duplicate copy of the issue is sent to a random selection of the publication's primary domestic circulation. Respondents are asked to go through the issue from cover to cover and mark with a red pencil all items they "found of interest." Complete surveys are returned to Readex, with the results usually reported on a base of 100.

Methodology. Readex readership reports are developed by mailing duplicate copies of the study issue along with copyrighted instructions to a representative sample of regular readers.

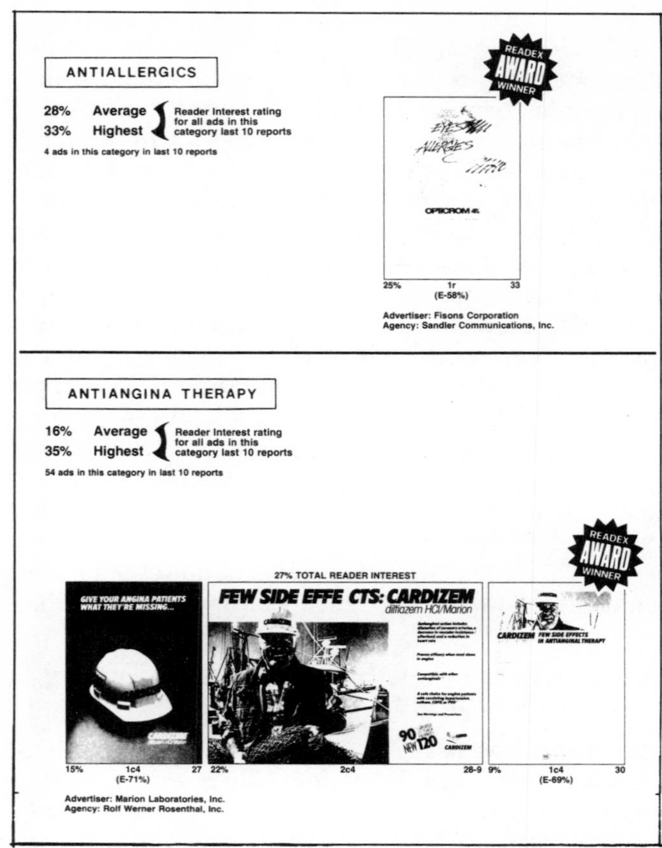

Figure 21–7. Award-winning advertisements analyzed by Readex. Both of these advertisements appeared in a professional magazine read chiefly by physicians.
Courtesy of Readex, Inc.

Study kits are timed to arrive approximately midway between regular issues. The marked magazines are then returned to Readex by business reply mail. Reports are based on approximately 100 responses, and most are identified by name, address, title, and industry.

Results are usually available three to four weeks after the study closes.

Advantages of the Readex Methodology

1. Mail surveys offer a cost-effective means of gathering data, allowing larger and more statistically sound samples.
2. Surveys go wherever the mail goes, reaching those respondents missed by personal or telephone interviews.
3. Respondents complete the surveys at their convenience; thus, no appointments or second calls are needed.
4. There is no interviewer bias in the results.

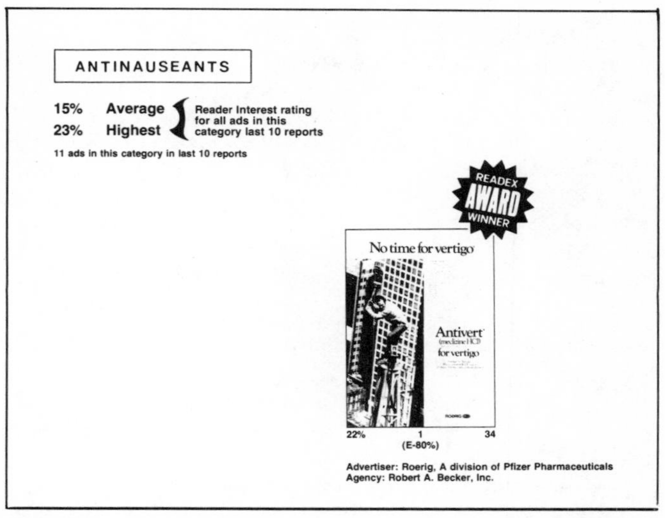

Figure 21–8. Readex-analyzed, award-winning advertisement. In this advertisement, aimed at physician-readers of a medical magazine, the Readex score for reader interest is significantly above average.
Courtesy of Readex, Inc.

Defects of Recognition Testing

Poor memory, dishonesty, false pride, either in combination or singly, reduce the believability. Sometimes magazine researchers attempt to measure the effect of the three factors by setting up a "confusion control." Thus, they ask people to point out advertisements they have read in a certain magazine. The advertisements have not yet appeared in any publication but have been so cleverly inserted in the test issue that the respondents think they are already-run advertisements.

The researcher finds out how much the reading of such advertisements totals and makes a statistical allowance for this confusion factor in the final figures.

So many people become honestly confused in readership tests that an allowance must be made for this "honest" confusion. Marlboro advertisements, for example, have a strong family resemblance. It is easy to think that you have seen a specific Marlboro advertisement when actually you are remembering not that advertisement but the impression created by the series. Other persons, ashamed to admit they read certain items, skip by them when being interviewed. Thus the accuracy of the readership percentage is reduced.

Not all reading is reported. Respondents may say "No, I didn't read that advertisement." In turn, the interviewer may accept the negative answer instead of making certain that the respondent has not actually read the advertisement. Much reading is not declared by the respondent. If respondents fail to tell you what they have read, you are helpless.

There is no way to correct for this factor, nor to validate your findings. The man conducting the test has

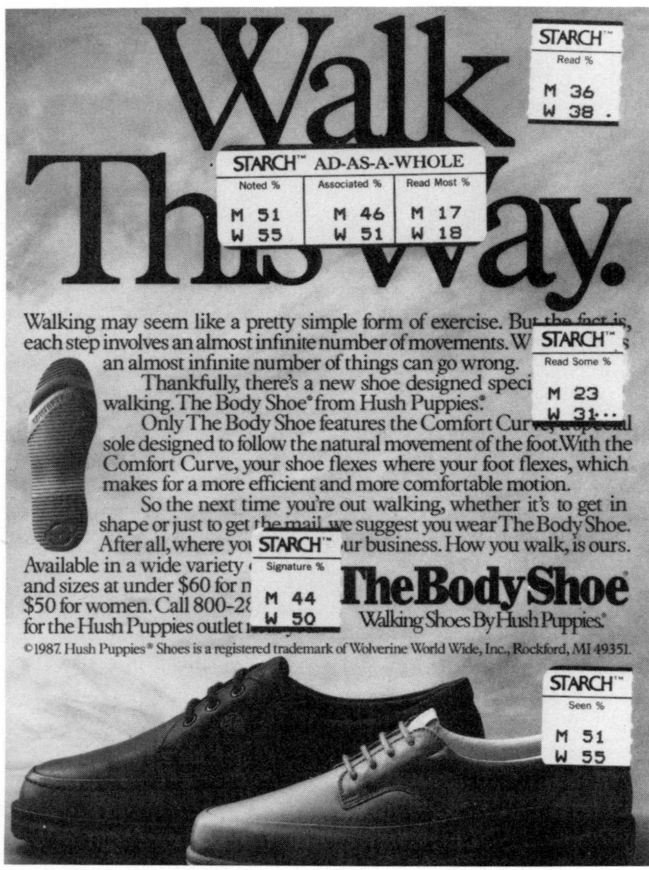

Figure 21–9. High readership advertisement. Starch figures for this advertisement are above average. Considering the amount of copy, the Read-Most figures are especially good. Likewise, the Advertiser-Associated figure is unusually high.
Courtesy of Starch INRA Hooper, Inc.

nothing to work from. As one researcher has ruefully said, "If certain product advertising gets no more readers than the surveys sometimes report, the products would have to be pulled off the market."

Recognition testing measures memory or observation; it does not indicate sales or conviction power. This is probably the strongest objection to readership studies as a whole. Proponents of recognition studies, such as Daniel Starch, have attempted to show that there is a relationship between high readership and high sales.

In *Factors in Readership Measurements*, Starch has said, "In general, the more readers an advertisement attracts and the more completely it is read, the more sales are produced by that advertisement—except that some types of copy treatment actually repel buyers. The more reading there is of such advertisements, the less buying there is."

Opponents point to many advertisements that obtained low readership but which pulled big coupon returns—and vice versa. "You can't sell 'em if they don't see your advertisement" is the usual retort. The answer to that is, of course, that a thousand persons may see your advertisement yet no one will buy the product.

Many times, too, short copy will rate higher in Starch's Read-Most figures than will long copy. Yet the lower-rated long-copy advertisement will often far outsell the other because the readers it sells it "hooks."

In a sense, high readership and sales might be in opposite corners of the ring. You may have devised your advertisement for high readership. Tricky, unusual features may get you your high figures, but you may have worked so hard for attention that you crowded out a powerful selling message. You may be full of pride when you see the Starch reports, but your sales manager may feel a different emotion when looking over falling sales.

The real readership is the readership of your sales story by people who may subsequently buy—not general, casual readership. You should ask, "How many prospects read our message?" A diamond advertisement, for instance, might get high readership among older readers sighing for romance. The diamond salesperson will trade a dozen older readers, however, for one young bride-to-be; she represents prospect readership.

Some Defects—Yes. But Recognition Testing Still Has Its Pluses

Regardless of weak spots, recognition testing can yield adequate measures of attention. Where gaining attention and readership are the primary purposes of an advertisement, recognition tests are usually a cost-efficient research solution. Even hard-boiled mail-order people, the kind demanding "direct results," use a form of advertising which they didn't try generally until readership studies proved it effective: the editorial technique. Yet mail-order people scoff almost in unison at readership studies. "Sales, not readership" is their motto.

As already mentioned, the recognition study measures actual reading behavior—a more reliable measurement than that obtained through opinion or what the respondents say they have read.

The method is useful for comparing readership of different campaign advertisements, or competitors' advertisements, too. Unlike mail-order advertising, newspaper or magazine advertising may run a long time before sales results show that advertisements are not being read.

A readership survey gives the advertiser a reasonably quick and accurate method of checking advertising effectiveness. Poor format, for example, might discourage readership. One advertiser provides backing for this point. Readership was poor on an advertisement he felt certain contained effective copy. When he examined the advertisement critically, he discovered the trouble: the format was dull, conventional, lifeless. Using the same copy but giving it a new dress, he tried again. This time he inserted several lively illustrations instead of one drab one. Copy was broken into small doses. Captions were plentiful. The advertisement was a success.

A warning should be made here. When comparing readership results—from a Starch report, for example—you should compare products in the same group. Your most valid comparison in readership is made with your competitor's advertising. Comparing your readership with that of a noncompetitor is meaningless.

Recognition Testing: Summing Up

Results from recognition studies have pointed the way to many techniques now used by copywriters. Recipes in food copy, for example, were shown from the first readership study to assure good attention from readers. Editorial techniques, shown by readership studies to get high readership, have been used more and more. Questions on layout and position have been settled through recognition studies. Such fundamental questions as "Will people read long copy?" "Does small type stop reading?" have been answered by recognition studies.

Not just one, but many studies have provided the answers. Questions are still being settled. A mass of evidence is becoming available as recognition studies pile up. Admittedly the conclusions are averages; they cannot be projected to every individual case. Still they point the way. The long-range value of the studies is obvious.

Consider vitamins, for instance. For years, advertisement copy that could squeeze vitamins in somewhere had almost automatically good readership. Then it was noticed through recognition studies that vitamins were not catching so many readers—the vitamin honeymoon was over and food advertisers began to think of other appeals.

Recognition studies are usually praised by those advertisers whose advertisements get high readership. They are often called unrealistic and silly by advertisers who happen to produce low-readership advertising.

Other Recognition Tests

Measurement of separate advertisements. Respondents are shown a number of advertisements clipped from a newspaper or magazine. They select advertisements they think they have seen published. They are then asked detailed questions about each of the advertisements. An advantage of this method is that the interviewer can thus lessen the influence of nearby editorial matter on the reading of advertisements.

Often, in recognition tests, respondents will answer that they have seen an advertisement simply because they have read the editorial matter near it. Also, since the advertisement is taken out of the usual reading sequence of the magazine, there is no chance for this factor to inflate the claimed reading. The method, of course, still has the usual disadvantages found in recognition testing.

Controlled recognition testing. A number of techniques have been worked out to correct the interview error occasioned by respondents' dishonesty or faulty memory. Some of these techniques require control groups. In a typical situation one group has seen the advertisements, the other has not. Reading differences are then balanced.

Another technique, the system of "confusion control" already described, uses the standard procedure of showing advertisements that have been run and others that have not. By applying a simple formula the researchers can weed out the unreliable interviews and come out with a close estimate of actual readership. The formula for this type of testing runs like this:

1. One hundred persons are interviewed.
2. Three persons claimed readership of an advertisement not yet published.
3. Thirty-three persons indicate readership of an advertisement that has run.
4. Subtract 3 from 100 (97).
5. Subtract 3 from 33 (30).
6. Readership is 30 persons out of 97 or 30.9 percent.

This method, used in magazine and newspaper studies, has also been used by the Traffic Audit Bureau (TAB) in analyzing poster reading.

Identification Test

In a typical identification test, a person is shown an advertisement in which all identifying features have been inked or pasted out. The person is then asked to identify the advertisement by indicating what company, product, or service is being advertised. The rest of the advertisements in the newspaper or magazine have been "masked."

Whether the results from identification testing are meaningful is debatable. Some advertisers feel, however, that high identification of their advertisements gives an important clue to the success of the advertising—especially in campaign advertising, where the advertiser wants assurance that the campaign idea and format are going over.

Recall Tests

A recall test tries to determine what you remember about an advertisement. Unlike in the recognition test, usually no advertisement is shown. The recall test aims at determining the positive, lasting impressions made by an advertisement some time after it has run.

Brand consciousness is probably measured better through recall testing than through any other method. Since no advertisement is shown, respondents must yank up facts about the advertising out of their minds without help from their visual sense. This form of testing is best administered by research experts, since the posing of the questions and interpretation of results are jobs for a specialist. Three forms of recall testing dominate:

- Unaided recall
- Aided recall
- Triple associates

Unaided recall. This form of recall testing is used very little. It consists of asking questions that provide no starting clue on which the respondent may base his answer. Information obtained from the vague questions that must be asked yield vague results. For instance, you might be asked, "What radio commercials do you remember hearing lately?" The same question might be asked about advertisements you have seen. Without any assistance from the interviewer, you are thus forced to pull out into the light some of the hundreds of advertisement impressions jostling themselves in your mind. Trying to attach some meaning to the answers is a nightmare for the researcher.

On an individual basis it is almost impossible to isolate the factors that would cause you, as the respondent, to name some particular advertisement and not some other advertisement. On a mass basis, it would take a terrific number of interviews to bring out any usable facts. Suppose, for example, you were asked, "What recent advertising copy has impressed you most?" Picture the possible answers to this question. Think of the interviews needed to develop any worthwhile facts. Then think of the countless variables that might have brought the answers. For practical copy testing you may forget the unaided recall.

Aided recall. Advertisers spend millions to create brand consciousness. This "burning" of the brand on the consumer is one of advertising's most important jobs. "How well is our advertising putting our brand across?" is a question of quivering interest if you want consumers to walk into a store to ask for Wheaties, or Ivory Soap, or Zenith. One purpose of aided recall is to indicate what brand a consumer thinks of when a certain type of product is mentioned, such as: toothpaste—Pepsodent; tires—Goodyear; canned soup—Campbell's.

Perhaps you feel that testing brand consciousness is quite apart from copy testing. In a sense your feeling is justified, since such testing doesn't delve deeply into the copy as do readership tests and checklists. Lack of brand recognition may, however, indicate that little association is being created between a type of product and a certain brand. Poor copy may be one of the reasons for lack of identification. Other reasons might be faults in the position of advertisements, illustrations, media, timing, and campaign continuity.

What is the principal importance of the aided recall test? Simply this: it indicates at least the beginning of an association between the brand and a product. Scientific illustrating, expert copy, and page advertisements are useless if such association isn't made.

If, when you want a blanket or chewing gum, you don't think of brands to fill your requirements such as North Star or Wrigley's Spearmint, then the copywriter, artists, and other advertisement creators have wasted their time. If they have succeeded, the recall test will indicate not only the success of your advertising but also the relative failure of your competitors in obtaining brand consciousness.

The aided recall using a question, "Can you name a brand of shaving cream you have seen or heard advertised recently?" is virtually useless for single advertisements but can be useful for measuring campaign impact. From the answers, you learn whether the campaign is moving forward or is failing to impress consumers.

Impact testing. One of the more interesting forms of testing is provided in impact testing in which respondents "play back" for interviewers what they remember of advertising they have seen in magazines read in a recent period. While a full impact report contains measures of recall, it contains also measures of persuasion and idea communication. Each measure is important to the full appraisal of communication effectiveness. Recall is only one element of impact testing.

Gallup & Robinson, a well-known advertising research organization, has led the field in impact testing. The company has some of the biggest names in American advertising as clients.

These clients, who pay substantial fees for impact testing of each product they advertise, are informed by Gallup & Robinson what has been good and what has been bad about their advertising as revealed in each impact testing procedure that has been carried out. This information is given to clients on a regular basis in "clinics" that are usually conducted by Gallup & Robinson in the client's offices.

The test itself consists of an interview that usually lasts 40 minutes. Persons are approved as respondents after first proving that they have actually read the magazine being used for test purposes. They are then shown names of all products which have been advertised in 30 full-page or double-page advertisements in the test issue.

The next job is to tell what they remember of the advertisements that they think they remember seeing in the magazine issue. When they tell what they remember they are, in research parlance, "playing back" the advertiser's message. What the advertiser hopes will appear in the playback are:

- Sales points or arguments
- The advertiser's principal message
- Reasons for buying
- What ideas were obtained
- What went through respondents' minds as they read

It is obvious from a glance at these points that impact testing goes considerably beyond recognition testing in that its objective is to measure the effect of exposure to advertising rather than to determine mere reading of the copy message. Idea registration (called Proved Name Registration [PNR]) and buying urge may often be determined from impact testing.

While the aims of impact testing, like those of motivational research, are to dig deeper than the surface to determine what to put into advertising or to determine what makes advertising work, the method has its difficulties. Expense of such research is one factor since costs of the method limit its use rather generally to the larger advertisers with big-budget campaigns. This limitation is unfortunate since many smaller advertisers are thus frozen out and, as is very often the case, they are the ones who could profit most from using impact testing.

Another criticism, often expressed by researchers, is that the method is too difficult. The procedure is "understimulating" which means that the clues given for recall are so weak that an advertising impression has to be massive before it can be recalled.

Those who criticize impact testing in this manner, on the other hand, often call the recognition method, as used by Starch, "overstimulating." This means that exposure to advertisements during interviews is often more intense and longer than during normal reading of the magazine. Although there is some validity in the charge that the impact method is difficult, the fact remains that a great amount of copy guidance is obtained from impact interviews. Advertisers who employ impact research use it for long periods and seem satisfied.

Another Gallup & Robinson print-testing service is Rapid Ad Measurement. An offshoot of the magazine impact program, RAM, as it is called, permits quick reporting of results on advertisements that are tipped into stripped-down copies of *People* or *Time*.

In addition to speed, major advantages are higher recall levels and greater number of verbatim responses for qualitative analysis. Other than for a reduced number of advertising cues, RAM interviews are identical to those used for magazine impact testing.

In addition to magazine print testing, Gallup & Robinson furnishes test results for radio, television, and newspapers.

Speaking of aided recall testing in general, it must be conceded that a single advertisement has so little chance to catch attention and sink the brand harpoon into the reader that you might well think of aided recall as used mostly for campaign testing. Yet the very success of a campaign destroys, to some extent, the chance of using aided recall testing to measure the effect of the campaign copy.

Take RCA, for instance. If you were asked what brand of television sets you had seen advertised recently, the answer might pop out, "RCA." Actually you may have seen more advertising by Zenith, G.E., Sylvania, or Silvertone. Over the years, however, RCA had possibly built more impact than any other single brand in your mind. Your answer, then, was not impelled by recent observation but from the piled-up impressions of years.

To use aided recall testing for current advertising of a leading product such as RCA, you would need to refer to some unusual feature that had not been used in past years such as a slogan, illustration, or headline. This kind of testing, although a form of aided recall, has been given a more impressive title, the "triple associates test."

Triple associates test. Suppose someone came up to you and asked, "What automobile advertises 'Big car quality at lowest cost'?" If at the time Chevrolet were so

30" NISSAN MAXIMA CARS
"Conversations"

PERFORMANCE SUMMARY

Sample Composition: 112 Men
106 Women

Indianapolis	Rockford Files	7:17 PM
Louisville	Family Ties/Cheers	7:13 PM
San Diego	Barnaby Jones	7:13 PM

	Men	Women
INTRUSIVENESS/PCR		
Proved Commercial Registration (PCR)	38%	23%
Norm: Domestic & Imported Cars	25%	18%
IDEA COMMUNICATION		
Lead Idea: Good Style/attractive/elegant	47%	55%
Norms: Domestic & Imported Cars	64%	64%
AVERAGE NUMBER OF IDEAS COMMUNICATED		
Average Number of Ideas per Respondent	2.4	2.1
Norms: Domestic & Imported Cars	2.8	2.7
PERSUASION/FBA		
Favorable Buying Attitude (FBA)	50%	60%
Norms: Domestic & Imported Cars	46%	47%

Figure 21–10. Summary report from Gallup & Robinson. In this report we have several measures of a television commercial's effectiveness: Intrusiveness. Idea communication. Number of ideas communicated. Persuasion.

advertising, and you answered, "Chevrolet," you would have made the three-way connection sought in the triple associates test. Here are the three factors:

- Product—low-price automobile
- Brand—Chevrolet
- Copy theme—luxury car quality at lowest cost

As you can see, you are given two elements: the type of product and the theme. Then you supply the brand, thus making the third association. You might not be given the theme exactly as it is used. The question might read, "What automobile advertises that it gives the value of a luxury car at a lower cost?"

Finding the extent of the association of brand with copy theme is the principal goal of the triple associates test. The information is used for determining campaign effectiveness only. Although advertisers want to develop high identification of the copy theme, they are even more hopeful that the triple associates test will connect brand and theme.

Consumer recognition of the theme for itself is of little value. In some campaigns, actual harm has been revealed when it was discovered that consumers associated the copy themes with the wrong products. Uncovering of such misinformation is another value of the triple associates test. If the advertiser discovers that a high percentage of the consumers are identifying the company's copy theme with a competitor's product, then the advertisers should scan the advertising carefully—especially if the campaign has been running for some time.

Sales increases may be due to many factors other than the effectiveness of current advertising. A rising sales curve may be the final result of good advertising that appeared a number of months ago. It may also be due to improved selling methods, a change in the price levels, a more favorable business climate.

Should your triple associates test show bad results, you might, in a view of the preceding, do some worrying about your advertising even though sales curves are going up. The upward trend might exist despite the advertising.

As in aided recall testing, you must be careful if you are the dominant advertiser. To illustrate, imagine that you are the first peanut advertiser to promote vacuum-packed peanuts. Imagine further that you are the only really big peanut advertiser. Suppose for your triple associates test you ask, "What peanuts are vacuum-packed?" How much reliability could you place in the findings when many persons could guess your brand?

To get around this difficulty, you can ask the consumers to indicate by brand which of several products are vacuum-packed. In this list you might name such products as coffee, soup, pickles, peanuts, and shoestring potatoes. If the respondents included peanuts among the several products vacuum-packed, you would know that your advertising of the feature was making an impression. Similar testing conducted at regular intervals should tell you whether your campaign theme and brand recognition were becoming stronger or weaker.

To sum up, think of the following in connection with the triple associates test: (a) It is an excellent way to determine brand and theme association in campaign advertising. (b) Through this test you can often obtain a more reliable indication of the success of your advertising than you will get from rising sales. Many times, moreover, you will find a strong correlation between sales and high brand and theme awareness and vice versa.

On the negative side, don't forget that, as in so many tests of copy, the results don't necessarily measure conviction or selling power. You can establish superb recognition of theme and brand, but the consumers may buy your competitor's product. Often it's easier to capture attention than conviction—especially if you depend on "irritating" consumers into becoming aware of you. In such cases the triple associates test results may look good despite what consumers actually think of your product and your advertising.

Tachistoscope Testing

The section on impact testing mentioned that critics have called the Starch technique "overstimulating" and the impact method "understimulating." Tachistoscope testing of advertising was begun because its originators believed neither recognition nor impact testing provided measurements sensitive enough to produce statistically significant differences among most printed advertisements.

A long-used testing device, the tachistoscope is a slide projector hooked to an electric timer. In the test situation, advertisements on slides are flashed rapidly before respondents who then play back what they have seen.

Backers of the method assert that respondents will be stimulated enough to remember whether they have seen the advertisements and what they remember about them, but they will not be overstimulated by having been given so much time to look that they "learned" the advertisement while the test was administered.

A criticism of such testing by those who favor recognition testing is that it is impossible to measure exposure to advertising and the influence of the advertising on those exposed to it at the same time. These critics add that the importance of memorability has been overstressed since it cannot be assumed that the reader who can play back the contents of an advertisement has necessarily been favorably influenced by the advertisement. Nor does failure to play the advertisement back prove that the advertisement has had no influence.

From the viewpoint of supporters of the impact method, tachistoscope testing fails to supply the interpretive data and analysis supplied by the former.

Sales Tests: Any Value for the Copywriter?

You will find sales tests mentioned in many books as a form of copy testing. It is true that the efficiency of different copy approaches is discovered in sales tests. Also, it is true that packaging, pricing, choice of media, labor conditions, income trends, salespeople, inventory controls, and other elements affect results of sales tests. The form of advertising—position, advertising size, frequency—are tested as much as the copy itself.

Since copy is just one of the forces being examined in sales tests, it does not seem necessary for this book to delve very far into the subject. Copy has been the principal object of analysis in other copy testing procedures—and the copywriter is close to such tests.

Sales tests, on the contrary, are closer to the market research people, or the sales department. You will probably not have actual contact with such tests except to supply the original copy for the campaign. After that, you lose sight of the test as the sales and marketing people move in.

A sales test, briefly explained, might be used if you decide to test the effect of your advertising in two markets. One of the market areas is considered a "control" area. The other is the "test" area. Three or more cities are usually found in each area. The new campaign will be used in the test section. In the control area you will either (a) run no advertising, or (b) continue to run your old campaign. Sales results in the two areas will then be compared by checking store inventories in selected stores before, during, and after the advertising is run.

Possibly you will run a different campaign in each of the test cities. The results will enable you to compare the campaigns against one another as well as against the control cities.

Some advertising people believe only in a sales test, because they look upon the test as operating under "actual" conditions as opposed to "artificial" conditions of other forms of copy research. Yet many factors make the sales tests extremely difficult to control. Results must be examined with great care to avoid erroneous conclusions. Some of the difficulties:

- Selection of appropriate control and test cities.
- Sales ability of salespeople in the different areas. Poor salespeople in the test cities and good salespeople in the control cities might throw the whole test off, since the new campaign might thus show poor sales despite effective advertising.
- Dealer reaction. Unless dealers cooperate equally in all the test areas, sales variations will occur quite apart from the advertising.
- Competitive advertising and sales efforts may vary from city to city during the test period.
- Media differences are hard to control. Some newspapers and radio stations are much more aggressive than others in their merchandising promotions. They do a vigorous job of backing up the advertisers. Also, they may vary greatly in the amount of reader or listening interest they command.
- Unusual weather conditions during the test may affect sales results. A paralyzing snowstorm affecting one of the cities might affect its sales record negatively.

Think of the factors named. When you realize that there are many other variables and that, in addition, a sales test is expensive and time consuming, you can see why it is not of great concern to you.

Surveys as a Source of Copy Claims

Surveys are among the favorite tools of marketers who wish to substantiate copy claims. "Let's do some research," is an often-heard preliminary to running a survey. It is hoped that the survey findings will supply support for sought-after claims.

Such surveys, based on an adequate and representative sample, are a legitimate means of furnishing material for a copywriter to use. While the copywriter's judgment and experience are respected, it is comforting to have the additional backing of survey research.

Unfortunately, too many surveys sponsored by advertisers are biased and do not, in other ways, meet the standards of good research. Most often the weakness is in the nature of the sample, and sometimes it is due to the interpretation of the findings. In the latter instance, the advertiser may conveniently pick out those facts that tie in with campaign objectives and ignore those that do not, or the advertiser may deliberately misrepresent, or misinterpret, the findings.

Comparative advertising often gives birth to such questionable surveys. An example is furnished in the case of a well-known manufacturer of microwave ovens. This company based comparative advertising claims on a survey conducted among its own authorized service agencies. The FTC, in an order against the advertiser, said that the limitations of the survey should have been made clear in the copy. This copy created an impression that the survey embraced *all* service technicians, not just the ones working for the company sponsoring the research.

What lesson is there for you in this situation? Simply that if you are furnished with such survey material you should study it. If it has shortcomings, they should not be overlooked in your advertisement. A legitimate advertiser should welcome such intelligent and ethical judgment that can well save the embarrassment of a legal judgment or FTC order.

There is no reason why you as a copywriter should accept such survey results unquestioningly even if they *are* supplied by the client. This is especially true in these days when the courts are holding agencies liable, along with the clients, for the truth of their advertising.

Copywriters and Researchers: An Uneasy Alliance

One of the factors in the frequent lack of harmony between researchers and copywriters is that the former live in a world of numbers and statistics. When they hand page after page of statistics to copywriters, the latter experience a profound unwillingness to plow their way through the figures in an attempt to unearth usable copy points, ideas, or phrases.

Such reluctance forms the basis of the possible resistance of creative departments to copy-testing. Still, the copy people can be won over if the researchers try to get on the creative plane and work harder to help writers in understanding and applying research findings.

Some creative types think of copy testing as a crutch that encourages laziness on the part of copywriters who tend to rely so much on the researchers that the latter begin to control or unduly influence the creative process. This causes them to depart from their advisory role to creative management.

Researchers are trying to break down the research/creative gap. They want to be viewed as helpers, not adversaries. Thus, we find such developments as VALS (Values and Lifestyles Systems) originated at Stanford Research Institute. The program stresses helping advertisers apply information about consumers' habits and tastes to evolve more accurate advertising strategies.

Behind the research is an effort to find the "why" of purchases and to explain it in a form readily usable by creative people. A copyperson may thus know before the copy is written just what engages consumers in the buying process.

Although some creative people are opposed to being guided by copy testing, the trend in recent times has been toward more copy-testing and more use of it, if for no other reason than that advertisers think it sensible for some form of testing to precede advertising expenditures, whether or not the creative people agree.

Keep an Open Mind

Copy research is valuable if it does nothing but reduce the margin of error in the guesses of advertising people. It can unkink the thumb in the famous "rule of thumb" measurement you have heard so much about. When you lose touch with the market and the consumer, copy testing may bring you back. If you were to be asked the principal values of copy testing, you might answer:

- To determine *before* publication what copy style, copy approach, or copy appeals are likely to obtain the greatest readership and/or sales conviction
- To determine *after* publication the quantitative and qualitative aspects of readership and thus to indicate what copy techniques should be continued, discontinued, or modified for future use
- To obtain through cumulative findings a body of information about copy that advertisers may use to produce advertising of the greatest efficiency—advertising that will cost the advertiser less in time, effort, and money because it avoids the mistakes of the past

Do Not Let Testing Replace Good Sense. Good Sense Must Be Used in Analyzing and Applying Copy Testing

Consider the Flesch formula, for example. Your copy will, according to the readability formula, receive an equally high rating if the copy is printed backwards or if the sentences are jumbled. Since the word count and personal references are the same in either case, the readability score will be the same. Good sense is the final determinant of copy effectiveness in this case—as it is in every copy testing method.

PACT Principles

Twenty-one major U.S. agencies, in 1982, established copy-testing principles under a designation of PACT (Positioning Advertising Copy Testing). Nine principles were designated as a foundation for the use of advertising research.

In the following, you will find the nine principles listed, with a brief explanation of each (the principles are provided in full by the contributing advertising agencies). The principles listed here will provide a useful guide in performing and understanding meaningful research.

- Principle I. A good copy testing system provides measurements that are relevant to the objectives of the advertising.
- Principle II. A good copy testing system is one that requires agreement about how the results will be used in advance of each specific test.
- Principle III. A good copy testing system provides multiple measurements. Single measurements are generally inadequate to assess the performance of an advertisement.
- Principle IV. A good copy testing system is based on a model of human response to communications—the reception of a stimulus, the comprehension of the stimulus, and the response to the stimulus.
- Principle V. A good copy testing system allows for consideration of whether the advertising stimulus should be exposed more than once.
- Principle VI. A good copy testing system recognizes that the more finished a piece of copy is, the more soundly it can be evaluated. Alternative executions are required and should be tested in the same degree of finish.
- Principle VII. A good copy testing system provides controls to avoid the biasing effects of exposure context.
- Principle VIII. A good copy testing system is one that takes into account basic considerations of sample definition.
- Principle IX. A good copy testing system is one that can demonstrate reliability and validity.

Addendum

Which Mexico Tourism advertisement (see page 269) was more effective?

Ad A. It had two times the stopping power of Ad B. Ad A's illustration had broader appeal, conveying the idea that Mexico offers a good climate for a vacation. Ad B's focus on history has narrower appeal for vacationers.

Which Prudential advertisement (see page 270) was more effective?

Ad A. It had four times the stopping power of Ad B. It was also more effective in increasing interest in the product or service. Ad A's benefit is more specific. This benefit is reinforced through headline, copy, and illustration. Many times, however, photographs will pull better than artwork; also, real people have a strong pull. Despite these two points, Ad A's strength was in its specificity in contrast to the general approach of Ad B.

22

ADVERTISING LAWS AND THE COPYWRITER

In a grumbling, put-upon tone, Pete Rowland said: "I swear, I should have gotten a law degree to be a copywriter. Why did I waste my time in marketing?"

His luncheon companion, Anita Metterin, smiled sympathetically but said nothing. She'd heard this speech before.

Pete continued: "Look at the record. No matter what the product or service, I've had lawyers all over me. When it was soap, the FTC legal beagles picked up my complexion claims. And they didn't fancy my handling of the antibiotic story for farm feeds, either. Later, there was that quibbling by the FDA over that pharmaceutical ad. Still later, they did a big number on me—and I mean a big number—for that contest copy.

"What a hassle! It's been a never-ending tug of war between my efforts to write strong, selling copy and the lawyers who want to keep out of trouble no matter what it does to the copy."

You may, if you're writing copy for certain types of products (such as headache remedies, cold cures, soaps, certain food products, and cigarettes) be working harder to please the lawyers than the clients. As you type, you have a haunted feeling. Just over your shoulder you can sense stern-visaged representatives of the Federal Trade Commission, the Food and Drug Administration, the Better Business Bureau, and others whose job it is to protect the consumer; plus, of course, your competitors may be complaining about what you've written.

Are they frowning as they read your copy? You fervently hope not because your clients will be less than enchanted if your copy drags them into the courts.

Before you worry unduly about legal trouble, however, remember that of the millions of words of copy produced each year, only a small percentage will get the writer into any kind of legal trouble.

Furthermore, if you find yourself assigned to products or services that *are* troublesome legally, you'll be given the first day on the job a set of legal "do's and don'ts" that apply. By observing these cautions, using common sense, and being guided by your innate sense of honesty, you'll keep yourself, your clients and your agency out of trouble.

The single most important principle is to get the facts and make certain they are correct. Any attempt to write copy about a product or service without knowing in complete detail exactly what it is and does will invite legal difficulties.

It must be emphasized, though, that even telling the absolute truth is not always enough. Each sentence in an advertisement, considered separately, may be literally true and yet the entire advertisement as a whole may be misleading. This can come about because statements that ought to be made are omitted, or because the advertisement is composed or set up in such a way as to create a misleading impression. If the copy can be understood in two different ways, the advertiser is not excused just because one of its meanings can be sustained as accurate.

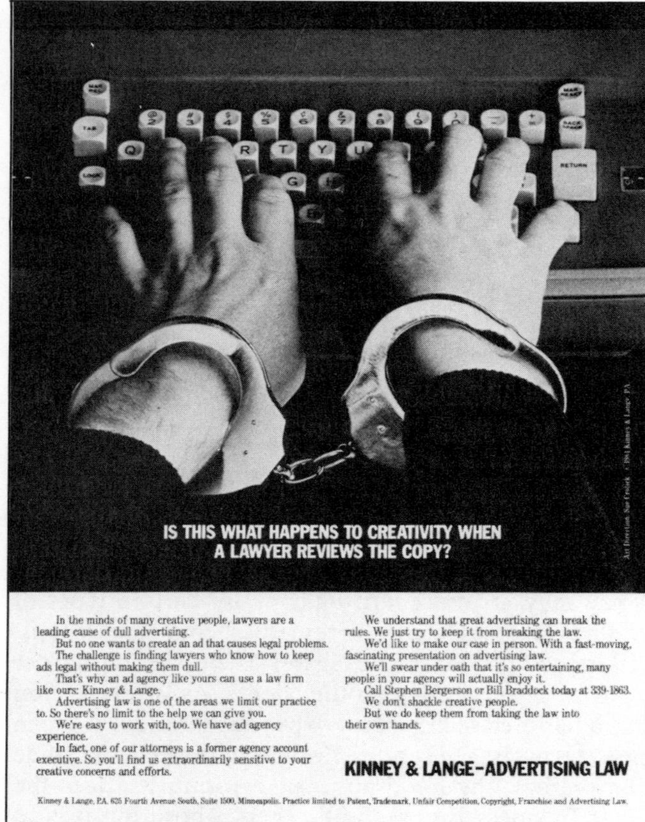

Figure 22–1. Advertisement of legal firm specializing in advertising law. You will find two other advertisements in this series in this chapter. This advertisement responds to a common complaint—that corporation lawyers are so conservative when they review copy that the corrected copy is without sparkle or sales power. Copywriters have long chafed against legal restraints. They want copy to be legal but they also want it to be bold and competitive. Lawyers tend to stress "safe" copy more than hard-hitting, daring copy.

Courtesy of Stephen R. Bergerson, Kinney & Lange.

It is essential to bear in mind also that most consumers are trusting and unsophisticated people. It is not a defense to a charge of false advertising to show that a particularly intelligent and acute reader should have been able to figure out the true meaning of the copy. The standard to be applied is not the level of intelligence of the average purchaser, but of someone even less knowledgeable than that.

Television creates its own special problems for the copywriter. The visual portion of a TV commercial may be misleading even though the off-camera voice is telling the exact truth; or the audio may be misrepresenting the picture that appears on the screen. Product demonstrations, in particular, must be genuine, and the accompanying dialogue must be honest and accurate.

Silly to Use "Tricky" Copy

There is no point in trying to be tricky when writing advertising copy. Short-term gains in sales possibly might result, but in the long run such a policy can do only harm to the advertiser. This can come about through loss of goodwill from disillusioned customers even though no government agency ever may get around to commencing a legal proceeding designed to force the discontinuance of the misleading copy.

Thus far in this introductory section, we have been dealing with the category of what generally are called "product claims." To show that the law is not completely arbitrary, there is another recognized category known as "puffery" or "puffing." Under this heading come the harmless exaggerations that are expressions of opinion rather than claims of some objective quality or characteristic for the product. For example, even the most gullible consumer is considered capable of grappling with the fact that such statements as "the best of its kind," "the most beautiful," or "the finest" might not be literally true. This does not mean that a false objective claim can be legalized by disguising it in the form of a statement of opinion. If an automobile will not get fifty miles to a gallon of gas, the advertisement still will be misleading even if the statement is put in the form of the manufacturer's opinion that, "I believe this car will get fifty miles to the gallon."

The difference is between a representation that induces the purchase and one that does not. Consumers who buy "the funniest book you ever read" can expect to be amused, but they don't really expect the advertiser to be able to prove the superlative.

Legal attitudes toward puffery have changed somewhat recently.[1] Many courts have become increasingly hostile to an advertiser's use of puffery as a defense. They are far less forgiving on this point than the FTC ever was. An example is furnished in the judgment (for $40 million) against Jartran (*U-Haul International, Inc. v. Jartran, Inc.,* 601 F. Supp. 1140, 681 F.2d. 216 USPQ at 1078 [D. Ariz. 1984]). U-Haul, a competitor, objected to such advertising claims as:

> Only Jartran can rent you trailers
> designed for the times.
>
> No one can rent you a truck like
> Jartran can.

In finding against Jartran, the court said:

> over the spread of time, and with increased (or perceived) reluctance of courts to resolve such claims, the rule of puffery had become a privilege to lie.

In its opinion, the court held that since the claims were meant to be believed and relied upon, a reasonable prospective purchaser would take them seriously. Accordingly, they exceeded the scope of permissible

1. Stephen R. Bergerson, Kinney & Lange. This discussion of puffery was influenced by suggestions from Mr. Bergerson. Likewise, he contributed up-to-date material on copyright, right to publicity, and corrective advertising, as well as material on the FTC. These subjects were covered in memos from Mr. Bergerson and in various speeches, most notably one on legal developments presented to the American Advertising Federation's Advertising Law and Public Policy Conference, Chicago, November 5, 1986.

puffery allowed by Section 43(a) of the Lanham Act. Section 43(a) is described later in the chapter.

Despite the fact that in many such cases advertising agencies are not named as defendants, the agency, in this instance, was named as a defendant and settled out of court. They testified that they had advised Jartran against making many of the claims that were questioned.

Product claims and statements of opinion, of course, are not the only areas in which legal problems arise in advertising. Permission to use copyrighted material, defamatory statements, the right to use a person's name or picture, proper trademark usage, and idea piracy are just some of the other areas where an awareness in advance of the possible legal pitfalls may save a great deal of trouble and expense that otherwise might be encountered. An attempt will be made here to discuss those topics that are most likely to affect the work of the copywriter.

Federal Trade Commission (FTC)

The one government agency most concerned with problems of advertising is the Federal Trade Commission (FTC). This agency, under the Federal Trade Commission Act, has broad authority to proceed against "deceptive acts or practices" in almost all kinds of commercial activity. The theory of the law is that misleading advertising, like other deceptive acts and practices, is an unfair method of competition. If a deceptive advertisement succeeds in its purpose, it will give the advertiser an unfair advantage over his truthful competitors. Such advertising is an offense even though no competitors are hurt, because the Federal Trade Commission Act is also designed to protect consumers.

The Federal Trade Commission is an administrative agency of the United States government that, like several others, combines the functions of prosecutor and judge. It has a staff that looks for violations and also investigates complaints sent to it by consumers and competitors. If the FTC staff believes that a particular advertisement or campaign is in violation of the law, it needs the approval of the Commission itself (there are five Commissioners) to proceed with the case. In recent years, the FTC and the courts frequently have filed charges against the advertising agency, in addition to the advertiser, when the investigation indicated that the concept for the allegedly misleading advertisement originated with the agency rather than the client.

A formal Federal Trade Commission proceeding is similar to a court trial, except that it tends to be interrupted for substantial periods and to drag on much longer. An administrative law judge presides; FTC staff attorneys represent the Commission; and the accused parties (known as "respondents") are entitled to be represented by their lawyers. If the administrative law judge decides the case in favor of the FTC, he will issue an order requiring the respondents to "cease and desist" their unlawful practices. The order can be appealed to the full five-member Commission. If affirmed there, a further review is available in a federal court of appeals; and some such cases have gone all the way to the U.S. Supreme Court.

Cease and Desist Orders

A cease and desist order may appear to be a mere slap on the wrist. Indeed, many FTC false advertising cases take so long to reach a conclusion that the challenged campaign has run its course and been discontinued. On the other hand, a violation of a cease and desist order can be punished with a civil penalty of up to $10,000 per day; and each day the violation continues can be treated as a separate violation, so that really substantial sums can be involved, on top of the expense of defending the proceeding from the beginning. Furthermore, the FTC has the authority to seek a preliminary injunction against an advertisement that is the subject of its regulatory proceedings.

Advertising cases often are settled at an early stage by the entry of a cease and desist order agreed to between the FTC staff and the respondents. A violation of such a "consent order" is subject to the same penalty of up to $10,000 per day.

In addition to the numerous cease and desist proceedings it is constantly bringing, the Federal Trade Commission also functions in several other and different ways. It issues advertising guides, trade practice rules, and standard rules. In addition to the Federal Trade Commission Act itself, which is phrased in broad general terms as indicated, the Federal Trade Commission administers several special statutes dealing with particular fields of commerce, including margarine, wool, fur, and textile products.

Two basic rules the FTC stresses are enough in themselves to give you a code to guide you in writing advertising copy: (a) laws are made to protect the trusting as well as the suspicious; and (b) advertisements are not intended to be dissected carefully with a dictionary at hand, but rather to produce an impression on prospective purchasers. Keeping these simple rules in mind will solve many of the legal problems in advertising copywriting.

FTC's Role in Policing Advertising Reduced in Recent Years

A change in the willingness, or power, of the FTC to police advertising created a regulatory vacuum. Because, consequently, it became unproductive to turn to the FTC with a complaint about a competitor's advertising, advertisers were forced to find a new way of dealing with such problems. The result has been an increase in private litigation between advertisers. Also, there has been a strong trend for advertisers to turn to self-regulatory bodies for help.

Along with the foregoing, another major development has occurred—the National Association of Attorneys General working together to regulate advertising at the state level. Individual attorney generals have also been active in bringing suits in their states. State regulation of advertising has serious implications for national and local advertising.

Section 43(a) of the Lanham Act. Once limited to trademark disputes the Lanham Act, through its Section 43(a), has been utilized heavily by advertisers who have persuaded federal courts to apply the section to advertising disputes. Section 43(a) reads:

> Any person who shall use in connection with any goods or services . . . *any false description or representation* . . . and shall cause such goods or services to enter into (interstate) commerce . . . shall be liable to a civil action by *any* person . . . likely to be damaged.

Application of 43(a) has resulted in an increase in private litigation because now advertisers may sue competitors for other than product disparagement or trade libel. For example, one advertiser can enjoin another's advertising when the other makes a "false representation" about its *own* product, even if the defendant advertiser has *not* made any reference to the plaintiff or its product.

Despite the diminished role of the FTC in policing today's marketplace, courts around the country draw upon previous decisions of the FTC in settling many cases under private litigation.

Also of increased importance in settling disputes between advertisers is the use of the National Advertising Division (NAD) of the Council of Better Business Bureaus and of the local Better Business Bureaus. The work of the NAD is described in detail later in the chapter.

Four Areas of Advertising That Might Involve You with the FTC (or Others)

The Federal Trade Commission is concerned with so many different varieties of false and misleading advertising that it is almost impossible to categorize all of them. There are, however, certain specific areas of difficulty that constantly recur in advertising cases brought by the Federal Trade Commission. Some of those of particular interest to advertising copywriters are discussed in the succeeding sections.

Premiums. When an article of merchandise is offered as a premium, it is essential for copywriters to learn as much as possible about the premium, just as they must learn about the product of the advertiser itself. A misdescribed premium is the responsibility of the advertiser, not of the manufacturer of the premium merchandise.

The most common problem arising out of the use of premiums is a misrepresentation of their value. Sometimes advertisers who are extremely careful when making claims about their own products are somewhat less careful in describing the premiums that they offer. If an advertisement states that a premium is worth a certain amount or has a value of a stated sum, that amount should be the price at which the premium merchandise actually is sold customarily when offered for sale on its own.

Premium offers also raise a multitude of problems under separate state laws. In order to make it practical to use premiums in national distribution, it is common to take two precautions. First, premium coupons have a cash value assigned to them. This ordinarily is a nominal sum like 1/10 of a cent, but the manufacturer must be prepared to redeem the coupons in cash at that rate on demand. Second, the coupon traditionally carries what is called a "nullification clause" reading somewhat along the following lines: "This offer void in any state where prohibited, taxed, or otherwise restricted."

Any premium offer on a large scale also may raise serious questions under federal and local tax laws, but these are not the responsibility of the copywriter and obviously are outside the scope of this discussion.

Contests, lotteries, and sweepstakes. A true contest is a perfectly lawful advertising method. Legal difficulties arise in two principal ways. The first is when the advertiser fails to give the full details of the contest. In such a case it frequently turns out to be some sort of a "come-on" device that will cost the reader much more than anticipated in extra fees for tie-breaking puzzles or some other hidden requirement. The second is when it is not a true contest at all, but a lottery, because the element of chance is present. This not only violates the Federal Trade Commission Act as an unfair method of competition but also is an offense under numerous other laws, state and federal.

The key to proper contest advertising is to make certain that all of the details are given clearly and unequivocally in the advertisements. This means more than a complicated list of rules in small type that a highly intelligent person might be able to figure out with close attention to detail.

A lottery is not a contest at all; it involves a payment (or other legal consideration) in exchange for the chance to win a prize. All three elements—chance, consideration, and prize—must be present or the promotion is not a lottery.

There ordinarily is no difficulty in determining whether a prize is involved. If no prize were offered, there would be no contest.

Chance means that the participant has no way of controlling the result. It may be understood as the opposite of skill. An essay contest in which awards are given for merit by impartial judges is perfectly satisfactory because there is no element of chance present; but a baseball contest that requires listing the standings of the teams in both the American and National leagues at the end of a particular month is something completely outside the possibility of control by the participant. It is guesswork, or chance, and not skill.

Consideration generally is found in the entrance requirements. For example, buying some breakfast cereal in order to get the coupon from the back of the box is enough to constitute consideration. It does not matter that the price of the cereal was not increased when the coupon was added to the back of the box. The consumer bought that particular box of cereal when otherwise he might not have purchased any, or have purchased a different brand, and that is sufficient to satisfy the requirement of consideration. The familiar provision for using a "reasonable facsimile" of the entry blank is included in order to avoid a violation of the lottery laws by eliminating the element of consideration.

A *prize* lawfully may be awarded by chance if there is absolutely no charge or obligation of any kind. So-called sweepstakes, with coupons distributed free to all comers, fall in this category. Conversely, if a prize is given for true skill as distinguished from chance, then it is not unlawful to charge a consideration for permission to enter the contest.

"Good purpose," incidentally, does not excuse a lottery. Although enforcement officials rarely crack down on fundraising drawings for charities, enterprises of this sort technically are lotteries just as if they were operated for advertising purposes or for private gain.

Testimonials and endorsements. An advertiser cannot escape responsibility for a false or misleading product claim by putting it in the mouth of an endorser. Testimonials and endorsements must be true and free from misleading statements. Merely because someone is willing to write a letter saying that a particular drug cured a disease does not mean that this necessarily is so, even though the author of the letter believes it to be true.

The Federal Trade Commission will take action against advertisements containing testimonials given by people who are not competent to pass judgment upon the accuracy of the statements of opinion that they are making There is a great deal of difference between a baseball player saying that he eats a particular brand of bread and likes it, and the same baseball player saying that eating a particular brand of bread has a beneficial effect upon his health.

There is nothing wrong about paying for a testimonial. The fact that the endorser receives some compensation for giving the testimonial need not be disclosed in the advertisement.

It is improper to take words or sentences out of context. A testimonial should be given in its entirety; or at least the portion that is used should not create a different impression from what the complete text would have implied if given in full.

When testimonials are used in advertising, they must be genuine. The natural tendency of any reader of an advertisement containing a testimonial or endorsement is to believe that a real person gave it. A fictitious endorsement, therefore, is an unfair trade practice.

The use of a testimonial also implies automatically that it is reasonably current. If the endorser no longer uses the product or if the product has been so changed since the date of the testimonial that the endorsement no longer fairly applies to the product that is advertised, then the testimonial should be discontinued.

A public opinion poll or market survey is the equivalent of a testimonial on a mass scale and its results must be used with corresponding care. In addition, reference to a poll or survey in advertising copy will be construed as a representation that proper sampling techniques were used and that the sample was of meaningful size.

Warranties. A special law on warranties for consumer products went into effect in 1975. It required a designation of whether the warranty is full, or a limited one. A full warranty must include a statement of the period of time it will remain operative. A limited warranty must set forth clearly what limitations are included.

These restrictions have teeth in them. For example, the law requires that the remedy (generally repair or replacement) must be provided to the consumer without charge and within a reasonable time after notice of a defect or malfunction. A warrantor cannot refund the purchase price as an alternative to repair or replacement unless the consumer agrees to accept a refund, or the warrantor can demonstrate that a replacement is not available and that repair is not commercially practicable.

In 1985, the FTC published its Guides for the Advertising of Warranties. (The subject of FTC Advertising Guides is taken up in the following section.) It is clear from the many pages of the Guides that any copywriter using the term "warranty," or its equivalent, must exercise special care and must be certain that the use of the term fits in with the advertiser's policies on the subject.

There are so many pitfalls and complexities attached to the use of warranty that the copywriter writing a warranty advertisement should study carefully the FTC's 1985 Guides for the Advertising of Warranties. It must be stated, however, that the FTC has the power to challenge warranty advertising that complies with the Guides but is deceptive in some manner not addressed by the Guides. Thus, while adhering to the requirements listed by the Guides will probably help a copywriter stay out of trouble, there is *still* a possibility for legal problems.

Advertising Guides

On several occasions, the Federal Trade Commission has issued what it calls "advertising guides." These are detailed statements that constitute basic policy developed by the Federal Trade Commission in specific business areas and compiled essentially for the use of its own staff. They are released also to the public, particularly for the guidance of advertisers, in the interest of obtaining voluntary cooperation and avoiding legal proceedings. Following are some examples.

Deceptive pricing. Claims of special savings, extra discounts, less than the usual price, and reductions from ticketed prices, have been among the most troublesome problems faced by the Federal Trade Commission enforcement officials. The Deceptive Pricing Advertising Guides go into these problems in explicit detail. Examples of both approved and disapproved types of statements are given, along with the basic principles that will satisfy Federal Trade Commission requirements.

A statement, for instance, that there is a reduction or saving from a specified retail price, or from the advertiser's usual or customary retail price, is improper if an artificial markup has been used to provide the basis for the claim of a saving. The claim is equally improper if it is based on infrequent or isolated sales, or on a price that was charged some substantial time in the past, unless, of course, these facts are stated clearly and adequately.

The saving or reduction must be from the usual and customary retail price of the article in the particular trading area where the statement is made, and the saving or reduction must be from the advertiser's usual and customary retail price charged for the article in the regular course of business.

Certain words and phrases are recognized as representations when an article is being offered for sale to the consuming public at a saving from the usual or customary retail price. Obviously, these should not be used unless the claim is true. Examples of words or phrases of this type are: "special purchase," "clearance," "marked down from stock," "exceptional purchase," "manufacturer's close-out," "advance sale."

Preticketing with fictitiously high prices comes in for special attention in these advertising guides. No article should be preticketed with any figure that exceeds the price at which it is sold usually and customarily in the trading area where it is offered for sale. In this connection, the Federal Trade Commission points out that those who distribute preticketed price figures are chargeable with knowledge of the ordinary business facts of life concerning what happens to articles for which they furnish the preticketed prices.

The same basic principle applies to the use of the preticketed price in advertising copy. The manufacturer may be held responsible for exaggerated prices in national advertising even though it is the retailer who misuses the figures; and the retailer will not be excused merely because it was the manufacturer who first advertised the fictitious price.

The key point to remember is that the word "price" itself constitutes an implication that the figure given is the usual and customary price charged by the advertiser in the recent regular course of his business in the trading area reached by the advertisement. This rule must be the starting point for all price advertising.

"Free" guide. The FTC guide "Use of Word 'Free' and Similar Representations" requires that all offers of "free" merchandise or services must be made with special care to avoid any possibility that consumers will be misled or deceived. This includes promotions of a similar type even though the word "free" may not be used, such as the "2-for-1 sale," "50% off with purchase of two," "1¢ sale," or "Buy 1—Get 1 Free."

The word "free" or its equivalent, such as "gift" or "bonus," indicates that the consumer is paying nothing for that article and no more than the regular price for the other. "Regular price" means the price, in the same quantity, quality, and with the same service, at which the advertiser has openly sold the product in the geographical area where the "free" offer is being made, in the most recent and regular course of business, for at least a 30-day period. In other words, the "regular price" may not be inflated in order to get back part of the cost of the "free" goods.

If there are any conditions or obligations attached to the receipt of the "free" merchandise, they must be stated clearly and conspicuously so as to leave no reasonable probability that the terms of the offer might be misunderstood. Disclosure of the terms in a footnote of an advertisement to which reference is made by an asterisk or other symbol is not considered adequate disclosure by the FTC.

In order to make certain that a "free" offer is meaningful, it should not be advertised in a given trading area for more than six months in any 12-month period. At least thirty days should elapse before another such offer is made in the same trading area. And no more than three such offers should be made in the same area in any 12-month period.

Tires and tubes. The Federal Trade Commission advertising guides for tires and tubes grew out of a long series of proceedings involving misleading terminology and various types of exaggerated product claims in this industry. One of the guides, for example, states that manufacturers should not use deceptive designations for the different grades of their products.

If the first-line tire of a particular manufacturer is designated "standard," then the same manufacturer's tires of a lower quality should not be designated as "super standard." If discontinued models or obsolete designs are offered, those facts must be stated clearly. Used products must be described adequately, so that it is clear they are not new. Terms such as "nutread" and "snow tread" do not constitute sufficient disclosure of this fact.

The unqualified use of absolute terms such as "skid-proof," "blowout-proof" and "puncture-proof" is improper unless the product really affords complete and absolute protection under any and all driving conditions.

The term "ply" is defined in technical detail. Tire advertising should contain an adequate statement of the identity of the fabric or other material used in the construction of the ply. Statements implying that tires possess a specified number of plies are not to be used unless this is the fact. The term "ply rating" is an index of tire strength and does not necessarily represent the number of cord plies in a particular tire. If a term such as "eight-ply rating" is used to describe a tire containing fewer than eight plies, then the statement must be accompanied by a conspicuous disclosure of the actual number of plies in the tire.

These technical provisions are included here as an illustration of the degree of detail into which the Federal Trade Commission goes on appropriate occasions. Obviously, it would be foolhardy to write copy for automobile tires without studying the Federal Trade Commission's Tire Advertising Guides carefully.

Trade Practice Rules

Still another function of the Federal Trade Commission is the promulgation of trade practice rules. Typically, these are quite complex and detailed sets of regulations worked out by members of the Federal Trade Commission staff in conference with representatives of a broad segment of the industry affected. They put the requirements of the Federal Trade Commission Act into concrete form as applied to that particular industry.

Over the years, trade practice rules have been issued by the Federal Trade Commission for dozens of different industries and practices. A few will be referred to here, largely for the purpose of indicating by example the fact that it is highly important for copywriters to determine whether trade practice rules exist in the industry with which they are concerned and to make certain they are familiar with them in detail if that turns out to be so.

Watches. A watch either is waterproof or it is not. In order to describe it as waterproof, the case must be of such composition and construction as to be impervious to moisture through immersion for the life of the watch.

The Federal Trade Commission trade practice rules include details of a specific test that requires complete immersion for at least five minutes in water under atmospheric pressure of 15 pounds per square inch and for at least an additional five minutes in water under atmospheric pressure of at least 35 pounds per square inch without admitting any water. If a watch does not pass this test, it may not be described as waterproof, although, possibly, it may be described correctly as "water-resistant" or "water-repellent." Here, too, a specific test has been promulgated by the Federal Trade Commission.

Similarly, the terms "shockproof," "jar-proof," "magnetic," and "regulated" are defined carefully. Improper use of any of these terms will be considered a violation of the principles of the Federal Trade Commission Act.

Products made of "gold." The use of the word "gold" creates a number of problems in the industry. The unqualified word "gold," or its abbreviation, cannot be used alone unless the part of the product so described is composed throughout of gold of 24 karat fineness. The word "gold" cannot be used at all to describe an alloy of less than 10 karat fineness. When the gold is more than 10 karat but less than 24 karat, the karat fineness must be shown in immediate conjunction with the word "gold."

Terms such as "duragold" or "goldene" may not be used unless the article is made of pure gold or of an alloy of at least 10 karat fineness. No phrase or representation indicating the substance, charm, quality, or beauty of gold may be used properly unless the article is of at least 10 karat fineness.

"Gold-filled," "rolled-gold plate," and similar terms also are described in terms of their technical definitions. It is an unfair trade practice to use any of these terms under circumstances where they do not meet the requirements laid down in the trade practice rules.

Luggage. The correct name of the material from which the luggage is manufactured must be stated. Luggage not made of leather, of course, must not be misdescribed. It is also an unfair trade practice to use tradenames that are misleading because they suggest the presence of genuine leather in a product made from imitation leather, or the presence of one variety of leather in a product made from a different variety.

Even genuine leather frequently is processed in such a way as to indicate that it is leather of a different type. The words "genuine," "real," "natural," and the like may not be used to describe leather that has been embossed or processed to simulate a different kind, grade, type, or quality.

The facts must be disclosed in detail when the product is advertised. For example, "top-grain cowhide," "simulated pigskin grain," or "split cowhide, backed with simulated leather" are appropriate terms that explain what the leather is and what finish has been applied to it.

Top-grain leather is the best grade. The trade practice rules provide specifically that leather from which either a layer of the top surface or grain, or a so-called buffing, has been removed shall not be considered top-grain leather. In addition, terms such as "waterproof," "scratchproof," "dustproof," and "warp-proof" should not be used unless they are literally true of the product.

Special Statutes

As indicated, the Federal Trade Commission is charged with the duty of enforcing a group of special statutes dealing with specific products or industries, in addition to its general powers under the Federal Trade Commission Act. During the past few years, it has become increasingly common to find specific statutes of this sort introduced into Congress, and there may be more of them from time to time. Some of the principal ones now in effect will be discussed briefly.

Wool products. The Wool Products Labeling Act defines "wool," "reprocessed wool," and "reused wool." It requires a clear and explicit statement of the true composition of any wool product and also a statement of other fibers in addition to wool if there are any such contained in the product. Although this law deals specifically with labeling, the same principles are applied as a matter of policy to the advertising of wool products and the rules and regulations under the Wool Products Labeling Act should be consulted in preparing advertising copy for any product containing wool.

"Wool" means the fiber from the fleece of the sheep or lamb, or the hair of the angora or cashmere goat. It may also include the so-called specialty fibers, which derive from the hair of the camel, alpaca, llama, or vicuna. Accordingly, it is proper to use just the word "wool" or terms such as "alpaca," "camel hair," "llama," "vicuna," "cashmere," or "mohair" if in fact the fiber is that type of wool. If, however, the fiber is reprocessed or reused, those words also must be included in order to avoid misleading the public.

The key facts that must be shown are the kind of wool involved and its percentage by weight. In addition, if 5 percent or more of any other fiber is included in the total fabric, the presence of this fiber also must be disclosed. And the weight of any nonfiber that is used as loading or filling must be disclosed with its proper percentage stated prominently.

Fur products. Since there are so many different types of fur and they come from so many different parts of the world, the principal objective of the Fur Products Labeling Act is to make certain that the true type of fur is named and that the country of origin is given in all instances. A Fur Products Name Guide has been issued by the Federal Trade Commission in which the name of the animal can be looked up and checked according to its scientific designation. The country of origin, of course, must be determined and disclosed.

Disclosure is required also if the product contains used fur; bleached, dyed, or otherwise artificially colored fur; or paws, tails, bellies, or waste fur.

Trade names or trademarks may not be used if they might create a misleading impression concerning the character of the product, the name of the animal producing the fur, or its geographical or zoological origin. The Fur Act specifically applies to advertising as well as labeling.

Textile fiber products. Another special statute in the series assigned to the Federal Trade Commission for administration is the Textile Fiber Products Identification Act. Like the Fur Act, this statute specifically applies to advertising as well as labeling.

If any fibers are mentioned at all, the correct generic name of each fiber present in the amount of more than 5 percent of the total fiber weight of the product must appear. Detailed regulations have been issued by the Federal Trade Commission, including a list of definitions of generic names for manufactured fibers.

In advertising any textile fiber product, all parts of the required information must be stated in immediate conjunction with each other, in legible and conspicuous type or lettering of equal size and prominence. The generic names of the fibers that are present in amounts of more than 5 percent must be listed in the order of their predominance by weight. If any fiber is present in an amount of 5 percent or less, then the list of ingredients must be followed by the designation "other fiber" or "other fibers" to make this fact plain.

Specific examples of various types of approved expressions are given in the regulations. The following statements, for instance, would be appropriate for use in advertising: 60 percent cotton, 40 percent rayon, exclusive of ornamentation; all nylon, exclusive of elastic; and all cotton except 1 percent nylon added to neck band.

An imported textile fiber product must be marked with the name of the country where it was processed or manufactured. This requirement applies where the form of an imported textile fiber product is not basically changed even though it is processed in the United States, such as by finishing and dyeing. However, a textile fiber product manufactured in the United States from imported materials need not disclose the name of the country where the textile was originally made or processed.

Red Flag Words

The watchful eyes of the Federal Trade Commission's alert staff are particularly sensitive to certain "red flag" words. The copywriter, too, must learn to recognize the danger signals. This does not mean that these words may never be used, but only that particular care is required because they are so easy to misuse. The presence of a red flag word frequently is an indication that the entire basic thought of an advertisement is wrong from the legal viewpoint. Of course, it is entirely possible to violate the Federal Trade Commission Act without using a single word on this list, but experience has shown that these are the ones most likely to create legal difficulties.

It would be futile to attempt a complete list of red flag words; there is no such thing and, even if there were, the passage of time would eliminate some old ones and add others. A few important examples will be discussed to illustrate the general principles involved in avoiding trouble. The fundamental idea is to make sure that you know just what the words mean and that your product can fulfill the promises contained in them.

Two such words have been discussed already: "free" and "guarantee" (or "warranty"). They are such troublemakers that they have been treated separately. The following are some additional sources of difficulty. Notice that a good many of these red flag words apply particularly to drug and cosmetic copy. Advertising for such products is watched with special zeal because these products affect physical and mental welfare. At one time, the Federal Trade Commission analyzed 915 of its cases and found that from all the different classifications of commodities, 65 percent of the questioned advertising copy related to drug products and 14.4 percent to cosmetics. In other words, almost 80 percent of all questioned copy fell into these two classes.

Banish, rid, stop, correct, end. Each of these five words says to the consumer, "This is the last of your trouble—it's all over now—permanently and forever." There may be times when you can use these words in their literal meaning. Too often, however, the Federal Trade Commission finds them used inaccurately—if not dishonestly.

Words in this group probably have been more used and abused in drug copy than in any other type of advertising. See if the following examples don't look familiar: Banish sleepless nights; Rid yourself of constipation; Stop psoriasis; Correct sluggish liver conditions; End headaches. Each of these statements promises relief to sufferers—permanent relief. It is the permanency feature that makes the Federal Trade Commission balk. Permanent relief means cure, and drugs seldom cure.

Cosmetics copy also often uses these words carelessly. It is too easy to write: "Acne sufferers—rid yourself of unsightly pimples" or "Ashamed of your hands? Banish roughness."

To generalize—think before you use these words. Consider whether your claims are truthful. Ask yourself, "Can my product cure, fix, or remedy *permanently* the condition under discussion?" If you can't answer that it does, you'd better use a different word, or qualify your statement with "may help rid you of. . . . "

Cure, remedy, therapeutic, curative. Millions of people suffer chronically from innumerable ailments: ulcers, varicose veins, eye trouble, headaches, arthritis. Each of these afflicted persons is anxious for relief. Some of them swallow gallons of patent medicines led on by unthinking or untruthful copywriters who promise "cure" or "remedy."

Unfortunately, real cures are rare. The proper procedure for the copywriter is to find out what the product actually has accomplished and claim only that it will relieve specific symptoms—not cure the disease (unless the manufacturer is certain that it really will).

"Remedy" is put in the same class as "cure" by the Federal Trade Commission. "Therapeutic" and "curative" are eyed suspiciously also.

Drug copy isn't the only type using these red flag words. Cosmetics, soaps, toothpastes, and foods are only a few of the other products that slip one of these words into their copy on occasion. All four of them are alarm signals.

Blemish-free, clear, smooth. There are few forms of mental suffering so acute as that felt by people who have bad complexions. Since they are so extremely susceptible to advertising promising them skin that is blemish-free, clear, or smooth, the Federal Trade Commission has been especially critical of such copy. Here are some points to remember in writing copy for a product used for skin care. If the product is applied externally and you promise that it will make the skin blemish-free, you must:

1. Establish the fact that the skin is blemished because of external factors and not because of a systemic condition.
2. Indicate that the product can be effective only if the cause of the blemishes is external.
3. Be sure your statements are based on proven facts. If the product is taken internally, then reverse the procedure of Steps 1 and 2.

"Clear," as applied to skin, is interpreted as blemish-free. Think of this definition when you use the word. Then set up conditions as you do when you use the expression "blemish-free" itself.

A "smooth" skin normally is difficult to promise unless you establish the fact that: (a) The skin is already rough because of some specified treatment or condition. (b) The regular use of your product will bring a change. Be sure that the manufacturer has support for your claim. It is better, incidentally, to stick to the comparative in this case. An outright promise of smooth skin through use of a product is easy to make but very difficult to fulfill. Many complexions will never become smooth through use of any product, but they may get smoother than they were. Be satisfied with that.

Safe, harmless. When you say unqualifiedly that a product is "safe" or "harmless," you are asking for trouble. Humans have a fiendish capacity for proving you're wrong whether you're writing about drugs, electrical apparatus, machinery, or even baby products. To say that a product is safe or harmless under all conditions is like saying a gun is unloaded. Too often you're mistaken.

Suppose a drug product is advertised as "safe" or "harmless." The Federal Trade Commission immediately wants to know (a) Isn't it possible that certain persons may be allergic to one or more of its ingredients? (b) Can all persons reading the statement rely on the fact that the preparation will not harm them?

Improper use of these red flag words in copy is more than just false advertising. Suppose a person does suffer from using the product because it turned out not to be safe or harmless. There is the basis for a possible damage claim.

So far as the law is concerned, when you say your product is safe you don't mean safe to a certain degree. You mean completely safe. The same thing goes for "harmless." If you're not sure, don't use either of the words.

Science, scientific, test, evidence, proof, research. Use these words, singly or in combination, and the credulous public conjures up visions of test tubes, microscopes, and long hours spent in the laboratory by white-coated men with Vandyke beards. If what you are writing is a television commercial, the picture may be right there on the tube to reinforce the impression created by the words. Yet this group of red flag words probably has been the most abused of all.

Scientists themselves use these words with great restraint. They imply a careful, systematic investigation conducted under unbiased conditions by experts who are trying to find out the truth, not to prove that their employer's brand has a slight edge over its competitors in some particular respect. Perhaps your company's laboratory discovers something about a product that you can translate into a copy claim. Do the findings of a couple of chemists become "science"? Because an informal poll of ordinary practicing physicians shows a slight favoring of your product, does this constitute "overwhelming scientific proof" that your product is superior? When you stop to think about the fact that even eminent scientists often honestly disagree, you can realize how extremely inaccurate and misleading an impression can be created by the careless use of these red flag words.

Approach "science" with humility and use "proof" and "evidence" sparingly. If you have substantial evidence to back you and if your use of the terms is literally true, then, of course, you would be foolish *not* to employ this very strong copy approach. Otherwise be careful.

Doctor, laboratory. These red flag words have much the same kind of built-in trouble potential as the group last discussed. A doctor's recommendation is considered a precious asset for any kind of product that can either help you or hurt you. "Laboratory" goes right along with it because that is where doctors frequently get their inspiration. But beware of the temptation to be anything but scrupulously accurate in your use of these terms. The Federal Trade Commission, knowing how gullible the public is about doctors' recommendations, is hypersensitive to copy of that type.

If you want to keep your "doctor" copy out of legal turmoil, here are a few points to bear in mind:

- Make sure the "doctors" to whom you refer are genuine physicians, licensed to practice medicine by a recognized governmental authority.
- If they are not such doctors, then make it very clear just what kind of "doctors" they are; for instance, doctors of naturopathy or chiropractors.
- Avoid the unqualified representation that a preparation is "a doctor's prescription." If true, the statement "formulated in accordance with" a doctor's prescription is acceptable. But be sure of your facts.
- Don't make a blanket statement of medical approval for your product based upon an informal survey which asked doctors for their personal preference or for a "less harmful than Product X" type of statement; these and similar limited expressions of opinion actually don't amount to recommendations.
- If an analysis by doctors reveals an insignificant advantage for your product over your competitor's product, don't blast forth with a claim of superiority. In the past, cigarette advertising sometimes was characterized by this kind of magnification of infinitesimal differences, without revealing to the public the fact that all brands contain substantial quantities of the substance involved in the analysis. Such things make cynics of the doctors and the public.

Often the word "laboratory" is used simultaneously with "doctor." The principal caution to observe with this word is that you must not refer to "our laboratory" when the client does not operate a control or research laboratory in connection with its organization.

At the same time, don't mention laboratory and doctors together unless the doctors actually did their research in the laboratory from which you assert they obtained their facts. Otherwise, you may have them approving research which they would not have endorsed according to their own ideas of research methods.

The word "laboratory" is viewed suspiciously whether or not doctors are mentioned in the same advertising copy. The strict attitude of the Federal Trade Commission is shown by a series of cases in which manufacturers were forbidden to use "laboratories" as part of a trade or corporate name because they did not actually operate any laboratory.

New. The Federal Trade Commission usually won't believe that if a product has been used for a time, it can be restored entirely to its original state through the use or application of your product. Whenever your copy asserts that the product stays "just like new" despite age, use, and abuse, get ready to defend your statements. "New" to the Federal Trade Commission means fresh—no different from the day you bought it. Remember that picture when you write "looks like new." Also keep in mind that the phrases "works like new" or "lasts like new" are subject to cynical legal scrutiny.

The scrutiny becomes especially watchful when the advertiser says that a process will make something old work like new. A "better performance" claim may very well be accurate and do a good selling job without ever getting attention from the Federal Trade Commission, while the little word "new" in the copy is waving the red flag and asking for trouble, which frequently comes.

Another facet to the use of the word "new" affects those advertisers who use "new" interminably in their advertising and on packages, thus giving the impression that the product is actually a new product, or a newly improved product. Generally, the Federal Trade Commission has taken the position that "new" should not be used to describe a product that has been in use for more than six months. Furthermore, it may be used properly only when the product is truly new or has been changed in a substantial respect. The word, moreover, does not apply to mere changes in packaging.

Although no more red flag words will be discussed, there are, of course, many more than have been presented here. The purpose in providing this partial list is twofold: to make you cautious in the use of these specific words; and to alert you to the necessity for honesty and accuracy that is the basic legal guide to all copywriting.

One of the dangers of running afoul of the Federal Trade Commission is that once they have discovered one product of a company to be advertised untruthfully, the Commission may then require that the company's other products live up to the regulations. This point is illustrated by a giant retailing firm whose advertising for a dishwasher was cited as being untruthful.

As a consequence, not only was the company enjoined to cease and desist making certain claims for the dishwasher, but also the company was told not to make claims for any of its major home appliances unless they were true and were backed up by reliable tests or strong substantiating evidence. Thus, if your copy brings the FTC down on you for one product, you can almost assume that your client's other products will be given a closer scrutiny in the future.

Food and Drug Administration (FDA)

Because of the constant jockeying for competitive advantage among advertisers of brand name merchandise, the FDA is ever vigilant in matters affecting labeling. In 1987, for instance, new FDA guidelines were issued that recognized the growing interest of the public in health and diet.

These labeling guidelines established standards for health claims relating to foods. Under the guidelines, a manufacturer of a high-fiber bran cereal that was promoted as an aid to an anti-cancer diet was given approval for its labeling claims. Heretofore, such claims had little chance of approval by the FDA. The change reflects not only increased responsibility on the part of advertisers to back up their claims, but also a flexibility on the FDA's part to recognize changes in the marketplace.

The Food and Drug Administration exercises control over a tremendously wide area of the entire American economy. Food is our country's single largest industry. Drugs are among the most widely advertised of all items. In addition, the Food and Drug Administration has jurisdiction over "devices," which are defined as instruments or apparatus for use in the diagnosis, cure, or treatment of disease or to affect the structure or function of the body of humans or animals. This definition includes everything from a fever thermometer to a massage machine.

And last but by no means least come cosmetics, which the law defines to include articles intended to be "rubbed, poured, sprinkled, or sprayed on, introduced into or otherwise applied to the human body or any part thereof for cleansing, beautifying, promoting attractiveness, or altering the appearance," with the single exception of soap.

Labeling Is the FDA's Chief Concern

The Food and Drug Administration is concerned primarily with the false or misleading labeling of products under its control. From the standpoint of the advertising copywriter, the principal problem, therefore, is package copy. In addition, any literature that accompanies a product has been ruled to be part of its "labeling"; and leaflets, brochures, or the like also come under the jurisdiction of the Food and Drug Administration when they are designed to accompany the product at the time and place of sale.

Other types of advertising for products controlled by the Food and Drug Administration are supervised by the Federal Trade Commission under its general powers over false and misleading advertising. But obviously it would be inviting trouble to make a statement in advertising copy that would go against the prohibitions of the Food and Drug Administration if it happened to appear on a label.

The statute under which the Food and Drug Administration operates deals specifically with the question of labeling that becomes misleading by failure to state what should have been included. The law provides that, in determining whether labeling is misleading, there shall be taken into account not only representations made or suggested, but also the extent to which there is a failure to reveal facts which are material in the light of any representations that are made.

There also is a specific provision that any information required to be on a label must be placed prominently, with such conspicuousness and in such terms as to make it likely to be read and understood by the ordinary individual, under customary conditions of purchase and use, for the particular product involved.

FDA Issues Helpful Definitions for Copywriters

Numerous detailed provisions are made for a great variety of specific products, some in the law itself and others in the voluminous regulations that have been issued from time to time by the Food and Drug Administration. Particularly worthy of mention is the fact that the statute provides for the Food and Drug Administration to issue definitions and standards of identity for foods, and many such have been published for a great variety of edible products. These definitions and standards of identity typically prescribe minimum quality standards that a product must meet in order to be entitled to bear that name. If the product for which you are writing copy fails to satisfy these standards, then it is not proper to use what you might think is its ordinary name. For example, if cocoa contains less than 10 percent of cacao fat, it must be sold as "low-fat cocoa"; and only if the product contains more than 22 percent cacao fat can it be called "breakfast cocoa." Obviously, this is the kind of factual detail that must be checked before copy is prepared.

If no standard of identity has been established for any particular food, then it must be labeled to disclose each ingredient by name—except for spices, colorings, and flavorings, which may be declared simply as such. There are provisions also for exemptions from these requirements, and the Food and Drug Administration has exempted various foods for various reasons. In a number of instances the indications are that these exemptions are only temporary, and definitions and standards of identity may be issued at a later date.

Drugs and Cosmetics Are Watched with Special Care by the FDA

Drugs and devices must be labeled with adequate directions for use. Special mention must be made where a drug is likely to deteriorate. New drugs may not be offered for sale at all unless they have been tested adequately and approved. Drugs listed in standard formularies such as the United States Pharmacopoeia must be labeled with their official names, and any differences of strength, quality, or purity from the official standards must be stated conspicuously on the label.

Cosmetics are subject to misbranding and false labeling restrictions similar to those affecting foods, except that there is no provision for definitions and standards of identity with respect to cosmetics. Note that a product may be both a drug and cosmetic. The claim on the label made by the manufacturer concerning its function will determine which set of legal requirements the product must fulfill. It is possible that the identical product can be sold under two different labels for two different purposes, in one case as a drug and in the other as a cosmetic.

Postal Service

The United States Postal Service exercises control over advertising in two main areas. The first of these affects advertising that depends on the use of the mails. This includes both direct-mail advertising and mail-order advertising. For example, a lottery or any fraudulent scheme—that is, a plan for obtaining money or property through the mails by means of false pretenses—is a violation of the postal laws. The Postal Service need not even take the offender to court. It can conduct an administrative proceeding, and if it finds a violation has been committed, the Postmaster at the local office is directed to stamp the word "Fraudulent" on all mail addressed to the offending party and return it to the sender. Postmasters also are instructed not to pay any money orders drawn in favor of such a party.

Second, in addition to this direct method of control, the Postal Service exercises indirect control over advertising carried in any publication that goes through the mails. This comes about because of the very valuable second-class mailing privilege which amounts to a government subsidy in favor of periodicals that have what is called a "public character"; that is, those that contain news, literature, scientific information, or the like, and have a legitimate list of subscribers.

Second-Class Mailing Privileges Can Be Revoked

The Postal Service has the power to revoke second-class mailing privileges if the periodical fails to maintain its so-called public character. It is theoretically possible that advertising misrepresentations might be sufficient to warrant this type of extreme action, although there seems to be no record of its ever having been done.

The particular concern of the copywriter with the second-class mailing privilege is that, while any periodical which has this privilege may contain advertising, the advertising must be clearly indicated as such. If an advertisement is written and set up so that it gives the appearance of being editorial matter, then the word "advertisement" itself must appear as an identifying symbol in sufficiently conspicuous type and placement so that it will be readily noticeable to the reader. Failure to comply may lead to revocation of the periodical's second-class mailing privilege.

Mail-fraud cases prosecuted by the Postal Service run into the hundreds of thousands and involve an estimated hundreds of millions of dollars in losses, possibly as high as between 60 and 100 billion dollars. Such fraud cases are an embarrassment to the media that run the advertisements in good faith only to find out through the Postal Service that the advertisers are dishonest.

These cases may be involved with misrepresented merchandise, false solicitations for charities, and telemarketing schemes. Another area for widespread dishonesty is in coupon redemption schemes operating through coupon clearinghouses. Millions of false coupons have been redeemed through legitimate clearinghouses, but the Postal Service is working hard to stamp out these fraudulent operators.

With the explosion in recent years of direct response advertising, the rulings of the Postal Service have touched many more advertisers than formerly and will continue to do so if advertisers are careless or dishonest.

Federal Communications Commission (FCC)

The Federal Communications Commission also exercises an indirect type of control over advertising. Radio and television advertising is subject to the general supervision of the Federal Trade Commission just like advertising in print media. The FCC, however, licenses every radio and television station, and it is one of the overall conditions of such a license that the station must operate in what the law calls the "public interest, convenience, and necessity."

If the Federal Communications Commission should find that, because of advertising misrepresentations or any other reason, a station has not been operating within this quoted statutory purpose, then it has the power to

These days, a lot more consumer advertising is bringing a direct response: lawsuits.

In fact, private lawsuits involving advertisers have increased at an undreamed-of rate in the last five years. And that can cause you nightmares.

That's why an ad agency like yours can use a law firm like ours: Kinney & Lange.

Advertising law is one of the areas we limit our practice to. So there's no limit to the help we can give you.

We're easy to work with, too. We have ad agency experience.

In fact, one of our attorneys is a former agency account executive. So you'll find us extraordinarily sensitive to your creative concerns and efforts.

We understand that great advertising can break the rules. We just try to keep it from breaking the law.

We'd like to make our case in person. With a fast-moving, fascinating presentation on advertising law.

We'll swear under oath that it's so entertaining, many people in your agency will actually enjoy it.

So call Stephen Bergerson or Bill Braddock today at 339-1863. And set up a time for Kinney & Lange to appear in your agency.

Believe us, it's a lot simpler than having your agency appear in court.

KINNEY & LANGE–ADVERTISING LAW

Kinney & Lange, P.A. 625 Fourth Avenue South, Suite 1500, Minneapolis. Practice limited to Patent, Trademark, Unfair Competition, Copyright, Franchise and Advertising Law.

Figure 22–2. Advertisement of legal firm specializing in advertising law. This striking advertisement uses a play on words in its reference to "direct response," the fastest-growing area of advertising. The reference is especially appropriate because this form of advertising results in more Federal Trade Commission actions than any other.

Courtesy of Stephen R. Bergerson, Kinney & Lange.

revoke or refuse to renew the station's license. This power obviously can be a potent one.

While the Federal Communications Commission has criticized false and misleading advertising, it is the Federal Communications Commission's general policy not to take any specific action with respect to this type of offense, but rather to bring the matter to the attention of the Federal Trade Commission. But the Federal Communications Commission has indicated its disapproval of advertising by persons offering advice on marriage or family matters. It also has disapproved advertising of lotteries and hard liquor. All such advertising practices jeopardize the licensee's chances of securing a license renewal, which ordinarily must be done yearly.

The Commission has been known to bring to the attention of a station (informally) what it considers objectionable advertising. This method of procedure can be extremely effective since few stations would care to risk the loss of their broadcasting franchises and some would be unwilling even to risk the publicity of a public hearing in connection with a renewal application.

Bureau of Alcohol, Tobacco, and Firearms

The Bureau of Alcohol, Tobacco, and Firearms is charged with the responsibility, among other things, of administering the Federal Alcohol Administration Act. On this basis, the Bureau of Alcohol, Tobacco, and Firearms imposes on the liquor industry what is almost without doubt the most detailed and severe set of controls that any industry in the country must face in its advertising practices.

The Bureau of Alcohol, Tobacco, and Firearms exercises supervision over distilled spirits, wine, and malt beverages. Its control starts basically with the labels to be used on the products. There are detailed regulations setting forth what must appear on the labels and no label can be used on an alcoholic product unless it has been approved by the Bureau of Alcohol, Tobacco, and Firearms in advance.

The next step is direct control over the advertising of the products. The class and type of the beverage must appear in every advertisement. These must be stated conspicuously, and the designation in the advertising copy must be the same as that on the approved label for the product. Detailed information about alcoholic content is required for distilled spirits, but statements of alcoholic content are prohibited in advertisements of malt beverages and wine. The name and address of the company responsible for the advertisement always must be included. It may be the distiller, the distributor, or the importer in proper cases. The name and address of the advertiser, the class and type of the product, and the alcoholic content (in the case of distilled spirits) are the so-called mandatories in liquor advertising.

The Bureau of Alcohol, Tobacco, and Firearms regulations also prohibit certain types of advertising statements specifically. These include false or misleading statements; disparagement of competing products; obscene or indecent statements; misleading representations relating to analysis, standards, or tests; and guarantees which, irrespective of their truth or falsity, are likely to mislead the consumer. Other prohibited types of advertising include statements indicating authorization by any municipal, state, or federal government; the use of certain words such as "bonded" (unless the product in fact is bottled in bond), "pure," and "double-distilled"; claims of curative or therapeutic value; misleading statements as to place of origin; and many others. In particular, no statement concerning an alcoholic beverage may be used in advertising if it is inconsistent with any statement on the labeling of the product itself.

Other Federal Laws

There are certain specialized industries in which still other federal agencies exercise specific control over advertising. For example, the Securities and Exchange Commission has the power to stop the sale of a security if its advertising contains an untrue statement of a material fact, or if it fails to state a material fact necessary to make the advertising not misleading in the light of all the circumstances. Another example is the Federal Aviation Agency, which has control over advertising by airlines of their passenger and freight services.

There are other federal statutes that apply to particular products and some of them contain labeling and advertising controls. Among these are the Economic Poisons Act, which governs insecticides, fungicides, and similar products; and the Federal Seed Act.

Another group of statutes deals specifically with the use in advertising of particular symbols or representations, including the laws which prohibit the use of the American flag, the Red Cross symbol, the 4-H Club emblem, Smokey the Bear as originated by the U.S. Forestry Service, and a number of others. A leading advertising agency once had to scrap a filmed television commercial because the magic letters "FBI" were mentioned in a flippant manner; the Federal Bureau of Investigation called the agency's attention to a law making the use of those initials in advertising a misdemeanor.

These statutes are so specialized in nature that it would be impractical to discuss all of them in detail. They are mentioned primarily to indicate the necessity for checking in each instance to find out before preparing copy whether or not some special law deals with the subject.

Obscenity

It is hardly necessary to point out that obscene advertising is improper. However, there are legal as well as moral objections to obscenity. The problem here is one of definition. Standards of taste vary from community to community and even more noticeably from time to time. Nevertheless, a writer should have no great difficulty in drawing the line between obscenity and acceptable copy. Although poor taste is not in itself unlawful, it certainly is disapproved by most advertisers. A copywriter who avoids poor taste almost automatically will avoid any question of violation of the obscenity laws.

Copyright

We are not concerned here with the technique of protecting an advertisement under copyright laws, but rather with the problem of using somebody else's copyrighted material as part of your advertising copy. There are many misconceptions about the right to use such material, whether in quoted or paraphrased form.

A copyright does not protect the basic idea of the author. Advertising copywriters therefore are privileged to use the basic ideas contained in anything that they may read. But copying the exact language, or closely paraphrasing the way in which the original author's idea is expressed, is an infringement if the original work is protected by copyright. The same rule applies to art as well as to copy.

It is sometimes thought that copyright infringement occurs only when the fact of copying is concealed; that is, when the copier attempts to pass off the work as his own. This is not so. The mere fact that the source is acknowledged does not prevent the use from being an infringement of copyright. Actual consent of the copyright owner must be obtained. A fee frequently is charged for this privilege, but that is something that must be arranged in advance because the copyright owner may decide to withhold permission altogether.

To obtain a copyright for a work, all that is needed is to publish it with a copyright notice. No filing is necessary. You will, however, lose your copyright claim if you publish the work <u>without</u> the copyright notice.

An issue that has become important recently is the "work for hire" doctrine of the Copyright Act. In the case of work made for hire, the employer or other person for whom the work was prepared is considered the author for purposes of this title. Unless the parties have agreed otherwise in a written instrument signed by them, the employer, or other, owns all of the rights comprised in the copyright. This doctrine is of obvious interest and concern to creative people.

Fair Use

The one basic exception to this rule is the doctrine of what the law calls "fair use." It is this exception that makes it possible, for example, for reviewers to quote passages from books that they are reviewing and for a scientist to copy from the works of others in the same field in order to be able to comment on scientific developments. It is important, however, to bear in mind that the purpose for which the copyrighted material is to be used is a definite limitation of the scope of the doctrine of fair use.

Specifically, to take even a small extract from a copyrighted work and use it in a commercial advertisement is not fair use. This point was made unmistakably in a case involving the Liggett & Myers Tobacco Company, which copied, although not in exactly the same words, just three sentences from a doctor's book about the human voice that made some favorable comments about the use of tobacco. Specific credit was given for the source of the quotation, but no permission had been obtained to use it.

The case went to court and the decision was in favor of the copyright proprietor. There must be "substantial" copying to constitute infringement, but this does not necessarily mean a large quantity. The court decided in this case that even three sentences amounted to a substantial copying under the circumstances because of the relative importance of the material that was taken. It was decided also that the use was not a "fair use" because it was for a purely commercial purpose.

Copyrighted Music

Another common misconception has to do with music, which is also subject to copyright if the proper formalities are observed. There is a wide-spread impression that so long as no more than eight bars of a popular song are borrowed, there can be no infringement of copyright. This is clearly wrong. The same basic standards apply to the infringement of a musical copyright as to a literary copyright.

In other words, was the part taken from the copyrighted work substantial and was the use a fair one? The distinctive characteristics of the melody or the lyrics of a popular song can be expressed in fewer than eight bars. It is, therefore, not safe to use the words of a song unless permission has been granted or it has been checked and found to be in the public domain.

Copyright does not protect the title of a work. On the other hand, this does not mean that everyone necessarily is free to use a title. The practice of commercial tie-ins of all types is so common today that titles of books, plays, motion pictures, songs, and even comic strips have become highly important commercial properties.

Although it does not constitute a technical copyright infringement to use someone else's title, this may be prohibited by general principles of unfair competition in order to protect its exploitation values. The legal test is whether the public is likely to infer that there is some connection between the title as used in advertising and the work on which the title originally appeared. If so, the title may not be used without permission.

Libel

To libel somebody means to injure the person's reputation by making a false statement that will subject the person to ridicule or contempt in the community, particularly if it would tend to cause damage to the victim in his or her business or profession. The penalties for libel can be severe. It is a complete defense to a charge of libel if the defamatory statement can be proved true in fact, but the possibility of such a situation developing out of advertising copy is remote. Most of the litigated cases in which individuals have been libeled by means of advertising involved false testimonials.

Libel can be committed by a radio or television broadcast as well as by a printed advertisement. Libel also can be committed by pictures. The use of a professional model is no assurance against a suit for libel. The usual form of model release, which will be discussed in the succeeding section, does not waive any rights under libel laws.

One particularly well-known case involved an advertising photograph. The angle at which the picture was taken and the way in which the light fell created an obscene impression that was not noticed by the people who prepared the advertisement. The model sued on the theory that this was damaging to his reputation and the court agreed that the photograph was libelous. Protection against this unfortunate kind of result can be obtained by having the model approve the finished layout.

It is possible to libel a business or a product as well as a person. While this is difficult to establish as a legal proposition under the laws pertaining to libel, disparagement of competitors and their products also constitutes an unfair method of competition within the meaning of the Federal Trade Commission Act and, therefore, may bring on a Federal Trade Commission proceeding.

Rights of Privacy and Publicity

The use in advertising of the name or picture of a person without consent constitutes a violation of the person's right of privacy. In New York State, this right is created by specific legislation which requires that the consent be in writing. In most other states, the same rule of law prevails through decisions of the courts, although oral consent may be enough. Utah and Virginia have specific statutes similar to that of New York. The New York statute, however, is limited to living persons. Utah and Virginia go further and give the heirs of a deceased person the right to complain about the unauthorized use of the deceased's name or picture. When preparing copy for national advertising, obviously the most restrictive of all these laws must be taken into account.

It is this right of privacy that makes it necessary to obtain a release from every model who poses for artwork or photography. Similarly, an endorsement or testimonial cannot be used without a release from the person whose name is to appear in connection with it. Anyone who is legally an infant must have his or her parent or legal guardian sign the release in order for it to be valid.

Releases frequently are limited in their scope. A model release, for example, may permit only the use of the picture of the person and not his or her true name. Furthermore, the right to use a picture does not always carry with it the right to use words in connection with the picture indicating that the model endorses a product or service. Even a release permitting a person's name to be used as an endorser does not necessarily include the right to create a statement praising the product and attribute it to the person as though it were the person's own words.

In addition, as indicated in the preceding section, the possession of a model release in the customary form does not excuse libel, so that a photograph covered by a release might be used in conjunction with libelous words in such a way as to violate the legal rights of the model.

Decisions of the courts have recognized that the right of privacy is somewhat out of step with the facts of modern commercial life. For example, figures in the entertainment and sports world frequently have no desire for privacy in the same way that an ordinary citizen does; they seek publicity actively. As a result of court decisions, therefore, the right of privacy of such persons has been limited on the theory that the person has given up his right of privacy by making himself into a public figure. This does not apply, however, to strict commercial uses such as advertising. A magazine or newspaper can use a publicity still of a motion picture star for editorial purposes, but it cannot be used as part of an advertisement without a release.

In recent years, the courts have considered the right of publicity as something distinct from the right of privacy. Only a public figure possesses this right of publicity. It is the law's recognition of the fact that the name and picture of a personality in the entertainment or sports world has a definite commercial value for endorsements, testimonials, and the like. Accordingly, the use of the name or picture of such a person for advertising purposes without written consent may give rise to a claim for substantial damages.

The right to publicity may be defined as the right to control the commercial exploitation of a celebrity's name or likeness and to prevent others from unfairly appropriating its value for their commercial benefit.

Unlike the right to privacy, it is a property right. Thus, it survives the death of its owner and descends to the owner's heirs.

As a copywriter, accordingly, you must realize that in a growing number of states you can no longer use the name, voice, or likeness of a deceased celebrity without the consent of the heir(s). For example, as of 1 January 1985, the California Civil Code defines the deceased personality as anyone who has died within 50 years prior to that date.

It will be desirable, occasionally, to use a personal name in advertising and the copywriter may devise a fictitious name for that purpose. This always creates the risk that unknowingly the fictitious name will turn out to be borne by some real person who will make a complaint. It then becomes a difficult, if not impossible, task, to prove that the name in the advertisement did not refer to the actual living person.

In order to avoid such problems, some agencies main-

XEROX

Once a trademark, not always a trademark.

They were once proud trademarks, now they're just names. They failed to take precautions that would have helped them have a long and prosperous life.

We need your help to stay out of there. Whenever you use our name, please use it as a proper adjective in conjunction with our products and services: e.g., Xerox copiers or Xerox financial services. And never as a verb: "to Xerox" in place of "to copy," or as a noun: "Xeroxes" in place of "copies."

With your help and a precaution or two on our part, it's "Once the Xerox trademark, always the Xerox trademark."

Team Xerox. We document the world.

Figure 22–3. Trademark protection advertisement. Notice the suggestions for protecting the trademark. Use the name as an adjective. Never use it as a verb or a noun. Many copywriters are careless in such matters. The illustration shows graphically what happens when trademark precautions are not followed.

Advertisement prepared by Backer Spielvogel Bates, Inc.

tain files of cleared names, generally persons on their own staffs or working for their clients who have consented to the use of their names in advertising. Even if a duplicate of such a name should turn up in the form of another person, the advertiser or agency always can go to the release file to establish that the cleared name is the one that was used in the copy. This will not excuse the use of a celebrity's name, even if by coincidence the agency has an employee bearing the same name who is willing to sign a release.

Proper Trademark Usage

Basic trademark principles were discussed in Chapter 9. The purpose of this section is to describe the proper ways of using trademarks and brand names in advertising in order to avoid the possible loss of the valuable legal rights that a trademark represents. Some trademarks have become associated so completely with the products to which they are attached that they are treated by the public as merely a name for the product rather than an identification of one particular brand of that product. When a trademark literally becomes a household word in this way, it has ceased to be a trademark and no single manufacturer any longer has the exclusive right to use it on his product. The tremendous investment that may have gone into establishing the trademark and creating a brand image through extensive advertising has been lost to the advertiser.

The question is an important one for advertising copywriters because the improper use of a trademark in advertising can give the public the impression that it is a generic term instead of a brand name, and that is what it will become very quickly under such circumstances.

Another indication of the seriousness of the problem is to list a few well-known products whose commonly accepted names today once were the valued trademarks of particular manufacturers. These include aspirin, lanolin, milk of magnesia, celluloid, kerosene, shredded wheat, thermos, linoleum, cellophane, and escalator. In order to preserve a trademark, keep in mind that it indicates only one particular variety of the product and is not the name of the product itself.

Proper trademark usage would become almost automatic if the copywriter recognized that, grammatically, a trademark is a proper adjective. A trademark tells the consumer something about the product; it modifies the name of the product and therefore is an adjective. On the other side, because the trademark is an adjective, there must be a noun for it to modify, and that noun is the generic name of the product. Remember, also, that because the trademark is a *proper* adjective, it is entitled grammatically to an initial capital letter.

The key principle in using a trademark properly is to make certain that it always is identified as a trademark and not treated as the name of a product. These five rules will help to make that point and therefore preserve the trademark.

1. *Use the generic product name with the trademark.* To avoid stepping on anyone's toes, let us imagine an Empire Manufacturing Company which produces washing machines under the trademark Gremlin. In its advertising, Empire should not talk simply about a Gremlin; it should advertise a Gremlin washing machine or a Gremlin automatic washer.

   A simple way to test your copy for this purpose is to omit the trademark from the sentence in which it appears. A complete thought still should be expressed as in the sentence "Get your clothes cleaner with a Gremlin washing machine," but not "Get your clothes cleaner with a Gremlin."

   When you use the generic name of the product every time you refer to the trademark, you help avoid a situation where the public will start loose usage of the term that eventually leads to loss of its trademark significance. If aspirin had been sold as Aspirin pain-relieving tablets instead of just as aspirin, it might still be the exclusive trademark of the Bayer Company.

2. *Use a trademark notice.* Designate the trademark with an appropriate notice at least on its first or most conspicuous appearance in any advertisement. If the trademark has been registered in the U.S. Patent and Trademark Office (and this requires a legal check), use the official circle-R notice®, the abbreviation Reg. U.S. Pat. & Tm. Off., or the full-length statutory version Registered U.S. Patent and Trademark Office. If it has not been registered, then use the abbreviation TM or the word "Trademark." The longer forms of notice obviously do not fit in body copy. Instead, put them in a footnote referred to by an asterisk. If you prefer, the note can appear at the top of the page or run along either side. Also, you may want to skip the asterisk, particularly if two or more trademarks are used in the same advertisement, and tell the whole story in a note; e.g. Empire and Gremlin are trademarks of Empire Manufacturing Co. Reg. U.S. Pat. & Tm. Off.

   Another way to indicate clearly that a trademark is not merely the name of the product is to use the word "brand" after it. Some well-known examples of marks treated this way by their owners are Scotch brand tape and Pyrex brand glassware. When the copy talks about the "Gremlin brand" of a certain product, there is no doubt that Gremlin is the brand name or trademark and not the generic name of the product itself.

3. *Use special typography for the trademark.* At a bare minimum, the mark should be capitalized. When a mark appears in lowercase letters, indistinguishable from the rest of the copy, it creates the impression that it is a generic name and not a brand name.

There are many other typographical methods to give distinctive treatment to a trademark so that there will be no doubt of what it is. It may appear in all caps, in quotation marks, in hand-lettered form, in a frame, in italics, in boldface, underscored, set larger than body copy, in a different typeface, or in a different color from the balance of the text; or the manufacturer's logo may be scaled down and included in body copy.

There should be a special form of display for the trademark, and it is important to stick to it. Many companies issue style sheets and specifications giving the exact proportions of the letters and the proper size relationships among all parts of the mark. The reason for establishing a standard form of trademark display is to avoid blurring the image of the trademark in the consumer's mind.

4. *Avoid incorrect grammatical forms.* Do not use the trademark as a noun. Specifically, do not pluralize it because that suggests it is a noun. Say, "a full line of Gremlin products," not "a full line of Gremlins." Some trademarks themselves end with the letter "s." Do not create a false singular form by dropping the "s."

   Never use the trademark as a verb. Do not say "Gremlin your clothes."

   Also, do not use a trademark in the possessive. It is wrong to say something like "the Gremlin's remarkable service record." Instead, invert the order of the sentence and introduce the generic term; for example, "the remarkable service record of Gremlin washers."

5. *Do not vary the trademark.* Don't change the spelling, insert or delete hyphens, make one word into two, or combine two words into one. Don't abbreviate the trademark or use it as the root for coined words.

   Going back to our imaginary clothes washer, an advertising campaign developed around the idea of "gremlinating" the household wash would quickly break down the distinctiveness of the Gremlin trademark. Changes in the form of the trademark detract from its status because they suggest to the consumer that it is just another word that is subject to variation or grammatical manipulation, and not a brand name.[2]

   Many companies publish manuals giving specific directions on how their trademarks are to be used. These manuals are prepared largely for the use of advertising copywriters, and it goes without saying that you should follow such a manual if one has been issued by the advertiser on whose product you are working.

2. Adapted from Sidney A. Diamond, *Trademark Problems and How to Avoid Them* (Chicago, Ill.: Crain Books, rev. ed., 1981), pp. 248–255.

Comparative Advertising

Direct reference to competitive products or services in advertising once was a rarity that people considered in bad taste or even morally reprehensible. In recent years, following a period when veiled references to "Brand X" were in vogue, a substantial amount of advertising has appeared in which competitors are mentioned specifically. No longer is a product or service simply "the best on the market"; instead, many advertisers do not hesitate to identify the competition and make direct comparisons. Philosophical questions of morals or ethics are outside the scope of this chapter, but does comparative advertising raise any legal questions?

In order to identify a competitor in advertising, it almost invariably is necessary to use the competitor's trademark so that the public will understand the comparison. For that reason, the legality of comparative advertising has been tested most often in the framework of lawsuits claiming trademark infringement. In one extreme case, a manufacturer of low-priced domestic perfume advertised that his product duplicated the exact scent of "Chanel No. 5," a famous and expensive brand of French perfume. When this use of the Chanel trademark was attacked, the court responded by ruling that there was nothing wrong about referring to a competitive product by its trademark, provided that the comparative advertising was strictly accurate.

This ruling came at a preliminary stage of the lawsuit. During the trial, however, Chanel proved that its competitor's statements were untrue. Scientific tests established that the chemical composition of the imitation was not identical to that of Chanel No. 5. The experts testified that it, therefore, could not possibly smell precisely the same. The false statements were stopped by court order. Nevertheless, the decision confirmed the right of the imitator to use the trademark Chanel No. 5 in its advertising, so long as it does not either misrepresent the facts or confuse the public into thinking that its product is manufactured or sponsored by Chanel.

Another famous comparative advertising case was the legal battle between the makers of Tylenol and Anacin. The pain-relieving ingredient in Anacin is aspirin, while Tylenol contains acetaminophen, an aspirin substitute.

American Home Products, the maker of Anacin, advertised that "Anacin can reduce inflammation that comes with most pain. Tylenol cannot." With the help of some consumer surveys, the court concluded that this and similar statements created the impression that Anacin was claiming to be a superior pain reliever to Tylenol. The scientific evidence, however, established the fact that acetaminophen is just as effective as aspirin in reducing pain.

By claiming greater effectiveness against inflammation, which may or may not have been true, the advertisements gave the impression to the consumer that Anacin was more effective against pain, which was not true. American Home Products was ordered to stop all

SUBJECTS AND TITLES:

1. ____________________
2. ____________________
3. ____________________

____
(date)

NAME AND ADDRESS OF ADVERTISING AGENCY

Attention: Mr. ____________________

Dear Sirs:

I am asking you to let me present an idea, suggestion, or uncopyrighted work which I think may be of interest to you or to some of your clients. This presentation is being made on my own initiative and not at your request.

I understand that the established policy of your company is to refuse to entertain or receive ideas, suggestions, or uncopyrighted works except on the distinct understanding that they may be used by you or your clients without any obligation whatever to the person submitting them. Anything I submit to you or your company will be on that basis; disclosure by me of any idea, suggestion, or uncopyrighted work is gratuitous, unsolicited, without restrictions and involves no confidential relationship between us.

Use by you and your clients of any ideas, suggestions, or uncopyrighted works submitted by me, and the compensation, if any, that I may receive therefore, are matters resting solely in your discretion.

Very truly yours,

____
(Signature)

____
(Print or Typewrite your name)

____
(Address)

____

Figure 22–4. Form to be filled out and signed by persons offering unsolicited ideas or material. Unsolicited ideas have been called "dynamite" by industry spokespersons. Big agencies get hundreds of such ideas each year. Usually, they are returned with a carefully worded rejection letter. In this example the advertising agency has not rejected the idea or material outright but makes it apparent that there is no obligation assumed if the ideas or materials are used and that compensation (if any) rests with the agency or its client. This form was used for some time, but eventually the agency using it decided to decline all opportunities to review unsolicited ideas.

advertising that represented Anacin as providing better pain relief than Tylenol. Again, there is no restriction on American Home Products' use of the trademark Tylenol in its advertising of Anacin, so long as the comparison is strictly truthful.

The prevailing view now is that comparative advertising is legally permissible so long as there is no misrepresentation. But if inaccurate or untrue statements are made, the advertisement can be attacked as false disparagement of the competitive product or service as well as trademark infringement and substantial damages might be awarded. Strict accuracy is the basic legal requirement a copywriter must bear in mind; that requirement must be observed with special care when the advertisement makes a direct reference to competitive products or services.

Unsolicited Ideas Cause Trouble

It has been explained that a copyright does not protect the basic idea of any literary or artistic work. Nevertheless, some ideas are treated as property by the law and, like other forms of property, they can be stolen.

One of the constant problems that plagues advertising agencies and advertisers alike is the unsolicited idea. An astonishing number of people constantly are engaged in attempting to present what they consider novel merchandising ideas, catchy advertising slogans, and similar helpful thoughts which they confidently expect will bring them substantial remuneration.

The fact is that professionals are much better at thinking up advertising ideas than amateurs. Even if the unsolicited idea has merit, it frequently turns out to be simply a duplication of an idea that is already in the company's files as the result of studies by its own staff or the staff of its advertising agency. Yet it is sometimes an impossible task to persuade the member of the public who submitted the unsolicited idea that it was not his or her brainchild that was stolen.

Generally speaking, there is no legal liability for using someone else's idea unless it was submitted and received in confidence, or in accordance with a contract that spells out the relationship between the parties. An unsolicited disclosure by itself cannot create a confidential relationship. Also, there is no liability if the idea is an old one, not originated by the person submitting it. Nevertheless, lawsuits claiming idea piracy—most of them unsuccessful—are constantly being brought against manufacturers, broadcasters, advertising agencies, and even universities.

Idea piracy suits are a nuisance and can be extremely expensive. Many large advertisers and advertising agencies have set up standard procedures by which they attempt to protect themselves from receiving unsolicited ideas in the first place; or, if they do, to receive them only when the submitter of the idea has signed a written release in advance that will protect the agency and the advertiser from the risk of litigation. It is important for a copywriter to learn just what system his employer follows for dealing with situations of this kind.

The copywriter may very well be exposed to friends or acquaintances from outside the profession who are sure they have a "wonderful idea" to submit. When faced with such a situation, the copywriter would be well advised to refuse to listen to the idea, but explain as politely as possible that the employer has a standard policy either not to consider ideas from the outside at all, or to consider them only when submitted in writing and accompanied by an appropriate standard form of signed release, whatever the case may be. Considerable difficulty, expense, and eventual hard feelings can be avoided through this precautionary technique.

State Laws on Advertising Must Be Observed, Too

The greater part of our discussion thus far has dealt with federal laws. These, of course, apply to all national advertising. The federal laws also apply to a great deal of local advertising because either the advertising itself or the product crosses state lines, and thus involves interstate commerce, which is under the control of the federal government.

It is necessary to know in addition that practically all of the states have their own individual laws dealing with advertising in one way or another. Writing copy for strictly local advertising, such as that for a retail store to run in a local newspaper, obviously involves the law of the particular state. Unfortunately, the situation is even more complicated than this, for states have the right to pass judgment on advertising that affects their local interests even though the same advertising simultaneously may be subject to federal controls.

To take one specific example, a number of states have their own advertising requirements for liquor. Advertising copy to appear in such a state must comply with the regulations of the Federal Bureau of Alcohol, Tobacco, and Firearms and also with the requirements of the local authorities.

Most of the states have enacted laws, based on the model statute recommended by *Printers' Ink,* prohibiting untrue, deceptive, or misleading advertising. These are criminal statutes which provide for a fine and imprisonment, as distinguished from laws such as the Federal Trade Commission Act, under which the typical penalty is an order to cease and desist. Because of the severe punishment, these state laws are not enforced very frequently. Local authorities seem to be reluctant to proceed criminally in such cases.

Some states are even stricter than the federal government in their legal approach to the lottery problem. There are parts of the country where the offering of a prize by chance is prohibited even if no payment or other consideration is required from the entrant. The theory of these state laws is that awarding prizes by chance is a form of gambling, which they consider both immoral and illegal whether the chance must be paid for or not. Today, however, most states are not strictly enforcing lottery laws and are more liberal in how they now define consideration.

Typically, a state also has a collection of other statutes covering specific areas of commerce that generally deal with advertising along with other phases of the business involved. Among the industries regulated in this manner in many states are small loan companies, employment agencies, optometrists and opticians, barbers and hairdressers, and real estate brokers. In addition, many states have their own Pure Food and Drug laws and practically all states prohibit obscene or indecent advertising. Intoxicating beverages are a special case, as already indicated, and the specific law of each state must be checked if liquor advertising is involved.

Work within the Consumerism Movement When Writing Copy

Sometimes laments are heard from creative people about the maze of legal regulations that have grown out of the consumerism movement. Fear is expressed that creativity will suffer as copywriters attempt to work within the limitations of the ever increasing rules, guidelines, and prohibitions.

An agency executive, Allen Rosenshine, president of Batten, Barton, Durstine & Osborn, had these words of comfort for creative people:

> Maybe the legal restrictions have become so stringent that we just can't do product demonstrations anymore.
>
> Well, I don't believe that.
>
> What I DO believe is that we are tending to shy away from the legal problems rather than trying to meet them head on. If we look long enough and hard enough, we will find something meaningful about the product that is worth saying, and can be said legally.
>
> If we can't, then we have a basis for a client recommendation to the effect that a product improvement is necessary. And even if it isn't the big breakthrough product improvement that will bring competition to its knees, as long as it makes sense conceptually, there is no reason why the creative department can't advertise it dramatically, but within the bounds of legal propriety.
>
> That's exactly the kind of creative imagination that clients have been paying for in the first place.
>
> And even if we can't make open-ended comparisons anymore, even if we CAN'T say a product is "better" without saying "better than what," that is not the end of advertising.
>
> Even if we CAN'T say "our product is the best you can buy," that's not the end of advertising either . . .
>
> I suggest we spend our time more productively if we work out our own set of guidelines that would enable us to work within the current—or even projected—legal restrictions.[3]

Corrective Advertising

Orders requiring corrective advertising are based on the theory that false and deceptive claims have a residual effect on the consumer so that conventional orders to discontinue the misrepresentations are insufficient to protect the public. Instead, the Federal Trade Commission now requests in many cases (and some advertisers have agreed to supply as part of the settlement of Federal Trade Commission complaints against them) positive statements that will dissipate the misleading claims.

A typical order requires that 24 percent of advertising expenditures for the product in question for a period of one year must be devoted to advertisements, approved in advance by the Federal Trade Commission, stating

3. Speech delivered to the Eastern Regional Conference of the American Association of Advertising Agencies, June 5, 1972, New York City.

Figure 22–5. Advertisement of legal firm specializing in advertising law. You've seen two other advertisements in this series. One significant line in the copy points out that a good copywriter may, in the interest of creativity, break "rules." If such breaking were not done, copy might develop a gray sameness. It is, however, totally undesirable to break the *law* in order in order to wring out a competitive advantage.

Courtesy of Stephen R. Bergerson, Kinney & Lange.

that previous claims were subject to misinterpretation and giving the true facts; for example, that "Profile" bread is not effective for weight reduction.

The Federal Trade Commission's advertising substantiation program was launched by a resolution adopted in 1971 that is based on the Federal Trade Commission's statutory authority to require the filing of special reports to aid its investigations. Orders calling for the submission of documents, including test reports and testimonials, to support advertising claims concerning safety, performance, quality, and competitive prices, have gone out to various manufacturers of such products as television sets, air conditioners, pet food, electric razors, toothpaste, and detergents.

These orders refer to specific product claims for which substantiation must be furnished; for instance: Sani Flush kills common household germs in 15 seconds; Tabby Canned meets 100 percent of a cat's daily nutritional needs; Ajax Liquid contains more ammonia than any competing product. The Federal Trade Commission reserves the right to make public any of the materials submitted in response to these special orders and also to release reports of its own to inform the public about the response or lack of response to its requests for substantiation.

An example of a substantiation case, widely reported in the media, occurred in 1977 when General Electric agreed to a Federal Trade Commission consent settlement. The agreement, published by the Commission for public comment, enjoined General Electric from claiming superiority over a competing product unless the nature of the superiority was specified or was discernible to the consumer.

The case stemmed from the company's statement that its television sets required less servicing than competing sets. Under the Federal Trade Commission settlement, the company could not claim greater dependability or reliability without giving particulars. Furthermore, it could not claim superiority if it knew of inconsistent or contrary evidence.

Advertisers View Corrective Advertising Seriously

That advertisers view corrective advertising seriously is illustrated by a giant pharmaceutical firm that threatened to stop all its advertising for one of America's best-known remedies if it were required to run corrective advertising. The company declared that compliance would ruin them in the hotly competitive market for this remedy. The reason for this statement becomes clear in the light of the court decision that would require that $24,000,000 of future advertisements containing a statement refuting an important and long-made claim for the product.

As a copywriter, you may do your client real harm if *you're* the one directly responsible for such offending claims. Evidence of this is research which shows that the reputation of the affected company is hurt when corrective advertising is run. According to Harold J. Kassarjian, researcher, attitude scores tend to drop significantly on the variables of honesty and sincerity when corrective advertising appears.[4]

Deceptive advertisements seemingly are perceived as a result of dishonesty and insincerity, and not as a mistake due to lack of experience.

One interesting sidelight, however, is that corrective advertising does not seem to reduce the credibility of all advertising in general.

You Have Much Help in Writing Legally Safe Copy

It may very well seem that the task of keeping up with this enormous array of legal requirements is beyond the capacity of any single individual. Fortunately, the basic responsibility ordinarily is not the copywriter's alone.

4. Harold J. Kassarjian, "Applications of Consumer Behavior to the Field of Advertising"; reprinted from *Journal of Advertising*, Vol. 3, Summer 1974, pp. 10–15, in Ronald D. Michman and Donald W. Jugenheimer, *Strategic Advertising Decisions: Selected Readings* (Columbus, Ohio: Grid, Inc., 1976), p. 73.

This is true particularly in a large advertising agency, which either will have its own staff of lawyers or use the services of an outside law firm to check copy for compliance with legal requirements.

It is, nevertheless, of great importance for the copywriter to have at least a minimal familiarity with the kinds of legal problems that do exist. A conscientious copywriter not only will acquire as much information as possible about the product or service on which he is working, but also about the kinds of legal restrictions that may apply to the particular industry involved.

The fundamental source of information about the product or service, of course, is the advertiser itself. The details may come directly, or more likely indirectly—through the account executive or supervisor in the place of employment. In the case of an advertising agency, information about legal requirements can come from the agency's own staff or from the client.

In addition, many industries have trade associations that provide quantities of helpful information. Better Business Bureaus also are sources of valuable assistance.

A number of industries have their own self-imposed codes of regulations. As a practical matter, although these do not have the force of law, it is essential that they be followed. Some well-known examples are the codes of The National Association of Broadcasters, The Distilled Spirits Institute, and The Motion Picture Association of America.

Another useful aid to advertisers, and thus to copywriters, is the AAF *Washington Report* that informs the industry of impending legislation. Often, the American Advertising Federation (AAF) files comments opposing new bills restricting advertising. In doing so, the AAF will take on such bodies as the FTC, the FDA, the Congress, and state legislatures. Located as it is in Washington, D.C., the AAF is quickly aware of any proposed regulations of advertising.

Self-regulation on the National Level—the NARC

Reasoning that it is better to regulate within the industry than to have the government issuing edicts, advertising people have long advocated self-regulation.

Most conspicuous and effective of the self-regulating bodies is the National Advertising Review Council (NARC). It is composed of representatives of the Association of National Advertisers, American Association of Advertising Agencies, American Advertising Federation, and the Council of Better Business Bureaus.

On the operational level, the National Advertising Division (NAD) of the Council of Better Business Bureaus scans complaints about advertisements. Advertisers may then be asked to substantiate their claims. If they cannot, they are asked to drop an offending claim or to modify it.

Occasionally, the NAD process fails to settle an issue. If so, the matter goes before a five-member panel of the National Advertising Review Board (NARB), that itself is made up of 10 advertising agency representatives, 30 national advisers, and 10 persons not connected with advertising.

If, by some chance, the panel's decision were to be ignored, the media will be told of the decision and, in addition to this publicity, the case will be sent to a government agency for action. To this time, no one has ignored a panel's decision. Only a tiny percentage, in fact, of NAD cases are referred to the NARB. NAD findings and challenges are reported regularly in the magazine *Advertising Age.* Generous space usually is given to such legal news. In some cases, the advertiser's claim is substantiated and thus reported. In other instances, advertisers either discontinue, or modify, claims. One example of this is a House of Fabrics advertisement for a direct-mail promotion that stressed a reduced price but did not make clear other charges. The company agreed to modify future advertisements with a disclaimer that listed all additional charges. Another example is an Avis television commercial in which listeners were told they could rent a Cadillac for $45 a day. The NAD felt that a qualifying statement included in the commercial changed the meaning, especially for viewers who might have missed the qualifier. Avis disagreed but clarified the modifier in future advertising.

So it goes. In the cases given in the foregoing, and in most of the other NAD cases, there is no dishonesty involved but simply a lack of clarity or lack of sufficient explanation. Advertisers, accordingly, are normally willing to go along with NAD recommendations.

APPENDIX

The Appendix contains helps and suggestions as follows:

- Copyfitting guide
- Type specimen sheet
- Proofreading marks
- Nine checklists, rating systems, and evaluation methods
- Layout suggestions
- Commonly misspelled or misused words

What you find in this section should be useful on many occasions. It is material for the working copywriter or for the student who is working at learning copywriting. Too often, material in a book appendix is never looked at. In this case, such neglect would be a pity since every item in *this* appendix should be useful to you at one time or another.

Copyfitting Guide

Even experienced copywriters can write too much copy for the space. Beginning writers consistently do so. Seldom does anyone write too little copy for the space, but this can happen, too.

There are complicated copyfitting systems that require mathematics, or call it arithmetic, that will help you. Then, there are crude word-count systems that are based on an average number of words per line, multiplied by the number of lines to achieve the total.

The first system is too time-consuming for the impatient copywriter, and the second too inaccurate. On the latter point, for example, "honorificabilituditadibus" is counted as one word. So is the article "a." Radio writers can be thrown off by multisyllable words, too.

Figure A-1 is a page from a type specimen book. You are given in this page type sizes from tiny 5-point type all the way to 36-point. Body type size usually does not exceed 12 points. For newspaper copy 10- to 11-point type is desirable, with 11-point type being especially good for easy reading.

You must remember if you use this type specimen page as a guide that 10- or 11-point type in one face may take more or less room than 10- or 11-point type in another face. Still, if you're careful enough to be guided by the pages reproduced here, your chances of being markedly wrong in your copyfitting for the usual advertisement are remote.

For a quick idea of how much copy you should write, find out the length of lines in your body text. Let's say that the line is four inches long. Assume, too, that you've decided upon 11-point size. Since you discover that 11-point type fits 15 characters to the inch, four inches will take 60 characters. Set your typewriter for 60 characters and then type away.

Naturally, you'll have to determine how many lines deep your copy is to go. Decide that and multiply 60 by the number of lines to get the total number of characters. Usually, however, all you need to know is the character count per line and then you simply type the number of lines needed. You normally don't worry about the total number of characters although sometimes you may be told to write a piece of copy with a limit of 780 characters, or 900, or some other figure.

Remember these type specimen pages if you're in doubt about how much copy to write. They can save you much reworking of copy, not to mention the embarrassment of having your copy returned for pruning.

Proofreading

You'll be asked to proof your own work, and sometimes, that of others. Likewise, someone may be proofing yours. When you use the standard proofreading symbols and methods, you're using a common language of the writer, editor, and printer.

Figure A–2 is a simple listing of proofreading marks. For most copywriters this listing is sufficient.

An incidental piece of information that might be useful to you is that there is no proofreading symbol for the

Figure A–1. Type specimen sheet.
Courtesy of Rochester Monotype Composition Co.
(see page 311)

Century Schoolbook Bold

Fototronic—Century Schoolbook Bold

5 pt. Printing has performed a role of achievement unparalleled in the revelation of new horizons, and in emphasizing t
he potentials of social and cultural development. The invention of printing stands at the peak of man's broad civiliz
PRINTING HAS PERFORMED A ROLE OF ACHIEVEMENT UNPARALLELED IN THE REVELATION OF NEW
PRINTING HAS PERFORMED A ROLE OF ACHIEVEMENT UNPARALLELED IN THE REVELATION OF NEW HORIZONS 1234567890
Printing has performed a role of achievement unparalleled in the revelation of new horizons, and in emphasizing in th
PRINTING HAS PERFORMED A ROLE OF ACHIEVEMENT UNPARALLELED IN THE REVELATION OF 123

5½ pt. Printing has performed a role of achievement unparalleled in the revelation of new horizons, and in emph
asizing the potentials of social and cultural development. The invention of printing stands at the peak of m
PRINTING HAS PERFORMED A ROLE OF ACHIEVEMENT UNPARALLELED IN THE REVELATION
PRINTING HAS PERFORMED A ROLE OF ACHIEVEMENT UNPARALLELED IN THE REVELATION OF NEW 1234567890
Printing has performed a role of achievement unparalleled in the revelation of new horizons, and in emphas
PRINTING HAS PERFORMED A ROLE OF ACHIEVEMENT UNPARALLELED IN THE REVEL 456

6 pt. Printing has performed a role of achievement unparalleled in the revelation of new horizons, and
in emphasizing the potentials of social and cultural development. The invention of printing stand
PRINTING HAS PERFORMED A ROLE OF ACHIEVEMENT UNPARALLELED IN THE REVEL
PRINTING HAS PERFORMED A ROLE OF ACHIEVEMENT UNPARALLELED IN THE REVELATION O 1234567890
Printing has performed a role of achievement unparalleled in the revelation of new horizons, and
PRINTING HAS PERFORMED A ROLE OF ACHIEVEMENT UNPARALLELED IN THE R 789

6½ pt. Printing has performed a role of achievement unparalleled in the revelation of new horizo
ns, and in emphasizing the potentials of social and cultural development. The invention of
PRINTING HAS PERFORMED A ROLE OF ACHIEVEMENT UNPARALLELED IN THE
PRINTING HAS PERFORMED A ROLE OF ACHIEVEMENT UNPARALLELED IN THE REV 1234567890
Printing has performed a role of achievement unparalleled in the revelation of new horizon
PRINTING HAS PERFORMED A ROLE OF ACHIEVEMENT UNPARALLELED IN 123

7 pt. Printing has performed a role of achievement unparalleled in the revelation of new
horizons, and in emphasizing the potentials of social and cultural development. Th
PRINTING HAS PERFORMED A ROLE OF ACHIEVEMENT UNPARALLELED IN
PRINTING HAS PERFORMED A ROLE OF ACHIEVEMENT UNPARALLELED IN T 1234567890
Printing has performed a role of achievement unparalleled in the revelation of new
PRINTING HAS PERFORMED A ROLE OF ACHIEVEMENT UNPARALLE 456

7½ pt. Printing has performed a role of achievement unparalleled in the revelation o
f new horizons, and in emphasizing the potentials of social and cultural develo
PRINTING HAS PERFORMED A ROLE OF ACHIEVEMENT UNPARALLE
PRINTING HAS PERFORMED A ROLE OF ACHIEVEMENT UNPARALLELED 1234567890
Printing has performed a role of achievement unparalleled in the revelation of
PRINTING HAS PERFORMED A ROLE OF ACHIEVEMENT UNPARA 789

8 pt. Printing has performed a role of achievement unparalleled in the revelat
PRINTING HAS PERFORMED A ROLE OF ACHIEVEMENT UNPARAL
PRINTING HAS PERFORMED A ROLE OF ACHIEVEMENT UNPARALLE 1234567890
Printing has performed a role of achievement unparalleled in the revelatio
PRINTING HAS PERFORMED A ROLE OF ACHIEVEMENT UNP 123

8½ pt. Printing has performed a role of achievement unparalleled in the re
PRINTING HAS PERFORMED A ROLE OF ACHIEVEMENT UNPA
PRINTING HAS PERFORMED A ROLE OF ACHIEVEMENT UNPA 1234567890
Printing has performed a role of achievement unparalleled in the rev
PRINTING HAS PERFORMED A ROLE OF ACHIEVEMENT U 456

9 pt. Printing has performed a role of achievement unparalleled in th
PRINTING HAS PERFORMED A ROLE OF ACHIEVEMENT U
PRINTING HAS PERFORMED A ROLE OF ACHIEVEMENT U 1234567890
Printing has performed a role of achievement unparalleled in the
PRINTING HAS PERFORMED A ROLE OF ACHIEVEME 789

10 pt. Printing has performed a role of achievement unparalleled
PRINTING HAS PERFORMED A ROLE OF ACHIEVEME
PRINTING HAS PERFORMED A ROLE OF ACHIEVEM 1234567890
Printing has performed a role of achievement unparalleled
PRINTING HAS PERFORMED A ROLE OF ACHIE 123

11 pt. Printing has performed a role of achievement unpara
PRINTING HAS PERFORMED A ROLE OF ACHIEV
PRINTING HAS PERFORMED A ROLE OF AC 1234567890
Printing has performed a role of achievement unparal
PRINTING HAS PERFORMED A ROLE OF AC 456

12 pt. Printing has performed a role of achievement un
PRINTING HAS PERFORMED A ROLE OF AC
PRINTING HAS PERFORMED A ROLE OF 1234567890
Printing has performed a role of achievement unp
PRINTING HAS PERFORMED A ROLE OF 789

14 pt. Printing has performed a role of achieve
PRINTING HAS PERFORMED A ROLE
PRINTING HAS PERFORMED A RO 1234567890
Printing has performed a role of achievem
PRINTING HAS PERFORMED A RO 123

Characters per pica: 5 pt–4.5; 5½ pt–4.1; 6 pt–3.8; 6½ pt–3.5; 7 pt–3.2; 7½ pt–3.0; 8 pt–2.8; 8½ pt–2.7; 9 pt–2.5; 10 pt–2.3; 11 pt–2.1; 12 pt–1.9; 14 pt–1.6; 16 pt–1.4

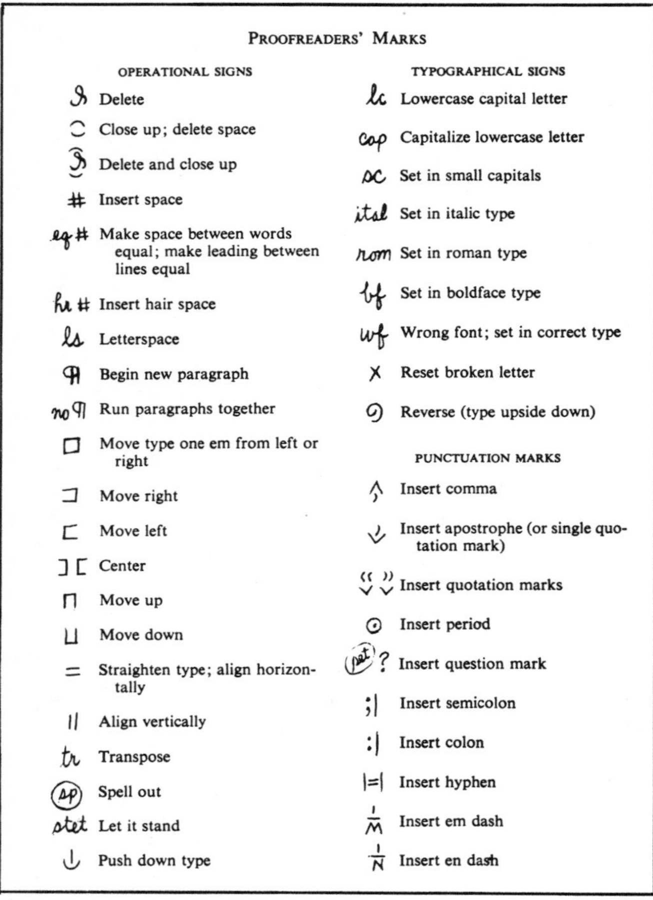

PROOFREADERS' MARKS

OPERATIONAL SIGNS

Mark	Meaning
	Delete
	Close up; delete space
	Delete and close up
#	Insert space
eq #	Make space between words equal; make leading between lines equal
hr #	Insert hair space
ls	Letterspace
¶	Begin new paragraph
no ¶	Run paragraphs together
	Move type one em from left or right
	Move right
	Move left
	Center
	Move up
	Move down
=	Straighten type; align horizontally
‖	Align vertically
tr	Transpose
sp	Spell out
stet	Let it stand
	Push down type

TYPOGRAPHICAL SIGNS

Mark	Meaning
lc	Lowercase capital letter
cap	Capitalize lowercase letter
sc	Set in small capitals
ital	Set in italic type
rom	Set in roman type
bf	Set in boldface type
wf	Wrong font; set in correct type
X	Reset broken letter
	Reverse (type upside down)

PUNCTUATION MARKS

Mark	Meaning
	Insert comma
	Insert apostrophe (or single quotation mark)
	Insert quotation marks
	Insert period
?	Insert question mark
;	Insert semicolon
:	Insert colon
=	Insert hyphen
M	Insert em dash
N	Insert en dash

Figure A–2. Proofreaders' marks.
Courtesy of University of Chicago Press, *The Chicago Manual of Style,* 13th edition (1982).

underline. When you underline a word, a printer automatically will set it in italics. To make sure that he understands that you want an underline, put a line under the word or phrase and then on the side of the sheet use these words: "Printer. Underscore, not *italics.*"

Checklists, Rating Systems, and Evaluation Methods

In the chapter on advertising research you read about checklists. For most copywriters, a checklist is merely a simple list of product points. For instance, if you were writing about a flashlight, you might list:

- Floats
- Casts beam half mile
- Waterproof
- Shatterproof plastic
- Three long-life batteries
- Lightweight
- Can be focused
- One-year guarantee

For the conscientious copywriter ever anxious to improve performance, there are many other useful methods. Many copywriters pay little attention to these. This is unfortunate because much is to be gained by using these suggestions either before, or after, writing copy.

1. Ad scoring systems. Some years ago, David Ogilvy, noted advertising man and author, offered the following scoring system for rating the mechanical or physical aspects of an advertisement. His suggestions are as valid today.

To use this, assume that the advertisement begins with a score of 100. Then deduct points according to whatever transgression has been committed. It is doubtful that any advertisement will obtain 100 points when you rate it in this manner. The scoring system has much merit, however, in making the copywriter and artist aware of some important principles.

On the content side, Mr. Ogilvy decries (a) any advertisement that is obviously dishonest; (b) an advertisement that would obviously be considered indecent or blasphemous by more than five percent of the readers of the publication in which it appears; and (c) any advertisement that is an obvious imitation of another advertiser's advertisement.

	Layout and Printing Factors	**Points Deducted**
1.	Graphic technique obtrudes itself between the copywriter and the reader.	17
2.	Illustration is lazy—it does not work hard at selling the product.	11
3.	It requires more than a split second for the reader to identify the kind of product being advertised.	10
4.	Brand name is not visible at a glance.	9
5.	Layout looks more like an advertisement than an editorial page.	7
6.	Illustration lacks "story appeal," something interesting happening.	6
7.	A drawing is used instead of a photograph.	6
8.	Layout is cluttered or complicated.	5
9.	There is more than one place to begin reading.	4
10.	Type is used self-consciously for purpose of design.	4
11.	Body copy is set in reverse or in a tint.	4
12.	Any illustration appears without a caption.	3

13.	Illustration is defaced in any way; for example, by having the headline run into it.	2
14.	Illustration is any shape other than rectangular.	2
15.	Headline is set in more than one typeface.	2
16.	Body copy is set in a sans serif face.	2
17.	Measure is wider than 40 characters.	2
18.	Long copy is not broken with crossheads.	2
19.	First paragraph is more than 12 words.	1
20.	Paragraphs are squared up.	1

2. Two-part copywriting system. You will find the following suggestions in two parts. In the first part you'll find major considerations to think about in your advertisement. By the way, this material applies to newspaper or magazine advertisements, but the suggestion about including telephone numbers and hours in item 5 would apply specifically to newspaper advertisements.

In the second part, the scoring sheet enables you to determine how well the six major considerations have been applied.

WARNING. Don't apply this too literally to all advertisements. In fact, you can't apply it to all advertisements. For example, there are splendid corporate, or institutional, advertisements that would rate poorly if judged by this system. There are image-building advertisements that would fare badly, too. In short, before you use this copywriting system, be sure that your subject matter, technique, or objective is suitable. If so, use. If not, don't use.

1. **Theme.** Can the sales message in the ad be stated in a simple declarative sentence?
2. **Headline.** A good headline includes the company name and a reader benefit. It should also be selective so the reader knows that the ad is directed at him or her. And, of course, the headline should be simple enough to be clearly understood.
3. **Illustration.** The illustration should attract readers and help tell the story or reinforce the main sales point of the ad. If possible, it should show the product in use.
4. **Text or body copy.** The text should follow the headline, amplifying user benefits, explaining and offering proof that the product or service being advertised is a good one. And the text should end with an action close. It should tell the reader what to do next and it should make it easy for him or her to do it.
5. **Signature.** The ad should end with the company name clear and visible. Address (complete with zip code), phone number, and hours open for business should be included.
6. **Ad layout.** The ad layout is nothing more than the arrangement of items two, three, four, and five. It should be planned to draw readers into the ad, guide them through it, and visually present the image the advertiser wants to present.

Scoring Sheet for Evaluating an Ad*

Item	Score
Can the main sales point be stated in a simple declarative sentence?	1
Does the headline mention company or brand name?	1
Does the headline promise a benefit?	2
Does the headline select the people the ad wants to talk to?	1
Is the headline simple and easy to understand?	1
Does the headline promise something new?	1
Does the illustration show the product in use?	1
Is the illustration attention-getting?	1
Does the illustration show user benefits?	1
Are there supplemental photos, drawings, or charts to add interest and help sell the product?	1
Does the text repeat the benefit in the headline and amplify on it?	1
Does the copy back up claims with proof?	1
Does the copy present the whole story?	1
Does the ad have an action close that tells the reader what to do next?	1
Are the company name, address, phone number, and hours included in the ad?	1
Does the ad attract the reader's attention?	1
Is there a logical visual path through the ad?	1
Does the ad convey the company's image?	1

16 or more	excellent
13 to 15	good
10 to 12	fair
9 or less	poor

*"Best Way to Judge Your Company's Ads: Score Them," *Sales Management,* September 18, 1972. Reprinted by permission from *Sales Management, The Marketing Magazine.* Copyright Sales Management, Inc., 1972.

3. Communications checkpoints. One major corporation established the following "communications checkpoints" as criteria for its review-rating program. The objective was to determine whether an advertisement was above average, below average, or average in qualitative terms. Many company advertising departments establish such guidelines to judge their own output and that of their advertising agencies.

1. Does the advertisement offer a reward for the reader's time and attention? A benefit to the user? News? Service? Does it entertain or amuse?
2. Does the advertisement avoid the necessity for mental work by the reader? Is the headline specific, clear, and direct? Does the illustration work hard to support the sales message? Is the layout simple and orderly, avoiding clutter?
3. Does it provide validation and support for the sales claim? By demonstrations? By tests? By case history or testimonial? By guarantee?
4. Does it exploit the principle of repetition? Is the story told in the headline? Again in the illustration? Again in the copy?
5. Does the treatment avoid the stereotype? Is it arresting? Fresh?
6. Is the total effect modern and advanced?

4. Essentials of good advertising. In Figure A-3 you will find material aimed especially at the copywriter who is creating newspaper advertising, especially advertising for retail stores. The basic ideas and the copy came from the Bureau of Advertising of the American Newspaper Publishers Association. The material had been published in the Bureau's *Annual Retail Advertising Plan Book.* It was also used as a mailer sent out by one newspaper to help local merchants and others prepare better advertisements. It is reproduced as it appeared in the February 1973 International Newspaper Promotion Association Copy Service Newsletter, edited by James B. McGrew, of the Lancaster Newspapers, Inc., Lancaster, Pennsylvania.

5. Ad evaluation checklist. In Figure A-4 you will find an elaborate advertising evaluation checklist that can be used: (a) to check your own work; (b) to check the work of others and thus provide a valuable critique. Used in this way, it eliminates the infuriatingly vague type of comment expressed in the words "I don't like it, but I can't tell you exactly why."

This checklist, thus, can be used by the copywriter or by the copy chief. It is not, as you can see, a casual, once-over-lightly evaluation because it embraces headlines, body copy, layout, illustration, and typography.

The person using this evaluation system on a regular basis might wish to work out a point scoring system and evolve a total for the "perfect" advertisement. Thus, advertisements could be judged in terms of how far or how close they are to a perfect rating.

6. Copywriting marketing code. Figure A–5 provides a detailed code useful for the teacher grading classroom copy assignments. By using the code designations the teacher can eliminate writing the same criticisms over and over again. As any teacher knows, a classroom of students will make the same mistakes. Just about every mistake that can be made in the layout, copy, headlines, and grammar is reflected in the code.

Dear Advertiser,

The increasing complexity of retailing — such as the rapid growth and diversity of competition, changing customer shopping habits and the continuing squeeze on profits — has made it vitally important that merchants get full value from their advertising dollars.

The newspaper ad is the retailer's best store window and salesman. Nearly everyone reads a daily newspaper, and readers shop the newspaper for good values. Yet, the effectiveness of advertising varies widely. In terms of readership and sales results, some ads are far more successful than others.

The most important single factor determining how many people will read any newspaper ad is the skill and technique used in preparing the ad.

The following suggestions for copy and layout are drawn from several studies. When effectively used, these techniques and rules generally increase readership

LANCASTER NEWSPAPERS, INC.
8 W. King St., Lancaster, Penna. 17604

essentials of a good ad

make your ads easily recognizable 1

Advertisements which are distinctive in their use of art, layout techniques and type faces usually enjoy higher readership than run - of - the - mill advertising. Make your ads distinctively different in appearance from the advertising of your competitors. Then keep your ads' appearance consistent. This way, readers will recognize your ads even before they read them.

A B C

use a simple layout 2

The layout should carry the reader's eye through the message easily and in proper sequence: from headline to illustration to explanatory copy to price to your store's name. Avoid the use of too many different type faces, overly decorative borders and reverses. These devices are distracting and reduce the number of readers who receive your entire message.

use a dominant element 3

— a large picture or headline — to insure quick visibility. Photographs and realistic drawings have about equal attention-getting value, but photographs of real people win more readership. So do action pictures. Photographs of local people or places also have high attention value. Use good art work. It will pay off in extra readership.

use a prominent benefit headline 4

The first question a reader asks of an ad is: "What's in it for me?" Select the main benefit which your merchandise offers and feature it in a compelling headline. "How to" headlines encourage full copy readership, as do headlines which include specific information or helpful suggestions. Your headline will be easier to read if it is black-on-white and not printed over part of an illustration.

SAVE

let your white space work for you 5

Don't overcrowd your ad. White space is an important layout element in newspaper advertising. White space focuses the reader's attention on your ad and will make your headline and illustration stand out. When a "crowded" ad is necessary, such as for a sale, departmentalize your items so that the reader can find his way through them easily.

NAME

make your copy complete 6

Sizes and colors available are important, pertinent information. Your copy should be enthusiastic, sincere. A block of copy written in complete sentences is easier to read than one composed of phrases and random words. In designing the layout of a copy block, use a boldface lead-in. Small pictures in sequence will often help readership. Don't be too clever, or use unusual or difficult words.

COPY

state price or range of prices 7

Don't be afraid to quote your price. Readers often overestimate omitted prices. If the advertised price is high, explain why the item represents a good value — perhaps because of superior materials or workmanship, or extra features. If the price is low, support it with factual statements which create belief, such as information on your close-out sale, special purchase or clearance.

$

specify branded merchandise 8

If the item is a known brand, say so in your advertising. Manufacturers spend large sums to sell their goods, and you can capitalize on their advertising while enhancing the reputation of your store by featuring branded items. Using the brand name may also qualify the ad for co-operative advertising allowances from the manufacturer.

BRAND

include related items 9

Make two sales instead of one by offering related items along with a featured one. For instance, when a dishwasher is advertised, also show a disposal, or if you're advertising a dress or suit you can increase potential sales by also including shoes, hats or handbag in the same ad.

A

urge your readers to buy now 10

Ask for the sale. You can stimulate prompt action by using such phrases as "limited supply" or "this week only." If mail-order coupons are included in your ads, provide spaces large enough for customers to fill them in easily. Don't generalize, be specific at all times.

NOW

Intelligencer Journal. LANCASTER NEW ERA SUNDAY NEWS

Intelligencer Journal. LANCASTER NEW ERA SUNDAY NEWS

Figure A–3. The ten essentials of good advertising.

Headline

Over-all, is the headline:	10-8 Strong	7-5 Average	4-0 Weak	POINTS
	____	____	____	____
1. Does the headline relate to the product?	Closely	Fairly	Poorly	
	____	____	____	____
2. Does the headline contain a benefit?	Strong	Fair	Weak	
	____	____	____	____
3. Is head lively and full of action?	Lively	Fairly lively	Static	
	____	____	____	____
4. Is headline tied in well with opening copy?	Very	Slightly	Not at all	
	____	____	____	____

Figure A–4. Advertising evaluation checklist.

5. Is headline tied in well with illustration? | Very ______ | Slightly ______ | Not at all ______ | ______

____
____
____

6. Is headline aimed directly at prospect-reader of publication? | Very directly ______ | Fairly well ______ | Not at all ______ | ______

____
____
____

Miscellaneous Comments

____
____
____

Body Copy

Over-all, is the body copy strong, average, weak? | 10-8 Strong ______ | 7-5 Average ______ | 4-0 Weak ______ | ______

____
____
____

1. Is copy well-organized in progressing logically from beginning to end? | Very well organized ______ | Fairly well organized ______ | Poorly organized ______ | ______

____
____
____

2. Does copy start out fast and interestingly?	Very well	Fairly well	Starts slow, uninteresting	
	____	____	____	______

____

____

____

3. Copy identifies company and/or product?	Strongly	Fairly well	Not at all	
	____	____	____	______

____

____

____

4. Copy stresses main benefit?	Strongly	Moderately	Poorly	
	____	____	____	______

____

____

____

5. Copy stresses subsidiary benefits?	Strongly	Fairly well	Poorly	
	____	____	____	______

____

____

____

6. Copy written in language of prospect-reader?	Very much so	Fairly well	Not at all	
	____	____	____	______

____

____

____

7. Can copy be called helpful?

	Very helpful	Fairly helpful	Not helpful	
	____	____	____	_____

____

____

____

8. Are copy claims believable?

	Quite believable	Fairly believable	Not believable	
	____	____	____	_____

____

____

____

9. Copy ending urge to action or some other positive manner?

	Strong	Average	Weak	
	____	____	____	_____

____

____

____

Miscellaneous Comments

____

____

____

____

Layout, Illustration, Typography

Over-all, is the total physical effect of the ad effective in achieving sales objectives, campaign objectives, or other objectives?

	10-8 Very	7-5 Fairly so	4-0 Not at all	
	____	____	____	_____

____

____

____

1. Is headline strong enough physically to achieve impact?	Strong impact	Fair impact	Little impact	
	______	______	______	________

2. Is main illustration strong enough physically to achieve impact?

	Strong impact	Fair impact	Little impact	
	______	______	______	________

3. Is main illustration interesting to prospect-reader?

	Very interesting	Fairly interesting	Not interesting	
	______	______	______	________

4. Is copy typographically easy to read?

	Very easy	Fairly easy	Hard to read	
	______	______	______	________

5. Is size of ad space suitable to accomplish ad objectives?

	Very suitable	Fairly suitable	Not suitable	
	______	______	______	________

6. Is layout technique (drawing or photo) suitable for purposes of ad?

Very suitable	Fairly suitable	Not suitable	
____	____	____	____

7. Does logo stand out?

Very well	Fairly well	Poorly	
____	____	____	____

8. Does layout "track" well in leading the reader logically through the ad?

Very well	Fairly well	Poorly	
____	____	____	____

Miscellaneous Comments

7. VALS. For many years, copywriters have thought in terms of *demographics* when writing copy. As you read in Chapter 3, it is valuable for writers to know such demographics as age, sex, income, and education in order to direct their messages intelligently.

Later, *psychographics* offered another useful tool with the emphasis centering on lifestyle and personality traits. A number of groupings were involved (see Chapter 3) that enabled copywriters to focus their copy on people they could visualize through psychographic descriptions.

Still later, we have *VALS*, a product of the Stanford Research Institute. VALS, while reminiscent of psychographics, makes some departures that have caused it to be widely used by advertisers and their agencies. In the following, you will find a skeleton of the system. This merely shows the groupings under VALS and the buying style of each.

VALS . . . Values and Lifestyles Systems (VALS—Breakdown by four groups)

Groups and types	Approximate % of population	Lifestyle	Buying style
Need-driven			
1. Survivors	4	Struggling for survival. Distrustful.	Price dominant. Focused on basics.
2. Sustainers	7	Hopeful for improvement over time. Concerned with security.	Price important. Want warranty.
Outer-directed			
3. Belongers	35	Preservers of status quo. Seek to be part of group.	Do not want to try something new. Heritage brand buyers.
4. Emulators	10	Upwardly mobile. Emulate rich and successful.	Conspicuous consumption. Sacrifice comfort and utility for show.
5. Achievers	23	Materialistic, comfort-loving. Oriented to fame and success.	Luxury and gift items. Like "new and improved" products but not radically changed products.
Inner-directed			
6. I-Am-Me	5	Transition between outer- and inner-directed. Very individualistic.	Impulsive. Trendy products.
7. Experiential	7	Seek direct experience. Intense personal relationships.	Process over product. Interested in what product does for them, not what it says about them.
8. Societally conscious	9	Simple, natural living. Socially responsible.	Discriminating. Want true value and environmentally sound products.
Integrated	2	Meld outer-directedness with inner-directedness. Mature, tolerant, assured, self-actualizing, often have world perspective.	Little importance to marketers from numerical standpoint but heavily represented in corporate and national leadership.

Layout and Typography

- L-1 sloppy lettering
- L-2 poor balance
- L-3 coupon badly designed (crowded, too little room to write, no sell)
- L-4 headline and/or logo too small to get attention
- L-5 headline is jammed against top
- L-6 illustration idea dull, or not appropriate
- L-7 too empty looking
- L-8 just generally amateurish
- L-9 use some small illustrations to liven up your ad, or to better explain the product
- L-10 your layout has no focal point
- L-11 your illustration is too small
- L-12 your layout is sloppy

Figure A–5. Copywriting marketing code.

L-13 copy lines are set in too wide a measure
L-14 copy blocks are too small
L-15 layout (or certain sections of it) looks crowded
L-16 too much solid, unbroken type
L-17 too much material run together. Don't obscure points by running them together. List for easy reading.
L-18 layout cut up into too many elements

Copy

C-1 poor writing
C-2 skimpy copy treatment
C-3 illogical writing; doesn't fit in well, or doesn't make sense
C-4 writing is confusing
C-5 take too long to get started
C-6 writing is awkward
C-7 trite, worn-out, or cliche-ridden language
C-8 too fancy or literary for audience
C-9 needlessly negative
C-10 language is artificial, unnatural, or stilted—or all three
C-11 you don't make clear just what you're selling
C-12 your writing is too impersonal
C-13 you don't get excited enough
C-14 don't jam too many ideas in one sentence or paragraph
C-15 dull, lifeless slogan
C-16 poor product name
C-17 you don't stress the U.S.P. or point of difference
C-18 copy isn't geared well to the medium you're using
C-19 you fail to stress the most important point
C-20 too sweeping a claim
C-21 statement is misleading
C-22 unbelievable
C-23 exaggerated

Technical and Grammatical Faults

C-24 unsupported comparative
C-25 grammar is incorrect
C-26 antecedent is not clear
C-27 bad punctuation
C-28 use paragraphs
C-29 your writing lacks transition
C-30 use active tense
C-31 avoid this backward "newspaperese"
C-32 write complete sentences
C-33 I'd prefer more cohesive writing rather than a mere listing of points a la catalog copy
C-34 wrong spelling

Headlines

C-35 weak headline—doesn't interest or doesn't sell
C-36 head (or copy) lacks benefit or direct personal appeal to reader
C-37 not a good tie-in of headline and opening body copy
C-38 you should use some subheads
C-39 headline isn't specific enough
C-40 headline doesn't involve the reader

General Faults

C-41 you fail to use principles taught you this semester (in writing, merchandising techniques, in physical form, copy style, etc.)
C-42 wrong form
C-43 too much copy for space (or paragraph, or point being made)
C-44 too much "we" or company viewpoint
C-45 company's promotional backing not sold hard enough, or specifically enough.
C-46 you're emphasizing the weaker appeal
C-47 not enough difference between your various ads
C-48 need more product details
C-49 need fewer product details
C-50 should use product name here
C-51 weak ending
C-52 doesn't end with urge to act

Analysis

A-1 superficial ideas or execution
A-2 you've aimed at wrong market(s)
A-3 analysis is badly-written
A-4 you haven't done a thorough job
A-5 no discussion (or not enough) of differences for different media
A-6 you fail to pinpoint your market(s) definitively
A-7 reasoning seems faulty here
A-8 too dogmatic here
A-9 you don't dig deeply enough

8. Client fact sheets. Most advertising agencies have worked up client fact sheets that are filled out by the account executives to serve as a guide to copywriters assigned to the account. Usually, the account executive will obtain the information in consultation with the client.

Such guides can be very elaborate. The following example (Figure A–6) is relatively simple but nonetheless useful to the copywriter.

Bloomhorst Story O'Hara Inc.

Creative Fact Sheet for Advertising Development

1. What major problem does the consumer have that the product/service can solve? Or, what major opportunity exists?
2. Advertising objectives? (Measured in changes in awareness, preference, conviction, etc.)
3. Creative Strategy/Considerations?
   A. Define our target demographic (age, income, etc.).
   B. Is there a current customer profile that differs from A? If so, explain.
   C. Who are the principal competitors?
   D. Explain the product or service:
      1. What is it?
      2. What will it do for the consumer? (primary & secondary benefits)
      3. How does it differ clearly from others?
   E. Now, give the reason why you can offer the consumer benefit stated in (D-2) by adding "because" to the statement. If evidence or research supports this claim, please note.
   F. Explain (or attach samples of) efforts made by competitors for a similar product/service. What executions by the competition do you feel are worth considering?
4. Mandatories & Policy Limitations (federal, regional, etc.).
5. In one sentence, what message are we trying to make to the consumer? (What should their perception be?)
6. Additional comments/information.

Figure A–6. Sample client fact sheet.

Copy Strategy

In Chapter 3 you read a brief discussion of copy platforms and copy strategy. The following is a much fuller discussion used by a marketing consultant with years of experience in marketing and advertising with leading advertising agencies and corporations.[1]

This, as you can see, is no mere checklist. It is a searching analysis of the reasoning and procedures involved in creative planning.

What Is a Copy Strategy?

- A copy strategy is a document which identifies the basis upon which you expect consumers to purchase your brand in preference to competition.
- It is that portion of the marketing strategy which deals with advertising copy. The fundamental content of a copy strategy emerges directly from the product and the basic consumer need which the product was designed to fulfill.
- A copy strategy should state clearly the basic benefit which the brand promises and which constitutes the principal basis for purchase.
- Although not mandatory, the strategy may also include:

  — A statement of the production characteristic which makes this basic benefit possible.
  — A statement of the character you want to build for the brand over time.

Characteristics of a Good Copy Strategy

Here are some of the things that characterize a good strategy statement:

- It's clear. The basis upon which the consumer is being asked to buy your brand in preference to others should be quite clear to everyone involved.
- It's simple. Key here is that the number of ideas in the strategy be kept to a minimum.
- It's devoid of executional considerations. The copy strategy identifies *what* benefits you are presenting to consumers, avoiding executional issues that deal with *how* these benefits are to be presented.
- It's inherently competitive. The copy strategy should provide the answer to the question, "Why should I buy this product rather than some other?"

Purpose of a Copy Strategy

- The copy strategy provides basic continuity for a brand's advertising. The copy strategy should be considered a long-term document, not subject to judgment changes.
- The copy strategy provides guidance and direction for the creative people. It prescribes the limits within which they can exercise their creative imagination, while being sufficiently flexible to allow latitude for fresh and varied executions.
- The copy strategy provides the client and agency a common basis upon which to evaluate and discuss the merits of an advertising submission in terms of intent and idea content.
- A clear copy strategy can save a great deal of creative time and energy because it identifies those basic copy decisions which you do not intend to review and rethink each time you look at a new piece of advertising.

Questions to Ask When Evaluating a Copy Strategy

A copy strategy is a basic document designed to provide direction for a brand's advertising over a long period of

1. Supplied by Larry Atseff, Alert Marketing, and Ogilvy & Mather Sales Promotion Services.

time. It is the translation of the marketing strategy into the area of copy. Because a copy strategy identifies those aspects of a brand's copy that are not subject to judgment changes, it should be developed with great care.

The precise intent of a copy strategy should be clear to everyone who reads it. This requires *focus*—the simplest possible statement of why you expect the consumer, long-term, to select your brand in preference to competition. A properly focused copy strategy means precisely the same thing to everyone who must work with it.

To evaluate the focus in your strategy, first conduct a realistic inventory of the benefit ideas to be found within it (or which you believe to be necessary to your sale). Then, ask yourself these questions:

1. *Are you prepared to accept the commitment to execute each benefit in every advertisement*? If your strategy contains more than one major benefit idea, is a *prioritization* indicated by the strategy?
2. *Examine each element in your strategy to make absolutely certain it is truly strategic rather than executional in nature.* Does each idea in your strategy represent the "what" you are selling rather than the "how" you will make that sale?
3. *If you have a strategic "reason-why," is it stated simply and precisely*? If you don't have a reason-why, don't invent one.
4. *Can you define a character for your brand which will provide long-term strategic direction for your advertising*? If you can't, don't invent one. If you can, state it simply and clearly. Avoid generalities and platitudes.
5. *Does the tone/mood reflect the brand character you are trying to create*?
6. *Is your strategy expressed as simply and succinctly as possible*? Do you really mean precisely what the words in your strategy say? Are there any excess words which could be omitted without changing the meaning of your strategy?
7. *In net, will it be instantly apparent to everyone who must work with your strategy precisely why the consumer is being asked to purchase your brand rather than any competitor's*? This is the *focus* of your strategy.

Suggestions—Major and Minor—for Preparing a Layout

No artist or professional copywriter will need these instructions. They are supplied here for beginning copywriters who prepare rough layouts. They are reminders of fundamentals.

1. Layout must be in actual size in which it will appear in the publication. Thus, if you are asked to do a 2-column by 10-inch ad for a newspaper, you will make a layout that is in that size. If you're asked to do a ⅓-page ad for a magazine, make the layout the size shown for ⅓-page in the magazine.
2. If your layout is less than a page, put a border around it.
3. For all parts of a layout, use a heavy, black pencil, or india ink with a speedball pen. This includes all lettering, your illustration, the lines you rule for your copy blocks, and your border.
4. In all retail ads, include price of product or service as a layout element.
5. *All* of the following must be lettered in your layout: Headlines, subheads, overlines, price figures (in retail ads *always*, and in national ads when suggested), logotypes, slogans (if any).
6. Headlines, price figures, logo, and illustrations should be big enough to be competitive with other ads and/or to stand out on the page.
7. If you use guidelines for your lettering, rule the guidelines lightly in pencil and then erase them when you've finished the lettering.
8. When lettering, don't try to letter in a type style such as bodoni, cheltenham, etc. And don't do script lettering. And don't letter in handwriting. Print in block letters.
9. For heads, capitalize the first letter of the first word. Other words should be lower case. But product name can be all caps.
10. Anything you letter on the layout should be in the size you want it to be in print. Also, if it appears on your layout, it should be on your copy page.
11. When you use subheads, and thus have separate copy blocks, mark the copy blocks neatly. Use a small, encircled letter: Ⓐ Ⓑ Ⓒ. Put the letter in the middle of the copy block.
12. Avoid the use of several small copy blocks. These chop up the ad too much. Ideal length of a line is 21 picas (3½ inches).
13. Don't box copy by running a line down each side of your lines.
14. When you rule your lines for copy blocks, remember that the copy must fit within the space occupied by the lines. Also, remember that the number of lines you draw for the copy block may differ widely from the number of printed lines that appear in the finished ad.
15. Avoid running copy block lines to edge of layout. Leave room on the side.
16. Somewhere in the layout there should be a dominant element. Usually, this will be the illustration. Sometimes it might be a very big, bold headline.

Spelling

Poor spelling is a national disgrace. If, by the time you reach the point where you are writing copy, you are a poor speller, there is probably not much chance that you will improve suddenly. The following collection of commonly misspelled or misused words (Figure A–7), however, might help you avoid mistakes that will embarrass you and your employers. Consult the list regularly and you may be surprised at your improvement. It contains many of the words you need to worry about.

Figure A–7. Frequently misspelled or misused words.

able—capable
accommodate
accept—except
achievement
acquire
affect—effect
all ready—already
all right
all together—altogether
allusion—delusion—illusion
among
amount—number
anxious—eager
apparent
apt—liable—likely
arguing—argument
aware—conscious
balance—remainder
beginning
belief—believe
between—among
bring—take
business
can—may
category
choose—chosen
clothes—cloths
complement—compliment
coming
comparative
conscience—conscientious
continual—continuous
controversial—controversy
council—counsel
criticism—criticize
define—definitely—definition
describe—description
disastrous
each other—one another
embarrass
environment
existence
experience
explanation
familiar
farther—further
fascinate
fewer—less
formally—formerly
grammar
guarantee
hear—here
height
imaginary
immediately
imply—infer
Indian
interest—interesting
irrelevant
its—it's[2]
lay—lie
learn—teach
led
lend—loan
loath—loathe
loneliness
loose—lose—losing
majority—plurality
marriage
may—might
mere
moral—morale
necessary
noticeable
occasion
occurred—occurring—occurrence
opinion
opportunity
paid
particular
party—person
performance
personal—personnel
possession
possible
practical—practicable
precede—procedure—proceed
prejudice
probably
professor
profession
prominent
proved—proven
pursue
quit—quiet—quite
raise—rise
receive—receiving
recommend
referred—referring
relevant
repetition
respectfully—respectively
rhythm
sense—sensitive—sensitivity
separate—separation
shall—will
shining
should—would
similar
sit—set
studying
succeed—succession
surprise
technique
than—then
their—there—they're
thorough
to—too—two
transferred
prepare
prevalent
principal—principle
privilege
unnecessary
villain
whether
will—shall
women
writing—written
your—you're

2. In the classroom, these are the two most commonly misspelled words.

INDEX

*Page numbers for definitions are in italics.

About the Author

Philip Ward Burton is the author of over 150 books and articles on the subject of advertising. A distinguished educator, he is professor of Journalism at Indiana University and former Chairman of the Advertising Department at Syracuse University.

Before pursuing a teaching career, Mr. Burton worked as a creative director, a copy chief, a copywriter, and a market and research director for a number of advertising agencies. He has also done consulting for General Electric, National Cash Register, and International Paper Products, among others.

Between semesters at Indiana University, Professor Burton continues to write on advertising-related subjects. A sixth edition of his *Which AD Pulls Best?* (along with coauthor Scott Purvis) will be published by NTC in the fall of 1990.

TITLES OF INTEREST IN
PRINT AND BROADCAST MEDIA
FROM NTC BUSINESS BOOKS

Contact: 4255 West Touhy Avenue
Lincolnwood, IL 60646-1975
800-323-4900 (in Illinois, 708-679-5500)

Essentials of Media Planning, Second Edition, by Arnold M. Barban, Steven M. Cristol, and Frank J. Kopec

Strategic Media Planning by Kent M. Lancaster and Helen E. Katz

Media Math by Robert W. Hall

Media Planning, Second Edition, by Jim Surmanek

Advertising Media Planning, Third Edition, by Jack Z. Sissors and Lincoln Bumba

How to Produce Effective TV Commercials, Second Edition, by Hooper White

Cable Advertiser's Handbook, Second Edition, by Ron Kaatz

The Radio and Television Commercial, Second Edition, by Albert C. Book, Norman D. Cary, and Stanley Tannenbaum

Children's Television by Cy Schneider

How to Create Effective TV Commercials, Second Edition, by Huntley Baldwin

Fundamentals of Copy & Layout by Albert C. Book and C. Dennis Schick

How to Create and Deliver Winning Advertising Presentations by Sandra Moriarty and Tom Duncan

How to Write a Successful Advertising Plan by James W. Taylor

Advertising Copywriting, Sixth Edition, by Philip Ward Burton

The Art of Writing Advertising by Denis Higgins

Strategic Advertising Campaigns, Third Edition, by Don E. Schultz,

Writing for the Media by Sandra Pesmen

The Advertising Portfolio by Ann Marie Barry

Public Relations in the Marketing Mix by Jordan Goldman

Handbook for Business Writing by L. Sue Baugh, Maridell Fryar, and David A. Thomas

Handbook for Public Relations Writing by Thomas Bivins

Handbook for Memo Writing by L. Sue Baugh

How to Write a Successful Marketing Plan by Roman G. Hiebing, Jr., and Scott W. Cooper